A History of Windsor Forest, Sunninghill, and the Great Park. [With illustrations.]

George Martin Hughes

A History of Windsor Forest, Sunninghill, and the Great Park. [With illustrations.]
Hughes, George Martin
British Library, Historical Print Editions
British Library
1890
x. 444 p. ; 4°.
10352.l.1.

The BiblioLife Network

This project was made possible in part by the BiblioLife Network (BLN), a project aimed at addressing some of the huge challenges facing book preservationists around the world. The BLN includes libraries, library networks, archives, subject matter experts, online communities and library service providers. We believe every book ever published should be available as a high-quality print reproduction; printed on- demand anywhere in the world. This insures the ongoing accessibility of the content and helps generate sustainable revenue for the libraries and organizations that work to preserve these important materials.

The following book is in the "public domain" and represents an authentic reproduction of the text as printed by the original publisher. While we have attempted to accurately maintain the integrity of the original work, there are sometimes problems with the original book or micro-film from which the books were digitized. This can result in minor errors in reproduction. Possible imperfections include missing and blurred pages, poor pictures, markings and other reproduction issues beyond our control. Because this work is culturally important, we have made it available as part of our commitment to protecting, preserving, and promoting the world's literature.

GUIDE TO FOLD-OUTS, MAPS and OVERSIZED IMAGES

In an online database, page images do not need to conform to the size restrictions found in a printed book. When converting these images back into a printed bound book, the page sizes are standardized in ways that maintain the detail of the original. For large images, such as fold-out maps, the original page image is split into two or more pages.

Guidelines used to determine the split of oversize pages:

- Some images are split vertically; large images require vertical and horizontal splits.
- For horizontal splits, the content is split left to right.
- For vertical splits, the content is split from top to bottom.
- For both vertical and horizontal splits, the image is processed from top left to bottom right.

WINDSOR FOREST

THIS EDITION is limited to 400 Copies, of which this is No. 241

A HISTORY OF
WINDSOR FOREST
SUNNINGHILL
AND THE GREAT PARK

BY

G. M. HUGHES

LONDON AND EDINBURGH
BALLANTYNE, HANSON AND CO.
1890

TO

HIS ROYAL HIGHNESS

The Prince Christian of Schleswig-Holstein, K G

(BY HIS GRACIOUS PERMISSION),

These Pages are Inscribed

WITH

EVERY FEELING OF RESPECT

This privilege is the more valued by the Author, as to no one could the Dedication of a Work,
Professing to treat of the Great Park of Windsor,
Be so appropriate as to him who holds its ancient office of Ranger,
And who has for many years resided in its principal Lodge.

"Art and history must go side by side in archæology to supply and illustrate each other; for what is history without poetry, and what is art without fact?"
—GAMBIER PARRY.

CONTENTS.

CHAP.		PAGE
	INTRODUCTION	1
I.	THE NEIGHBOURHOOD	5
II.	THE PEOPLE	15
III.	THE FOREST	26
IV.	TRADITIONS OF THE FOREST	60
V.	THE FOREST HUNTING	69
VI.	THE ENCLOSURE OF THE FOREST	80
VII.	SUNNINGHILL	91
VIII.	LOCAL DERIVATIONS	97
IX.	SUNNINGHILL IN NORMAN AND PLANTAGENET DAYS	104
X.	SUNNINGHILL IN STUART TIMES	113
XI.	SUNNINGHILL AND THE NEVILLES	120
XII.	THE VILLAGE UNDER THE COMMONWEALTH	125
XIII.	SUNNINGHILL IN THE EIGHTEENTH CENTURY	134
XIV.	VALUE OF LANDS	151
XV.	POPULATION AND MORTALITY	154
XVI.	OUR ROADS	158
XVII.	THE CHURCH	167
XVIII.	THE VICARS AND THEIR VICARAGE	187
XIX.	SUNNINGHILL PARK	200
XX.	SILWOOD PARK	214
XXI.	KING'S WICK	223

CONTENTS.

CHAP.		PAGE
XXII. THE CEDARS	.	233
XXIII. BEECH GROVE	.	240
XXIV. COWORTH	.	245
XXV. SOME OTHER HOUSES	.	250
XXVI. THE WELLS	.	260
XXVII. THE CAMPS	.	269
XXVIII. THE GREAT PARK AND VIRGINIA WATER	.	278
XXIX. CRANBOURN TOWER	.	298
XXX. ASCOT	.	312
XXXI. BAGSHOT AND WINDLESHAM	.	324
XXXII. THE NUNNERY OF BROOMHALL	.	343
XXXIII. THE ROMAN ROAD	.	358
XXXIV. OCKWELLS	.	374
XXXV. THE ASCOT RACES	.	384
XXXVI. THE GEOLOGY OF THE DISTRICT	.	393
XXXVII. THE FAUNA	.	402
XXXVIII. THE FLORA	.	416

APPENDIX.

CHARITIES AND ENDOWMENTS	.	429
TOMBSTONES	.	433
INDEX	.	443

LIST OF ILLUSTRATIONS.

FULL-PAGE ENGRAVINGS.

	PAGE
POPE'S WOOD, BINFIELD, *engraved by E. Radclyffe*	9
CLAUDE DUVAL'S COTTAGE, *from a drawing by Miss Louisa Wale*	17
COOPER'S HILL, RUNYMEDE, *engraved by E. Radclyffe*	38
SWINLEY FOREST, *from a drawing by Miss F. C. Fairman*	48
CROMWELL MEETING MR. WINWOOD FOR A DAY'S HAWKING, *from a drawing by Hugh Thomson for this work*	69
COWLEY'S HOUSE, CHERTSEY, *engraved by E. Radclyffe*	136
OLD SILWOOD HOUSE, *from a drawing by Miss Louisa Wale*	217
THE MANOR FARMHOUSE—THE NEW HOUSE OF 1668	219
THE AVENUE, KING'S WICK, *from a drawing by R. Jones*	225
THE OLD WELLS INN, *from a drawing by Miss Louisa Wale*	261
CLIEFDEN WOODS, *engraved by E. Radclyffe*	277
THE GREAT PARK, BISHOPSGATE, *engraved by E. Radclyffe*	279
THE DUKE OF CUMBERLAND SHOWING THE NEW MANDARIN BARGE TO THE HEIR APPARENT (IT IS BELIEVED), *from an engraving of picture by T. and Paul Sandby*	291
THE DUCHESS OF MARLBOROUGH	285
THE DUKE OF MARLBOROUGH	288
OLD CRANBOURN LODGE, *from a drawing early in this century*	298
BAGSHOT IN THE COACHING DAYS, *from a drawing by Hugh Thomson for this work*	324
ASCOT RACES IN THE LAST CENTURY, *from a picture by Paul Sandby in Her Majesty's possession*	384
OCKWELLS, *from a drawing by Edward Hughes*	375
MAGNA CHARTA ISLAND, *engraved by E. Radclyffe*	366
SCOTCH FIRS ON THE LAWN OF EVERSLEY RECTORY	424
MAP OF THE FOREST COUNTRY SHOWING THE ROMAN ROAD	

LIST OF ILLUSTRATIONS.

ENGRAVINGS IN TEXT.

	PAGE
THE GIBBET	25
WILLIAM THE CONQUEROR'S OAK, CRANBOURN CHASE, WINDSOR, *from a drawing by G. M. Hughes*	31
SUNNINGHILL OLD CHURCH, *from a copy of a water-colour drawing made towards the end of the last century*	91
COTTAGE IN THE BACK LANE, *from a drawing by G. M. Hughes*	94
OLD STAINES BRIDGE, *from a copy of an old engraving*	161
THE OLD WINDMILL, *from a drawing by Miss Louisa Wale*	165
YEW TREE IN SUNNINGHILL CHURCHYARD	169
TOMBSTONE IN SUNNINGHILL CHURCHYARD, *from a drawing by G. M. Hughes*	170
OLD SUNNINGHILL CHURCH BEFORE 1827, *from a model of the Church made in 1827*	171
NORMAN DOOR-ARCH OF THE OLD CHURCH, *from a drawing by G. M. Hughes*	177
THE OLD CHANCEL, *from a drawing by Miss Louisa Wale*	179
THE VICARAGE, SUNNINGHILL, *from a drawing by Miss Louisa Wale*	189
ARMS OF CAREY, *from a map made about 1630, in the possession of General Crutchley*	201
ARMS OF CRUTCHLEY	213
THE AVENUE, KING'S WICK	225
CRANBOURN TOWER, PRESENT STATE, *from a drawing by R. Jones*	311
THE SEAL OF THE NUNNERY, *from the original at the Record Office*	357

WINDSOR FOREST.

INTRODUCTION.

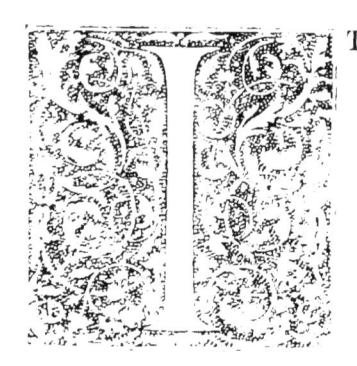

IT has been said that the history of Berkshire has hardly been so well investigated as that of most other counties. The learned Elias Ashmole, the quaint Fuller, Camden, Aubrey, Hearne, and others, have all contributed to it. Mr. Lysons, to whose valuable labours we are most indebted, has dealt with it more fully. But when we turn from the wider area of a county history to the more limited one of a particular parish or district, an ample field for research is open to us.

Of Sunninghill, for instance, we have scarcely any account. A few lines from some of these earlier writers have sufficed for its description. These have become stereotyped in the pages of all subsequent compilers, and have been handed down from one to another, until their very errors are so sanctioned by time as to be accepted without question as veritable facts.

I may well, therefore, attempt a more particular account of our parish; and although the facts connected with it may not be very important, they may help to clothe the dry bones even of parochial history with a more real life, and give a warmer colouring to many of its incidents. The little pictures of the social doings of our ancestors, which it is the province of archæology to reproduce, are not without interest, nor altogether unprofitable as studies. They help to show the gloom and the lights and shadows that fell upon the chequered lives of our forefathers; and by fair comparison, make us, it is to be hoped, the more contented with our own.

In an account of a forest parish, it will be essential to give some idea of the forest of which it forms a part; but of that I can venture only on a general sketch, my space not permitting me to notice some of the most interesting places within its limits. Of Windsor, for instance, the most important of all, I do not propose to speak, for it has had many historians already; but of the Great Park I may well give some account, as very little has been written of that.

In thus endeavouring to raise the ancient parish out of the oblivion in which it has long been buried, I have made it a labour of love to gather together its relics. These I have collected, as far as I have been able, from the Record Office, the British Museum, St. John's College, Cambridge, and other places open to my research; and although I cannot hope to breathe a new life into these scattered remains, it is something to bring them to light, and to preserve them for the use of others.

Very soon, however, in my explorations, I was reminded of that amusing incident related in Darwin's Life, how two newspapers in Kent, and one in Yorkshire, announced the remarkable fact that all the beans that year had grown on the wrong side of the pod! Darwin was appealed to as to this wonderful phenomenon, and on inquiry he found many most intelligent farmers and gardeners ready to bear testimony to its truth, but one of them went a trifle too far, and declared it was quite a mistake, for they only grew so in leap-year! Nevertheless, over a wide breadth of England people were found as convinced of the fact as some sailors are that whistling raises the wind. Just so in my researches, I found a prolific crop of little historical assertions which seemed almost all of them growing, as it were, " on the wrong side of the pod."

We have been told, for instance, that our church bells had been given to us by Queen Elizabeth; that our yew tree was a Domesday landmark; that the Ascot Races were founded by the Duke of Cumberland in 1752, and the very forest itself was created only by Henry VIII.; that Lord Ranelagh built Cranborne House; that the Duchess of Marlborough never lived at Cumberland Lodge; that the Old Wells Inn had been but a superior tea-garden, "neatly designed;" and that the Manor House was the home of the eccentric author of "Sandford and Merton," as Sunninghill for a time was of the "baby" queen of Richard II.

But for this wrong-headedness or wrong-sidedness of the beans, the Lime Avenue of King's Wick would never have been haunted by the ghost of Nell Gwynn; nor King Charles' spaniels have reposed (as was really believed by some) under the Stone Vase in the meadow there; Sunninghill Park need not have had that "herd of sixteen head of deer" to guard it from tithes, as so often related; and Charters would not be mistaken for the site of a Carthusian Monastery.

I have been compelled in my ruthlessness, one by one, to sweep away this crop of the curiosities of parochial literature, although by doing so I lose that piquant flavour of which my account may stand so much in need.

But why have troubled about these things at all? Having taken some interest in our ancient history, and having from musty old records, and the lips of intelligent old people, gleaned facts that I thought ought not to be entirely lost, I ventured to publish them.

I sat down to work, "surveyed the plot, drew the model, and found," of course, "the cost of the erection to outweigh the ability," and then perhaps it would have been better had I "desisted to build at all." But here is the result of my work, and whatever it may be, I must not omit to acknowledge the courtesy of those who have rendered me assistance.

The more especially am I indebted to Mr. R. F. Scott, the Bursar of St. John's College, Cambridge, for his kindness in facilitating my inspection of the records and papers of that college; to Major Holmes, for his attention in affording me help at the Royal Library at Windsor; to the Dean of Westminster, for his courtesy in reference to my search for the Seal of the Nunnery of Bromhall, supposed to have been in the Chapter Library; to Mr. Alan Stewart, for obtaining for me the perusal of the Manor Court Rolls, always so valuable in such work as this; and to Mr. Ferard also, for so kindly allowing me access to his manorial papers; to Mr. Kensington of the British Museum; Mr. Hellard of the Office of Woods and Forests; Mr. Atthill of the Heralds Office; and Mr. Thompson and Mr. Salisbury of the Record Office, for their unvarying readiness to help me on many occasions. I must on no account, too, forget to thank Mr. W. Barr Brown, Miss Louisa Wale, and my other local friends, who have been most kind in affording me information.

Where I have differed from, or presumed to correct other writers, I hope I have not done so with any show of discourtesy, for I have entertained no such feeling, but, on the contrary, gratitude for the help their labours have afforded me. To Messrs Tighe and Davis' valuable work on Windsor I am especially indebted. An important history recently published deals so similarly with the subjects of my chapters one and two, that in self-defence, to avoid the charge of plagiarism, I think it right to say that those chapters were written twelve months at least before the volume I allude to was brought out.

For the errors which my book contains I must ask the indulgence of its readers, trusting to their good-natured criticism. I may here observe that I shall be grateful for the sight of any old drawings, or for information that will throw further light on the subjects I have treated.

CHAPTER I.

The Neighbourhood.

FROM WINDSOR, towards the south and south-west, extends for many miles an open country, remarkable for its salubrious climate, its wild beauty, and the poverty of its soil.

A cluster of royal forests, and the innumerable heaths and commons that ran into them, formed until lately almost one continuous uncultivated waste to the very shores of the Solent. Windsor, Alice Holt, Wolmer, Chute, Pamber, East and West Bere, were as a wedge, on the one side of which lay the New Forest and the chases of Waltham and Cranborne, and the wide tract of Salisbury Plain; and on the other side, Ashdown, and those numerous woodland patches which still remain of the great Wealden forests of Sussex. Eastward of us extended far over the hills of Norwood, and the chalk downs of Kent, an equally barren country. From Ascot Heath to Bexley Heath, a distance of about thirty miles, it was, but with few inconsiderable exceptions, all waste.* Our neighbour, General Crutchley, remembers his uncle telling him of having ridden across the country from Sunninghill Park to Topham Lane, beyond Basingstoke, thirty miles in another direction, without touching upon a high road. We were surrounded, it was estimated, by 100,000 acres of wild heathland.

Without going so far back as when after the signing of Magna Charta, the Barons, to do honour to the occasion, held a tournament in a glade of the forest at a place called "Stanes Wood near Hounslow," in Ogilby's time (about the middle of the last century), the open lands began at the very outskirts of London; Kennington and Walworth

---

* See Marshall's Rural Economy of Southern Counties, vol. ii. p. 82. But Bexley Heath is in Kent, not Sussex, as the author states.

Commons led out to Battersea Heath, two miles across, and to Hounslow, with its 4000 acres of waste.

It is of the north-eastern portion of this area, comprising what was formerly the great forest of Windsor, that I now propose to speak.

A bold sweep of the river Thames, as it flows from Reading by Windsor to Chertsey, encloses this district on the northern and eastern sides; while on the south it is margined by the range of chalk hills known as the North Downs.

Through the centre of this country, which formerly formed part of the Saxon kingdom of the Bibroci, ran the Roman road from London to Silchester.

But of this I shall speak more fully hereafter, and only notice now the interesting encampment at East Hampstead, near Wellington College, as forming a characteristic feature of our forest. On this beautiful spot we must linger awhile. From the top, although encroached on by recent planting (which I trust ere long may be removed from the immediate proximity of the hill), peeps are still left that show how glorious the view must once have been of the wide expanse of open heathland, and of the great forest adjoining; for on the north of this Roman road lie woodlands covering hill and dale for many miles, once the home of the wild boar and the ox, and, until quite recently, of roaming herds of the red deer. Hard by the primeval oaks of Swinley still exist in all their ancient glory.

From an elevation such as this, or from the loftier one of High Curley Hill, above the village of Bagshot, a view of our forest country may be obtained, as beautiful as it is interesting. One may even now traverse its woodlands in perfect solitude. Rambling across these high ridges on a fine summer morning, the air, so pure and bracing, comes to us a moving atmosphere of light and freshness.

"Beneath a broad and equal blowing wind"

we look over this wide expanse of heath-land, and the innumerable wavelike undulations in which it fades away in the distance, and agree with Lacordaire that "the mountains, the sea, and the forests, are the three great works of Nature."

Even in winter, when the sun-gleams pass over the dark heath like cloud-shadows over the sea, it is beautiful—on the warm tints of the withered brake, and the white stones that crop up on the moorland, with their patches of rich orange lichen, the eye rests, it may be, with relief; but in summer, and on through the autumn, when these sandy slopes are carpeted with heather and ling so soft in colour, they are especially charming.

But what a change this country has undergone! It resisted innovation for many hundred years, but surrendered at last to the great enclosure movement of the early part of the present century.

The deer were killed off, or removed, and the land was allotted for cultivation. Plantations of Scotch fir and larch were soon made, as the most profitable way of utilising the land; and even where man did not plant, if he only enclosed and cleared, Nature, in her own silent way, worked back to her original forest state. A clump of Scotch firs, as Kingsley observed, soon showed a line of youthful descendants, rising up towards the east like a great comet's tail, the cones borne, of course, by the prevailing westerly winds; seedlings also of the oak, and birch, and beech, no longer browsed and kept under by cattle and deer, spread over every protected spot, till the whole face of the country has changed; the clay districts are cleared for agriculture, while the heathlands have become more thickly wooded. Many old men are now struck with its altered aspect; where, in their boyhood, they could see for miles, now thick foliage shuts in the view.

In ancient times, so bare were certain portions of the forest, that a clump of trees or bushes was a noticeable object, and gave name to the spot; as Burley Bushes, Beggars-bush Heath, Wickham Bushes, Hag-thorns, Shrubshill, Beech-hill.

Our climate is fine, and the air on the hills pure and bracing; but in the valleys the white mists hang when not fifty feet above, the air is warm and dry. The Thames fogs rarely reach us.

The rainfall has probably not much increased, though by drainage the surface water has diminished, and the climate has improved. Our pine woods, although known here only during the last two or three centuries, have become a very striking and beautiful feature of the neighbourhood: in winter, by their evergreen foliage, giving warmth; and in summer, breathing forth a balmy aroma. Dr. Granville, who in 1841 reported on the capabilities of Bournemouth, dwelt on this aroma as a great advantage. But the physical character of the country has not changed more than the taste of the nation has in its estimate of wild scenery. Eighty years ago, the love of Nature in its wilder aspects, so characteristic of the present age, was not known as a national taste. The epithets applied to the moorlands or the recesses of the forest were "desolate or dreary wastes," "savage woods."

Our remote ancestors loved Windsor Forest only for the great game, and as a splendid hunting ground. Our more immediate forefathers had very little to say in admiration of it, and some of them very hard things to its discredit.

Three of the most active and intelligent men of the seventeenth century were, probably, Nicholas, the Secretary of the Navy to Charles I.; his successor, the ever memorable Samuel Pepys; and John Evelyn, the accomplished diarist. They all paid visits to our forest, and what did they say of it?

Nicholas, we know, liked it so much that when he fled from the plague it was to Sunninghill he came to live for awhile.

Pepys made some eventful journeys to Cranborne Lodge, noticed hereafter.

Evelyn also visited it; but what did they think of the forest?

Mr. Pepys admired Cranborne for "its most noble prospect; but otherwise," said he, " it is a very melancholy place, and of little variety save only trees."

Evelyn is quite silent as to our scenery, but we can well imagine what his opinion of it was from the description he gives us of Fontainebleau—a forest, he says, "so prodigiously encompassed with hideous rocks of whitish hard stone, heaped one on another in mountainous heights, that I think the like is nowhere to be found more horrid and solitary." Seeing them now, one thinks those horrid rocks the most beautiful features of the scene.

There is an amusing notice of our country, however, by an eminent personage, who, although in nowise of æsthetic tendencies, loved her rubber of whist, and did not despise good ale!—the celebrated Sarah Duchess of Marlborough, happy possessor of all the good things that royalty could bestow, and among them the Rangership of Windsor Great Park, with its lodges. Writing to dear Mrs. Jennens in 1717, she says—"I mean to make this place your home when the weather is warme, and they all come to settle here. You may go as often as you please to London, and I am sure this air will do you good, and no place can be more agreeable than this is in the three warme months." Again she writes, and I cannot omit this, as it shows so characteristically the fashion of the age—"Lady Pembroke will play but half-crowns. I won't desire you to dine here if it is uneasy, but we never go to dinner till half-an-hour after two. All I can say is, you will both be very wellcome, and I have wonderful good ale!"

But there was one of bright and gifted fancy who dwelt in the solitudes of these very woods, and a poet too. He must have left us glowing pictures of it? No; he lived in an unpoetic age—the beginning of the eighteenth century; and though his life here was as a transient

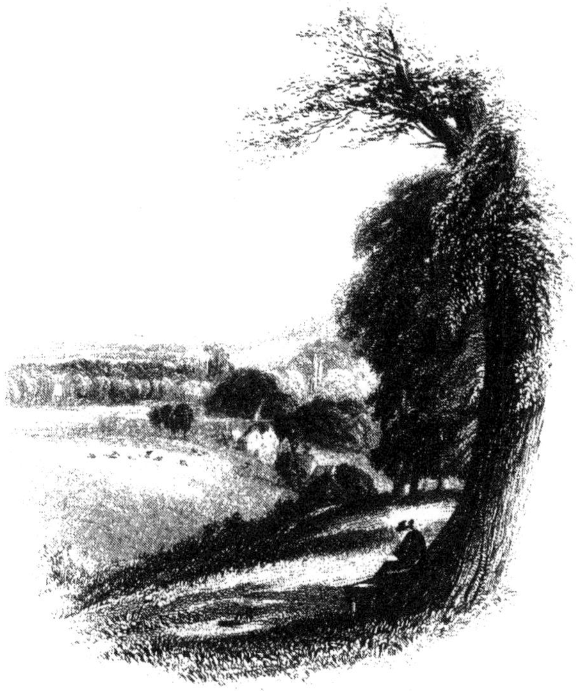

gleam of light across the gloom of the forest, he was hardly a true lover of Nature. His narrow-minded old father, who would never trust his fortune to such an apostate government as that of Protestant William, little knew what he did for English literature when he brought his bright-eyed, weakly boy to wander among the glades of Binfield. Alexander Pope, as we are told, wrote his "Ode to Solitude" before he was twelve, and part of his "Windsor Forest" at sixteen. He speaks of the

"Inspiring shade,
Scene of my youthful loves and happy hours;"

yet he talks of the pines diffusing a "noxious shade," and of the "dreary desert" and the "gloomy waste," and finally

"Crowns the forests with immortal greens!"

This love of Nature was inspired by Virgil; and his "Windsor Forest" ever seems but a beautiful incongruity. His fancy found a more congenial home in the fashionable drawing-rooms of Queen Anne's time than in the shades of Binfield.

How different to Pope's artificial admiration is the genuine love of Nature that Chaucer everywhere reveals. He tells us of

"The green laurel and the wholesome pine."

Pope was much in our neighbourhood. His friend Bridges writes to him from East Hampstead, in July 1715, that he had received a proposal to meet an acquaintance of Pope's at dinner at Sunninghill, and that if he could spare a few moments from Homer, his company would be reckoned a favour by the gentleman. This unnamed gentleman was probably Sir George Brown "of Berkshire," as he is invariably described, the "Sir Plume" of "The Rape of the Lock," for he was certainly residing at Sunninghill early in the century, and in 1703 had a son baptized in our Church. Mrs. Rackett's residence at Hall Grove also drew him to this side of the forest, and when Mr. Rackett (or Ragget, as it was usually spelt here) died in 1729, Hall Grove was let, and the widow (Pope's sister) may have come to Sunninghill to live, for in October 1738 our Registers show the marriage, by banns, of "Ann Ragget of this parish, and John Leicester of the parish of Yately."

That Pope was often here is clear from Dennis's retort—"Inquire between Sunninghill and Oakingham for a young, short, squab gentleman, the very bow of the God of Love, and tell me whether he be a proper author to make personal reflections." That he did not enjoy his seclusion is seen in one of his letters to Parnell, wherein he says—"I can easily imagine the solitary hours of your eremitical life in the mountains from some parallel to it in my own retirement at Binfield; we are both miserably enough situated."*

But while disparaging Pope's ideas of natural scenery, I quite admit his genius in other directions. To prove that the new field to which his tastes inclined was the right one, we have only to turn to that inimitable effort of his fancy, "The Rape of the Lock," which he wrote, however, while he was in our forest, sighing for the gay world. The old house at Binfield in which he lived is gone. On its site stands a more imposing successor, that in no way, however, enables us to realise the Poet's own description of—

> "My paternal cell,
> A little house with trees a-row,
> And, like its master, very low."

These trees were elms, as stated by Mr. Bowles in 1806, and again by Mr. Carruthers, who tells us two remained in 1852. I mention this because Mrs. Oliphant (followed by Mr. Courthope in his able work) describes them as a row of big-branched, storm-worn firs, with great trunks gleaming red in the sun. But this, however poetical, is entirely imaginative—suggested, no doubt, by the fact of there being Scotch firs there now—but had these been Pope's trees, they would be nearly 250 years old now; and I venture to say that when Pope lived at Binfield, there was not a Scotch fir of any size in the parish. The trees now there are indeed noble trees, and of great age for Scotch firs in this country, but hardly 150 years old. It would be interesting if it could be shown that they were planted by Pope. It is more likely they were planted, and the present house built, by William Pitt, Esq., who purchased the property of Pope's successor.

Pope's or Priest's Wood, too, is gone. The trees were all beeches, and on one of the largest, twelve feet from the ground, were the words, "Here Pope sang." They were cut by George Lord Lyttelton, who was often a visitor in this neighbourhood. (See Gent. Mag., vol. lxxxvi. part ii. p. 200.)

---

* Pope's chief patrons here were the Dancastles, who brought his father to Binfield; and Sir William Trumbull, an old gentleman of much culture, who lived at East Hampstead, and after an important official career, weary of State affairs, he came back to "enjoy the glory to be great no more," and died at East Hampstead in 1716.

Here Pope lived for the first fifteen years of the century. Just a hundred years after, in 1814, the *Windsor and Eton Express* announced, "that beautiful green Knoll and Glade called Pope's Wood, and 125 acres of waste, for sale in building lots, by order of the Enclosure Commission."

Swift knew this country well. He writes to Stella, reminding her of their call at the Golden Farmer, in his walk once from Moor Park to London, but he has left us no eulogy of the prospects that lay open to him on his way, nor, although we find him riding out from Windsor round Sunninghill, has he said a word of what he thought of our neighbourhood. He did say what he thought of Windsor, and perhaps remembering his uncomplimentary description of that place, we may have lost nothing by his silence.

Earlier than all these, we have Denham and Cowley, both dwellers in this forest country—the one at Egham, the other at Chertsey; but they said nothing in praise of it.

Gay was a frequent visitor to the forest; but he thought nothing of its beauties or its dangers, save of that paragon of beauty, the belle of Oakingham, "Sweet Molly Mog" of the Rose. Poor Gay fancied he had no chance against the Vicar; but the lovely Molly smiled so charmingly on all the customers, that he was "nowhere" in particular in her affections. She was the "toast" of the neighbourhood, yet died unmarried at an advanced age in 1766. Her memory is preserved in Gay's ballad.

Mr. Lysons says that the favoured swain was Mr. Standen of Arborfield, who died in 1730, and who lived at the old manor house sketched in "Our Village" as the old house at "Aberleigh;" and the same author gives us, on the authority of the current talk of the neighbourhood, another version of the story: that Gay and some poetical friends, detained at the inn by the weather, proposed that they should write a song, each contributing a verse—the subject was to be the Fair Maid of the Inn; that by mistake they wrote in praise of Molly, but in fact it was intended to apply to her sister Sally, who was the greater beauty, and that a portrait of Gay, still in Lysons' time, remained at the inn; but I can see no reason to depose Molly from the pedestal on which Gay so distinctly placed her. This ballad is also attributed to Swift, but its authorship is hardly worth contention. The Doctor, it is quite likely, was one of that happy party. Indeed, it is said to have consisted of Gay, Swift, Pope, and Arbuthnot.*

Defoe, writing in 1722, says—"I took the Winchester coach, and crossing the Thames at Stanes, dined at a small village called Egham, and from thence through the worst heathy country I ever saw: in eighteen miles more got to Farnham. If a stranger should be brought

---

* See English Poets, Chalmers, vol. x. p. 488.

asleep out of London, and awake in the forest, as they call it, he would think himself in Westphalia, it being all over heath and furze as there, and not a house to be seen all the way except a hunting seat of the Earl of Anglesea's, called Farnborough, which makes the better appearance standing in so coarse a country!"

Again he says—" I took the coach-road over Bagshot Heath, a horrid barren country. Through this desert, for I call it no better, we came into the great western road leading from London to Salisbury, and pass the Thames at Stanes." *

This must have been from Ascot by Virginia Water, now considered a lovely piece of road.

Another wayfarer, one fine June morning, about 1776, trudged over these breezy commons from Farnham—a poor country lad, William Cobbett, seeking his fortune with thirteen halfpence in his pocket, with his blue smock frock and his red garters tied under his knees. Having refreshed himself with twopenny-worth of bread and cheese, and one pennyworth of small beer, he found himself at Richmond, on his way to Kew, to seek work at those famous gardens. On his journey he had somehow lost a halfpenny, and had only threepence left, when he espied in a shop-window a little book, "The Tale of a Tub." He could not resist it, so away went his supper. He got over into a field at the upper corner of Kew Gardens, sat under a haystack, and read till he fell asleep.

Now, what said he of this beautiful country? He could see clearly enough a charm in the woods, and in the flowers of the field, but he had no taste for the artistic beauty of the desert. So late as October 1822, he wrote—" On leaving Oakingham for London, you get upon what is called Windsor Forest—that is to say, upon as bleak, as barren, and as villainous a heath as ever man set his eyes on. However, here are new enclosures without end." But in the New Forest he found one spot " than which there was not a poorer in all England, nor, he believed, in the whole world: it was more barren and miserable than Bagshot Heath."

But poor disappointed man, at the close of his journey, he wrote very savagely—" At the end of this blackguard heath, you come (on the road to Egham) to a little place called Sunninghill, which is on the western side of Windsor Park. It is a spot all made into ' grounds' and gardens by taxeaters."

Nothing could justify such a description.

---

* See Tour through Britain by a Gentleman, 1742.

We must come to a later time, when one could roam over these wilds without fear, and when the refining influences of natural scenery had become the antidote to the turmoil of modern life. Then we no longer hear of the "noxious shade," but of the fine "aroma of the pine;" and by the aid of an improved artistic culture the "desert" is made to "blossom as the rose."

Civilisation creates its own compensations.

Mrs. Carter was one of the early writers of the eighteenth century who evinced a love of wild scenery. She wandered alone over the Sunninghill Commons with real enjoyment, in the same way that Miss Mitford afterwards did over the breezy commons of Silchester.

Scott, some forty years later, develops this better taste in his own happy way.

And when the tide had well turned, let us hear how the *Reading Mercury* sings our praises. In 1784, when a house was to be let, it is described as "in that beautiful and enchanting country which may be truly called the Montpelier of all England!" And again in 1792: "Sunninghill—to be let, apartments, situation the first in the kingdom; the celebrated waters, the air pure, the summit of the most delightful country, equal to the German Spa." Robins himself could hardly have exceeded this!

Of more modern authorities, Dr. Arnold, writing to Coleridge from Laleham, says—"Of the country about us, especially on the Surrey side, I have explored much; but not nearly so much as I should wish. It is very beautiful, and some of the scenes at the junction of the heath country with the rich valley of the Thames are very striking." Nor was our country unknown to one of all modern poets perhaps the most passionate worshipper of the woods, whose tall trees

> "Kept ever green
> The pavement and the roof of the wild copse,
> Chequering the sunlight of the blue serene
> With jagged leaves,—and from the forest tops
> Singing the winds to sleep."

But on no finer nature did the wild scenery of our forest ever leave its impress more tenderly than on that of Charles Kingsley; and how lovingly he bore testimony to it.

The first glimpse of the fir-forests and the moors, "those delicious self-sown firs," filled him with deep emotion. "Truly beautiful, grand indeed," he says, "to me it is to see young live Nature thus carrying on a great savage process in the heart of this old and seemingly all-artificial

English land; and reproducing here, as surely as in the Australian bush, a native forest, careless of mankind."

And lastly, and as practical as any of our certificates, is that of the *Lancet* paper, for June 6th, 1874, in which the writer describes this country as "one of the healthiest as well as one of the most beautiful in our island." He repeats the anecdote of Sir James Clark, who spent the last years of his life at Bagshot, and while speaking to Mr. Waterer there on the subject of winter resorts, declared, as he thrust his umbrella into the ground, that "in the circle of five miles round my umbrella you have the healthiest spot in the world."

CHAPTER II.

The People.

BUT from the pleasant aspect which this country affords to one looking upon it from the vantage ground of the last quarter of the nineteenth century, if we turn to the eighteenth, and inquire into the social condition of its people, we must admit that the picture has a very gloomy reverse.

A forest has always been the home of the lawless, from Will Scarlet and Allen-a-Dale to Claude Duval and Dick Turpin. When a man did something wrong he fled to the woods, so it is not very surprising to find that the social condition of our people, and their morality, should afford but a sorry picture.

Our forest of Windsor in this respect has been no exception to the rule. So early as the time of Edward II. we find the great preserver of the peace in these parts, the Abbot of Chertsey, who kept the King's Gaol there, complaining of the difficulty he had in removing his prisoners to Guildford, "per vastum et nemora foreste de Windsor," by reason of the attempts made by their accomplices to rescue them on the journey; and petitioning the king to allow another coroner, as there were only two for the whole county.*

Again, in the time of Queen Elizabeth, Maidenhead Thicket was so notorious for its highway robberies, that a special Act† was obtained, to relieve the poor inhabitants of Sunninghill and others of the Hundred of Beynersh, *alias* Benhurst, from the whole burden of the compensation they had to make to the unfortunate wayfarers who were robbed there. The Hundred is described as consisting only of "five small villages and three small quillets or hamlets," against whom there had been recovered within one year the then large sum of £255 for robberies committed,

---

* About the same time the warden of the great fair of St. Giles, at Winchester, paid five mounted serjeants-at-arms to keep the pass of Alton during the continuance of the fair, "according to custom." See Turner's Dom. Arch., vol. i. p. 107, and comp. Feriæ. S. Egidii Winton, 17 Ed. II., chap. Ho. West. † 39 Eliz. c. xxv.

"to the utter impoverishment of the unoffending people." Just at this time, when there were no monasteries to resort to for "casual relief," vagrancy greatly prevailed, and we were in quite as bad a way as our neighbours of Surrey, where, in 1585, we are told there were "a great stoare of stout vagabonds and maysterless men (able enough for labour) which do great hurt in the county by their idle and naughtie life." They were dealt with, however, in a most summary fashion—sent to the Port of London, and shipped off to the Low Countries.

The period following the Restoration was one of unusual turbulence and crime, and highway robbery very much increased; insomuch that by a statute 4 and 5 William and Mary, 1692, it was enacted that any one apprehending a highway robber to conviction, should be paid £40 by the Sheriff.

Our forest country was in fact, as it were, classic ground. The very *élite* of the profession made it the field of their exploits. It was the favourite district and home of that most chivalrous of highwaymen, Claude Duval, the son of a respectable miller of Domfront, in Normandy. He came to England in the service of some young travellers, became page to the Duke of Richmond, and finally took to the road. An expert swordsman and shot, he prospered in his new calling, and pursued it with all the courtesy of a cavalier. The well-known story, told at the time, of his having ransomed Sir —— Richardson, by taking only £100 out of the £400 which he knew was in the carriage, on condition of his fair lady dancing a coranto with him on the heath, is apparently authentic. It is alluded to at the time of his execution.*

Another exploit of his was the robbing of Esquire Roper, the Master of the Buckhounds to King Charles II., as he was hunting by himself in Windsor Forest. He took fifty guineas, and bound him hand and foot, and quietly departed, leaving him to the chance of being released by the foresters.

The trade was so lucrative that it enabled him soon to retire to his native country, but he could not resist its fascinations, and rather than die of ennui, returned to finish his career at Tyburn, in January 1670. He had been taken at the "Hole in the Wall,"

---

* Mr. Frith, in his interesting picture, which has made this incident so familiar to us, assumes, I fancy, a little too much artistic licence in his details, and his autobiography, if not noticed, may transmit rather an incorrect version of the facts. The fainting lady of the picture is hardly justified, as there were in the coach "the knight, his lady, and only one serving-maid." And as to the heroine having been the beautiful Aurora Sydney, whoever she might be, that rests, we are told, only on an old story. From the best contemporary authority the facts were as I have stated them. See Memoirs of Duval, 1670, Brit. Mus.; also Harleian Mis., vol. iii. p. 308, 1744; Frith's Reminiscences, vol. i. p. 306.

CLAUDE DUVAL'S COTTAGE.

in Chandos Street; and such was his reputation with the ladies—a brave, handsome young fellow of twenty-seven—that several women of position are said to have visited him in prison, and would have obtained his pardon, but that Mr. Justice Morton declared he would resign his office if this notorious criminal was reprieved. After his execution he lay in state in the Tangier Tavern, St. Giles, and was buried at St. Paul's, Covent Garden, where the epitaph of "Old Tyburn's glory, England's illustrious thief," tells us—

> "Here lies Duval—Reader, if male thou art,
> Look to thy purse; if female, to thy heart.
> Much havoc has he made of both."

Now in one of the most beautiful parts, and the wildest, of Western Surrey, where the Frimley Ridges slope away towards the north in broad masses of heather and gorse-covered moorland, lies what is left of the once terrible Bagshot Heath, which on this side extended to the Grand Stand at Ascot, and thence round as far as Cæsar's Camp in the forest. On this breezy waste, rather more than a mile from the village from which it takes its name, the Guildford road is crossed by Lightwater Lane. Down this about a quarter of a mile stands what was once (for it is now slated) a picturesque reed-thatched white cottage, or small farmhouse, the abode, you might well suppose, of pastoral peace. The cackling of the geese, or the wild plaintive cry of the lapwing, as it draws you from its nest, are the pleasant sounds that redeem its solitude. This was the residence of Duval. On a visit we paid it once, its present owner very kindly showed us the interior, pointing out especially, although now much altered, the site and remains of the old fireside and chimney, in which the hiding-place was so contrived, that its only access was through a trap-door in the back, which, when closed, was obscured by the smoke. Here the great "bandit" lay concealed, as the host told us, when the soldiers were after him.

The same immediate locality, it is generally believed, was the favourite haunt of another notorious character, who in the early part of the last century is supposed to have been the leader of a gang of highwaymen that infested this Bagshot and Sandhurst country, and levied "black mail" on all who traversed it, and that he, the notorious Dick Turpin, resided at this same house; but although Bagshot Heath, just outside the forest boundary, and yet within touch of so many points of the great western road, was admirably suited to his nefarious trade, and may now and then have had a flying visit from him, I may confidently say the tradition is a mistake, and that "Black Bess," and Turpin's wonderful ride to York, are simply myths. Epping Forest and the Hackney Marshes were his principal haunts, and Yorkshire his last place of business and concealment. He was hung at York in 1739.*

Sunninghill was in the midst of a most lawless district. A daring gang of ruffians were plying a brisk trade on the heaths around; and in January 1783 some of them were tracked to our village, and were carousing here, doubtless at "The Wells," when young Edward Lane, the son of Mr. Edward Lane of Coworth, endeavouring to arrest them, was "shot to death," as our Church Registers tell us. On the 20th March 170¾, they also record that "a certain highwayman, whose name we know not, attempting to rob the Salisbury stage-coach near the King's Wick beech in this parish, was shot through with a brace of bullets by a gentleman who was in y[e] said coach, and was buried here on Wednesday following." The unknown adventurer has a lasting monument in this simple register! He was probably one of the Dibley Gang, so-called from Dibley, a notorious highwayman, the terror of the whole county of Berks, who was condemned at Reading in 1702. Such outrages were of common occurrence; and as to poaching, in spite of the Duke of Cumberland, who took much interest in preserving the game here, it was carried on by organised gangs who set all law at defiance. The powers of the Legislature, however, were at last brought down on them with terrible vengeance. Indeed a more graphic picture of the lawlessness which prevailed round our retired village early in the eighteenth century cannot well be afforded than by simply relating the incidents which gave rise to that sanguinary statute called the "Black Act."

The earlier outrages of Waltham Cross in Essex were more than repeated at Bishops Waltham in Hampshire; and thence a spirit of depredation soon spread over the whole of our forest country. The practice of "blacking," as it was called (resorted to in Tudor times), was here revived.

Early in 1722, a gang of daring poachers and smugglers, known as the "Waltham Blacks," traversed the country, robbing parks and fish-ponds, and demanding money, regardless of all authority. The band

---

* The real incident on which this story was founded occurred, I believe, about the year 1676, long before Turpin was born. One Nicks robbed a gentleman on Gadshill at four o'clock in the morning, crossed the river with his *bay* mare as soon as he could get a ferry-boat at Gravesend, and then by Braintree, Huntingdon, and other places, of all which we have a very circumstantial account, reached York that evening; went to the Bowling Green, pointedly asked the Mayor what time it was, proved an alibi, and got off. This account was published about the time of Turpin's execution, but it makes no allusion to him whatever. It required the romance of the nineteenth century to change Nicks to Turpin, and the bay mare to Black Bess. See Defoe's Tour through Britain, 3rd ed., 1742, p. 135. See also *Morning Advertiser*, 1750, I.

was at first composed only of "owlers" or smugglers, but was soon reinforced by deer-stealers. Their leader, William Shorter, whom they called "King John," was a small farmer. A royal proclamation was at first issued, but the "Blacks" were more daring than ever. One of their body had been fined £10, and his guns had been taken from him by a keeper, Holmes of Old Windsor; and on the 11th April 1723, some of the gang paid him a visit, threatening that unless the money were refunded, and the guns returned, they would burn his house and himself in it. His son, a young man of twenty-two, put his head out of the window to remonstrate with them, when one of the gang at once shot him. Sir John Cope of Bramshill incurred their anger, and they revenged themselves by cutting down over £500 worth of his young plantations.

The Government had no alternative—the gang must be suppressed; and as a preliminary, on the 25th April, a Bill was ordered to be brought in, and the "Black Act," 9 George I., was passed, and came into operation on 1st June 1723. Two messengers were sent down to arrest the ringleaders, who were supposed to be at Oakingham; but not finding them there, the officers attended the Reading fair on the 1st May, and took them by a successful ruse. Some of them, it seems, had laid an information on a charge of high treason against a clergyman, a Mr. Power, who had offended them. The officers caused it to be believed that they had come down to get evidence against him, and prevent his getting out of prison. Three witnesses were required for this purpose to go with the officers to London, and they were to be handsomely rewarded for their trouble. The bait was a tempting one—revenge and money both. Three of the principal leaders volunteered to go, and fell into the trap.*

On Saturday, the 5th of May, twenty-one more of them were brought to London under an escort of eighty horse Grenadier Guards. A few days afterwards two more of the band were brought up for deer-stealing out of Cranborne Park, and over forty were ultimately secured. A Special Assize was held at Reading. Four of the worst were executed, and hung in chains in Windsor Forest, including the man who shot young Holmes—others were transported; and thus the gang was broken up.

This local incident is doubly interesting as showing how even in the most conscientious hands history becomes sometimes distorted. Since

---

* See *British Journal*, May 4th and 11th, 1723; *Weekly Journal*, same day; *London Journal*, 25th May. Also State of Great Britain, by Bowyer; Lord Primate Boulter's Letters, 1725; Brit. Mus. Add. MSS.

writing the above I have read Mr. Lecky's version of the affair.* He says —"The long quarrel between Archbishop Boulter and King arose in a great degree from the bitter language in which the latter prelate censured the conduct of the Primate, who had ordained and placed in an Irish living a man named Power, who had been one of the famous Hampshire deer-stealers, known as the Waltham Blacks, and had only saved himself from the gallows by turning informer against his comrades." The historian supports his heavy indictment against the English Government for its treatment of the Irish Church by this scandalous charge of ordaining to the priesthood a common felon who, having saved himself from the gallows by informing against his comrades, was then presented to a good Irish living! A more monstrous transaction could not have been found in the records even of the eighteenth century. But fortunately it is all a mistake.

I have carefully examined Mr. Lecky's authorities.† He takes the account from a letter of Dr. Coghill, an Irish partisan, who says it came from Lord Fane, who talked of Power as "one of those fellows," and that Archbishop King, having "heard the story," attacked the Primate on it very bitterly. We are told that he did this "in language of such vulgar scurrility as to preclude transcription."

King, with all his energy for good, was evidently an unscrupulous politician, and not very particular about his facts. He talks of the Primate having given a living of £200 per annum "to one of his Walton Blacks, whom he since ordained;" but passing over the fact that the living was of about £150, the last allegation was simply untrue. Power had never been a member of the gang, but its great enemy.

Swift, equally reckless, in a letter to Dr. Stopford, 1725, repeats the story, and adds to it by making Power the leader of the gang—"The A.B.D. attacked the same for giving a good living to a certain animal called a Walsh Black, which the other excused, alleging he was preferred to it by Lord Townshend. It is a cant word for a deer-stealer. This fellow was leader of a gang, and had the honour of hanging half-a-dozen of his fellows in quality of informer, which was his merit. If you cannot match me that in Italy, step to Muscovy, and from thence to the Hottentots." That the facts were as I have related them, any one may see on reference to the London papers of the time.

Poaching could never be entirely suppressed, and after some years the removal of the deer from Wolmer Forest was decided on. Gilbert White

---

* Lecky's History of the Eighteenth Century, vol. ii. p. 236.
† See Mant's Church of Ireland, p. 443; Boulter's Letters, i. p. 32.

tells us that the Duke of Cumberland sent down a huntsman and six yeomen prickers with the staghounds to take every deer in Wolmer, and convey them in carts to Windsor.

The Legislature thought to forge, in its sanguinary criminal laws, fetters strong enough to keep down starving criminals, but with what effect? Had we walked from Sunninghill within the time of living memory across the heath towards Bagshot, we might have seen by the roadside an ugly wooden frame, from which in days of yore dangled in chains the bleached bones of some highwayman or sheep-stealer.* Throughout the whole line of road from London to Portsmouth these hideous spectacles were common: intentionally so, perhaps, for we were bounded by three of the most notorious places in the kingdom —Bagshot Heath, Maidenhead Thicket, and Hounslow Heath. The periodicals of the time show plainly what our social condition was.

Old General Hawley not inaptly described it as a kind of "snivelling rebellion." In 1769, a formidable gang of gipsies, highwaymen, and smugglers made Knaphill Wood their headquarters, and the inhabitants of Guildford and Knaphill set out armed to dislodge them, and after a sharp onset they took fourteen of them, several having fled.

Aubrey, at the end of the seventeenth century, speaks of Shrubshill as infamous for its frequent robberies. Gay, too, leaves us his impression of our neighbourhood—

> "Prepared for war, now Bagshot Heath we cross,
> Where broken gamesters oft repair their loss."

Windlesham Common might well have been the "crack-skull common" of Goldsmith.

In 1773 a band of highwaymen had been particularly active in this neighbourhood, and the innkeepers of Hounslow, Cranford Bridge, and Salthill, united in their own defence, and employed four horsemen to scour the heath, and endeavour to disperse them. The little "Brummel" Hut, elsewhere described, was a very suspicious beerhouse in one of the loneliest parts of the heath, and a favourite haunt of highwaymen, with whom landlord or ostler, or perhaps both, were often in league, as seems pretty clear from an outrage committed there one day in January 1774. A London rider (as he was called then) stopped there to rest for three-quarters of an hour, and asked the landlord if his bags would be safe. He took them off, and soon resumed his journey, but was never heard of again. His horse only

---

* 14 Geo. II. made sheep-stealing punishable with death.

was found the next morning riderless in a field hard by. Walpole was robbed twice—once, in 1781, under rather amusing circumstances. As he and old Lady Brown were going to play a rubber with the Duchess of Montrose at Chiswick, at seven o'clock in the evening, a mounted highwayman took their purses, raised his hat, and departed. Walpole had nine guineas in his. The old lady being in a great hurry to get on, Walpole exclaimed, "Why, what's the use, Madam, now that he has got your purse?" "Oh!" she replied, "get on, for there's nothing but bad money in it. I keep it on purpose!"

These outrages were increasing, for Walpole tells us he had lived at Strawberry Hill thirty years, and could go about anywhere, but then in 1782 he could not stir a mile from his house after sunset without one or two servants with blunderbusses. In June 1787, Mr. Gregory Wale, the uncle of our late Vicar, was one night returning from a ball at Windsor, attended by his servant. He was attacked near Egham by four footpads, who robbed him of his watch, gold snuff-box, and £3. He was so beaten that he never really recovered. In broad daylight it was no better, for in January 1799, Major Gore and two ladies, passing over Bagshot Heath at twelve o'clock at noon, were robbed of their watches and a considerable sum of money.*

> Indeed this prevalence of outrage was perhaps the most striking characteristic of the age. The newspapers of the day give us a very black picture of it all. Their sheets are full of the sensational histories of great criminals. Men of all grades rushed to the "road." Here a ruined gambler held a pistol to your head, and raised his hat like a courtier when he rode away with your purse. In one case, where a gentleman valued his sword especially, it was returned to him with the chivalrous remark, that had it been set with diamonds he should have it, and with an apology that actual want alone had prompted the outrage! But there were ruffians of a coarser nature who took life with brutal indifference. At times, however, they had too warm a reception, as when a gentleman, stopped by two fellows, exclaimed, "You're quite welcome to what I've got," which turned out to be a blunderbuss, with which he shot them both dead on the spot.

Our neighbourhood at this time was one of the most wild and lonely, and its population very scanty, and mostly settled about the villages; but there was one portion of it not settled at all—the gipsies—who were very numerous here. Windsor Forest was a favourite resort of theirs. Ben Jonson speaks of the gipsies of Windsor as quite a characteristic of the place; but the forest of Norwood† was their king's chief stronghold. They were long the objects of prejudice and suspicion. Every petty theft from the common or the hen-roost was laid to their charge; and the vagrant laws were executed against them with merci-

---

* See *Reading Mercury*, 1799. † See Deddington's Diary, June 1750.

less severity. Even so late as 1827, but little mercy was shown to this unfortunate race. Mr. Norwood tells us that he heard two men sentenced to death at Winchester for horse-stealing. To one who was a gipsy no hope was held out, although he piteously implored that his life should be saved. "No," said his Lordship, "I and my brother judges have come to the determination to execute horse-stealers, especially gipsies, because of the great increase of the crime." Harsh times were those even half a century ago.

But we must leave the gipsies for the rural class dwelling round our forest villages. Many of these were outcasts to some extent by reason of their inability to obtain regular employment, or through their unwillingness to yield to its restraints. They eked out a precarious existence by occasional labour in summer, especially in harvest times, and by less commendable pursuits, when hunger pinched them in winter. The poor laws, as then administered, allowing outdoor relief to every man, able-bodied or not, kept the race alive, and produced great mischief. Ignorant to the last degree, for they could neither read nor write, and shut out from the better influences of civilisation, they were as hardy and brave and reckless as savages. Kingsley calls them "Nature's gentlemen;" and many a fine nature, though fierce withal, was covered by the "clouted shoe" and suit of velveteen they sported at the village fêtes. The pastimes of the age were sadly demoralising. A boxing match or prize fight on the village green, when high festival was held in honour of the patron saint of the church, was a common event; while a bull-baiting or a badger-baiting at one of the forest towns was especially attractive. Wokingham, or Oakingham, as it was called, was famous for these exhibitions, as also was Bracknell; and if it be true that bull-baiting was continued there until 1840, our forest must have had the honour of being the last place in England, surely, in which that noble pastime was practised.[*] George Staverton, in 1661, gave rent of a house for the purpose of buying a bull to be baited and killed at Wokingham at Christmas; and thus it became an established institution—advertised as any other sport might be. It was held in the market-place, and honoured with a public dinner. In 1786 a better feeling was beginning to prevail, and both the pulpit at Wokingham and the press at Reading denounced the inhumanity of the sport, but it lingered long afterwards. The revels, again, were even more revolt-

---

[*] See Col. Cooper King's History of Berks, p. 243. It would seem not, for Macaulay, in his celebrated letter to Mr. Adam Black in 1841, on his declining to subscribe to the Musselburgh Races, says—"The members for Beverley still, I believe, find a bull for their constituents to bait."

ing and demoralising. Instead of dogs and bulls, human beings were the gladiators; and as in the one case the dog that pinned the bull oftenest won the prize, so in the other the man who broke most heads was the greatest hero.

In ordinary times our villagers often joined on foot in the chase with the gentry in the daytime, and too often indulged the irresistible propensity by following the game on their own account at night. The population was starving, and for a hare or rabbit a man would risk his neck! And after all, they were only following the example of their betters. Clandestine deer-stealing, we are told, was not considered at all a disgrace. Many respectable persons followed this nocturnal amusement—for such they really considered it; and if discovered, they had £30 in their pocket to pay the penalty, and repeat their exploits on the following night. But when the second offence was made felony, the sport was abandoned, for they were called no longer deer-hunters, but deer-stealers.*

All this shows a deplorable state of things; and yet when one looks at the root of the evil, one can hardly wonder at it.

In 1792, just at the commencement of the war, wheat was from £13 to £14 a load; agricultural wages, 8s. per week—not enough to supply a family with bread, and no other food was cheaper.†

Cobbett tells us how the labourers round Salisbury joined four or five together and cast lots to see which should have a fire on the winter nights, and the others came to boil their kettles at it and warm themselves.

Little wonder that our poor deluded rustics became "Waltham Blacks" when "King John" gave them 2s. 6d. a day.

What availed it that the gibbet bore aloft the skeletons of the stealers of sheep, or of some youth who might have broken open a dwelling-house and stolen a pocket handkerchief.

But time goes on, and change works its silent way, improving, we hope, and refining. The past fades like our Surrey Hills in the blue distance, losing perchance in the eyes of some of us of the present much of its grossness in the light of romance; but in truth it was very gloomy.

Yet the time came when the bleached bones fell from their chains.

---

* See Chaffin's Anecdotes of Cranborne Chase, 1818.

† In 1800 wheat rose to £9, 12s. a quarter, more than four times what it was at the beginning of the war. It averaged for that year, £5, 12s. 1d., and for 1801, £5, 18s. 1d., both years being years of scarcity. In 1812 a peck loaf, which was bound to weigh 17 lb. 6 oz. avoirdupois, cost 5s. 6d. to 6s. 8d., and swallowed up more than half a week's wages.

The poor fellows, some of whom would probably have hung there, were drilled round our village, and made into splendid soldiers, marched off to the sound of the drum and fife to fight the French, and help to build up a glorious history for their country. Romilly played havoc with the criminal statutes; Howard and Neild with the gaols; the coarse pastimes of our fathers have passed away; and although much still remains to prevent our boasting of any superior refinement, we may look back, without shame or dread of comparison, on those "good old times" of our ancestors.

CHAPTER III.

The Forest.

"There are few things more full of delight and splendour than to travel during the heat of a refulgent summer in the green district of some ancient forest."—CONINGSBY.

WE will now consider this country as "Forest" in its technical sense. Over a large extent of the forest there were no trees!—hill and dale of heath-land and morass, for many miles together, formed some of its most beautiful portions. It was so with Wolmer, which, Gilbert White tells us, "had not a tree upon it, all moss and muir, heath and fern;" and here, on our Surrey borders, one might have rambled for miles without seeing more than a few clumps of Scotch fir, or a lone holly, or silver birch, with here and there a little pool on the waste called a deer "slade," at which the deer were accustomed to drink. Yet in no part of the world can we find woodland scenery more enjoyable than our own, as at Burnham or Swinley; that of the New World may be more grand, but its very grandeur is oppressive; in the dark pine-woods of the north reigns a silence so intense as to fill the mind with gloom. Mr. Drummond, in his recent travels in tropical Africa, tells of thousands of miles of vast thin forest, shadeless, trackless, voiceless; with trees like our own, "only seldom so large, except by the streams, and never so beautiful." Old English writers have differed in their appreciation of the woods as much as they did as to the note of the cuckoo. The Greeks had rather a pleasant idea of the forests, while to Dante, on the other hand, they are said to have been repulsive. He tells us of their horrors in the opening lines of his great poem; but I think the picture he gives of that celestial forest in the twenty-eighth canto of the "Purgatory" amply refutes this idea. For whole days he had rambled amid the pine-woods of Ravenna, as in a beautiful dream; the warbling of the birds reminds him of the gathering melody of the wind as it stirs

"From branch to branch
Along the piny forests on the shore."

Although the very word "wood" is from the Saxon "wode," wild, yet in England the green woods had no very dreadful associations in the minds of our earlier poets. Chaucer delighted in them; and Shakespeare loved them too. In his later life, when far away in his City haunts, their pleasant memories lingered in his mind in all their purity; the forests were to him the home of the wild and the free. "The Two Gentlemen of Verona" and "The Midsummer Night's Dream" alike attest the deep love of the woods which the dingled recesses and open moorlands of the Forest of Arden had impressed on his youthful imagination. In his delightful play of "As You Like It" he sends his gentle maidens unguarded to the forest for meditation; but they are the creatures of poetic fancy, but little in accord with the stern facts of reality. Spenser has a greater dread of the forest, and Milton better still realises its dangers when he makes his benighted maiden in "Comus" fear to encounter the rude wassailers of the woods:—

> "The nodding horror of whose shady brows
> Threats the forlorn and wandering passenger."

The time had not come when they could sing:—

> "One impulse from a vernal wood
> Will teach you more of man,
> Of moral evil and of good,
> Than all the sages can."

But whatever diversity there may be in our æsthetic view of the woods, there can be no doubt of the horror in which they were regarded when under the ægis of the terrible Forest Laws. This feeling, indeed, is forcibly expressed by the universal sympathy extended to the brave outlaws who set them at defiance; Robin Hood and his merry men of Sherwood were not less the popular favourites of mediæval times than, in the fancies of our childhood, they have been ever since; we rejoiced in the thought that—

> "The fish of the lake, and the deer of the vale,
> Were less free to Lord Dacre than Allen-a-dale."

It is not well for the laws when he who steals the king's deer is the fascinating hero of our nursery tales and the impersonation of all manly virtues.

Now, a "forest," as our old black-letter lawyers tell us, is "a territory bounded by unremovable marks or by prescription, in which wild beasts, and fowls of forest, chase, and warren, abide under the protection of the king;" and, as Manwood describes it, "is the highest franchise of princely pleasure." A "chase," like the forest, was an open ground; the park, an enclosed one; but there was one terrible distinction between the superior and inferior franchises, as the poor miserable natives knew to their cost. In the inferior ones offences were punishable by the common law of the land; but in the forest, by its arbitrary forest laws and in its own courts. The next great distinction was in the animals protected in them; the wolf and the boar were safe in the forest from all but privileged arrows, but beyond its bounds, even in park or chase, they might be destroyed.

So late as the eighteenth century Brigadier-General Howe endeavoured to stock the Holt Forest with the wild hog, but the country rose upon them and destroyed them.* James I. turned out half-a-dozen wild pigs at Egham.

For the origin of Windsor Forest we look back in vain through centuries of a changeless existence into a past almost too remote for history.

As the forest of Nature, this wide tract of waste and woodland was primæval; a remnant of it still survives at Swinley, to show how beautiful its primitive condition was.

When, two thousand years ago, on its dry hillocks the earliest Celtic tribes pastured their flocks, and guarded them by their watch-fires at night against destruction by the wolves, they called it the great "Frith," the deer forest, and so it was designated more than fifteen hundred years afterwards in the manorial records of a neighbouring parish.

The Romans opened up the great Frith by their western road, but it was not until the Saxons and Scandinavians established themselves on its borders that this wilderness of Nature assumes its new character as the "forest" of man, and then its history properly commences. Canute, we know, made laws for his hunting; and Kings Edward and Harold had their open "walds" and "deer-falds," or enclosed parks. It was of these that Canute spoke when he declared:—"I will that every man be worthy of his hunting in wood and field, on his own estate; and let every man abstain from my hunting: look, wherever I will that it should be freed under full penalty."† The perfect realisation of this idea, however, with all its privileges and penalties, was reserved for Norman times. But meanwhile the monastic orders were beginning to bring their civilising influence to bear on some of the recesses of our woods. Edmund, the Saxon king, by his

---

* See White's Selborne. † Canute, Sæc. 80. See Stubbs' Charters.

Charter in 942, granted the meadow of Hockesham (probably Cookham) to the Monastery of Abingdon, and the Abbot did homage afterwards to the king at the Manorial Court at Bray. Harold in 1047 gave them the Hundred of Hornmere, and these gifts were followed by several others. Edward the Confessor built a royal palace in the adjoining parish of Old Windsor, and emparked it, before the Castle was erected on its present site.

Mr. Freeman, in his "Norman Conquest," states that Windsor Castle was begun where it now stands in the Conqueror's time, or even earlier; but others, referring to his description of Oxford and Windsor as "Motœ" and not "turris," as London was, think he was mistaken in this, and point out that the ancient palace at Windsor, in which the death of Earl Godwin and the quarrel of Harold and Fostig are said to have occurred, was at Old Windsor, on a moated spot there, since known as the Moat Farm; * but the truth, I think, is, that although the present site may have been an earlier earthwork, which the Conqueror adopted and strengthened, possibly by the erection of a keep or tower, there was no palatial residence on that spot till Henry I.'s time, nor even a fortress of any magnitude.†

The Castle stands in the parish of Clewer, and formed part of the possessions of Harold. The Conqueror gave it to Ralph, the son of Seifride, minus, however, half a hide; and Domesday records that Harold had 5 hides, and Ralph 4½, "et Castellum de Windesores est in dimidio hida;" the Conqueror thus retaining in his own hands the chalk-hill or Mota, and the ancient earthwork that crowned it. We have no mention, however, of any important fortress there at that time, and not a vestige of masonry remains to suggest it. What has been discovered is rather of the time of Henry I. than William I.

In 1110, we are told, "In this year King Henry I., at Pentecost, for the first time held his court in the *New* Windsor." And in the earlier part of his reign, about 1104, he dates a writ from *Old* Windsor; but after 1110, when the Castle was more finished, in the grant of lands at Bagshot to the monks of Abingdon, he uses the words, "apud Castellum Uuildesores." ‡

It was not until the time of Henry III. that Windsor became of much extent. In 26th of that sovereign £7 were paid "to our good men of Windsor in recompense for the damage they sustained in taking down their houses, for a fosse which we ordered to be made round our Castle of Windsor."§ And again, 4 Edward I., £200 paid "to Geoffrey de Pycheford, Constable of Windsor, to expedite our works there."

It has been suggested that the name of Windsor, or, as it was anciently called, Windlesores or sora, was derived from the rill or

---

* See Tighe and Davis' History of Windsor, and Loftie's Windsor Portfolio, 1885.

† No argument can be drawn from the use of the word "Mota," or "Motœ," for that, of course, has no reference to a moat of water; but is derived from *mota* or the French *motte*, a mound or hillock, often artificial. It was the central stronghold of our early English or Saxon earthworks, the pallisaded mound supplanted in Norman times by the stone keep. It naturally became the place of open air assembly of the tribe for political or judicial purposes, and thus became known as the Moot-hill, from the Anglo-Saxon "Mōt," a place of meeting; the assembly taking its name from the hill. At Downton in Wiltshire we have a most interesting example of this. In later days when a building for convenience was used it became known as the Moot-hall. See Muratori's Italian Antiquities.

‡ See Chronicles of Abingdon. § See Exch. Issue Roll. 26. Hen. 3

streamlet called Vindeles, or Windles, which gave name to Windlesham: Windlesora, the place beyond or adjoining to Windles, in the forest.

In 1065, two days after Christmas (it could not have been on 5th January 1066, as some authorities state, for the king was dead then), Edward made a grant of Windsor and Stane, and all their surroundings, to the Abbey of Westminster.

The poor king's hunting days were over. At the end of 1065 he was in his dotage, and fast sinking into the grave; he seemed only anxious to witness the consecration of his new Abbey before he died. He did so at Christmas of that year; and not forgetting its endowment—

> "Splendid manors, *lands* and *woods*
> He gives, confirms (the gift) at once;
> And according to his grant, he intends
> For his Monastery royal freedom." *

He died a few days afterwards. The monks of Westminster held their possessions but a short time, for in the following year a dark cloud hung over the land, but only metaphorically, for it would seem to have been a glorious summer; in fact, a comet year!

Halley's comet, which had shone so brightly eleven years before the Christian era, blazed with ominous splendour in the clear sky night after night for two or three weeks. The people were terrified, and soon came the crowning disaster of Senlac; and if you look into that wonderful piece of historical evidence in the Museum at Caen you will see the comet; and a very cogent fact it appears in proof of the genuineness of that valuable work.

William, after burning Southwark, marched by this forest to cross the Thames at Wallingford. He saw what a fine hunting-ground it was, and so as soon as he had established his conquest he remembered and coveted it. He quickly persuaded the Abbot of Westminster that some fertile land in Essex would suit his purpose much better than this, and accordingly in his Charter he says: "With the consent and by the favour of the Reverend Abbot of Westminster, I have agreed for Windlesora, for the royal use; that place appearing proper and convenient, on account of its nearness to the river and the forest, and its suitableness for hunting, and many other royal conveniences; in exchange for which I have given Wokendune and Feringes."

And what thought the Saxons?

---

* La Estoire de Seint Ædward le Roy. Printed in 1858 under the editorship of Mr. Luard. See Hook's Lives of the Archbishops of Canterbury.

"He made large forests for deer," says the Saxon Chronicle, "and enacted laws therein, so that whoever killed a hart, or a hind, should be blinded. As he forbade killing the deer, so also the boars; and he loved the tall stags as though he were their father. He also appointed, concerning the hares, that they should go free."

WILLIAM THE CONQUEROR'S OAK, WINDSOR FOREST

A new phase, and a terrible one, now set in for our forest history. Its scattered people were driven off, and the wild boar's lair and the roaming grounds of the deer were to be sacred precincts, not to be molested — girt about by a system of newly-created forest laws, thoroughly characteristic of the tyranny of our Norman rulers. Severe enactments were so blended and interwoven with the figments of law and custom as to form a vast network of feudal despotism; special courts were created, one above another, to administer this terrible code; the Court of Attachments for small trespasses sat every forty days; the Swainmotes, for more important ones, were held three times in the year; and for the highest offences the Supreme Court of Justice-seat was convoked once in three years. Over this latter the Chief-Justice in Eyre, aided by the first judges of the realm, himself presided.

The keepership of the Forest of Windsor was always committed to one of the chief royal favourites, and with it was generally associated the office of head-steward of the household and governor of the Castle. Under him various persons, of more or less importance, were appointed under-keepers; and with the rangers, the foresters, and verderers, regarders, agisters, and beaters, formed an organisation equal to the governing of a province. It had its own prison, too, "the coal-house" at the Castle.

Not only the courts and officers, but the very laws were especially created for it, to supersede the common law of the land. No subject could possess a forest, but the king only; within the afforested district all private rights were subservient to those of the Crown; a private owner could not cut his own woods without the royal licence, nor build a shed upon the waste; that would be an encroachment on the royal demesne, and called a "purpresture."

He could not grub up for cultivation a rood of his lands; that was one of the greatest offences. It was bad enough to cut the trees, but to tear them up by the roots, or, in the old language, to "assart" the lands, so that the wood could not grow up again from the stubs, was a far more heinous offence. In earlier times no wayfarer was allowed to traverse the forest without paying toll, called "chiminage," or "chearinage," but to this there were certain exceptions. One going to attend the king might, as of right, shoot a stag or two on the way, both going and coming; and others of proper rank might do the same by courtesy, first blowing a horn to show the keepers it was not done by stealth.

This right of toll for chiminage continued to be exercised in all its vexatiousness even so late as the sixteenth century. There is an instance of a petition to the king from the Corporation of Windsor which runs:—

"Hitt is so that now of late Wm Staverton keep^r of Cranborne & Henry Staverton his brother by his comāndem^t within the said Borough upon Midsom^r day last passyd in their open fayer attached and distreyned Thomas Engely, Wm Smith of Egham, Ric. Bishop of Dorney, Wm Smith servant of Henry Stiward of Houndeslow, comyng wth a pakke at his bakke and divs other, for chymynage contrary to their old usage and custome and to the grants and confirmations to them granted by the king our sovereign lord" (undated, but in sixteenth century).

The Conqueror and his sons, as is well known, caused their laws to be held, by nobles and people alike, in the most intense hatred; and whenever they were able to wrest from the Crown any guarantee of their liberties, these detested laws were the first to be restrained. When Rufus required his barons' support, he promised them the liberty of hunting in their own lands, which they had by Canute's laws long before. Henry I. was very jealous of his forest rights, but the people gained ground at times, even against his rule; and at his death, before the succession became settled, they revenged themselves by a wholesale slaughter of the beasts of the chase; hardly a stag was left. By and bye Henry II. came, and showed himself as tyrannical as his grandfather. "He was a mighty hunter," as Peter of Blois says of him, "having always in his hands bows and arrows, swords and hunting-spears, save when he is busy in council or over his books." Richard and John were no better; when the latter was made, in this very neighbourhood, to grant his famous Magna Charta, the provisions of the more ancient Charta de Foresta were also confirmed.*

But when Henry III. became king, he was only a boy nine years of age, and then came an opportunity, not to be lost, for restraining the outrageous encroachments of his predecessors. They had virtually afforested nearly the whole counties of Berks and Surrey; and what can more eloquently prove the justice of the people's complaints than the language of the statute then enacted, 9 Hen. III.:—

"We will that all our Forests, which King Henry our Grandfather afforested, shall be viewed by good and lawful men, and if he have made forest of any other wood, more than of his own demesne, whereby the owner of the wood hath hurt, forthwith it shall be disafforested." †

In pursuance of this declaration, wrung from the young King, direction was given for the better defining the forest boundaries, and a careful perambulation was made here for that purpose, showing

---

* The magnitude of the evil, too, is apparent when we consider that Henry II. possessed sixty-eight forests, sixteen chases, and 781 parks in different parts of England.
† It may here be noticed that the Great Charter of John was in fact superseded by this of 9 Hen. III., which has ever since been recognised as the Great Charter. See Dr. Vaughan's "Revolutions of English History."

exactly the Surrey bounds;* and in the face of which it is difficult to see how so much contention about it could afterwards have arisen.

The line in our immediate neighbourhood was:—"De Coleford usq. ad Bredeford; De Bredeford p regia st^{a}tam usq Bagset; De Bagset usq. Bromhal; De Bromhal usq. Sorbeshult; De Sorbeshult usq. Harpesford; De Harpesford usq. la Cnappe; De la Cnappe usq. Lodereslak; De Loder usq. ad Tamis.†" This clearly proves that no part of Surrey was in the forest.

Of this forest of Windsor the earliest keeper or warden of whom we hear was the Conqueror's Minister, Walter Fitz Other. This Walter was the son of Otho, a Florentine, who settled in Normandy, and came to England in the reign of Edward the Confessor. Domesday describes him as castellan of Windsor, and warden of the forests in Berkshire, and of thirty-two lordships in various counties, all which "Dominus Otherus," his father, "held in the time of Edward the Confessor." ‡

The same post was confirmed by the Empress Maud, at Oxford, to his son, William Fitzwalter, and he then assumed the name of De Windsor. Their principal seat was afterwards at Stanwell. Hubert Walter, Lord Chancellor and Archbishop of Canterbury, was keeper under King John in 1201; and Engelard de Cygony, one of that king's foreign mercenaries, was afterwards appointed. But he was hated, and when the people of Windsor complained of him, Hugh de Neville was sent down to investigate and redress their grievances.

Edward I. on his accession conferred the keepership on Geoffrey de Picheford, with these manors, "and the seven hundreds appurtenant thereto." And after him came Richard de la Bataille, until 30 Ed. I., when John of London (who was Queen Marguerite's chronicler) in 1302 had a grant of them for three years, at the same rent as Geoffrey de Picheford paid. § But during part of this reign, the great outlaw, Adam Gurdon, held office in Windsor Forest.

We next find the Gascon influence, which Edward II.'s connection with Guienne induced, strongly asserting itself in the forest.

Oliver de Bordeaux, enriched with the keepership of Guildford Castle and enclosures from the waste at Ascot and Winkfield, was in 1319 promoted to the high office of chief forester of Windsor. Another of his Guienne countrymen followed him, and we are then introduced to a family which rose to still greater influence here. Their

---

* See Rot. Lit. Claus., vol. ii. p. 57.
† See also Register of Chertsey Abbey.
‡ See Chronicles of Abingdon.
§ Rot. Orig., 21 Ed. I.

names survive to this day in the Brocas Lands and Brocas Elms at Eton, where, as also at Windsor, Clewer, and Bray, they possessed large estates. John de Brocas, the founder of the family, was chief forester of Windsor in 1334, and surveyor to the works of the castle in 1351. The family migrating from Bray, became seated at Beaurepair and Roche Court, in Hampshire.

These De Brocases were descended, as we are told in their history, which Professor Burrows has so pleasantly written, from an ancient Gascon family, of which one Arnald de Brocas was "valettus" in the household of Edward II. (groom of the chamber, we should call him, as Norreys and Weston afterwards were to Henry VIII.). This worthy fell in the field of Bannockburn; whereupon the King brought his young sons to England, and provided for them. John, the eldest, was made "Custos equorum regis," or, as he was sometimes called, "Gardein de nos grands chevaux," of which there was a great stud then kept at Windsor; but after the battle of Poitiers, retrenchment was thought of, and he, and Edmund Rose, and the famous William de Wykeham, were appointed Commissioners to realise all they could of the royal property here; they sold several houses in the forest, and were now busy selling off part of the stud in the park. The central figure in this family was Sir Bernard Brocas, the third son of the royal studgroom. He was a great friend of William de Wykeham, and also of the Black Prince, whose friend he was alike in love and war. He achieved much distinction at Poitiers, and when he came home expected great rewards; and here we have the most amusing incident of his career. The brightest star of the court just then (a little too blazing a star perhaps) was the beautiful widow of Thomas Lord Holland, who had been known as "the Fair Maid of Kent," and many of the young gallants, just fresh from the wars, were soon at her feet; among them was Monseigneur de Brocas: to make sure of his prize, he asked his young master to be his friend, and plead for him, "to get the said lady and Countess for him to wife." She was, we remember, the Prince's cousin.

A French chronicle, of which Professor Burrows gives us a translation, affords a quaint history of the wooing. "The office which the young Prince had undertaken was," the chronicler tells us, very agreeable to him; and he went often for his own pleasure to see her for her beauty and gracious presence; "but the lady said she would never marry, and then she wept," for, says the chronicle, "she was very subtle and clever." She soon laid the ambassador himself in chains, the Prince fell violently in love with her, of course, and to soothe her tears, "took to kissing her," and then, at that most inopportune moment, opened his commission for "one of the most perfect knights in England;" but the weeping beauty declared "she had already given herself away to the most perfect knight in all the world," and so was the Black Prince caught by the fair lady. They were married on 10th of October 1361.

Sir Bernard, however, consoled himself for his loss by marrying the great heiress of the De Roches family. He died in 1395, and was sumptuously buried in Westminster Abbey.*

Here we get an instance of the way in which our great forest families, such as the Trussels, the Lovels, De Brocases, De Foxles,

---

* See Patent Rolls, Ed. II. and Ed. III., and Rot. Orig. Ed. II., and the "Brocas Family" by Professor Burrows.

and Norreys, intermarrying one with another, became recruited and established. It clearly shows, too, how at times in our history, and especially in this Edwardian period, we are indebted to the fresh blood of foreign races for the maintenance of our own. These Gascon knights, there can be no doubt, brought over, with their Southern vivacity and talent, a certain culture and refinement that tended to enrich and polish our national life.

Edward III. was very fond of the forest; he built the more important portions of the castle, and he also erected a hunting-lodge at Easthampstead, where, until the beginning of the present century, the old moated mansion remained.

His grandson, Richard II., stayed there to enjoy the hunting in August 1381, and Sir Simon de Burley, K.G., was chief forester in 1377. To him, if not to his great namesake, the Lord President Burleigh, we probably owe the name of the well-known spot called Burley Bushes.

From the earliest times portions of the forest were made over to private owners, subject to the paramount hunting rights of the Crown. Henry III. granted to Peter de Rupibus, Bishop of Winchester, "all felons' goods, &c., in the manors of Wargrave, Waltham St. Lawrence, Warfilde and Billingbere, and that no Sheriff nor Bailiff of the King should have any power or entrance into the same, except only in case of attachments."

Edward I., in like manner, granted to John de Pontifera or Pontois free chase or free warren in all those his lands, both within and without the forest (only he was not to take nests), also freedom from expeditation of dogs, from the power of the king's foresters, and from "chearinage," and also power to assart his lands.

It is remarkable to how large an extent the religious houses were interested in the forest. The first sixteen great tenants in Berkshire mentioned in Domesday were ecclesiastical or monastic bodies. Athelhelm, the Saxon ally of the Conqueror, was made Abbot of Abingdon, and endowed with no fewer than thirty manors in Berkshire. But besides Abingdon, Winchester, Waltham, Chertsey, Stratford, Westminster, Reading, and our own Bromhall had possessions and privileges in it.

The Abbot of Chertsey, as we have seen, was an important guardian of the peace of that wild corner of the county. In the manor of Heywood, in the forest, which belonged in ancient times to the Abbey of Waltham, Holy Cross, Essex, the Abbot had the privilege of "cutting his woods without licence, putting his hogs therein, hunting the hare, ox, and wild cat;" and these privileges appear from a petition of Sir Edmund Sawyer in February 1633, to have been enjoyed since the time of Edward III., with a liberty called "Staffherd," which is to keep sheep on the waste, in consideration whereof the lords have been at the charge of a dinner for the officers at the Swainmote court every third year, and also pay yearly a "metchome" to the keeper of the bailiwick. The Attorney-General, at the great court of justice-seat at Bagshot, objected to the privileges, but required the dinner to be continued. Sir Edmund also claimed the right to enclose his woods with as great a ditch and high hedges as he pleased, but the court at once disallowed this, as injurious to the king's hunting, and fined him for the trespass.

Sir Sampson Darrell was, at the same justice-seat, fined £5 for erecting a windmill on his own ground within the forest, for the reason that it "frightened the deer, and drew company, to the disquiet of the game."

But all this great Abbot's privileges were not of so innocent a character, for in ancient times he exercised the terrible right of "Furcas," and he hung up now and then his refractory tenants; for in the report of Edward I.'s commissioners (circa 1272) we read, "That the Abbot of Waltham, that now is, erected a gallows in Heywood in this year, and hung there, at a certain time, a woman, against the law of our lord the king, and without warrant."

The tithe of venison taken in the forest was especially granted by Henry I. to the Abbey of Abingdon, and in 1158 Henry II. confirmed this tithe to the monks.

Some of the old tenures of the forest estates were very curious. For instance, in 1634 Sir Edward Zouch died seised of the office of forester of Windlesam Walk and Frimley Walk, in the purlieus of the forest, and of an annual fee of forty shillings, holden of the king by the service of "calling the deer to the king's window at the castle of Windsor on the first morning after his Majesty shall come thither, after the feast of St. James next following the decease of any preceding lord of this manor, and of winding a horn-call on the day of the king's coronation, yearly in the walks, in lieu of wards, and all other services." *

As to the extent of the forest, it comprised at one time parts of Buckinghamshire and Middlesex, nearly the whole of Surrey, and the eastern part of Berkshire, as far as Hungerford; while the Vale of

---

* See Manning and Bray, "Surrey: Woking."

Kennett was anciently deemed within its limits, but much of this was illegally added, and was disafforested by Henry III. in 1226.

For centuries afterwards, the country for many miles round the castle, and over which, from its lofty towers, so fine a prospect is to be had, formed part of this great hunting domain. Beyond the river, on the north and east, lay the manors of Upton and Burnham (so famous for its woodland scenery), Langley, Datchet, Farnham Royal, and Eton in Buckinghamshire. In Surrey the hundreds of Oking and Godley, including Chobham and Chertsey, and the lands almost up to the town of Guildford, were, according to Norden, within the radius of the forest; but although practically so treated, they were not legally forest, but merely chase in the crown, and so continued as late as 1673.*

Its original circumference was computed at 120 miles, although, according to Norden, in 1607, exclusive of the Buckinghamshire portion, it was only seventy-seven miles; year by year, however, some grant or secret encroachment lessened its area, till at the time of the enclosure, in 1813, its circuit had been reduced to fifty-six miles. One can well understand how the forest disappeared. William Trussel had his lands at Folyjohn, Winkfield, and Ascot, as on our borders at Bramshill Sir Thomas de Foxle obtained 2500 acres for a park.

A large tract close to us, called in an ancient map the Charterlands, comprising the Bailiwick of Fynes, came into possession of the Nevilles.

Potnol Park, near Virginia Water, must have been enclosed at an early date; it was held of the King by the nominal rent of a "red rose" annually. It took its name from the very ancient family of De Podenhale, formerly seated in these parts; one of whom, William Podenhale, citizen of London, in the time of Edward III., acquired certain lands in Coworth and Sunninghill.

But old as it was, it was not ancient in the legal sense, for as early as 1485, 1 Henry VII., there was a grant for life to Richard Pigot, one of the yeomen of the King's guard (for faithfull service doon unto us of tyme passed, aswele beyond the see as on this side), of the office of keeper of the park of Potnall, co. Surrey, within the precinct of the forest of Windsore; but there seems to have been an omission in the grant, and accordingly we find Pigot petitioning for its rectification, "for as moche as the said office was not auncient,† according

---

* See Prince Rupert's Book, Windsor Royal Library. Particulars collected by Sir Bulstrode Whitelocke; also Norden's Maps and Gomme's Maps of about 1663. Brit. Mus. MSS.
† See Materials for Hist. of Henry VII.

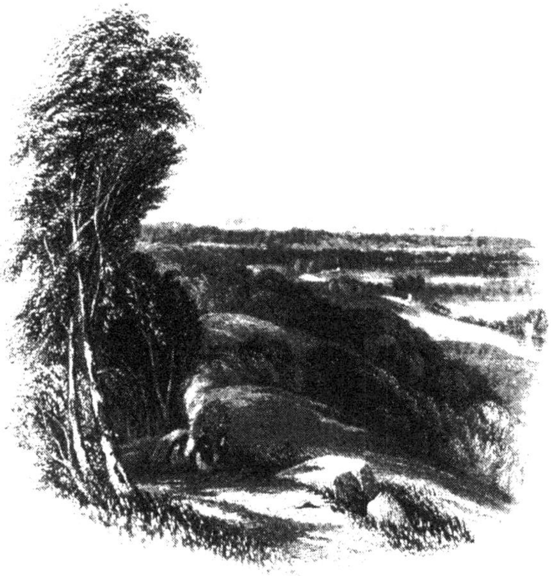

to the lymytaciouu of the statute made of Edward III. and Richard II., some time kings of England, therefore your besecher can no wages have allowed in your Escheker, beseeches your most noble and abundant grace to grant new letters patent, with express wages of iiii^d a day, as oone John Molle late had by the graunte of King Edward IV."

In 1528 Henry VIII. granted to Sir William Fitzwilliam "his park of Potnall, then not inclosed, but as waste, but which late was inclosed within the forest of Windsor, paying a Red rose to the Sheriff of Surrey." *

It would appear that the name Windsor Forest was applied to a wide district which had been more anciently an assemblage of forests; and in two inquisitions in the Tower Collection we get the names of some of the places within it; thus—"Altewode, Bechehulle, Halsham, Herne, Harpesford subtus parcum, Inewoode, Le Layenne, Le Loge, Le middle Loge, Le north Loge, Le Rowehull, Sandhurst, Le Symtherugge, Undermull, Wolvelegh, and the old park at Windsor."

On the west and north-west lay the forests of Swinley, Colynrugge, Ashrugge, Twichen, Blackmore, and Bray. Towards the north and east was Windsor. On the south the Surrey marshes and heaths added a wide stretch of country to the forest as its purlieus or chase; this included Bagshot, and was called the bailiwick of Surrey. These ultimately all became known as the great forest of Windsor. This extensive district had been from early Norman times divided into bailiwicks, of which there seem to have been three, Fynes, Finchampstead, and Battles, which last included Sunninghill. Fynes was also long known as Twychen, as from an inquisition held at Windsor in 12 Edward III. we find that "John Brocas was the forester in chief, J. de Fienes forester of the Bailiwick of Hyewychen, Henry Battaile forester of the Bailiwick of Ascot or Battles." †

These divisions were again parcelled into "walks," each one ruled over by a keeper or under-keeper, who exercised, within his particular jurisdiction, all the privileges of ownership. They were very great men indeed in their way; and although the official allowances were not large, a good house, with various perquisites, and sport at all times, made these posts enviable possessions. It was of these the poet writes—

> "I read you by your bugle-horn,
> And by your palfrey good,
> I read you for a ranger sworn
> To keep the king's green wood."

---

* Pat. 9 Hen. VIII., and see Rolls of Parliament, vol. vi. p. 374.
† See Exch. Rolls, vol. xv., Henry III. to James I.

But the keepers were always quarrelling among themselves, and, as Old Norden observes, there was "contention between every neighbour keeper for intruding one into another's walke, for not one of them truly knoweth his own bounds."

This was so from the earliest times. In Edward I.'s reign, Geoffrey de Picheford had a quarrel with the Bishop of Worcester, who had the manor of Wargrave, about trespass. So again when poor William Brun was caught hunting in the forest, he was pursued all the way to Reading, where the Abbot gave him sanctuary.* Geoffrey demanded the prisoner, but the Abbot refused to give him up, and the King sanctioned his act. Each of these little potentates—for as keepers of these walks they were little less—held his own court, and dispensed "justice" without practically much interference or control; the only safeguard at all was afforded by the Verderers, officers who ultimately became elected by the county to sit as judges in the forest courts.

During the York and Lancaster troubles the rulers of the forest were ever changing; as one faction or the other prevailed, so the favourites for the time were installed in power; and the Stavertons, the Noreyses, and the Nevilles were alternately in the ascendant.

Of Henry IV. we hear but little; but that he hunted here we know, for on one occasion, in April 1406, he was laid up at the manor-house in the Great Park from an accident to his leg.

Henry V. was too busy with his foreign wars to take his pleasure in the woods; and Henry VI. either too much engaged in his home ones, or too much indisposed to enjoy forest pursuits.

Edward IV., however, was much addicted to his hunting, as we learn from the opening verse of the old ballad of "The Tanner of Tamworth:" †—

"In summer, when leaves grow green,
And blossoms bedeck the tree,
King Edward would a hunting ride,
Some pastime for to see."

We find him often at Windsor indulging in the chase.

It was here, about 1472, that, having invited the Archbishop of York, the Earl of Warwick's brother, to hunt with him in our forest, he committed one of the basest acts of his false life. In the midst of their good sport and conviviality, the host invited himself "to hunt

---

* See Tighe and Davis, History of Windsor.
† Percy Reliques, vol. ii. p. 83.

and disport him" with his guest at his beautiful manor of the Moore; whereupon the Archbishop, right glad of this evidence of royal friendship and good-will, "went home to make purveyance thereof, and sent out of London, and divers other places, all his plate and other stuff that he had hid after Barnet field and Tewkesbury. The day before the King should have come to the said manor of Moore, which the said Archbishop had built right commodiously and pleasantly," the King sent for him to Windsor, where he was arrested, and all his carefully collected treasures were swept by this adroit piece of deception into the King's coffers.* All his vast estates were forfeited, and the King even broke up his "mitre, in which there were full many rich stones and precious, and made thereof a crown for himself."

The wars of the Roses left men but little time for the pursuit of pleasure; but we get one or two glimpses of our forest country in the days of Henry VII. that are interesting; for although he had enough to do to restore order and fill his treasury after those terrible dissensions, while

> "The King was in the counting house
> Counting out his money,"

his young sons were disporting themselves with their bows over these wooded heights of ours, or trying their hands at hawking for a heron over the swamps and pools in the Great Park and Swinley.

The elder of the two youths, Prince Arthur, we know was here about 1500, from the interesting letter noticed more fully in our account of the manor. And as so little is known of him, I may well repeat one of the last incidents of his short history. He was then about fourteen years of age, his brother Henry ten; the elder boy was too delicate to excel in athletic pursuits, but the younger was especially strong and robust, and was thenceforth much in our forest, enjoying perhaps the happiest, at least the most innocent, years of his life.

In 1501 Prince Arthur and his father made a journey through this country, of which we have a graphic account left us; and a very momentous journey it was.

The young Prince, roaming in such wild freedom between Sunninghill and Easthampstead, had been, at the interesting age of two years and seven months, the subject of a matrimonial engagement.† His scheming father and his Catholic Majesty King Ferdinand of Spain were the high contracting parties.

---

* Annals of the White Rose.   † See H. Dixon's Two Queens.

For the fulfilment of this arrangement the time had now come.

The King had set out on the 4th of November from his palace at Shene to meet the young Infanta of Spain, who having arrived at Plymouth, was now on her way to London; but the weather had been so wet and boisterous, and the roads so bad, that he could get no farther that day than Chertsey, where they rested for the night with the Abbot. The next morning, we are told, "the king's grace and all his company rose betimes to urge their coursers" over the barely passable roads towards Easthampstead, where they were to meet the Prince; and toiling up over the ridge from Chertsey might have been seen a muffled cavalcade of knights and men-at-arms, journeying by way of Windlesham to Bagshot and Easthampstead, and there beneath the royal pennon rode the King. He spent the evening with the Prince at Easthampstead, and on the following morning, the 6th, they journeyed to Dogmersfield, Hants,* a little village round the mansion-house of Oliver, the Bishop of Bath and Wells, where the Spanish cavalcade had arrived with its precious charge.

The illustrious Elvira Manuel, to whose care Katherine had been consigned, on hearing of the King's coming, sent to stop him, and to explain the solemn injunction which had been laid upon her not to allow the face of the Princess, as was the fashion of a true Moorish bride, to be gazed on, no, not even by the Prince himself, until he drew aside her veil in church.

It is difficult to imagine how such an astounding intimation would be received by a king of England in those rude times. However, they discussed the dilemma in the road: the Spanish grandees soon found out they were in England; for the Infanta and the Prince met that evening, and danced together.

For the next seven or eight years the younger boy was often in our forest; he certainly was on the 1st of August following his father's death, for on that day we know he was at the Lodge at Sunninghill, where, in the intervals of pleasure, he held a Council.†

Henry, passionately fond of the chase, drew round him here a few friends as ardent in it as himself. Chief among them was Sir William Fitzwilliam, with whom he had been much brought up; the coarse-natured Hercules, Suffolk, who afterwards married his sister Mary, was also much with him; Sir Henry Neville, Henry Norreys, and Richard Weston were great favourites; the last

---

* See Leland's Collectanea, vol. v. pp. 352-355, and Miss Strickland's Queens of England.
† See Brewer's Letters, vol. i. p. 54.

especially, whom he loaded with gifts, and in 1511 made keeper of his forest of Windsor, and soon afterwards knighted. It was he who in 1520 built that interesting mansion of Sutton Place near Guildford. In 1514 he secured for Fitzwilliam the next vacancy of the office of keeper of Bagshot Park, which he granted to him with the herbage and annual fees out of a messuage called "le Crown" in Bagshot; no doubt the inn there.* In 1518 he made a further grant to his friend "of a piece of waste land called Potnoll Parks," and in 1527 Fitzwilliam and his half-brother, Sir Anthony Brown, were made bailiffs of Bagshot.

Henry, in 1526, was in a restless state of mind; unpleasant thoughts were agitating him, for now, for the first time, doubts about his marriage were suspiciously stimulated by his passion for Anne Boleyn; and here, the victim at once of an uneasy conscience and dread of the sweating sickness, which his father had brought into England, and which now kept him continually moving from place to place, unable to take interest in state affairs, he came for the solace of his favourite sport.

At the end of July, Fitzwilliam, hunting with him somewhere, says, "I received a packet of letters addressed to the king, which I took to his Majesty immediately; but as he was going out to have a shot at a stag, he asked me to keep them till evening."† In April 1528 he was at Windsor with Anne Boleyn.

Sir Thomas Heneage writes to Wolsey, who was doing all the king's work, "Every afternoon when the weather is fair the king rides out hawking or walks in the park, not returning till late in the evening."‡ "To-night the king sent me down with a dish to Mistress Anne for her supper." "She wished she had some meat from you, as carps, shrimps, or others."

This was in the hawking season; later in the year he was at Easthampstead after the greater game, and "Hennege" writes again to Wolsey in the autumn, "The King's Highnes commendith hym heartely unto your Grace, and sends unto your Grace by thys berar the grettyst red dere that was kyllyd by His Grace or any of hys honters all thys yere. Yesterday his Highnes toke mervelous grett payn in hontying of the red dere from nine of the clock in the mornyng to seven of the cloke at nyght, and for all his payns taking he, nor all his servauntes coud kell no more but this oon."§

---

* See Cal. State Papers, 1518.
† Brewer, vol. iii. p. 253.
‡ Brewer, Hen. VIII., vol. iv. p. 1049.
§ State Papers, Dom.

He sent an invitation from the King for Wolsey to come to Easthampstead for "pastyme together for two or three days." A most critical time this in the great Cardinal's career, the dead calm before the eruption. His mind was ill at ease; the Legate was contriving how not to arrive from Rome; and Anne was doubtless at Easthampstead, so poisoning the King's ear as to make pastime with the deer a doubtful pleasure to the Cardinal.*

In August 1534 Fitzwilliam writes to Cromwell: "At my coming this night to the Great Park, my keepers of the forest met me, and put me in comfort that the king should have great sport. When you come to Charsay [Chertsey], Ocking or Guildford, bring your greyhounds with you, and I trust you shall have sport after your abetyd." [Cal. State Papers.]

Apropos of Sir William Fitzwilliam and Anne Boleyn, there is a slight incidental allusion to our forest worth preserving. On her appearing before the council, the Duke of Norfolk would not listen to her, and, as she said, handled her very cruelly. Fitzwilliam, although he had been very active against her, seemed the whole time to be absent in mind; Sir William Paulet alone treated her with courtesy.

She exclaimed against the unfairness of the proceedings, alleging, among other things, "that as to my Lord Treasurer [Sir William Fitzwilliam], he was all the time in the forest of Windsor." Now this has puzzled historians, for he was known to have been actually present; but Mr. Friedmann has pointed out the true meaning,† I have no doubt, of this speech. Anne, as we know, was very French in her education and style; her remark is simply an adaptation of a Parisian idiom,—"être dans la forêt de Fontainbleau,"—for being absent in mind.

The author, however, hardly seems to have known of Fitzwilliam's residence in, and love of the forest, which gave double point to the allusion.

Miss Strickland (in her Lives of the Queens) tells us that this was spoken of "my Lord Treasurer," and says he was her father; but

---

* It is amusing to see what in the eyes of a great Minister of that age the qualifications of a good Abbot were. In 1533, Sir W. Fitzwilliam writes to Cromwell: "I am informed of the death of the Abbot of Beaudeley (Beaulieu), Bishop of Bangor, who was in the king's displeasure for offences in these parts against the king's game. I chanced in communication with the king to mention one who was a virtuous man and a good husband, and had ever been good to his game, though the forest of Wolmer, and Windsor, and other places are about his house, and I thought he would make a good Abbot of Beaudeley; on his asking who he was, I replied the Abbot of Waverley." Dated Windsor, August 20. [See Cal. State Papers, Dom. 1511.]

† See Gairdner's Letters of Reign of Hen. VIII., 1536, and Friedmann's Anne Boleyn.

she is in error as to this, for Sir William Fitzwilliam was "my Lord Treasurer" of the household at that time, and to him the allusion is clearly made. I am the more desirous of correcting this, as it would otherwise involve the miserable sight of a father sitting in judgment on a child, and seeing her perish with thoughtless indifference. Her father, who was Earl of Wiltshire and Lord Privy Seal, did not sit on the trial, nor did Fitzwilliam,—this incident occurred at the committal of the Queen by the Council at Greenwich.*

We must now go on a few years, until the King, that once gay forester, was becoming corpulent and inactive.

What a picture we get of the morality of the age from the little evidences we come upon now and then. There is a piteous letter from Erasmus Forde complaining of the Dean of Kingston (Wolsey) having cut down a stately row of elms at his mansion of Norbiton Hall for use at Hampton Court. The Cardinal had but little respect for the rights and feelings of others when he levied blackmail on all around for the stately house he was raising at Hampton; but its mortar was hardly dry when a greater tyrant still came one fine day to see him at his "most wholesome manor." We can well imagine how fair the place looked in that beautiful bend of the river. The visitor was so well pleased, that Wolsey, to save his head, gave up his house; and the King was no sooner installed at Hampton than he required a forest more accessible even than Windsor.

To achieve this, he paid a visit to Lord Windsor at his manor of Stanwell, which had belonged to his family from before the Conquest.

He was handsomely entertained, and soon proposed an exchange. Lord Windsor pleaded in vain that it had been the home of his ancestors for several centuries; he hoped his Highness was not in earnest; but he was referred to the Attorney-General, who had already prepared a deed of exchange; and Bordesley Abbey, in Worcestershire, was substituted for the ancient inheritance of the Windsors![†]

Henry resolved to lay the whole country between Hampton and his palace of Nonsuch, near Epsom, into forest; but even he could not do this in the face of the statutes of his predecessors; he could afforest no man's estate against his will, and therefore he had to make private arrangements with the owners. These he managed in his own violent way, and finally by statute accomplished

---

* See Cal. State Papers, 1535 and 1536; Surrey Archæological Collections, vol. viii. p. 197; and Ellis' Original Letters, Letter 66.

† See Loftie's Hist. of London, and *Quarterly Review*, 1550.

his object, having laid waste and depopulated a vast tract of fertile land, and destroyed its churches and villages; on the Surrey side of the river alone nine manors were absorbed. He conferred on the district forest rights and privileges, and called it the Honor of Hampton Court, although it is doubtful whether, even by such means, it became legally a "forest."

In the following year he obtained "an Act for uniting of divers lordships and manors to the Castle of Windsor," and another "for the uniting of the manor of Nonsuch and divers other manors to the Honor of Hampton Court."

There can be little doubt that the Conqueror's mythical atrocities in the New Forest pale beside those of Henry in *his* new forest.*

While on this subject, I must refer to a curious error which the learned Sir William Blackstone made in his Commentaries, and Serjeant Stephen continued, and which has remained unnoticed through all the numerous editions of that celebrated work. They say "some of the royal forests still exist, and with some few exceptions, such as the New Forest in Hampshire, founded by the Conqueror, that of *Windsor by Henry VIII.*, and that of Richmond by Charles I., are of such remote antiquity, that no trace is said to be found in history of their first creation." †

Henry had nothing whatever to do with founding or afforesting Windsor; that was a forest several hundred years before his reign; in fact, it was never anything else. Coke in his Institutes, iv. p. 317, is a direct authority against Sir William's statement; and more remarkable still, in Domesday it is one of the few forests mentioned by name. Oliver Goldsmith's noisy parties overhead at 2 Brick Court may have disturbed the learned student.

Soon after Henry's death the Honor of Hampton Court was *dechased*, and the deer were removed to Windsor Forest: this word, *dechased*, confirms the view that it really never was a forest, but merely a chase.

About this time poor Surrey, a prisoner in the castle, sighing no longer for his fair Geraldine, mourned in sad reality the loss of his beloved forest, in which so many happy hours of his boyhood had been spent.

Of Edward VI. we have but little to say. In physique he was not made for a huntsman.

Mary was still less inclined to the pleasures of the chase, although

---

* See Wise, Hist. of New Forest.   † Stephen's Blackstone, vol. i. p. 668, 7th ed.

on the Tuesday after her marriage she was at Windsor, and a new or but little practised method of hunting was resorted to for the Court's entertainment; toils were raised in the forest four miles in length, and a great number of deer were slaughtered.* When she died the Great Park even had no keeper.

Her sister Elizabeth, however, under the guidance of her favourite, Sir Henry Neville, had many a day's sport in our woods. In 1602 she shot a "great and fat stag," as Dudley described it, with her own hand, and sent it to Archbishop Parker; but as the journey between Windsor and Lambeth then took so long, the venison was partly boiled to make it keep.

Little Court schemes were proposed to the Queen about this time. Lord Howard in 1592 wrote to her that some one had offered £40,000 for all the herbage and pannage and dead trees of all her forests. This he dissuaded her from, remarking that the line between the living and the dead trees might easily be mistaken, and showing this little proposal in its true light by adding that "her Majesty has a hundred and eighty parks, forests, and chases on this side Trent and beyond"

Elizabeth frequently visited this country to see her Latin secretary, Sir John Wolley, at Pirford, near Woking, who was Roger Ascham's successor, and to whom in 1590 she gave the manor of Thorpe, which had remained in the Crown since the suppression of the monasteries.

With James I. a new state of things arose. He had neither the power nor the tact of his predecessors, and acts of his were deemed tyrannical, although not half so outrageous as those which they had committed with impunity.

One of the first things he did, however, after he came to his new inheritance, was to acquire a knowledge of it; and he sought the help of his surveyor, John Norden, a very superior man, who soon produced the Survey to which I so often refer: it is still preserved, a most valuable historical document, for which the archæologist should ever be grateful. It was finished in 1607, and was a great performance for that age. The fee paid for it, I find, was £200.

It describes the various walks, and gives us the names of their keepers. Sir Henry Neville was the keeper of Swinley Walk, in which Swinley Pringles was a place for the red deer; Sir Richard Crosbie was at Easthampstead; Sir Charles Howard at Sandhurst and Bigshott Railes (the present Ravenswood); Sir Charles's underkeeper was one Hankin or Hanykin, which explains the older name of Ravenswood, "Hannican's Lodge." Sir

---

* See Miss Strickland's Queens of England, vol. iii.

Richard Weston was of Ashe, with Linchford ; Sir Francis Knoles of Bearwood Walk ; Sir Richard Lovelace of Cranborne Walk ; "Nafordton" of New Lodge, a home of the fallow deer ; Creswell of Egham ; Walters of Windlesham ; Twitcher of Brookewood ; Hobson of Purbright, and Taylor of Frimley.

The whole forest is set out, with its boundaries defined ; but on this two things are important to note : first, the qualified way in which the bailiwick of Fiennes is alluded to ; the ownership was evidently a matter of delicacy. Norden speaks of it as "Binfield Walk, verie spatious—Sir Henry Neville's by patent, as is sayde, called Fynes Bailiwicke." Secondly, the Survey indicates a large part of Surrey as in the forest ; and declared part of Byfleet to be in the forest, and part out.

James's son Henry, Prince of Wales, soon began to take an interest in the forest. The keepership of Folijohn Park had been bestowed on his gentleman usher, Walter Alexander, and after him on Sir Francis Wolley. About this time the king was employing Sir Cornelius Vermuyden to drain the Great Park, which we are told was full of morasses ; and thus were set to work "divers poor men," at a cost of £300. He was also just then at Bagshot taking great interest in his hunting expeditions ; and a spice of danger was not at all distasteful to him ; for in 1613 we find the Earl of Suffolk writing that "order has been taken with the keeper of Egham Walk for the king's six wild pigs, until they are fit to be turned out ;" and in September 1617 we find him at Bagshot for three nights after his return from the North ; and towards the end of the month we learn that he was there with the Prince "to the hunting of the wild boar."[*] His last visit was in 1624, of which he himself has given an amusing account in a letter he wrote on 1st September from Oaking to the Duke of Buckingham, then keeper of the forest. "Having chainged my purpose," he says, "in resolving to staye heere till Mondaye, so earnist I ame to kill more of Zouche's greate staigues, I summone thee to come heere to-morrowe, and lette Kate and Sue goe to Windsore and meete me on Mondaye after noone at Harrison's Heath hearde, with thaire bowis."[†] Those who say that James's pleasure was only "to shuffle after conies with a stick or bring down partridges with a hawk," and that "he had no nerve for going at the wilder game," have not given him his due.[‡]

---

[*] Nichol's Progresses, p. 492.
[†] Harl. MSS., cited in Nichol's Prog. of Jas. I., vol. iv. p. 1004 ; and Dr Goodman's Court of Jas. I., vol. ii. p. 382. [‡] Dixon's Royal Windsor.

SWINLEY FOREST BEECHES

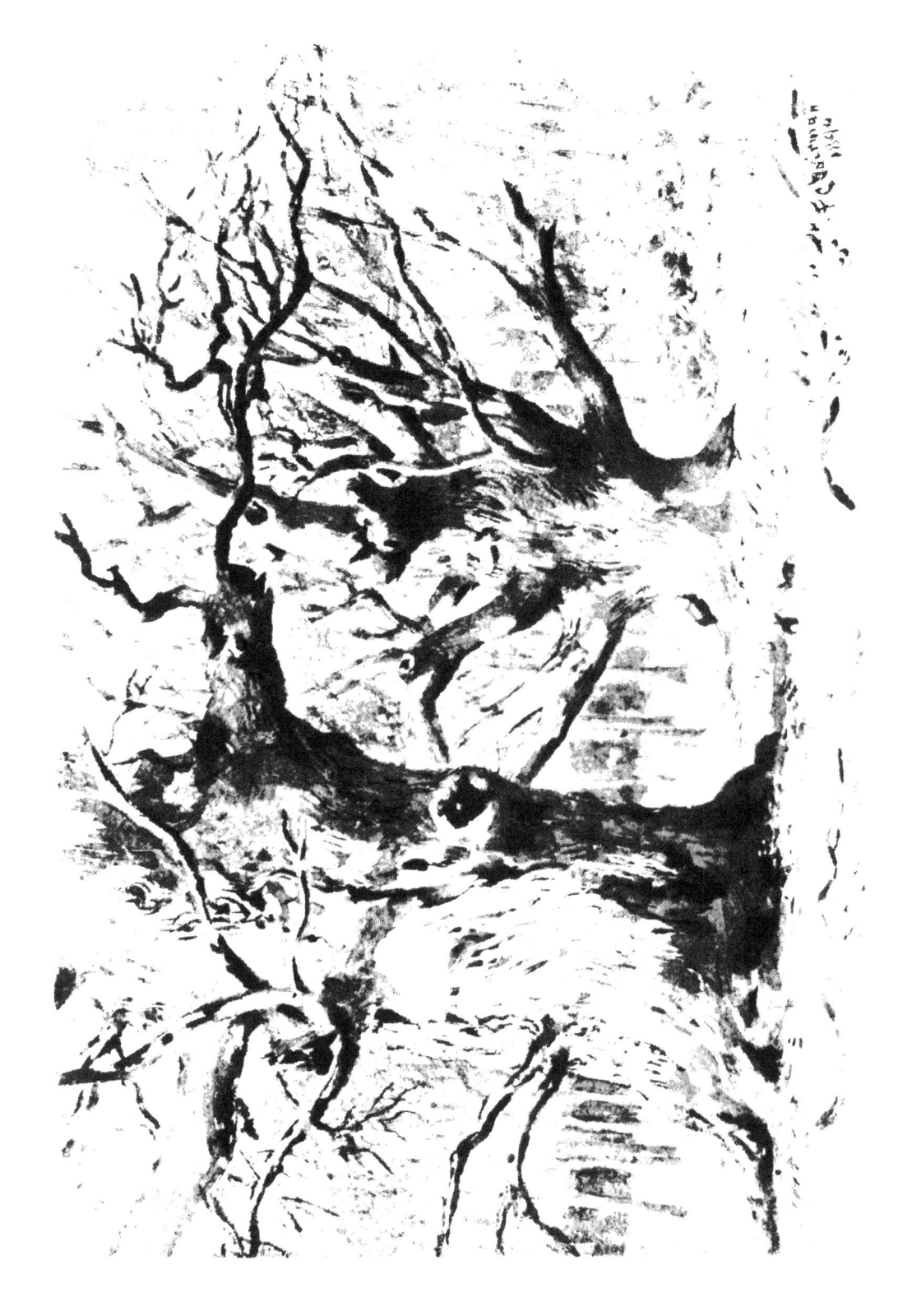

But James knew little of the temper of the people he had come amongst; he had closed the little park, and Cranbourn Chase, and not an hour of peace had his officers since enjoyed;* the gates were locked, "the squires and better sort made private keys, and entered like the gentlemen of highest quality; the locks were exchanged, and they broke the fences with as little scruple as the tramps."

Henry Rich, Lord Holland (the son of the profligate Lady Rich), had been appointed ranger, and was utterly incapable of appeasing the spirit of resistance and lawlessness which his own indiscretions had done much to arouse; he was incessantly worried, and little wonder that we hear, in 1635, "Lord Holland is gone to Tonbridge to drink the waters for fifteen days." It was he who through his wife, the heiress of Sir Walter Cope of Kensington, became possessed of the fine mansion since known as Holland House.

Charles I. followed his forest hunting, early in his reign, with much energy. His great subjects too sometimes craved permission to enjoy a run in the forest, for in 1629, the Marquis of Winchester writes to Secretary Dorchester,† "to move the king for warrants to hunt a brace of stags this summer with the Marquis's hounds in Windsor forest after the king has left the forest."

But affairs were assuming a terrible condition of chronic disorder. The King was exacting, while the dwellers in the forest were more and more restless and defiant. And now commenced an agitation of considerable importance on the part of the men of Surrey, who resolved to have long-standing doubts removed as to whether any portions of their county were within the forest, as shown by Norden.

In 1632 Noy, the King's Attorney-General (of shipmoney notoriety, and Carlyle's "invincible living heap of learned rubbish"), insisted that the western part of the county was within the forest;‡ and the Earl of Holland, as Chief Justice in Eyre south of the Trent, held a Court of Justice-seat at Bagshot in August of that year. He was assisted by Lord Richardson, the Chief Justice of the King's Bench, and Baron Denham of Egham, who were there to advise on the points of law that might arise, "so that the abuses, happening for due observance of the forest laws, might be reformed."

The Court sat also at Windsor, where Lord Chief Justice Finch was sent to assist. The old formalities were observed.§ Every forester

---

* Dixon's Royal Windsor.   † Cal. State Papers.   ‡ Brayley's Surrey.
§ See MSS. notes taken at the Court, in possession of Mr. H. G. Poulter of Bagshot.

when first called was bound on his knees to deliver up his horn to the Chief Justice in Eyre, and every woodward in like manner to present his hatchet, and they paid a fine of six shillings and eightpence before they were re-delivered to them. Sir Edmund Sawyer, and several other lords of forest manors, were presented for various offences, as also were some of the smaller people. Noy, full of forest-law learning, and ready with all the ancient precedents, secured a decision in the king's favour of course, in almost every case. This gave great offence, and alienated the affections of the people, as Lord Clarendon afterwards pointed out, so that when the help of our brave foresters was so sorely needed, they held back. But the Surrey men would not accept this as final; they knew their history too well to submit to these arbitrary pretensions.

No part of Surrey had been treated as royal forest, until the time of Henry II., who gradually reduced nearly the whole county into an afforested district. Richard I. was compelled to throw open again all eastward of the river Wey (except the royal park of Guildford and its manor), leaving the rest of the county, afterwards termed the "Bailiwick of Surrey," to be regarded as forest.

This arrangement lasted till King John's Great Charter restored the county to the state in which it stood before the time of Henry II., that is to say, free.

Queen Elizabeth was evidently very tender on the subject, for she granted to several of the parishes, in the Bailiwick of Bagshot, exemption from purveyance, and liberty to cut coppices, to induce them to preserve the deer. The gentry of the county were now becoming very outspoken, and in July 1640 the Grand Jury of Berks presented a petition against "the innumerable increase of deer, which if allowed to go on a few years more would leave neither food nor room for any other creature in the forest,"[*] and setting forth as their final grievance "the rigid enforcement of the forest laws."

The King's difficulties were increasing; and now was the opportunity for the Surrey folk to stand to their guns; the whole country was in a ferment. Edward Nicholas, in a letter to the king, dated 31 August 1641, writes — "There hath been some of yor Maj^{ties} deer killed in Windsor For^{est}, neer Egham, by ye inhabitants of that towne, and of ye parishes adjoining, who hunted in ye day-tyme by eighty or a hundred in a company:

---

[*] Harl. Colln. 1219. Brit. Mus. MSS.

Sr A^r Maynwaring hath been amongst them, and wth good words, and promises, hath made them forbeare for ye present;" but it was too late for "good words."*

In September 1641 the sheriffs were ordered to repress the riotous proceedings, that were so ominous at this time. Every village in the forest had some daring spirits to stir up their fellows to revolt; the Smiths of Sunninghill, Henry Bannister of Oakingham, Aminadab Harrison, and George Godfrey of Easthampstead, Richard Hayworth, and Richard Gason of Warfield, were notorious leaders.

Harrison and one Patey were imprisoned; yet the riots continued, and in the following May, Lord Holland held an important meeting with the Sheriff of the county, and the officers of the forest at Egham.

Parliament had now taken the matter up seriously, and an Act was passed declaring, that no forests should be adjudged to extend further than they were known to extend in the 20th James I., and by virtue of a further provision of this statute, a writ was issued in September 1641 for an inquiry into the bounds of the forest of Windsor within the Bailiwick of Surrey, to see how they stood then: it terminated, in 1642, in the recognition of the freedom of the whole county from the forest laws, except the royal park at Guildford, a decision equally "of course," at so critical a time!†

After the restoration of Charles II., the question was again opened, but the attempt was defeated by the landowners; and the Bailiwick of Surrey, ever afterwards, was deemed as "purlieu"‡ only of the forest: so that when any of the king's deer strayed thither, they might be destroyed by the owners of woods or fields in which they were found, but by no other persons; and in order to secure the preservation of such deer as might escape from the forest into the "purlieu," an officer called a ranger was appointed by Letters Patent, "to retrace and drive them back again."

---

* Evelyn's Diary.

† Charles I. in his speech to the two Houses on taking away the Star Chamber, July 1641, says:—"I have bounded the forests not according to my right, but according to late customes."—The Works of Charles I., a rare book.

‡ The "Purlieu" was an adjunct of the forest which became "disafforested" when against the owners of the soil the forest laws ceased to have effect, they still prevailed against the rest of the world. The derivation is said to be simply from the old words "pur luy," the land remaining forest to all the world except the owner. See Nath. Boothe, steward of Forest Court, Windsor, 1719. Brit. Mus.

The lands beyond the forest bounds from which the straggling deer could thus be reclaimed, were called the "percursus" of the forest; and into these no keeper could enter with bow or arrow, or kill the game there.

The King now wanted money, and for other good reasons thought it well to realise what he could, and Bagshot, Sunninghill, and Folijohn Parks, were severally disposed of.

The storm-clouds were gathering. The King raised his standard at Nottingham, and the keepers fled, and left his glorious forest in the hands of the mob. The vagrants and poachers, now unrestrained, committed all kinds of depredations on it. Once roused, it was impossible to keep them in check.

The Parliament had great trouble with them. What had been going on ever since James had failed in his indictment against Richbell and Buckeridge, two substantial burghers of Windsor, had now become chronic. Banister, Harrison, and Godfrey were as active as ever, snaring the King's deer, of which the Parliament were now "taking charge," until they could persuade Charles to part with his evil counsellors (how delicate the early language of revolution often is). They had been warned, but were not deterred; so in April 1643 Earl Holland had to inform the House of Lords, "that he had lately received letters advertising him that the people in Berkshire adjoining the forest of Windsor, have a resolution speedily to come in a tumultuous manner, and pull down the pales of the park at Windsor."

The House took measures to secure the preservation of the peace, but the populace were too excited to be readily awed. Their local rulers, the keepers, had fled, and unknown men supplied their places. The odious Pembroke became Governor of the Castle, and one Oldsworth was ranger.

Old Denham the judge, one of those who gave judgment for Hampden, in the celebrated ship-money case, died at his seat at Egham, and his son the poet, on coming into possession of the estate, was made Sheriff of Surrey, and was quietly indulging in his poetical effusions, so successfully as to cause Waller to exclaim, that "Denham had broken out, like the Irish rebellion, when no one expected it;" but being a staunch Royalist, the Parliament confiscated his estate, and gave it, as the most cruel of sarcasms, to the Puritan poet George Withers! He, however, was retaliated on in his turn, it is said, when Sir John Denham observed, "Please your Majesty, do not hang George Withers, that it may not be said I am the worst poet alive."

Waller, like his friend Neville, took a leaf out of the book of the

Vicar of Bray, and adroitly enough wrote a panegyric on the Protector, and afterwards another on the King.

Before we quit this period, I cannot but recall that memorable journey through the forest, the most melancholy, and, when its ulterior results are regarded, probably the most momentous, that it ever witnessed;—that of Charles I. on his way from the Isle of Wight to Windsor.

It was on a wet, gloomy day, the 21st December 1648, that over the hill by the Golden Farmer, a large body of cavalry came down into the village of Bagshot :* "Le Crown" and the other inns were soon full of the dark troopers of Major-General Harrison, who had in charge the deposed monarch. A proud, dejected prisoner, he was entertained by his faithful adherents, Lord and Lady Newburgh, tenants of his royal lodge there. They were staunch Catholics, and the lady a woman of high spirit; her first husband, Lord Aubigny, was killed at Edgehill. A rescue of the King had been resolved on. He was to have lamed his horse, or complain of his paces, and this he did all the way from Farnham to Bagshot; the fastest horse in the neighbourhood was in their stables as a mount for the intended fugitive; but the array of troops filled all hearts but the lady's with dismay. The King could not be induced to make the attempt, and unfortunately that best horse had been disabled by a kick overnight: the fates were against the project; and surrounded as the King was by troopers, with their pistols "ready spanned," it was hopeless.

Over these roads, accompanied for some miles by Lord and Lady Newburgh, the cavalcade made its way into Windsor, where Charles—a prisoner in his own palace—kept, as Heath expresses it, his last sorrowful Christmas.

This journey to Bagshot is very particularly set out in an old newspaper called "The Moderate Intelligencer," published at that time.†

"FARNHAM, *December 20th*.

"His Majesty came yesterday from Hurst Castle on horseback, dined at a ladies, and afterwards to Winchester to bed.‡ This day he reposed at Alton, and came to this place to bed; to-morrow he will betimes

---

* See Clarendon's Hist. of Rebellion, vol. iv. p. 525.
† At Guildhall Library.
‡ The Lives from the Clarendon Gallery, vol. iii., says, "He slept that night (29th Nov.) at Letley Abbey, a country-seat of Lord Hertford's near Southampton." This date is wrong, and it was doubtless Netley Abbey.

at Windsor Castle, to the Governor of which, Colonel Harrison (who performed this business, being assisted with about two thousand horse), will deliver up his charge. The king, who is not to be spoken to or visited, is indifferent chearful." "21st. This night the king came to Windsor." The town was full of Cavaliers, who had flocked in on the King's arrival, some of whom drinking the King's health too loudly, were set upon by the soldiers. Three were killed, and many others secured: thereupon came out a sensational account, dated from Windsor, Sunday, 24th December 1648. "Terrible and bloudy newes from Windsor since the bringing in of the king's majesty, by the army, and a dangerous fight on Saturday last, between the Parliament's forces and the Royalists, who, by a strange design and unheard-of stratagem, would have rescued the king from the power of the army."

This is confirmatory of the story of the proposed rescue. It was in this journey, while at Winchester, that the King cured the innkeeper by his blessing; at least Dr. John Nichols, the warden of the College, vouched for that fact.

But as to the poor forest, that was having a very hard time of it; and if inanimate Nature ever does weep, as the poets tell us— the forest of Windsor must have shed bitter tears at the downfall of royalty. It was now everybody's game: of deer it might be restocked—but of trees it could not be so quickly. And although the King had laid low some of the best oaks for his navy, the Commonwealth laid to still more lustily for theirs: the powder-mills and arms-factories at Hounslow made incessant demands on it; every hearth in the neighbourhood blazed with royal logs. Humphrey Broughton, yeoman of Hurst (our neighbour of Ascot), was a great offender; he and Captain Aldrich had been helping themselves too liberally, and had to answer for it to the Council;—Broughton was brought up in December 1650, and was bound over in £500 to appear when required—and good behaviour.

As soon as the war broke out, Colonel Venn had been placed in command of the Castle:* his garrison not receiving their pay with regularity, helped themselves to the timber and all else they could lay hands on, and burnt up the park pales; the soldiers of General Cromwell were regarded at the time as terrible poachers.

Of the sport of the forest, that "diversion of princes," no more shall scenes so frivolous offend the virtue of the nation, or the dignity of the Commonwealth: the hateful laws of course; the abused

---

* See Petition of Alex. Thayne at the Restoration.

privileges; the very beasts of chase, would all now be swept away!

No! The feudal claims and rights were suppressed, but the sports of the forest, attacked and beset though they were, still survived;—the Cavaliers were frightened away, and so were most of the deer, but the huntsman's horn still resounded through the forest glades; the royal guardians were all dismissed, but Puritan magnates reigned in their stead.

After 1648 the great Roundhead notability, Sir Bulstrode Whitelock, figured as Constable of the Castle and Custodian of the Forest; nor did any of his courtly predecessors support authority with more ostentation or display. He was quite the great man of the neighbourhood, and when he went into Windsor the church bells rang out, just as they had been accustomed to for the King; scarcely a consistent homage to the sovereignty of the people.*

This Sir Bulstrode Whitelock was Lord Keeper for the Commonwealth, "a man," as Hume says, "of great abilities and power, and a man of honour, who loved his country, although in every change of government he always adhered to the ruling power," but it was a mercy, when we think what some of his colleagues were, that there were a few calm, enlightened men to guide the state in its confusion, and we must forgive him for talking of "one Milton, a blind man, who was employed in translating a treaty with Sweden into Latin," when we remember that when the Parliamentary generals had sold King Charles's pictures, the most precious collection in the world, it was this Sir Bulstrode, who, at the instigation of his friend Selden, stepped in to save the library and medals; but for him, they would have been sold by auction, to pay the arrears of some regiments of cavalry quartered near London. Sir Bulstrode came of an ancient forest family, whose ancestral property was near Wokingham, and although he sided with the Parliament, he had but little sympathy with the narrow-minded, canting element of the party; in earlier life he had been the author of a very lively musical air known as Whitelock's Coranto; and had kept, at Fawley Court, a pack of hounds, the pride of the county. He fell back with especial relish to his rubber of whist, and his forest sports, as soon as he dared to do so.

His early life had been embittered by an incident, that we may search in vain, through even the pages of fiction, for one more terrible, and as it involves also another family to which I have had occasion to allude, I will tell the sad story. Humphrey May, Groom of the Chamber to Charles I., rose to a high position at Court, was knighted, and became a member of the Privy Council. His descendants Hugh, Adrian, and Baptist, all held offices under the King after the Restoration. Sir Humphrey had a sister, and between the young royalist maiden and the rising lawyer, Bulstrode Whitelock, an attachment sprang up; the gentleman's democratic inclinations had hardly become developed then, or, as it was with Dorothy Osborne and her Puritan lover in later days, love triumphed over political differences. The day was named, the wedding party assembled, but when they expected the bride to appear, they were all startled by dreadful shrieks from her chamber. There she lay in a terrible fit. The case was not then understood, and after a time the marriage was permitted. It was but a delusive hope, soon fit after fit followed, and the poor creature

---

* See Memories of Bulstrode Whitelock, by R. H. Whitelock.

was committed to the hands of a keeper, and died some years after. He subsequently married a daughter of Lord Willoughby of Parham.

No royal sport was ever more enjoyed than that which some of these Puritan gentry had under Sir Bulstrode's keepership, which lasted in fact as long as the Commonwealth. On 22nd August 1649, Whitelock writes, "I sent my keepers into Windsor forest to harbour a stag, to be hunted to-morrow morning, but I persuaded Colonel Ludlow, that it would be hard to show him any sport, the best stags being all destroyed; but he was very earnest to have some sport, and I thought not fit to deny him, and on the 23rd accordingly, my keepers did harbour a stag. Colonel Ludlow, Mr. Oldesworth (member for Salisbury), Mr. Thomas (member for Oakhampton), and other gentlemen, met me at daybreak. It was a young stag, but very lusty and in good case. The first ring that the stag had led the gallants was above twenty miles."

No wonder that the deer were scarce, for they had been assailed by poachers, civil and military; every inhabitant of the forest made free with them. On one occasion, as we have seen, a hundred were slaughtered. When the Great Park was surveyed by the Commonwealth in 1649, it was reported that "in the said park there is noe deare." In 1652 a coolness was beginning to arise between Whitelock and Cromwell, and the former frequently retired to the Manor Lodge, Virginia Water, to enjoy his hunting, and brood over the state of the nation.

Great havoc was still made with the timber. In 1652 Lord Commissioner Whitelock had more than he could do to stop the depredation, and Mr. Neville was associated with him to look after it. The forest was one of the principal sources for our shipbuilding, and in 1649 I find an order of the Council to "deliver timber to Paul and Everard Ernions, strangers, for the repairs of the mills for making sword blades at Hounslow heath."

The wharves on the river were overcrowded with timber, and the state of things well realised that after-thought of the poet—

> "Thy trees, fair Windsor, now shall leave their woods,
> And half thy forests rush into my floods."

Not only were the deer all gone, but the forest lodges, as well as the forest, were all going to wreck; and we have a report from Colonel Christopher Whichcote and Thomas Reading in 1653, complaining of great trespasses "since the forest laws were suspended," and "that the seven Lodges are a great burden, and claim as much wood for their firing as when the forests were furnished with deer." They found themselves powerless to stop all the mischief that was going on, and so they request "that William Hyde, an active, knowing gentleman, that lives near the forest," might act with them. They reported that Cranbourne Lodge was much out of repair, New Lodge much decayed; worse and worse, for "Bearwood Lodge, house and barns, are ready to fall." They speak of a Milton's Lodge, belonging to Cramborne, as a poor house held by John Bennett, "and of Swinley Rails Walk, in possession of Henry Neville, Esq., by commission of the Committee of the Revenue, as being "house, barn, and rails very much decayed."

Evelyn drove through the country in the summer of 1654. He "saw my Lord Craven's house at Causam [Caversham], now in ruins, his goodly woods felled by the rebels."

The Commonwealth at last had come to an end—it never really took root in English soil; the whole country was in ecstasies of delight to welcome back a king; the Windsor bells ceased their peals of honour to Sir Bulstrode, who in 1660 resigned his office into the hands of Lord Mordaunt, the new warden, to whom he wrote, that the post was "a place of very great antiquity, honour, power, and pleasure, but of very little profit." *

Charles II., although not much given at first to hunting, so far interested himself in the forest as to set about the re-stocking it with deer soon after his restoration. Trumball, of Easthampstead, had entered into a contract for supplying the park there, and the forest, with deer, but was, it seems, unable to perform his contract; for in November 1661 there was an order releasing him from it, and a warrant for payment of £1000 on account, to Sir William St. Ravy, for expenses of transporting red and fallow deer, from Germany and elsewhere, to replenish Windsor and Sherwood forests.†

In March 1662 Earl Holland pretended a right to the granting of the offices of Constable of the Castle and Keeper of the Forest, but so flagrant a claim could not be admitted; the House of Lords declared the right to be in the Crown.

During the summer of 1665, a pleasant excitement arose in the neighbourhood, by the supposed discovery of coal here; London was

---

* See Bulstrode Whitelock's Collections, Windsor Castle.
† The king was restored to all his estates, notwithstanding any sales thereof, by order of the House of Lords, in July 1660.

to have a supply at its doors; and Windsor Forest was to supersede the coal-fields of Newcastle.

Edward Hyde, Lord Cornbury, like his name-sake, "the active knowing gentleman" of the Parliamentary Committee, was alive to his opportunities, and in July obtained a licence of monopoly to himself, Sir George Cateret,* Sir Thomas Draper, and six others, to dig for coal, paying a royalty to the crown of sixpence a chaldron. But it was all a failure, the black treasure never turned up; and so our beautiful country remains to us still, unsullied by that golden harvest! "No woods were allowed to be felled this year on account of the destruction in the late rebellion."† The king was now beginning to take more interest in forest sports, and was very anxious to get the Surrey gentlemen to help in the preservation of the game, and in March 1664 he wrote them a coaxing letter, to preserve the deer and heath-poults, which had always been kept there.

In this reign was abolished one of the most important and obnoxious prerogatives of the Crown, that of "purveyance," an ancient privilege, which I must not dismiss without a few words, although in the same way that our Church through its very poverty had some exemptions, so our parish on account of its barrenness was relieved from this burden.

Purveyance, it will be remembered, was the right of purchasing necessaries for the King's household, at a fair price, in preference to every other competitor, and until altered by statute, without the consent of the owner; carriages and horses might be impressed for the King's journey, and lodgings must be provided for him and his attendants; his harbinger was an important officer, the herald of his coming, and oftentimes a very unwelcomed one. But when we remember the state of the roads in those days, and that the King could not travel without a small army of attendants, who would certainly have starved but for some such provision, this prerogative seems simply a necessity. What, however, was in theory just, was in practice a standing grievance of the people, not so much from the nature of the right as from its abuse.

In the adjoining parish of Winkfield, a curious practice prevailed to lessen the intolerable inconvenience of the system; the inhabitants there made a list of all those liable to this burden, to work out a voluntary rate per acre to meet it, and thus, "doing his Majesty a service in an improved way," as they expressed it; and the reasons given, so well show the evils of the ordinary plan, that they are worth recording.

"1. To provide sufficient teams for his Majesty's service in removes.

"2. Whereas in many cases, where good teams have been kept, there are none, whereby the burden lay very heavy upon poor men that kept weak teams.

"3. At the coupling together the horses of divers men, an unequal team was made, many times, six horses of so many men; much discord, and contention, very long before they set forth; many words against the Constable, concerning *Indifferency* (partiality is meant), and so in fine the service delayed."

---

* See Docket Book at Rolls, 1665. † Cal. State Papers.

From all this, and the vexations of purveyance, Sunninghill seems to have been exempt, the damage done by the deer being burden enough.

In 1633 the inhabitants of the forest, having carried 1200 loads of timber from Alsenholt (Alice Holt), Hants, to Harnhaw, Surrey, last year, with a great deal of difficulty, the greatest part of the country through which it is to pass being within the forest of Windsor, and freed from carriage by charter, "pray relief from the other 1200 loads required."

In March, the Justices of Surrey, being eased by the council of a third of the 1200 loads, decided that the foresters could not claim exemption as against the state for service and defence of the kingdom, and that the county must carry the remaining 800 loads. What that meant in those days of bad roads, may be gathered from a remark of Gilpin's, who says, some of the great oaks, that used to be felled for the navy at Chatham, sometime occupied two or three years for the journey [out of Sussex], a score of oxen was often required to draw them; and the wain used for the purpose was expressively called "a tug." *

Charles I., it would seem, was not above the pursuit of the smaller game, and spent a bright autumn day now and then in the woods round Sunninghill squirrel-hunting, a pastime exciting at least, if not dignified. One Thomas Symonds, page of the presence to Queen Ann, (James I.'s widow), presented a petition in 1660, for the keepership of the Great Park, as granted to him by the late king, "who used to come to his lodge when squirrel hunting." †

After the Restoration, on the King resuming possession of the Great Parks, the rangership of it and of the forest was given in reversion, after the death of Nicholas, to Lord Mordaunt, Prince Rupert, the Duke of Norfolk, and the Earl of Portland in succession.‡ When Queen Ann came to the throne she gave the rangership of the Great Park to Sir Edward Seymour, with a promise of the reversion to her beloved Sarah Duchess of Marlborough, who eventually obtained possession of it in 1709. In 1716 Lord Cobham was appointed, and in 1746 it was given to his Royal Highness William Augustus, Duke of Cumberland, George II.'s son; from him, in 1765, it passed to his nephew, Frederick, Duke of Cumberland, who died in 1791, when it reverted to his Majesty. But the keepership of the forest seems in 1766 to have been conferred on Edward Augustus, Duke of York, and in 1767 on William Henry, Duke of Gloucester.

---

* See Turner's Dom. Arch., vol. i. p. 185.

† Hunting the squirrel on Christmas day was an old Suffolk custom, within the memory of persons still living.

‡ James II. was a mighty hunter of the "greate staigues" as his grandfather called them, and rode furiously. Burnet tells us that when Prince George of Denmark complained that he was growing fat, "Walk with me," said Charles, "and hunt with my brother, and you will not long be distressed with growing fat."

CHAPTER IV.

Traditions of the Forest.

ALTHOUGH our forest has never had any great wizard of the south, to clothe its wild glades with the interest of romance, or repeople its old houses, as Scott did those of his beloved border-land, yet it is not altogether devoid of interesting incidents, and it has associations which not even the most prosaic enlightenment will ever efface.

Between Truth and Romance, however, the line of demarcation is often but a thread. They are both fair maidens forsooth, so that we are placed in as great a dilemma to choose between the two, as our young Berkshire friend was in the garden of Cupid, where we are told, in true old Berkshire dialect,*—

> "T'other young may-den looked shy at me,
>   And vrom her seat she ris'n,
> Zays she, Let thee and I go our own way,
>   And we'll let she go shis'n." *

So while "she goes shis'n," let us ramble with Romance for awhile into the forest. It is true that such rude foresters as the Miltons and the Smiths, "rooted squatters," whose savageness no poetry can redeem, are but miserable representatives of those worthies of fact or fiction, Robin Hood and his "merry men" of Sherwood.

Mabel Lynwood, whom Mr. Harrison Ainsworth has made as "sunshine in a shady place" in our forest, I may soon dispose of. She would certainly have made an admirable foil to the dark eyes of Mistress Ann, so mischievous to Wolsey's fortunes, but she is but a myth, a mere vision of modern fiction. Of the ballad of King James and the Pedlar, the locality is uncertain, and I will not repeat the many-times-told joke of King Henry and the Abbot of Reading.

Gay, and his innocent flirtation with his beautiful Molly of Woking-

---

* Scourings of the White Horse. T. Hughes.

ham, supply us with only an ordinary picture of eighteenth century life. I will do no more than allude to the ancient legend of the Bleeding Well of Finchampstead, or to that old English metrical romance of Guy of Warwick, which perhaps, dating only from the thirteenth century, is considered to be of Saxon origin, for although the hero, Sir Guy, is said to have dwelt at Wallingford on our borders, and the slaying of the huge wild boar of Windsor Forest is mentioned as one of his especial exploits, we can hardly lay claim to this as a local production. Nor must we reckon among our legends, as history might be offended, that memorable instance of trial by battle that occurred in 1163, on an island in the Thames, when Henry de Essex was proclaimed traitor, and, vanquished by Robert de Montford, was left for dead on the field, to be rescued by the monks of Reading.

We cannot tell of any stray arrow that slew a king in our woods, although William III. was intended to have been similarly disposed of in the Great Park, we are informed; but that was indeed a sorrowful bolt that killed the keeper at Bramshill, and robbed of all their joy the remaining years of poor old Archbishop Abbot. But of all our legends none is so well known as that of Herne the Hunter, a weird creation of the great poet's mind, an uncanny spirit possibly of Scandinavian origin, that has haunted many another wood, ere Shakespeare enchained him within the Forest of Windsor, or rather let him wander within its bounds on parole; and there, in the imagination of some of us, he may have been wandering ever since; but,

"Beautiful fictions of our fathers,"

why need we meddle with them at all? Pilgrims have come from the world's end to visit Herne's Oak, and have almost looked down upon the grass to see the magic circle of his elfish sprites; hundreds have gazed on the venerable tree, whose bare stem for a long time was shown as the identical oak; and what mattered it to them if, at last, as some wicked wits have asserted, it turned out to be a beech!

King George the Third was very angry when they told him he had allowed it to be cut down. It seems that it was dead, and with others was inadvertently marked for destruction, and felled in 1796. It was a pollard tree in the Little Park, near Queen Elizabeth's Walk, in the classic fields of Frogmore. Paul Sandby had made a drawing of it, as also had Mr. Ralph West, a son of the painter; a copy of this last was made by Mr. Delamotte, in 1800, and engraved in Knight's Shakespeare. Acorns were taken from it as late as 1783.

Mr. Jesse, however, is quite confident that he saw in its decay, still standing, that venerable tree which, Shakespeare tells us, Herne the Hunter, according "as the old tale goes,"

> "Doth all the winter time, at still midnight,
> Walk round about,"

and he gives us a sketch of it; but this evidently must have been some other tree, so that its identity is doubtful.

Now, did Shakespeare know much of Windsor or its neighbourhood? For all that "The Merry Wives of Windsor" shows, his knowledge might easily have been picked up during a brief visit to the locality, and a supper with mine host of "The Garter." In the original sketch of this play, Falstaff was to appear as "Horne" the hunter, in the shape of a stag with great horns on his head—an apparition with which women, since Horne the hunter died, frightened their little children. This story of Horne's death is mentioned then as one of comparatively recent occurrence, and, curiously enough, we are able to trace foundation for it. In a MS. of the time of Henry VIII. in the British Museum, we find "Rycharde Horne, yeoman, among the names of the hunters whiche he examyned and have confessed" for hunting in his Majesty's forests; and on one of the trees, as the legend goes, he hung himself. But the play, which Queen Elizabeth required for her delectation within a fortnight, was a great improvement on the original, and more marked by local colouring.* Datchet, the Castle ditch, the pit hard by Herne's Oak, and the Oak itself, are there for the first time mentioned. Horne becomes "Herne," for some reason, probably to avoid offence to relatives of the deceased keeper. The vision was made of more remote origin, for he says "there is an old tale goes."

No trace or record whatever is known of the existence of such a person as "Herne," at any time "keeper here in Windsor Forest," nor was the tree so christened in the original edition—there Mrs. Page has to describe it as an oak, no particular one. Where did Shakespeare get the substituted name?

Just before the appearance of "The Merry Wives of Windsor" Norden's Maps of the Parks and Forest were published, and must have been well known to Shakespeare. With one of these before him, when he came down to Windsor to complete his knowledge of the locality, he might have seen marked in that very part of the forest, near Frogmore, which was the scene of Falstaff's adventure, a wood called "Herne's wood." Was this the origin of the name? It had in

---

* See Tighe and Davis' Hist. of Windsor.

truth, I think, no reference to any human being. Close by was shown the Heronry—yet it is quite possible that it was this Herne's or Heron's wood that stood sponsor to the tree that Shakespeare immortalised.

I will now notice a ballad, in Norman French, dating from about the time of King John, reciting how the hero of the story, Fulke Fitzwarine, and his younger brothers, were brought up with the children of the King (Henry II.), and how one day, when Fulke was at chess with Prince John, the latter was so enraged at losing, that he broke the chess-board over his young friend's head, who repaid him so well that he fled to complain to the King. John's character was well known, and he only got another beating for his pains. Fulke went abroad; and when he came back, John was on the throne. Fitzwarine, in disguise as a charcoal-burner, sought him in Windsor Forest, drew him into an ambush, and made him vow to forgive and restore him to his forfeited possessions; the king, however, fell into his power again, in the New Forest, before a public pardon was granted and his estates restored. This ballad was at first, before the end of the thirteenth century, in English verse, but a prose rendering of it only has been preserved.*

The chronicles of the period confirm the main circumstances of the story. I may also speak of the exploits of Adam Gurdon or Gordon, a famous outlaw of the time of Henry III., who was considered the strongest man of his age, and ravaged the counties of Berks, Hants, and Bucks at the head of his daring bands. It is stated that the Prince Edward made him prisoner in Alton Wood, Buckinghamshire, after engaging him in single combat; but such was his valour that the King pardoned him and took him into his service. This incident, however, occurred at Alton in Hampshire, not Buckinghamshire, for the prince in his magnanimity introduced the great rebel that very evening to the Queen, who was lying at Guildford. Adam's home was Temple Manor at Selborne, of which place he and his wife Constantia were benefactors. There he ended his days in peace, after having served the King for many years as keeper of the forest of Wolmer as well as Windsor for a time.

We must not forget, among the legendary stories of the forest, that which gave rise to the mulct of "White-hart Silver," imposed by Henry III. as a penalty for the destruction of a favourite white hart, by Thomas de la Linde. Camden, and other grave writers after him, vouch

---

* See Tighe and Davis' Hist. of Windsor.

the reality of this incident, but they place the scene of it in Whitehart forest. A local authority, Mr. Waterson, fixes it in our neighbouring forest of Blackmore; but it does not seem clear whether it was imposed, as he asserts, on the four or five and twenty tenements mentioned by him in that locality, or on any wider area.

But by far the most interesting romance which we possess is also one of the earliest—the metrical Ballad of "The King and the Shepherd," a gem in its way. Whether founded on fact or not, it is impossible now to say; nor is that very material: it was probably in the nature of a political skit at a grievance of the age.

It is supposed to have been written in the reign of Edward III. or very soon afterwards, by whom is not known; but whoever may have been the author, it affords us a rare picture of forest life and manners, and shows a shrewd insight to human nature, and especially rustic nature, which the writer possessed. The manuscript is in the University Library at Cambridge; but was published by Mr. Hartshorne in his "Ancient Metrical Tales."

The poem opens with a scene, in which the King, wandering along the river side one fine May morning hawking, becomes separated from his courtiers, and meets a shepherd; a characteristic greeting ensues; for the poet tells us

> "The shepherde lovyd his hatte so well,
> He did hit of never a dele [He did not take it off in the least]
> But seid 'Sir gudday.'"

He soon, however, becomes friendly and pours out his miseries:—

> "I am so pyled with the Kyng,
> That I must flee fro my wonyng,
> And therefore wooe is me.
> I hadde cattell, now have I non;
> They take my bestis and don them slone,
> And payon but a stick of tre.
> Thei take my hennes and my geese
> And my schepe with all the fleese
> And ladde them forth away."

He suffered many other wrongs and indignities at the hands of the King's men. The King asked his companion's name. "Adam, the Shepherd," said he; "and men call me," said the King, "Joly Robin," and assured Adam that the King "wot it not;" but the shepherd insisted that he owed him by the stick of hazel, (the usual method of scoring the reckoning), as he could show £4, "odd two shillings;" and with worldly wisdom promised Joly Robin seven shillings of the amount for himself if he would get it for him; and then Jolly Robin said

> "I was borne
> The t'other Edward here beforne
> Fful well he louyd me,"

and that he had some interest at court, and had a son with the queen; and that if he came on the morrow he should be paid: they become excellent friends. Adam tells of his wonderful skill with his sling, no wild fowl that flies that he cannot hit, and ends in asking Jolly Robin to dinner.

> "The shepherde's house full merry stood
> Under a forest fair and good."

They saw so much game about, that Jolly Robin said he would have some of it, "evening or morning," but Adam advised him not.

> "Let sech wordes be
> Sum man myst here the;
> The were bettur be still;
> Wode has erys, felde has siȝt,*
> Were the Forstur here now right
> They wordis shuld like the ille †
> He has with hym yong men thre
> Thei be archers of this contré,
> The King to serve at wille
> To kepe the dere both day and nyȝt,
> And for there luf ‡ a loge is diȝt
> Full hye upon an hill."

Not unlikely to have been the ancient forest lodge on St. Leonard's hill near where the scene is laid. However, arrived at the cottage, there is soon set before the guest

> "Brede of whete bultid § small
> ii penny ale he brou't withall
> He broȝt a heron with a poplere
> Curlews bocurs both in fere,
> The mandlart and hurmech,
> And a wylde Swan was bake,
> Sich fowle can my slyng take."

Then as they warmed to their work, a jovial game ensued, which consisted of alternate draughts of the twopenny ale; but we must let the shepherd himself explain it.

---

* "Wood has ears, field has sight."　　† "You would repent of."
‡ "Luf"—love.　　§ "Sifted small."

" When thou seest the cuppe anon,
But thou sei 'passelodion'
Thou drynks not this day
Sely Adam shall sitt the hende *
And answer with 'berafrynde'
Lene upon my ley
Passilodion that is this
Who so drynks furst I wys
Wesseyle the mare dele.
Berafryne also I wene
Hit is to make the cup clene
And fylle hit full wele."

" When the cuppe was come anon
The King seid 'Passylodion'
When he the cuppe hade;
Hit was a game of great solas,
Hit comford all that ever there was
Thirof theri were noght sade."

" The scheperde ete till that he swatte,
And then non erst he drew his hatt
Into the benke ende,
And when he feld the drynk was gode,
He winkid and strokyd up his hode,
And seid 'Berafrynde.'
He was qwyte as any swan
He was a wel begeton man,
And comyn of holy kynde,
He would not ete his cromys drie,
He lovyd nothynge but it were trie,
Nether for ne hende."

The rustic game was played with great zest, the cup made Adam wax very confidential, and Jolly Robin drew him out the more successfully. He said that to be fed on such dainties in a town would "have cost dear; there is no meat I love so much as buck or doe." Good fare is produced, three conies "all baken well in a pasty." Adam is the more complimented on his skill with the sling; but were he as perfect with the use of the bow what could he not have?

" Then seid the scheperde 'no thing soo,
I con a game worth thei twoo,
To wynne me a bridde,
Ther is no hert ne bucke so wode
That I ne get without blode,
And I of hym have nede.

---

* " Sitt the hende"—sit near thee.

> I have a slyng for the nones
> That is made for great stonys,
> Ther with I con me fede;
> What dere I take under the side,
> Be thou siker he shall abide
> Til I hym home will lede."

To the cup again; and the shepherd, as he warms to the king, wishes before he leaves to show him

> "A litull chaumber that is myne,
> That was made for me,"

and leads him to a secret place dug far under the earth, out of sight, and "clergially wrought," and in it they found plenty of venison and wine. Then

> "The Kyng rode softly on his way,
> Adam followyd, and wayted his pray;
> Conyngus—saw he thre—
> 'Joly Robin, chese thou which thou wytt,
> Hym that rennys or him that sitt,
> And I shall gif him the,
> He that setts and will not lepe,
> Hitt is the best of alle the hepe,
> Forsoth so thynkith me.'
> The scheperde hit hym with a stone,
> And breke in two his breste bone,
> Thus sone ded was he.
> The Kynge seid 'Thou art to slow,
> Take hym also that rennyth now,
> And thou con thy crafte.'
> 'Be God,' said Adam, 'here is a stone,
> It shall be his bane anon—
> Thus soon his life was rafte
> What fowle that sitts or flye,
> Whether it were ferre or nye,'
> Sone with hym it lafte.
> 'Sir,' he seid, 'forsoth I trowe,
> This is behette any bowe
> For alle the fedurt schafte.'"

So far as it goes, for the ballad was never entirely finished, the end of it is, that Adam is made to promise a visit to the court on the morrow, to find out Jolly Robin, and get his money, and receive a return of his hospitality. He goes; and the game of "passilodion" and "berafrinde" is repeated: Jolly Robin discovers his rank; and all ends in an orthodox fashion.

Now, how full of sly wit, and shrewdness, this simple tale is, and of morality too; not even Nicholas Nickleby could have accomplished more good. It was levelled at the extortions of the King's bailiffs and their servants, and let us hope successfully.

Whoever wrote it must have known the forest intimately, and the ways and very language and manners of the rudest foresters.

We are apt, in this democratic age, to lament the neglect of the respectful salutation of touching, or raising the hat; here we get a wholesome hit of the poet that shows us it was not invariably observed, even in the fourteenth century. "Sir, gudday," was all that was to be had of the shepherd.

With one as wary as a wild stag, how natural the caution—"wode has ears; field has sight." There are dwellers in the forest now, with all Adam's cunning of hand, although not so practised, and with all his sly discretion; no beast of the field, from the weasel upwards, but they can capture, nor wild bird they cannot take, "an they will;" they may probably be able neither to write nor read, but can fell a tree with wonderfully few strokes, and have rare skill in all their rustic crafts.

But as to the translation, I would venture to suggest, that the word "and," in some places, should be rendered "an," as a better reading: but my principal criticism must be on Mr. Hartshorn's rendering of the word "qwyte" as white; it seems to me to spoil the passage altogether; "white as any swan," I cannot but think is meaningless here, and peculiarly inapplicable to a sunburnt shepherd, carousing at such a feast: now the Anglo-Norman word, "qwyte," or "quyte" is an adjective, meaning, among other things, quiet, and surely in this sense it is used here. It would then give life and character to the whole passage; the writer wished to show that our friend of the forest was not quarrelsome or noisy in his cups; and he could hardly have paid him a higher compliment or selected a better image whereby to convey his meaning. The swan is the most silent of birds, and was even called the mute swan.

But who was the author? Might it not have been written by Chaucer; and, for obvious reasons, not published till after his death? None knew our forest better than he, for he lived some years at Windsor; none could better supply the worldly wisdom and sly sarcasm of this little poem. And the style is his, as well as the very expressions in many instances. In answer to Adam's inquiry as to who the bystanders at the court were, it says

> "The Erle of Lancastur is t'on
> And the Earl of Waryn Sir John."

And just before 1347 there was a John Plantagenet, a descendant of William de Warrenne, Earl of Surrey. The date would not be inconsistent with such a theory.

CROMWELL MEETING MR. WINWOOD

CHAPTER V.

The Forest Hunting.

OUR forest hunting has had many fashions, most of them of Norman origin, as are also many of our hunting terms; the word forest itself was unknown till after the Conquest, and chase, archer, forester, view — are all from the Norman French. The forester blew a "pris" when the stag was taken, a "mort" when he was slain, and a "furloin" to show that the deer was far away. For many ages the wild boar was hunted in our forest with hound and spear, as the canvasses of Snyders and Rubens have made so familiar to us. The red and fallow deer were stalked with bow and arrow; while for feathered game hawking was a favourite pastime. This most picturesque of all our forest sports prevailed from very ancient days to the end of the Stuart period. It was followed by the ladies of the household as well as by the lord and his pages; and of those joyous scenes of the olden time very pleasant pictures have also been preserved to us.

It is difficult, however, to realise what hunting was in mediæval times. Not only was it the pastime of princes, and even of great abbots and ecclesiastics, but it was really one of the most important affairs of life. When Henry VI. of Germany was waited on by his courtiers with the announcement of the death of his father, the Emperor Frederick Barbarossa, he said, "The day is fine, gentlemen, allow us to put off serious affairs until to-morrow;" and, as we have seen, Henry VIII. asked his minister to keep a packet of state letters till the evening, as he was going to have a shot at a stag. Poor Archbishop Abbot never smiled after his last day's hunting.

No forest, with the exception perhaps of Fontainebleau, has ever been so famous for its sport as Windsor, or so illustrious in its sportsmen; its very officers were magnates of no mean order. The earliest notice of any of them I can find is of one William Twici, who was the king's huntsman in chief at a very early period; he was a great hunter, and wrote a treatise on his craft in Norman French. It is true that he mentions the fox as a beast of venery, altogether an inferior object of sport; but it cannot be said that its special hunting is only of recent introduction, for the following entries, in the wardrobe accounts of Edward I., show that it was established at that time under an officer especially appointed for the purpose.

"Anno 1299 and 1300.

"Paid to Wm. de Foxhunte the King's huntsman of Foxes in divers forests and parks for his own wages, and the wages of his two boys to take care of the dogs, £9, 3s.

"Paid to the same for the keep of twelve dogs belonging to the king, &c.

"Paid the same for the expense of a horse to carry the nets."

It is mentioned that the hunting season commenced on the 1st September after the dead season.* The method of taking the beast was totally different to that now practised. The present orthodox fashion of the chase came in during the eighteenth century after the Black Act had virtually rung the knell of open deer forests. But none of these forest functionaries affords us a more interesting history than that ancient hereditary one, the Master of the King's Buckhounds, of whose office Professor Montague Burrows has given us so full an account in his history of the Brocas family.

In the days when Rockingham Castle was a favourite royal hunting seat, the small Manor of Little Weldon, in Northamptonshire, was put aside for the support of the Master of the Buckhounds; and in 1216 a grant of it was made for that purpose to Hamon le Venour. On the death of John Lovel, who held the office in 1316, the Escheator reported, that he "held one messuage, and one carucate of land, in Weldon Parva, of the king, in capite, by service of keeping and feeding at his own charges 15 canes currentes of the king's, for the forty days of Lent in each year." This estate did not comprise the whole of the Royal Manor, but only that part of it known as the "Hunter's Manor." It was an inheritance descendible on the heirs as any other freehold would be; and strange to say, on daughters as well as sons; and accordingly we find it soon in the possession of a singularly appropriate representative, Thomas de Borhunte, who no doubt brought from his forest home, on the northern slopes of the Portsdown hills, in the wealden of Sussex, all the qualifications for such an office; he acquired this coveted post by having married Margaret Lovel, the daughter of its former owner. After his death Margaret with this dowry did not long remain a widow. She married Wm. Danvers, and to him carried her Manor and Mastership of the Buckhounds. On their deaths they passed to the widow of Sir John de Borhunte, Margaret's son, who had predeceased her.

"Hunter's Manor," and its valuable appurtenant, became by purchase the property of Bernard de Brocas, the favourite of Ed. III., and in spite of all the fluctuations of fortune that characterised those terrible days of the Wars of the Roses, so adroitly had these acute Gascons tied up and settled their possessions through the medium of trustees, just

---

* See Encyclopædia Britannica, title "Hunting."

then introduced, that when the great Sir Bernard, "Squjer Maister of the King's Buckhounds," had been laid under his stately tomb in Westminster Abbey, and the crash fell on the second Sir Bernard, who was hung as a traitor at Tyburn, the bulk of his estates and the Mastership were found secure against escheat; and so through many generations, this curious privilege in "grand serjeanty," devolved with the patrimonial acres of Beaurepaire and Roche Court; and growing more and more a nominal office, and more and more the subject of family litigation, it descended at last on so profligate a representative, in the person of Sir Pexsall Brocas, that it virtually became extinguished; and although the shadow of right was sold in 1633 to Sir Lewis Watson, afterwards Lord Rockingham, it then in reality ceased to exist. There is hardly another instance of such a "serjeanty," save, perhaps, the Dymoke royal championship, lasting in one family for over 267 years.

This interesting account, however, rather implies that the hereditary Mastership had reference to all the King's forests, but it is clear that the "serjeanty" was local for the keeping of a pack of hounds on Hunter's Manor, and for use only in the neighbouring forests: no member of the Brocas family ever exercised authority in the forest of Windsor, except when appointed its forester in chief, in 1334. At the very time that Hunter's Manor was in the hands of the Lovels, William Twici, Richard de Bataille, and Oliver de Bordeaux severally held the office of Chief Forester of Windsor. In 1623, Hastings, Earl of Huntingdon, was Master of the "Hart-hounds" or Buckhounds, as John Carey was in 1661; but we never hear a word of the De Brocases. This was probably the reason why the support of the Master of Hunter's Manor was thrown on the issues of Sussex and Surrey, and not on Berkshire, already burdened enough with its own forest. To return to the fashion of the hunting—that has had many changes. At no very remote period, the stag was roused from his lair with blood hounds, or harboured by the huntsman on foot, whose fleeter dogs, held in leash, were then slipped for the chase.

The sport began at five or six o'clock in the morning, and it was often at the break of day

"The wild horn, whose voice the woodland fills,
 Was ringing to the merry shout."

A faster age succeeded, when the horse was used, and the hounds hunted much as at the present time. The fox, that had always been a beast to slay and get rid of as vermin, with net or trap, became a favourite beast of chase, to be pursued less for destruction than pleasure.

So early as Charles II.'s time a pack of harriers was kept by the king, at a cost of £700 a year in the whole.*

But although the fashion of sport has changed, the love of it has

---

* Cal. State Papers, 1667 and 1673, and Docket Book at Rolls.

always been a mighty ingredient in our English nature; how true were the words of the old ballad—

> "The horn, the horn, the lusty horn,
> Is not a thing to laugh to scorn."

Even the Roundhead gentry were not superior to the pastimes of the forest; that truly perfect English gentleman, Hampden, did not deem it unworthy to "harbour an exceeding propenseness to field sports;" and Bulstrode Whitelock's passion for it was equally strong. A new era for our forest hunting set in towards the close of the seventeenth century; and so important was it in its influence on our neighbourhood that I may be pardoned a little digression here.

Mr. Pepys tells us of his amusing journey to Cranbourn Lodge, when he had to scramble up a ladder to see Sir George Carteret, who was rebuilding the old house. One room was spared because Sir Thomas Aylesbury in 1637 had a granddaughter born in it, who afterwards became Anne Hyde, Duchess of York, and mother of Queen Anne. Now the little lady Anne was left a motherless child at the age of seven; but she never forgot her mother, and was very fond of our forest, because it was her mother's birth-place. She was taken out from Windsor to see the old room when it belonged to Lord Godolphin. She and her play-fellow, Sarah Jennings, passed many pleasant days in the fine air and scenery of this wild country.

Sarah, we know, was appointed to her household, and married the far-sighted handsome Colonel Churchill; while her young mistress, when she was twenty years of age, had to take as her husband Prince George of Denmark.

Queen Anne had two dominating ideas—the Protestant Church, and her husband and his forest pastimes. She lived only for these, for her children all died.

Of this first object of her care, what a noble monument remains in "Queen Anne's Bounty"—to commemorate the other, we ought to put up a statue to her at Ascot.

I will not speak here of her character save in that aspect of it which most concerns us, its energy in the pursuit of pleasure. Her husband liked nothing so well as his horses and hunting, except, perhaps, his dinner; and in these tastes, at least, the husband and wife agreed very well.

Their earlier married days, it is generally supposed, were spent much in obscurity. They were really in this neighbourhood, riding or driving after the hounds, building their new kennels at Ascot, and laying out the drives that facilitated their favourite pastime.

The only event that occurred to upset her much was the birth of a baby brother, whom she at once disowned. It made a pretty family quarrel, and Lear and Goneril and Regan were seen in sad reality.

The King, in the moments of his anguish at the ingratitude of his daughters, perhaps the only moments of his life which command our sympathy, shows us his estimate of his son-in-law's worth. His desertion to the Prince of Orange only evoked the exclamation, "So 'Est-il-possible' is gone too!" He was valued, it seems, at something less than a common trooper. But Anne subsided into her quiet life. She lost all her children save one, the little Duke of Gloucester, and he died before he was twelve.

Hunting then became a greater passion than ever with her. She infused a new spirit into the sporting annals of our neighbourhood, although we cannot admire the way in which she pursued her pastime, for it was very unsportsman-like, according to our views. Like Queen Elizabeth she hunted under the blazing suns of July, regardless of the standing crops; but fortunately, round Sunninghill, she was not troubled much with these.*

Swift, in his letters to Stella, tells us that on August 7, 1711, "The Queen hunted the stag through the meridian heat, till four in the afternoon. She drove forty miles that day, and being beyond her dinner hour, the board of green cloth did not dine until the late hour of five o'clock." A calamity we should not think so much of now!

When the "quarry" was taken, the death was celebrated by a "mort"—a "double mort" for a hart, or "triple mort" for a royal hart—with a great blowing of horns, when a hunting-knife was presented to the principal man present, to cut off the stag's head;† this was a great ceremony, especially when witnessed for the first time. Thus about 1696 the Queen's poor little son, the Duke of Gloucester, underwent his "baptism of blood" on first seeing a deer slain—his face was smeared all over with its blood. But it was a miserable affair; the deer was not hunted, but brought into a yard and killed for the purpose.

Luttrell tells us that the Queen pursued her pleasure after her accession to the throne, when she was no longer able to mount the saddle. "In Aug. 1702, she was at Windsor, where she takes the divertisement of hunting almost every day, in an open calash in the forest," i.e., she drove down the long rides, and saw what she could of the hunt; and Swift adds, 31st July 1711, "The Queen was abroad to-day

---

* Miss Strickland, vol. viii. p. 44.   † Ashton's "Social Life of Queen Anne."

to hunt, and finding it disposed to rain, she kept in her coach. She hunts in a chaise, with one horse, which she drives herself, and drives furiously like Jehu, and is a mighty hunter like Nimrod."

She spent most of her summers at Windsor, taking her pleasure, as far as she could, in spite of her great enemy the gout. She restocked portions of the forest; in 1712 her keeper, William Lowen, was paid for bringing up a hundred red deer from Houghton Park to Windsor.

It was to render easier this style of hunting that she commenced the drives that are so striking a feature in our forest country; nine of them radiate from the Soldiers' Pillar, at Ascot, and others from different points of the surrounding heath-lands. George III. completed these roads, actuated to a great extent by a similar inability, in his later years, to follow the chase otherwise than in his carriage.

Neither George I. nor George II. cared much for hunting,* but the young Prince Frederick, father of George III., took great delight in it, and in 1739 was lauded as the hero of Somerville's poem, "The Stag-Chase in Windsor Forest."

But "Fitz is dead!" and his brother, William Augustus, the young Duke of Cumberland, comes on the scene: of him I have spoken so much in connection with Virginia Water, that I need only say here that he threw himself ardently into forest sports, and found his youthful nephew, George III., who inherited his father's taste for it, a very apt pupil in the field. So, too, was the Princess Amelia, who hunted two or three times a week with the Dukes of Grafton and Newcastle, to whom she paid much attention. The society of the former, it is said, was very agreeable to her. On one occasion they became separated from their companions, lost their way, and had to seek help at some house in the forest, to the great indignation of the Queen. ["Georgian Era," Vizetelly & Co.]

Under such royal patronage hunting became very fashionable, and at no time was it practised with greater zest than during the latter half of the eighteenth century.

Under George II. Mr. Jennison held sway, as Master of the Buckhounds; he was a thorough representative of the excessive conviviality of the age—"a five-bottle man," who would not let his friends walk away from the table; but, as "A Forester"† tells us, on his ceasing to hold the office, "They changed the torrid for the frigid zone," for when

---

* In 1740, in the Earl of Jersey's time, the deer had become so reduced that there was an order to spare them for twelve months. [See Forest Book, Windsor Castle.]

† A Forester of Windsor, 1818, in verse.

Lord Bateman came to Swinley he threw a gloom over all its sports, and was a very unpopular Master.

> "No sportsman now was to the mansion led,
> No corks were drawn, no social tables spread;
> 'Twas blank and dull till Jersey's cheerful light
> Dispersed the gloom of long incumbent night."

He was not only considered, but considered himself, the King of the Forest, his Majesty at this time having absolutely never hunted a day with his own hounds. The appointment was then one for life, but soon became a mere political reward, and changed with every Ministry.*

When it was asked in Coningsby, what sacrifice some one had made that he should have the Buckhounds, "Past sacrifices," replied Lord Eskdale, "are nothing, present sacrifices are the things we want; men who will sacrifice their principles and join us." A story is told of Lord Bateman that, on his asking George III. when the hounds should be turned out, was answered, "I cannot exactly tell, but I *can* inform you that your Lordship was turned out about an hour ago!" After Lord Jersey came Lord Hinchingbroke (son of Lord Sandwich, the "lively Hinchingbroke" of Pope's letters), who filled the office with much spirit. He found things in a bad way; the Yeomen Prickers were very ill-mounted, which is hardly surprising, as their salaries were but £98, 10s. 8d., and out of that they had to provide and keep two good horses! An extra £25 a year was soon obtained for them by their new master.

Walpole, writing to Sir Horace Mann in 1750, gives us an amusing account of his devotion to sport. "Lord Sandwich," says he, "goes once or twice a week to hunt with the Duke, and as the latter has taken a turn of gaming, Sandwich, to make his court and fortune, carries a box and dice in his pocket; and so they throw a main whenever the hounds are at fault, upon every green hill, and under every green tree." In 1751 the Duke was thrown from his horse while hunting, and was nearly killed. He was given over by his physician, but recovered. The salary attached to the post of Master was large, and ranged, it is said, from £1200 to £2000 a year; but out of this public breakfasts were supplied at Swinley Lodge, the official residence of the Master, to every gentleman who chose to attend the meets.

The open-handed owner of Hinchingbroke doubtless shone in such a capacity, and did the honours with great liberality; this was John, the

---

* *Sporting Magazine*, 1794, vol. iii. p. 315.

fourth Lord Sandwich, the "Jemmy Twitcher"* of the Parliamentary wits of that day. He was a hard worker, and is supposed to have invented "sandwiches," to save his time, possibly, while throwing one of those mains with the Duke. But his name will ever be associated, if not tarnished, by his connection with poor Margaret Ray, whose melancholy fate threw a gloom over the remainder of his life. After Lord Sandwich, the Earl of Albemarle was Master of the Hounds, but hunting was not much to his taste. He was followed by the Marquis Cornwallis.

Of Swinley Lodge nothing is left but its laundry, which has been converted into a house for the paddock-keeper; but as one drives by it, the avenues of limes and elms tell their tale of other days. The old mansion, at which so many joyous gatherings took place, stood exactly where the avenues cross one another; the present road passed in front of the house, and the cross-road went through it under an archway; on the west were the lawn and gardens, and on the east the offices. It was a red brick house, and was pulled down, I believe, about sixty or seventy years ago. In H. Walters' map of 1823 it is marked as then standing. Although in this "Grove of Swinley" there has been a lodge for centuries occupied by the Master of the Buckhounds or his underkeeper, it seems that the freehold of the enclosures was only acquired by George III. in 1782. It never probably had a gayer time than when the King reviewed the troops on the eve of their departure from the camp at Swinley in August 1798, of which I speak elsewhere.

The King, the Prince of Wales, and his brother the "Bishop of Osnaburgh," the Princess Royal, and the Princess Sophia, were all enjoying their hunting in the autumn of 1779. The meets were more numerously attended than they had ever been: on one occasion three hundred people were present, and fields of 150, or 200 horsemen were not uncommon.

The practice of turning out the deer instead of "harbouring" it was then adopted. The last meet of the season was in Easter week, when they hunted Monday, Thursday, and Saturday. The opening day, Mrs. Papendick informs us, "was invariably one of much ceremony. The stag was turned out in great style, and the Queen and Princesses were present, and all the nobility and gentry of the neighbourhood; the King always made it a point of attending." On one occasion, after the service at the Chapel Royal on Easter Sunday, as they could not easily have reached the ground by ten o'clock on Monday, to Bishop Porteus' great

---

* Jemmy Twitcher was one of Macheath's gang in the "Beggar's Opera."

umbrage, they entered their travelling carriages in the afternoon for Windsor.*

At this last meeting arrangements were always made for the running of the King's Plate; which of the Yeomen Prickers were to run, and the horses they were to ride.† My lady readers may like to know what the hunting costume of that day was like. In 1779 Her Majesty and the Princesses wore "blue habits faced and turned up with red, white beaver hats, and black feathers."

The gentlemen, also, had their fashions. The old fox-hunting dress at one time was a red flapped coat, with broad white or yellow lappet collar, showing a full frilled shirt, frills at the wrist, leather gaiters, and black jockey cap, or a close felt cap and high top-boots. A costume of 1756 shows the rider in close curled wig and short three-cornered cocked hat, frock coat with leather waist band, and leather breeches. The groom here had a small round jockey cap. The horses were invariably dock-tailed.

In 1786 a very conspicuous change occurred in their costume. The old Duke of Grafton, and the then late Lords Godolphin and Pembroke, and Mr. Grenville, had always worn the small jockey cap, and the King had adopted it also. The whole Hunt now determined, in compliment to his Majesty, to do the same, and the picturesque three-cornered cocked hat was accordingly doffed in favour of the close-fitting black velvet one, which then came generally into fashion, and which after a century's use is retained now only for the huntsman and his whips.

Some of the finest runs on record were had at this time. I need hardly allude to the remarkable one which occurred in the time of Charles II., when, we are told, a deer was hunted here, went away, and was taken at Lord Petres' seat in Essex: only five came in at the end of this seventy miles' run—the King's brother, the Duke of York, being one of them. There was a wonderful run in November 1780, when after five hours' chase over Bagshot Heath, and crossing the river at Staines, the stag came back again, and got away. In the following year there was another, when, of nearly two hundred that started, only ten or twelve came in at the finish. His Majesty rode above eighty miles,

---

* See Mrs. Papendick's "Court and Life of Queen Charlotte."

† The Yeomen Prickers were ancient officers of the Hunt. In 1667 there were five of them had a salary of £40 a year each, and a horse livery. They derived their name from the old English "Pricker," a rider urging his palfrey with the prick or spur. Chaucer constantly uses the word and Spenser too:—

"A gentle knight was pricking on the plain."

several horses were killed; but one can hardly read the details of such exploits with unalloyed pleasure. Thus in 1783 a contemporary account is given of a fine run of six hours, at the end of which "the stag dropped down dead before the hounds; not twenty of the horses out of 150 were in at the death; several horses died in the field, and tired ones were seen crawling away to every village."

On the 17th April 1797 a deer was turned out at New Lodge, ran above sixty miles, and was taken at Tilehurst near Reading. His Majesty followed and returned in a postchaise. And again, on the 5th December of the same year, the Hunt had great sport; his Majesty tired three horses.

Still the sport flourished; the more dangerous or distressing the more gallant the day! But our tastes have improved; such scenes no longer mar the good old English sport that has had so beneficial an effect on the rural life of the country. May it long prosper.

In 1790 large additions and alterations were made to the dog kennels which Queen Anne had erected at Ascot, and for which the Duke of Cumberland obtained a large piece of "their common," as the parishioners expressed it.

An anecdote* that shows the King's good nature and love of a little fun is vouched as authentic. Two young Eton boys were spending their holidays with a friend at Sunninghill (who, is not stated), and had wandered into the forest, where they met a fresh-looking old gentleman in the Windsor uniform, who jestingly asked if they were playing truant; they gave an account of themselves, and said, "They had come to see the King's staghounds throw off;" it was replied, "He does not hunt to-day, but when he does I will let you know; but you must not come to the ground by yourselves lest you should meet with accident." Two or three days after, while the family was at breakfast, a royal yeoman pricker rode up to the gate to announce that the King was waiting till he brought the two young gentlemen to a place of safety to see the hounds throw off.

But this fresh-looking old gentleman was not always so amiable, as General Conway found out when he voted in Parliament against him, and lost his regiment and appointments.

The King continued fond of his sport as long as he was able to enjoy it, but the state of his health early in the century put an end to it for a time.

The poor hounds were soon dying of ennui, for want of work, and in

---

* See Scott's Life.

1812 we have the curious announcement that "the King's staghounds are gone to the coast of Sussex, for the benefit of bathing, and, attended by the huntsman, regularly take their morning ablutions."

This was followed in June 1813 by the statement that the Royal Hunt has been discontinued, and a suitable provision made for the huntsmen, the expense of it being justly held unnecessary during the illness of his Majesty. The hounds have been disposed of to form a pack in Sussex.

But although the King's kennels had been sold, the Prince of Wales hunted this country with his own staghounds for some years, and the Duke of York had his foxhounds, and one or two other packs were kept in this neighbourhood.

A living link, connecting these bygone days with the present, was old Tom Woods, of the Royal Hunt Establishment, who died only in 1862. He rode with the Duke of Cumberland, who had a fine black horse, which no one could ride but Tom; and this is how he managed it. "I took un right away to the back of Ascot-stand as is now, and down to Sunninghill Bog, and when he had 'splunged' about in it that till he had pretty well settled hisself, I got on un, then, and gave him my way on it; ever after that when he tried on any of his games, I gave un another turn in Sunninghill Bog, until I tamed un." *

Old Tom must have outlived many masters, as he was about ninety-three years of age.

Johnson, the huntsman, died in 1812, after nearly thirty years in office. He was succeeded by George Sharpe, his son-in-law. After him, in 1824, came Charles Davis, who grew old in the service, died in 1866, aged seventy-eight years, and was buried at Sunninghill. King held the post for a short time, and his resting-place is also in our churchyard. Frank Goodall followed in 1872, remaining till 1888, when he was succeeded by Harvey, the present huntsman.

---

* Menzies' Windsor Forest.

CHAPTER VI.

The Enclosure of the Forest.

"Dubbut, loook at the waaste, theer warnt not feead for a cow;
Nowt at all but bracken an' fuzz, an' loook at it now."

A VERY unromantic, matter-of-fact chapter opens, when I describe how the Windsor Forest Enclosure Act received the royal assent in 1813. In a moment the ancient forest ceased to exist; the woods were there, the waste, the great "frithe" remained, but as "forest," no more. All its dreaded laws were repealed, its rights and privileges were swept away for ever; the vast unenclosed area, which had been hedged in only by its legal fictions, antiquated customs, and black-letter laws, was in reality "no man's land," for although many, from the King down to the peasant, had rights over it, the absolute property was not, except theoretically, in any one. Stripped of all its poetry and romance, and of half its beauty, it was changed in a moment, as it were, by Parliamentary magic into a multitude of separate commonplace freehold allotments. A few years of agitation, two or three of routine work, transformed it into private ownerships, bounded and defined by straight lines of ditches and turf banks.

But how did such a transformation come about? When goods increase they increase that eat them, we are told, and during the war the manufacturers and farmers prospered, and the labourers in the fields, the mines, and the factories, multiplied exceedingly; but unfortunately they did not participate in the general well-being—they were in truth on the verge of starvation.

In 1812 and 1813 the Luddites were smashing the looms that were destined to feed their children; as, in 1832, the rustic labourers were burning corn ricks, while they themselves were clamouring for bread. How were the people to be fed? Enlarge the grain-growing area;

enlarge the commons—that became a cry throughout the country—cultivate the wild wastes and heaths, and the desert shall be crowned with waving corn. It was a good cry, but to some extent fallacious. For a few years it produced labour, but not a vast quantity of food. It was a benefit to the rich, but a very qualified boon to the poor; a great social blessing nevertheless. The advantage, I believe, was the amelioration, not of the irreclaimable soil, but of its irreclaimable population. The social problem was a difficult one, and the poor-laws aggravated it. The forests throughout the country had become nurseries for crime. The Black Act of George I.'s reign tells its own miserable tale. The love of sport is so inherent in the English rural mind that a forester would choose the barest existence in his native woods to almost any life of regular labour elsewhere. What inhumanity then could be more refined than to place a half-starved rustic in one of these "Alsatias" of the eighteenth century, a very garden of Eden to him, and tell him not to eat of the wild animals which were its fruits. His rights and perquisites, loppings and toppings of trees, peat for firing, and other privileges, were easily and excusably abused. Such was the actual state of things—want, and irresistible temptation—when the Black Act was passed in 1723; its error, no doubt, was in attacking the consequences, rather than the causes of the evil. The statute made it death for a man disguised to kill a rabbit, or even when disguised to be seen in a rabbit-warren; or unlawfully take a fish out of a pond; or, whether disguised or not, to kill a stag in a park or other enclosure. Well might Bishop Hoadley of Winchester, when asked to restock Waltham Chase, say, "No; the Act has done mischief enough already."*

In January 1773, at Reading, two young men underwent a flogging at the public whipping-post in the market-place, "By order of a justice, under a [then] recent Act, for killing a hare;" the announcement at the time added, "As the Act now stands, the offender must be punished (*i.e.* whipped) within three days after his commitment, and on the fourth he may bring an appeal." It had become a practice to place man-traps and spring-guns in plantations; and on a poacher's being killed by a spring-gun, so little was the law understood, that so late as 1816 a case was laid before Mr. Gurney for his opinion of their legality, when he pronounced against them.

The Government attention had been called to our forest abuses as early as 1805, and a commission was appointed to inquire into the subject; but their proceedings were deemed so arbitrary and despotic, that

---

* See White's Selborne, *note*.

a violent opposition arose, and the matter was dropped for a time. The inquiry was afterwards continued. The Commissioners sat at the Wells, Sunninghill, and other places; evidence was taken, and ultimately, after four several Reports had been made in 1807-8-9-10, the case for Parliamentary action was fully established. The inquiry brought to light some interesting facts: the whole affair revealed a state of dilapidation and abuse. The Commissioners at the outset " were astonished to find not a single paper in the castle that afforded any complete information on any one right of the forest, or of the Crown within it "— no original documents, save books of proceedings in " Court of Swainmote and attachment," the earliest of which were of the years 1606 and 1607. " They were informed that a great quantity of the forest papers were deposited in a room which was afterwards used as a Guardroom, and had been within the memory of persons then living, removed, but to what place no one knew!" With some of them Cromwell's soldiers are said to have lighted their pipes! Many, we know from other sources, were designedly burned.

However, it soon appeared that of the twenty parishes and thirty-five manors of which the forest consisted, 500 acres had been enclosed without authority; and there were 340 " purprestures " or encroachments on his Majesty's soil.

But which aspect of the case presented the most deplorable state of things it is difficult to decide—the condition of the deer or their keepers, of the lodges and woods or the inhabitants of them.

As to the deer, they had dwindled down from 1300 in November 1731 to 318 in 1806; " poor dappled fools," they were in as melancholy case as Jaques' friend. The " native burghers of this desert city " were languishing and starving for want of food; many died of hunger, and the surviving does had not strength to rear their fawns. This arose from other animals having been turned into their feeding-grounds, and from failure of the supply of hay in winter; because in some cases, the Report observes, and the truth must be told, " the allowance granted for this purpose having been perverted to private advantage."

But while the poor deer were breathing out such an attenuated existence, the poor keepers were hardly in better case. I do not allude to the office of Master of the Buckhounds, which had of late years become a highly paid post of a political character, but to the keeperships, which were never of much pecuniary advantage, for in 1609 we find Sir Richard Weston writing to Salisbury that " his place as a forest keeper is painful without profit; he solicits a grant of fifty acres out of lands now to be taken into the park." About this time (James I.) the salary of the keeper of the great park was but £12, 2s. 6d., and that of ranger of the forest £9, 2s. 6d., but the perquisites were large. At a much later date the out-ranger, Lord Cranley, was allowed £600 a year for himself and his drivers; they could not, therefore, have had very fine places. There were twenty-seven other officers and keepers, who were paid £511, 8s. 11d. per annum, out of which they had to spend £80 a year for hay for the deer in Bigshot and Swinley Walks, which averaged about £15 a year each. No wonder the poor animals—the lower ones, I mean—were starved. The steward of the Forest Courts had no salary, and his fees amounted only to about thirty shillings a year! What would the grand steward of olden times have said to such a state of things as this, when he saw his successor superseded by the village constable? Nor can it be a matter of surprise that with stipends so slender the keepers' houses and lodges had now become dreadfully dilapidated.

These houses were Cranbourn Lodge, New Lodge, Swinley Lodge, and Bigshot Lodge, also Try's Lodge (annexed to the office of out-ranger), near Chertsey, out of the forest, in possession of Admiral Sir Richard Onslow, Bart. Cranbourn Lodge had then been occupied by his late Royal Highness the Duke of Gloucester. New Lodge, with twenty acres of land, was granted for life to Her Highness Princess Sophia of Gloucester in 1798. Not the first time, be it remembered, that a lady assumed the responsibilities of forestal duties; but the Report adds, "it was in a most dilapidated state, and scarcely habitable by the servants." Poor Princess! the office, after all, was not a grand one! Swinley was always inhabited by the Master of his Majesty's Stag-hounds. Now as to Bigshot Lodge. This, the Report says, "is much more ruinous than even New Lodge," and that was not fit for the servants, "this is in no degree whatever habitable." It had been for many years occupied by the late Major-General Cox. The poor general was not happily located, for we are told "to the north of it a piece of waste land has been enclosed, with a bank and rail, but no pains have ever been taken to redeem it from the swampy state occasioned by a stream-head immediately in it." Nature was regaining its ground, evidently, in its physical, if not in its animal, energies here; but I must not generalise too quickly, for the woods were in a deplorable state. The Government demand on them, and the lawless depredations—committed in the time of the Commonwealth—had destroyed the forest timber almost beyond recovery. The timber then growing in the forest was valued at £200,000, but from neglect only a small portion was useful for naval purposes. Of the 2230 acres of wood scarcely a sapling or young tree was left to succeed those which had been cut down or were decaying. They were open to every species of depredation, but the worst "species" were, I fear, the officers of the forest, the principal of whom were all honorary, and "cannot," as the Report continued, "be expected to attend to it." "The inferior ones on whom the labour depended are so ill-paid that they cannot devote the necessary time to it," not even to observe the continual abuses and depredations that were practised; and if they could, and here lay the difficulty, "the forest laws are inadequate to correct the mischief."

A woful account this, but of the people we have no better. They, too, were in a destitute state, it would seem; for the Commissioners, after alluding to the fact that the rights of Turbary, or of cutting turves, could not strictly exist in a forest, said, that it had been long enjoyed, and the wants of the poorer inhabitants of the district sufficiently convinced them that (consistently with humanity) it could not be prevented.

They were strongly impressed with the conviction that nothing more favoured irregular and lawless habits of life among the inferior class of society, than scattered and sequestered habitations; and it is on this account that in parishes bordering on any extensive forests it is hardly possible to find a collected village. "The inhabitants of all the parishes around the forest (Windsor and Oakingham excepted) live in widely scattered dwellings, affording means of committing their various depredations with the least chance of detection. They recommended the removal of these scattered cottages to the utmost extent possible, and collecting them into close hamlets, the habits of each individual becoming thus known to the whole community, and the consequences wholesome to every one, as restraining a propensity to thieving, and wholesome to the community at large." All opposition having been overcome, the Act passed in 1813. Much time was then spent in obtaining the award, appropriating the allotments, and carrying out various exchanges between owner and owner, which the Act made provision for. What became of the deer? Hardly had the forest ceased to be than a daring rustic, calling himself "Robinhood," appeared at the head of a gang of marauders, who made sad havoc with these gentle denizens of the waste; but the nineteenth century was too late for such exploits, and "Robinhood" was soon brought up before the Maidenhead magistrates, and "extinguished" with a fine of £50. Then came their reclamation, not the reclamation of the deer-stealers, but of the deer; and they were all driven from "their assigned and native dwelling-place," the forest, to the park—a place of safety alike from the apple-baited hook or the stealthy moonlight shot, to be preserved for the orthodox chase. This driving was a great affair—a two days' business; and it enlisted a very gallant band of drivers. No less than a troop of the Royal Horse Guards, and a detachment of the 5th Infantry, were employed early in September 1814 to assist the Yeomen Prickers to sweep the wild heaths and dells that so late were forest; they had warmer work at Waterloo a few months later! In this case "the poor affrighted herds," we are told,* "fled before their pursuers, plunging into the toils spread for them; many were chased to places of safety, many escaped, and some were killed." And thus were they driven from the plains they had browsed for ages!

The result of this measure to the neighbouring landowners was very beneficial. They acquired large accessions to their estates, every parish on the average getting something like a thousand acres of land; for of the 60,000 of which the forest consisted, about 34,000 were enclosed lands belonging to the Crown and other owners, and over 24,000 were open heath and moorland, to be divided among about twenty parishes. Our parish had a good share. To the larger landed proprietors extensive allotments were made; in fact, every owner was more or less enriched.

This was not all settled, however, without considerable discussion and many conflicting claims. "The King's most excellent Majesty" claimed the manors of Old Windsor and New Windsor, but so also did Henry Powney Isherwood; George Simpson alleged that he was lord of the manor of Sunninghill; and the Master, Fellows, and Scholars of St. John's College were seized of the manor of Chawridge, and also of the manor of Broomhall; and Daniel Agace claimed some right in the waste lands in Sunninghill and Winkfield, in respect of the manor or reputed manor of Ascot, otherwise Escott;—but they settled it all at the Wells and Windsor, and divided the spoil. The King's majesty intimated that he would like to have Ascot Heath racecourse, of about 206 acres; which, however, it was understood should be kept as a racecourse for the public use. This was really for the public welfare, and was readily acceded to. Then it was resolved as a basis of general division that the Crown should take one third of the residue;† the lords of manors and other owners another third; and the remaining third, after providing for the expenses, should be made over for the benefit of the poor.

---

* *Windsor and Eton Express*, September 1814.
† Speaking more precisely, his Majesty took 9.32 parts.

It would be invidious to consider at this distance of time how far the inferior interests were properly "taken care of," for the real position of matters, stripped of all technicality, was rather amusing. The Crown had of this open forest the most ample enjoyment, perhaps, but, except in the demesne lands, it possessed no interest in the soil; the lords of manors and owners had the legal estate or interest in the land, but had no right to use it; the poor had no right whatever in the soil, but just such rights and privileges over it as prevented any one else appropriating it.

It was more in the award, and the allotments made under it, that any grievance could be found; it was what is called a "public benefit," but the poor were sufferers. The small neighbouring farmers were so in a still greater degree; for, as the inquiry showed, "all the inhabitants proved long enjoyment of right to turn cows, horses, sheep, and pigs into the forest without stint;" and now the cow lost her grazing, the pigs their acorns, and the poor donkey even its roaming-ground and thistles. "The boon that such extensive open lands had been to the young cattle at certain times in the year can hardly be over-estimated. Warning voices were not wanting at the time. A country gentleman, as early as 1772, wrote a pamphlet to prove who the gainers and the losers would be; but as to the small commonfield farmer he must, it was predicted, become a hired labourer. The value to the poor of firing from the heath and its turves and wood may well be imagined, when we consider the price of coal at that time in Sunninghill. In a memorandum among the papers of St. John's College, dated at the beginning of the present century, I find it stated that "coals in summer are £3, 3s. or £3, 10s. per chaldron, mutton and beef about 9d. or $8\frac{1}{2}$d per lb., butter 16d. or 17d. per lb." These must have been war prices.

Besides this, the right of the poor to "browse wood" was a great comfort to them. This was, when the keepers cut the "lops and tops" from the trees for the deer in winter, after the deer had stripped off the bark, the inhabitants, by long custom, had the right to take the wood for fuel; but no branch came within this perquisite that was larger than a deer could turn over with its horns.

To some the compensation made on the enclosure was not at all equivalent to what they lost. Indeed, to that valuable class in the country, the yeoman or small farmer, cultivating his own freehold, the measure was simply destruction; a few of the richer ones took rank with the gentry, but the bulk of them ceased to be. Their farms were not large enough without that most valuable privilege of turning out their cattle on the waste.

With regard to the allotments to the poor, the Act was absurdly drawn, in not recognising the possibility of any change in circumstances. It directed "that the Commissioners were to allot to the churchwardens and overseers of the poor of Sunninghill a piece of waste land lying within the said parish, called Sunninghill Bog, containing 112 acres, to be held in trust for the poor, and the turves, fern, and other fuel arising from such land shall be taken and used by the poor inhabitants occupying houses or lands of not higher rent than £5, in such manner as such churchwardens and trustees shall from time to time in each and every year direct."

Now, under certain restrictions, they had all these privileges before over nearly 2000 acres. The turves on 112 acres would not have lasted a generation, had it remained the fuel of the people; but the time came when wood and coal superseded it, and their possession was valueless. A cold, miserable, undrained morass; in winter the haunt of the bittern and the snipe, and in summer the home of the frog—a beautiful wilderness of heather and gorse!

Time went on; no £5 a year houses were to be found in the parish. The pleasant hills above this poor man's domain were crowned with charming houses; the swamp over which they looked became a vineyard of Naboth! Some of the residents would buy it, but would not give enough for it; and then came the cruellest cut of all, it was made "beautiful for ever" by Act of Parliament. A little clause in the Act of 1876 (39 & 40 Vict. c. 56) declared that the land should never be used for any other purpose than those mentioned in the original enclosure statute. That was only for gardens, then but little in demand, and for fuel, for which it soon became obsolete and useless. The trustees endeavoured to get it turned into pasture, that every poor family in the place might have fresh milk at a moderate cost—a blessing quite denied to them. But, no, this strange clause stood in the way; the Charity Commissioners were powerless against this terrible enactment. But worse was still in store. Could that be possible, one would exclaim, when under the old Act this undrained, untrenched, land could not be let for longer than seven years, and for so short a period it would pay no one to take it. But, yes, instead of releasing the land from the shackles in which it had been bound, for some unknown reason, they were at the end of this enlightened nineteenth century actually tightened. Another Act * was passed which prevented the letting of any allotment for more than one year, and at the best rent that could be obtained for similar land in the parish. The result of this is that a

---

* Allotments Extension Act, 1882.

large part of the allotment is as useless as it was sixty years ago.

Now, it is curious to see how, during a single generation, the national opinion has changed on the subject of commons. At the beginning of the century we were mad for their enclosure and destruction, before the end of it our views are entirely reversed, and we are equally vehement for the preservation of what remain.

If the student of social history will dispassionately review the subject, he will come, I venture to think, to a very qualified judgment as to the manner in which this great enclosure scheme was carried out.

As to the question of food for the people, our forest was not, it is to be hoped, a fair example; for very little corn has been grown on the 24,000 acres during the last fifty years. Nature laughs at our efforts. In many and many a field you may still trace, if you like to look for them, the little ridges which the ploughshare has raised in the vain hope of a future harvest; year after year it now again produces only wild crops of heather and ling. Man gives up the unequal contest, for it will not pay! The great value of the measure was, doubtless, not in its agricultural so much as in its social and jurisprudential aspect. Its disadvantages have been made the subject of recent public discussion.* An eminent politician, without understanding the law of the case, states much that is perfectly true as to the loss which the enclosures entailed upon the poor, but he spoils his advocacy by roundly asserting that the enclosed lands belonged to the community. This incorrect and reckless statement brings down upon him the sledge-hammer of a doughty champion, a great legal luminary. "Belonged to the community! Nothing of the kind," says he, "the commons and wastes belonged to the owners of the soil. Rights in the poor people there were none." "Those living on large commons were the most lawless and ill-behaved in the kingdom."

The acute lawyer, however (if I may presume to say so), in his turn overreached himself; he deals with the strict technicality of the law as it stood, or rather was supposed to have stood, at the date of the enclosures. But see what a curious fact is involved in this, and which, no other system of jurisprudence in the world can show the like of. The learned judge only went back three hundred years for his law! The pure fountains of inspiration were not to be reached at so shallow a depth! Another eminent authority rushes into the arena, and declares that "the law on the subject must be carried back at least to

---

* See *The Times*, 1885.

the Statute of Merton!"—that is, for six hundred and fifty years! What a wonderful system of law we possess, and how abstruse a science it must be! The result of all this learned discussion establishes the proposition I started on, that neither Lord nor Commoner alone could deal with the common without the other; and brushing aside all the refinements as to whether only the socage tenants, or all the free tenants, the "liberi tenentes" of the manor, were entitled to the common rights, it would seem that the unscientific disputant, hitting at random, chanced to hew out the true spirit of the law as accurately as the skilled jurist who was trammelled with the armour of its technicalities, for this latter did not give sufficient weight to the long usages which had in many instances established as a custom the enjoyment of rights over the common in favour of every householder of the village. Our forest was but a conglomeration of commons and lands over which the Crown had forest rights. The Commissioners who reported to Parliament in 1808, having the full evidence before them, declared that all *the inhabitants* proved certain "rights" over the waste. This is not quite consistent with the assertion that they had none; and it is needless to analyse the origin or nature of their title. It is sufficient that they and their forefathers for ages had enjoyed these rights without question, and but for the enclosures, would have enjoyed them to this day. In confirmation of these views, it must not be forgotten that the Committee of the House of Commons in 1825 deplored the extent of the enclosures.

Now, what was thought of the measure at the time? It was considered a great reform, and worthy of the support of all men of progress. Bentham says—"In England one of the greatest and best improvements is the division of commons. In passing through the lands which have undergone that happy change, we are enchanted as by the sight of a new colony. Harvests, flocks, smiling habitations have succeeded to the dull sterility of a desert." He thought that although it gave facility to the wealthy towards the augmentation of their wealth, it equally benefited the poor by raising their wages.

On the other side we get an equally earnest and more violent partisan, William Cobbett, a sincere friend of the labourer, reprobating the enclosures, especially of such land as he saw round Highclere, Berks, "worth as tillage land not one farthing an acre, and never will, and never can be;" and of the down lands round East Meon, Hants, he thought the same. "Yet not one single inch of them but what is vastly superior in quality to any of these 'great improvements' on the miserable heaths of Hounslow, Bagshot, and Windsor Forest." "Villainous enclosures," as he calls them. Timber growing is generally the only profitable way of using these lands.* In 1836 came the first recognition of the desirability of preventing enclosures on public grounds.

---

* The magnitude of these enclosures throughout the country was very great. The first Act for the purpose was that of Ropley, in the county of Southampton, in the years 1709 and 1710. Only one other passed in the reign of Queen Anne ; 16 in that of Geo. I. ; 226 in the time of Geo. II. ; and 1532 in that of Geo. III. up to the year 1797. Then was the great rush to Parliament for powers of enclosure. Nothing like the energy of this movement has been seen, save the road-making fever at the commencement of that century, and the railway mania of the present one. According to the First Report of the Committee on Waste Lands, published in 1797, England was supposed to contain 46,000,000 acres, of which about 6,600,000 remained waste, about 1,200,000 were common fields and of Lammas tenure, so that we may assume prior to 1800 nearly 2000 Acts had been obtained, and from that date up to 1845, 2000 more ; and altogether between 6,000,000 and 7,000,000 acres have been redeemed up to the present time by these means. I will not enter further into statistics. [See Annual Register for 1797, and the *Times*, November 1885.]

CHAPTER VII

Sunninghill.

IN the south-eastern corner of the forest lies Sunninghill, of which I propose more especially to speak. It was essentially a forest parish, surrounded on all sides by wild heaths and woodlands. On the north lay the ancient forest of Blackmoor, and the woods of Cranbourn and Winkfield; on the west Swinley and Bagshot formed a still wilder border; while the wide sandy wastes of Windlesham and Chobham, and the marshy woodlands of East-moor, Selmoor, and Blackness-moor fringed it on the south and east.

Thus was our village "hersed about" by its dark woods, and buried in a long lasting isolation.

The natural boundaries of the parish are to a large extent formed by streams. That from Englemere by the Ascot schools (shown in Norden's map as going down to Lord's Mill) is its northern border as far as the bottom of Hatchet Lane, where it leaves our parish and flows into the lake at Ascot Place. Hodge Lane and the stream from Sunninghill Park to Virginia Water then define our boundaries, the line passing through China Island and the centre of the river to Highbridge and Blackness, where from the Broomhall stream we turn westward over Beggars-bush Heath by the Larch Avenue to Englemere Lake again, the eastern corner of which we include. South of this lies the curious, isolated portion of Broomhall Manor (the site of the Nunnery), which was until quite recently, " for all purposes of rating," a part of our parish.

We are in the Hundred of Cookham, and of that ancient group of the " Seven Hundreds " into which this district was divided, and which formed one of the five great divisions of the county. In its fiscal arrangements Sunninghill was exceptional, for being a royal manor, under special obligations to Windsor Castle, and subject to peculiar forestal disadvantages, it did not come within the sheriff's ordinary jurisdiction; and as early as the time of King John, we find Engelhard de Cygony, in 1220, writing to the Sheriff of Berks that he had no right to collect tallages within the Seven Hundreds of Windsor.

The village is about six miles south-west of Windsor Castle, twenty-four from London, and fifteen from Reading. It stands in one of the most beautiful parts of the forest, where the land slopes from the Great Park towards " Surrey's pleasant hills " on the south. It has a fine site on its warm, sandy ridges, which, although dry and healthful, are clothed with luxuriant foliage. A ridge of elevated land, the continuation in reality of the Frimley range, runs from Bagshot towards Ascot, round to Sunninghill, and thence towards King's Beeches and Earlywood, thus enclosing a large depression of morass called Sunninghill Bog. This within living memory was quite untraversable, except by the causeway made across it in the time of Queen Anne.

The village is situated mostly on the eastern portion of this range. It is rather anomalous, however, to call its scattered houses a village at all. One would expect to look for it nestling compactly under the grey tower of its Norman Church, but why it is not there we shall see hereafter. A few isolated houses are the only remnants now of old Sunninghill.

Time has wrought great changes in the place. New houses, new roads, and new families render it rather difficult to realise its old features or its old associations. But let us endeavour to recall them.

There is no pleasanter spot in the parish than that which the Norman builders chose for their little forest church. It is surrounded by green meadows, extending towards the east to a streamlet flowing into what is now the Silwood Lake, and westward to a stronger moorland stream that drains the low lands of Swinley and Sunninghill Bog, and thence rushes onward to the same lake and Virginia Water. This stream was bordered in its course by those ancient pastures, the "denes," the "long deans," and the "lither deans," whose Saxon names tell us so plainly of our first "innings" of the great forest.

Adjoining the churchyard on the north, opposite to the Cedars, was the ancient church green, on which stood a small building called "the Church House," an adjunct rather of a lay than an ecclesiastical character. It was used for parochial meetings as well as for the transaction of ordinary public business, and was to the parish, I imagine, what the vestry was to the church. The "porringers" and other things used in the parochial festivities were kept there. We get an excellent description of these places from Aubrey, who, writing in the middle of the seventeenth century, says—"In every parish is or was a church howse, to which belonged spitts, crocks, &c., utensils for dressing provision. Here the howsekeepers met and were merry and gave their charitie: the young people came there too, and had dancing, bowling, shooting at buttes, &c., the ancients sitting gravely by looking on." In the earliest deed we have relating to this property (5th September 1632), a transfer from Robinson to Gwynn and others, it is described as the church house, consisting of a building and half an acre of land on or near the ancient church green, and as being "assart lands," and "purpresture" of the forest of Windsor. It was to be held in trust for all the parishioners of Sunninghill. The church green, also an enclosure from the waste, had doubtless been a gift to the parish by the lord of the manor or by the King as lord paramount. A quit rent was paid for it, as for all other assart lands. Almost every village, in the olden time, had its green, the "locus ludorum" of the villagers. Selborne, we may remember, had its "play-place," a level area near the church, which was known as the "Plestor."

But this church green of ours was evidently not public property exactly, but the private property of the parish, and I find one of the neighbours claiming a right of footway across it. It became, as one can well imagine, a "Vineyard of Naboth" to an owner of the Cedars, the Hon. John Yorke, who managed to acquire it by exchange for fourteen acres of land on Chobham Common. At the north-east corner of the church green stood a small house, described at the beginning of the century as a "genteel cottage," near to the Cedars, and now forming part of the stable buildings.

Beyond this, northward, we look across to the pleasant bank on which stood the ancient manor house of Eastmore; and below it to the right another old mansion known as "Farrants," and the farmhouse still standing in the valley by the lake. Westward of these is Tetworth, from which towards Cheapside (the market-place) we touch on what was once the old Lammas Lands, and come to Lord's Green, where now is the Tun Inn. East of that was the mill, not long since burnt down—a very ancient property, held of the lord of the manor, at the rent of a "red rose." Still further on we strike the borders of Coworth.

At the crossways the Lime Avenue of King's Wick contributes to the charm of a piece of roadside scenery not often surpassed.

COTTAGE IN THE BACK LANE.

It was still more beautiful in olden time, for within living memory the Wells Lane was but a narrow country way, with sloping banks covered in the spring-time with wild flowers; and the Church Lane had a row of trees on each side, meeting overhead, and forming one of the prettiest features of the village.

In the valley, towards Ascot Heath, stood the old Wells Inn, of which I shall have much to say. These places were isolated in the great common that on all sides surrounded them, and which even until the present century ran up with its wild gorse-covered heathlands into the heart of the village itself, so that King's Wick, the village green, and the Cedars were on the margin of the waste. A farm or two had arisen in the valley by the Wells, and on the southern slopes of the Blackwick or Kingsbeech ridge patches had been cultivated in places on the grain-demand which came with the great war.

Opposite to the King's Wick meadow is what was called "the General's Piece," in earlier times a portion of the waste, which the good folk of Sunninghill also used as their green, and a charming spot it was. Overlooking the swamps towards Swinley Forest in the distance, and open to the full light of the setting sun, the forester from his hovel on the hillside may have listened to the belling of the deer, or to the welcome note of the Ruff and the Reeve in the bog below.

It has been the scene of many a festive gathering. Here were celebrated the "Donkey Revels," an annual festival of great repute with the villagers, generally held on a Sunday, and was a great feast. On the east of this was a piece of the common afterwards allotted to King's Wick, called the "Donkey Laurels;" and not far from that was "the Roundabout," where still stands a mound crowned by a clump of Scotch firs, and scaled by a winding path. It is now part of the Frognal property. This, too, was the scene of many a joyous gathering of the young men and maidens of the forest.

Beyond this lay Beggars'-bush Heath,—why so called? Was it the trysting-place or altar of the gipsies and beggars? For such a custom at one time prevailed, as is shown by friend Jacques, in "As You Like It," asking, "And will you, being a man of your breeding, be married under a bush like a beggar?"

This part of our common was one of the pleasantest spots in the parish. Before Silwood Cottage and Oakleigh were built, the wayfarer from the King's Wick crossways, leaving Ashurst and its fish-ponds on the one side, and a smaller house on the other, would come to the butcher's shop in the valley where Fir Grove now stands. Here the common widened, extending for miles southward, and bending round towards the east to where now Silwood House is, and so to Lord's Green; but keeping straight over the hill he would come to the intersecting road to "Sunninghill Dale," and to a cluster of cottages—"Farmer Brown's," Morton's, and Portsmouth's. General Frederick's old house was over the brow on the southern margin of the waste, and facing the common in the present Mill Lane, Lady Harewood's. On the top of the heath before you come to Titness Wood was the residence now known as the Oaks.

But how changed it all is! Then there was hardly a tree in that direction to intercept the distant prospects over the heath, so that the Surrey hills beyond the dale greatly added to the beauty of the view.

Our village has never been the seat of any flourishing trade, nor is it even agricultural, for Nature has given it a soil as inimical to cultivation for profit as it is delightful for residence.

To its balmy air and wholesome soil, as well as to its wild beauty, it owes much of its fair fame; but to the pleasures of the chase it is still more indebted. Its dowry was, being "proper and convenient," as the Conqueror deemed it, "for a royal retirement, and its suitableness for hunting."

Sunninghill lay wide of the chief thoroughfares, in complete seclusion, buried in what was once the depths of the great Bearroc Wood, through which neither the lonely traveller nor the many armies which have made this country the path of their inroads ventured to advance.

The wonderful road which the Romans constructed has long been abandoned, although here and there still clearly discernible above the swamps and hills which its undeviating line encountered. Ages, however, passed before any modern road struck into the forest.

Should these perambulations excite curiosity to know more of the earlier history of the ancient village, I will endeavour to explore it. I ought at once, however, to anticipate the alarm which anything like a "dry-as-dust" dissertation will occasion, and recommend those who have no archæological taste to turn over the next few pages.

CHAPTER VIII.
Local Derivations.

"I hate such old-fashioned trumpery."

"I love it, I love everything that's old: old friends, old times, old manners, old books, old wines."—*She Stoops to Conquer.*

HOW eloquently our local names remind us of our forest origin. That of our county, the derivation of which has been so variously rendered, is very characteristic. Some derive it from its Beechwood, but I am inclined to think it comes from the Gaelic *Barrach*, "the birch," so prevalent here—hence the Barrach or Berroc wood that anciently occupied so large a part of the forest, and ultimately Berroc-scire, and Berkshire. The Saxon was *Beorce*, "the birch," I think, not *Beoce*, "the beech." Swinley, like Frogmore, speaks for itself. The Saxon Charter of King Edmund calls it *Swinleia*, in like manner Eversley, from *Eofer*, a wild boar, with the Anglo-Saxon *leia*, a sort of bosky open pasture; Wolley or Wolvely, from *Wulver leia*, the place of wolves; Cranborne, the Crane burn or stream, that bird having been common here at one time; Bearwood, from *Bare*, the Old English for boar. Then Englemere and Englefield, the very name of their early Saxon possessors, the "mere" signifying here, probably, the lake or water, and not, as in many other cases in the neighbourhood, the boundary of forest or county, as in Haslemere and Winchmere. Bromhall and Bramshill, otherwise Bramselle, from the broom so flourishing there; Ockholt, the Oak-wood; Bracknell or Brackenowl, or as in the Saxon it was written *Braccan heale*, from its bracken; Hagthornes, from the Old English *hag*, a haw or berry; Coworth, the Cow warth or farm; Egham, Windlesham, pure Saxon terminations; Ashridge, Holly-hull, Beech-hull; Shrubshull, described at one time as Thornhull, but afterwards in several old charters called "Sorbes-hull," signifying merely shrub or scrub.[*]

---

[*] See old translation in MS. note-book in possession of Mr. H. G. Poulter of Bagshot. See also Mr. Corner's paper "Surrey" (Archaeological Collections, vol. i. 1858).

But it is in these ancient forest and manorial charters and perambulations that we get the earliest as well as the most interesting and authentic notices of our country. The Charter of Frithwald to the Abbey of Chertsey, A.D. 666, that of King Alfred about 889, and of Edward the Confessor in 1062, are well worthy of our study.*

These alleged Saxon Charters are in Latin, but the description of the land limits are in Anglo-Saxon. They were transcribed from a manuscript in the Cottonian Library of the British Museum, written, it is supposed, about the time of King Stephen; and although the names of the places may have been mostly those of Saxon days, several were Norman. In more than one instance this is clearly the case. The charter is from the Chertsey Register of the twelfth century, and was doubtless interpolated at that time. How strikingly it pictures to us the desolation of the country, in which, there being but few villages or homesteads, natural objects are the principal landmarks—old trees, streams or hills, with here and there some ancient road or weird monument of a still older race, spoken of as ancient many centuries ago.

Mr. Corner gives the following translation of one of these.

The landmarks in "Alfred the wise king's day, of the 15 hide of land in Egham. First at the Shigtren above Halsham"—the Shigtren, it is said, was probably the tree of victory, but it is quite as likely to have been the hollow tree, used as a drain for a small watercourse—"and so forth right to the Thren Burghen"—clearly the three remarkable barrows near Egham called the Three Bury Hills—"from the Burghs to Eccantricwe"—an oak tree—"forthright extending to the south end of Sire Giffrens Heath de la Croix. From the heath forthright almost to the further end of Herdies,† and so forth through the Thornie Hull to Hertleys nether ende of the Menechene Rude.‡ From

---

* Our "fords" are very numerous, but in the adjoining county of Hants they assumed another form (from another tribe probably), and we get the interesting termination "stoke," as in Basingstoke, Ilchenstoke, Laverstoke, derived, as Mr. T. W. Shore, I think, well points out (Archæological Review, Ap., 1889), not from a stockade defence, as doubtless in some cases it was, but from the fashion adopted to cross a stream or bog by throwing in materials secured by stakes, and thus called a "stoke." Every place bearing this termination is found on a stream. When the stones could withstand the rush of water it remained simply a "wade"—Ed. I. perambulation speaks of the "wade" near Romsey. The "wades" or fords were ultimately mostly spanned by bridges, and the places altered their names, as "Redbridge," anciently "Reodford," over the Test.

† This, I doubt not, was the herd-pastures of Coworth, from the Gothic *Hairdeis*, "herds."

‡ This ancient name of Hertleys (now Broomhall) is probably from the Saxon *Hert*, "the stag," being the sunny glade where the wild deer sunned themselves on the margin of the wood.

LOCAL DERIVATIONS.

the Rude down rightaway on the west side of Poddenhall almost to Winebright"—now Potnall Warren. From this the line went "westerly to a way that goeth to Winchester, that is called Shrubbestede, between the Shrubbes and Winebright going adown northward under the Park gate (or road), and so forth from the gate going along by the Park hedge to the new hedge, from the hedge along the Frithesbrook to the Hore Aepeldure." Which stream was this? A note in the Monasticon says it was a stream where peace was made, but surely it meant only the forest stream? "From the Hore Aepeldure to the Knepp by the Quelmes, from the Quelmes under the stonie held, and so going down by Tigelbeddeburn." This may mean the stony incline down by a stream that Norden shows flowing from near the spot in question eastward "down to that eyte that stands in the Thames at Lodders Lake"—probably the famous Magna Charta Island*—"and so forth along Thames by mid stream to Glenthuthe"—easily identified as a creek at the entrance to Egham racecourse—"from Glenthuthe by mid stream along Thames to the Huthe before Negen Stone"—the Hithe before the Nine Stones? Egham Hithe opposite to Staines. These were doubtless Druidical stones, the number nine being very significant in connection with ancient Pagan rites. The name of "Nine Stones" is given in Cornwall to groups of standing stones, although numbering more than nine; and through the Maen Tol of that county the patient was sometimes drawn nine times to cure deformities or pains in the back. "From the hythe along Thames by the mid stream down to Nippenhale, from Nippenhale to Wheleshuthe over right to the Black Withege"—the black willow tree—"into Fulbrook, from Fulbrook into Sirepol, from Sirepol into Whelegate." The strangers' way or road, as some think, is meant by this; but here we are getting away from our forest country, so I must leave the remaining names. Now I cannot admit for these interesting descriptions any earlier date than that given to the MS., the time of King Stephen, or Henry I.

Just then a Saxon origin of title was becoming of value, and when the monks did not possess such a charter they sometimes fabricated one, or reduced into writing their oral traditions; and we must not forget that the ancient charters of Chertsey may have been destroyed when the abbey was burnt. The heath of Sire Geoffrey de la Croix, for instance, is a Norman name, and establishes the date, surely, as that of the transcript.

---

* The name Lodders Lake may, I think, have come from the Saxon *Lád*, the raised causeway-path through the marsh there.

This is the earliest notice I have found of Shrubshill; and Hertley's the most ancient name of what is now Broomhall Farm.

The "Hore Appeltree" was a favourite boundary mark in early times. In the Saxon Chronicle it is said that the dire conflict of the battle of Senlac took place at the "Haran Apuldran."

We get here two names which lasted for ages, the "Knepp" and the "Quelmes," the latter especially to the present day. I have noticed it in an old purveyance list of 1617, as a property in Winkfield in the hands of Sir Richard Lovelace. The word is sometimes thought to be a corruption of *almes*, and to signify a gift or possession in "frank almoigne" to a church, and this was the view Mr. Waterson in his account of Winkfield took of it; but it has also another and much more terrible meaning, derived from the Anglo-Saxon *cwellan*, "to kill;" *cwealm*, "death;" and thence *cwalm-stowe*, a place of violent death—in fact, the place of execution; and that, I think, was its meaning here. It was on a spot long known as "Gallows" Farm. The other place, the "Knepp," occurs as the forest boundary through the Norman and Plantagenet reigns as *La Cnappe*—the "Knepp by the Quelmes." It was clearly a hill, from the Anglo-Saxon *cnap*, "a knob."

> "Hark! on knap of yonder hill
> Some sweet shepherd tunes his quill." *—BROWN.

The Tigelbeddeburn is simply, we are told, the tile-bed stream.

Again in Frithwalds Charter describing the boundaries of Chertsey, we get an interesting allusion to the *antiqua fossa* "Fullingadich" which Mr. Salmon conjectured to have been the causeway between Staines and Egham; but in this he must have been mistaken, I think, for in this charter it is said, "up endlong Waie to Waigebrugge of Waigebrugge innan the ælde muledich: midennerde of there dich on there ælde herestræt; andlange stræt on Woburnbrugge."

Now the *ælde muledich* is, I conjecture, the old "mud-wall," and the *ælde herestræt* was the ancient military way there. Then we get as a boundary mark the *Curtenstapele*—the gibbet, in truth—this being another name for it, from *Cwerten*, "a prison," and *stapele*, "an upright post." †

---

* There is a curious instance of a similar hillock at Selborne, which, although surrounded by arable fields, was always left unploughed. It was called Kite's Hill, and close to it was another eminence known as Gally [Gallows] Hill. The kite was ever to be found sailing above the gibbet. Over old London Bridge, where the traitors' heads were hung in the fifteenth century, they were especially numerous.

† After 1076 this word *Cwerten*, or *Cwcartern*, gave place to *prisun*. See T. E. K. Oliphant's Old and Middle Eng.

Since writing the above, I have been favoured with the perusal of an old MS. commonplace book, bearing date about the latter end of the seventeenth century, and in it are translations of these charters, varying in several interesting particulars from the foregoing. In the Egham boundary the *Eccantriewe*, "oak-tree," becomes ye Holme tree or Holly.

Poddenhall is given as "a village called Woodenhale, at a bridge called Winbridge almost," and continues the translation thus, "from Winbridge westward to ye way by wch they goe to Winchest^r wch is called Shrubbshead" (that is to say, a head of young twiggs), "between ye young twiggs and Winbridge going down northward beneath ye gate or way of a hedge full of oakes, and so forward from ye gate going by ye hedge of oakes to a ford called Harpisford to a Mill. from ye Mill going forward by ye hedge of oakes to a new harbour, from thence all along Frithesbrooke" (that is, a river where peace was made) "to an old apple-tree, from thence to a little Hillock neere ye Gallowes or Gibbets," and then continuing much as in the other translations.

The "new harbour" may have been the first enclosure there of the Great Park.

But this old account was the more especially interesting, as completely confirming the surmise as to the meaning of the "Knepp by the Quelmes." It is there identified most satisfactorily as the little hill by the gibbets.*

To these ancient derivations I will add only one more, not however the less interesting, as having occasioned a pleasant interchange of thought between Charles Kingsley and his friend the Rev. Isaac Taylor, a great authority on such matters—the termination "shot" in Bagshot, Aldershot, which it was suggested was from "holt" as a prefix; but this, as Kingsley himself admitted, was hardly satisfactory.

I cannot accept it at all. We get "holts" all over the country; while "shot," I believe, is local. I have never heard any plausible derivation of this termination. The Scandinavian *Sceoppa*, a "treasury," has been suggested; and we are told of the Danish *Kirk-shot*, and of the *Shot-flagon* which Boniface presented to his departing

---

* This word *Cnappe* has passed through several languages, with but slight variation, for many hundred years. It is a remnant of the dialect of our earliest British inhabitants, of whom we are reminded by the neighbouring tumuli at Ascot. It is a pure Gaelic word, *Cnap*, a knob or hillock. The Anglo-Saxon was *Cnæp*. In the south of England the C was long retained, but in the north it ultimately gave place to the Teutonic K, and it became "Knap" or "Knepp," as in Knepp Castle, standing on its Sussex knoll. The Normans recast the original word in a French mould, and made it *La Cnappe*. See M'Alpine's Gael. Dict.; Macleod and Dewar's Gael. Dict.; T. L. K. Oliphant's Old and Middle Eng.; and Maclean's Hist. of Celtic Languages.

customers when they had "drunk above a shilling." But it is not from that, I think, but from the old Saxon word *sceat*, a portion or corner of the sea, a bay,* in our case, meaning a corner or angle of the waste, usually enclosed by turf banks, so commonly practised in this country. The Norman form of this word was *sceat, sete*, or *shete*.

Domesday speaks of "Holesete" for Holdshot, and Norman Charters call Bagshot "Bagscete;" while the Testa de Nevill writes "Bakeshete" and "Bacshet." These afterwards became "shote" and "shot."

We get the very word in "Shete" Street, Windsor; and close to that town in ancient days there were places called "the great shete" and "the little shete," situated in a corner of the larger common known as "Le Worth;" and in 1393 a deed describes a piece of ground as "in campo dicto le shete."

In a Forest Boundary Inquisition of 1327, before referred to, we have the line described as running from Shrubshill to Horton, and "abinde per medium *la Shete* usque Gomerychford" exactly where it crosses the border-land of Bagshot and Bigshot.

Here, then, we have the exact word, as it was used in Norman days, applied to the locality of Bagshot. I am the more convinced that this is the true derivation by observing that all the places having this termination are curiously enough on the border of the county or district in which they are situated. I can find no exception.

Our nearest is Lavershot, the Windlesham Nursery, close to the Berkshire border. Then Bagshot is in an angle of Surrey; Bigshot at the junction of three counties; Bramshot, Grayshot, and Lodshot in an angle of Hampshire, between Sussex and Surrey; and Aldershot in a complete corner of the same county on the border of Surrey. Nor must I forget Calshot, with its grey castle, in a remote corner between Southampton Water and the Solent.

All these, anciently written in the same way, have been, I believe, corrupted by broad pronunciation into "shot." We may trace this origin of the word in its application to that little projecting angular window of mediæval architecture called a "shot-window," of which Chaucer tells us—

> "And stille he stant under the schot wyndowe;
> Unto his brest it raught, it was so low;"

---

* See Bosworth's Anglo-Saxon Dict.; Halliwell's Dict. of Archaic Words; Carlisle's Account of Charities, p. 305.

and again in that finer picture given us by old Gavin Douglas, who speaks of the "shot-wyndo that he unschet one litel on char," to look out over the wild northern sea from the walls of Tantallon. The shot-window was a projection from the wall, as the land shot was a projecting corner into another territory. Shakespeare still more clearly supports my derivation in a very poetical passage of Henry V., sadly misunderstood by some commentators, wherein he says—

> "I will sell my dukedom
> To buy a slobbery and a dirty farm
> In that nook-shotten isle of Albion."

Singer explains this, I think, correctly, *shotten*, anything projected, an isle, that is, that shoots out into capes, promontories, and necks of land—my meaning exactly.

In an ancient Inquisition of the Forest, 16 Ed. III., I meet with a place known as "La Morhulle." It may have been the Quelmes or the hill near Virginia Water, afterwards known as "Hangman's Hill," the site now of the Clock-case, or perhaps the Quelmes in Winkfield.

CHAPTER IX.

Sunninghill in Norman and Plantagenet Days.

OF Sunninghill it is surprising to find how little has ever been written. Mr. Lysons disposes of it in a few lines; and yet nowhere else is there to be found more than a repetition of his account. Local information amounted hardly to a tradition, but rather to the expression of a current belief, that our village was a *vill* in Saxon times; that the church contained Saxon memorials, and was of Saxon origin; and that the ancient yew-tree in the churchyard was a landmark alluded to in Domesday.

I began in hope that I might be able to confirm these statements; but after some little research I can come to no other conclusion than that they are all without foundation.

The last with regard to the yew-tree may be first dismissed. There is not a word in the Domesday Survey referring to it.

That the church had a Saxon origin is not so easily refuted. The fact has been assumed, probably, on the strength of the inscription which is known to have been carved on the impost moulding of the old chancel arch; but this is fully gone into elsewhere, and, I venture to think, disposed of.

It is almost, however, involved in our third question. Was Sunninghill a village in Saxon times? I believe not. Everything I can discover tends to the conviction that in the time of Edward the Confessor Sunninghill was but the name of a wild spot in the heart of the forest —an early clearance on these sunny hills especially favoured by the Saxon shepherds and swine-herds.

Had a village existed here, then, it could hardly have been effaced so utterly, not only from off the face of the earth, for that would be quite possible, but from the records of history, and from the still more lasting evidences of tradition. Not a vestige can I find, not a ruin nor a stone to mark its site, nor the slightest allusion in any ancient writer to give colour to the fact of its existence.

The negative evidences are strongly against it. What says that most valuable of all our records for such a purpose, the Conqueror's Great Survey? Mr. Lysons and all other writers who allude to Sunninghill tell us that it is not mentioned in Domesday at all.

But we know it was royal demesne, and as such must have been mentioned, if not exactly described, in Domesday under the heading "Terra Regis."* Yet by its own name it certainly is not there—a fact that strongly confirms the theory of our non-existence as an inhabited village at that time. Our identity may have been lost, but I think we may trace it, if we look in the right place. Now Sunninghill had no separate manorial existence—it was parcel of the Manor of Cookham; and there we must look for it. "The King," says Domesday, "holds Cookham in demesne—King Edward held it." It is described as containing, besides its home lands, a certain outlying forest tract separated from them. The words are—"It answered for 20 hides, but was never taxed, it had pannage for 100 hogs, and another part is in the forest of Windsor."

Now this isolated district, this "other part in the forest of Windsor," was precisely what is now the parish of Sunninghill, and has been always to this day treated as a detached parcel of the Manor of Cookham.

So we are, after all, in Domesday; and although thus incidentally, it was the only way in which, under the circumstances, we could have been described.

It is even doubtful if at the time of the Conquest we had any parochial existence, and I must fain believe that those rude shepherds and their flocks, and the swine-herds and their happy pigs, were the sole tenants of the warm sandy banks that ere long became the site of Sunninghill.

In support of this view it may be added that in the Nomina Villarum (9th Ed. II.), Sunninghill is not mentioned, although Winkfield and Ascot are.

The very first notice I can find of our Sunninghill country is in the Saxon Charter of A.D. 666, in which the Chertsey lands are said to be bounded by another province called "Sunninges," and this is one of the earliest forms also of the name. In the records of Broomhall we

---

* Elton's Tenures of Kent.

shall meet with the name of "Isabella de Sunninges" as presiding over the Nunnery.

The word "Sunninges," like "Wokinges" (Woking), was probably a patronymic giving the name of a tribe to the district they inhabited.

It is in connection with the Nunnery of Broomhall that we hear next of Sunninghill. We probably owe the existence both of the Church and the Nunnery to that great burst of religious enthusiasm and general culture which so remarkably characterised the middle of the twelfth century.

This house was not long established before it obtained, as a necessary adjunct, to aid in its work of civilisation, the royal gift of our Church. This could hardly have been raised by the Prioress and her nuns, whose slender means were quite inadequate to such an effort, for had it been so we should doubtless have seen it nearer to the Nunnery walls.

King John, by that all important Charter of 1199, gave the Church of Sunninghill and its belongings to the Nunnery of Broomhall, thus clearly establishing the fact that the Church, whether erected by the "King's ancestors" or not, was then in his hands—an independent, and, in all probability, an earlier foundation.

I think its date, for reasons elsewhere explained, may be put within a few years of 1130. However that may be, it is interesting to see the gradual process of the Nunnery's growth. Its first grant of the Manor of Broomhall, the wild tract of heath-land on which the house was erected, was soon added to by enclosures from the surrounding waste and marshes. In exactly the same way the village itself arose. The ruling figure in the scene was that of "our Lord the King," in whose vast demesne these new elements came into existence. The nobles, his bailiffs, or knights in capite; the nuns, his dependents in Frankalmoigne; the Bordarii and the Villani were all obtaining a footing in their several ways, and laying the foundation of "fixity of tenure" and our modern system of land ownership.

Long and arduous was the "struggle for existence" which these rude tillers of the soil waged, not only against the forest and its denizens, but, far worse, against the forest laws by which they were so jealously guarded.

Encroachments were dealt with by the forest courts; the purprestures condoned by fine or favour became "assart lands," and were paid for by an annual assart rent in the nature of an acknowledgment or quit-rent, the payment of which thenceforth secured the ownership, rather than the occupation merely of the land. In fact, these tenants

SUNNINGHILL IN NORMAN AND PLANTAGENET DAYS.

in ancient or royal demesne became, as has been well said, a kind of copyholders of free tenure.*

The fines and rents together, however, were sometimes fully equal to what was then the value of the freehold; † but the quit-rents, although originally important, became in after times trivial as against the rising value of the land, and at last altogether ceased. The cost of collection eventually rendering the rent valueless, the Statute of Charles II. reduced the services due by the tenants of the Crown to a form, which left them merely nominal.

Thus the holding became virtually the freehold of the yeoman or the villager who had grown up upon it—a curious contrast to what is now taking place. The increment which now inures to the benefit of the landlord then inured to the advantage of the tenant.

The earliest name I can find associated with the infant village is that of William de Cumba, who conveyed certain lands in Sunninghill to Gilbert, the son of Blackeman, as early as the 9th of Richard I.‡

This name occurs again in later times at Winkfield, where in a list of those liable for purveyance in 1617, the Quelmes estate is described as belonging to Sir Rd. Lovelace, late "Blackman's."

But the name curiously has much earlier and almost romantic associations, reminding us of one of the great Saxon families of Berkshire, to which there is reason to believe our ancient parishioner belonged. Mr. Freeman, speaking of the consternation at the approach of the Conqueror, tells us of one " Blæcman " or Blackman, a wealthy secular priest of Berkshire, a tenant of the Abbey of Abingdon, and himself founder of a goodly Church in its neighbourhood, "who risked all his possessions, temporal and spiritual, to share the fortunes of the widow of Godwine." He is supposed to have fled with her to Exeter. He is spoken of in the History of Abingdon as " Presbiter pecuniosus." Now we must remember that the Manor of Winkfield, adjoining our parish, belonged to the Abbey of Abingdon; and there we find the family of Blackman remaining centuries after.

---

* In 1606, in a conveyance of three acres of land from the Feoffees of the Crown to John Robinson the Vicar, the limitation was "to him, his heirs, and assigns holding of the King and his successors in fealty only in free and common socage, and not in chief or by knight's service; and yielding to the King's Majesty in the name of a fee-farme 4d. at the feast of St. Michael the Archangel."

† Thus in 1606, Rd. Furbanck and Sir Francis Wolley and others were found to have "assarted" ninety-seven acres of the forest, and they were fined £70, 9s. 8d., and left at a rent of 11s. 9d. And again in 1633, Thomas Perry of Winkfield was fined at the Swainmote £5 for grubbing up half an acre of coppice ground near Fernhill. These were considerable sums at that time.

‡ Fines 1195 to 1214.

The next information we meet with of local interest is from the Inquisition post-mortem on the death of Galfrid de Baggesete, 39 Henry III., who is shown to have been possessed of the Manor of Chobham.

"*Bageshote ballivat Shunghill er Coworthe terr.*—A certain serjauntia which belonged not to Bagshote but to Shunghull and Cowirthe held of our Lord the King in capite. Said serjauntia worth 75 shillings. Said Geoffrey pays to our Lord the King 60 shillings annually for the said Bailiwick. He also holds Byrell in capite of Lord Wm. de Wyndlesore by seizin of half a knight's fee paying ½ a mark."

This return then continues—"That Alicia de Fraxle, daughter of a certain aunt of the said Galfrid, who was senior, is one heir; and Alicia de Tywe [et] Johanna de Hurul? aunt of the said Galfrid, are the nearest heirs of the said Galfrid, of whom "Alicia" the younger aforesaid is of the age of forty years."

The jury were always particular to specify which was the eldest heiress; and in this case it was the more necessary, as, although by the law of England all the daughters take equally their father's estate, the "serjeanty" devolved, as an office or possession of honour requiring personal service, on the eldest in exclusion of the others.*

It is singular, however, that in our Manor of Cookham a custom prevailed for the eldest daughter to take in ordinary descent in exclusion of her sisters.†

This Inquisition also shows the connection which has always existed between Sunninghill and Coworth. From this Alicia de Fraxle or Foxley we get notice of a family that soon after rose to great distinction in the forest. Professor Montagu Burrows, in his interesting History of the Brocas Family, says that the first member of the family of De Foxle who can be traced is Sir John de Foxle, Baron of the Exchequer in 1308, and that his only son Thomas succeeded to his mother Constantia's Manor of Bray in 1333. This Thomas held the high office of Constable of the Castle of Windsor, and is still better known to us as the builder of the old mansion of Bramshill, portions of which remain worked up in the magnificent Jacobean house still standing on its noble site at Eversley, which Lord Zouch erected in 1604. But I think this Inquisition carries back the family history to a still earlier generation. The mother of the above-mentioned Alice de Fraxle or Foxle was an aunt, it seems,

---

* Thus by Inquisition post-mortem, John de Pecham, 21 Ed. I. 35. It appears that he left three daughters, of whom the eldest was heir to his land in serjeanty.

† See trial of Slaverton and Logan, Exch., vol. vi. p. 220.

of the Norman knight Galfrid de Baggesete, this showing the existence here of the De Foxles at least a century earlier than the time stated. They afterwards intermarried with the family of De Brocas.

But the most important personage here at that time was the Norman knight Richard de Battaille, chief forester of Windsor, bailiff of the Bailiwick of Bagshot, and also of that in which our parish was situated, and which for ages afterwards was known as Battles Bailiwick. He and his ancestors were probably the first great lords of our village, and owners of the whole clearance. The family afterwards resided at Winkfield, where the Battles Aisle is to this day a record of their ancient existence there.

The first time we meet with this Richard is in the 51st Henry III., and the Inquisition post-mortem shows his death in 1271. In the following year John of London was invested with the lands which Ricus Bataille held of the King.

It must have been of him that the Hundred Roll speaks when it reminds us of that ancient practice of the "Frank-pledge" or engagement of neighbour for neighbour, and gives us the names of the five freemen who were then answerable for the great man of Sunninghill.

The same document goes on to report "that Richard de Batayile junior had made a 'purpresture' at Sunninghill in the Manor of Cocham of ten acres." But by what authority they knew not.

We again meet with Henry Battaille, junior, as forester of the Bailiwick of Ascot in the 12th Ed. III.*

The Patent Roll, 51st Henry III., introduces us to the next great family with which we were connected, when it tells us that Richard Battaill the forester granted to John de Sunninghull an acquittance for his dogs having been taken in the forest.

This Hundred Roll also mentions the name of Isabella de Sunninghull, and records her amusing litigation with another lady in the neighbourhood, Johanna, the widow of John de Wolvely. When ladies quarrel they often carry things to extremities; and so did they, for they carried the case to Windsor on petition to the Queen herself. Why not to the King? Was he away on his Palestine adventures? or was it not rather because the manor had been settled on the Queen.

This was doubtless the same Isabella de Sunninghull who in 1295 presided over the Nunnery of Broomhall.

John de Sunninghull, and Johanna his wife, in 1363, purchased of

---

* 3 Cal. Rot. Pat.

one John Holm the Manor of Sunninghull, with the appurtenances, one messuage, and one carrucate of land, and twenty acres of wood in Twytenham, or as it is also therein called, Whytenham; but how John Holm acquired it does not appear. And in this same year James de Colewell, St. John Brocas's bailiff, purchased 16s. worth of timber of this John de Sunninghull,* who is mentioned as owner of the wood called Red Grove, Coldwellhurst. In 1376 we find a John de Sonynghull transferring the same estate to "Wills le Venour." †

This is the first time that we hear of the *Manor* of Sunninghill, as in courtesy it was also described in 6th Ed. IV., when the Inquisition post-mortem on the death of "John Noreys Armiger" states that he died seized of the "Manor" of Sunninghill.

But the survey of James I. at the Land Revenue Record Office clearly shows it to have been only parcel of the Manor of Cookham, as described in the Hundred Roll, and as such it was always held in demesne of the King, or rather the King himself held it as of his demesne, and committed its management to a bailiff. ‡

I must here correct a little error into which Miss Strickland has been led in her Lives of the Queens of England, and has evidently led many others. She gives Sunninghill as the abode for a time of the young Queen of Richard II., but she has mistaken the place. § Her words are :—

"While this revolution was effected the young Queen was removed to Sunninghill. There she was kept a State prisoner." Again—"Isabella took an extraordinary part in this movement for the restoration of her husband. When the Earls of Kent and Salisbury came with their forces to Sunninghill, where she was abiding, they told her," &c. In the note she gives her authorities, which at once disprove the statement—Guthrie and Froissart; Sir John Hayward, p. 127, ed. 1599. He says—"The insurgent lords came to the Queen from Colnbrook to Sunning, a place near Reading." That was not to Sunninghill, but to Sonning, often spelt Sunning, where the Bishop of Salisbury had a beautiful manor house, to which another Isabella was once removed from Leeds Castle in Kent.

Sunninghill was always from the earliest times famous for its timber, which here, as in all the other parts of the royal demesne, belonged to the King.

Sunninghill, East Hampstead, and Foly-John Park supplied large quantities for the repairs of the Castle, and for the building of Eton College; and Sunninghill in particular was resorted to for oak for the

---

* See Brocas Family, Professor Burrows, and also Inquisition post-mortem, 6 Ed. III.
† There was a Jo. de Venur, a man of property, at Oakhanger, who made a grant of land to the Priory of Selborne in 1233.
‡ Roll 1608, lib. 2, fo. 9.
§ Vol. iii. p. 26.

building of St. George's Chapel at Windsor. And in the time of Philip and Mary, Sunninghill Park sent its quota for the poor knights' houses which were then erected.

From a very ancient period there has been a close connection between our parish and the Castle at Windsor.

In the time of Edward II. Sunninghill was held by the Queen Isabella as her own private estate; and this may account for Isabella of Sunninghull's appeal to the Queen. We find Sir John de la Beche, the powerful Berkshire knight, whose effigy now lies mouldering in the interesting old Church at Aldworth, "did suit and service to Isabel, Queen of England, once in three weeks, at her Court at *Cookham*." For several reigns it would seem to have formed part of the peculiar appanage of the Queens of England.

During the Wars of the Roses, Sunninghill as a royal manor shared, at least nominally, the various changes of fortune of its royal masters; and soon a time came when it knew not, from day to day, who its chief lord was. But the storm that brought down so many of the great families of England, and "left riderless many a Berkshire steed," helped to secure in their holdings the actual tenants of the soil. It gave a death-blow to the feudal system, but a new life to the inferior tenures, which were becoming the freeholds of a later day. The lower tenants felt but little of the shock, so long as they paid their quit-rents.

Henry IV., at the outset of his reign, settled on his youngest son, Humphrey, Duke of Gloucester, "the good Duke Humphrey" of history, the Manors of Cookham and Bray, including Sunninghill, in tail general; and William Fyenles or Fyennes was his "forester of our Bailiwick of Twychen."

On Henry's death, these manors were doubtless part of the large dower with which his widow, the Queen Joanna of Navarre, had been endowed. Her stepson, the young King Henry V., left her in the enjoyment of her wealth and his palaces to go off to the wars in France, which opened with the great victory of Agincourt; and, strangely enough, he sent home as a prisoner Joanna's own son. But an ill state of things was brewing up between Henry and his stepmother. Her money was a fearful temptation to one who thirsted for every farthing he could lay hand on to prosecute his glorious campaigns. She at that juncture (and the coincidence is peculiar) was accused of witchcraft, sent off prisoner to Leeds Castle, and deprived of all her dower-lands. Meanwhile Henry was helping himself to her ready-money to pay his soldiers and even his own servants.

But as soon as Henry V. died in 1422, these lands were restored to her, subject to conditions as regards improvements, by those to whom the Crown had granted them during her imprisonment.

Our great Lord of Gloucester became Protector to his little nephew of ten months' old. The profits of the Manors of Cookham and Bray, Binfield and Sunninghill, were devoted to the repairs of Windsor Castle, and in 1447 stood charged with the payment of one hundred marks per annum for these repairs; and on this account, when in that year various royal manors were charged with certain sums by way of dower for the late Queen, these manors were especially exempted.

Henry VI. had now grown up, and had married Margaret of Anjou. The "good Duke of Gloucester" is made away with at the bidding, it is thought, of the Queen and her accomplices. William Perkins, his bailiff here, was dismissed, and John Norres reigned in his stead.

Shortly after Norres' appointment was passed the Statute 28, Henry VI., the quaint preamble of which is worth noticing, to show some of the grievances of which our forefathers of Sunninghill had to complain :—

"Whereas the King having understood that his pore Liege peple by full long tyme have been grevously charged with continuell takyng of theire goodes and cattell for the dispenses of his honourable household whereof they have not been sufficiently contented nor paied to their grete empoveryshyng, he therefore assigned or charged for these purposes on the Seven Hundreds of Cookham and Bray among others viii[li]. * "

In 1454 a hundred marks yearly were charged on the same manors for payment of the King's household.

Edward IV., in 1468, confirmed to the Queen for her support the profits of the Manor of Cookham and Bray, and the Seven Hundreds and the lands in the forest, which had then lately belonged to Humphrey, Duke of Gloucester, deceased; and Henry VII. continued the grant to her with other estates in lieu of her dower.†

These royal manors continued to be set apart for the advantage of the Queen Elizabeth (Woodville), and were administered by her bailiffs.

Sir William Norreys, who resided at Ockwells, succeeded to that office on the death of his father.

Henry VII., however, on his accession in 1485, appropriated these estates. But in 1488 we hear of Sir William Norreys again as "bailiff for the Queen," his former mistress's daughter; and in 1501 the old commander's son, Sir Edward Norreys, took his father's place, and held the stewardship with Robert Bray.

---

* 25 Henry VI. Rotuli Parliamentorum. † 1 Henry VII.

CHAPTER X.

Sunninghill in Stuart Times.

WE will now pause for awhile and endeavour to realise what Sunninghill was like when Elizabeth's great reign had closed, and her Puritan keeper, Sir Henry Neville, was the principal man of the place.

In the barren heathlands around us but few enclosures had yet been made.

Broomhall had fallen, and was now dismantled; its ruins had been turned into dwellings for the College tenants; and its barns and buildings gave shelter to their corn and cattle. It was the only farm in the neighbourhood.

The homesteads of the Norman De Baggesete and De Battaille * had passed to other hands, as also had the Cow-farm of Galfrid at Coworth. But ere long arose a still more important place, the Royal Lodge in Sunninghill Park, of which I speak so fully hereafter.

We must not forget the mill provided probably by the lord for his tenants. It was called Lord's Mill, and stood on the eastern side of Mr. Savory's lake. It was just within our parish, but the mill house stood in Winkfield, and Humphrey May, the tenant, was included in a list of those liable for purveyance for that parish in the seventeenth century. From the Manor Court Rolls I find that as early as the time of James I. this water-mill is mentioned, and also another then known

---

* In 1795 the Vicar exchanged a piece of land for another in Sunninghill which is described as abutting on a meadow called "Battle's Innings." Battle's Bailiwick, we may remember, included Sunninghill, and took its name from Richard de Battaille, the King's Bailiff in the time of Henry III.

The Innings was the enclosure reclaimed from the forest and marshes, and thus we get confirmation of the fact suggested by the Hundred Roll that Sunninghill was the homestead if not the place of residence of this great Norman lord and of his serfs and tenants. Several Statutes of Eliz. (5, 8, 23) speak of the recovery and "Inning" of Plumstead Marsh; and in 1531 a piece of ground was taken out of the "King's ferme" and "ynned" to enlarge the Little Park of Windsor.

as the Old Mill, which would carry us back to a remote period. The one was probably only the reconstruction of the other, "with all modern improvements." It was held of the lord at the rent of a red rose annually, if demanded—a pretty form of nominal rental (adopted, probably, from the Lancastrian badge), which became afterwards the less poetical peppercorn of our day. Potnal Park was also held in the same way.

This mill was a very important property, a "vested interest" in the owners, and in early times would have required the King's license for its erection; but once established, it had a monopoly in grinding the corn of all the tenants of the manor.*

Broomhall had a mill of its own. Out on the open waste stood the little Norman Church, with its low massive tower, grey even then with age. The roads which led to it were but little better than bridle tracks, over which now and then a good couple rode "pillion" to their devotions on high days and festivals. The family coach of the squire which figured in later years was not then known in England, and the farmer's cart could with difficulty travel over our roads.

The estate of King's Wick had existed for ages, probably, although the old house pulled down at the beginning of this century might not then have been built.

The Wells' Inn, which at a later date played so conspicuous a part in the history of the parish, may have been a woodman's house or underkeeper's lodge at that time, but neither Beech Grove nor the Cedars was erected, although on the last-named site there was a cottage. In truth, two or three mansions, and the mill, with one or two other houses of less importance, as many farmsteads of the yeomen, and a small colony of foresters and squatters, whose cottages and hovels were arising on the patches of "assart" lands which they had obtained, made up the Elizabethan village.

But this primitive community was in a state of restless growth, and on the eve of great changes. With the Stuarts a new order of things set in, and we begin to get a clearer idea of the parish and its people. Our documentary evidences become much more circumstantial. Norden's Survey, made for James I. in 1607, affords us an excellent account of the forest.

It was followed in 1608 by another survey of all the royal manors;

---

* See Serjeant Thorpe's charge at York, 1648, wherein it is stated to have been a crime "for any Milner to take excessive toll for grinding corn, viz., above a 20th part or 24th part, according to the strength of the water."

and that which relates to our parish, now at the Land Revenue Office, is interesting, although very indifferently executed. It tells us that "The Commonable and waste ground in the parish of Soninghill conteyne in the whole by estimation 1550 acres," and that "The bounde of the parish of Sonynghill first beginneth at Dornford towarde the east, and from thence southward to Kingswick, thence westward to Englemore Pond, thence to a conduit in Hedge Lane, and from thence to Dorneford before mentioned." It then tells us that Robert Hedge and Francis Broughton held lands in Sunninghill as of the Manor of Cookham.

Dornford, the starting-point, was some spot in the eastern corner of the parish, the old name of which is now quite forgotten. It was undoubtedly near Blackness Gate, probably on the Coworth stream, for we find the name as early as 1372, when William Drerenford of Coworth, and Johanna his wife, conveyed certain lands in Coworth and Sunninghill. The ford probably took its name from him.

It is curious to find the boundary line going thence southward to *Kingswick*—the earliest actual notice I have met with of that name. Where was it? It was certainly the name of the old mansion I have described; but if that is the spot alluded to, the jury was ill-informed on that subject, for the survey left out a large strip of land lying to the south which was the true boundary of our parish, and takes no notice of the isolated estate of Bromhall; and that they made this mistake is rather confirmed by the fact of their putting the extent of the waste at 1550 acres, while in the more accurate survey five years afterwards it was given at 1985. This omission would to some extent reconcile the two accounts. I incline to think it was the boundary of the manor, and not of the parish. Besides the waste there were the Lammas lands, reminding us of the olden time when agriculture furnished no roots for the cattle in winter, and when therefore, through half the year, no meat graced the lord's table save what had been salted down before Michaelmas. The great forest that lay at their doors supplied in its woods and waters the principal part of the subsistence as well as the pleasures of the people, yet the Manor House required its demesne, and the small Vicarage its "earable" closes, but what were the poor tillers and foresters to do? They all clubbed together, and cultivated their Lammas lands—those pastures and arable fields that were used by the little communities and townships throughout the country in common, as in early times nearly all the cultivated lands in the kingdom were, before the separate system of farming was adopted.

They were called Lammas* lands because on Lammas Day (1st August) every one had a right of common enjoyment of them. The fields were open to the cattle to graze till the following April, when they were again shut up for the purpose of cultivation. Every third year one of the fields was left fallow.

<small>This co-operative agrarian system was of Teutonic origin, upon which the Feudal Manorial arrangement afterwards became engrafted. Until the end of the fourteenth century there were no separate holdings in England. Then the stimulus given to sheep-farming struck the first fatal blow to these village communities. A worse one followed on the dissolution of the Monasteries; but it was not until the end of the eighteenth century, when war and an increasing population demanded a better system, that the common field cultivation ceased. See *Edinburgh Review*, October 1887.</small>

In Sunninghill the Lammas lands were near Cheapside. In the neighbouring parish of Winkfield they were very extensive, and in the Survey of 1613 they were described as containing 532 acres, consisting of three very large arable fields called Winkfield Common, Millfield, and Wellfield. There was also one great waste of 4533 acres, but scarcely any separate arable fields in the parish. In Sunninghill we had nearly 2000 acres of waste. In Chobham, adjoining us on the south, there were 11,000 acres, so that in these three adjoining parishes there were more than 17,000 acres of uncultivated land. These facts are most important in giving us a clear idea of the state of our neighbourhood and its agriculture.

The King in 1606 sold the quit-rents of the Sunninghill portion of the manor for £629, 10s. to Sir John Norreys, William Prydys, and William Derson, and from this we obtain our first introduction to the names of the "forefathers of the hamlet." We learn that the principal estate is described "marsh lands containing eighty acres with the woods upon the same, vocat Eastmore, in the occupation of William Day." This was the only single holding of any size. In the whole there appeared to be rather less than 150 acres of enclosures within the manor, and some twenty cottages, "all which," the grant states, "were reputed to be parcel of the assart lands and purprestures in the forest of Windsor." They were held in socage subject to the small quit-rents, 2s. 2d. only, for instance, being charged on the eighty acres of Eastmore. It is rather singular that

---

<small>* The word Lammas some have thought had reference to the command, "feed my lambs," but it had nothing to do with lambs. It is the "hlaf-mass," *i.e.*, "loaf-mass," because it was customary to celebrate mass on that day with a wafer made from the newly gathered corn, the festival occurring at the commencement of harvest, to implore the blessing of Providence on the ingathering. See Chas. Brown's pam., p. 282.</small>

SUNNINGHILL IN STUART TIMES.

no mention is made of any house there, although even cottages, where there were any, are named. The old black and white timbered house now standing by Silwood Lake was not then built, although probably erected very soon afterwards, as it is mentioned in the next survey.

But a much more searching inquiry was shortly to follow this, and a report was made, of so much value as a record of what Sunninghill and its people were at that time, that it is worth setting out fully.

It was a survey of "assart," purpresture, and other lands within the forest of Windsor, taken by virtue of a commission under the Great Seal of England directed to Otho Nicholson, Esq.,* and others, A.D. 1613, and contained the following:—

	Acres.	R.	P.
St. John's College, one house and 15 closes of pasture and arable (near Coworth) called Bromhall	136	1	23
Do. Do. called Titness	98	0	23
Richard Hodd, a cottage			
Wm. Morgan, house and	15	0	0
Robert Lloyd, house and meadow	2	3	11
Henry Lane, one parcel of woodground adjoining upon Lord's Green called Clark's	7	2	35
Wm. Pursell, land	12	2	0
Robert Hodge	18	3	6
Homfrey May, part in Winkfield with a water Mill	15	2	21
Robert Hodge, grounds and house	17	2	28
Cheapside Cottages there	17	0	0
Homfrey May, one Water-Millne and pond	1	0	28
Philip Farant, three house and two meadow	7	0	33
Nicholas May, 2 closes and meadow ground called Modhill [or Medhill]	6	0	39
Philip Farant, one parcel of woodground Adams and Denbrook [or Tenbrook]	23	2	26
Do. pasture near Tetness Hill	23	2	26
Nicholas Milton, 1 house and 2 closes	3	3	0
William Slann, house and land	7	3	7
Henry Milton, 3 closes	13	0	0
Robert Milton, 1 close	2	1	30
Do.	3	3	34
John Searle	3	1	13
Mr. Matthew Day, 12 closes and a house called Eastmere	63	3	34
Mr. Robert Hodge, 4 closes called Pickreste near —— and Blackwater	17	0	1
Richard Slann, 3 closes near Sunninghill Park	7	2	30
Mr. Robinson, small pasture	1	0	8
Daniel Slann			
The Vicaridge, 8 closes of arable and meadow ground called the Vicaridge with a house	14	1	13

---

* Otho Nicholson built the old Carfax in the High Street at Oxford in 1590 for a conduit.

	Acres	R.	P.
Mr. Robinson, 1 house	1	0	33
Thomas Milton, 5 closes and a house	14	0	0
Widow Milton, 1 house and close	3	3	29
Haman Attlee, 1 house and little close	0	3	18
Do. Do.	3	2	13
Rex Sunninghill Park with part in Winkfield containing together	472	1	38
Wm. Baker, house and land lying near Sunninghill Park	13	0	23
John Cottrell	22	1	39
Rex Wast, one waste belonging unto Sunninghill containing	1985	1	23
Francis Broughton, coppice wood called Dene lying on the bounds of the ——	8	1	14
Do. Do.	13	3	19
William Pither, pasture ground	3	3	19

There would seem to have been about sixteen or eighteen houses as they are called, and eight or ten cottages.

From this we get an excellent account of the place and its people, whether within the manor or not.

Eastmore is reduced from eighty acres to sixty-three; but a house appears on it. Hedge or Hodge had increased his holding. He was of a Winkfield family, and Hedge Lane still preserves his name there. But probably one of the most important personages resident in the village was the Philip Farrant who appears as the second largest landowner in the place. His family had been people of consequence here in the days of the Tudors. He lived in a house which for ages afterwards was known as "Farrants," of which I shall speak more fully in the account of Silwood.

The number of houses and cottages here altogether in the time of Henry VII. did not probably amount to more than a dozen, the manorial house and the surrounding farmsteads and cottages constituting the village; and at the time of which we are now speaking would not have amounted to over thirty, although estimated (by the Vicar in 1801) as high as forty-three.

Lord's Green is mentioned, as also Cheapside, and the seventeen acres of the cottagers there were doubtless part of the Old Lammas lands. The greater part of the parish was waste; not more than about 700 acres were pasture and 100 arable.

How slow its agricultural progress was we shall see hereafter. Its population could not at this time have much exceeded 100 people.

Of this primitive state of the parish we find a curious confirmation in the State Papers of 1636. It was a time, we may remember, when Charles I. was urging the collection of his unconstitutional ship-money tax, and poor as our little village was, it was not poor enough to escape the pressure of that terrible "screw." The parishioners felt that they were unjustly assessed, and in January of that year they presented a petition (at the head of which was Philip Farrant) showing—"That the Hundred of Cookham and Binfield upon all taxes had charged them (the petitioners) with a *sixth* part, whereas they were not above the *twelfth* part, according to a Survey taken for his Majesty, which showed of manured lands in Cookham 5201[a], in Binfield 2907, and in Sunninghill but 799."

The Justices at Oakingham in the following year admitted the complaint of our good folk, and declared "that Sunninghill was not a *tenth* part of the Hundred, and that it consisted of barren heath overlaid with deer, whereas Cookham and Binfield were very good land and freed from deer."

This was, in 1637, confirmed at Reading, and its share fixed at one-*tenth* only.

CHAPTER XI.

Sunninghill, and the Nevilles.

"Ye think the rustic cackle of your bourg
The murmur of the world! what is it to me?"

WHAT! is not the bourg or the little village but the world in miniature? As the "ripple washing in the reeds" responds to the great waves of the ocean beyond, so do the heart throbbings of our secluded life beat in unison with those of the outside world.

Let us now turn for awhile to the social aspects of the parish, and consider its people and their doings.

What the Norreys were at Ascot and Bray, a secondary branch of the still more illustrious family of the Nevilles was at Sunninghill.

The Nevilles at a very early period had possessions in the forest, and one of them married into the family of Windsor, which had owned estates here from Saxon days.

The Bailiwick of Fiennes, an extensive district, including Bray, Winkfield, Bracknell, and Wokingham, became the property of the Nevilles. By the Crown they were called "keepers by inheritance." They themselves would have said "owners by inheritance" had they ventured to do so.

Henry Neville was gentleman of the chamber to Henry VIII. and Edward VI. In 1551 he obtained a grant of the Manor of Wargrave, and was recommended by the King for Sheriff of Berkshire. He married Elizabeth,* daughter and sole heiress to Sir John Gresham, lived at Billingbere, and lies buried at Laurence Waltham. Now the Nevilles were staunch supporters of the new learning and the new religion, and rose accordingly into particular favour with Edward VI. When Mary came to the throne, however, she annulled the grant which her brother had made to them, and gave the estates to the See of Winchester, of which her favourite, Dr. White, was bishop.

---

* See Rouse's Antiquities of Sussex; also James I, Progress, Nichols.

But under Elizabeth the Nevilles came again to still higher favour. It was then that Sir Henry resided at Sunninghill Park as its keeper; and in that locally important post commenced his connection with our parish.

He was here as early as 1560, for in that year I find him writing from Sunninghill to Sir Thomas Parry, "desiring to have the timber-work of an old house at East Hampstead to repair his stables," and also in the midst of his busy occupation with the musters, "wishing for a quiet day to go a wooing in."

The Nevilles were fair specimens of the true old Puritan character, although hardly of that high perfect type of it seen in such men as Hampden, Vane, Hutchinson, or Capel—earnest and withal inconsistent. They were lovers of liberty and freedom of conscience, yet in 1585 we find Sir Henry very active in arresting and examining a Romish priest on whom certain Popish relics were found at Henley; and in 1588 he was still very energetic in persecuting the "Recusants"— in fact, he was a firebrand among some of his Romish neighbours round Sunninghill.

In January 1593, this Sir Henry Neville died, and was succeeded by his son, Henry Neville, Esq., who was knighted shortly afterwards. He was at Sunninghill Park when the Queen, about to send him as ambassador to France, wrote to him in January 1599—"You are to give orders for restraint of killing game and deer in Mote and Sunninghill Parks in Windsor Forest during your absence as ambassador resident in France."

In December of that year a letter from Antwerp alludes to the French ambassador (Sir Henry) as a "Puritan," and he was jealously watched by the Papal party. The celebrated Dudley Carleton was his secretary about this time.[*]

In 1601, Sir Henry, as the State Papers show, "did lie in the Lodge in Sunninghill as Master of the Game." He dearly loved his forest home, and the hunting in his native Berkshire woods. But with his mental endowments, which were of no mean order, he had inherited a restless, intriguing disposition. In certain London taverns, where some of the ablest men of the day were beginning to air their political aspirations, he was well known as an eloquent advocate of liberal and somewhat hazardous principles.

And now a cloud came over his bright prospects. He had started for Paris in 1601, and had got as far as Dover, when the Earl of Essex

---

[*] Clarendon's Hist. of the Rebellion, vol. iv.

accused him as a party to the "confederacy of Drury House," as they called his mad attempt at revolution when he lost his "sweet wine monopoly." Thereupon our ambassador was sent for, and in May he found himself in the Tower. Cecil writes as to his "being in displeasure with the Queen" for not revealing his acquaintance with Cuffe. "I am," says Cecil, "grieved for him, as he married my cousin-german." He was dismissed from his office, worth, we are told, £5000 a year, and fined £10,000, afterwards reduced to £5000. There is a piteous letter from him to Cecil in April 1602, proposing part payment and security for the balance of this fine.

This was a great blow to his fortunes.

In 1605 the new King, although personally not liking him, gave signs of relenting, and intimated the grant which we find was made "to his son, Henry Neville, after himself, of the office of keeper of Sunninghill Park and Mote Park, and riding forester of Battle's Walk,"* so that had been left to him. At the same time a license was given for them both to travel for three years. However, next year he is again in his beloved forest; and on the 15th September 1608, he writes to Sir Thomas Windebank, excusing himself "for not returning home to dine with him, having been carried as far as Cranborne in chase of a deer."

He was evidently now in pecuniary difficulties, but his busy scheming mind was never long at rest; and as His Majesty was almost as poor as himself, he hit upon a happy idea, as he thought, of recruiting their resources. He proposed "a project to raise a present sum for His Majesty's use without any wrong or just cause of grievance to any man, by exempting two men in every parish from serving as jurors or constables;"† and this suggestion, it seems, was actually adopted, for in January 1607, he was arranging for William Day and others to pay £10 apiece to exempt them from juries. In 1609 he applied to Salisbury in a more practical way "to forward his suit for farm of land or annuities to his younger sons in compensation for £4000 spent by him in the public service in France." This may have been true; and but another instance of his royal mistress's peculiar habit in such cases.

Then, in 1612, he endeavoured, through the powerful influence of Rochester, to obtain the Secretaryship; but we learn from the State Papers of the time that he failed in this "because of the flocking of

---

* Cal. State Papers, July 8, 1601. Lodge's Illustrations, vol. iii. p. 200.
† Lodge's Illustrations, vol. iii.

Parliament men to him. The King says he will not have a Secretary imposed on him by Parliament."

This flocking of Parliament men to him may be explained perhaps by his having been an able and popular party man, and just about this time returned with Sir Thomas Parry as member for Berkshire, and probably against the Court influence.

In this affair of the Secretaryship we begin to get a glimpse of the rising storm, and the King's jealousy of the "Parliament men." The spirit of the time, too, is well shown in the heavy forfeitures which were in this particular year inflicted on the Recusants.

In 1615 Sir Henry died; but the family troubles were not over. He left an heir still a Henry Neville, who was soon plunged into litigation with the Crown respecting the right to Ashridge, Sunninghill, and other lands in Windsor Forest, upon which an inquisition was taken in September 1618. Kind friends, however, were now undermining him in the King's favour.

The Mote Park keepership was in 1617 given to one Hugh May, groom of the chamber, and Adrian May, his nephew, on surrender of Sir Henry Neville; and two years afterwards that of Sunninghill Park was conferred on Alexander Levingston. The Ashridge lands were restored on being "compounded" for, and pardon was given for "past trespasses."

Incidentally we get a curious confirmation of the antiquity of the Nevilles in this neighbourhood, for in 1627 Sir Henry Neville writes from Billingbere to Secretary Conway about a small business between Sir Richard Harrison and himself concerning their walks, and doubts not he can give him satisfaction, and will sooner relinquish the privileges he has had for three hundred years by inheritance than give distaste to His Majesty. He would not have written so in his better days. This was in reply to a letter to him, "that the King desired them to be reconciled, and His Majesty's game preserved." He died in 1629, leaving two sons—Richard, who resided at Billingbere; and Henry, born in the same year, it would seem, 1620.[*]

The heir married Catherine, daughter of Lord Grey of Werke, and Henry, in 1633, married Elizabeth, sole heiress of the ancient family of Staverton; and in the same year we find an amusing allusion to the marriage in a Petition of Henry Neville of Billingbere, gentleman, in which he says—" Having taken to wife Elizabeth Staverton, by whom he has an estate of copyhold lands in the Manor of Warfield in the Forest

---

[*] The Swainmote at Windsor in 1633 shows that the heir was then a minor.

of Windsor, and a house that cannot be made fit to live in without being new built, and having also to pay a great fine to Richard Neville, Gentleman of the Chamber, all which will amount to £1500 at the least, prays liberty to fell six hundred trees."

No wonder the forest disappeared! This family afforded one of the many instances of antagonism which the Civil War brought out.

Richard became a staunch Royalist and Colonel of Brigade to Charles I., while Henry threw in his lot with the Roundheads, represented Berkshire in 1650, and in 1651 became a member of the Council of State, till Cromwell alarmed him, and he ended his days as a strong political writer.

The Colonel, meanwhile, joined the Royalist camp, and was ruinously fined, as we shall see, with our parishioner, William Gwynn, as a delinquent. He had placed his family, it would seem, at Croydon, where their temporary residence is recorded in the following quaint entry in the Church Register there :—

"1646. Henry Nevell, the son of Colonell Nevel. The Colonall's name is Richard Nevill of the bill and beare in barkshere."

The clerk must have taken him for a publican!

The following is from a register of Waltham, St. Laurence, Berks :—

"Henry, son of Richard Neville, and Anne his wife, was born at Croydon in Surrey, Jan. 2, 1646. He died young."

This entry was doubtless made on their return after the Restoration.

In 1630 Sunninghill Park ceased to be a Royal Lodge. It was sold to Thomas Carey, Esq., or Carew, as the name was then often written, and in the west is still sometimes pronounced. But this did not entirely sever the connection of the Nevilles with our parish, as some of them remained for years afterwards.

CHAPTER XII.

The Village under the Commonwealth.

A NEW phase now opens in the history of our parish. Dark clouds were gathering. The poor parishioners were beginning to feel the serious pressure of taxation. King Charles' "Petition of Rights" was doubtless a sham, but his imposition of the ship-money tax was a terrible earnest.

Our villagers had not only to pay their taxes, but were assessed in an unfair proportion. Everything was going wrong. Oppression had roused a spirit of resistance, and provoked at the same time aggression.

Lord Holland, whom James had appointed Constable of the Castle, found things in the greatest confusion.

Sunninghill was a hot-bed of insubordination.

The year 1636 was a most important one to our village, as well as to the country at large. The ship-money tax had been resolved on, and the Sheriffs were pressed in all quarters to raise it at once; but it met at last with opposition in the neighbouring county of Buckingham, where John Hampden, the popular Squire of the Chilterns, challenged its legality. The case, however, took a long time to decide, and Sunninghill had meanwhile a fresh subject of excitement.

The plague was raging in London. It was the most terrible visitation that had ever been since the Black Death.

Where better than to this little forest village could one fly from such a scourge? and hither came the indefatigable Secretary of the Admiralty, Edward Nicholas, Clerk of the Council, the hardest working man in the kingdom; and to this visit of his we owe several little peeps into the social life of Sunninghill.

It has often been observed that these great epidemics generally appeared in hot summers. That of 1666, the worst of all, was remarkably so. The very birds appeared to languish in their flight.

"The 7th June," Pepys says, "was the hottest day that ever I felt in my life;" and from a letter I have met with it was evidently the case in this instance, for in May, John Robinson, the Vicar, writing to "his brother" (brother-in-law, in truth) says—"Never man saw such want of rain in their parts. All are well at East Hampstead." But after the dry hot summer came the deluge! and on the 16th November Nicholas' father writes to him at Sunninghill—"Have not had one fair day nor night almost three weeks together. I have not known more rain fall together in all my memory." How similar to the year 1885—as hot a summer, probably, and as wet an autumn; and the same scourge has visited even in these days several continental cities.

In May, the Vicar writes again, "that the sickness was increasing. Nicholas' man tells the writer that three houses are shut up in Smithfield Bars, one in the old exchange, and it scatters dangerously."

In June Sir Charles Harbord, Surveyor-General, writes to Nicholas—"I had not time to visit you at Sunninghill, but if God send me health, I and my wife purpose to ramble into your forest this summer to find you out, and see our friends at East Hampstead. In the meantime do me the favour to write how you like your new habitation there. Pray commend me to your sister and neighbours."

It is uncertain which house this new habitation was, but I think it must have been King's Wick. The friends at East Hampstead were the Trumballs. Nicholas married a daughter of Sir Thomas Aylesbury, who lived at Cranborne Lodge. In 1631 I find him writing to Sir Thomas Aylesbury as his father-in-law, and therefore Nicholas and Edward Hyde, afterwards the celebrated Chancellor, were brothers-in-law.

We get an idea of our isolation in the fact that while staying here in September 1636, a messenger with important despatches was sent down to Bagshot to find Nicholas out at Sunninghill.

In March 1637, Nicholas informs Wolley (who was an under-keeper of the forest, and resided at Sunninghill) that the sickness is much dispersed in London. All his goods are already carried from Sunninghill to Thorpe, whither he purposes to remove his wife and children at least.

The plague still raged on into the spring of 1638, for Wolley's son, Robert, writes to his father—"The sickness increases at London. There died two of the King's corochmen [coachmen]. Mr. Nicholas is in the west country. Present my duty to my mother, and love to my brother and sisters. I hope to see you all at Sunninghill this year."

THE VILLAGE UNDER THE COMMONWEALTH.

A Sir Francis Wolley was keeper of Foli John Park about this time. One Jo. Wolley, Esq., had been lessee of Bromhall under the College in 1581, and in 1638 a John Wolley was residing here, and married Dame Helen Wolsley, the widow of Sir Thomas Wolsley.

Of Sir Francis Wolley the literature of that age will ever preserve to us a pleasant memory, in relation to young John Donne, whose clandestine marriage got him into such trouble with his father-in-law, Sir Geo. More of Loxley. It was the generous help of Sir Francis that saved the young couple from starvation.*

The King and his courtiers in 1636 had fled to Hampton Court, the great Cardinal's "wholesome manor;" and the Sheriffs of the several counties had been enjoined not to let the plague in, or more correctly, not to allow any Londoners to come within ten miles of the Court! † Similar precaution was taken in 1540, for when the plague appeared at Windsor, the infected persons were removed to a distance, "the King's Highness bearing the expenses." ‡

We have referred elsewhere to the dispute just at this time between the Vicar and the new proprietor of Sunninghill Park, which ended in litigation—it was more than a "nine days' wonder" for the village; but the severity and vexatious proceedings of the new Governor of the Forest, Earl Holland, excited the inhabitants a great deal more. The lower orders, and the better people too, were alike roused against this hated official.

In April 1640, Sir Arthur Mainwaring reported to Earl Holland on the encroachments in the forest. "The cottagers," he says, "are the ruin and destruction both of the woods and game, and the shelter of deer-stealers and all disorderly persons. Among them are specified "William Milton, junior, a cottage and rood of land in Windlesham, paying to Sir Charles Howard 6s. and two pullets." "In Sunninghill, Elizabeth Milton, one cottage erected on His Majesty's waste, by what rent we know not; value per annum, 5s." "Robert Milton, a similar case, value per annum, 12d." Several others of this extensive Sunninghill family are reported in the Survey of 1613 to have had holdings in the parish; and earlier still, as we have seen, they abounded here. But the most degenerate of them all seem to have been four "squatters," male and female, who got a hold in the forest, and refused to be expelled. Grubbing under the roots of trees, they stood at bay with pike and gun. No verderer liked to tackle them, for blood was certain to be shed.§

We were living on a volcano, the rumblings of which were clearly audible to every one but the King. The torrent burst over the land at last. In every parish in the kingdom civil strife was now to rage. Every man's hand was raised against his neighbour: in some cases, brother

---

* See Walton's Life of Dr. John Donne.   † See Cal. State Papers, Dom 1636.
‡ Nicholas' Proceedings, Privy Council, vol. vii. p 56.   § Dixon's Royal Windsor.

against brother, and parent against child. Sunninghill felt the shock at once. Windebank, the Secretary, fled in December, and reached Calais in safety, although Hyde said it was not in the wit of man to save him.* Nicholas succeeded him, following the fortunes of the King in banishment. The Nevilles, as we have seen, took different sides.† Windsor was strongly Republican. The Days, connected with Sunninghill, held municipal honours there throughout the Commonwealth. The Aldridges and the Broughtons were also that way. In Chertsey it was the same. The family of Hammond there gave the Republican army its Lieutenant-General, Thomas Hammond, and the Isle of Wight its Governor, while Dr. Henry Hammond was a Royalist and Chaplain to the King. The Mays and the Gwynns, Auditor Gwynn, and our parishioner, William Gwynn, were Royalists.

In the list "of Loyalists Compounders for their Estates, printed at London, 1655," may be found the names of

William Gwynn of Sunninghill, gentleman . . .	£112 13 0
Richard Neville of Billingbere, Esq.	887 0 0

William Gwynn's delinquency was "the leaving his house and attending the King in Oxford." He was summoned before the Committee which sat for Berkshire, at Reading Abbey, in August 1646. He claimed the benefit of General Fairfax's Articles, granted on surrender of the city, and was discharged in 1651; but he was afterwards fined, as we have seen, and Harbottle Grimston, Esq., was ordered to enter upon his lands at Sunninghill, and take the profits until £280, 7s. 8d. and interest should be raised thereout. The lands were in mortgage to one Harvey, which might account for this difference. On the original letter at the Rolls, dated March 1647, I find a note—"Mr. Slan, you ought to attorn tenant to Mr. Grimston, according to this order." ‡

Now came the strain for means to carry on the war. Everything that could be turned into money was seized on and converted. The Royalist nobles and the Universities sent their plate to the melting-pot for the King's use; and the Parliament was equally vigorous.

Even the fees of the Manor Courts were not overlooked. "The head silver of Sunninghill, and the tithing silver of Ascot, infra Winkfield," were sold during the Commonwealth.

---

* Cal. of Clarendon State Papers in Bodleian.

† Henry Neville, Esq., was associated with Lord Commissioner Whitelock and others during the Commonwealth to look after the timber in Windsor Forest. In 1651 he was elected one of the Council of State, but resigned rather than sanction Cromwell's proceedings.

‡ 1655. There was a license for a "William Gwynn to come and reside in London, the late proclamation notwithstanding."

During all this time, at Sunninghill, as at most other places, the people were scattered. Some, siding with the Parliament, saved their estates, while others suffered for their loyalty. Among those who had nothing to lose, lawlessness revelled in its opportunities. William Smith of the village, with divers others, were in 1643 summoned as delinquents for destroying the king's deer. This Smith family was a bad one, as we shall presently see.

Sunninghill was in a ferment; lawlessness was coming too close, even to the cottage doors, to be pleasant. When Colonel Richard Neville and Mr. Gwynn were the victims, it was not of so much consequence to the public weal, but when the "three acres and the cow" were also threatened, it became quite another matter. The wildest notions of equality prevailed and were setting foot in the forest. On the beautiful St. George's Hill across the common, a band of "Levellers" in 1647 raised their standard, and were breaking up the land and planting it with beans, as it was as much theirs as any one else's! They proposed to live in the simplicity of a state of nature; but a troop or two of Roundhead cavalry soon brought them to their senses.

Our own people did not view these Socialistic doctrines quite favourably, and accordingly all who had anything to lose in Sunninghill and the neighbouring forest parishes made formal protest in support of their rights. In February 1653 they filed their claim, alleging—

"That the Masters and Fellows of St. John's College, Cambridge, being seised of several Manors, lands &c. in Sunninghill, and also Mrs. Margaret Osborne, widow, Matthew Day, Francis Broughton, gentleman, John Robinson, clerk, Thomas Roberts, Edw. Laine, Wm. Morgan, Robert Lloyd, Thomas Holgeathly, Wm. Henry Zichford, the heires of Stephen Edsall, Jacob Baker, Widow Pursell, Thomas Farrant, the heires of Wm. Wapshott, Wm. Slan, Robt. May, Wm. Trigg, Robt. Milton, John Robinson, clerk, Ralph Jenkins, John Slan, Robert Attlee, John Barnes, Wm. Boult, Wm. Pyther, and Henry Savage being seised in their several demesnes, as of fee in the several lands and tenements in Sunninghill in said Forest, Do by their Attorney claim the said several Manors and the Commons, Franchises, &c. to the same belonging, for that they say that they and those whose estates they have in them have time whereof the memory of man runneth not to the contrary, enjoyed common of pasture for all their commonable cattle levant and couchant at all times of the year in the waste grounds within the parish of Sunninghill, and have used and enjoyed common of turbary, yeate heath and pannage, with liberty to cut, dig, and carry away gravel, loame, and sand in and out of all the waste grounds aforesaid without hindrance of the Lords Bailiffs or Officers."

The ancient folk of Sunninghill were very conservative of their rights, and their energy was attended with success, and this although the laws were practically suspended and license everywhere prevailed: the holiest rites were neglected or abandoned, and we cannot sum up the disasters more eloquently than the simple entry in our Church Register does:—

["Memorandum.—Y^t for ye space of twelve years, viz. from 1641 to 1653, there was no care taken for ye registring any births, burials, or marriages in this parish of Sunninghill, by reason of ye tumults and confusions of the civil warr, which then raged in England.—J. M." *

The storm, however, was now spending its force. The nation, stunned, was beginning to breathe again; the people found the evils they had suffered so to avert were but exchanged for another series even more irritating and obnoxious.

In their homely life their feelings were outraged and their innocent pleasures prohibited. Christmas was no longer the beloved festival it had been. "It was a sin," says Macaulay, "to hang garlands on a Maypole, to drink a friend's health, to fly a hawk, or to hunt a stag." And although this gives a truthful picture of that doleful time, it is hardly consistent as a matter of fact with the well-authenticated hunts in which Sir Bulstrode Whitelock and the very heads of the party indulged in our forest, as we have elsewhere seen, unless, indeed, for such sinful indulgences the great ones were allowed absolution of some sort not hitherto supposed to have any place in their creed. Even the Lord Protector himself yielded to the temptation. One can hardly imagine Cromwell hawking; yet in September 1651, on his journey from Aylesbury, we find him going a little out of his way to meet Mr. Winwood, the Member for Windsor, for a day's hawking.†

For setting up a birchen tree called a Maypole, or for playing at an unlawful game called football, one might in 1650 have been indicted at the Quarter Sessions.‡

The nation at last found the state of things intolerable: they had changed one tyrant for a legion; and the Restoration came. The people were—and no wonder—intoxicated with joy. The intensity of their former gloom can hardly be more forcibly proved than by the outburst of delight at getting back a king, even Charles II. The church-bells rang out merrily, the Maypoles were set up again, and our village green was made glad once more with morris-dance and "donkey revels." Even the sedate parishioners, "the ancients," rejoiced not the less in their quiet homes, and, with true reverence, brought out again the family Prayer-book, hidden during the troubles; for between 1654 and 1660 its use had been prohibited under a

---

* The account Boyle gives us of a journey he made in 1650 through Egham, Bagshot, and Farnham well shows the state of lawlessness to which our country had been reduced. See Works of Honble. R. Boyle, 1772.

† See Carlyle's Cromwell, vol. iii.   ‡ See Hist. of Maidstone, by J. M. Russell.

penalty of £5 and £10, or for a third offence a year's imprisonment. The vicars in most cases brought out again their surplices, which they had been compelled to abandon for some years.

The bonfires on the green for Gunpowder Treason were lighted up again, and for generations our young foresters, with but little idea of the meaning of the custom, keenly enjoyed it, as justifying license and giving them the jolliest night of the year. The merriest peals from our old church-tower rang out on that anniversary. Thus so long afterwards as in 1728 it was agreed by the parish that "the ringers be allowed for two hours, one in morning and one at night, 3s. and no more, viz., on the King's birthday, and on the 5th November."

In some places long afterwards, the bells rang out for the victory of Culloden for a year or two, but then died out, while on the Fifth of November they never failed to be heard.

In 1661 our poor old friend Neville was again in trouble. The state papers contain the following ominous statement:—"Stopped the Reading letters to find information about Henry Neville, but failed; has written to the postmaster a friend of his to ask after him, on pretence that a friend wishes to visit him, and is told that he is at home eight miles from Reading."

Just at this time he was an active member of the celebrated Rota or Coffee Club, a kind of debating society for the dissemination of republican opinions. Round its table, says Aubrey, "sat Milton and Marvell, Cyriac Skinner, Harrington, Neville, and others," discussing political questions. Aubrey himself was a member, as were also Charles Wolseley and John Wildman.

In 1663, however, Neville was in prison under examination as a "suspected person," and in December of that year he was again examined, with Major Wildman, Whitelock, and others; they appear to have met at Leeds, no doubt the old castle in Kent.

In February 1664 he was a prisoner in the Tower, petitioning the King "for liberty and a pass to go abroad; that he had been fourteen weeks in close prison, though not having offended even in thought since the Restoration."

In June 1667 we still hear of him. One Hicks, writing from Billingbere to Williamson, thinks it better, considering the condition of the King's affairs, to send a letter coming out of the country for that grand rebel in Rome, and encloses one from R. Neville to his brother Sir Henry Neville, Rome.

The "grand rebel" lived, however, till 1694, and was buried at Warfield. He was the well-known political writer.

The family estate, the property of his elder brother, the Colonel, devolved on the Colonel's heir, Richard, and afterwards passed to Henry, the second son, who, by Act of 5th Anne, took the name of Grey, from his grandfather, Ralph, Lord Grey; and he dying without issue in 1740, the property was transmitted to a son of his sister Catherine, who assumed the old name, and took the estate on the death of the widow of his uncle, Henry Neville Grey, in 1762.

I have gone fully into this pedigree because it has been so much confused. Ashmole, Lysons, and others call Henry, the political writer, the son of the Ambassador; but in truth he was the grandson; and it is doubtful too if they are right in stating, as for consistency's sake they were bound to do, that dying without issue, he bequeathed the estate to his nephew, for I cannot find that Sir Henry ever had the estate, and his nephew would take direct from his father Richard, the Colonel.

When things began to settle down after so terrible a convulsion, it was soon perceived how completely all social order had been destroyed.

At the end of one of our old church books is recorded—

"Vicessimo nono Charles II. that at a General Quarter Sessions at Newbury the grievous state of the country was taken into consideration, on account of the great increase of rogues, vagrants, and sturdy beggars, grown now so insolent and presumptuous as to extort money from those that live in remote places by threats, and through fear they will fire their houses and steal their goods," and the vagrant laws were ordered to be strictly enforced, "and that where such rogues are apprehended with forged or counterfeit passes, the constable, headborough, or tithingman, assisted by the minister and some others of the parish, shall cause to be stripped naked from the middle upwards and to be openly whipped until their bodies bee bloudy."

"Then the offender was to have a certificate of such whipping and passed on to his native place."*

Such was the state of the country, and such the barbarous remedy. It was, however, a strange duty of a parish "minister"† to be present at the public whipping of a criminal. It would appear that as the vagrant laws punished any man found in a parish, without his certificate, an offender might have been whipped, but for the certificate mentioned, in every parish he passed through until he reached his own.

It must not be forgotten, however, that this was rather a time of special disorganisation, it was the first year of King William; and

---

* This was an ordinary practice. I find from the notes of a Surrey justice in 1608 that Richard Jenkyns and Susan his wife were taken vagrant at Taudridge, and "because he knewe not certeynely where he was borne, I caused them to be whipped."

† I find an instance at an earlier date of the Archdeacon of Salisbury himself officiating in person, for an ecclesiastical offence.

THE VILLAGE UNDER THE COMMONWEALTH.

James's troops were still, some of them, roaming about the country under arms, but under no discipline.

Sunninghill had reason, I fear, to record this warning in its books. Her people were a rough set.

Highway robbery, deer-stealing, and horse-stealing were common offences here.

I find a case of the latter in 1685, where one James Smith of Sunninghill was convicted for horse-stealing, and received sentence of death: he stole a horse in March, and two others in April, sold them, and would give no account of how he came possessed of them. There seemed to be a total absence of affirmative evidence, but in those good old times they did not trouble themselves about that so much. Now we must prove the crime; then in any suspicious case it was assumed, and the prisoner had to exculpate himself.

The Assizes were then held at Windsor, it seems, and Baron Gregory opened them on 27th July at seven o'clock in the morning. The weather was intensely hot, and he adjourned the court from the Town Hall, on account of its closeness and the heat, to the market-place.

CHAPTER XIII.

Sunninghill in the Eighteenth Century.

"The wild wind rang from park and plain,
And round the attics rumbled;
Till all the tables danced again,
And half the chimneys tumbled."

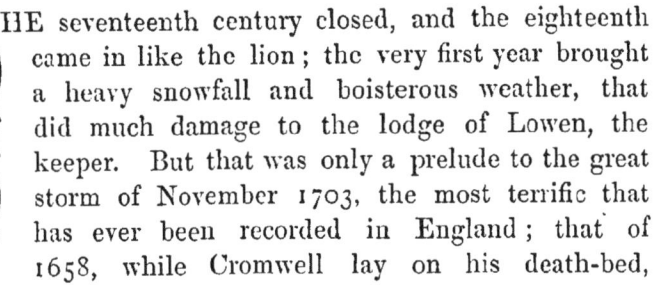

THE seventeenth century closed, and the eighteenth came in like the lion; the very first year brought a heavy snowfall and boisterous weather, that did much damage to the lodge of Lowen, the keeper. But that was only a prelude to the great storm of November 1703, the most terrific that has ever been recorded in England; that of 1658, while Cromwell lay on his death-bed, amid the howling of a tempest that overthrew houses and tore up the great trees at St. James's, was nothing to this; nor probably was that earlier one of 1251, that swept over our forest on St. David's Day, doing such havoc among its trees and destroying the mills and houses about.

This of 1703 passed over the southern and western counties with fearful violence, but I must not notice its ravages except as they touch this country. At West Horsley, the wife of John Nicholas (Edward Nicholas' son, and daughter of Spencer Compton, Earl of Northampton) was buried in her bed.

The great Plestor Oak at Selborne, the pride of the village, fell beneath its fury, and the famous Magdalen Oak at Oxford lost one of its huge limbs.[*]

At Oakingham the houses and market-place were greatly damaged, and hundreds of trees were torn up by the roots; at Bagshot most of the houses were shattered and four hundred panels

---

[*] See Great Storms, a Collection of Casualties, Brit. Mus. 1136 i.

of the park pales were thrown down. At Windsor a coachman was actually blown out of his seat and had his neck broken. Such an impression had it made on the nation, that a day of public humiliation was appointed.

But bright days followed, and the proverbial forty fine summers of the first half of the century were in store as a glorious compensation. But curiously enough, while the general population doubled, the agricultural stood still, and yet it is said to have been the golden age of the English peasant. The climate seemed to change after 1764, and the harvests were as unprosperous as they had previously been favourable. Sunninghill, however, always exceptional in its fortunes, must look back to this time as one of its most favoured periods.

Queen Anne and her husband, Prince George, took a fancy to this country, and were laying the foundation of much of our future welfare. The new kennels, the new rides, the new races, all tended to increase the prosperity of the place. A few more new houses had been built here during the seventeenth century; the picturesque timbered farmhouse I have mentioned as still standing by the Silwood Lake appeared, and another soon rose on the site of Tetworth. General Frederick's old house in Sunninghill Dale was of about this date, I should think. The Cedars had been enlarged; the Wells Inn had been largely added to; the farmhouse in the lane near, another (long since pulled down) on Bangor Lodge property, were new. These, with "Lady Baber's brick house," for which Sir Thomas Draper was assessed to the Church rails in 1672, as well as Brook Lodge, were all, I believe, one by one added to our village during the latter half of the seventeenth century. Besides these, a few rude huts and thatched cottages had been added to those on the pleasant ridge that overlooks the Bog.

And now let us endeavour to realise the state of our community during the Georgian era.

There are some who look back on those good old times, and regret their loss; they recall the picturesque village; those thatched cottages covered with roses, as they would fain believe; the few better houses on their own fair lawns; with those springs hard by that drew the gay world to their waters for promised health if not for perpetual youth. What an Arcadia they fancy it must have been! But, alas! it is as delusive as that poetic age so mischievously described—

"Ere England's griefs began
When every rood of ground maintained its man."

No, it is only a dream. The pastoral pipe, if we look for it, will be found to have become transformed into that other pipe—

"Blown by surmises, jealousies, conjectures,"

as we shall presently see. Most of the inmates of these rustic dwellings depended on the better houses for support, or were employed by farmers, but there were still some among them who preferred the precarious livelihood which the forest induced, and eked out an existence (as I have before noticed) by a little labour at harvest-time and a little depredation at others. With turf and wood in abundance for their fuel, their wants were few; and when in hard weather hunger pinched, they fall back on the modicum of relief which the State in its unwisdom provided even to the able-bodied. As to clothing, the women with their spinning-wheels made nearly all of it, and the parish supplied the rest; a few rushes dipped in grease gave them what light they required after the sun went down, and this was indeed but little, as the education at their command enabled very few of them to read or write. The only schooling within their reach was to be had at the night-school in the Vestry, held at times by the parish-clerk. But what could one expect of these poor villagers when in 1712 Dr. Johnson was taken as a child to London to be touched by Queen Anne for the evil? That this account of our villagers is a truthful one, I have fallen, since writing it, upon the following confirmation. Mrs. Carter in 1769, speaking of her friend Mrs. John Pitt, says: "She has been exerting herself with zeal and activity to relieve the wretched state of the poor people in this place, and to awaken a sense of industry among them, which will be a great blessing to them if it succeeds."

With such a state of things it is not very surprising to find that ignorance and lawlessness were still the characteristics of our village. The labourers' wages were less than half what they are now here: a single man received 8s. a week.

The same pilfering propensity that poor Cowley was so soon made the victim of, when he came amongst them to end his days at the Porch House, Chertsey, actuated them still.* I am afraid, if there was no horse to steal, they stole the grass, for he wrote, it will be remembered, "I can get no money from my tenants, and have my meadows eaten up every night by cattle put in by my neighbours." †

---

* The "porch" which gave name to this house projected ten feet into the highway, and was pulled down in 1786 for the safety of the public. See illustration.
† Chalmers' Lives: Cowley.

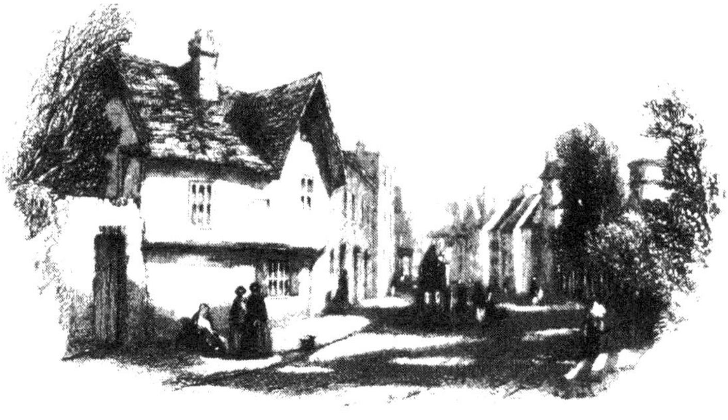

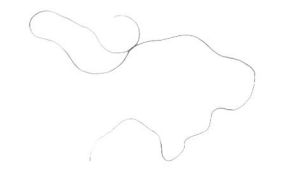

We have seen how Smith took the horse, how another poor fellow obtained his quietus by a brace of bullets from the Salisbury coach, and how we smarted for the robberies in Maidenhead Thicket and other places in the Hundred.

Some of our parishioners were having a lively time of it with the royal game, for in 1749, "Thomas Lloyd having been proceeded against for keeping lurchers, not being qualified, His Royal Highness the Duke of Cumberland agreed to stop proceedings on condition that the parish would for the future noways encourage the *pouchers*, but endeavour to detect them to the best of their power."

The forester was then what he continued to be down to the time when Charles Kingsley says of him—"The clod of these parts is a descendant of many generations of broom-squires and deer-stealers. The instinct of sport is strong within him still, though no more of the Queen's deer are to be shot in the winter turnip fields, or caught by an apple-baited hook hung from an orchard bough;" but after reciting his weaknesses, he adds—"But when he grows old, a thorough gentleman!"

Sunninghill was the scene of great political excitement in January 1715, for at the general election after the accession of George I., party feeling was never known to run so high—indeed it was as bad as, or worse, than in 1710, when these contests first assumed the acrimonious character which has since so much disgraced them. The great fight was between the Whigs or Ministerialists and the Tories or High Churchmen. Sir Henry Ashurst, who lived at Sunninghill, contested Windsor, and John Aldridge, his busy neighbour, of whom we shall hear much more, seems to have been the most active partisan against him. A tremendous fight it was.

The poll was declared—

Christopher Wren . . . 141	Sir Henry Ashurst, knight . 136
Robert Gayer . . . 137	Samuel Travers . . . 135

But the first two were petitioned against, and the others returned. Sir Henry seems to have been a Ministerialist, while Aldridge worked for the Church party.

Let us now turn to our parish records, and we shall find, as I feared, that the romance of our history fades away as we scrutinise it closely. Yet here and there between the dark shadows we get glimpses of a brighter life.

The musty minutes and account-books of a parish during the eighteenth century afford, it may be, a dry study, but certainly not an unprofitable one. They reveal the social history of the time, and of the life especially of the lower classes, and bring back to us a very melancholy picture.

I must be careful, however, not to attribute to any particular class a discredit attaching to all alike. It was a national state of things, a general coarseness of the age. The tastes of the people were cruel, and their pastimes often degrading.

The most striking fact shown by these old records is the intensity of the principle of "Local Government." It was far more comprehensive and important than it is now. The parochial officers were especially influential. The Vicar's churchwarden was often the principal man in the place, and the overseers of the poor sometimes county magistrates. Thus in 1768 "Mr. Schutz and Edmund Cook, Esq.," were overseers; and in 1775 John Pitt (who was Lord of the Manor), and Jeremiah Crutchley, served that office.

The Vestry was the Commons house of the parish, and the Vicar its permanent Speaker. The Constable was its Serjeant-at-arms, and most important executive officer. He was assisted by others whose position is scarcely known, and whose duties are quite forgotten—the "Tithingmen," I mean, whose province seems to have been very similar to that of the constable. Some authorities assert that the Tithingmen were appointed to hear and determine all lesser causes between villages and neighbours, but latterly, at least, they had no such judicial capacity, and it is doubtful if they ever had. They appear to me to have been rather in the nature of public prosecutors in trivial offences, which they "presented" to the Court Baron. Thus an amusing instance of their duties occurs in our superior Manor of Bray, where in 1517 "the Tithingmen presented that Alice, the wife of William Smythgate of Bray-wick, is a babbler, and has an unruly tongue, wherefore said Alice is commanded to refrain herself under penalty of 40s. and bodily punishment."*

This important Parliament was convened sometimes from the pulpit;† and its mandates were required in many cases to be obeyed on Sunday. Thus in 1723 it was announced in our Church that certain certificates required by the Poor Laws were to be brought to the Vestry on Sundays. Again, in 1717, it was ordered that certain accounts be brought to the Church "next Sunday," and that they should come to a resolution on that day as to how the money is to be raised to repair the

---

* See Kerry's Hist. of Bray.
† In 1634 the meetings of the Corporation of Maidstone were usually so announced.

Church house. And still further, on 7th September 1735, notice was given that "a Vestry would be held on next *Sunday* at the *Wells.*" In 1756 I find—" Sunday, June 6th, agreed at a Vestry by all persons then present, that a rate be granted to John Slann, the acting churchwarden for the year 1755, of 3d. in the pound."

This was the year of the great litigation with Egham over the question of whether Broomhall was in our parish. Egham had laid claim to it, but we had a Vicar who would not have his rights trampled on, and the challenge was quickly accepted. Victory, as we know, declared itself for us. The parishioners were intoxicated with delight, if with nothing else. They rang the Church bells for two days, save, of course, when they were having "refreshers" at the Wells.

On the appointment of certain of these parochial magnates, particular privileges were expected by the rest of the House, for in May 1761 it was "agreed at a Vestry this day that every overseer shall spend at the Vestry one shilling on the first time that he enters the Vestry-room, over and above the shilling allowed by the parish as an old custom." This implies that pipes and refreshments were introduced, which probably helped to counteract the acidity of the debates, and certainly to prolong their duration.

There was some reason, then, after all, in meeting at the Wells!

But this "good old custom" required a little qualifying, it seems, for in 1760 it was resolved that no money be spent at the parish expense at any bye Vestry, and only 5s. on Easter Monday.

And what were the duties of the parochial officers? They looked after the boundaries of the parish, in a good old-fashioned way, a very necessary thing when maps were scarce. Thus at this time I find an entry—" We unanimously are desirous to go in procession and visit and beat the bounds of our said parish on Holy Thursday, at eight o'clock in the forenoon, and all persons occupying houses, messuages, or tenements, are desired to make ready and pay their usual customary fees, as belonging to bound houses, on or before the above day."

Not only was the condition of every poor man and woman in the parish considered, especially if they were likely to come upon the rates, but the very wardrobes of the boys and girls were publicly turned out, as it were, and restored.

The Vestry attended to the well-being of their humble parishioners in other respects. Their domestic arrangements were overlooked, and it was seen that the girls went out to service in due time. In 1736, for instance, it was agreed "that the officers of this parish give notice to William Lloyd, Edith Lloyd, John Lloyd, Thomas Humphrey, jun., Sarah Humphrey, John Cordey, and Thomas Lloyd to appear on Thursday next before His Majesty's Justices to show cause why they don't go to service."

There was not then any poor's-house (that was not built till 1795). The infirm and invalid and infant poor were placed under the care of some of their neighbours, at a certain agreed weekly sum.

Thus in 1713 it was agreed that Elizabeth Banfield, now having lately had the smallpox, is to go to William Scarlett's till she is "aired," and the overseers to pay Scarlett 2s. 6d. a week for two weeks.

Another important duty of the Vestry was to take care of the interests of the parish by keeping paupers out of it. Its boundaries were jealously guarded, and not even on the wide expanse of the waste was a settler permitted to encamp. There was then as much difficulty for a labourer to move from one parish into another as one has now to pass from England into France or Spain.

What should we now think of such a resolution as the following:—

"1713. Agreed that there be a warrant taken out by the Churchwardens and Overseers to carry Francis Bell before the Justices touching his intruding himself into this parish contrary to law."

And again in January 1717:—

"Whereas the parishioners have been put to great trouble by permitting persons to come and live in this parish in tenements under £10 per annum, agreed that whoever shall come to settle there contrary to law, the Officers belonging to this parish do within 28 days of their coming procure a warrant to remove them back to the parish from which they came, unless they bring a certificate."

And worse still in 1723:—

"It was agreed to pull down the cottage John Robinson hath begun to build on the waste unless he takes it down in tenn days."

And later in 1763:—

"Agreed that any person or persons whatsoever that shall for the future erect or build any cot or cottage in the parish of Sunninghill without the consent of the whole parish, that they shall be immediately pulled down."

But we must not be hard on our forefathers of Sunninghill, for building on the waste certainly required some regulation; and we must remember that the enlightened inhabitants of the capital were not much farther advanced in social science in 1611, when a proclamation there forbade any additional building in London, although its population was fast increasing.

But by far the most daring of the privileges assumed by this august power "the parish" was that of disposing of what did not belong to it, portions of the waste; and the most amusing thing in this was that they had no right or even semblance of right to justify them. The Lords of the respective Manors might have made such a claim with some reason, but for the parish there was none. However, the practice became established, and as the Enclosure Commissioners at a later date reported, "the owner of the soil received no compensation, or was even consulted."

The method of proceeding was to apply to the parish officers for leave to enclose a parcel of the waste. This they granted generally at a price which at Sunninghill was £12 an acre, and elsewhere in the neighbourhood between £20 and £28.

One can only account for this curious practice on the principle that "there was nothing else to do!" Plots of land were coveted by one and another, and neither the Crown, the Lord of the Manor, nor the foresters could legally sell an acre without an Act of Parliament, and that was quite out of the question, and so they all seemed to have agreed to be blind to each other's little irregularities; and when a few acres were wanted it was a most ingenious legal fiction to suppose that the parish possessed the power of selling it, for if they had not this power, who had? If you got on the right side of the local authorities, the thing was done! The funniest part of it all was that the Crown itself, although having more right than any one else (especially in Sunninghill, of which it was Lord Paramount of the Manor), fell into this happy arrangement, for when His Royal Highness the Duke of Cumberland required two or three acres near his dog-kennels at Ascot, he applied to the parish for it, and had the land, but forgot to pay for it. An opportunity, however, soon occurred for putting this little omission straight. In November 1793 another piece at Mill Gate was wanted, and the parishioners having been asked what compensation was expected for it, sat in conclave, and came to the following characteristic resolution:—

"The inhabitants having taken the premises into consideration, and likewise that a larger piece of *their* common has lately been enclosed for the purpose of a dog-kennel for His Majesty's use, for which no compensation has yet been made, they are unanimously of opinion that the sum of one hundred guineas is a very reasonable compensation, and ought to be paid to the overseers of the poor of this parish, and that the said sum of money be laid out in erecting cottages for the poor."

Many others availed themselves of this practical solution of the impossible, and the parish in this way sold many acres of the waste; but as it was rather an ugly state of things to look back on, when at the time of the enclosure its illegality was made clear, the enclosure scheme only obtained local support on the understanding that "bygones should be bygones," and an Act was accordingly passed (47 George III.) to close up all inquiry into the past.

The Vestry thus not only guarded the parishioners against inroads from without, but it also took cognisance of their internal morality; and we shall discover that it was not exactly a bed of roses on which our ancestors reposed, guarded although it were by that supreme authority.

As early as 1703, our electioneering friend, Mr. Aldridge, an important personage here, was squabbling with the Vicar about the road through the Vicarage yard. The difficulty cropped up several times afterwards.

But a most eventful circumstance occurred about this time, and one which I fear cast its shadow over the fortunes of the parish during the remaining half of the century.

The Rev. Joseph Thistlethwaite was appointed to the living in 1748, and a terrible firebrand he proved to be. Able and vigorous, he saw at once that the living had been neglected by his non-resident predecessors, and lost no time in setting it to rights, and the parishioners too! The fine seasons of the earlier part of the century had promoted cultivation, and of course, the tithes, as Macaulay and other writers point out as having been the case generally, were just then largely increased.

The new Vicar, I find, on coming to the living, let the Vicarage house, furnished, with three-quarters of an acre of garden, for six years, at £80 per annum, and began to claim and get in the augmented tithes. This he did without discretion, or apparently any leniency. The whole parish was roused, but the Vicar exacted his dues. The old question of the Church Lane too, which had been so long a matter of dispute, was not likely now, with so watchful a guardian, to slumber long, and in 1756 it became a more serious contention, and was discussed in Vestry.

The strife evidently continued, for on the 2nd of May in that year, the following curious entry appears, and seems worth quoting at length as a curiosity in parochial literature :—

"Whereas the inhumanity and malice of some men has been made very apparent in commencing and carrying on very vexatious and cruel law-suits, to the disturbance of the public peace, and to the ruin of the fortunes and the ease of mind of particular persons; and whereas many other good and honest men are afraid of speaking freely and openly on behalf of themselves and their neighbours, lest the same malice and revenge should fall upon them; we whose names are underwritten, being a majority of the inhabitants of Sunninghill, present at this public vestry, from a desire of promoting as much as in us lies the good and welfare of our said parish, do agree to pay out of the money levied for the relief of the poor the whole expenses of every action at law which shall hereafter appear to be maliciously brought against any person residing within our said parish : Provided if the said action at law shall be adjudged by a majority of the inhabitants in full vestry to be malicious. And also in case any person shall spitefully and maliciously defame and scandalise the good name and reputation of any inhabitant, or shall in any other respect injure his person or property, we do further agree to support such inhabitant in prosecuting the injurious person at law, if it shall be judged needful, in order to recover a full satisfaction for the defamation and injury, and do consent to pay as aforesaid the whole expenses of the said prosecution.

(Signed)   JOHN BABER,
J. THISTLETHWAITE,
and sundry others."

This league against malice does not appear to have been successful in crushing out the offenders. The war was continued, and burst out again with increased violence, and in the autumn of 1763 an ominous fire broke out and swept off the Vicar's barn and all his outhouses. The dwelling-house only very narrowly escaped. All this I find, in the Vicar's own words, in a letter to the College, in which he estimates the loss at £232; and as a reason for obtaining their bounty towards its restoration, he lets out quite enough to account for his misfortune, for, says he, "without reckoning the house at anything, now I live in it, I have doubled the value of the living since I came to it, by raising ye rents of ye tithes, which you will readily believe could not be done without much difficulty and trouble, and should the farmers take this advantage of my having no barn, or other convenience for taking them in kind, I do not know how far I might be obliged to sink the rents again. 22nd October 1763."

About this time a Mr. E. C., whose family had been ancient freeholders and parishioners of Sunninghill, on coming to live in his own house, contributed to the bad spirit which raged in the parish. He soon fell out with the Vicar, who, as he alleged, "had stopped up in 1750 the old ancient coach road to Church, which leads through part of the Glebe land, and through the Vicarage yard," and in 1764 laid his complaint before the College.

The letter has the following indorsement :—

"*N.B.*—Mr. T. was indicted for ye offence, traversed and tried ye indictment at Reading Assizes. Mr. C. carried two waggon loads of witnesses, *every one* of whom proved they had seen the gates to this road locked. The Court did not examine a witness for Mr. T. The above letter was sent me by Mr. Cordale the Bursar.—J. T."

The next year a Mr. Davis, who lived at the Cedars, and the Vicar were quarrelling about another path, and a small piece of land, and the College was again appealed to, but they thought it was not worth fighting for. In 1765, having been threatened with trouble about the way through the Glebe lands again, the Vicar got the Vestry to agree to pay his law expenses out of the profits of the Church house, or other parish estates. The infection was spreading, and an action was brought in the Court of Exchequer against one Byrne and others for tithes which they refused to pay. Byrne was a tenant of Mr. Pitt.

But the worst case of all was to come. Mr. C., to whom allusion has been made, appears to have been Overseer of the Poor, with a young farmer, Edward Brown, in 1763, the year of the fire, and the parish, in Brown's name, took exception to C.'s accounts, and the Quarter Sessions found that he had charged 30s. a month to the "weekly" poor more than he had paid. C. thereupon, as his opponents alleged, determined, in revenge, "to ruin Gentleman Brown, and make him as poor as a Church mouse." How was this to be accomplished? It seems that Edward Brown, who was a younger son of a respectable farmer of Sunninghill, in 1761 purchased for £25 half an acre of freehold land abutting on Sunninghill waste, called Beggars'-bush Heath. He built a house on it for his own residence. We are told, it was two storeys high, with four rooms, and was rated at £5 per annum.

To supply himself and John Pourtsmouth and other neighbours with water, he dug a well on the common.

For all this he was persecuted by Mr. C., who discovered an old obsolete statute of Elizabeth, requiring every one to lay to his cottage at least four acres of land; and on this monstrous charge he was indicted at the Reading Lent Assizes for 1767. I have not been able to discover what became of it, although I can hardly doubt the result of so malicious a proceeding, as the statute alluded to (31 Elizabeth, c. 7) contains exceptions for cottages in "market towns, works, and quarries, and in any forest or chase."

On this case some one, doubtless the Vicar, has left us his observations. "There were," he says, "near 500 persons in the parish, mostly legally settled therein, and not therefore at liberty to move to other places! and if the contention were right, all those are worse off than the beasts of the field, for they may not roam to find food, but are neither able to stay where they are nor roam away!"

It was not until the end of this year of 1767 that the dispute with Mr. Davis about the Church way was finally set at rest by an award of

Sir Anthony Thomas Abdy (who lived at Chobham Place, and was a barrister), to whom the whole case had been referred. It was virtually in favour of the Vicar.

But a terribly vindictive litigious spirit still prevailed in the parish; and Mr. Aldridge, and a Mr. Bromley, a yeoman, both among the "well-to-do" folk of the place, were especial enemies of the Vicar. After some litigation in Court, Bromley attended at a Vestry which he had previously "packed" for the purpose, and publicly denounced the Vicar, declaring "Our Parson hath forsworn himself in the Court."

This could not be endured, and "Our Parson" was equal to the occasion. He at once brought actions for libel against them, which were tried at the Assizes at Reading, and the result is explained by the following order of the Court by consent:—

"In 11 year of George III. That Defendant John Aldridge pay costs; and that the following acknowledgment be signed by him in the Vestry book.

"Mr. Aldridge hereby asks pardon of the Reverend Mr. Thistlethwaite, Rector of this Parish, for having indecently charged him with the crime of perjury, in which accusation Mr. Aldridge acknowledges himself to have been grossly mistaken, and as an instance of his sorrow for the same has signed this acknowledgment in the Vestry book."

The same was repeated exactly in the action against Bromley.

All this shows that the spirit and tone of the social life of this retired little forest village were in nowise pleasant at this time. It was not Arcadia at all. But another dark shadow is thrown over this century by the system of Poor Laws that especially characterised it. No dispassionate inquirer can review that great legislative achievement without a feeling of humiliation. If, as we must believe, it was the best remedy that the wisdom and philanthropy of that age were capable of devising to meet the emergencies of the case, all I can say is that the case was very bad.

It was in or about 1733 the Poor Laws were introduced, and without further noticing the impolicy of affording outdoor relief to able-bodied men, one cannot peruse the minutes of a parish vestry and overseer's book of the time without amazement at the costliness of the system of settlement which was then adopted, and the wasteful litigation between parish and parish that ensued from it. Paupers were fought over, and carried about from place to place, sometimes from one end of the kingdom to the other, and more money was spent in these proceedings than would have kept them for years.

So early as the year 1662 we have the following entry:—

"John Wise, a vagrant, taken up at Totnum Higheros in Middlesex, and ordered to be sent to Ramsey in Hampshire, died here and was buried the 19th August."

Let me notice here a few other less unpleasant entries which struck me in our books:—

1678. *October 24th.*—Collected at Sunninghill for and towards the rebuilding of the Cathedral Church of St. Paul's in London—

Sir Thos. Draper, Bart.	. . . . .	£3 0 0
Mrs. Dawson	. . . . .	0 11 0
And sundry others, amounting altogether to	. .	0 9 0
		£4 0 0

1683. *January 1st.*—Henry Milton, Susanna Bonfrey. "When these two died ye frost was so hard and so deep in ye earth y^t their graves were made wth beetle and wedges."

"John Lane, son of Ed. Lane. John Lane was shot to death while employed in taking some Highway-men that were drinking here."

1692. Receipt for cure of bite of a mad dog taken out of Calthorp Church, Lincolnshire. Almost the whole town being bitten with a mad dog, and all that took the medicine did well, and those not died mad.

1707. Paid Mr. Hall for curing Winkle's boy of a broken leg and *arme*, £2, 5s. "Goody Milton was then receiving relief."

1710. Ringing the bells for the victory of Mons, 2s.; Gunpowder Treason, 3s.; Thanksgiving, 2s.; The Queen's Coronation Day, 2s. In all, 9s.

The following is expressive:—

1712. *July 5th.*—"That the Overseers pay 16s. 6d. agreed for a kilderkin of beer to be drunk out on the thanksgiving day after ye church service, and that the churchwardens pay 3s. for ringing on that day."

1720. The Overseers of the poor to provide badges according to Act of Parliament for those that receive weekly collections!

1731. Agreed to repair the Stocks!

1732. John Aldridge to be paid £10 towards expense he has been put to in the Law suit brought against him by Edward Dickenson.

1810. Bill for shaving the paupers, a halfpenny each.

But to return to the village. Its progress had not been great during the seventeenth century—the Civil War had stopped all advancement; but with the opening of Queen Anne's reign Sunninghill was awakening to a new life.

The Springs were attracting fashionable visitors, who bruited far and wide the praises of our salubrious soil and climate. That we had a choice society here in the forest is evident from a letter Pope wrote in 1716 to his friend Thomas Dancastle, in which he tells us "that good Mrs. Racket found Chiswick a very lonely place in comparison of Hall Grove [near Bagshot], where and whereabouts there are kept above twenty coaches, besides stages on the heath without number."

During the eighteenth century several new houses appeared—Beech Grove; the Oaks; Harewood, or Sunninghill House, as it was called at first; the new Silwood House (since supplanted by a newer one); Silwood Lodge; Oakleigh, or the White House, as it was christened by its builder, Mr. Gregory; and lastly, Silwood Cottage, which was built at a later date, and became the residence in turn of Mr. River, Sir Charles Wentworth, Mrs. Ann Dawson, Captain, and afterwards Vice-Admiral Hardyman, as it is still of his daughters—all these, and some others, among which I must not omit a new public house, the "Thatched Tavern," erected in 1780, appeared upon the borders of the waste, and the nooks and corners of the village. One of these houses became the property of Pelham Clinton, Duke of Newcastle, and he died here in May 1795.

But about the end of the century the growing demand for corn brought about a striking change. The wild heath-lands over which the scholarly Mrs. Carter had rambled, as she said, like a solitary goose, doubting in her reveries whether she would not soon be sighing for the sight of a cornfield, became now dotted with them.

The bank to the north of the Silwood Lake, now part of the park, was destined ere long to stand thick with shocks of grain, and bring to us that scene of all others the most eloquent of homely, happy English life, a harvest-field. Again, across the common to the south of us, on the ridge of Blackwick Hill, was the Belleview or Child's Farm.

It is curious that in the old surveys not a single arable field in the whole parish is mentioned, except at Broomhall. Now that wheat had doubled in price, it was to be seen endeavouring to grow even on our sandy slopes; but a time came when the farmer found that in growing corn he buried gold.

But nothing shows our advancement, or at least the expansion of our ideas, more than the expansion of our houses. Every habitation grew larger—the hovel became a cottage, the cottage ere long was transformed into "a villa," and the farmhouse into a grander mansion. The Belleview farmhouse, for instance, had its beautiful addition of the octagon drawing-room, and almost every house in the place some similar extension.

The "grounds," as Cobbett contemptuously calls them, were equally ambitious. Nearly all those little patches of meadow and garden enclosed from the forest were by the force of an inevitable law bought up one by one and thrown into the larger estates, to form their pleasure grounds or parks. Here may the tame deer be seen enclosed, where once not long ago the wild ones roamed at will.

Old Fuller's facetious allusion to the skittishness of the Berkshire steeds is curiously borne out with us. Not one of the principal families, save that of the worthy possessor of Sunninghill Park, has been here much more than half a century. Even of our smaller houses the tenants have been constantly changing. This is owing not only to the increasing value of the properties, but also to the military occupation of the place at the time of the camps, which has left its impress on our society even to the present day. Our village, however, may still boast of some ancestral distinction among its lesser worthies. These not having been troubled with "restive steeds," have been able to "keep their feet" in the place a long time. Passing over those no longer here, the foremost of whom were the Nevilles and the Norreyses, whose blood flows still in honourable channels elsewhere, the Babers, Farrants, Drapers, Days, Merricks, Lanes, Atlees (a very ancient family here, and at Winkfield, where Haman-at-Lee figures as an important yeoman), Buckworths, Cowderys, Ashursts, and Parsons, we come to those who are still amongst us.

Of the respectable tradesmen, none have so ancient a connection with the place as the Mortons. They may have shod the horses of Queen Mary, for all we know, as they were here in her time. The name of Pither, too, is of very long standing, and in Winkfield a Pither is mentioned among the owners of assart lands and purprestures in the Survey of 1613, and during the Commonwealth.

Of the old yeoman class, while in the adjoining county are to be found the direct descendants of the forester who carried into Winchester the dead body of Rufus, here close on our borders we have a still more remarkable instance, a family occupying the same position as yeomen from the days of King Alfred to the present time. At Almners Barn, near St. Ann's Hill, at Chertsey, the Wapshots have dwelt for centuries. Another branch flourished at Shere, and I find them also in our parish, and at Winkfield. They took their name probably from a place called "Wopshete," in Chobham, a very ancient enclosure, spoken of as a boundary in the Saxon Charter to Chertsey.* It is a little remarkable, however, that in a still lower sphere we have families in Sunninghill whose ancestors might have seen Henry VIII. hunting in the parish; witnessed all the changes which three dynasties, the Tudors, the

---

* See Surrey Collections, 1858, p. 90; Hunter's Hist. of Windsor.

Stuarts, and the Hanoverians, have brought about; helped to pile up the bonfires for Gunpowder Treason; danced round the Maypoles set up to welcome back Charles to the throne; and are here still the liege subjects of Her Majesty Queen Victoria in the year of her jubilee.

They have survived the years of famine and the years of fatness, and in spite of the Tithingman and all other adverse influences, here they are in the nineteenth century just what they were in the sixteenth.

The families of Milton were here before the reign of Henry VIII., and in that of Elizabeth they comprised nearly half the parishioners. Some of them occupied a respectable position. In 1552 a Robert Milton was churchwarden, while others of them were the "subvagatores" of Charles I.'s time, and some were vagrant squatters, the dreaded outlaws of the forest, and the particular horror of Lord Holland and his keepers. "Goody Milton" was a recipient of parochial relief for many years, and the name has only quite recently disappeared. The Slanns are of equal antiquity, and are still here. The Cottrells, the Lloyds, the Bowyers, and the Turners are of no less ancient standing. Some of these families have lived at Sunninghill in a long line of unbroken succession over 300 years, with but slight variation in the same humble position of life throughout. Kingsley's "gentlemen," with the same love of freedom and dislike to change, they cling to the soil in very much the same fashion of primitive holding that enabled them to settle upon it. Labourers then, they are labourers still.

The Turners, although of rather more importance in the seventeenth century, have been singularly consistent, and when one of them rose to become a gentleman's servant, although he may have lost caste a little, he was always afterwards known as "Gentleman Turner."

On looking back, we find every indication of a low social condition of the villagers. Few of them probably could read or write. Nor can we much wonder at it. There was no opportunity for learning. The first educational suggestion—we cannot call it effort—in the parish was a very meagre one—a night school was occasionally held by the parish clerk in the vestry.

It is very amusing to look back on the views of our ancestors on the subject of education, and in the face of which the unenlightenment of our village is hardly to be wondered at. See what our county town was equal to in 1630. The King writes to Bishop Davenant of Salisbury—"Andrew Bird, master of the Free School of Reading, states that the inhabitants have long enjoyed one free school without any molestation of any other attempting to teach Grammar in that town, but such only as have been tolerated to initiate children for the public school. Yet of late there has been a license granted by his Chancellor to one to teach Grammar there, which tends to the prejudice of the Borough and school. It is the King's pleasure that he cause that license to be revoked." In the same enlightened spirit, when Henry VI. built his college of Eton, he directed that no other school should teach within ten miles of it.

Our first step towards improvement was probably in 1732, when it was ordered that a vestry or schoolroom be built on the north side of the Church. This went on till 1819, when Mr. Augustus Schutz supplied the want, and laid the foundation of our schools, at the instigation, it would seem, of his wife. He made over a small piece of land in the village, and a cottage which had been built on it, to the trustees for the purpose of a school for the children of the poor inhabitants, and endowed it with a sum of £1154, 0s. 5d. Consols towards its maintenance. The Dawson gift of £102, 2s. Stock followed this. In 1866 St. John's College was induced to give a small piece of land adjoining to that of Mr. Schutz for a playground. In 1880, the trustees finding the buildings quite inadequate to the very largely increasing demands of the parish, the question had to be considered how best the requirements could be met, and to avoid the introduction of a Board School the inhabitants subscribed a considerable sum, and the present schools were erected at a cost of over £2000. They were opened by the Princess Christian in 1881.

CHAPTER XIV.

Value of Lands.

OUR history shows no exception to the general rule in this country as to the gradual rise in the value of land. From ancient times, when it was almost a drug for want of cultivation and want of money and a grant of waste land was often a common medium of payment for personal and menial service when coin was scarce, until now, when it has become the most coveted of possessions, its increase has been, not perhaps constant, but with certain periods of stagnation continuous. Never for any length of time has it gone seriously back.*

The earliest instance I have met with throwing any light on values in our immediate neighbourhood is that of a license to alienate ten acres of land in Bagshot to the Prior and Convent of Newark (near Woking). In 32nd Ed. III. it appeared that the lands "were held of the Prior doing suit at his Court at Send, and were worth one half-penny an acre yearly, and no more, because the land was heath lying next the King's forest of Colyngrigg."

In 1630, Sunninghill Park, with 472 acres, "450 of it good land," sold for £2700—that is, not £6 an acre—including the mansion; but this might have been an exceptionally favourable purchase, for in the following year Folyjohn Park, with only 239 acres, fetched £14 an acre,

---

* In Saxon days the rent of land was mostly paid in kind, and at a rate which, if reduced into present money, would be about 1d. or 2d. an acre, which may account for the Royal Commissioners at a much later date selling the lands right out at 12d. or 18d. an acre. In the thirteenth century, 6d. an acre seems to have been the average value of arable land, though meadow was double or treble that sum. (Elton's Tenures, p. 71.) In Fitzherbert's time, owing to the scarcity of manure, there being no stall-fed cattle, and the expense of its cultivation, arable land became of less value than meadow. He estimates that an acre of common on a hillside, with a sprinkling of gorse or furze which could be cut for fuel, was worth two acres of arable. (Eng. in Fifteenth Century, W. Denton.) The price of certain land at Hungerford, in 29th Eliz., was 40s. an acre, as nearly as possible what it would now let for per annum, and ten acres sold for 43s., and a coppice at £4 an acre. (Hall's Society in Elizabethan Age.)

or more than double the last. The old mansion of Eastmore, with its "four score acres," shortly afterwards realised less than £1000, while Fernhill in 1706 was sold to Thomas Hancock, Esq., for £4000. In 1796, 8½ acres, now the most valuable of the Silwood Estate, which was then part of the common, and close to the house, sold, as we know by our parish accounts, for £100, exactly £12 an acre; and although in some of the adjoining parishes £20 and £28 were obtained for the waste, we find the Enclosure Commissioners a few years afterwards alluding to this as a most unreasonably high price. At the beginning of the century, King's Wick, an extensive but dilapidated house, with nine acres of land, sold for £830.

But while progression has been continuous and slow, it has not been regular. Its first great bound was probably after the reign of Elizabeth, when the influence of Spanish gold and English enterprise began to tell upon the country. A lull then came, and values increased very slowly. Our agriculture hardly improved at all.

Sunninghill in 1613 contained about 700 acres of pasture, and 100 acres of arable which was at Broomhall, for strange to say, with that exception, there was not an acre of ploughed land in the parish.

It could have made but very slow progress in its arable farming during the next 150 or 200 years, for in 1769 Mrs. Carter, we may remember, was sighing for the sight of a cornfield. A considerable advance, however, was at hand. The French War that broke out in 1793 sent up the price of all agricultural produce, and with it, of course, the price of land. Under these influences Sunninghill nearly doubled its arable cultivation, and yet the corn-growing area was but small, notwithstanding that stimulus, for in 1813 we have the means of knowing exactly its extent, as in that year I find, from a statement by the Vicar to the authorities of St. John's College, there were but "about 200 acres of arable land in the parish, and half of that in the occupation of James Sibbald, Esq.," who "had perhaps 150 acres besides of water and woodland. All the rest of the parish, except the heath, is in small patches, the largest 40 acres."

This shows a very slight increase, when only 100 acres were added to the plough lands in two centuries! The pasture lands had not, I believe, increased in a much greater proportion. From some notes of the Vicar of Winkfield, it seems that the tendency to plough the pastures had set in towards the end of the century, and was deemed to have led to the impoverishment of the farmers. It was a wrong step, no doubt.

The first quarter of this century, however, brought a serious reaction,

VALUE OF LANDS.

and to the general influences a local one was added when the enclosure of the forest came. This threw on the market a large quantity of land, which was saleable only at a very low price. The depression lasted thirty or forty years, when another accident sent up land to the highest price it had ever touched—the construction of the railway from Staines to Reading caused a very considerable and sudden rise in its value. That which had been almost valueless for agriculture remained undeveloped as a "residential" district for want of facility of communication with London. This being supplied, it at once doubled in value.

Every year since circumstances have tended to add to this increase. Twenty years ago, although then but little was to be had, £100 would hardly have been expected for the most valuable acre in the parish. Forty years ago five acres in the best part of Ascot, adjoining Mr. Magniac's property, realised only £26 an acre; and so lately as 1873, 612 acres, with roads already made over it at considerable cost, realised but £100 an acre.

Since that time, land in Sunninghill has again greatly increased in value. The best acre in the parish would not then have realised so much as the worst would now! And although from external causes the highest prices have hardly been maintained in some cases, in which they had risen unduly, it cannot be said that the price of land here generally has materially fallen.

Now of this sketch the main facts are entirely borne out by the parochial rating assessments which have been made from time to time. Thus in

1707, the rateable value of the whole parish was but about	£518 0 0	
1796, it was	1062 0 0	
1803, it had risen to	1622 10 0	
1831, it stood at	4310 0 0	
But coming to the present time, in		
1884, our estimated gross rental was £25,039 2 1		
and the rateable value	20,779 15 0	
1886, the figures were . . £31,465 0 7		
and the rateable value	25,416 7 0	
1889, the figures were . . £33,917 14 7		
and the rateable value	27,418 13 6	

So that, roughly speaking, the estimated value of the parish has increased
    50 fold during the last 180 years
    25 ,, ,, 90 ,, and more than
    15 ,, ,, 83 ,,

And during even the last five years it has increased at about the rate of £1500 a year—in other words, almost three times its value in Queen Anne's reign is now added every year. Something of this increase may be owing to the greater activity of the assessors.

CHAPTER XV.

Population and Mortality.

ONE can hardly omit in an account of a parish some inquiry as to its population and its mortality, for who knows but like the waters of some sparkling fountain of wonderful repute, which, when analysed, are found to be impure, so our boasted salubriousness might vanish on accurate investigation.

In the days of Queen Elizabeth, I gather (from the meagre sources of information open to me) that the houses, with the hovels and turf huts around them, numbered only about twenty; and on this basis I assume a population of not more than eighty or ninety people.

The Church Registers, which begin in 1561, show only two deaths in the year; but that was exceptional, and for the succeeding ten years the average was about three. From the same source it would seem that 1 in 30 of the population died annually, which very closely confirms my estimate, and gives us fair reason to believe that at that time there were not more than ninety inhabitants sparingly scattered over the district comprising what is now Sunninghill, Ascot, and Sunningdale—an area of nearly 3000 acres.

In 1613 I believe the houses had increased to about thirty or thirty-four, and taking $4\frac{1}{2}$ as the fair average at that period, we get a probable population of 150 or thereabouts. From that time it took nearly a century and a half to double these figures.

I fix this number per house, although our churchwardens in 1801 put it at four.* In 1871, taking the whole of Berkshire, including the towns, it was five.

---

* The Rev. Mark Noble, Rector of Barming (a competent authority), gives $5\frac{1}{2}$ as the average of his parish in that year, but he regarded more than five as crowded. White, in his History of Selborne, takes five as the fair average. In Maidstone, in 1782, a census was taken, which showed $5\frac{6}{10}$ as the number of persons to a house; but that was in a town, and nearly five to a family. The mortality was but 1 in 37, which was considered very low.

In 1705 I find a steady increase, shown by a statement which Mr. Morris, the Vicar, left, to the effect that the parish contained about fifty families; and on our basis of calculation we may assume therefore that the number of inhabitants was about 225. In 1748, Mr. Thistlethwaite estimated that there were then at most sixty families, and putting the houses at fifty-five, we get 247 as the population.

Confirmatory of this, it seems that in 1750 there were sixty-five houses; but then for some reason, possibly the works in the park and the construction of Virginia Water, a sudden increase occurred, for in 1767 there were 107 houses and 120 families, and thus as the increase was mostly in the small cottages, I take four as the average, which gives us 428 as the number of the people at that time.

In 1780 we are told there were 115 houses, which would raise it to about 460. From that time a rapid increase set in. The establishment of the camps here stimulated work, and thereby added to the population, which amounted at the end of the century to just about 700. In 1801, when the first national census was obtained, we get a very accurate statement made by the churchwardens and overseers. They gave the number of inhabited houses as 154, uninhabited 20 = 174; the inhabitants exactly 699, or four to a house. There were 158 families. They add this note, very characteristic of our parish, "That so many residing in London in winter at this season of the year makes near 200 population less than in summer." The deaths at this time were 23 per annum (taking an average of five years), or 1 in 30 of the population, or 33 per 1000; but this was an unfavourable calculation, as the 200 absentees were not included, although several deaths from visitors during the summer would swell the rate of mortality; but making due allowance for this, it confirms our general basis of calculation.

In 1811 again the population was 913 (males 451, females 462); the deaths 22 (25 on an average of five years, or 1 in 36 = 27 per 1000). In 1831 the people numbered 1520.

But the greatest bound of all that the place has made was during the last half of the present century, on the opening of our railway.

At the time of the last census in 1881 the number of houses in the parish was 631, and the population had risen to 3040. In the ecclesiastical district the houses were 451, and the population 2207.

From 1881 to 1885 we show the following low rate of mortality :—

	Deaths per 1000, Sunninghill Parish.	Mean Rate of Combined Districts.
1881	12.1	14.9
1882	12.4	16
1883	8.7	16.8
1884	10.6	16.3
1885	13	

It is thus seen that, roughly speaking, it required nearly a century, between 1607 and 1705, to double the population, although between 1748 and 1767 the same was almost achieved in a quarter of that time. In the thirty years between 1780 and 1811 it again doubled. A similar remarkable rate of progression was maintained during the next thirty years after 1811, and this notwithstanding the national depression that followed the great war. In 1881 both the houses and their inhabitants had more than quadrupled.

The death-rate in London in the reign of Elizabeth was over 40 in the 1000—Macaulay says 43; and in 1685, 1 in 23 of the inhabitants of the capital died annually. With us it was not probably higher than 1 in 35.*

As far as I can judge during the seventeenth and eighteenth centuries the rate of mortality here varied but little—that is to say, Sunninghill seems to have been as healthy in 1600 as it was in 1800. Of sanitary precautions there were few or none adopted in either century. Our soil and climate were very favourable to life, and our natural drainage so excellent as to require but little artificial aid. About 1 in 30, or 33 per 1000, of the people died annually. The few sanitary improvements resorted to appear to have enabled the community to combat the evils of increasing numbers with tolerable success.

Indeed with our scanty population, porous sandy soil, and good spring water for drinking, there was, fifty years ago, but little to be desired for purposes of health, nor any great occasion, as there is now, for sanitary regulations, of which we were then almost entirely ignorant.

Local medical experience confirms this. I am assured that for the last fifty years there has never been an outbreak of typhoid fever here until about ten or twelve years ago, when it was traced to the use of some impure milk.

Under such favourable natural conditions the old cesspool was

---

* See *Times*, 14th December 1885.

really as safe as the improvements of modern science became in the more artificial existence that we have now to contend with.

And when to these our natural advantages we now add the improvements of modern sanitary science, we are still able to maintain and even increase our ancient reputation. These have vastly lessened the effects of those terrible epidemic and infectious diseases so prevalent in olden times, and tend more and more to equalise the death-rate of town and country.

They have doubtless contributed to produce our present enviable condition. The mean death-rate of our country between 1841 and 1876 was 1 to every 45 persons (*Encyclopædia Brit.*, vol. viii. p. 222), and that of the capital between 1871 and 1880 was but 1 in 47 = 21 per 1000, and is still decreasing. Sunninghill shows now only about 11 or 12 per 1000, facts which amply support its claim to be regarded as a remarkably healthful place.

CHAPTER XVI.

Our Roads.

IT has been well said that if you wish to read aright the history of a district, you must begin by learning the alphabet of its roads. I have already alluded to the isolation of our village, as shown by the incident of the Queen's Messenger being sent to Bagshot to find Nicholas out at Sunninghill, but the full measure of our insignificance can hardly be realised until we come to consider our roads; and what a flood of light, or rather of darkness, this throws on the scene! We who know what the roads of the nineteenth century are, find it difficult to imagine what they were in the early part of the eighteenth. How shall we define a high road? It has been called an invention of the time of George I., to enable carriages to travel from one parish to the next, and a stage waggon from one county town to another.

Before that period some of the most important roads in the kingdom were merely bridle ways. Ruts two or three feet deep were not uncommon in them, and in a long journey it was not a question of whether the carriage had broken down, but how many times! The roads were so narrow that two vehicles could not pass at some points even of the best of them; and the bells, those picturesque adornments of the farmer's teams, which some of us remember, gave out their melodious and very necessary warnings in most country lanes. The travelling in olden times tells us unmistakably what the roads were. Thus when the Mayor of Plymouth sent a despatch to Sir Edward Conway with "haste-haste-haste," the journey was accomplished at the speed of $3\frac{3}{4}$ miles an hour!—the fastest stage being in our country from Hartford Bridge to Staines, where the pace was got up to over five miles an hour.

And in 1637, Secretary Coke, writing to Sir Edward Osborne, dates from Bagshot, 5th September:—"This day I received at Bagshot yours dated from York the 2nd, whereby you may see what expedition is now used in the carriage of letters." * This improved postal service was at about the rate of five or six miles an hour. But when the King went to York in 1642, and the service was undertaken by gentlemen, the journey was performed with really wonderful expedition.

Well might Charles II., when admiring the naturally good roads of Norfolk, suggest that that county should be cut up to provide highways for the rest of the kingdom. It is difficult to realise Young's well-known statement, that in a road between Preston and Wigan he saw ruts four feet deep, and passed three broken down carts.

A more graphic account of their state can hardly be found than from the pen of an attendant of Prince George of Denmark, who was staying at Petworth in 1703, and joined King Charles of Spain in his journey through this very country from Portsmouth to Windsor and back. "The coaches," he says, "were ordered at six o'clock in the morning, and set out by torchlight (it was Christmas). We did not get out of our coaches again, save only when we were overturned, or stuck fast in the mud. It was hard service for the Prince to sit fourteen hours in the coach that day. They were thrown but once indeed in going, but in returning they were overturned twice. Both our coach, which was the leading one, and his Highness's body coach, would have suffered very often if the nimble boors of Sussex had not frequently poised it up or supported it with their shoulders from Godalming almost to Petworth. The last nine miles of the way cost us six hours time to conquer them!"† What could poor "Est il possible" have thought of this!

Even down to the present century we could hardly realise the excellence of our own roads without knowing something of the horrors of these Sussex ones. They were quite proverbial.

In 1794, January 7th, Gibbon, in the very last letter he ever wrote, tells us that he was "almost killed between Sheffield Place and East Grinsted, by hard frozen long and cross ruts that would disgrace the approach to an Indian wigwam."

This may explain Sir Thomas Gorges' forethought, when in 1609 he wrote to Salisbury, to know if the King was coming to hunt in Cranborne Chase (Wilts), "that the ways may be prepared."

How those large stage waggons, drawn by eight powerful horses, which at one time traversed the forest, tell of a bygone day!

We get an idea of our roads, too, from the statutes that regulated

---

* See life of Ed., Earl of Clarendon. p. 116.   † Archæologia, vol. iv.

their traffic. Thus in 1753, the wheels of waggons were required to be nine inches wide, and in 1757 the trustees of turnpikes were allowed to charge one-half more for those having the fellies of their wheels less than that width; and as late as 1776 waggons with wheels of that width might be drawn by eight horses, carts by five; while if the wheels were but six inches broad, not more than seven horses were to be employed; but if sixteen inches, they might be drawn by any number.

But of the roads of Sunninghill. Norden shows none of any kind through our parish, nor had we then any other than bridle-tracks.

What visions of the past do these recall! The Squire on his roadster, with well-holstered saddle, and with pistols ready for any emergency; the yeoman with his wife riding pillion behind him to market or to church; the pack-horses of the traders, lawful as well as contraband, winding their laborious way through the by-lanes of the country, were well-known pictures of the times of our forefathers.

Perhaps the earliest way that entered our forest was that ancient British one which crossed the Thames near Laleham, thence by Chertsey, Egham, and Ascot, held its course over the dry ridges to Silchester and the west. Then came the Roman road, the finest of all our forest ways. These have been for ages abandoned. De Lacy's Charter to Broomhall shows that there was a royal road, a *via regia*, or highway, in Plantagenet times from Bracknell to Reading, but it did not extend to Sunninghill.

The principal roads were suggested by the points at which the Thames could be conveniently crossed by travellers from London to Reading, Salisbury, and Portsmouth.

Among the earliest of these "through" roads was one by the terrible Maidenhead Thicket, another from Windsor over Binfield Heath to Reading, by which we hear of the contending armies making their way in the time of the Commonwealth. At a later date the "forest road" was made, traversing much the same country by a somewhat different route. And lastly came the Virginia Water road through Sunninghill, Bracknell, and Wokingham, over Loddon Bridge. These passed through Berkshire. But another really more important to us was that which struck into the southern part of the forest through Surrey, leading from the passage of the river at Staines, following almost the line of the Roman road by Egham to Virginia Water, where it crossed the stream at a well-known spot, called in Norden's map the Watering-place, and more anciently Harpesford; thence over Shrubshill to Broomhall, where in ancient times it passed by the gate-

OUR ROADS.

way of the Nunnery to Bagshot, and so over the hills through Frimley and Farnham to Winchester, but this till within the last century was little better than a bridle road—the more frequented route was that which ran from Chertsey and Staines through Thorpe, and so over Chobham Common through Windlesham village to Bagshot, which may explain the anomalous position of Windlesham in the present day, standing as it does quite out of the high road, although so ancient a place.*

Of more local ways Sunninghill had but few. That which connected Bagshot with Windsor passed the old gibbet on the right, Swinley rails on the left, then by Englemere Pond, Burley Bushes, and

OLD STAINES BRIDGE.

Sunninghill Park, and so on between the Mote Park and St. Leonard's Hill to Windsor.

* Here, although space will not allow of my touching on the history of Staines, I may say a few words of its bridges, by which so important a route was opened into the forest. After the British and Roman ways, the most ancient we hear of was Oxenford's bridge of wood, for the making and maintaining of which Windsor's oaks paid ample tribute. At the foot of this, Lord Ashley tells us, stood the old Vine Inn, at which he stopped in 1646 (see Christie's Life of First Earl of Shaftesbury). This in 1790 was supposed to be worn out (see Manning and Bray's Surrey, vol. iii. 256), and a new bridge was commenced, under the superintendence of Thomas Sandby, at a point eastward of the old one, and was opened in 1796. But a strange fatality hung over the bridges of Staines. This one did not last a year. The centre arch cracked, and in 1801 an iron bridge was erected of a single span of 180 feet, which was opened in 1803. That within a twelvemonth shared the same fate, caused by the excavation of a cellar under the Bush Inn on the Staines side. Fortunately the old one of heart of oak remained, and did duty until another

One of the earliest roads that entered our village was from the Nunnery of Broomhall. It passed the stream where in the time of Henry III. we read of the "new brugge towards Sunning," thence to a spot near the schools at what was afterwards called Sunninghill Dale. From this it went up over the common by the old house in Sunningdale Park, crossing the Larch Avenue to Pembroke Lodge, then directly through the village down by Coombe Meadows to the Wells Inn, passing close by the old farmhouse in the lane, and there dividing, one road going over Ascot Heath and the other bearing round (as still shown by the trees in the hedge-row, where now is a sharp corner opposite the inn) to Sunninghill Park, by the old Manor House, and so on to Cheapside, Lord's Green, and the Mill. But this road through the village disappears altogether in a map of 1800, wherein it is shown turning off through "Sunninghill Dale," but the track from that point to the village, now the station road, was still used.

The old thoroughfares to Bagshot and Swinley rails are perhaps more altered than any. That to Bagshot was much more direct and convenient than the present one. It came from the north of Bagshot Park by the gallows, which stood where Mr. Waterer's nursery is now, a little off the road, not far from the Cricketer's Inn, and thence in its straight easterly course to King's Beeches or Blackwick Hill, passing through Berry Stede down the valley to Pembroke Lodge, up through the wood, and out opposite to Silwood Lodge; thence crossing the western side of Beggars'-Bush Heath by the door of old Silwood, it went on to Lord's Green and the Mill.

There was also at the beginning of the century a road straight from King's Beeches through Sunningdale to Shrubshill.

The Church road certainly presents the most difficult problem for explanation.

It is a strange anomaly that the earliest building in the parish, placed out in the waste, with uninterrupted access to it from all quarters, should have met so hard a fate as to be shut up and approached now only by one "blind lane"—the "Church Vere"—from the Crossways. It is a most unnatural position, if I may use such a term. I have no doubt at all that "once upon a time"

---

iron bridge was being constructed. This was supported by eight rows of strong wooden piles, six in a row, dividing it into several arches, of which, however, three only were serviceable for barges, the others only by very small boats. Of this I give a drawing, taken from an old engraving. On this being finished in 1807, the old wooden bridge was removed. Finally came the present one, built about 200 yards higher up the stream than the preceding, and opened by William IV. and Queen Adelaide in 1832, making the fifth within half a century.

tracks led directly to the Church from all the principal places I have referred to, and one probably from the Church Green to the Manor House and the Mill, very much on the site of the present footpath; but one by one they have all become changed and destroyed. Some may yet be traced by the curious, although all vestiges of them are now lost to the ordinary observer.

We must not forget the one for which, as John Aldridge made use of it to the trouble of the Vicar, he paid him the "fat pig at Christmas." This way ran from the Church directly through the Cedars garden, as described when speaking of that place. It was the subject of much quarrel and litigation, but was finally decided to be the private road of the Vicar. At the hearing of the case, one John Pickering, born in 1724, gave evidence "that he worked at Mr. Baber's for five years. The coach usually went to Church through Brook Lane, but when they went through the Parsonage Lane, it being the nearest way, that he used to go with the footman behind the coach; and though in the five years it often went through the Parsonage Lane, they did not once find the gate at the bridge open, but always locked, and the coach and family in it waited whilst ye footman ran to Mr. Bentley's for ye key, which he carried back on returning from Church, with ye family's compliments. Y^t at other times he has often seen the heathgate locked, never heard it was a common cart-way; that when his father was carried from Cheapside to be buried in 1745, though it was a very wet day, they went to ye Church though Brook Lane, a worse way, and much about, because the people said they must not carry him through the Parsonage Lane, it not being an allowed carriage way."

The present Church Lane must be the one referred to in the following resolution of Vestry:—

"Nov. 1745. Agreed to give Captain Farrell the Church Lane that now is from the 'Comon' Gate as far as his own land reaches, which is as far as Mr. Bentley's orchard, upon an exchange for ever. The said Captain Farrell to give the parishioners part of his field adjoining to the Church Lane for to make a new Church Lane down to the Church for ever. It is also agreed that the parishioners *is* to make a good ditch and hedge on both sides of the new lane, and after the said fences *is* made good, Captain Farrell is to repair his for ever. And it is further agreed that the piece of ground which is at the end of his field he gives the parishioners is to be laid to part of the old lane facing Mr. Bentley's."

Captain Farrell lived at Ashurst's, where Mr. Shutz afterwards did. The present Church Lane was much altered and widened in 1745, as above described. The common ran up to the cross-roads, so that it would come from the "Comon" Gate.

The time at last came when these forest tracks were to be improved into "roads." The increasing wealth of the country demanded quicker communication between one part of the kingdom and another, which was impossible on such roads as then existed, and with such vehicles as alone could travel on them. A great burst of energy set in for road constructing during the earlier part of the eighteenth century, just as in the latter part came the enclosure of the commons, and in the nineteenth the rage for gas and railways.

We owe our first good road very much to the great Government powder mills and factories at Hounslow Heath, and which we hear of as in full work during the Commonwealth manufacturing arms under foreign experts. For these works a large supply of timber was necessary, and to facilitate its transit, an Act was passed in 1727, "for repairing the road from the powder mills, Hounslow, to a place called Basingstone, near the town of Bagshot, in the parish of Windlesham." This place was near the "Golden Farmer."

Subsequently, in 1753, the way on from Basingstone through Frimley and Farnham to Winchester was taken in hand; and in 1757 that from the "Golden Farmer" to Hertford Bridge Hill.

The road from Virginia Water was repaired and in great part made in 1759. It was then described as leading from a place called the Old Gallows, in the parish of Sunning, through Wokingham, New Bracknell, and Sunninghill, to Virginia Water.

No sooner were the roads made traversable than the coaching enterprise of the country responded to their invitation, and in 1769 this neighbourhood, although accustomed to the western stages which traversed it earlier in the century, and to the six or eight-horsed forest waggons, was startled by an apparition on wheels called the "Reading Flying Machine," soon to be followed by the "Wokingham Flying Machine," which "sets out at six o'clock to London, and returns the same day!" In 1774 a "new Wokingham Machine" was started, "setting out from Wokingham through Sunninghill to London, stopping at Sunninghill Wells.

In a map of 1798 we see the proposed alteration of the old western turnpike road over Bishopsgate Heath to Windsor, and the new proposed road by Priest's Hill to Windsor; and the present road through Egham, above described, is called "the new road to Windsor that is made and completed." It crossed a common called Wick Heath, containing twenty-seven acres, near Virginia Water, then proposed to be purchased, passed round the corner of the park at Blackness Gate by a spot called Crocks Hole, "and thence up Titness Hill over Beggars'-Bush Heath straight to the Church Crossways. But these improvements soon raised up in the village two gates or tollbars—one on the hill at King's Wick, and another on Beggars'-Bush Heath near the Post Office; and in 1811 there seems to have been a turnpike gate at Blackness. When the great road changes took place, the old way from Bagshot to Sunninghill, which we have described, was changed very much for the worse. From King's Beech Hill it was carried quite out of the way due south towards Windlesham into the Egham road to the Windmill Inn (so called from an old windmill which stood out on the common near to that spot), and making the journey to Bagshot a mile further for us. Here we turn at a right angle to the west, and after a few rods are traversed, again as sharply to the south towards Windlesham.

This is simply an awkward break in the old straight drive from King's Beeches to Windlesham.

At a place in Sunninghill called Mill Gate there were at the beginning of this century two wooden bridges across the brook. But these being much out of repair, the Crown Surveyor, John Robinson, seized the opportunity of obtaining rather more than two acres and a half of the waste to throw into the park, in consideration of his building a good brick bridge and making the roads to it convenient. This Mr. Robinson was engaged in 1811 in surveying this neighbourhood, and left a few measurements that may be of local interest, as showing the distances from Sunninghill to Windsor by different roads—

	M.	F.	P.
To Windsor through the Park by Blackness Turnpike	6	2	35
By Mill Lane and Blackness Gate by Mill Gate	6	1	3

	M.	F.	P.
By Sunninghill Park through the Great Park by Sandpit Gate.	7	2	20
By Sunninghill Park, crossing the Holly Walk by S^r. And^w. Hammond's	5	3	11
N.B.—The place whence the above are measured is the house at the N.E. point of the common, late Mr. Barker's.			
From the Wells to the house, late Barker's .	1	0	38
From Wheatsheaf, at Virginia Water, to Barker's, by Blackness old road	2	2	32
From the end of Col^l. Heartley's road, where it joins the great road to the Wells	0	4	20
From late Barker's to Dog at Belfont, through Blackness Turnpike .	9	6	35

I may mention that "late Barker's," from which these measurements were taken, is now Harewood, Colonel Hay's.

CHAPTER XVII.

The Church.

IN our Churchyard there is but little to interest us. The tombstones are not very remarkable. The best fragment of work, perhaps, is in one on the south side of the Church, to the memory of William May. This, it has been said, stood at one time in the Church, and was covered with a black marble top, but how or when its removal and transformation took place I have no information.

We have certainly changed for the better in the style of our monumental inscriptions.

I must notice, at the outset, a curious custom, which seems to have prevailed in our parish for several hundred years, with regard to the maintenance of the Church pales. From the earliest times to which our records go back, it has been a practice for the inhabitants, at a Vestry especially called for the purpose, to award to the owners of the principal properties the repair of a certain number of the Church pales. Thus in 1671 I find "a list of those bound to uphold the rails of the Churchyard." Among others, "the rails called the Queen's rails, now Sir Thomas Draper, Bart., 5 panells." "Thomas Rawlins, for Farrant's, now Mr. Aldridge's, 7 do."

In 1672 we have a similar list, headed by the curious words, "beginning at the great old oake tour on ye north side of ye gate, and so forward." Could this have referred to the Church House, or to the turret shrine in the north-east view of the Church? Among the names in this are:—

	Panels.		Panels.
Francis Broughton	3	Mr. Thos. Rawlins for Farrant's, now Mr. Aldridge	7
Sir Thos. Draper for Robinson's	3	Edw. Lane of Coworth for Robes	1
Richard Atlee		Broomhall	6
Sir Thomas Draper, Bart., for ye brick house	3		

The Parson always has to do the gate.

In 1714 the Vestry agreed "that notice be given next Sunday at the Church that all the inhabitants meet to settle the repairs of the

Church rayles, and adjust the severall proportions of the inhabitants thereof." Again, in 1721, I find another list, as follows:—

	Panels.
—— Baber for his Park	18
John Aldridge for Sylmore	4
Sir Henry Ashurst, Bart., for the brick house, *alias* stony lands	2
Do. for new bridge	2
John Baber, Esq., for Broomhall and Tittenhurst	7
John Aldridge for Eastmore	5
Mrs. Barbara Jordan, Widow	5
Mr. Edward Lane	1
John Pitman, late Edward Lane	4
Thomas Hatch for the Wells	3
The gate is maintained by the Minister	3

But the list for 1766 shows so great an increase of the inhabitants, that for local information it may be worth setting out:—

	Panels.	Foot.	Inch.
T. D. Baber for his Park	18	144	4
Late Worth, now Cooke, Esq., a little gate, &c., leading into the Church Green, &c.	2	13	2
Mr. John Aldridge for Bronsvelt	2	10	10
Do. for Sylmore	4	28	4
Late Attlee, now John Bartholomew	3	19	9
Late Ashurst, now William Farrell, stony land	2	14	6
W^m. Farrell for New Bridge	2	13	10
Late Jacob Edwards, now John Johnson, J. Pearman, Saml. Sawyer	1	8	1
Mr. Deane and John Simons	1	8	6
Thomas Elliot and John Fernhead	1	7	10
George Cacutt	2	18	8
W^m. Slan and Mr. W^m. Davis	1	8	5
John Aldridge, late Whapshots	1	9	5
Geo. Hatch and John Johnson	1	8	3
Widow Ann Staples	2	11	10
John Aldridge, late Edward Lane	1	6	1
John Baker and others	1	8	6
Ed. Atfield	1	7	9
Thos. Baber for Broomhall and Tittenhurst	7	54	5
Widow Deed and James Grace	1	10	6
John Pitt, Esq., for Eastmore	5	36	3
Edm^d. Cook, Esq.	5	38	11
Sir John Ellwill, Bart.	1	10	7
Mrs. Schutz pannell and style	1	7	0
Mrs. Lane Hatch for careless	1	8	6
John Skillings, &c.	2	14	10
Thomas Tilbury and others	1	8	2
Thomas Platts, landlord	2	14	0
Mr. Lane, or Ed. Lane	4	23	4
Geo. Hatch for the Wells	3	19	10
Rev. T. Thistlethwaite for the gate			
	79	594	5

It seems to have been usual for the Vicar to let the grazing of the Churchyard; and an old paper, dated about 1798, showing the income from the Vicarage, includes in the estimate, "Churchyard, 10s. 6d." I need hardly say that the ancient graveyard lies round the Church. That on the other side of the road is a modern addition.

Before we enter the Church, let us notice one of the most interesting objects in the parish, testifying in its silent eloquence to our great antiquity—the ancient yew-tree in the Churchyard; that hale old living witness, whose cradle may have been rocked in the time of the

Confessor, or in that of Henry II. at least, has only just now taken to crutches in the reign of Victoria. This venerable record of Norman times still flourishes in the enjoyment of a vigorous old age. Its huge clustered-column trunk is hollow and worn, but thanks to the care which has filled up with a metal covering the gaps which time has made in it, bids fair to last many centuries yet. Now and then a bare red muscular limb yields to the tempest, but still its head is green.

The circumference of the stem at 3 feet from the ground is 18 feet 3 inches, and at 5 feet, 23 feet 3 inches. Why yew-trees were so commonly planted in churchyards will never perhaps be conclusively settled. Ray says it was because as an evergreen tree it was regarded as a symbol of immortality. But the Statute 53, Edward I., bears upon it, the more especially when we consider that in ancient times building was often bad, and but ill able to stand the force of violent gales; and coupled with this, it may be observed that the tree is usually planted at the precise spot at which the Church is most exposed to the wind. The Statute anno 1307, s. 2, runs, "And yet seeing those trees be often planted to defend the force of the wind from hurting of the Church, we do prohibit the parsons of the Church that they do not presume to fell them down unadvisedly, but when the chancel of the Church doth want necessary reparations."

The idea of their having been planted in such places for archery purposes is hardly worthy of serious consideration.

However that may be—

> "The seasons bring the flowers again,
> And bring the firstling to the flock;
> And in the dusk of thee, the clock
> Beats out the little lives of men."

And still—

> "At noon the wild bee hummeth
> About the mossed head stone."

THE CHURCH.

Our Church is dedicated to St. Michael and all Angels, or rather more correctly speaking, to God and His service to the honour of St. Michael.

It is a curious fact that nearly all the churches dedicated in early times to that saint were built on hills; and even that those erected on lofty situations were almost always so dedicated. Although the origin of this practice is traceable to an old monkish tradition or legend, it became almost a general rule.

"The churches on the great Mont St. Michel, off the coast of Brittany, and on that lesser one in Mount's Bay, Cornwall, are well known instances. On the high rock of

OLD SUNNINGHILL CHURCH, SOUTH-WEST VIEW.

Brent Tor, on Dartmoor, we have another of the many similar examples. Even St. Michael's, Cornhill, is no exception to the rule, for it occupies the highest spot in that locality, the bank of a wider river that once rolled by." *

King John's grant of the Church of Sunninghill to the Nunnery of St. Margaret of Broomhall does not mention the name of its patron saint, but strange to say, on the judicial farce of its dissolution, under Henry VIII., the inquisition describes it as the Church of St. Margaret at Sunninghill. This, although in a legal document, was probably the mere carelessness of the officials. I have no reason to think

* Dedication of Churches, by Charles Brown, M.A.

that our Church was re-dedicated when St. John's College, Cambridge, became its patrons. Instances, however, are not wanting of such a change.

The existing building was erected in 1827, on the demolition of the ancient Norman Church that occupied its site; and there it stands, a monument of the "munificence" of Augustus Schutz, Esq., and the "liberal donations of His Majesty and the inhabitants of Sunninghill." In the Church may be seen a board proclaiming this fact, and a very fair rustic rendering of "Ego et rex meus" it seems to be. Still more does it stand a monument of the taste of the people, and the architectural degradation that then prevailed. In an archæological point of view, I can say nothing in praise of our Church. Of original work there are no fragments remaining, except in the chancel, and those are covered by plaster and modern masonry. Yet as a specimen of the very worst period of English architecture it is, at least, instructive. The village carpenter was apparently called in to advise the good folk of the place in the great work they had undertaken, and the result is ludicrous in the extreme—a curious anomaly. The plain plastered arches in the nave are the carpenter's realisation of their Norman predecessors. No longer resting on their massive rounded pillars, but on wretched iron shafts, not even fair apologies for clustered columns, the hammer-beam roof is suggestive of fifteenth century style, and the windows are of no style at all. It will accommodate, the gallery included, about 500 people. Of the seats in the body of the Church 204 are free, and 234 appropriated; but of these latter forty-nine are faculties, or are claimed to be such.

We must hope that at some future day the Church may be rebuilt in a manner worthy of a better age and of the beautiful site it occupies.

Let us now endeavour to recall the past, and see if we can reproduce the old Norman Church of our fathers.

We get a very early representation of it, slight though it be, in an old map which belonged to Lord Burleigh, and was engraved probably in the time of Queen Elizabeth. It shows a typical Norman Church, with chancel and nave divided by a square low tower rising from the centre.

It was very small, and as soon as the population began to increase much, more accommodation was essential; and in 1712 one Edward Watson was paid for building six new pews on the north side of the Church. Pews in a Church were the exception rather than the rule at this time. Convocation in this very year 1712 enjoined that all churches about to be consecrated should be previously pewed. In 1732 a vestry or schoolroom was built on the north side of the Church.

The next notice we have of the building is an exceedingly valuable one, for in 1768 it fortunately attracted the attention of Dr. Milles,* the President of the Society of Antiquaries, who, on the 25th February in that year, read a paper on the very curious inscription it contained, of which I will presently speak more fully. He incidentally exactly confirmed the suggestion of the old maps, describing the Church as "a specimen both in its form and size of the earlier parochial churches which were built in this kingdom, consisting only of a nave and small chancel divided by a square belfry tower."

Mr. Lysons also similarly describes it, adding that the south door was Saxon. This remark is mentioned because it indicates the site of the ancient door; but as to its having been Saxon, I need only say that in Lysons' time it was the prevailing opinion that all circular-headed doors were of that date, an opinion now quite exploded.

Shortly after this, in 1779, its condition and the requirements of the parish alike demanded attention. The Hon. Mr. Yorke, who lived at the Cedars, and was most anxious to purchase the ancient Church green in front of his house, "proposed to the parish to pull down the vestry room, and allow the parish a sum equal to the expense of building a new one, and give the parish all the materials of the house called the Church House, as well as those of the present vestry." "And the parishioners, judging that it may be necessary to enlarge the Church, ordered that estimates be obtained of value of materials, also of an additional building to be placed at the west end of the Church: the lower part to be used as a vestry, and the upper to be formed into a gallery, and laid out in seats, for use of parishioners, and a staircase leading to same." In April 1807 Mr. Thistlethwaite, the Vicar, died, and it seems from a letter at St. John's College that he left by his will £500 to be laid out on the Church. It was that legacy that gave rise to the alterations then made. A contract was obtained for "adding an aisle to the Church;" and in the next year John Milton, George Lee, and James Slanne were paid "for erecting an additional part to the Church, with one gallery, five seats, and a pew under the same, and eighteen other new pews, at a total cost of £827." This was a considerable addition, and included that "part of the north aisle" which was the

* See Archæologia, ii. 129.

only exception to the rebuilding in 1827. It was important also as having been the origin of our faculty seats.

Thus it was that the old Norman Church was patched about before its final demolition. There still exists in the village a rude model of it, a copy of one made at the time it was taken down; and although it gives no ornamental details, it shows the main plan and character of the building as I have described it. From this it appears the entrance doorway was at the south-west corner, shut in by a porch of later date; and the tower was surmounted by a dwarf shingle spire. There is also a water-colour drawing of the Church in the possession of General Crutchley, and another belonging to old Mrs. Morton, which gives us a view of the eastern end, showing a curious turret at the north-eastern corner of the tower, an extremely interesting feature. This drawing was made by a Mr. W. H. Parr, some time apparently during the last century, before the Cridland tomb was erected, or the road made to the Cedars stables. These representations all agree in their main features, and enable us to realise what the old Church was; but of actual details, all, it was supposed, had long since gone to mend the roads! It is difficult, therefore, to say that the Church was Norman, and not Saxon. The yew-tree, supposed to be over a thousand years old, might suggest the earlier date; and the ancient inscription, before referred to, has given rise to an opinion in favour of this view.

Dr. Milles, Dean of Exeter, in his valuable dissertation, which I cannot do better than give at length, says—

"On the impost moulding of one of the arches of this tower is carved the following inscription:—

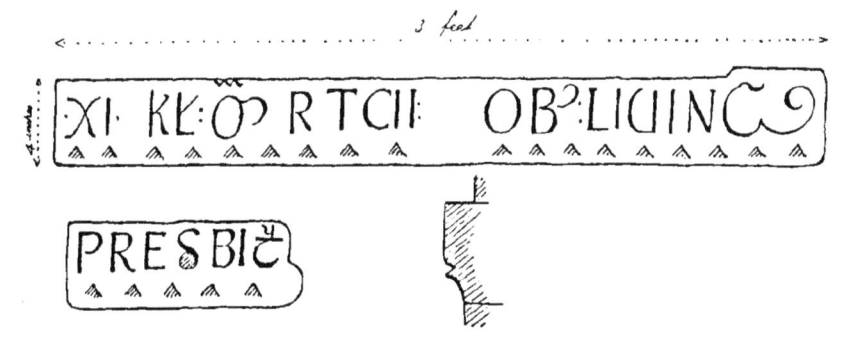

which I read thus:—

'Undecimo Kalendarum Martii obiit Livingus Presbiter.'"

"The last Bishop of Devonshire, before the removal of the Episcopal See from Crediton to Exeter, was called by this name. He held the See of Worcester at the same time, and died in the reign of Edward the Confessor.* The style and situation of the inscription show it to have been rather commemorative than sepulchral." "The body might have been interred under the tower, at that time perhaps the entrance to the Church, but there not being any year mentioned seems to show it was rather intended as a memorial for his successors and the parishioners of the day on which his death was to be celebrated or a mass said for his soul." "It is precisely the style in which entries are made in the Roman Calendars for the celebration of the deaths of their saints or founders or benefactors." "The simplicity and conciseness of the inscription is another proof of its antiquity, and so is the use of the Roman numerals, and the form of the letters, which are Roman capitals, except the ꝺ in Martii ; and the E in Presbiter, which are Saxon letters." "I must observe likewise that the inscription is perfect, and fills almost two sides of the impost moulding. It appears also to have been cut subsequent to the building of the tower, the distance between the words being unequal on account of some cavities and imperfections in the stone which rendered it unfit for the inscription."

Now this careful inspection by one so competent, followed by so excellent a description, affords us a most valuable contribution to our history of the Church. But it would seem to me that if there were only two Saxon letters in this inscription, we must conclude that it was carved at a time subsequent to that in which Saxon characters were in common use; or why not all in the same style? And then if cut on the stones after the tower was built (and not inserted simply), it clearly proves that the tower (taken down in 1827) was not earlier than of Norman times.

However inconclusive such reasoning may be, these records in stone are the most faithful we possess, for, as we have said, documentary evidence quite fails us in arriving at the date of our Church; but fortunately archæology again comes to our aid—that handmaid of history, as it has well been called; and certainly in this case I have found the handmaid more reliable than the mistress.

The daughter of our late Vicar remembered having heard it said that when the old building was pulled down, the entrance doorway was removed, and put up in the garden of a neighbouring house, Tetworth. Thither one day we made a voyage of discovery. No such thing was known of there. But a little exploration soon revealed, built up in the doorway of the kitchen garden, the object of our search. There, almost covered with ivy, stood before us, clearly enough, when the festoons by which it was so much concealed were stripped off, the stones of a veritable Norman door-arch. The capitals, if ever there were any, were gone; but the other remaining stones of the arch, with

---

* The Saxon Chronicles state 1047. This year died Living, the eloquent bishop, on 10th of the Kal. of April (March 23), and he had three bishoprics—one in Devonshire, one in Cornwall, and one in Worcester.

their zigzag mouldings, and the double-billet roll, were there all perfect. It tells us as clearly as though written in a charter of vellum that this doorway, taken down in 1827, was erected by Norman hands during the twelfth century, and, we may safely say, somewhere about the year 1120 or 1130, for although the work is rude, the mouldings hardly indicate very early Norman work. We find the double-billet in use about this date. Thus we establish the erection of a Norman Church, or at least an important part of it, in the twelfth century. I cannot say that a Saxon one had not previously existed on that site, but I know of no vestige of authority for the supposition. Besides, the very dedication to St. Michael is of Norman suggestion. That saint was not held in much veneration in England till the Norman Conquest, when Duke William happened to arrive on the eve of St. Michael's mass, as the Saxon Chronicle tells us, and the dedication became a very popular one. St. Michael's effigy was borne on the Conqueror's banner.

Since writing the above I have taken some pains to learn whether we can determine the date of this inscription from the style and formation of its letters, for it seems to be the very keystone of our Church history. The most eminent authorities at the British Museum have kindly given me their opinion. They think, that rude as the work was, it was not older than about the early part of the twelfth century. At the Record Office I have been equally fortunate. Some of the best opinions there entirely confirm this view; and, what is more important, they point out that the two Saxon letters, the M in Martii, and the P in Presbiter, were used in that identical form in the twelfth century, and down even to the thirteenth.

This appears conclusive, as removing the only ground on which the argument in favour of a Saxon Church could be supported.

But why then, it may be asked, is the name of Levingus thus honoured, if he were neither priest nor benefactor of our Church? I think with Dr. Milles that it was simply commemorative. Living was a monk of Winchester, and afterwards abbot of Tavistock. Before he held his bishoprics he was a great friend of Godwine the Sheriff, and was present at his death. He was held in great esteem by Harold, in whose earldom our lands lay; and was remarkable especially for his eloquence, as well as for his learning and piety. Beloved by all, he was regarded with little less than saintly reverence.

I cannot but think that our Church was built, as I have said, about 1120 or 1130, during the reign of Henry I., and under the auspices either of his first Queen, "the good Queen Molde," or of her

THE CHURCH.

daughter Matilda—their Saxon lineage accounting for the honour done to the memory of Living, their beloved Saxon bishop. These ladies were well known for their piety, and much given to religious endowments, and it is not improbable that one of them, or Adeliza, Henry's second Queen, founded the Nunnery. The royal family of Scotland, from which they sprang, was intensely Saxon in feeling and tastes. Maude's brother, David I., founded Holyrood, Melrose,

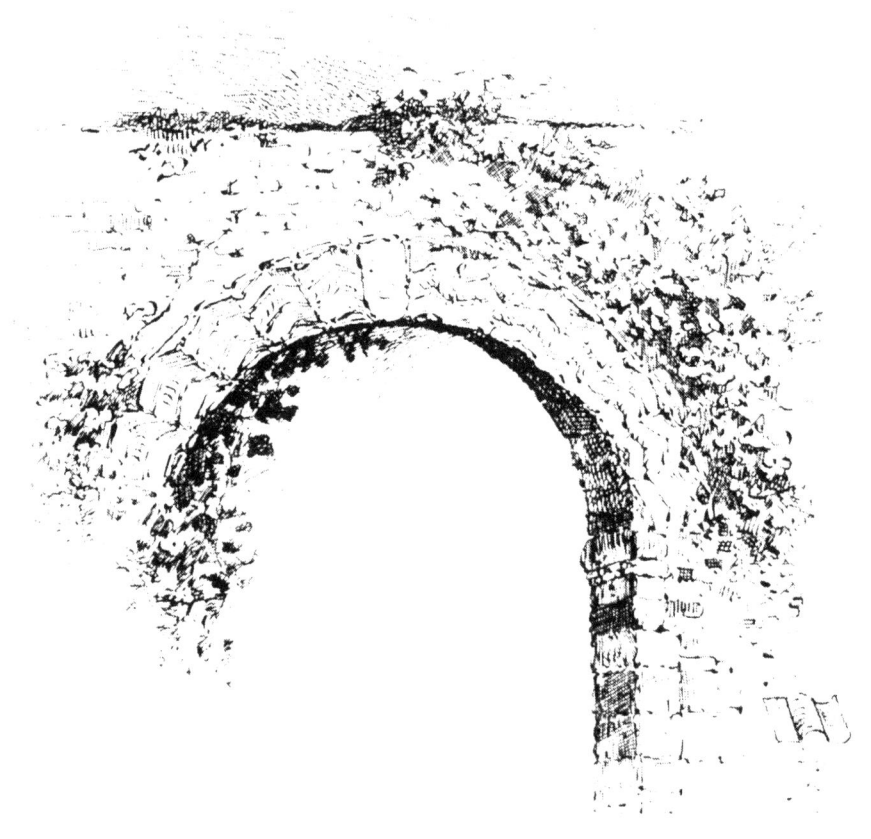

DOOR ARCH.

Dryburgh, and several others of the most famous religious houses in that kingdom. This connection would account for its dedication to St. Margaret, as Molde's mother was Margaret, Queen of Malcolm, King of Scotland, and sister of Edgar, and became the most venerated of Scottish saints. We must also remember that of both these ladies Roger, Bishop of Salisbury, the great minister of Henry I., was a powerful ally, and without his assent neither Church nor Nunnery is likely to have been erected in his diocese; and moreover, such was the jealousy of all that was Saxon, that it may be assumed no one in England, before the marriage of Henry I. to Matilda, would have ventured to do such public honour to a Saxon bishop; and the very Norman Latin form of the word "Livingus," instead of the Saxon "Living," shows surely that its cutting was done in Norman days.

The Church was given, we remember, by King John, in 1199, the very first year of his reign, to the Nunnery of Broomhall, which shows at once a different origin for the two institutions. Henry I. probably built the Church in his own forest demesne; and soon afterwards possibly his second Queen, Adeliza of Louvain, who, after the King's death, married William de Albini, founded the Nunnery; but of this elsewhere.

With regard to the interior of the Church, so lately as 1873, it was an example of an unrestored Church, then, however, becoming scarce; and although, like Amos Barton, one may say, "Mine is not a well-regulated mind, and has an occasional tenderness for old abuses, and lingers with a certain fondness over the days of nasal clerks and top-booted parsons, and has a sigh for the departed shades of vulgar errors," yet, methinks, there were formerly some abuses—an old-fashioned want of reverence being one of them—that we can hardly regret the loss of. Thus here the aisles were paved with ancient memorial stones of parishioners buried there, I assumed, ages before. Some of them having sunk more than others occasioned a rather uneven surface. One might look down, and read with becoming reverence, "Here lyeth the body of——;" but a little further research discovered how terribly the stones had been torn up, muddled together, and replaced, of course in the wrong places. We are told on a board at one time affixed to the wall of the north aisle that the Church was paved in 1706 by Richard Elliot and Nath. Phillips, churchwardens. Where did they get the stones? Had they not been placed there one by one as each person whose name is recorded had been buried? No; it seems they were all laid down in 1706. But what we can hardly believe of 1706 is still more difficult to realise of 1827; and yet a worse thing happened then. The building contract, fully discussed as it was by the parishioners "in Vestry assembled," stipulated that the builders might use or sell as they liked all the old materials, and might use for paving the aisles all the old tombstones that had been removed, and were then in the Churchyard; and so the poor restless stones were made to lie, in more senses than one, in very different places from those in which the piety of our fore-fathers had originally placed them.

But this pavement was to serve but a little longer. Up it was torn again in 1876, when the stones finally disappeared!

There is nothing remaining in the Church of archæological interest. I may notice here, however, a record in our registers, that "in 1786, Mrs. Elizabeth Clayton was buried *in* the Church in a *common grave*, close to the brick grave in which Lady Buckworth was buried in 1767. It does not now appear to be known that any other vault or grave has been made under the pews, between the tower and the west end of the Church, on the north side of the 'Isle.'" This lady was the widow of General Clayton, who was killed at Dettingen, and was a daughter of Lady Buckworth.

The Church seems to have been built of a dark ferruginous conglomerate stone, still found on the heaths around, of the same kind

OLD CHANCEL.

probably as the "heath-stone from Cranborne" taken to Windsor in 1476 for the re-erection of Chaucer's ruined chapel there. Here it was used in large masses, and remains to this day a very hard durable stone. Some of it, when the Church was pulled down in 1827, was made useful to support the Beech Grove bank in Wells' Lane. In 1861 a large portion of the north wall of the chancel was taken away for the introduction of the organ. It was found to consist of the same material, and it may still be seen in the Vicarage garden. The wall was destroyed with difficulty.

Since writing the above, the chancel has been rebuilt (1888). The old work was found to be of this same stone, and was very substantial. The coigns were here and there large blocks of chalk, harder than marble.

But a more interesting alteration was made by the Vicar about 1873, when he restored the chancel. The old roof has been described to me as having been a low timber one, of barrel form, with wood ribs to support it. It was of very rough planks, exceedingly decayed, and was painted blue.

It is likely to have been the original roof.

At the same time the old pavement of common bricks was taken up, and a new one laid down. Beneath the east window a wooden coffin, or the mouldering fragments of one, was found, and a skeleton, sufficiently perfect to allow of the bones being measured. Their length indicated the remains of a man over six feet in height. In the centre of the eastern wall, on the removal of a board on which the commandments were written in yellow letters, a more ancient inscription was revealed, showing the creed, in old English characters, with very beautiful ornamental capitals. On the same eastern wall, in the northern compartment, a fresco was laid bare, showing a figure with very pointed shoes, and with cross-bandaged chausses or hose; but this, unfortunately, on exposure to the air, perished, I am told, before it could be carefully examined.

The pews of our Church were narrow, box-like enclosures, with doors, some of oak, others of deal, and many of them patched with odd pieces. The more important pews showed by their imposing dimensions the superior position of their occupants.*

---

* Fixed seats, it would seem, were rented before the Reformation, but it was not till the seventeenth century that they were commonly adopted in churches. The earliest dated pew (according to Heale's Hist. of Pews, vol. i.) is 1530, at Bishop's Hull, Somerset; and I find that Dursley, Somersetshire, was first pewed and the seats paid for in 1579. There is an early instance of one in 1599, at Cartmel, Lancashire, where there was assigned to one Killet "a place or queare for him and his wife several to themselves, in consideration of his having kept and continuing to keep the Church booke." The sermons of the sixteenth century led to pews, but they did not become general till long after that. Locks to the doors came still later. We have an amusing allusion to this subject in the time of Queen Anne. Bishop Burnett could not secure the attention of the young ladies at St. James's to his tremendous orations, while their eyes found more interesting employment elsewhere, so he prevailed on the Queen to have the pews heightened. This brought out a squib, supposed to be by Lord Mordaunt—

"And now Britain's nymphs, in a Protestant reign,
Are locked up at prayers like the virgins in Spain."

In the centre of the nave stood the stove for heating the building, with an iron flue making its exit through the roof. Nothing could be more hideous. On the right hand side, nearly opposite to it, was a wooden construction, used as the font, which was replaced by one of stone when the Church was reseated. Under this wooden font, on a white freestone, was the following inscription:—

"Hoc Baptisterium amoto veteri
Positum est, anno Dñi, 1703.
John Morris   Vic.
John Aldridge } Gard."
Nath. Deller   }

What the ancient Norman one was I do not know. But these two were certainly unworthy successors to it.

Before 1876 all the seats, except those under the gallery, were appropriated; but then on the reseating of the Church more than half of them were made free. With regard to our faculty seats, there has been some slight misapprehension. In 1807, when the new north aisle was built, five faculty pews were made in it, and appropriated (by faculty, dated 23rd Sept. 1807) to Sir James Sibbald of Silwood; George Ellis of the Cedars; James Mann of Tetworth; and the Right Honourable Lady Harewood. No other faculties are to be found in the Registry at Salisbury. But on the rebuilding of the Church in 1827, the Incumbent left a note to the effect that there were no faculty pews in the nave except the Vicar's, and one for the owners of Titness; and this statement was no doubt substantially, although not strictly, correct. They were not faculties, but held by as good a title in the nature of prescription. The chancel belongs to St. John's College, owners of the advowson, and the only seats there, three in number, were used by them or their tenants, and the Vicar. Titness Farm and Broomhall were the representative houses. When the chancel was wanted for the choir, the College only gave consent on the understanding that their tenants should have similar accommodation in the nave; and that would give the owners of Titness, as well as the Vicar, a prescriptive right to their seats. Memorial windows have recently been placed in the nave to the memory of the Rev. Alexander Malcolm Wale, by the parishioners; of Samuel Grove Price, Marrianne Grove Price, and Lettsom Grove Price, by their relatives; of Thomas Holloway, by his kinsman, George Martin Holloway; and one by Lady Stepney, to the memory of her sister.

Here I may say a few words as to the Church plate and other

effects.* There is not to be found among the parochial papers or registers any list of what the Church possessed of this kind; but at the Record Office I have found an interesting account of what we had in the time of Edward VI. The wholesale plundering of plate and treasures from the churches and other religious houses, which the King had set the example of on so grand a scale at the time of the Reformation, had been followed by his faithful subjects with great alacrity; so much so, indeed, that in the reign of Edward VI. it was deemed necessary to adopt measures for the safe custody of Church effects, if they were any of them to be preserved. Royal Commissioners were sent into each county to take inventories of what the different churches contained; and among others in the Hundred of Benhurst so visited was Sunninghill, and in respect of which they made the following return:—

"*Sunninghill.*—This inventory indented, and made the 1st day of August in the sixt year of the reign of our sovereign Lord Edward VI., between the Commissioners of the said sovereign Lord, for the viewe of all the goods, plate, jewels, belles, and ornaments of every Church and Chapel in the county of Berks, belonging or appertaining to the said parish of the one part, and Robert Milton and Thomas Kaye, churchwardens of the said parish and Church of Soninghill, of the other part, Witnesseth that the said Commissioners have delivered to the said churchwarden all parcels hereafter particularly written, viz., a chales of silver, in valew by estimation 40s.; thre belles in the stepull, one cope of red damask, two vestments of saten of burges, with all things to them belonging, and too aulter clothes of lynen, one towell with a draper towell, a sepulcre of timber, and too brass candlesticks, too crewitts, and all the said parcels sauflie to be kept and preserved, and all and every parcel thereof to be forthcoming at all times hereafter when it shall be of them required. JOHN SMYTHE
RICHARD SLANN
did deliver for the churchwardens above-named."

This is interesting in several particulars. The "chales of silver," valued at 40s., equal to about £20 of the present day, must have been a handsome piece. It may have been disposed of in the days of Edward VI. or Elizabeth, when such articles were proscribed as superstitious, and were in many places only spared by their conversion into communion cups.† As late as 1569, in many places the chalices were hidden away in hope of the mass being restored. At Sunninghill,

---

* See Church Goods, Berks, Ed. VI., F. H. 296. Index, p. xii., 4 Ed. III. to 30 Eliz.

† At Dursley, in an inventory of 1643, the "silver gilt chalice" disappears, and is replaced by "2 pewter communion boules." So complete was their destruction, that there are very few ancient chalices left in England. At Sanderstead, Surrey, the "chalys was changed for a cuppe," while our neighbours at Chobham and Horsell sold theirs, and bestowed the money "upon weapons and artyllery for the King in his wars," as Aldford did on "bows and arrows" for his service. At Thorpe they had an eye to local improvements, and spent the produce of two candle-

THE CHURCH.

however, it could hardly have escaped the vigilance of Sir Henry Neville or the Commissioners who in 1641 were sent out to destroy all such "reliques of idolatry." But even had it done so, it was far too valuable to have survived the melting-pot during those twelve terrible years of chaos in the Civil Wars.

Then we are told there were three bells—this was in the time of Edward VI.; and I may be excused a slight digression to dispose of a little error of long standing, for which, I fear, our fair gossip tradition is responsible. She has set it about the village that Queen Elizabeth presented us with a peal of six new bells! How could that be when we have only three? Yes, but the old tower was too weak to bear them all, and three were given away to Winkfield. Now as to the Winkfield bells, of all their six, one only is of so early a date as 1597; the others are of the time of James I. and Charles I., and our own are none of them so early. One bears the inscription, "William Eldridge made mee 1662;"* another has "S K 1705." The last is quite modern, "Cast by John Warner 1786." We cannot even fall back on the suggestion that the royal bells have been recast, and I must fain believe that Mistress Tradition has in this case been romancing a little. In 1707 we had a catastrophe in the belfry, for under that date a parish meeting is recorded "when ye bell was mended."

"Saten of burges," or of Bruges, the place from which the best satin was imported. "A sepulchre of timber" reminds us of the ancient forms of worship which had been carried on in our parish churches. These sepulchres, it will be remembered, were representations of the entombment set up at Easter. They were generally of wood, and movable, although sometimes they were permanent stone structures, but they were always placed on the north side of the chancel, near the altar. The crucifix was placed in the

---

sticks "upon the reparacion of the hie waye." At Egham some of the Church effects had been made away with by the churchwardens; and worse still, in another case in Surrey, they were "imbesyled and sold by one Sir Thomas Berington, late Vicar of the pariche, who is now ded, and nothing worth at his death"! The title of "Sir" for the priest had survived till then. At another place the valuables were said to have been " brybed away."

* An old family of bellfounders at Wokingham, and afterwards at Chertsey. The churchwarden accounts of Winkfield and Bray show Thomas Eldridge at Wokingham in 1565, and that the foundry was still there in Richard Eldridge's time, 1602. Richard, Brian, and William were at Chertsey from 1592 till after 1704.—See Church Bells of Sussex, by Amherst Daniel Tyssen, p. 6.

sepulchre on Good Friday, with great solemnity, and watched till Easter day, when it was taken out and placed on the altar.*

Much that was interesting in our Church having escaped the Reformation of the sixteenth century, had a worse assault to withstand in the bigotry of the seventeenth. In January 1641 Commissioners were sent into every county "for the defacing, demolishing, and quite taking away of all images, altars, or tables turned altar-wise, crucifixes, superstitions, pictures, monuments, and reliques of idolatry out of all churches and chapels."

The only wonder is that anything was preserved, knowing the latitude with which these ample words and injunctions were construed.

Nothing of silver plate appears to have been left in our Church. Its place was supplied by a pewter service, consisting of a flagon with lid, alms dish, and paten. The latter appears to have been purchased in 1665, as there is an entry in our registers of that date, "Disbursed for a communion patten, £10. Other portions show the date 1675. This service is still in our possession. But the one now used is silver, and consists of—

1. A chalice, with cover, engraved, "Given to Sunninghill Church by H. C." London Hall mark, 1676. Arms on a lozenge shield, chequy, vert, and argent a fesse ermine. The cover of this chalice is of later date, 1711.
2. An alms dish, Hall mark, 1715; engraved, "A gift to Sunninghill, 1716," with the strange addition, "with the number of ounces, 33." Coat of arms argent, a double-headed eagle, displayed, sable within and bordure sable verantee, an escutcheon of pretence of same arms.
3. A paten, engraved, "Empt in usum Ecclesiæ de Sunninghill com. Berks anno Dom. 1704. J. H. } Gard. N. D. }
4. A small paten, 1834.
5. A flagon, glass, silver mounted, 1876. I have failed to identify these arms. Those on the chalice are a lady's, and are very like those of the Tubervilles. It is a coincidence, however, that in this very year, 1676, Colonel Richard Neville died, leaving a son, Henry, and a daughter, Catherine, his only surviving children. Their initials might represent the H. C.

As to those on the alms dish, they are not unlike the arms of Killigrew of Cornwall; and the fact of our parishioner, Sir Henry Neville, the ambassador, having married Ann, daughter of Sir Henry Killigrew, might explain the connection. But the double-headed eagle may simply be the emblem of the Holy

---

* In the accounts of St. Helen's, Abingdon, occurs an entry, "A.D. 1558, Payde to the sexton for meat and drink, and watching the 'sepulture,' according to custom, 22ᵈ." And at Bletchingley in Ed. VI.'s time, "Paid to Brand for watching of the sepulker, viiiᵈ." The use of lights or tapers before the sepulchre was one of the three cases in which lights were suffered by Cromwell's injunctions in 1538.

Roman Empire, as in the coat of Fielding, Earl of Denbigh, who was a Count of that Empire. William married Mary, daughter of Henry Carey, Earl of Monmouth. I must leave this for future solution.

Before we leave the Church, let us have one more peep into the old registers, to notice some entries of curiosity in reference to the ecclesiastical affairs of the parish.

It is noteworthy, how when the orthodox practice of marrying by banns had been abandoned or neglected in the revolutionary times, it became recognised again; and some of the entries carefully record the fact of the banns having been duly published. This occurs first in the year 1653, on the marriage of Ursulia Robinson, a daughter of the Vicar.

In 1653, during the Commonwealth, an Act was passed for better registrations, and the following entry occurs in our books:—

"John Robinson [who was the Vicar at the time] is nominated by the parishioners and approved by the next Justice of Peace to be the Parish Register according to the Act of Parliament 24 August 1653 and hath taken his corporall oath for the true registering of all marriages, births, and burials according to the Act.

WILLIAM TRUMBULL.
FRANCIS SAYER."

This, it will be remembered, was the last of the twelve melancholy years in which "there was no care taken for ye registring any births, burials, or marriages in this parish of Sunninghill by reason of ye tumults and confusions of the civil warr which then raged in England."

From this our entries are duly continued. In October 1678 we meet with another curious entry which is as follows:—

"Hic incipit Register eorum qui sepulti fuerunt in amiculo ferali ex lana ovina solūmodo composito."

On the occasion of every burial, an affidavit made before a magistrate was required to verify the fact that the corpse was interred in a shroud made of sheep's wool only! The Act of 18 Chas. II., 1666, explains all this. That statute was intended "for lessening the importation of linen from beyond seas, and for encouragement of the woollen trade;" but not having been so strictly enforced as was thought desirable, the 30th Chas. II. was passed to strengthen its powers, enacting that from the 1st August 1678 "no corps shall be buried in any shroud or other thing than what is made of sheep's wool only," or be put in any coffin lined with anything but sheep's wool only, under a penalty of £5.

After a few years the statute became a dead letter. Cromwell's instructions for the general adoption of Parish Registers was in 1538. They were especially enjoined by Statute of 6 and 7 Wm. III., c. 6, "for carrying on the war against France with vigour," and a tax was laid upon marriages, births, and burials! In 1783 a duty of 3d. became payable on every christening. In 1757 it was customary for the Foundling Hospital in London to send children into the country for change of air, and many from that institution were buried here. It was the want of strength in the poor little children, and not in the air, let us hope, that explains this otherwise equivocal compliment to our climate.

CHAPTER XVIII.

The Vicars and their Vicarage.

"Some years ago, ere Time and Taste
    Had turned our parish topsy-turvy;
When Silwood Park was Sunning waste,
    And roads as little known as scurvy,
The man who lost his way between
    The Bucket Hill and Sandy Thicket,
Was always shown across the green,
    And guided to the parson's wicket."—Praed.

THE Living of Sunninghill is a Vicarage in the Deanery of Reading, and was for several centuries in the Diocese of Sarum,[*] until transferred to that of Oxford in 1836.[†]

"Sunninghill,"[‡] wrote Dr. Ducarel, in an opinion he gave some years ago, "appears in the King's books to be only a curacy." The entry in the Liber Decimarum stands:—

Diocese of Salisbury, not in charge.

Sunninghill Cur. or V. (St. Michael) Prox 5s. 1d., a Terrier in 1704. Olim. Pri. Broomhall, St. John's College, Cambridge Patⁿ. and Prop^r. £10 certified value."

The earliest notice we get of the Church is in the Charter of King John giving it to the Nuns of Broomhall; and it was thenceforth

---

[*] More anciently, however, before the erection of the Bishopric of Sarum, we were within the province of Dorchester, out of which was carved that of Ramsbury, and the bishops were sometimes called the Bishops of Sunninges. At Sonning on the Thames they had a complete establishment, although it was never more than a Peculiar of the Dean, who was Ordinary, and held his visitations there, exercising episcopal jurisdiction. It was not in itself a separate bishopric.

[†] By 6 and 7 Wm. IV. c. 77.

[‡] Sunninghill is not noticed in the Valor Beneficiorum, nor in the Taxatio Ecclesiastica Angliæ, c. 1291, nor in the Valor Ecclesiasticus temp. Hen. VIII. In the Liber Decimarum, 1709, it is described as in the Dec. of Newbury, and discharged from first fruits and tenths, "non in onere." See Ecton's Thesaurus Rerum Ecclesiasticarum.

served by their curate at a very small stipend or wage for his labour. This at first was a mere discretionary payment, and until the statute 4 Hen. IV. c. 12 might have been revoked at any time, and the curate discharged without more ceremony than in the case of any ordinary servant.

After many days came the great event of its history, the suppression of the Nunnery; and in the Inquisition taken at Windsor in March 1522, it was found "that the Convent was seized of the Church of St. Margaret and the churchyard," which it went on to say are of "no value, because set apart for divine service." At the instance of Bishop Fisher the advowson of the Church was then granted to the Master and Fellows of St. John's College.

At this time there was evidently a small house or cottage for the curate, for in Baker's History of the College (Mayor's ed.) is noticed a lease in 1565:—"To Robert Sherrington, clerk, curate of Sunninghill, of 9 acres, Priestes-more and Pristes ground, with the *Pristes house* there, for twenty years, at a rent of 5s., and other 5s. for the curate." To this is added a note—"M$^{d.}$ that be not leased but to the Vicar."

In the important survey of 1613, the Vicarage is described as consisting of "eight closes of arable and meadow ground with a house."

This house or cottage stood on the site of the present Vicarage, and forms what are now the offices. George Dawson, early in his incumbency, and prior to 1677, substantially repaired this cottage, the College finding timber.

I have been informed that a date was discovered in one of the lower rooms of 1747. This would rather suggest that a considerable addition was made to the cottage at this time, and my surmise is confirmed by an undated memorandum among the papers of St. John's College, written after 1807, in which it is stated that "the *new part* of the Parsonage is in good condition, and consists of two good parlours, and a small sitting-room below, and two good bed-rooms with light closets, and a small bed-room above, no garrets. The old part forms the offices."

So that in fact the principal part of the present Vicarage may be attributed to the middle of the eighteenth century. The house was virtually rebuilt on the appointment of Mr. Thistlethwaite the very year of the date above mentioned. The part now comprising the offices is much older, as we see it was *repaired* before 1677.

This poor little forest living, if dependent only on its Vicarial or small tithes and glebe, would have afforded but a very scanty subsistence to its Vicar; but the College at once recognised its duty and bestowed on him the Rectorial tithes also; and this was probably done from the first, as we have seen that the Priests-moor and land were leased by the College to the Vicar as early as 1565, and they have ever since been enjoyed by the Vicars under similar leases from the College at a nominal rent.

It is not improbable that we owe this to Fisher's influence, as it would seem his conscience was not at all easy as to the part he had taken in the dissolution of the Nunnery.

THE VICARAGE.

The earliest Terrier with which we are acquainted is one of a date some time earlier than 1654, in which year John Robinson, junior, died. It was, I believe, the Terrier of 1654.

Terrarium Vicariæ de Sunninghill.

A Terrier of all those things which belong unto the Church of Sunninghill, in the Countie of Berks, according to the knowledge and best enquirie of the Minister, Churchwardens, and Sidesmen of the said parish. Impri^s We have tithe of all corne and hay, woole and lamb, calf and Whitege, tithe of copices, tithe honey, tithe goose, tithe eggs, Pigge and fruite, offerings, morts, buryings, marriages, and churchings, according to the custome which hath been used (vid) for buryings vi^d marriage vi^d churchings vi^d. And one annuitie or set portion of money per annum 40s. payed half yearly out of a certain farme called Bromhall, which ye College of Saint John's at Cambridge hath lying near unto our Church, and is of our parish in all taxes and rates whatsoever, though not in our parish. And this is all we can learn is properly due and belonging unto our Church.

 W<small>M</small>. B<small>ONDILL</small>, *Churchwarden.*
 S<small>TEP</small>. E<small>DSALL</small>, *Churchwarden.*   By me, J<small>OHN</small> R<small>OBINSON</small>, *Cler.*

A much more full and interesting one is the next:—

A true and perfect Terrier of the Glebe-land tithes, portions of tithes, and other possessions belonging to the Vicarage of Sunninghill, An. Dom. 1677.

The Vicar of Sunninghill hath right unto all tithes whatsoever, as of corne, hay, wool, lamb, wood, fish, pig, goose, &c. But ye right he hath to ye Rectory-tithes is from the bounty and goodness of his patron, viz., ye worthy Mr. Fellows, and scholars of St. John's Coll., Cambridge, holding of them as ye undoubted owners thereof ye said impropriate Rectory by Lease, as also his glebe-land, paying as an acknowledgment 5s. per annum.

His glebe-land consists of about 14 acres lying together, and is at this day divided into 3 earable closes and 3 meddows. It is bounded upon ye west by ye house and land of John Aldridge and John Church; on the south by the lands of Sir Thomas Draper; on the east by the lane leading to ye Church green; and on ye north by ye land of Will Buckle, and a lane (which also belongs unto it) y^t leads out into ye heath by ye house of ye said John Aldridge. And because the said John Aldridge maketh use of the lane to the trouble of the Vicar, he pays him therefore yearly a fat pig at Xmas.

The aforesaid Will Buckle also for a little piece of ground by the brook and now laid unto his meddow pays 2s. 6d. per annum.

There is an house and stable and an hay house upon the glebe-land and lately well and substantially repaired by the bounty of the Patron y^t gave some timber and ye cost and charges of the present incumbent. No land in this parish is exempted from paying tithes in specia except ye lands of Bromhall and Titenhurst, and such as lie in the Park of Sir Thos. Draper, the first of which did anciently belong to the Monastery of Bromhall and now to Saint John's College Camb., and for the other Sir Thos. Draper pretends and pays a modus decimandi of 13s. 4d. per annum. A Mill also (not because of any ancient composition, but because the tithe cannot without great trouble be taken in specie) pays 5s. 8d. per annum. He hath for marrying 1s. 6d., and for publishing the bands 1s.; for churching of a woman 6d., for burning a corps 6d., for registring 4d. He hath 1d. for ye herbs of ye garden, a penny for ye white of the Cow, a penny if ye calf be weined, but if sold ye 10 p^t of ye price. He hath of hony and wax ye 10th pounds, or if ye bees are sold ye 10th p^t of ye price. He hath tithe of eggs, which is most commonly compounded for at some final rate. The offering of each person is 2d. unless they please to give more. If a corps be buried in ye body of ye Church, ye vicar's fee is 6s. 8d., and ye churchwardens are paid for breaking the ground. But if in the chancell, his fee is 10s., and he is paid for breaking the ground. He hath mortuaries of 10s., 6s. 8d., and 3s. 4d. as ye inventory is in value according to the Statute 21 Hen. VIII.

This small Living hath some immunities and priviledges, for by reason it is worth little or nothing without ye bounty of its patron, and when that is extended not worth £50 per annum. It is not in the King's book, and so pays neither first fruits or tenthes to ye king or procurations to the Bishop. But it pays the Archdeacon for sinodals 1s. 6d. per annum.

There is a Church house adjoining to ye churchyard, one room of which serves, as oft as occasion is, as a vevestry for meetings about public affaires, and ye other mean profitts y^t are made of it are accounted for by Feoffees intrusted by ye parish for such like matters.

JOHN WAPSHOTT } *Churchwardens.*   GEORGE DAWSON, *Vicar.*
HEN. TRIGG

N.B.—A copy of this Terrier among the Church papers is not verbally correct, though not differing in any material points. The Terrier exhibited in 1704 differs very little from the above, except that it mentions that double fees are required for the burial of any person who is not a parishioner. The churchwardens also observe in the conclusion of it that they were not able to find the Terrier which was exhibited in Archbishop Laud's Metropolitan Visitation, Anno Dom. 1634, and have therefore copied very nearly that exhibited in 1677.

Now there are many little noteworthy points in this quaint document.

It was not often in such forest districts as this that the Vicar had tithe of wood; it was probably only of coppice. In the weald of Kent, the old forest of Anderida, the woods were not titheable. Lamb and pig, and goose, however, were important items. It sets quite at rest, too, the question of his having at this time the "arable" closes of the glebe at a nominal rent.

Then how characteristic of that simple age is the accommodation rent of the "fat pig" at Christmas! It also shows that there was a Vicarage house then of some age requiring substantial repair. The sly hit at Sir Thomas Draper, who "pretends" and pays a modus decimandi of 13s. 4d., refers to what then still continued "a thorn in the flesh." The notice, too, is curious of the annuity of 40s. per annum payable out of the Broomhall lands, which "are of our parish in all taxes and rates whatsoever, though not in our parish."

But above all, in point of interest, to us of the present day, is that part of it relating to the tithes "in kind" which were payable to the Vicar. Thus 1d. for the herbs of the garden, 1d. for "ye white of the Cow, a penny if ye calf be weined, and if sold ye 10th part of ye price." What a quaint expression "ye white of the Cow," meaning, as many of my readers may not be aware, the milk of the cow.

In an old Terrier at Hurley of 1704, it also occurs.[*] There it runs —"Our Vicar hath ye tithe of 'Rod Yeots,' *i.e.*, Osiers on the islands, calves, white of cows." We find a similar term in ancient use, "white meats," which were milk, butter, cheese, eggs, and any composition of them which before the Reformation were forbidden in Lent, as well as flesh, till Henry VIII. published a proclamation in 1543 allowing the eating of *white meats* in Lent. Some think it is connected with the

---

[*] See the Rev. F. T. Wethered's letter to the *Guardian*, March 31, 1886.

derivation of "Whitsun Day." The famous Gerard Langbain, in a Latin letter, observes—"It was a custom among our ancestors upon this day to give all the milk of their Ewes and kine to the poor for the Love of God in order to qualify themselves to receive the gift of the Holy Ghost, which milk being then (as it is still in some countries) called Whitemeat, &c., therefore this day from that custom took the name of Whit Sunday." Tusser, in his "Five Hundred Points," p. 47, writes:—

> "Slut Cisley vntaught
> Hath whitemeat naught."

We can only wonder how such a system could have lasted for hundreds of years; what friction it must have produced between Vicar and parishioners; what little heart-burnings must have arisen even with the most orthodox among them, when with every small mercy of increase on the farm, the Vicar and his rights were to be thought of. The rustic going to the tithe feast with the tithe pig under his arm is a well-known picture of those times. The old hen could not lay an egg without giving that reverend gentleman a vested interest in it, "for he hath tithe of eggs;" even the very bees that hovered over the flowers of the cottage garden were contributories to his scanty maintenance. The last Terrier would imply that there was tithe of honey as well as of the bees, but that would be illegal, for where tithe is paid of the honey and wax it would not be due of the bees.

Generally a clergyman might claim the tenth calf when it was known, or when it was not, then an average one. It could not have been so with pigs, or we should hardly have had the joke which has survived to the present day among the rustics, who will still with a laugh point out "as the Parson's" pig that diminutive one which is almost always to be found in every litter. To what can we attribute the survival of respect under such frictions, and under such a strain? There must have been a deeply seated love of Church among our forefathers, an affection that grew up between those whom the holy offices of the Church brought together in the most important events of their lives, and the joys and sorrows of the family circle, to account for it.

It is well indeed that the parson's pig has been compounded for. I may here refer to a custom in the neighbouring parish of Winkfield, which shows the primitive character of some of a Vicar's emoluments in those earlier days. There was a practice there for all young per-

---

* Cro. car. 404.

sons, before receiving their first sacrament, to come to the Vicar and offer him two pence and receive a ticket. Here it was probably the same. "The first annual offering, according to custom."

Consisting, as the parish did, so largely of forest land, we can well understand how the living was worth little or nothing; and indeed, when "the bounty of its patron was extended, it was not worth above £50 per annum." In the frugal times of our ancestors, however, Vicars—men, too, of a superior class to the ordinary incumbents of their day—were always found ready to serve it; and little as it was, it reflects credit on the College that they have from the first bestowed on the Vicar all that the living produced.

It was a great blow, of course, when the 13s. 4d. modus was established, as it deprived the living of tithes over the largest estate in the parish. It became a question, on the enclosure of the forest, when so much land was brought into cultivation, whether this modus relieved the redeemed lands; and in 1826 counsel's opinion was taken on the point, there having been 168 acres awarded in respect of the park, and seventy-one in respect of the titheable lands. It was thought that for certain things the land was exempt, and for certain others not so.

In the time of Queen Anne we have a statement of the value of the benefice forwarded to Mr. Archdeacon, with a view of getting an augmentation from the newly instituted endowment called Queen Anne's Bounty. Mr. John Morris, the Vicar in 1705, states "that the small tithes of this parish, to which only yᵉ Vicar, as such, has a title, are not worth £10 a year." What an amount of unpopularity he must have incurred to get that! He further states, "That in addition to these he enjoys yᵉ major part of yᵉ great tithes also, and moreover, that our Church without this bounty of the impropriators is so slenderly endow'd, yᵗ we might ever despair of having any fit person to perform the service of it; and now that it is extended, it continues to be a poor benefice, hardly amounting to the clear value of forty pounds a year." *

And so here we find a Fellow of his College literally "passing rich with £40 a year!" Yet, if we compare it with the state of things now, there is not much to choose between the present and the past. It would be equal to nearly £300 a year in present money, and there

---

* When Queen Anne's Bounty was instituted, there were over 5500 livings under £50 a year, and some hundreds not over £20.

were ten acres of glebe to keep two or three cows upon. And in estimating the Vicar's duties, although—

"Wide was his parish, and houses far asunder,"

yet we must not forget that there were only about fifty families to attend to. In truth, it was a little too good to obtain the augmentation asked for.

The neighbouring livings, however, were no better. In 1656 we find William Rayner, minister of Egham, in a petition to the Protector, alleging, "I have bestowed forty years in this parish, which is of large extent, and the people numerous, but the living only £40 a year. I have nourished up a people who are so earnest for me to stay with them, that though I have had many better offers, I dare not leave them. I am now disabled, and need an assistant,"—"begs enlargement."

This William Rayner, B.D., ejected from Egham in 1662, was offered by the Parliament the Presidentship of Magdalen College, Oxford, or a Fellowship of Eton, but declined, because his conscience was against pluralities. He was an eminent Church historian, Fellow of Corpus Christi College, and honoured by Archbishop Usher.[*]

In the case of Sunninghill, it was not till 1723 that the Commissioners were successfully approached. Dr. Palmer, who had just the year before been appointed to the living, was too well off, apparently, to reside upon it. But he succeeded in getting a grant of £200, and Dr. Palmer himself to this added a like sum of £200 (of which £100 was part of a legacy from Ed. Colston, Esq.). This £400 was in April 1762 invested by Mr. Thistlethwaite in the purchase of two closes of land in Sunninghill, called "Further Long Deans" and "Searle's Meadow," containing nine acres, let to Mr. Henry Aldridge for £12 per annum. In February 1792, Further Long Deans, containing five and a half acres, was exchanged by Mr. Thistlethwaite for five closes of land near Bullbrook, Winkfield, "Heathfield of the Moor," containing twenty acres. Searle's Meadow was in October 1795 exchanged by Mr. Thistlethwaite for a close of meadow ground called Winfant Mead, containing four and a half acres, abutting on a meadow called "Battle's Innings," and on the common or waste on the north.

These properties were subsequently disposed of.

I must not omit to mention that on the Vicarage lawn three trees are said to have been planted by three illustrious men. A horse-

---

[*] See Calamy's Nonconformist Memorial.

chestnut by Chesterfield, an elm by Bolingbroke, and a beech by Burke; but on what occasions they were planted I cannot ascertain; it must have been, I think, at different times, and doubtless during the incumbency of Mr. Thistlethwaite. The beech is the only one standing; the elm was blown down within the last ten or twelve years; it was, I am informed, 111 feet in height. Another version attributes the planting of one of these trees to Chatham, and that I could well understand, for Mr. Pitt and Lady Hester were living at Sunninghill somewhere about 1754-55, and the Vicarage was let at that very time. If we can suppose the great Minister to have been its tenant, we may conclude that these trees were planted by him or his friends.

THE VICARS.

Of the Vicars themselves I must now say a few words, for although I do not find that they left any remarkable reputation in the outer world, the parson of a parish, for good or evil, must always be a most important, if not the most important, person in it.

The following is a list of the Vicars. Mauritius Scrill and those following him are entered in our Church Register, thus leaving the earlier ones unaccounted for, until, through the courtesy of the Bursar of St. John's College, I have been able from their books to complete the list by adding the names of Gates, Ranerd, and Sherrington.*

22 years.—JOSEPH GATES, presented by the Master and Fellows of St. John's College in 1535 as "Vicariam mobilem."
    THOMAS RANERD, clerk, presented to the Vicarage 14th July 1557, vacant by the deprivation of Jo. Gaites.
    ROBERT SHERINGTON, clerk, was in 1565 Curate of Sunninghill.
    "MAURITIUS SORRILL, *primus, quantum constat, Rector ecclesiæ de Sunninghill, sepultus fuit secundo die May* 1594." Elsewhere written "Scrill." 38th year of Elizabeth.
41 years.—"JOHANNES ROBERTSON, *A.M., Rector ibidem proximus, sepultus fuit* 17 *die Julie* 1635." This is a mistake; the name was Robinson; he was inducted May 24, 1594. His son
19 years.—"JOHANNES ROBINSON, *Rector, filius prioris Rectoris. Sepultus fuit* 22 *die Augusti* 1654."
9½ years.—"FRANCISCUS SAYER, *A.M., per* 10 *annos Vicarius hinc in Rectoriam de Yatingdon in Comitatu Berks commigravit anno* 1664." Inducted October 24, 1654, but left for Yatingdon, December 4, 1663.
37 years —"GEORGIUS DAWSON, *A.M., prox. Vicarius, sepultus fuit* 5th *die Oct.* 1700,"

---

* The words are shown as they stand in the Register, the additions are from other sources.

at Sunninghill. "Inducted April 12, 1664, the 11th year from the glorious revolution."

1½ years.—"GULIELMUS FORKINGTON, A.M., menses (plus minus) 18 *Vicarius hinc in Vicariam de Chatteris in Com*^k^ *Cantab. migravit* 1702." Inducted February 16, 1701, but migrated to Chatteris, in the Isle of Ely, March 22, 1702, a few days after the commencement of Queen Anne's reign.

20½ years.—"JOHANNES MORRIS, A.M., *hinc in Parochiam de Brentwood in Com*" *Essex, migravit Octr.* 8, 1722." Inducted May 8, 1702. He was married in 1709 by M. Vaughan, Canon of Windsor, to Anna Dawson.

25 years.—"ROBERTUS PALMER, D.D., *obiit Decr.* 23, 1747."

59 years.—"JOSEPHUS THISTLETHWAITE, A.M., *sepultus fuit April* 20, 1807." Inducted June 18, 1748.

10 years.—MONTAGUE HEBELTHWAYTE never resided on the living. Mr. Neve was his Curate till August 18, 1816, when migrating, he was succeeded by Mr. Morris. Mr. H. died February 4, 1817, at Bridlington in Yorkshire. On his death

13 years.—. . . . AINGER succeeded. Mr. Hitchings was his Curate in charge in 1826, and the Rev. P. E. Boissier had charge of the parish from 1826 to 1830. This gentleman founded St. Peter's Church, Malvern Wells, and died in 1888, at the advanced age of 98.

54 years.—ALEXANDER MALCOLM WALE, B.D., inducted in 1830. Died May 1884.

JAMES SNOWDON, A.M., inducted 1884.

The history of some of these earlier incumbents is curious. The Bull of Pope Clement VII., confirming the gift of the advowson to St. John's College, was obtained in 1524. But I cannot find that any Vicar was appointed till 1535, up to which time a stipendiary curate was probably engaged to serve the church.

Our first Vicar's fate well illustrates the troubles and vicissitudes in the life of a country parson of that age.* In the depths of the forest, in the adjoining parish of Winkfield, stood an ancient moated Vicarage-house approached by two wooden bridges, which, however, were altered by Mr. Waterson, who died in 1759. These moated parsonages were not then uncommon in wild woodland districts; there are a few still to be found.

The Vicar was one Joseph Gates; and I find that in the year 1535 he was also appointed to the Vicarage of Sunninghill.† This little charge was not a very serious addition to his labours, for it involved the care of scarcely fifty souls. In 1542 he was acting with John Norris, Esq. of Winkfield, and others, as referee in a dispute about the Rectory of Aldesworth. About the time of Gates' appointment to Sunninghill, his great fellow-collegian Parker was enjoying his charming abode at Stoke by Clare, and pondering over the propriety

---

* See MS. papers of the Rev. William Waterson.
† See Baker's Hist. of St. John's.

of the marriage of priests, against which fearful innovation, as in the minds of the orthodox it was then considered, he was preparing a defence. As soon as Edward VI. ascended the throne, Parker in 1547 married the estimable Margaret Harlestone. The Archbishop had already brought home a Mrs. Cranmer, although the enabling statute only passed in 1549. With these eminent examples, our Vicar, Joseph Gates, seems also at the same time to have brightened his retired moated home with the presence of a wife. He was happy enough while the young King reigned; and indeed was, I am inclined to believe, honoured with royal patronage; this I infer from an entry I find in the household book of Edward VI. in 1547, and which I cannot but think refers to our Vicar. It runs, "Paid to John Norris, gentleman vsher, for himself and one grome for riding and geaving attendance vpon Mr. Gates, the King's deputy at the christening of Mr. Symbarbes childe at Bray by the space of two days xxx^s and viii^d." Was he of the family of the Sir John Gates who, in the time of Edward VI., purchased the Bishop's Palace at Wells for its materials, and stripped the great hall of its lead and timber?

But when Mary came to the throne, all was changed, and a fearful persecution burst on these conscientious men. Cranmer was soon brought to the stake. Parker was deprived of all his valuable preferments, but was solaced in his retirement by the society of his accomplished wife. Our poor country pastor was equally unfortunate. He was obliged to give up his Vicarage or his wife; and to his honour, he ran away from the former, and was not heard of here again. Among the muniments of the College I found the appointment of his successor in 1557, " on the deprivation of Jo. Gaites."

With this untoward termination closed the career of our first Vicar. Of the second I know nothing; nor much more of his successor, Sherrington, except that on 1st September 1565 the College leased to him the rectorial glebe and house at a nominal rent, as it was customary to do on the appointment of a Vicar. Of the third incumbent we are equally in the dark.

These Vicars of Sunninghill, most of them Fellows of their College, were in scholarship and general position above the ordinary type of the country clergy of their day. Macaulay's well-known description of them would certainly not apply to our parish. Our Vicars clearly exhibited Puritan proclivities, but this would be expected when we remember how strongly Cambridge has always reflected those views.

The Robinsons, father and son, were well connected, and maintained a social intercourse with some of the best families in the neighbourhood. Robinson, the father, I find seems also to have had the small tithes of the little Chapelry of Horsell, if not of its parent church, Woking. These, having anciently belonged to the Priory of Newark, had been on its dissolution leased by the Crown to Christopher Villiers, Earl of Anglesey (younger brother of the first Duke of Buckingham), and by him granted in 1630 to John Robinson of Sunninghill, who held them till the year of his death.

Francis Sayer, A.M., has left no mark on the "sands of time"— at least the Bagshot sands—and stayed here only ten years. George Dawson, A.M., held the living thirty-six years. William Forkington, A.M., venit, videt, et migravit in the course of eighteen months.

John Morris, A.M., stayed with us, as we have seen, twenty years, and then left for the better living of Brentwood, Essex. Robert Palmer, D.D., held the living just a quarter of a century, but was non-resident all the time.* His wealth and position apparently rendered such a forest home unattractive to him. He gave back to Sunninghill something of his receipts. His endowment of £200 remains a memorial of him. The rebuilding of the Vicarage occurred the year that he died. Possibly Mr. Thistlethwaite called upon his executors for dilapidations.

But of all the Vicars, Joseph Thistlethwaite, A.M., held the living longest, and left his mark upon it more indelibly, if not more pleasantly, than any of them. He seems to have been a man of great force of character, and the Bursar of the College of that day spoke of him favourably. But he was unquestionably the very personification of restless energy. His perception of his rights was only equalled by his activity in maintaining them, as shown elsewhere. We find him busy repairing the breaches occasioned by the neglects of his predecessor, settling the disputed question of the church way, and laying out the church funds in good purchases, and afterwards in exchanging them to advantage, two acres for four, and five acres for twenty. Then comes the culmination of his fierce encounters with his parishioners, and we have him crushing his slanderous foes by two indictments at the Assizes at Reading for libel; and there again he prevailed, dragging the offenders before the Vestry, to make them publicly "eat their own words," and sign apologies in the minute-book. I must not, however, forget to add that he seems to have been the champion of the

---

* In 1810 Parliamentary Returns show that the clergy who were non-resident then actually constituted a majority of the incumbents in England and Wales.

oppressed. When the young farmer was so cruelly persecuted by his wealthier neighbour, our fighting parson threw in his powerful help for him. There exists a statement of this case so pregnant with force and sarcasm, that to no one in the parish can it be so well affiliated as to our sword-tongued Vicar. This incident reflected to his honour, although on the whole he did much mischief; and not only obtained a bad reputation in the parish, but lowered his office in the eyes of his parishioners; and to some extent alienated from the Church the affections of the people. He may have been a scholar, but had no tact or knowledge of the world, and was "too fond of the right to pursue the expedient."

Montague Heblethwaite never resided on the living.

Alexander Malcolm Wale (Chancellor's B medallist and 16th Wrangler, St. John's, B.D.), whose incumbency lasted so long as to be second only to Mr. Thistlethwaite, was an accomplished scholar and an orthodox Churchman. Those who knew him in his younger days speak of him as a faithful friend and most pleasant companion. I, who knew him only in his later life, could perceive the influence of these qualities in moulding an old age alike genial and worthy of respect.

James Snowdon, A.M. (Crosse Theological Scholar of Cambridge University, Tyrwhitt Hebrew Scholar, and Fellow of St. John's), is still our Vicar. May he long remain so.

CHAPTER XIX.

Sunninghill Park.

IF this estate but little has hitherto been written, and that unfortunately is very inaccurate. I will endeavour from independent research to supply some account of it.

As before observed, we have no large properties in our parish; this, however, is the most important one. It was for ages a royal deer park, and its lodge was the residence of the keeper and riding forester of Battles Walk. There is a tradition that there was a cell or religious house of some kind here, but I am unable to give any information about it, although I have been assured that in the garden near the lake there are remains of such a building.

Be that as it may, a considerable enclosure from the forest was made here at an early period, probably about the time of Richard II., and on its being emparked a lodge of some kind was built. This was doubtless merely the residence of an underkeeper, and was clearly the same as that which afterwards became known as Jewett's Lodge. Norden shows it as standing on the Sunninghill side of the park, near to, if not on the exact site of, the present farmhouse, which then stood on the park boundary towards the waste.

This carries us back to the remote days of the Wars of the Roses, or even earlier.

The ancient family of Stafferton or Staverton were staunch supporters of the cause of the White Rose, and while that was in the ascendant William Stafferton enjoyed the office of keeper of Sunninghill Park and Swinley; but to him the fatal field of Bosworth was a catastrophe that shattered all his fortunes.

As soon as Henry VII. came to the throne, a new keeper was of course appointed to the place which "William Stafferton our rebelle," as he is described, "late had," and on the 8th July 1486 a grant was made, "for life, to Henry Jewett, of the offices of one of the foresters of Windsor Forest, called the 'ryding Forster,' and of parker of Sunnyng Park, *alias* Sunninghill, within Windsor Forest, with wages of 3d. a day as forester, and 4d. a day as parker, out of the issues of Windsor Castle."*

How long Jewett held it, or who followed him, I am not able to say; but searching the Royal Treasury payments,† I fell accidentally on the following interesting entry:—" 1511, July.—H. Smythe towards making a stable at Greenwich, a watch-house at the Tower of London, repairs at Nottingham Castle, *setting up a new house in Sonnynghill park*, rails in the great park at Windsor, £300."

The words "setting up a new house" are clearly suggestive of the existence of an earlier one, and that undoubtedly was Jewett's, which, from another source, I learn was in 1535 out of repair. This new house was the ancient mansion, which stood on the hill near to the end of the present avenue, almost on the boundary-line of the parishes of Winkfield and Sunninghill, but actually in the former parish. It is shown in Norden's map of 1607 as a large place, with its four sides surrounding a courtyard, which was entered by a gateway in the main front of the house, facing south, and looking down on two large ponds in the park now included in the lake.

Henry VIII., as I have shown, when a youth of eighteen, signed, in the Lodge of Sunninghill Park, one of his first official documents, while hunting here on the 1st August 1509. Now this visit might possibly have been to the new house paid for in July 1511, or, if the old one, he must then have made up his mind to build another, and set about it at once; for we see it was finished, and paid for to some extent, within two years from that time.

The families of Staverton, Norris, and Ward were in succession the great men of Winkfield about this period, and it was in that parish that the larger part of this estate lay. But it is as the home of the Nevilles, whose family had been so long connected with the forest, that Sunninghill Park became first associated with us.

Sir Henry Neville, the gentlemen of the chamber to Edward VI., was appointed its keeper. He also had the bailiwick of Fiennes, and the keepership of Swinley Walk in Battles bailiwick.

During the reigns of Edward VI. and Elizabeth, Sir Henry was altogether the most important man in our district. But in 1619, as we have seen, his grandson became involved in litigation with the

---
* P. S. No. 982. Pat. p. 4, m. 23.   † Cal. State Papers.

Crown, and was deprived of his offices; and Sunninghill Park was granted to Alexander Levingstone, the Prince of Wales's tutor.

While residing here, the Nevilles took much interest in our parish. Both Sir Henry and Sir Edward, sons of the first keeper, occupied the Park-house, and the births and burials of several of their children are recorded in our Registers.

Norden tells us that "Sunninghill Park hath 260 fallow deere, about eighty of antler; about thirty buckes; circuit by the pale $3\frac{1}{4}$ miles; it contained about 450 acres good ground." He shows the house and water, and south-west of it two other large ponds, called "Brewer's ponde," near "Reditche" gate; "red ditch" no doubt, from the colour of the water from the moor; while "brewer's" pond is probably but a corruption of the old word "brueria," a marsh, *i.e.*, the marsh ponds.

As the seventeenth century advanced, the royal troubles were beginning, and the extravagances of the Court soon led to emptiness of exchequer. Many of the Crown properties were sold, Sunninghill Park amongst them. We have an old memorandum in the church, purporting to be an "extract from the grant of Soningwell," *alias* Sunninghill Park, by Charles I. to Thomas Carey, Esq., November 1630, of £2700. Such was the value of money in those critical times: 450 acres of "good ground" and an old mansion for exactly six pounds an acre! Royal properties in those days were excellent investments to get hold of; the purchasers were generally those who were in close attendance on Majesty, and knew the happy moments in which their suit might be most favourably preferred. Thomas Carey and Endymion Porter were both grooms of the chamber, and both are recorded as purchasers of Crown lands in 1627. One William Calley, writing to Endymion Porter, who had just purchased some park of the King, says "he is glad to hear it, as he *presumes* Porter has no ill bargain."

This first private ownership of Sunninghill Park brings to our parochial history a very interesting personage; but his genealogy and the devolution of his estate have been so sadly confused by all the writers who have touched upon it, that I have had great difficulty in working out the real facts.

Banks tells us that Thomas Carey, groom of the chamber to Charles I., died of grief on the execution of his royal master in 1648. But his death, in truth, occurred fourteen years before that event.

Again, Ashmole, Lysons, Banks, Burke, Richards, and Hakewell all say that this estate passed to Sir Thomas Draper on his marriage with an heiress of the Carey family; and this statement, although quite inaccurate, has been handed down as an unquestionable fact for over a century. What a tenacious life a genealogical fiction has!

By means of the arms on an old map in the possession of General Crutchley, I have identified our purchaser of 1630 as a member of the Devonshire and Guernsey branch of the ancient Carey family. His great-grandfather married Mary, the elder sister of Anne Boleyn. Her son Henry was accordingly first cousin to Queen Elizabeth, who tantalised him, as Fuller tells us, by not offering him the Earldom of

ARMS OF CAREY.

Wiltshire until he was on his death-bed, when he replied, "Madam, seeing you counted me not worthy of this honour whilst I was living, I count myself unworthy of it now I am dying."

His son Robert, our man's father, was more fortunate. It was he to whom, while endeavouring to soothe the old Queen's last hours, she said, "No, Robin, I am not well."* He left her to ride off to her successor with the announcement of her demise. He was afterwards created Lord Carey of Leppington and Earl of Monmouth. His second son, Thomas Carey, the purchaser of Sunninghill Park, was groom of the bed-chamber to James I. and Charles I.

* See Memoirs of Robert Carey, Earl of Monmouth.

He married Margaret, daughter and heir of Sir Thomas Smith of Parson's Green;* a portion of the old house is still standing—its gardens were very celebrated. The State Papers show that "Thos. Carey and Margaret his wife held lands in Soninghill in 1633."

He was destined, however, to enjoy his new house but a very short time, for he died at Whitehall in April 1634, and was buried in Lord Hunsdon's vault, in St. John the Baptist's Chapel, in Westminster Abbey. His widow seems afterwards to have married Sir Edward Herbert, the Attorney-General.

From the will of Carey I find many little particulars throwing light on his affairs. He left to the King, as a memento, "his best andirons;" and after providing for the bringing up of his infant children, and for clearing off what remained due of his purchase money, he directed that Sunninghill Park should "be converted to the best profit that could be made thereof by good husbandry, and not used for pleasure." He had previously by deed settled it on certain trusts for his children. He left no son, but three daughters. They are mentioned in a grant in 1635. "To Margaret Cary, relict of Thomas Cary, late of the bed-chamber, for the use of Philadelphia, Frances, and Elizabeth his daughters." Neither of these married Sir Thomas Draper. Philadelphia married Sir Henry Lyttelton, Bart., and died without children in 1663 at Tunbridge, where she had gone to drink the waters.† Frances died in childhood, and Elizabeth, the youngest, married Mr. John Mordaunt, afterwards Viscount Mordaunt,‡ which disposes of the idea of "the sole heiress" having married Sir Thomas Draper.

Elizabeth Carey was a woman of singular piety,§ and of great personal beauty and accomplishments. One of the rhymers of the day writes of her—

"Betty Carey's lips and eyes
Make all hearts their sacrifice."

It was owing to her energy and address that her young husband was saved when tried for high treason to the Commonwealth in 1658, for having taken part in the rising of Lord Holland.

---

* See Heralds' Visitation.

† Their old family mansion of Frankley, Worcestershire, had just been burnt to the ground by Prince Rupert, to prevent its falling into the hands of the Parliament. Sir Henry, at the head of his tenantry, joined the King at Worcester, and was there taken prisoner.

‡ Heralds' Visitation; and see Register Extracts, Appendix, Surrey Archæological Collections, vol. ix. pp. 2, 413.

§ See her private Diary, which, after being lost for two centuries, was printed by Lord Roden in 1856.

She had contrived to influence several of the judges, and especially to gain over the President. Pride, through sudden indisposition, was obliged to leave the court, and in his absence the verdict was taken. Nineteen of the judges voted for conviction—twenty for acquittal. To this accident Mordaunt owed his life, much to Cromwell's disgust.

Viscount Mordaunt was constable of the castle and keeper of the forest and parks of Windsor, and died in 1675, when Elizabeth Carey's son Charles, that fiery romantic spirit, whose eccentric career was destined, as Macaulay says, to amaze Europe, succeeded to the title.

On this subject it is curious to notice the mistakes that have been made; but however inaccurate the earlier writers are, the later authorities are certainly no improvement on them; Burke in his Extinct Peerage, followed by the Dictionary of National Biography (vol. ix. p. 63), generally so accurate, mixes up in this instance the history of two distinct persons, mistaking the purchaser of Sunninghill Park and groom of the bed-chamber to James I. and Charles I. for the scapegrace "Tom" Carey, gentleman of the privy chamber to the last-mentioned King; not recognising, apparently, the fact that these offices were quite distinct. The former was the second son of Robert, Earl of Monmouth, as before described; the latter was the son (not the brother, as Chalmers says) of Sir Matthew Carey of Chertsey, and the same whose service with Sir Dudley Carleton terminated so much to his discredit in 1616.[*] He seems afterwards to have sown his wild oats in song, and become a poet, and through his wit to have gained service with the King. He is probably the person referred to in the State Papers as going with Lord Herbert to France as secretary in 1619, and again "4th Dec. 1624, Tom Carey is sent to France with a love-letter and jewel for the bride. She is expected in the end of January." He was a friend of Sir John Suckling and of Ben Jonson, and is spoken of in January 1638, in a letter from "Madam Ann Merrick to the fair Mrs. Lydall," which speaks of the "Alchymist" as having then been revived, and of a new play "sent to Sir John Suckling and Tom Carew to correct."

Our Carey was dead at that time. But what became of this estate after Carey's death? In 1638 we get an incident throwing light on its history. In that year the Vicar of Sunninghill raised the question with Carey's executors as to the amount of tithe payable to him in

---

[*] See State Papers, Dom. 1616, September and October; also Pedigree at Heralds' Office, I. c. i. p. 29.

CAREY PEDIGREE.

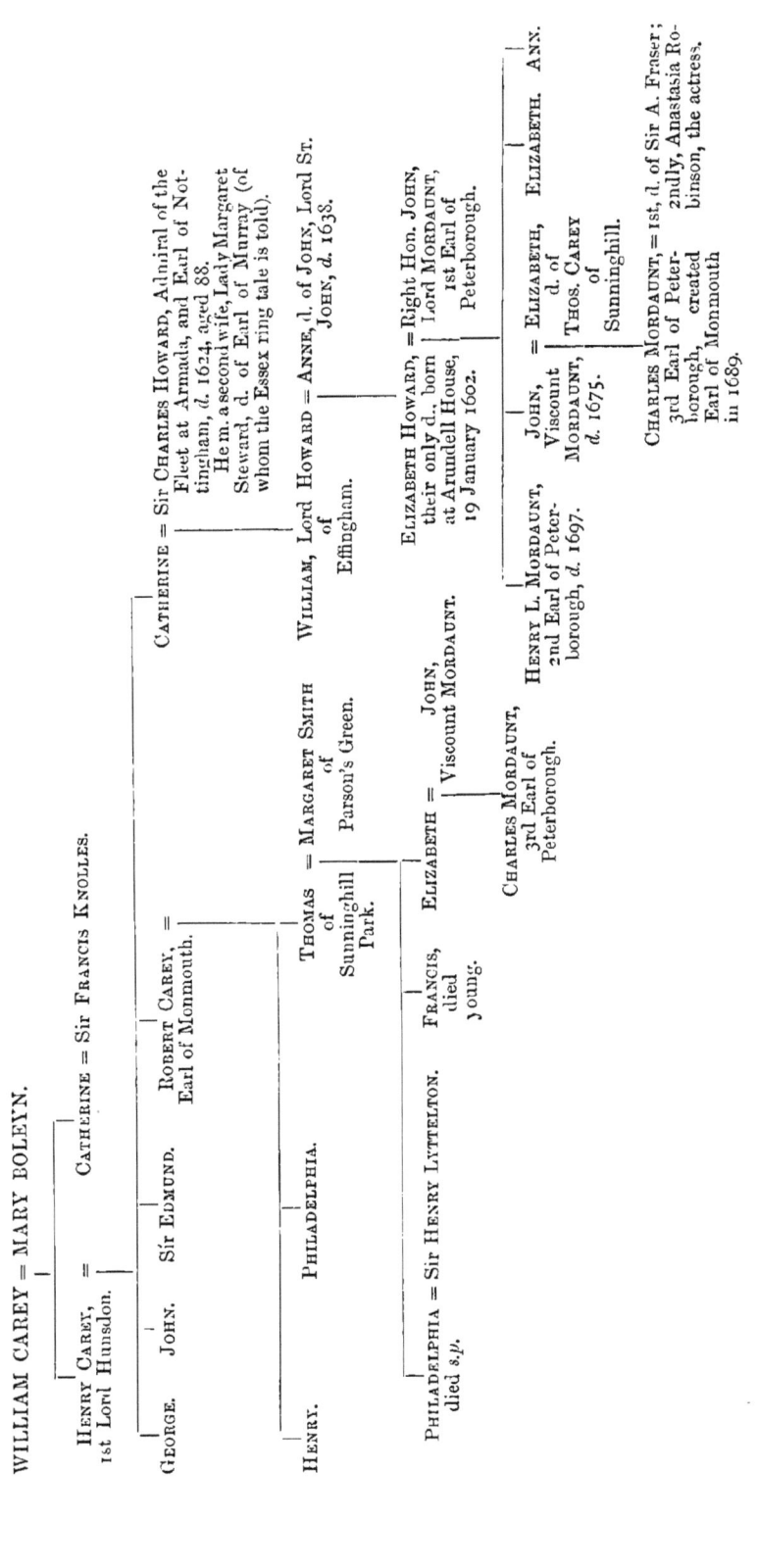

WILLIAM CAREY = MARY BOLEYN.

- HENRY CAREY, 1st Lord Hunsdon.
- CATHERINE = Sir Francis Knolles.

Children of Henry Carey:
- GEORGE.
- JOHN.
- Sir EDMUND.
- ROBERT CAREY, Earl of Monmouth.
- CATHERINE = Sir CHARLES HOWARD, Admiral of the Fleet at Armada, and Earl of Nottingham, d. 1624, aged 88. He m. a second wife, Lady Margaret Stewart, d. of Earl of Murray (of whom the Essex ring tale is told).

- HENRY.
- PHILADELPHIA.
- THOMAS = MARGARET SMITH of Sunninghill Park.
- WILLIAM, Lord HOWARD = ANNE, d. of JOHN, Lord ST. of Effingham. JOHN, d. 1638.

- PHILADELPHIA = Sir HENRY LYTTELTON. died s.p.
- FRANCIS, died young.
- ELIZABETH = JOHN, Viscount MORDAUNT.
- ELIZABETH HOWARD, their only d., born at Arundell House, 19 January 1602. = Right Hon. JOHN, Lord MORDAUNT, 1st Earl of Peterborough.

- CHARLES MORDAUNT, 3rd Earl of Peterborough.
- HENRY L. MORDAUNT, 2nd Earl of Peterborough, d. 1697.
- JOHN, Viscount MORDAUNT, d. 1675.
- ELIZABETH, d. of THOS. CAREY of Sunninghill.
- ELIZABETH.
- ANN.

CHARLES MORDAUNT, = 1st, d. of Sir A. Fraser; 3rd Earl of Peterborough, created Earl of Monmouth in 1689. 2ndly, Anastasia Robinson, the actress.

respect of this property, and the Calendar of State Papers sets out the petition of the Vicar, John Robinson, to the King.

"Before the King parted with the park of Sunninghill to Mr. Thomas Carew, his Majesty, when it was full stored with deer, gave to the Vicar of Sunninghill 20s. for one Lodge, and 3s. 4d. for the other per annum, and the keeper, knowing the Vicarage to be worth but twenty marks, allowed the Vicar the going of a nag for nothing, and six or eight cows for 'six a week.' Since it came to Mr. Carew, notwithstanding, as it may be said, it has been disparked (for there are only some eight or ten deer kept to colour the keeping of the tithes from the poor Vicar), the ground being let out to tenants in several parts, they not only deny the tithes due to petitioner upon the improvement of the lands, but also the former benefit allowed by his Majesty and the keeper, and will only give him a mark, saying, if he will have more, he must get it by law. The petitioner being unable to wage law, prays a reference to the Archbishop of Canterbury and the Lord Keeper, authorising them to call the executors of Mr. Carew, and settle a course for relief of petitioner and his successors."

An order, it would seem, was made in accordance with the tenour of this; but in the following May it was alleged against the petition that 13s. 4d. used to be paid in lieu of tithes, and that the heirs were under age, and it was therefore ordered "that the petitioner should bring his action, under the statute of Edward VI., for not setting forth tithes, against Mr. Carew and Mr. Fisher, to be heard at the next assizes whether there be such a rate or no, and if so, whether it will bar the petitioner, the park being now employed for tillage and other uses." *

To law they went, and the result is clearly ascertained, not only from the State Papers, but from a memorandum left by the Vicar in his parochial archives. It was decided, apparently on an affidavit of one Barnes in 1637, first under-keeper, afterwards keeper of the said park, affirming that 13s. 4d. was paid to the Vicar of Sunninghill by Mr. Carey, and afterwards as a modus decimandi and no more.

It is sufficient for us to know that the case was thoroughly investigated; for in the State Papers is a record dated September 1639 to the effect that "the Council do write to the Chief Baron of the Exchequer (Sir Humphrey Davenport) with the petition of John Robinson, Vicar of Sunninghill, showing how he was surprised

---

* Cal. State Papers, Dom. 1639.

and ill-dealt with by some witnesses at the trial at the last assizes before you at Abingdon, and desiring that he take it into consideration, that the poor man or the church may not suffer." So we may assume that, having been reconsidered, it was deemed a just and final decision.

This too is somewhat confirmed by the MS. notes of Mr. Waterson, the Vicar of Winkfield, who died in 1759, from which I find that Winkfield, much to his regret, was in the same case; but he also tells us that his Vicarage received from Swinley, also a royal enclosure, only a modus of 6s. 8d. Sunninghill Park, a larger property, paid 13s. 4d.

These are the facts which have given rise to the tradition, so often repeated, that it is tithe-free so long as sixteen head of deer are kept upon it.* It is needless for me to say that there is no magic in numbers, or any foundation for the assertion beyond what I have mentioned.

The details of these proceedings are interesting, independently of the main question involved, for they clearly prove that Thomas Carey, the purchaser, left not only an heir, but "heirs," who were minors at the time of his death. It confirms the fact of the park having been let out for husbandry and abandoned as a place of pleasure, although still kept in hand. I find also at the Rolls another little fact, that, in accordance with the practice of the time on sales of the royal demesne lands of the forest, there was reserved to the King on his sale to Carey a fee-farm rent, as well as the timber and privileges of the forest; and this rent of £10 was sold by the Commonwealth to a Thomas Carey in September 1650. Now who was this Thomas Carey? The original purchaser was dead, and it must clearly have been some one interested in the estate. We may, I think, fairly conclude that it was a trustee of that name, some relative of the deceased. He contemplated probably a sale as soon as the heirs came of age and the dreadful troubles of the civil war were over, and, as a wise trustee, redeemed this rent-charge. The extensive old mansion had already been let on lease to Thomas Draper, Esq., and on the two daughters coming of age, they sold it to him in 1654 for £3300, as is evidenced by the existing title-deeds, confirming Mr. Waterson, the neighbouring Vicar of Winkfield, so far as showing that Draper *purchased* the property. It was this gentleman, moreover, who (he further tells us)

---

* Moule's English Counties Delineated.

"pulled down the old mansion-house that stood upon the hill, and rebuilt it where it now stands."

Having now brought the devolution down to Sir Thomas Draper (who was only Thomas Draper, Esq., at the time of his purchase), let us inquire who he was, and who he married.

There were in our parish at this time two families of Baber, a Thomas and a John Baber, who came of an old race of Somersetshire gentry; and Ellen Baber, a daughter of one of these, was married in 1655 at Sunninghill Church to Thomas Draper, Esq.

This lady was a relative of Sir John Baber, Knight, of Little Syon, Middlesex, some time physician in ordinary to King Charles II., by whom he had been made very useful in certain negotiations with the Puritans. But whether this was the Thomas Draper in question I do not know. If so, she must have died early, and he must have married again, for his widow *Mary* survived him some years.

Thomas Draper evidently stood well at court; his connection with the King's physician may have assisted him. He was made a Baronet by Charles II. on 6th June 1660—or 9th, as Burke says—very soon after his restoration, and Baber was knighted the same year.

The Visitation at the Heralds' Office, however, although attested by Mr. Baber in 1819, gives only the Christian name of Sir Thomas Draper's wife, "Mary."

Of this marriage there was no son, but two daughters, Elizabeth and Mary. Elizabeth married Sir Henry Ashurst, Bart.,* who for many years resided at Sunninghill; and Mary married John Baber, Esq., eldest son of Sir John, the King's physician. They had a son, John Baber, born in 1684, and buried at Sunninghill in 1765, and he married Ann, only daughter of the Right Honourable John, Lord Stawell. Now as Elizabeth, who had become Lady Ashurst, had no family, old Lady Draper settled the Sunninghill estate, on this marriage of her grandson, John Baber, the son of her daughter Mary, in what is termed strict settlement, subject, however, to her own life, and that of her husband, Sir Thomas.

In 1668 a royal visit was paid to Sunninghill Park by Charles II. and his brother; and the *London Gazette* of September 9th announced that on "Thursday His Majesty, accompanied with His Royal Highness, arrived at Bagshot, and have spent the time in hunting hereabouts. Sunday last His Majesty did Sir Thomas Draper the honour

---

* Knighted in 1688.

to dine with him at his house at Sunninghill, when he was very handsomely entertained. In the afternoon he went thence to Windsor."

Sir Thomas and Lady Mary Draper lived out the century and beyond it at Sunninghill Park. In 1703, however, he died, and is described in our Church Register as "Honoratissimus Dñus Thomas Draper Baronettus" in the record of burials for that year. Dame Mary, his widow, survived until 1717.

It appears from her will that at the time of her death her daughter Elizabeth, Lady Ashurst, her grandson William, and granddaughter Elizabeth, were all living with her at the Park, having each their rooms, the furniture of which she left to them. Her neighbour John Aldridge was one of her executors and trustees; and she mentions the fact that her late husband had purchased the property at Sunninghill known as late John Robinson's, and also another of R. Osborn. Under the settlement the estate passed to her grandson, John Baber; he resided upon it many years, and dying in 1765, let in his heir-at-law, Thomas Draper Baber, the great-grandson, and not, as Burke in his Extinct Baronetages calls him, the grandson of Sir Thomas and Lady Draper. It was this gentleman who, three or four years after he came into possession of the estate, sold it in 1769 to Jeremiah Crutchley, Esq.

We thus bring the estate into the family of its present worthy possessor. And here I cannot but notice how the literature of one century throws its light over the interesting little incidents of another, and scenes of a hundred years ago become as fresh as though they were of to-day. The home-life of the wealthy brewer Mr. Thrale at Streatham stands out as a pleasant picture. Himself, with his own sterling good sense; his talkative wife, whose good-nature made her frivolity even charming; their daughter and their protégée, the sparkling clever authoress of "Evelina," Fanny Burney; and above all, the great genius of the age, Johnson, whose ponderous wisdom under that roof lost half its asperity and nearly all its rudeness, make up a group of singular interest. Of this family party young Jeremiah Crutchley was also a member: he was Mr. Thrale's ward.

Soon after attaining his majority he purchased the Sunninghill estate; and without intruding into private affairs, I may refer to a visit that Dr. Johnson paid to his young friend in July 1781, for that is a matter of history. He came down with Mrs. and Miss Thrale. Between the great scholar and the young country squire there seemed to exist a genuine esteem; the guest himself acknowledged "that he had never been happier in his life than in those two days." The old Doctor left this flattering record of his visit to Sunninghill Park, in words, curiously enough, almost identical with those of Scott on his visit to the Cedars. The stone piers of the gateway which Miss Thrale presented to her host are still standing at the farm, in what was then probably the chief entrance to the park.

The Babers continued to reside in the parish for many years. Thomas Draper Baber died in 1783; Mrs. Barbara Baber in 1794; and an Edward Baber was buried here so lately as 1827; while a James Smith Baber was living at Coworth in 1835.

Mr. Jeremiah Crutchley sat as Member of Parliament for Horsham; and after thirty-five years' enjoyment of his Forest home, died unmarried in 1805, when the property passed to his nephew, George Henry Duffield, who took the name of Crutchley. This gentleman served the office of Sheriff of his county in 1807, as his uncle Jeremiah had done in 1773; from him it devolved on Mr. Percy Crutchley; and is now, and we hope will for some years continue, in the possession of our much-respected parishioner General Charles Crutchley.

Let me now, before I close, say a few more words about these houses. The first, as I have said, was Jewett's Lodge. That which Henry VIII. "set up" was a very different place; it occupied unquestionably the most beautiful site on the estate; its shubberies crowned the hill-crest, where now the knoll rises above the present house, and it looked westward over the lake. Not a vestige of it remains; the fountain is gone that once sparkled on its lawn, but the site of it is marked by what is still known as the "Fountain Close." This rather explains its relation to the beautiful Lime Avenue, which seems now to occupy a somewhat incongruous position; for the old house and its courtyard extended some distance northward; and the end of the avenue would thus be brought to the garden entrance, and justify the idea, which I cannot abandon, that it was planted as an approach to the old mansion. When this was done I cannot quite ascertain.

Mr. Waterson, writing before 1759, says, as I have mentioned, that Sir Thomas Draper pulled down the old house and rebuilt it where it now stands, "but whether for conveniency I know not, but surely not for pleasure or prospect." If he be right in this, it would have been about 1655 or 1660. But the avenue was not laid out for the new house; had it been so, it would have approached it differently:

and when that was built the trees were probably too well established to permit of removal, and so the line was cut through to afford a view from the new house. It was hardly a happy adaptation. The trees appear to be of the same age, and are almost exactly the same distance apart, as those at King's Wick.* I am altogether inclined to think that they were planted as early as 1632 by Carey, the grantee. We may fairly assume that it was not earlier; for in a map made when he bought the estate, the old house is shown where I have described it, but there is no avenue. It is most unlikely that the executors or trustees would have planted it, considering the testator's directions; and when Draper purchased the estate, the old house was doubtless much dilapidated; it had been standing empty probably throughout the troubled years of the Commonwealth; and the new owner, I expect, found it better to build a new mansion, as suggested by Mr. Waterson, on the site of the present one, than restore the old house.

It was probably in the new mansion that the King was entertained in 1668. When I consider the fine position of the old place, I cannot but admit sharing, to some extent, Mr. Waterson's views as to the change of site; and it is difficult to imagine that in a park abounding with beautiful foliage, the spot selected for the new house should be one which, to give a view from it, necessitated the defacement of those trees. But fashion is supreme.

Just then the new Dutch style of gardening was coming in, and flat formal lawns and water were its essential features. William, and his great gardener, the Earl of Portland, in the Lodge close by, may possibly have influenced this choice of site.

Erelong this fashion had to yield to another, in which only the wildness of Nature could be tolerated; and to this many a fine avenue owes it destruction: those at Cobham Hall, Kent, were terribly victimised by it.

The first successor to the royal Lodge here was a red brick building by the lake, with two wings extending towards the water; a draw-

---

* The lime was not used as an avenue tree in England until about the time of Charles I. Johns says the custom was adopted in the time of Louis XIV. Evelyn regarded it as a scarce tree, and one not so much planted as it ought to be. But it could not have been first brought over, as some have stated, by Sir John Spelman, for single specimens had existed here before that. Sir Thomas Browne sent to Evelyn an account of a famous tree at Depeham, near Norwich, which then measured 46 feet in circumference. The Fulham Palace Lime Avenue was planted, probably, by Bishop Compton, about the year of the Revolution. [Faulkner's Hist. of Fulham.]

ing of it still exists; but when Mr. Crutchley purchased the estate in 1769, these wings were pulled down, and the house was almost rebuilt under the direction of Mr. Wyatt as it now stands.

At the time of the enclosure of the forest, this property was largely added to, and the boundary extended towards Sunninghill.

CHAPTER XX.

Silwood Park.

SUNNINGHILL has for ages past been called a manor even in ancient writings, although, strictly speaking, it was only a parcel or member of the royal manor of Cookham. The waste and all the timber on it accordingly belonged to the King, as lord paramount.

We have seen how, from time to time, patches of the waste were enclosed and "assarted," the trespasses condoned by a fine, and the lands then held at an annual quitrent payable to the lord. These manorial rents, accruing from the forest or Sunninghill portion of the manor, seem from a very early period to have been separately dealt with, and their owner or lessee regarded as lord of a separate manor, so that his residence was not inappropriately termed the manor-house.

Within the manor there would seem to have been both free and customary tenants, freehold as well as copyhold.

I find it described as a separate manor so early as the conveyance of it by John Holm in 36 Edward III.; and curiously enough, four hundred years after John Holm's time a plot of this estate was known as Holm's Close.

John Norris, too, is stated in his Inquisition post-mortem, 6 Edward IV., to have died possessed of "the manor of Sunninghill."

In the time of Henry VI., a grant was made of it to Edmond Hungerford, Knight, John Norris, gentleman, William Norreys, Roger Norrys, and Thomas Bakham, "to be held in capite," at a small rent, "according to custom."[*] Thomas Hasely then seems to have held it with lands in Ascote and other places. Subsequently it became the property of Henry, Lord Norris, and from him it passed to the Lanes

---

[*] 27 Hen. VI., pars. 2, m. 11.

of Coworth. In 25 Elizabeth there was a deed made between "Henrie Lane of Coworth, in the parish of oulde Windsor, yeoman, and Wm. Daye of Eton, gentleman," whereby, in consideration of £210, Henrie Lane sold to William Daye "all the manor of Sunninghill, with all its rights and appurtenances, late parcel of the possessions of the Right Honorable Henreye Lord Norreys, together with all the freehold and copyhold rents." From William Day of Eton it descended to his son, Matthew Day, a person of much consequence at Windsor, of which he was five times mayor. He served that office through the troubles of the Commonwealth, and died in 1661, at the age of eighty-eight.

The first manor court of which I have been able to find any record was one held by him in 15 James I. He remained lord of the manor for many years—indeed until his death. It was shortly afterwards sold to John Aldridge of Sunninghill, farmer, who held a court here in 1675. He in 1700 made a family settlement of it on his son John Aldridge, who died about 1737, and whose widow, Elizabeth, appears then as lady of the manor. In 1747 another John Aldridge devised the manor to trustees in trust for his son George, a minor; and in 1752 a court was held by Henry Stephens and George Bellas as trustees under that will.

In 1764 they sold the estate to John Pitt, who held a court in that year. In 1784 he sold again to James Hartley, who disposed of it in 1787 to James Sibbald, Esq. In 1813, or very shortly after, it was the property of George Simpson; from him in 1824 it passed to Michie Forbes; in 1855 again to John Hargraves; and about 1875 to Charles Patrick Stewart, whose representatives held it until 1888, when it was purchased by its present owner, Thomas Cordes, Esq.

This accords substantially with the account given by Lysons in his MSS. in the British Museum, for he says, "John Pitt purchased the manor of John Aldridge, attorney at law, the son of John, a proctor in Doctors' Commons, which last-mentioned John Aldridge was the son of John Aldridge, a tanner of Sunninghill."

Long ere this the heriots and other manorial rights and the fees and fines had all died away, and the quit-rents become no longer worth the expense of collection. The "Hayward"* of Cookham told me, not long since, that he remembers going over to Sunninghill to collect the rents, but after two days' work all he

---

* The Hayward or Heiward was a very ancient officer of the manor, who looked after the hedges and roads, collected the rents and fines imposed by the bye-laws, regulated the number of cattle put on to the waste by the various tenants, and discharged other similar duties.

could get together was fifteen shillings! They are now only things of the past.

But where stood the manor-house? This brings us to a very interesting letter which Professor Montague Burrows has fortunately discovered and brought to light from the archives of All Souls' College, Oxford, and which has not been noticed before in connection with Sunninghill. It was written by Prince Arthur, son of Henry VII., when he was fourteen years of age, and is dated from "the manor of Sunninghill." It is said to be one of the only three letters of his known to be extant; there is one to the Princess Katherine, and one to Ferdinand and Isabella as to meeting his bride, which are both in Latin; this one, in English, is addressed to the authorities of All Souls College, and concludes:—

"We desire and right affectionately pray you that the rather for o^r sake, and at the contemplation of these o^r l^{res} [letters], ye wol have o^r right and well beloved William Pickering, scoler of lawe, inasmoche as he is of alliaunce unto the founder of y^{or} place, and that his fadre also is in ye right tender favor of o^r derrest modre the quene, especially named in y^{or} next election, as we especially trust you, whereynne be ye ascertayned us to be [be assured that we will be] unto you and y^{or} said place, the more good and gracieux Lord in eny y^{or} reasonable desires hereafter.

"Geven under o^r signet at the Manor of Sunninghill the XVIII day of November."[*] This could not have been written later than 1499 or 1500. His suit, for some unknown reason, failed, as Pickering's name is not on the College Register.

Professor Burrows thinks it must have been written from the house in Sunninghill Park, or from the Nunnery; but, with all submission, I must dissent from this conclusion. The Nunnery was never so called; and the Royal Lodge in Sunninghill Park, which preceded the present house, had not then been built; nor were either of them even in the parish. So intelligent a youth as the Prince is known to have been would hardly have made a mistake in the proper designation of the place from which he was writing.

It was much more likely to have been from the manor-house of which I am speaking.

The affection always understood to have existed between mother and son is strongly shown by the language of this letter. Although I have not been able to find any account of a manor-house here so

---

[*] Worthies of All Souls, p. 38.

OLD SHAWOOD HOUSE.

early as the reign of Henry VII., one no doubt existed. William Day of Eton certainly possessed a place here in the days of Elizabeth, for he is described in the Heralds' Visitation as "of the manor of Sunninghill;" and he paid, as we know, a quit-rent of 2s. for it. No other estate here has paid so much.

In the Survey of the manor in 1606, this property, in the occupation of William Day, is described as containing eighty acres, and is therein called Eastmore, but no house is mentioned; while in the more accurate Survey of 1613 we find it in the possession of Matthew Day, William's eldest son, and "a house called Eastmore" is there specially noticed. With this manorial rights were long enjoyed and transmitted. In the conveyance to Mr. Aldridge again in 1673, the mansion-house of Eastmore is particularly described. This ancient homestead, sometimes called Eastmere, from the mere which it overlooked, but generally Eastmore, from the great moor that stretched away towards the east, stood on the bank near to its old garden, in which the famous vine now flourishes. It looked southward over the lake, and possessed a beautiful site. Within living memory its foundations might have been seen, and on its deserted lawn the arbor vitæ and other evergreen shrubs long lingered to mark where the old house stood.

It was abandoned as the owner's residence on the estate, being sold to Mr. Sibbald at the end of the century, when he built himself a new house at the other side of the property, on the margin of Beggars'-Bush Heath. This last has again in its turn been pulled down, to give place to the present Silwood. The old mansion was not, I think, destroyed for a long time, but was used as the homestead of the farm; for on the sale to Mr. Forbes in 1824, it is described as "all that capital messuage or mansion-house, then or then late called Eastmore Farm," showing that the old house was then still standing.

This was the origin and nucleus of the Silwood estate, and in tracing its gradual enlargement we find another instance so characteristic of our neighbourhood's development. In 1613 we have seen it consisted of sixty-four acres; when disposed of to Aldridge, it is described as fourscore and ten. This was added to considerably, and when sold to Mr. Hartley it was advertised as of 184 acres. It was again increased by Mr. Sibbald and Mr. Simpson, and finally almost doubled by the enclosure allotments.

Of the Aldridges, who had become the owners of this manor, we hear as an enterprising family of the forest, who sided in the

Civil Wars with the Parliament. They were large timber-merchants and tanners. One of them is spoken of in 1638, by Harvey, a servant of Endymion Porter, as "John Aldridge the keeper." In June 1649, I find a minute of the Council, "Mr. Aldridge to have the beeches and oaks in Windsor Forest, fit only for firewood, cut and sold to the use of the State;" but he seems to have used his opportunities recklessly, for in December of the next year, "Captain Aldridge and others were ordered to answer for spoiling the woods of Windsor Forest." The Aldridges were parishioners here certainly as early as 1668, when several of their children were baptized in our Church, and different members of the family were at various times churchwardens of the parish.

In 1672, John Aldridge purchased the manorial estate, with its old mansion of Eastmore, from the Days. It was in the occupation, apparently, at this time of one Mondy, or Mundy.

Not far distant from the manor-house, and of scarcely less antiquity, stood an old mansion in the valley below, or on the ridge immediately rising from it, the home of the Farrants, an ancient Berkshire family of yeomen, who in the days of Elizabeth appear, after the Nevilles, to have been our principal people. One Philip Farrant had a son Thomas baptized here in 1575, and in 1605 there were three Philip Farrants living in our parish at the same time—father, son, and grandson; and altogether they mustered quite a numerous tribe.

Philip, the grandfather, is described in the Survey of 1613 as holding about fifty-two acres of land here, with three houses. Rather more than half a century afterwards this property descended to Judith, the only daughter of one Thomas Farrant; and she in 1668, being then the widow of Jefcoat of Shoreditch, sold it to a Mr. Rawlins, by the description of "all that mansion-house" at Sunninghill, and one other messuage known by the name of "the new house," with sixty acres of land, of which Selmere Hill and Long Deans were portions, as also were two fields described as "lying between the great coppice and the mansion." The great coppice was the "Selwood" which still partly exists to the south of the stream, and from which the whole estate of Silwood now takes its name. The Denbrook of the Survey of James I., and the Little Dean, and hither Long Dean, are all clearly identified as lying by that same stream, and derive their names from the Saxon den or dene, signifying a valley, or a place in a valley by a wood, exactly describing the spot in question. This old Tudor mansion of the Farrants, which for ages afterwards, as our Church

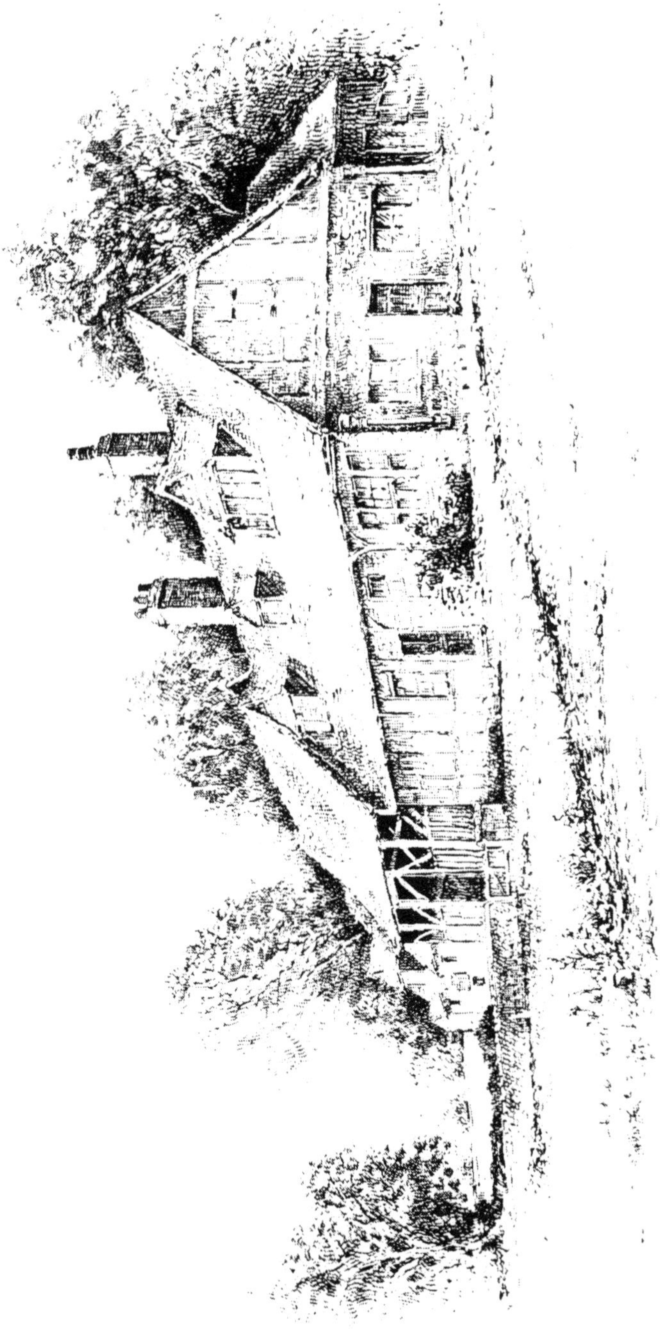

books show, was called "Farrants," must have stood near where the farmhouse now stands. It has long since disappeared. But where is the house which thus in 1668 was called "the new house"? This, doubtless, was the present old timber farmhouse, so picturesque an object by the lake, which conforms very closely in its character to that date. It was then occupied by one William Edsall, yeoman, who was also the tenant of Farrants; the owner, Mrs. Jefcoat, residing in London. Mr. Rawlins held the property only a short time, and sold it to Mr. Aldridge in 1671 or thereabouts. In the Church-rail list of 1672 we find mention of "Farrants," as the most important property in the place, liable for seven rails, while Eastmore was answerable only for five, but Sylmore is not named; while in 1721 "Farrants" is gone (pulled down probably), and for the first time "Sylmore" appears as the home of Aldridge, the son, he occupying the farm, and carrying on his business of a tanner (as the outbuildings, I think, still show) at "the new house," which outgrowing that name, became known as Selmore, after the land it stood on.

It is very difficult to realise and trace out all these changes, and to identify the meadows by the stream, the moors, the wastes, and the arable closes on the bank between these two mansions, with what are now the smooth park lands of Silwood.

The road which, as a pathway only, passes to the north of this house, until Mr. Stewart turned it in 1876, passed to the south of it. Much nearer to the water another road, a cartway, led up over the hill to the old mansion of Eastmore.

This name of Selmore is very suggestive of one of the earliest reclamations from the moor. It is derived doubtless from the Saxon "Sel," great. The "Selwood" retained, as we have seen, the name of the great coppice for several hundred years. The old place Farrants is the more interesting to us, as having been, I am inclined to think, if not the birthplace, the residence of the family of Richard Farrant, one of the fathers of our English Church music.[*] He was gentleman of the Chapel Royal previously to 1564, and organist of St. George's as well, I believe, as of Eton College. He died, some say, in November 1580; other authorities not until 1585. But very little is known of him, save from the few pieces of music he left us. But the beautiful anthem, "Lord, for Thy tender mercies' sake," at one time attributed to him, is pronounced now not to have been his. In 1725 Mr. Aldridge, it would seem, was not himself residing

---

[*] See Hawkins' Hist. of Music, and Grove's Dict. National Biography, vol. xviii. p. 227.

in the manor-house, but let it; and it was there, I have no doubt, the Buckworths lived during the time they were our parishioners. Several of them lie buried in a vault in our Church.

They were descended from the learned Sir John Buckworth of Sheen, who died in 1709. His son, John, died unmarried, and Sir Edward succeeded to the title in 1758. He was Master of the Horse to their Royal Highnesses the Princesses, and assistant gentleman usher to His Majesty George III. These appointments probably brought him into our neighbourhood.

In 1764 the Aldridge family sold the estate to Mr. John Pitt, the Surveyor-General of His Majesty's Woods and Forests, who in 1782 was busily engaged in extending the park towards Egham, and negotiating for the purchase of certain waste lands there, and in helping to enlarge Virginia Water. It was his wife and daughter who, Mrs. Montague and Mrs. Carter tell us, were endeavouring to help the poor villagers, and educate them a little. Mr. Pitt was living at Eastmore when those ladies were staying at King's Wick. He held the manor for twenty years, and then it ultimately passed to James Sibbald, head of the banking house of Marsh, Sibbald, and Co. of London. Having purchased several small properties on the eastern side of the estate, he abandoned the old mansion, and, very nearly on the site of the present house, built himself a new one, the first Silwood, under the direction of his architect, Mr. Robert Mitchell.

The old road from King's Beeches to the mill then ran by the door of the house, and was in fact the southern boundary of the property, as that from the Wells to Cheapside had been its northern line. But Mr. Sibbald was an enterprising man. He soon acquired the angle of Beggars'-Bush Heath, which he overlooked towards the east, and then addressed himself to getting the road turned. In 1790 he obtained a resolution in Vestry, "changing the road leading from the south corner of the land belonging to John Charlwood over Beggars'-Bush Heath, so as the road shall pass on the south side of the ancient gravel pit on the said heath, on condition that he kept it in repair;" and subsequently, in 1796, as our Vestry book shows, "James Sibbald, Esq., enclosed 8½ acres of the waste in front of his house by consent of the parish, he paying its value, £100."

On this estate, close to Silwood House, there stood, overlooking the common, until it was pulled down by Mr. Stewart about 1877, a pretty rustic house, known as Silwood Lodge. It was here about 1792 that the Honourable Mr. Grenville resided. It was advertised for sale in that year as then lately inhabited by him. This gentleman was of the family of the Honourable George Grenville, the first William Pitt's brother-in-law, the "gentle shepherd" of Parliamentary history.*

In 1806 Mr. Sibbald was made a baronet, and as he had no family, the title was conferred with a special limitation in remainder, in default of male issue, to his wife's nephew, David Scott, who, on Sir James Sibbald's death, became the second baronet. This gentleman had a son, James Sibbald David Scott, born at Sunninghill in 1814, who afterwards became the third baronet, and died in June 1885.

Previously to 1813, however, the estate had been sold to Mr. George Simpson, who was the owner at the time of the enclosure.

Sir James Sibbald's retirement saved him from the wreck of his banking house, which had a terrible collapse, not in the general crash of 1825, but in 1824. It had no great reputation, but an amazingly clever young managing partner, who entered the firm in 1807, when the Bank stood as Marsh, Sibbald, Stracy, and Faunteleroy. It became a struggling concern, and to save it in its hopeless condition the daring manager resorted to forgery. He was in the habit of making notes, and a very ominous one found among his papers ran thus:—"The Bank first began to refuse our acceptances, thereby destroying the credit of our house. The Bank shall smart for it."† They did smart for it, to the amount of £360,000! This was in 1824. Faunteleroy was hung for this at Newgate in that year.

Mr. Simpson, it seems, was ruined by the great panic of 1825, and thereupon Mr. Michie Forbes became owner of Silwood.

I may here observe that Mr. Lysons must have been quite mistaken when he told us that this place belonged to Day, the author of "Sandford and Merton," for Thomas Day, the eccentric author of that book, was born in 1748, died in 1789 from a fall from his horse at Laurence Waltham, and was buried at Wargrave. He resided at Anningsley in Chertsey, and I have sufficiently accounted, I think, for the ownership of Silwood between these dates. He may have been a descendant of the Days, its earlier owners.

I have been told by a daughter of Mr. Forbes that she had often seen in her father's possession an ancient map on which was the representation of an encampment showing tents and soldiers, and under it an inscription, "The Battle of Selwood;" but I cannot find any such battle recorded in history, nor can I hear that Sunninghill was ever known to be so distinguished.

---

* See Lecky, vol. ii. p. 471.   † See Gent. Mag., 1824.

Mr. Hargreaves having purchased the estate, disposed of 612 acres of the outlying lands on the south (as also of the Belleview and King's Beech farms, which had been formerly added to the property), retained the mansion and about 250 acres of the home property, which he eventually sold to Mr. Charles Stewart. This gentleman, however, had hardly pulled down the Silwood House of Sir James Sibbald, erected the present one, and cleared away Silwood Lodge, when in 1882 his death occurred, and a few years later the estate was sold to its present owner, Mr. Cordes.

CHAPTER XXI.

King's Wick.

"I sometimes think that as men, when they die, do not die all, so of their extinguished habitations there may be a hope—a germ to be revivified."—CHARLES LAMB.

THE next place I have to speak of is the old mansion of King's Wick, that once stood at the cross-roads near the Church, almost on the spot on which a stone (a specimen from some quarry) has since by chance been placed. Not a vestige of it now remains to mark even its site—nothing but a slight elevation in the meadow, scarcely perceptible, indicates the spot; and like the Findern flowers, that for centuries preserved the tradition of that ancient Derbyshire family when all else had passed away, so here, in spite of utter neglect, in the meadow in which sheep and cows have grazed for over eighty years, the snowdrops, those "garden-flowers grown wild,"* are still to be found forcing themselves up year after year in the spring-time on what was once the ancient garden; and the cherry tree, the old English small black cherry, that can only be found in such sites, despised as useless by our modern improved tastes, still at least gives a rich banquet to the birds and a globe of snowy blossoms to the bees.

The word Wick is probably Danish (the Latin Vicus), the Anglo-Saxon "Wic" signifying a camping-place or habitation. It afterwards came to mean a cluster of huts or a vill, which may account for its application to those little fishing vills in ravines or bays on the seashore still called "Wykes" (in Yorkshire there are several); but the King's Wick at Sunninghill suggests doubtless, in accordance

---

* Referring to the flowers, Jesse tells of a curious fact of a similar kind. On removing the peat, some six or eight inches thick, round an old castle formerly belonging to the Regent Murray, near Moffat, from the ancient garden-bed flowers and plants sprang up of various kinds, some of them but little known in Scotland at that time.

with its original meaning, the habitation that arose in the forest called Wica—the farm of the King's bailiff. There were many such houses known as the Wick or Wicke, and in this neighbourhood others besides the King's Wick.

It is supposed to have been a hunting-lodge of the Crown, and as tradition asserts, at one time the residence of Nell Gwynne, whose name its avenue of limes bears to this day. Tradition also tells us that it was for a time the home of some of the French refugees who were driven away from their country at the time of the Revolution, and that, when the old house was pulled down at the beginning of this century, the materials sold for enough to pay for the whole property. These, like most other traditions, are very near the truth, although not quite.

I have met with but one person who remembers the house. He was the oldest man in the parish, nearly ninety years of age—"Jemmy Stevens," *alias* "Blackbird." He managed to walk up from his hovel in the bog to tell what he knew of the past, and so perfect a type of the class to which he belonged (one of Kingsley's "gentlemen"), that I may digress a little to describe him. Once perhaps a stalwart, wiry man, he had become almost a walking skeleton, bent nearly double with age and hardship, yet his bright piercing eyes lit up his yellow, sharp-cut features with wonderful life. Dressed in his holiday suit—a low-crowned beaver hat, a red neckerchief tied in a bow loosely round his bony throat, without any collar, a brown velveteen short coat, and blue waistcoat, knee breeches, and grey worsted stockings. Of his legs only skin and bone seemed left, and his head was bent almost to the stick that supported him. He remembered the house, he said, and where it stood—between the road and the avenue, where the stone now stands; but could not tell which way it faced! The idea occurred to me that he was drawing on his imagination; but one of those little flashes of truth in a moment set one's doubts at rest. "He knew he remembered it. He was a boy," he said, "and remembered skirmishing about after the dancing was over, and picking up the pins." This idea had not been suggested, and we shall see its truth. "George IV., when a young man, used to come there. He had seen the carriages as thick as they could stand in the road, and remembered running in and out among the horses." He called the avenue "the bowling-green alley." The bowling-green extended from the pond to the road, which was shut out by a high broad wall. At the sale the very wall was sold—marked off in lots. His father bought one to build a cottage with. Between the road and the bowling-green alley was all garden, with "serpentine walks, you know, where the quality walked." "General Fitzpatrick lived at the corner; he *was* a gay old chap!"

Such was the last of the eighteenth-century rustics of Sunninghill;

THE AVENUE, KING'S WICK.

a first-rate poacher, but, as he told a neighbouring clergyman, "he had been a hoggish man in his time." He admitted having spent a night once in the woods endeavouring to shoot the keeper! He slept in the one little room in which he lived, and probably never had a day's illness in his life, unless hunger is illness; but his end, poor old fellow, arrived at last. A present of flannel had pleasurably excited him; the "mainspring" snapped; he rolled from his little bed against the door, and all was over.

There is some reason to believe that the "new habitation" in which Nicholas, the Secretary of the Navy, took up his quarters when he fled out of London from the plague, was King's Wick. The old house is described in the title-deeds as "a capital messuage or mansion-house called by the name of King's Wick, with two acres of land belonging thereto, and also several other pieces of land formerly enclosed out of the common or waste ground belonging to the parish of Sunninghill in the forest of Windsor, by virtue of several licenses for that purpose granted to Mrs. Olivia Porter, containing three acres, and which, with its gardens and buildings, belonged to her." She devised it by will to Mrs. Mary Baron; and she again to Elizabeth Willis, afterwards the wife of Joseph Windsor, of whom it was purchased by Sir Edmund Elwill, Bart., previously to 1740. I have not been able to fix exactly when the house was built; it may have been about 1625 or 1630. Norden's map does not notice it, nor can it be identified in the Survey of 1613; but very curiously the manorial survey of 1608 gives "King's Wick" as one of the boundaries of the parish, although I think erroneously. It was probably the manor boundary; it was not within the manor. This is interesting, however, as being the earliest mention of the name I have met with.

The tradition, to which I have referred, assigning the avenue to Nell Gwynn, and the house as a hunting-lodge of the Crown, may be true, although I cannot find any authority for it; and the trees are, I think, older than her day; but at the time this house must have been built, there was one William Gwynn, a person of some consequence, residing in the parish. In 1632 he was made a trustee of the Church Green property; he was a staunch Royalist, and was afterwards mulct of a considerable sum as a "delinquent" in the time of the Commonwealth. It might have been Gwynn's Avenue from him, and the Nell subsequently added to the tradition.*

---

* A Matthew Gwynn was Mayor of Windsor in the time of Edward VI., and in a Survey of Windsor Park in 1649, Auditor Gwynn is mentioned as the lessee of Frogmore farm-lands. The lease was a renewal of a former one of 4 James I. His name was William, and he or his ancestor, a William Gwynn, had been lessee in Henry VIII.'s time.

William Gwynn sold some property, "his house and lands" at Sunninghill, to a Mr. Thomas Osborn during the Commonwealth before 1654. The widow, Margaret Osborn, we hear of as a lady of some position residing here shortly afterwards, and she was succeeded by her son, Thomas Osborn.

The house then became the property of Mistress Olivia Porter, whose husband was an interesting historical character; and, if only to preserve a few facts about him, I may be allowed to digress a little.*

Mistress Olivia Porter was the fourth daughter of John Lord Butler (or Boteler, as it was then written) of Bramfield. She married about 1620 Endymion Porter, a young man of great promise, in the service of the Duke of Buckingham.

In August 1621 we find him writing to her an affectionate letter on Buckingham not letting him go to her on some particular occasion.

On 20th February 1623 the State Papers record a pretty excitement. The Prince Charles and Buckingham, pretending to join the King at Newmarket, slipped off through Essex disguised with false beards, crossed to Gravesend, and on to Canterbury. The Mayor stopped them, as they were thought to be Barnevelt's sons, but they got on to Dover, and there being joined by Sir Francis Cottington and Endymion Porter, they sailed for France. There was consternation at Newmarket; the Council met on special business; the clerks even were excluded; the courtiers knelt to implore the King to tell them if it were true, and His Majesty had to admit it, apologetically reminding them how he, his father, and his grandfather had all gone from Scotland to fetch their wives. In 1622 we find the young married folk were still separated; she did not like it, and she evidently let him know her mind; for he writes to Olive, "Fears her love does not equal his; hopes nothing will make her repent her choice, but she must know that he must govern her, not she him; blessings on their babes." In April 1623 he was still at Madrid, they were most handsomely received; he writes home to his wife describing the Princess and her ladies, and hopes she (his wife) is not jealous. She replied sharply, no doubt, for in May he wrote again "wishing not to be put in mind of any unkindness between them; sends her a jewel which she may pawn, if she has no more credit." On the return of the Prince from this romantic expedition in 1623, the Windsor bells were set ringing at a cost of 3s.

In 1636 Endymion had become groom of the bed-chamber, and Mistress Olivia was becoming a great lady; she speaks of ordering three suits, two of blue, and one of "Ezebelah" colour. My lady readers may remember the incident of the Infanta Isabella's † vow in 1602, not to change her garments till Ostend was taken. Dreadful to relate, the siege lasted three years, which made this colour fashionable. Shortly after this, heavy jewellery bills appear for the "Right Honourable Mrs. Porter." The husband was meanwhile patronising the arts on his own account, as well as that of the King, and in March 1638 we find him delivering on His Majesty's behalf to Sir Peter Paul Rubens a chain of gold weighing 82½ ounces and £1170, part of £3000 owing to him.

---

* Endymion Porter was a friend of Thomas May, of Mayfield, Sussex, an accomplished man of the day, who, through disappointment, left the King and went over to the Parliament.

Porter possessed a good estate, on which he lived, at Aston-under-Edge, Middleton, Gloucestershire. He is somewhere described as son-in-law to Mountjoy, Earl of Newport, but that was his younger son, Thomas, who married the Earl's daughter.

† Daughter of Philip II, and wife of the Archduke Albert.

Van Dyck painted Endymion Porter several times; and in the possession of Viscount Strangford is a fine picture of him, his wife, and three of his sons; it is said to be one of Van Dyck's finest productions.

One little incident I may record, as it shows what the resources of Durham were in those days. Porter, who was there in May 1639, writes to London asking for half-a-dozen quires of paper, for he could get none there.

The sons were evidently living riotously, and the good mother's religious feelings were much wounded. Sometime in 1640 she wrote a characteristic letter to her son George:—

"I am very sorry you continue still your disorder, without having any sense of Almighty God, who has preserved you from so many dangers; and if that would not move you, if you had any good nature, or sense of the affliction your father and I suffer, you would not do it." Prays him to make haste home. Father and son were both with the King at York in September of this year. George Porter, trumpeter to His Majesty, had been wounded, and in December was very ill. His mother induced the Queen to write to the King to send him home.

Then followed the terrible civil war, and in the year that his master was beheaded Endymion died. He had been an especial object of hatred to the Parliament, and one of the very few to whom pardon had been denied. He had been stripped of all his possessions, and reduced almost to beggary.* After the Restoration, the widow obtained the office of surveyer of petty customs and subsidies in the Port of London, a profitable appointment.

Here I must leave Dame Olivia Porter as the owner and occupier of her Forest mansion. She gave it by her will to a Mrs. Mary Baron, who left it to Elizabeth Willis, afterwards the wife of Joseph Windsor. They sold it to Sir Edmund Elwill, Bart.; from him it passed to his son Sir John Elwill, who represented Guildford in the Parliaments of 1747, '54, and '61.†

At this time, thanks to the light literature of the day, we get a pleasant view of the old mansion, and what it had come to. Sir John Elwill, the owner of King's Wick, was not, for some reason, himself residing in it in 1769, and it was used as assembly-rooms for the gentry of the neighbourhood, for which its spacious apartments were well suited. Every Monday there was a great gathering, with music and dancing, and during the rest of the week it was inhabited by lodgers, who came hither for change of air and to drink the waters. On the 28th of July of that year, Mrs. Elizabeth Carter, writing to Mrs. Vesey, says, "I hope soon to have the happiness of spending many delightful hours with Mrs. Montague at Sunninghill." These two ladies were among the most accom-

---

* His will is dated March 26, 1639. I cannot find, although I have carefully searched in London, that it was ever proved, but a creditor's administration was taken out for his estate in 1649, to enable his assets to be realised.

† Sir John Elwill, Bart., married Selina, widow of Sir Arthur Cole, Lord Ranelagh [Hoare's, Wiltshire]. Sir John Elwill, Knight, the father of Sir Edmund, was made a Baronet in 8th Queen Anne.

plished women of the age. Mrs. Carter was the more learned, but Mrs. Montague, with her accomplishments, possessed affluence, which made her the leader of fashionable and literary society. And it was here that this promised happiness was to be realised; a charming country, delightful society, improving health, all contributed to bring it about in this tumble-down old mansion and its quaint gardens.

We get a further insight into the life here in a letter from Mrs. Carter to Miss Talbot (a niece of Lord Chancellor Talbot), her great friend, and this I give at length as it so well describes the country :—

"SUNNINGHILL, *August 16th*, 1769.

"It was thought most desirable that I should remain here drinking the waters, of which I can only say they do not disagree with me, although I am not yet arrived at drinking a full dose. Here I am struggling about by myself over these lone commons, very like a solitary goose. We are lodged in a house lately a Baronet's seat, so it is very spacious, and has a good garden, partly laid out in wood walks, &c., which are pretty, though not extensive. At present we are the only lodgers, but the largeness of the house, if it was full, would be as inconvenient and as noisy as an inn. The breakfasting-room is in the garden, but as it is filled only one day in the week, this is no great grievance. The spring is about half a mile from us, and I rise early and walk there, and am back about the time Mrs. M. is stirring, and then accompany her. I am extremely pleased with all I have seen of this country, though whether before I leave it I may not wish for the sight of cornfields is not clear. We dined on Monday at Mrs. Dunbar's,[*] and it gave me great pleasure to find it so sweet a place; it answers the idea of a ferme orné more exactly than anything I ever saw, and has an air of tranquillity and cheerfulness which makes it appear like the abode of virtue and contentment, and is perfectly adapted to the mind of its sweet mistress. It is about three miles from here; Mr. J. Pitt's about half a mile. We dined one day at Mr. Wilmot's at Farnborough, about ten miles from Sunning, and I dare say you will think us very intrepid heroines to travel over Bagshot Heath by moonlight, but our valour was not signalised by any adventures. I think there are not above a dozen water-drinkers. We are mighty

---

[*] Now Lady Aitsas.

quiet and rural, except of a Monday, when a public breakfast and fiddles collect all the Misses round the country."

Again on the 23rd of August she writes:—"At Sunning with Mrs. Montague. This country is a perfect new scene to me, and, so far as I have travelled over it, appears very delightful." She speaks of her late friend, "dear Lady Ann Dawson." "Mr. Dunbar is going to Ireland, but lovely Mrs. Dunbar does not accompany him."*

Confirming all this, I find the Dowager Countess Gower writing to Mrs. Delany:—

"BILL HILL, 30th August 1769.

"Ffortune has bless'd ye fforest wth ye genius's of ye age. Mrs. Montagu, Mrs. Carter, Mrs. Dunbar, &c. &c., and Lord Littleton,† are at Suñing wells, and sport sentim^{ts} from morn till noon, from noon to dewy eve; I molest 'em not, contenting myself in my rustic simplicity."‡

A few years pass, and Sir John Elwill, then living, I find, at an old family house at Egham, of which Paul Sandby has left a drawing, wished to dispose of the King's Wick property, and in 1774 it was advertised for sale as—

"At Sunninghill, a very commodious house, with all convenient offices, coach-house, and stabling for upwards of twenty horses; a large garden, wilderness, and pleasure-ground walled in; late the assembly-house."

This entirely confirms the tradition as to the extent of the house, and as to its having been used as assembly-rooms. Davis, the proprietor of the wells, died about that time, which may account for the assemblies not having been at the wells that year; it especially corroborates old Stevens as to the garden-wall. The wilderness was at the south and east of the pond, and probably opened into the Nightingale Dell mentioned elsewhere. Within the last twenty years vestiges were to be seen there of the iron arbour-work of the "wilderness."

A few years more elapsed, and in 1778 Sir John Elwill died, and by his will gave King's Wick to trustees for his only child, Selina Mary, who married Felton Lionel Hervey, Esq., and afterwards the Right Honourable Sir William Henry Freemantle, K.G.H., and they subsequently went to reside at Englefield Green.

---

* Vol. 1., 2nd series, p. 236. † The literary Lord Littleton, born 1709.
‡ Brit. Mus. Reading Mercury.

The old mansion had been falling into disrepair, and during the minority of the daughter had probably again been used as the assembly-rooms for the neighbourhood; and in 1780 Miss Talbot visited Sunninghill again, and writes to Mrs. Carter recalling old times, and tells of the change eleven years had brought about. Mrs. Carter replies on the 14th August: "Why did you not name in what part of Sunninghill the spot which you so charmingly describe is situated, that I might try to recollect it? I think the change of the house where Mrs. Montague lodged must be greatly to its advantage. It could never look well but in a ruin."

When Prince George was living at Bagshot Lodge, he often doubtless came over to the balls here, as mentioned by old Stevens; but that part of the old man's narrative must have been clearly traditional, as he could not have remembered those earlier visits, although probably some of later date may have impressed his boyish memory.

About 1792 King's Wick became the home of some of the French refugees; and a friend tells me of another old man who knew the house then. "Gentleman Turner" informs him that he remembered it very well, and that it was a very large place; he well recollected climbing up to look in at the windows to see the dancing when the French refugees were living there. These facts explain the picking up the pins.

It became soon afterwards the birthplace of a little Prince, as the following entry in our parish register shows:—

"1793. Charles Just Francois Victurnien, the son of Mark Etienne Gabriel de Beauvau, Prince de Craon, and of the Holy Roman Empire, and of Nathalie Henriette Victurnienne de Montemart, was born March 7th.

Witness my hand, JAMES STEVENSON, *Accoucheur*."

Our young Prince, if not the most exalted of royalties, came of two of the most illustrious families of Anjou and Lorraine; their later associations, however, were not so entirely unsullied.

The young Prince de Craon, the last of a long line of nobles, was killed at the head of his regiment at the battle of Fontenoy;* but a young lady of his family became the favourite of Leopold, Duke of Lorraine; at the same time a M. de Beauvau, a descendant of one of the noblest families of Anjou, was "Governor," as he was called, of Leopold's son Francis, the future Emperor.

Between this Mark de Beauvau and the young lady a marriage was arranged; he was created Prince de Craon and of the Holy Roman Empire, thus reviving the ancient title. He died in 1754. Then came Charles Juste Victor, Prince of Beauvau, who was a man

---

* Walpole's Letters, Dom.

of some ability, and the friend and patron of St. Lambert and of other men of letters of the time of Louis XV.; he served as a volunteer in the armies of France with much distinction; received a marshal's baton, and was made a Minister of State in 1789. He was very staunch in his devotion to Louis XVI., and died in 1793, having survived the murder of his royal master only three months.*

His son, Mark Etienne Gabriel de Beauvau, Prince de Craon, born in 1773, sought refuge in England; and took up his abode at King's Wick, where the year his father died, and ere he could have had the title a month or two, his son Charles Juste Victor was born on 7th March 1793—not 1792, as sometimes stated.

The fashionable gambler Fitzpatrick, who had purchased the property, soon pulled the old house down and turned it into money; sold the materials in lots, even to the very garden-wall. A present parishioner's grandfather purchased the greater part of them; some went to build a house that stood in the grounds of Bangor Lodge, and, on its demolition, that in which Mr. Barr Brown now lives at Ascot, and a cottage near St. George's School there. Lead was just at that time at a very high price, and it is quite likely that the tradition alluded to was correct in this respect.

General Fitzpatrick included this property with his own house at the corner in his gift to Mrs. Caroline Price, settling it on trustees (Uvedale Price, of Foxley, Hereford, and Robert Price) in trust for the lady for life, and afterwards to his niece, the Honourable Caroline Fox, daughter of his sister, Lady Mary Holland. This gentleman, Mr. Uvedale Price, was the friend and travelling companion of Charles James Fox, and with him visited Voltaire at Ferney. On the death of Lady Caroline Price, the tenant for life, in July 1826, the Honourable Caroline Fox, of Little Holland House, Kensington, became entitled, and in 1838 conveyed the property to Michie Forbes, Esq., of Silwood Park.

On the enclosure of the common by the Act of 1813, several acres were added to the property, and were soon planted. It next passed by purchase to the Hargreave family, in whose possession it remained until 1873, when the writer bought it, and built the present house on the margin of the forest land, preserving the old name of King's Wick.

---

* Walpole's Letters, vol. i. 202 and 204, Wright.

CHAPTER XXII.

The Cedars.

"A noble lord affirms I like his plan;
I never did, my lords, I never can:
Plain words, thank Heaven, are always understood;
I could support, I said, but not I *would*."—ROLLIAD.

CLOSE by the Church stands the house known as the Cedars. The property may have belonged originally to the Nunnery of Bromhall, and on its dissolution have come into the hands of St. John's College; for so early as the days of Queen Elizabeth there seems to have been a cottage near where now the Cedars stands; and in the possession of St. John's College is an indenture of lease, "made in the twentieth and one year of our Sovereign Lady Elizabeth," to one Michael Slade, "of a tenement and of a piece of land abutting on Fernie field on the north, on the churchyard on the south, and upon a little lane over against the Vicarage on the west, for twenty years at a rent of ten shillings. This little lane was that, doubtless, which became the subject of the memorable acknowledgment of "the fat pig at Christmas."

The Cedars was afterwards the property of a Mr. William Buckle, who possessed it in 1677; and early in the eighteenth century we find a Madam Elizabeth Squire residing there, who was apparently its owner. From her it seems to have passed to a Mrs. Scott, under whom Sir David Lindsay may have held as tenant, for he was there in 1763. His daughter married Mr. Augustus Schutz.

Mrs. Scott sold the property, consisting of the house and garden, to Mr. Davis, who in 1765 had a dispute with the Vicar about the road. Part of the land was then described as "Buckle's meadow, now Davis' garden."

The road in dispute was one which led direct from the church down by the Cedars on its western side through part of the present kitchen-garden; it passed to the north of the glebe meadow (formerly called the Barn Close and the Hill Close), over the stream at a bridge there, and so up the meadow on the other side out on to the common, between Tetworth and the old manor-house, which was then John Aldridge's. The piers of the bridge may still be seen on the banks of the stream. The Cedars garden did not then extend to the brook; and the angle which was thus left between the road and the stream was an osier-bed, particularly noticed in the litigation, and for the use of which the Vicar was afterwards paid 2s. 6d. a year. When Madam Squire lived at the Cedars in 1731, she hired, with the sanction of the College, the Vicarage meadows of Dr. Palmer, who was non-resident, and she then turned the road away from her garden and caused it to pass from the present stile opposite the church down the western side of the hill meadow, where the path is now. Traces of the old road may still be seen. Subsequently in 1779 it belonged to the Honourable John Yorke, who by exchange with the parish acquired the ancient Church Green, which lay directly opposite to the house. This gentleman was the fourth son of Philip, Earl of Hardwicke, the Lord Chancellor. The estate was advertised for sale, however, in 1787, as "an elegant freehold villa, with eighteen acres of meadow, the residence of Mrs. Yorke, deceased;" but probably was not sold then, for the Honourable John Yorke was still living there in 1794, and died at the Cedars in 1801. By him or his representatives it must have been sold to Mr. George Ellis, who lived in it till his death in 1815. His brother, Charles Ellis, succeeded to his estates, and in 1827 was created Lord Seaford. A Mr. Franks was there for a short time, and in 1829 a Mrs. Munnings seems to have been its owner. She sold it, I believe, to Mrs. Parry, who was there in 1843; from her it passed to her son, Major Parry, and to his son it still belongs. In 1801 the property also comprised "a newly erected genteel cottage near the church," before spoken of as still forming part of the stable buildings. Very pleasant associations will ever be connected with the Cedars.

We get a delightful picture of it as the home of the refined and cultivated Mr. George Ellis and his charming wife. Rare must have been their attractiveness to have drawn around them such men as Heber, Scott, Canning, Leyden, Douce, Rogers, and bound them together in the closest friendship. Heber was Richard, the elder brother of the future Bishop, an accomplished man, to whom the sixth canto of "Marmion" was dedicated. He brought his friends Scott and Ellis together, and Ellis introduced Scott to Canning.

In 1830 Scott writes, "My friend the late George Ellis, one of the most accomplished scholars and delightful companions whom I have ever known."

When the "Border Minstrelsy" came out in 1802, a parcel was despatched to Sunninghill with vols. i. and ii. They were thus acknowledged:—

"SUNNINGHILL, *March* 5*th*, 1802.

"MY DEAR SIR,—The volumes are arrived, and I have been devouring them; not as a pig does a parcel of grains (from which simile you will judge that I must be brewing, as indeed I am), putting in its snout, shutting its eyes, and swallowing as fast as it can without consideration,—but as a schoolboy does a piece of gingerbread; nibbling a little bit here and a little bit there, smacking his lips, surveying the number of square inches which still remain for his gratification, endeavouring to look it into larger dimensions, and making at every mouthful a tacit vow to protract his enjoyment by restraining his appetite."

He then goes on to threaten that Mrs. Ellis must, at the risk of pulling caps with Mrs. Scott, set off for Scotland if he will not come to England soon. At Scott's instance, Ellis had shown much kindness to Leyden, who has left us in a few quaint lines a lasting impression of the sweet nature of that "gentle dame," Mrs. Ellis :—

> "To speak not of his gentel dame,
> Ich wis it war bothe sin and shame,
>   Lede is not to leyne;
> She is a ladye of sich pryce,
> To leven in that dame's service
>   Meni wer full fain."

She was a daughter of the famous Sir Peter Parker, who lived at Ongar Hill, Chertsey, and she died at the age of ninety so recently as 1862. Leyden was one of the most eccentric characters of the age, a shy vain youth, with the learning of a dominie, loving the legendary lore of his native dales, which he poured forth in snatches with all the boisterousness of his fervid nature.* In the fourth canto of the "Lord of the Isles" he is thus lamented :—

---

* Wordsworth speaks in 1803 of passing through the village whither Leyden, the author of "Scenes of Infancy," and Scott's intimate friend, walked over several miles of moorland country every day to school, a poor, barefooted boy. "He is now," says Wordsworth, "in India, applying himself to the study of Oriental literature."

> "Scenes sung by him who sings no more;
>   His bright and brief career is o'er,
>   And mute his tuneful strains,
>   Quenched is his lamp, of varied lore,
>   That loved the light of song to pour;
>   A distant and a deadly shore
>   Has Leyden's cold remains."

In writing to Ellis in May 1803 Scott says, "How often do Charlotte and I think of the little paradise at Sunninghill and its kind inhabitants," and, "We sincerely hope Mrs. Ellis and you will unrivet yourself from your Forest, and see how the hardy blasts of our mountains will suit you for a change of climate."

But the brightest picture of all is where we find Mr. and Mrs. Scott, Heber and Douce, going down to Sunninghill "to spend a happy week with Mr. and Mrs. Ellis at the Cedars;" and one day in May, all seated under an oak in the Forest, the great Wizard of the North read to them the two or three cantos just then completed of the "Lay of the Last Minstrel." But of this happy party one noted individual must not be forgotten; he lay on the grass, gazing intently at the reader, seeming, as it were, to devour in silence his every word. This was Camp, the favourite bull-terrier, more to Scott than Bounce had ever been to Pope, or Spot to Hogarth.

We want the pencil of Watteau to realise to us this interesting group.

Scott parted from his dear friends at Sunninghill, and, accompanied by Camp, went under Heber's guidance to spend a week at Oxford, which he had not then seen. He spoke afterwards of his never having enjoyed two weeks more in his life. Now as to the question whether a portion of "Marmion" was not written at the Cedars, there cannot be the slightest doubt.

Scott himself says, "I remember with pleasure at this moment (1830) some of the spots in which particular passages (of "Marmion") were composed; it is probably owing to this that the introductions to the several cantos assumed the form of familiar epistles to my intimate friends." The fifth canto, it will be remembered, is addressed to George Ellis. For several weeks, in March 1807, Scott was at the British Museum working out his facts; but Lockhart says, "He uniformly reserved his Saturday and Sunday either for Mr. Ellis at Sunninghill, or Lord and Lady Abercorn at their beautiful villa near Stanmore." He returned to Edinburgh in May, and in the December following wrote the introduction.

> "When such the country cheer, I come
> Well pleased to seek our city home;
> For converse, and for books to change
> The Forest's melancholy range,—
> And welcome with renewed delight
> The busy day and social night."
>
> . . . . .
>
> "Dear Ellis! to the Bard impart
> A lesson of thy magic art,
> To win at once the head and heart,—
> At once to charm, instruct, and mend,
> My guide, my pattern, and my friend."

He still more pointedly alludes to our country when he writes—

> "Till Windsor's oaks and Ascot plain
> With wonder heard the Northern strain."

In the garden at the Cedars is a spot which, as a stone erected there tells us, was a favourite resort of Sir Walter; it bears engraven on it a few lines from "Marmion," and close by a bright spring trickles from the bank, marked by another stone, put up, no doubt, by Ellis, with the lines

> "Behold her mark
> A little fountain cell,
> Where water clear as diamond spark
> In a stone basin fell;
> Above, some half-worn letters say,
> Drink, weary pilgrim, drink and pray."

It was from this retired shelter, as is mentioned, I am told, in one of his letters, that he used to watch the deer at evening as they came from Swinley to drink at the Silwood lake. It was all open forest then.

Here, too, in the garden is a monumental stone vase to the memory of "Tuscan," bearing the word "Fidelity" on one side and "Sagacity" on the other; but this canine favourite of somebody's died in 1837, and judging from the inscription, which recites his virtues in thorough orthodox fashion, could not be of Camp's race, but a hound of larger breed.

Returning, however, for a moment to Ellis's earlier life; those who are familiar with the literary history of the last century will know how important a part in the political warfare of that time

"The Rolliad" and "The Antijacobin" played; but who could have imagined that those periodicals, teeming with all the "fire and brimstone" of personal invective, had their inspiration to a great degree from the inoffensive occupant of that "little paradise" at the end of our Church Lane, and that the amiable Mr. George Ellis was one of the principal forgers of those thunder-bolts?

The chief contributors were Canning, Richardson, Tickel, Ellis, his neighbour, afterwards General Fitzpatrick, and Lord John Townshend.

During the French revolutionary war Ellis took the part of the Government, and was the writer of some of the best verses in the "Rolliad;" but he made a blunder in speaking of Pitt as "pert without fire, without experience sage."* He did not know him personally till his return from Lille in 1797 with Lord Malmesbury. At their first interview, one night at supper, some friends asked for the story of the origin of the "Rolliad," much to Ellis's embarrassment; when Pitt, hearing the request, leant forward and said—

"Immo age, et a primâ dic hospes, origine nobis,"

leaving to be implied

"Casusque tuorum, errores que tuos."—*Æneid*, Lib. 1.

In these squibs at that time personal peculiarities were thought fair game for attack; so a worthy Alderman's wooden leg was made game of; and Dr. Prettyman the future Bishop of Winchester's squinting was not spared:—

"Argus could boast an hundred eyes, 'tis true,
The Doctor looks an hundred ways with two;
Gimblets they are, to bore you through and through."

A neighbour of ours also figured in its pages as a follower of Sir George Howard, the commander-in-chief:—

"Erect in person, see yon knight advance,
With trusty squire, who bears his shield and lance;

---

* See Gent. Mag., 1815, p. 371, and Russell's Life of C. J. Fox.

The Quixote Howard! royal Windsor's pride!
And Sancho Pança Powney by his side!"

But nothing it contained would be more instructive to some worthies of the present than the lines at the head of this chapter, which were written to satirise Lord Shelburne's casuistical way of speaking.

CHAPTER XXIII.

Beech Grove.

"Well, well—the world revolves upon its axis,
And all mankind turns with it—heads and tails;
We live and love—make war and pay our taxes,
And, as the veering wind shifts, shift our sails."

AT the cross-roads at the beginning of the Church Lane stands a house called Beech Grove, which, although of no great antiquity, is not at all a modern one. Like many others in the place, it has been enlarged. It was originally a small, pretty, rustic residence, more especially noticeable for the fine trees on its lawn, and the evergreen foliage and rhododendrons, now of unusual size, with which it is surrounded.

Its associations are not without interest to the local historian, and recall a phase of eighteenth-century social life very characteristic of that age, if not altogether flattering to it. Could you look back to the year 1800, you might perhaps have seen its owner as he stood by his gate, a very tall, handsome man of military bearing, tottering in a premature old age, and in that "battered old beau," as Wraxall calls him, you would have seen the idol of society during great part of the last half of the century, and one of the most brilliant ornaments of its fashionable life.

The greater lights of the age, Dr. Johnson and the immortal few who worshipped him in the smoke of his beloved City taverns, are familiar enough to us; but we have almost forgotten that knot of lesser wits and politicians that made literature fashionable in the drawing-rooms and clubs at the West End.

The old gentleman referred to was General the Right Honourable Richard Fitzpatrick, second son of the Earl of Upper Ossory, the constant companion and friend of Charles James Fox, whose elder brother, Stephen, married Fitzpatrick's sister, Mary. These young people

began life in a blaze, for they were very fond of private theatricals; and after distinguishing themselves in that way at Winterslow House in January 1774, that beautiful mansion of the Hon. Stephen Fox was burnt to the ground: they were acting "High Life Below Stairs." Richard Fitzpatrick, however, I think, before this had not been altogether unknown to fame as a ringleader of the "half-price" theatre riots in 1763; but he became a man of considerable culture, high courage, and elegant manners. He was one of the most reckless libertine set of gamblers and spendthrifts that the age produced. The wit and pleasantry of the time expended themselves in intellectual fireworks of a small kind, bon-mots, love ditties, prologues, smart anonymous pamphlets, and for excellence in these he was without a rival.*
Very early in life he was initiated into Parisian society. Madame Du Deffand, writing in 1769, speaks of Fox, Spencer, and Fitzpatrick as staying to the end of her supper. "I think the last is my favourite, for his soft and tractable manners;" and again, "There was play at my house on Sunday till five in the morning; the Fox lost 150 louis. I fancy this young man will not get off for his stay here under two or three thousand louis." Trevelyan, too, speaks of him and Fox as both delightful talkers. Lord Lyttelton also thought him scarcely behind Fox in talent, "and in the article of colloquial merit at least his equal."

Walpole goes still further. "He writes," said he, "as easily as his friend, and is a more genuine poet." "In controversy I have too high an opinion of his parts and wit to think myself in any degree a match for him. I have always spoken with enthusiasm of Charles Townshend, George Selwyn, Charles Fox, Mr. Fitzpatrick, Mr. Gray, Mr. Gibbon, and of anybody of singular capacity and parts." Brilliant company this to excel in. Not even George Selwyn, with all his inexpressible drollery, could rival this "battered old beau" in his prime.

The American war brought him into active service; and the idol of the ladies was in no way deficient in the field. He returned in time to assist his friend Fox in the duel he fought with one Adam, and which very nearly extinguished that eminent life. Wraxall speaks of him as in person "tall, manly, and extremely distinguished; he possessed no mean poetic talents, peculiarly for compositions of wit, fancy, and satire, in all which he far exceeded Fox." Sir James Mackintosh was of the same opinion. The lines

---

* Fitzpatrick wrote a prologue for his friend Sheridan in 1794, on the opening of his new theatre.

in the Temple of Friendship at St. Ann's Hill are his. How unfortunate that the incomparable *jeux d'esprit* that Sheridan once struck off while waiting for dinner should have been accidentally burnt! The subject, not the most promising, was the appraisement of an old worn-out gig belonging to Fitzpatrick, which Lord John Townshend was to purchase at Sheridan's valuation. "You can have no idea," said his Lordship in a letter to Samuel Rogers, "what fun he made of this. Fox used to say it was the most comical thing ever written. Fitzpatrick, though it was not a little severe upon him, was delighted. But no one cared so little about a joke against himself as Fitzpatrick, who was as remarkable for his immovable good-temper as he was for his excellent understanding and polished wit." *

In 1781, after a description of the dresses at the Opera, we have the important announcement that Mr. Fitzpatrick had very little powder in his hair!

He was now at the height of his fortunes. In 1783 General Conway was delighted at his being made Secretary at War. He was not, however, a statesman, like his illustrious friend, but politics found plenty of employment for him in those famous political squibs and lampoons for which he was celebrated.

The General came to us for repose after his gay life, to which I need only allude as exemplifying the predominant vices of the century.

Deep play was the curse of the nation; even the ladies, said Walpole, "game too deep for me." Fox, as all the world knows, piled up his debts at the card-table, which his rich infatuated old father made it the pleasure of his life to discharge. In the "hottest" places the two friends were ever to be found or expected immediately. What a cameo is this of 1782! "The Prince of Wales dined with Mr. Fox yesterday by previous engagement; they drank royally. Charles went thence to Brooks's, stayed till four in the morning, and it being so early, finished the evening at White's with Lord Weymouth, and the evening and the morning and the next day were the first day!" and so be it, says Horace Walpole.

Fitzpatrick on one occasion wrote, "I won £400 last night, which was immediately appropriated to Mr. Martindale, to whom I still owe £300, and I am in Brooks' books for twice that sum." Well might George Selwyn exclaim, when he heard that a waiter at Brooks' had been arrested for felony, "What a horrid idea he will give of us to the people in Newgate!" The old General lost almost

---

* Rogers and his Contemporaries. P. W. Clayden.

his last shilling at Brooks', and then, in partnership with Lord Robert Spencer, set up a faro bank there, by which he recovered something of money, but not credit, to end his days on. Was it then his good friend Ellis drew him away to vegetate at Beech Grove? His tastes, certainly, just then took a milder turn; he amused himself with botany, and enjoyed the quiet social intercourse with his charming neighbours so near him — the most enviable time of his life.

Even now, however, improvidence brought its vexations, as is shown by a little entry in our parish vestry-book: "Resolved that a letter be sent to General Fitzpatrick, stating the great inconvenience that has arisen to the parish from the arrears for the years 1799 and 1800 on account of the income-tax left unpaid by him."

We get a glimpse of the "old beau" in his later years while on a visit at Foxley from a letter (just published) from Wordsworth to Sir George Beaumont in 1811. "When in Wales last autumn," he says, "I contrived to pass a day and a half with your friend Price," but he admits having been in a very ungenial frame of mind; his host's daughter, he remarks, "put me out of tune by her strange speech, looks, and manner; and then, unluckily, Fitzpatrick was there, a torch that once may have burnt bright, but is now deplorably dim." *

It was then that he pulled down the old mansion of King's Wick to turn every brick of it into money. He lived a gay life, and remained, as the old poacher described him, "a gay old chap" to the last. Both he and Fox, ardent admirers of French institutions, had imbibed the free-thinking irreligious notions so prevalent then; they paid but little thought to the conventionalities of life, and their domestic arrangements were alike irregular. The lady to whom he left his house and furniture, and the King's Wick land " to boot," Mistress Caroline Price,† was an inmate of Beech Grove, whose position there, in the eyes at least of our friend "Blackbird," was a very equivocal one. Lady Lade was her particular friend, a lady of strange character and a great whip of the day, excelling even her husband in the art of driving; she was in the "Tommy Onslow" set, and attracted the Prince's notice at the Windsor Hunt.

Beech Grove as well as the King's Wick property was left to her

---

* See Memorials of Coleorton.
† She is called in the Manor Rolls "Caroline Price, wife of Uvedale Price, and mother of Robert Price." Her husband became Sir Uvedale, and she, therefore, Lady Price.

for life, and afterwards to the General's niece, the Hon. Caroline Fox, the daughter of his sister Mary, Lady Holland. General Fitzpatrick died in 1813, and was buried at Sunninghill; he wrote his own epitaph.

Beech Grove afterwards became the residence for a short time of Dr. Baillie, the eminent mental physician of the day (brother of Joanna Baillie), who wished to be near the castle on account of his royal patient, George III. It had several temporary tenants, and ultimately became the property of Mrs. Burt, afterwards of Mr. Toller, and its present owner, Mr. Hichens.

CHAPTER XXIV.

Coworth.

I HAVE already alluded to the ancient estate of Coworth. Delightfully situated on the western slope of Shrubshill and the Warren, it is sheltered now by its almost overhanging woods, and looks down over Sunningdale towards the south and west. Its name is derived from the Saxon "warth," a farm—the cow-warth or pastures of the tribe. This is confirmed by one of our most ancient records, the Chertsey Abbey lands boundary, where this spot may be identified with a place called "Herdies" near the "thornie hulle" or Shrubshill of to-day. Herdies from the Gothic "hairdeis," herds.

It forms the eastern boundary of Sunninghill, and although only a small portion of the property is in our parish, it has always been very closely connected with us—indeed, more so, probably, than with its own parish of Old Windsor.

Here we have another of the many instances of the open character of our country in former times. One of Paul Sandby's drawings shows the Belvidere a century and a quarter ago; it then stood on a bare moorland hill; the only trees upon it were a few apparently newly planted round the tower. Wide views were to be had in all directions over the common.

The earliest notice I find of this place is in the Inquisition taken on the death of Galfrid de Baggesete in the time of Henry III., from which we learn that he held of the King in capite certain lands towards "Cowurthe." These, as before mentioned, he held in serjeanty, in conjunction with lands in Sunninghill.

Again, in 29th Ed. III. a fine was levied in relation to a house "at Coworth by Johnes le Neve and Johes Fraure and his wife;" on a sale probably by them to Le Neve.

The principal estate here was for several centuries in the possession of the ancient family of Drerenford or Derenford, afterwards called Danford. For in 45 Ed. III. "Wm Derenford of Coworthe and Johanna his wife conveyed to Wm Podenhale, citizen of London, one messuage and forty acres of land and four acres of marsh in Coworth and Sunninghill;" and in the same year this William Podenhall also had a conveyance from "Laur, the son of Wm Derenforde," of certain lands in those places.* This family was located at Coworth for generations afterwards, and was still flourishing there through the reigns of Elizabeth and her Stuart successors.

In 1667, John, the son of Richard Derenford, was baptized at Sunninghill; in 1688 a John Danford of Coworth was buried there; and so lately as 1726 a James Dernford was regarder of the forest at Sandhurst.

Having established the existence of this family here, I am enabled to throw light on a puzzling reference in the Survey of James I., for there, at the eastern end of the parish, a place called "Dornford" is mentioned; but all local knowledge of it has been lost; no one here had ever heard of it. It was evidently a ford on the stream running through Coworth, which was anciently a much more important one than now; and was probably at the point at which the present road crosses it. It took its name naturally enough from its owners, the Darnfords.

I have not yet been able to fix the site of any old manor-house at which this family resided. Indeed, I am inclined to think that Coworth never was a manor of itself. I can find no trace of it. It may have been a member of some other manor, as of Old Windsor, for instance, and became, as it were, its outlying manor-farm. By this title it is noticed in our parochial Registers as far back as they go, early in the reign of Elizabeth, when it was called "the manor-farm Coworth," and was the home for several generations of the family of Lane.

This name brings to Coworth some interesting associations. The first of the family here was a Henry Lane, whose son was baptized in our church in 1571. He seems to have been a good type of the Berkshire yeoman, such another as Farrant of Sunninghill, Attlee of Winkfield, or Atfield of Windlesham, and rivalling, in truth, the boasted yeoman of Kent, of whom it is well said—

"The Gentleman of Wales,
The Knight of Cailes,

---

* See Fine Rolls, 45 Ed. III., p. 107.

And the Laird of the North Countree;
But the Yeoman of Kent,
With his yearly rent,
Will buy them out all three." *

This yeoman of Berks owed his advancement probably to his marriage into one of our great Forest families; for it was he, doubtless, who, as the Heralds' Visitation tells us, "attended Henry VIII. as a voluntier at the taking of Bulloigne;" and married "Anne Norris, descended of ye noble family of Norris, and near kinswoman unto Sir John Norris, Generall of ye Forces in Ireland." This must have been Sir John of Fifield House, Queen Elizabeth's famous captain, who took to heart so much the slight of being superseded in his chief command. On Lane's return from this glorious expedition he probably settled at Coworth; and some years later, being then described as of that place yeoman, he purchased of Henry Lord Norris the manor of Sunninghill, but soon sold it again in 1583 to William Day of Eton.

In 1573 a Henry Lane, his son, I believe, was married at Sunninghill to Amis Stoke. He would appear to have lived to a very advanced age, and died at Coworth in 1641, as shown in almost the last entry in our Registers before the civil war. His second brother, George, inheriting only the valiant spirit of his mother's race, left his quiet home in the Forest to seek fortune in the service of his great kinsman in Ireland. There, among the wild chieftains of the island, he fell in love with the fair daughter and sole heiress of Cormock O'Farrell, Esq. of Killincroobagh. Their son, Richard Lane of Fulske, was made a Baronet, and married the only daughter of Gerald Fitzgerald of Clonbolg and Rathaman, thus allying himself with one of the most patriotic of the old native families, and reminding us of a history perhaps as romantic and as terrible as any that even those fierce times could show. This turbulent race of the Geraldines, after being almost exterminated by MacCarthy More, rose to a princely position, until its chief, the Earl of Kildare, was practically the ruler of all Ireland. Henry VIII., to crush them out, got possession of Gerald, the ninth Earl, his son, "Silken Thomas," as, from the splendour of his dress, he was generally called, and his five uncles, and hung them all at Tyburn. Two children only were saved, "Silken Thomas's" half-sister, a bright beautiful girl, the fair Geraldine of poor Surrey's dream, who was sent to England, and brought up with the royal children at Hunsdon, and at the age of nineteen was given in marriage to a wealthy widower, the great Lord of Cowdray, Sir Anthony Brown, the King's standard-bearer. Her little brother escaped, and, under the protection of Cardinal Pole, wandered about the Continent in poverty. Queen Mary restored him to his estates, and as the eleventh Earl he married Mabel Brown, the daughter of his sister's husband by a former marriage. To this great family in its adversity Richard Lane was thus united, while his sister became the wife of

---

* Mavor tells us that at the beginning of the century there were more yeomen farming their own lands in Berkshire than in any other county of the same size, although Kent, I think, had more. Pitt used to say that no Minister of this country could command ten votes in Berkshire. [*Scouring of the White Horse, Quarterly Review*, vol. cvi. p. 203.]

† Reg. 2, L. 2, p. 58.

John O'Farrell of Terlichin. Richard, son of Sir George Lane, Bart. of Fulske, was Charles II.'s principal Secretary of State for Ireland, and was created Viscount Lanesborough. By a second marriage with Lady Frances Sackville, daughter of Richard, Earl of Dorset, he had a daughter, married to Henry Fox, through whom he became ancestor of George Lane Fox, M.P.

Meanwhile in the elder branch the old homestead of Coworth remained for over two centuries. Our Registers show four or five Edward Lanes in direct succession living there from the days of Queen Elizabeth, contemporaneously with the Danfords. This branch is now represented by Captain F. G. Vigor, of the Duke of Cornwall's Regiment of Light Infantry.

Lysons speaks of this place as a kind of scattered hamlet, and Norden's Survey confirms this. His map shows a few houses standing apparently round about the site of the present mansion: at that time it was also called the "Warren Hill." Persons now living can remember some of these cottages; and their foundations have quite recently been struck on.

The old manor-farmhouse, in which these Lanes resided, is still standing, and although now sadly defaced by some former owners with incongruous additions, and an entire encasement of fir slabs to make it pretty as a cottage orné, it affords to the curious an excellent example of the farmhouse of the substantial yeoman of the period.

It occupies a pleasant site facing the west, and was built of oak and brick and plaster-work, with picturesque gable wings, and primitive unporched entrance in the centre; from the high roof rose a good chimney stack; the rooms were low-pitched, with the usual heavy beams across the ceiling; the kitchen had its ample fireplace, with walls tapestried, as George Eliot says, with flitches of bacon, and ceiling ornamented with pendent hams. The upper chambers were very small, and approached by narrow passages of different elevations. The walls are very thin, but the ancient rough-hewn oak beams still show how abundant that material was with our forefathers.

Formerly a main road from Shrubshill and Sunningdale passed close by the front door of the farmhouse and present mansion, and so on through the little hamlet down to "Dornford" and Blackness Gate; this has been slightly altered and turned by the gardens.

In this house lived, and in all likelihood was born in 1616, the Edward Lane who lies buried in our churchyard, and who spent his patriarchal life here, where he died in October 1714, at the age of ninety-eight years! He accomplished what could not have been possible in any other period in the whole course of our history from the Conquest; he witnessed the reigns of no fewer than ten sovereigns or sovereign rulers, for he lived in the time of James I., Charles I., the Commonwealth, the Protectorate of Cromwell, and his son Richard, Charles II., James II., William and Mary, Anne, and George I. Good testimony this to the salubrity of our neighbourhood. He always regarded Sunninghill as his parish, and was indeed at one time our churchwarden. Another Edward Lane succeeded him, and is remembered as the donor of Lane's charity, a small gift to our parish.

Little change took place here till towards the end of the century, when, in 1796, James Barwell, Esq., son of William Barwell, formerly Governor of Bengal, was the owner of Coworth. He virtually erected the present mansion by adding two wings to an older house which stood on its site, and thus more than doubled the size of it. He or his brother also built Buckhurst.

> It was this William Barwell who, it will be remembered, was Warren Hastings' staunch ally at the Council-table throughout the whole of that struggle at the Board which led to the well-known duel between Hastings and Philip Francis. He never failed to support his friend, who was thereby ultimately enabled by his casting vote to secure the supremacy.

When his great trial was over, and all the passion and excitement had died away, Hastings purchased and came to reside at Beaumont Lodge, and Barwell, the son of his old colleague, came to Coworth, where he died in 1811. From him it seems to have passed to James Smith Baber, Esq., of the Sunninghill Park family, who held it in 1835. His tenant of the house was Mr. G. Nettleship. Mr. Arbuthnot bought the estate about 1840, and Mr. Farmer, the present owner, in 1884.

CHAPTER XXV.

Some Other Houses.

ASHURSTS.

ASHURSTS is the name of an estate in the Church Lane, now the property of Colonel Blundell, M.P. The present residence was built, I think, by Mr. Schutz. Like most of the houses here, this took its name from its owner, Sir Henry Ashurst, Bart. I find this gentleman a parishioner of Sunninghill for many years; he married Elizabeth, the eldest daughter of Sir Thomas Draper.

Of a portion, at least, of this property we hear at an early period, when it was granted to John Robinson, the Vicar, by the feoffees of the Crown in 1613, as three acres of the waste, afterwards known as "Stony Lands." From him it would seem to have been purchased by Sir Thomas Draper, who built on it a house known for many years as "the brick house;" a description possibly at that time sufficiently distinctive among the timber houses of the Forest; in 1672 he was assessed for three panels of the church rails in respect of it.

After Sir Thomas's death, Lady Draper was assessed for it in 1715. It was in this year that her son-in-law, Sir Henry, contested Windsor in the great election before referred to, and he appears to have been in the midst of all the party strife that it aroused. His political views seem to have been in opposition to those of Dame Mary, his mother-in-law; but I cannot say whether that at all influenced the gift over of the property to the Baber grandson, or whether "the head and front" of poor Elizabeth's "offending" was her not having a son. Lady Ashurst at the time of her mother's death, however, was living with her at Sunninghill Park. By her will the old lady left this property to her daughter and her husband, Sir Henry, for life, and afterwards to her grandson, William Baber; but Lady Elizabeth Ashurst ultimately acquired the absolute interest in it, and in 1740 left it by will to Mr. Thomas Hatch, from whom it passed to his widow, Mrs. Lane Hatch. She sold it to a Captain Farrell, who entered into an exchange with the parish in 1745 in relation to this very Church Lane.

From Captain Farrell it came to his son William Farrell, who in 1766 was rated for "Stony Lands" as "late Ashurst's, now William Farrell's." He sold it to Thomas Birch, Esq., and he again to the Hon. John Yorke.

A Mrs. Schutz was residing in our parish in 1766, and was assessed for the "panels and stile," doubtless the side entrance to the churchyard, over the wall of which a stile may have led from this property, as the road did not then go round the churchyard, as it does now, but straight by the Cedars door.

This name, however, suggests the founder of the family, one Baron Schutz, envoy to the Court of Queen Anne, who offended her Majesty by alluding a little too plainly to her successor, and she requested his immediate recall; but on the accession of George I., Schutz accompanied him to this country, and was often visited by him and his son at his fine mansion of Shotover, four miles from Oxford. Pope makes several allusions to him:—

"If honest Schutz takes scandal at a spark,
That less admires the palace than the park."

And again—

"Alas! like Schutz, I cannot pun."*

Augustus, the elder of the two sons of the Baron, was Equerry to George II. when Prince of Wales, and Master of the Robes and Privy Purse to him when he became King: he was a great personal favourite with his Majesty, and died in May 1757. His wife in 1736 was Lady-in-waiting to the Queen.

However, the place eventually became the property of Mr. Spencer Schutz, on whose death in 1806 it was advertised for sale as "for many years the residence of Mr. Spencer Schutz, with twenty-four acres of land and three fishponds." It then passed to Mr. Augustus Schutz, who in 1803 had married Elizabeth, daughter of Lady Lindsay. He died in 1826, and was buried in our church. It was this gentleman who took so much interest in the parish, established and

---

* Hervey's Memoirs, vol. i. p. 411.

endowed its schools, and became a large benefactor to the church. From this Mr. Schutz it passed through various hands. Sir William Norris lived here for about two years, and was buried at Sunninghill, as was also his son, who fell in the Indian Mutiny. His son, the novelist, leaves mementoes of his residence with us in some of his books. In "My Friend Jim" we have the Marquis of Staines, Lord Sunning, and Lord Bracknell.

Ultimately, in 1874, it was purchased by Colonel Blundell, M.P., in whose possession it is still.

KING'S BEECHES.

On the beautiful ridge, anciently known as Blackwick Hill, which divides our common from the great wastes of Windlesham and Chobham, there formerly stood a fine grove of beeches, from which, doubtless, the place took its modern name. Tradition tells us that King Charles II. planted these trees, originally seven in number; but I can find no authority for it. When the present owner purchased the estate, this account of their origin was mentioned to him: three of the beeches were then standing, but the stem of one of them is all that now remains. It was undoubtedly a favourite spot with King George III. from which to review his troops as they lay encamped round it at the end of the last century, and to this point accordingly may still be traced the straight drives to Ascot, Virginia Water, and other places. Some of these, however, had been previously laid out by Queen Anne.

I am altogether inclined to think that it is to King George, and not Charles II., that we owe the origin of the name. In a large-scale map of the neighbourhood of 1788, a small house is shown here, and a cross to which the drives converged; but there is no indication of the beeches, and the hill is marked, "King's Beech Hill," as though one tree only had been so especially distinguished.

On the top of the hill a small house had been erected, of which I have but little more to say than that it became the property of a Mr. Round, and by him or his executors was sold to Dr. Locock, but he did not reside there. It has since been much enlarged or rebuilt, and now belongs to our esteemed neighbour Mr. Barnett.

CHARTERS.

We have already seen how, at the beginning of the century, from the Blackwick Hill to King's Wick in the village it was all common. Down the valley ran a stream forming four ponds, one below the other, on what are now the properties of Mr. Morrison, Mr. Mackenzie, and Miss Fairman. A large one was drained away by the railway cutting. On the hill ridge to the south, nearly on the site of Mr. Hamilton's shrubberies, stood a farmhouse, barn, and rickyard, with three or four cottages, near a spot known as "Hancock's Mount." There were Hancock's parishioners here since the middle of the sixteenth century. Was it from them it took its name, or from some encampment there of General Hancock? The farm was also called Belleview, and afterwards Child's farm, from the name of its occupier, an uncle of Mr. Barr Brown; this earlier name was suggested by the fine prospect it had over Windlesham and Chobham common and the surrounding country, when the farmhouse assumed a new phase of residential importance; for towards the end of the last century a fine octagon drawing-room, with chambers over, was added to the little low-pitched cottage.

The property in 1784 was advertised for sale, and when we read the eloquent description of its charms as then proclaimed, we can only hope that its present possessor may find in a green old age a perfect realisation of its truth. It ran—

"Sunninghill.—A cottage and fine octagon drawing-room in that beautiful and enchanting country, which may truly be called the Montpelier of England; three bed-chambers, &c, barn, and one hundred acres."

The property was purchased by the owner of Silwood and thrown into that estate. On the enclosure of the Forest, the strip of waste in the valley was allotted, in respect of it, to Mr. Michie Forbes, who was accustomed to hold his harvest-home festival in alternate years in this octagon room, and at the home-farm in the old black-and-white farmhouse by the lake.

About 1868, Mr. Hamilton bought the property, and on the site of the cottages (the farmhouse had been previously pulled down) he erected the present house, calling it Charters, I believe, from the pond below it on the southern slope of the ridge. The name had no connection, however, with the Nunnery, as it is often supposed to have had—a mistake supported by the still more recent one of a neighbouring owner giving the name of Bruno to a new house near; thus very inappropriately associating the name of the founder of the Carthusian Order with the ancient Nunnery of Broomhall, which was a Benedictine, and not a Carthusian foundation.

In the valley to the north, on the site almost of Pembroke Lodge, stood a smaller farmhouse belonging to the Belleview property, and called sometimes Belleview Cottage; its stabling still remains. From King's Beech Hill by this first-mentioned house ran the road to Shrubshill before spoken of, and by the latter the older way from Bagshot, still to be traced passing up through the wood by Silwood House.

BUCKHURST PARK.

Although there may have been an ancient house of small character on this spot, the present one as it now stands is comparatively modern. It was built by Mr. James Barwell at the end of the last century. After his death in 1811, his brother, Mr. Smyth Barwell, I think, resided there.

In April 1798 it was advertised to be let for a year as a modern and excellent family house, called "Bucket Hill," having stabling for ten horses, and thirty acres of land.

In 1804 it was sold to Mr. John Vernon, who soon extended its boundaries, especially by the purchase of the Mill property, which anciently comprised the mill in Sunninghill, the house in Winkfield, and fifteen acres of land between Mill Lane and Buckhurst Hill. This little estate belonged to the family of May, who were millers here for many generations. One of them left it by will to Henry Emblin, who sold nine acres of it to Mr. Vernon. A cottage and garden in the lane were also thrown in by exchange with the parish at the time of the enclosure.

The hill so early as 1662 is described in the Windsor map as Bucket Hill, and the mill below as "Bucket Mill." A windmill is marked as standing on the top. In another map at the Royal Library of about 1753, and also in Roque's map of 1762, it is likewise so called; but in 1687 the manor rolls mention the Hill as Buckhurst Hill. It acquired its present name before 1833, for in that year Greville in his Memoirs writes: "11th June 1833.—Was at a place called Buckhurst all last week for the Ascot races; a party at Lichfield's racing all the morning, then eating and drinking and play at night. I may say with more truth than anybody,

> 'Video meliora proboque, deteriora
> Sequor.'

The weather was charming, the course crowded, the King received decently."

Mr. Vernon must have lived here some years, for he was at Buckhurst in 1825. From him it seems to have passed by sale to the Rev. George Hunt, who sold it to the late Mr. Savory, the father of its present owner.

The old mill has not long disappeared; it was burnt down only a few years since, and the property all now forms part of Buckhurst Park.

SUNNINGDALE PARK.

Not far from the road which runs from Lynwood to Sunningdale, at the end of the Larch Avenue, there stood in the valley towards the south-east an old house nearly on the site of the present stables. We must remember that at the end of the last century a military road, much used at the time of the reviews here, ran from King's Beeches along the ridge in a line with the Larch Avenue to Shrubshill and Virginia Water; while the old trackway from Bromhall to our village came up through the centre of the present Sunningdale Park estate, passing close by the house I am speaking of on its western side. Whether it was here or at some other house in the "dale" that General Frederick resided between 1787 and his leaving "Sunninghill-dale" in 1798, I do not quite know, but in the former of those years his house is described as a "compact villa" at Sunningdale.

It is not unlikely that this property came into the possession of Lord Uxbridge, and that it was here he entertained his Majesty during the reviews, as elsewhere described.

A Mr. James Stewart afterwards purchased it, and he dying

a bachelor, it passed from him to his brother, the Rev. Charles Stewart. Old Patey, the herdsman in the Park, told me he remembered the place very well.

The Rev. Mr. Stewart built the present house, a little higher on the hill, about 1830 or rather later. He was at one time curate of Sunninghill.

It was again sold about twenty-five years ago to Sir Charles Crossley, and by his executors, in 1883 I think, to Mr. Mackenzie, who has much altered and enlarged the house.

HAREWOOD LODGE.

Among the oldest of our remaining houses is one erected, probably about the beginning of the eighteenth century, in Mill Lane, on the border of Beggars'-Bush Heath, looking over the mill in the valley and across the common towards Silwood.

In 1713 it was the residence of the Cowderys, and at the end of the century it came into the possession of a Mr. Barker.

<small>This name recalls that of a family of considerable antiquity here, connected with the Days of Eton, and incidentally it reminds us of the still more ancient race of the Oxenbridges; for so early as 1532 John Oxenbridge died seised of land in Sunninghill, and in 1572 one Robert Oxenbridge had a suit against the Rev. William Day, Dean of Windsor and Provost of Eton, who died in 1596. This gentleman's daughter Rachel married Robert Barker, and was so connected with the Bulstrodes.*</small>

In 1806 it was occupied by Lady Harewood, with only an acre of land, and took its present name from her, instead of Sunninghill House, by which it had been previously, as it has since been, sometimes called.

It was here that "Gentleman Turner," while in the service of Sir James Sibbald at Silwood, remembered walking with his old master and mistress, lighting them with a lanthorn across the common to play a rubber with Lady Harewood.

Lady Harewood could not have been there long, for in 1811 (then known as "late Barker's") it was the residence of John Robinson, the Crown Surveyor, and in 1815 was in the possession of William Towry, Esq., whose family held it for many years.

---

* See Gyll's Hist. of Wraysbury

George Philip Towry in 1771 purchased Folly John Park, which he possessed till about 1798, when it became the residence of his son-in-law, the first Lord Ellenborough. From William Towry Harewood passed to George Edward Towry, who was living there in 1829, when it was known as Harewood Lodge. He seems to have continued his occupation till so lately as 1843. He was buried at Sunninghill. A larger amount of land has since been added to it, and it could have been but a short time after this that it came into the possession of its present owner, Colonel the Hon. Charles Hay, who has largely increased the size of the house.

TETWORTH.

This, although not a large house, has a most pleasant situation on the bank beyond the stream, north-west of the church, not far from the straight-mile entrance to the Ascot Racecourse. The estate is now the property of Lord Harlech. It has had many owners. Mr. James Mann, Mr. Desborough, and a Mr. Carter—of a family, I presume, long resident at Shrubshill—resided there; then a Mr. Meyrick Fowler seems to have had it, and after him the Rev. Mr. Peart became its owner; he sold it to a Captain Foley, who having an estate called Tetworth, gave that name to this house. How long it was in the possession of Mr. Meyrick Fowler I do not know. The name, however, recalls that of an old parishioner, the Right Hon. Lady Lucy Meyrick, who was buried in our church in 1802, in the brick grave made for her husband, Pierce Meyrick, Esq., in 1752.

THE OAKS.

This place, built, I believe, early in the eighteenth century, before Silwood House came over to become its *vis-à-vis* on the common, occupies a pleasant position on the eastern edge of the old Beggars'-Bush Heath.

It was the residence for a long time of the Churchills, one of whom, a Charles Churchill, Esq., son of old General Churchill, and therefore grand-nephew of the great Duke of Marlborough, lived here for many years; he is frequently mentioned, with Lady Mary, his wife, by Horace Walpole and by Mrs. Montague in their letters as residing at Sunninghill in 1748, and later in the century. This reminds us of that amusing incident when the Princess Royal, in conversation with Mrs. Oldfield, the celebrated actress, inquired of her whether it was true, as reported, that she and General Churchill were married. "Oh," replied the lady, "it may be so reported, your Royal Highness, but we have not acknowledged it yet."* This gentleman married Mary, daughter of old Sir Robert Walpole by Miss Skerret, his second wife, the Phryne of Pope's Epistle to Bathurst. When Sir Robert was created Earl of Orford, she had the King's letters to rank as an Earl's daughter.

Her daughter Mary became the second wife of Lord Cadogan in 1777, and her son Charles married Joanna, eldest daughter of Sir Patrick Murray of Ochtertyre, and resided here many years, until after 1829. The widow, Mrs. Joanna Churchill, continued to reside at the Oaks till her death in 1846, at the age of ninety-five.

In later times the Blaines had it, and it is now the property of Mrs. Entwistle.

BANGOR LODGE.

This house has been greatly enlarged by its present owner, General Michael—almost, in fact, rebuilt. It was originally a small cottage residence erected towards the latter end of the last century by a Mr. Baldwinson, whose wife, Mrs. Jemima Baldwinson, had formerly been in the service of Lady Harewood. Their niece, Mrs. Holmes, subsequently resided there. The Hon. Miss Warde, who lodged at the house for some time, became the purchaser of it. She left it to her nephew, Lord Bangor, from whom it was bought by General Michael.

The road to Swinley through Sunninghill Bog passed nearer to the house, but has recently been turned more to the south and much improved.

---

* See Journal of Miss Berry, by Lady Teresa Lewis, also Walpole's Letters, cix., and Fielding's Life of F. Laurence.

A large tree there, known as the Queen's, or some say King's Oak, is said to have been planted by a member of the royal family after breakfasting at the Lodge, while in the occupation of one of the royal yeoman prickers; but I am assured, on the authority of a Mr. Holmes, a son of the niece referred to, that this is erroneous; he is certain that Mr. Baldwinson built the house, and that there was nothing previously on the site. This would dispose of the planting tradition, because the tree is several centuries old. The story which Mr. Holmes received from his great uncle was that George IV. once took shelter beneath it from a storm, and that while waiting there, Mr. Baldwinson dried his coat, and the tree was always afterwards called the King's Oak.

Independently of the old farmhouse now standing in the orchard below, there was, I am told, a still older cottage there, which was pulled down in 1832, and the materials used in the erection of a house on the Ascot Road, now the residence of Mr. Barr Brown.

CHAPTER XXVI.

The Wells.

> "And I have shadowed many a group
> Of beauties that were born
> In teacup times of hood and hoop,
> Or while the patch was worn."

THERE is another house in the parish that must not be forgotten—the old Wells Inn. It was in the valley below the church, on the margin of Ascot Heath, or, more correctly speaking, of Bagshot Heath, as it stands on the left-hand side of the road.

This old roadside inn, of the seventeenth century, was pulled down only about five or six years ago, and a new sham Gothic house, with modern "tap," received its license and its name, but can never sustain its old associations. Before, however, they quite fade away, let us endeavour to preserve them; for

> "Imagination fondly stoops to trace
> The parlour splendours of that festive place."

What a flood of old traditions this fragment of our history brings to light! Round it gather some of the most lively memories of our quiet village.

As to the date of the house, I have been informed that the old fireplace in the kitchen was the most ancient portion of it, and somewhere showed the date 1557; but that may have been merely a farmhouse, for I can find no notice of any place of entertainment here so early as that; the house we remember was of a later date.

The first person who kept the Wells that I can trace was John Hatch, who was there in 1721. In 1754 Davis was its proprietor; he seems to have been succeeded by one Richard Hodges, who was there in 1770; then came David Bronsveldt, who had it

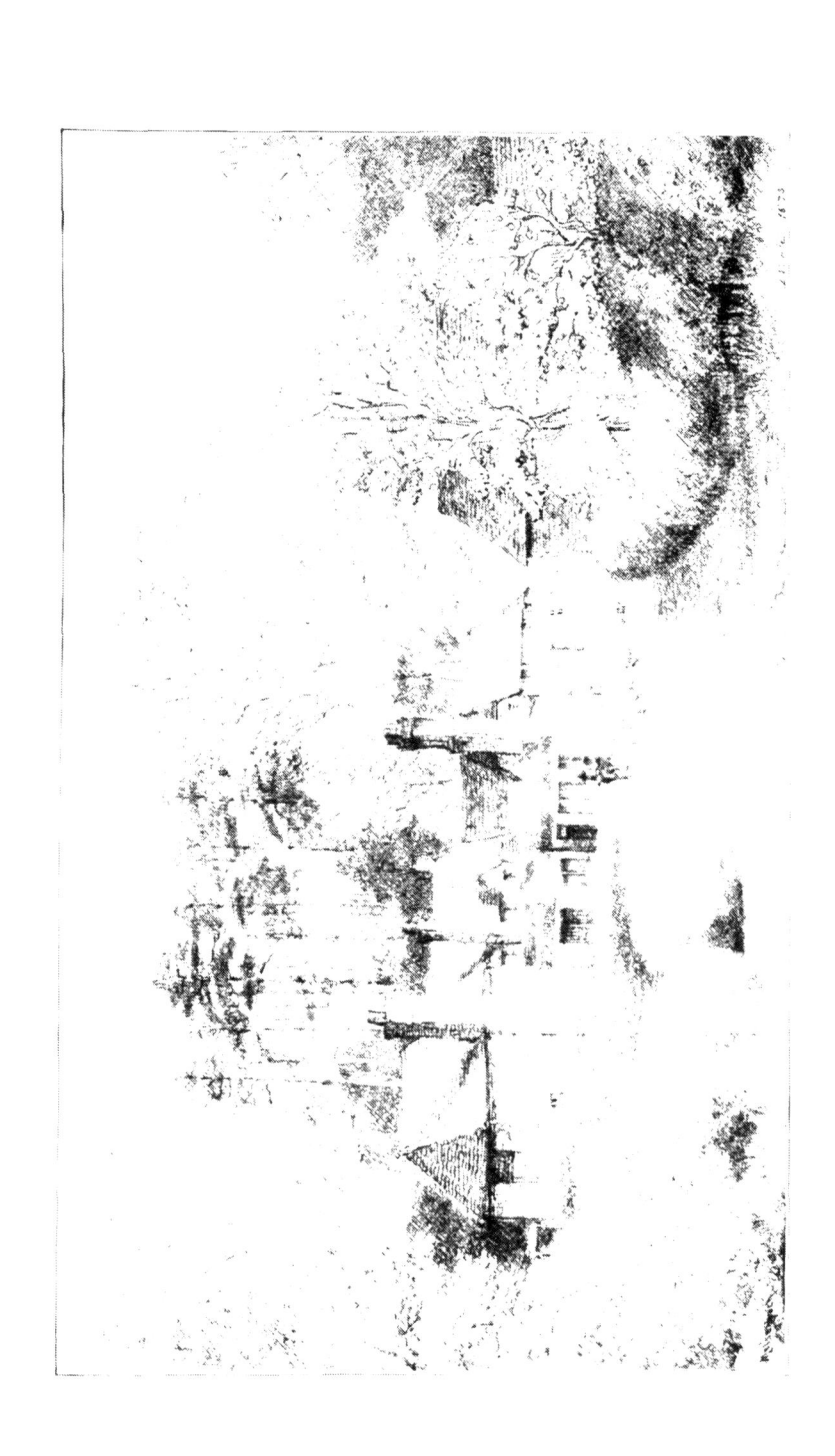

for many years, but failed there. In 1794 J. Marshall took it, and held it during perhaps its gayest time; in 1802 came Larmer, and afterwards Dellar, Dilly, the Walpoles, and lastly, in its fall, Stevens.

It doubtless owed its earliest notice to its springs. The "Wells" by the red stream of Swinley attracted in some way, I imagine, the notice of royalty or royalty's physician, and the fortune of the little Forest house was made.

But of these "Wells" how little do we know beyond the fact of their being held in great repute during the eighteenth century.

Bath and Tonbridge Wells were earlier, and more famous, but not so select in their company as Sunninghill. At Bath the pump-room was practically open to all, and you might find yourself dancing with your own footman, or at least your tailor; a state of things which Humphrey Clinker describes as "a monstrous jumble of heterogeneous principles," and "was worse than debasing the gold coin of the nation!" But at Sunninghill there was no accommodation for the million.

The grave and the gay, the learned student from his college, the blue-stockings from their salon, the bright young beauties from the drawing-rooms of the capital, and the fops from the gaming-table at White's, all came to this fountain in the Forest, and were made whole, or believed they were.

Now all its glory is departed and forgotten.

I once thought I should like to taste the water; but when the landlord brought me to it, we found, alas! that nature had covered the well over with a gauzy veil of bright verdure. Its history has been covered up almost as effectually, and no one has thought it worth while to reproduce it. You must toil through the letters and diaries of the last two centuries, and from the most unlikely corners pick out the fragments that will throw light on it, and then *cui bono?*

At the outset of my inquiry, I thought perhaps we might trace the origin of these Wells to the reign of Queen Anne, for her Majesty evidently believed in the efficacy of the "water-cure." Her father, strangely enough, just before her little brother's christening was to come off, advised her to go to Bath! It was an age of quackery. Look into any old newspaper of the day, and so marvellous were the certain cures of the eighteenth century, that the only wonder is that a single disease has come down to us of the nineteenth.

For every malady, too, water was the remedy. In 1702, when Queen Anne was touching a crowd of infatuated creatures for the evil at Bath and Whitehall, a common quack medicine was advertised for its absolute cure, in presumptuous competition with royal beneficence. Wells were all the rage. Bath, Tonbridge, Sunninghill, Hampstead, and Epsom were the most fashionable, but in 1700 a new one was opened at Richmond, and a spring at Kingston Wood was being tried by the Faculty. It was then, no doubt, I at first thought, that the excellent virtues of our Wells were brought to the notice of royalty, just at that time taking its pastime in our forest, and terribly assailed now and then by attacks of the gout. I find Sunninghill Wells noticed in a pamphlet giving an account of England by the Rev. Francis Brokesly of Shottesbroke, dated 1711, wherein, referring to the mineral waters of the country, he says, "To omit the celebrated springs at Tonbridge, Epsom, &c., I shall not need to tell you of the Sunninghill waters, which are of the finest kind; nor of Holy John, commonly called Folly John, waters of the second sort." After searching, however, the old papers for some years previously to that time, I could find no mention whatever of our Wells, nor are they included in a pamphlet on the natural history of the chalybeate waters of England by Benjamin Allen, M.B., in 1703, although he describes thirty-two places famous for them.

But a little further research has established their much earlier existence, and brought to light an interesting incident in their annals.

So early as 1666 two of the most brilliant of seventeenth-century worthies came as pilgrims here. We may smile at their credulity when it leaves us such pleasant associations.

At that time there was residing at Oxford one Dr. David Thomas, an eminent physician, and member of the celebrated "Invisible College," so glorious in its after career.* In 1666 John Locke became

---

* During the turmoil and trouble of the Civil War a few kindred spirits met, almost by stealth, for interchange of thought in experimental philosophy, at first in London, till the plague drove them to Oxford, where they assembled at the lodgings of Dr. Wilkins, the Warden of Wadham. Here these "learned and curious" gentlemen, who became known as the "Invisible College," or, as they termed themselves, the "Philosophical College," applied themselves to the study of nature, and became the Royal Society, under the auspices of which they laid the foundation of that splendid edifice of natural philosophy, of which we are all now so proud. They survived the torrent of ridicule and contempt with which their first essays were met, and although they seriously countenanced the theory that the barnacle-shells on the rocks gave birth to barnacle-geese, that was not to their shame, but the contrary, as showing what our knowledge of natural history was, on which they worked out so splendid a result.

his assistant or junior partner.* Locke's fellow-student, Richard Lower, had just discovered the medicinal value of the Astrop Wells in Northamptonshire; and Lord Ashley, afterwards first Earl of Shaftesbury, then suffering from a serious malady, wrote to Thomas for a dozen bottles of this water. Through this Locke became introduced to him. They met, and were charmed with one another. On his Lordship's leaving Oxford, he went to Sunninghill, and made Locke promise to follow him thither; and here in our village the brilliant talker and the thoughtful unimpassioned student spent together the first fortnight in August 1666. And the most momentous fortnight it was, probably, in Locke's life; for then, alternating between two opinions, it finally determined him to physic instead of divinity, and made Lord Ashley's London house his home for sixteen years—indeed till the Earl's death. Momentous was this visit in every way, for it nourished a friendship damaging to Locke's reputation, and opens an interesting question as to whether Macaulay and others, who have painted Lord Shaftesbury so utterly black, have troubled to inquire whether his character had no bright spots as well as black ones in it. Surely so acute a mind as Locke's could hardly debase itself so low as to contract a lifelong friendship with a man who had no redeeming virtue whatever in his nature. When the patron fell, Locke stood by him, when he might have thrown him over. There must have been some latent unsuspected kindliness in the man's breast hidden away for his friends, or we shall make Locke as base as the Chancellor.

Now although this shows that the Sunninghill Wells were famous before 1666, it does not clear up the question of their discovery; it might have been in the gloomy days of the Commonwealth, or the time of Charles I., or even earlier. Lord Holland, we know, had faith in waters; but I should rather incline to attribute it to Sir Thomas Aylesbury, or some of his science-loving friends. Warner, one of the original members of the Royal Society, was in the habit of spending his summer with his patron, Sir Thomas Aylesbury, at Cranbourn. In 1632 Edward Hyde was often there courting, and in after life became Locke's particular friend when Chancellor of the University. Viscount Mordaunt was also his patron, while Prince Rupert was at the old tower, which later on was the home of Boyle's nephew, "poor old Ranelagh." Locke must here have met his old Somerset-shire-country folk, the Babers, who were then living at Sunninghill;

---

* See Fox Bourne's Life of John Locke; Spratt's Hist. of Royal Society; Life of Hon. R. Boyle, first Earl of Shaftesbury, by W. D. Christie; and Philosophical Transactions.

and Cowley was not far off at Chertsey, "writing up," at Evelyn's request, the poor languishing Royal Society, that had a King for its founder, but sadly lacked a Mæcenas; for this object could he only find an inspiration, " it would hang the most heroic wreath about his temples," as Evelyn well prophesied. So altogether Sunninghill may be said to have had an atmosphere strongly charged, as it were, with the electricity of science.

However, resuming the more recent history of these Wells, in 1767 the Vicar writes: "Sunninghill is and has been of late years much resorted to by persons of great rank and fortune for its salutary waters, for ye wholesomeness of ye air and its agreeable situation."

When houses in the neighbourhood were to be let, they were invariably described as being near to "the celebrated Wells," and apartments were secured for the season wherever they could be found.

In a letter from Mrs. Carter (Miss Carter) to Mrs. Vesey in June 1763, she says: "Mrs. Dunbar is very busy settling herself at Lovell farm; Mrs. J. Pitt is at Sunninghill, much improved in her health, less probably from drinking the waters than from seeing Miss Pitt much better than she was in town."

Between the old Wells house, at the left hand of the illustration, and the road stood, until about twenty years ago, a long ballroom or breakfast-room opening into the garden. I find it noticed so early as 1754, when it is advertised that "On Monday the 20th of this instant will be a public breakfast and music at Mr. Davis's long room, and will continue every Monday during the summer season. Each person to pay one shilling at coming in as usual." In after years, when a band was added as an attraction, it was especially notified that there would be "nothing extra for the music." It must have been on to the lawn from this room that the powdered fops of the day led forth the high-heeled beauties to the dance. They "did" the waters, stopped to breakfast, and then a few fiddles, as Mrs. Carter tells us, set all the girls dancing. What charming simplicity of manners! Shall we ever get back to it?

It was here, I daresay, in one of these leafy alleys, that a little incident occurred—we must not call it scandal—of which, as Charles Lamb truly says, all true history is full; but it caused some sensation among the fashionables at Sunninghill and in society.

In 1746 the Lady Mary Campbell, youngest daughter of the Dowager-Duchess of Argyle, was staying here, and here accordingly came Lord Coke, her admirer, to urge his suit for her hand.

Now the writers of fiction and the painters of the time have made us quite familiar with the exquisite way in which, on bended knee and with the lady's hand to his lips, a well-instructed cavalier made his "declaration," but history has not handed down to us how the ladies acted their part. Not often, I am sure, as this fair young Scot did, if that interesting old gossip of the century, Horace Walpole, is correct when he tells us,[*] "Since he [Lord Coke] has been at Sunninghill with Lady Mary, she has made him a 'declaration' in form, that she hates him, and always did, and always will." "At White's he has been advised to shoot himself, and has promised to consider of it."

They were afterwards married, however, in 1747, and a pretty life they led; there was a duel or something like it at Sunninghill, and a lawsuit somewhere else. He died in 1753, and the title became extinct in that family in 1759.

We can almost re-people the place by the help of contemporary literature, say in 1769. There were the Babers from Sunninghill Park; hardly the Crutchleys, for it was in this very year Mr. Jeremiah Crutchley, a young bachelor, purchased the place; General Lindsay from the Cedars; the Pitts from the manor-house; the Churchills from the Oaks; and now and then the great folk from Cumberland Lodge and Cranborne Lodge, and the other houses in the Park. The Buckworths had just left; but perhaps the largest party of all came from the old mansion of King's Wick, just above the Wells. This old place was at that time the seat of Sir John Elwill, the Member for Guildford; but for some reason he vacated the house for a time, and let it, as is so fully described elsewhere, and we find the visitors who were lodging there in daily attendance at the Wells—Mrs. Montague, Mrs. Carter, and others of the best literary society of the day. Lady Grey too was there, as "melancholy as ever," we are told.

Colonel and Mrs. Dunbar brought over a houseful of friends, among them Lord Irnham (then in the decline of life), and with him one of his daughters, a young lady of some note or notoriety. This was probably Elizabeth, the younger, no great beauty. She was a sister of that Colonel Luttrell whose name is best known as the Government candidate against Wilkes in his celebrated contest for Westminster.

"Junius" has transmitted to us Lord Irnham's character, with which, therefore, I will not meddle. But never to these garden

---

[*] Walpole's Letters, vol. ii. p. 114.

assemblies came a more dangerous young beauty than this Miss Luttrell's elder sister, Ann, who had married —— Horton, Esq., of Catton, Staffordshire, and soon became a widow; and here very probably too it was that in 1770 she met our royal neighbour of Cumberland Lodge, Frederick, the second Duke, brother of George III. She was then, we are told, "a young widow of twenty-four, extremely pretty, not handsome, very well made, with the most amorous eyes in the world and eye-lashes a yard long; coquette beyond measure, artful as Cleopatra, and complete mistress of all her passions and projects." *

By these long eye-lashes and other charms, Frederick, royal Duke though he was, soon became entangled, and, much to the consternation and anger of his royal father, he married her in November 1771.

The Royal Marriage Act soon followed.

In a letter from Mrs. Carter to Mrs. Vesey, 23rd August 1769, she describes, while staying at King's Wick, her "rambles without any companions but my own reveries over these wild heaths all day long;" and then people attributed all the benefit to the "waters!" She had been down to her morning's devotion at the springs; the Dunbar family had gone back to breakfast with Lord Irnham and Miss Luttrell, and she had come home to prepare for attending Mrs. Montague to Lady Frances Coningsby's, who was also here.

In little clusters on the lawn we can imagine others of a very different stamp: Mrs. Montague, a fine old lady of considerable attractions, was doubtless the object of much attention; in frequent attendance was Mr. Stillingfleet—Benjamin Stillingfleet (a grandson of the great Bishop), who wrote some tracts on natural history, an accomplished gentleman, the great friend of Mr. Aldworth Neville of Stanlake, and of Mr. Uvedale Price, and related to Windham. It was of him that Mrs. Montague said he attempted to destroy "the false shame that attended the devotee to ornithology."

Then there was the eccentric genius Lord Lyttelton, the Trumballs of Easthampstead, and many others of the neighbouring folk. Shortly before this one might have seen another group of some note here, for Mr. Pitt and Lady Hester and their children, including the great little William, were doubtless often here during their residence at Sunninghill.

These Wells were patronised for some years, and in 1780 the "Faculty" thought the waters necessary for Mrs. Vesey.

---

* Walpole's Letters, vol. v. p. 347.

But as the century advanced, a change came over the fortunes of the little inn: the water-cure became a failure; and the fashionable world, more skittish than old Fuller's Berkshire steeds, had turned its back on Æsculapius; the water-drinkers lost their faith, and the waters therefore their virtues, and so the dilettanti of the earlier part of the century were elbowed out by the sportsmen and the soldiers of the later time.

The decline is alluded to by the author of "Les Délices des Chateaux Royaux" (Pote) in 1785. He says:—

"The Wells are neatly designed, and the gardens laid out with some degree of taste, and here were wont to be held public breakfasts and assemblies; but we are sorry to add these meetings have of late been much lessened."

An old lady, still living, tells how she was brought as a child to Sunninghill to "drink the waters."

But in 1792 it was only a case for advertising; and the *Reading Mercury* proclaimed their virtues as equal to the German Spa; and Mr. Larmer in 1802 announces that "the waters are in the highest perfection."

Now the picturesque costumes of the age are gone, swept away in the revolution of fashion, with the dances at the Wells. "The heir with roses in his shoes;" his fascinating representative with flapped waistcoat, silk stockings, and brand-new buckles; and later on, the beau, with that most artistic of hats, the three-cornered one, with which little Samuel Rogers chased the butterflies at Stoke Newington in 1772. All are gone! Of the ladies' toilettes, we need hardly lament the loss of the head-gear, towering at one time so "elated," at another so "exceedingly reserved," and those amazing hoops,* against which all that poor Addison and the caricaturists could do was useless; although we may have a lingering regret for one or two charming compensations, on thought of which even the horrors of the "patch" may be forgiven. How becomingly did many a fair face rest on the studied disarrangement of the "Steinkirk," with its folds of fine Mechlin lace; a dainty foot, too, in high-heeled shoes and buckles, looked daintier still; and how wonderfully effective was that choicest baton of the coquette, the fan, so fashionable at the beginning of the eighteenth century!

---

* See Addison's Papers, No. 129.
When the beauty of Handel's "Messiah" was first recognised in Dublin in 1742, such crowds were drawn, that an advertisement was issued begging the ladies for the occasion to discard their hoops.

With all this, a few fiddles on the lawn soon worked a disenchantment: a minuet or a country-dance showed that there still breathed beneath this mimic stateliness a genuine nature.

But it is all gone now. Half a century passes, and this is how the young Peninsular heroes, of whom we shall presently speak, were attired when they shone in the ballroom at the Wells—say a Colonel of the Old Blues* :—

"A swallow-tail coat, with large red facings, collar and cuffs elaborately covered with gold lace, epaulettes, white kerseymere breeches, white silk stockings, evening-shoes, or 'pumps,' as they were called, and a huge cocked hat and feathers."

To all this we must say adieu. Adieu to these country-dances, and a long adieu to the old inn itself.

---

* Lord William Lennox's Recollections, 1814.

CHAPTER XXVII.

The Camps.

"Ah! then and there was hurrying to and fro,
And gathering tears and tremblings of distress,
And cheeks all pale, which but an hour ago
Blushed at the praise of their own loveliness."

BY far the most stirring period of our quiet history, and the most prosperous for the "Wells," was that of its military life. From the earliest establishment of our standing army, this neighbourhood was selected for its training ground. The first great camp was that formed on Hounslow Heath, when King James massed thirteen thousand of his troops there, as the Londoners thought only to overawe them; but that ominous cheer that rose from the ranks, and smote the royal ear so unpleasantly, when the Bishops were released from the Tower, made him and his court also think that the camp should be farther away.

Ashford Common and Bagshot Heath were afterwards chosen. One of the first in this district was at Ascot in 1739, when George II. was alarmed at the prospects of the Pretender, and we were on the eve of war with Spain. The encampment was on the hill a little to the north-west of the Ascot Schools; its lines are still visible. On the return of the army from Culloden in 1746, several of the regiments that came south were encamped in this country. Lord Albemarle, the Duke's aide-de-camp, was then living at Bagshot Lodge, and Johnson's dragoons and Hawley's "ragged" fellows were quartered about the village.

Ten years later came war with France, and troops were mustering on our heaths. In 1755 and 1756, Colonel Honeywood's regiment, and Colonel Wolf's, so memorable in after time, were quartered at Bagshot and Windlesham. In the neighbouring county, twelve thousand

Hanoverians lay encamped on Coxheath. The Black Hole at Calcutta reminds us of our struggle in the East, while in the West we were disputing with the French the possession of our American colonies. Another ten years brought us into a much more serious conflict with the Colonists themselves, and then again we were surrounded by camps. Our early naval successes, too, caused an outburst of delight in this neighbourhood. Egham was illuminated in 1762 on Admiral Keppel's taking the Havannah. The King in 1777 reviewed the Royal Horse Guards Blue on Ascot Heath, and in 1781 the Inniskillen Dragoons were at Maidenhead Thicket. Soon afterwards the peace with America brought our soldiers back, and in 1784 our village was beginning to feel the excitements of a new life. On the sandy hills around, the little white field-tents began to appear; and on the 17th May in that year Prince George of Wales attended a review of the troops on Ascot Heath. The gaiety of the place was much increased by the residence of the Prince at Bagshot, which also gave an impetus both to the hunting and the racing here; but the camps established every year in the neighbourhood still more enlivened it. Thus in September 1786 we get an account of a breakfast at the Wells by "our own correspondent" of the day, in language which I will not spoil. He says, "The public breakfast at Sunninghill Wells on Monday last was uncommonly brilliant; more than two hundred ladies and gentlemen in the first families in the counties of Berks, Surrey, and Bucks were present. The band of music belonging to the camp in the neighbourhood of Sunninghill, consisting of near twenty instruments, played all the time, which added to the personal charms of so many of the ladies, and the gentility of the whole company rendered the celebrity very highly and universally pleasing."

The fiddles did wonders at the beginning of the century, but how "the light of other days" must have paled before such a military band!

In 1788 new regiments were being rapidly formed and trained here; for now from all quarters came rumours of war. The nations were gathering their forces; the raw levies of the country were assembling round our village; and Bagshot Heath, Swinley, Ascot Heath, Winkfield Plain, and Windlesham were becoming the nurseries or training grounds of our infant armies. The whole of our forces did not at the beginning of the century number twelve thousand men,[*] and it was with difficulty in 1738 that the Government induced Parliament to

---

[*] See Debates in Parliament, 1738.

raise them to eighteen thousand. But the storm-cloud, long impending, burst at last; the French Revolution startled the world, and sounded a general note of war throughout Europe.

In May 1792 we were all excitement. The Duke of Richmond and Colonel Moncrieff surveyed the ground at Bagshot Heath for the encampment of seven thousand troops, who were to take up their ground on the 2nd July, and be inspected by the King on the 5th. The objects aimed at were practice in erecting redoubts and field-fortifications, and giving instruction to our young officers, but especially to practise the artillery and engineers in new tactics, which were to be generally adopted throughout the army.

At that time we were not actually at war with France, although on the eve of it, and a rumour was raised that this military activity was only induced through a scare. In the House of Lords, Lord Lauderdale fell with fury on the Duke of Richmond. "There is a camp," he cried, "to be formed at Bagshot, to overawe the people of the capital and to stifle their efforts for reform. I declare I am glad the noble Duke is to command that camp. If apostasy can justify promotion, he is the most fit person for that command, General Arnold alone excepted."* It is not surprising that a duel was arranged on this outburst, but it was prevented. The old cry was enough, at least, to postpone the encampment from the 2nd to the 23rd July. On that day, from all quarters there was a gathering of troops; the artillery from Woolwich and regiments of all arms mustered on the various eminences of Bagshot Heath, which extended then for many miles round. The place of rendezvous was at Wickham Bushes, three miles from Bagshot, and the right of the camp rested on the hill which the ancient Roman legions had chosen seventeen hundred years before, the earthworks of which are still to be seen. On the 24th there was a brilliant review and sham-fight before the King, surrounded by a staff of the highest officers. By his side rode a young civilian, not then thirty-three years of age, to whom much deference was paid. This young man was William Pitt, the Prime Minister, who was there scrutinising with his own eyes the early organisation of England's newly-trained levies. But the great display was to be on the 7th of August, when for three days this little army was to manœuvre before the royal family and a most distinguished company, military and civilian. Over two hundred thousand persons were estimated to have been present. The people showed an intense loyalty; and in the midst

---

* See Great Governing Families of England, by Sandford and Townsend.

of their excitement the Duke of York produced to the Queen a letter he had received announcing that the Prussians had actually marched on the 4th to attack the French.

The nation and its young Minister knew well what was coming; they did not know, however, that on that very day, the 10th of August, while they were storming the heights of "Cæsar's Camp" in bloodless fury, the Parisian rabble were storming the Tuileries in frightful earnest. The tocsin had sounded, and the camp broke up the next day, to find that war was now inevitable. In the following spring it came. As early as the 25th February 1793 a body of troops left their camp at Swinley, marched to the Horse Guards, and were there paraded before the King and the Queen, the royal Dukes and the three elder Princesses, who all accompanied them on their march as far as Greenwich, where they embarked under the Duke of York to join the allies in Holland.

In June the King was inspecting a camp at Ascot, riding along the lines with the royal family, fostering the high spirits of the troops. The Guards distinguished themselves in the campaign, although it was a failure. That of 1794 was still more disastrous. We began, as usual, badly; but a latent power was about to exert itself, that soon set things right again. The great naval fights were coming that saved England from destruction and established her supremacy on the seas.

The French were preparing to invade England, and the people were at the "red heat" of patriotism. Subscription lists were opened in every village. The patriotic pulse beat faster here than in most places, owing to the fact that almost every cottage hereabouts had sent some inmate to the ranks, and almost every house of the better class was the home of some naval or military captain.

Several infantry regiments had been quartered in our neighbourhood, and Ascot Heath, New Lodge Green, near Braywood, and Warfield were cavalry stations.

In June 1798 another camp was ordered in the Forest, and a battalion from each of the three regiments of Guards camped close to our village, near to the recently erected Nunnery; their well may be seen, I am told, to this day in the garden of one of the new houses there, which has accordingly been christened "Guards Well."

Here, on the 29th July, the King reviewed them at seven o'clock in the morning from King's Beech Hill, which overlooked their encampment, and afterwards started off to St. James's. This beautiful hill was then crowned with a clump of fine beeches. The spot was a favourite one with the King for military evolutions; one of the straight drives from Ascot led directly to it.

Ascot Heath had been very early chosen as a review-ground for the cavalry; but on the 30th of July 1798 an unfortunate accident happened there. As the 1st Dragoon Guards were delivering their last "grand charge" at a review, three of the men fell and were ridden over, and one was killed. On account of this, His Majesty ordered the place of review to be changed to Winkfield Plain, "the ground on Ascot Heath not only being rough, but very swampy." At this eventful time, the King and his sons were working hard with the army, and inspecting troops everywhere. On the 10th of August he was out at half-past seven in the morning on horseback to review the 11th and 15th regiments of Light Horse, on what was then called, not Sunninghill, but Bagshot Heath, "where the Duke of York met His Majesty for a grand field-day round King's Beech Hill." "The troops," we are informed, "made an excellent appearance on the different heights of the Heath, both cavalry and artillery."

On the 16th of August the encampment on Walton Common was inspected; and the next day His Majesty reviewed the 7th Dragoons on Winkfield Plain, accompanied by the Prince of Wales, the Duke of York, the Prince of Orange, and the Princesses. At the close of the proceedings, "the royal party paid a visit to the Earl of Uxbridge, at his seat at Sunninghill, and there partook of an elegant entertainment."

The Wells was meanwhile having a famous time of it. Every Monday there was a public breakfast at one o'clock in the day, and, as an attraction to the young ladies, it was advertised that there would be "a band of martial music in the gardens."

Every week or two a ball was given there in the evening; and "mine host" did not omit to announce when the nights were moonlight.

But amid all these festivities, we never, perhaps, witnessed so gay a time as in August of that year, and Thursday the 23rd was the gayest of the gay. All the cavalry regiments encamped at Swinley, together with the Staffordshire Militia, were ordered to take up their ground near Hatchet Lane, where the general officers met the royal family; the troops then marched to the top of King's Beech Hill, where the Staffordshire regiment of foot was planted to defend it against the heavy cavalry, supported by the 7th, 11th, and 16th Light

Horse; the troops on the hill were supposed to represent the English, and the attacking cavalry the French. A spirited action ensued; the French, of course, were repulsed. It was an imposing spectacle, and gave great satisfaction, we are told, to an immense concourse of spectators, especially as the French were beaten. To us now it would be a fine sight, but we can hardly realise the pitch of frenzied excitement with which the people, who believed their homes and hearths were in jeopardy at that moment, witnessed such a scene. The King and his splendid staff shone out that day in the new Windsor uniform, which just that summer had been altered, and very handsome it was; a light blue frock, with black velvet collar and cuffs, trimmed (in full dress) with gold. After this review the Duke of York gave a great entertainment to the royal family at Swinley Lodge; a pavilion was erected in the pleasure-grounds in which they dined; the King stood up at the height of their enthusiasm and drank health to them all, and hoped to see them there again next year. Dances followed, the servants and rustics dancing on the lawn.

The King took particular notice of an old man, a baker at Swinley, seventy-two years of age, who said he could dance till twelve o'clock, and walk twenty miles afterwards. He told His Majesty and the Duke of York that he remembered the camp at Windsor fifty-eight years before.

Lord Uxbridge was living at Sunninghill; his high-spirited son had early shown his patriotism by raising on his father's estate this very regiment of Staffordshire Volunteers, which subsequently became known as the 80th foot. He served with distinction under the Duke of York, and on his return to England was transferred to the 16th Light Dragoons, which had also taken part in our review; but he had left it the year before for the 7th Light Dragoons, also in action that day. He practised on these wild commons a new method of cavalry evolution, that soon covered his men with glory in all the encounters they were destined to have, and most of all in that great day at Waterloo that lost him a leg, but gained him a Marquisate. It was thus this young soldier, Henry William Paget, Lord Uxbridge, became Marquis of Anglesea.

On the last day of the month the King visited the troops again to say adieu to them before they broke up their camp; they were drawn up in line on the roadside on Ascot Heath, and there His Majesty passed them in review, and thanked them for their good behaviour.

Sunninghill was all gaiety in the evening again, with a ball and supper at the Wells, given by the particular desire of the officers of the Swinley camp.* They danced in the long room I have mentioned, which was pulled down only about five-and-twenty years ago. What a variety of scenes, grave and gay, that inn on the heath must have witnessed! In the dances here our young soldiers made life go merrily enough through the summer, and distinguished themselves in many a field to which they were hurrying. Among them was a dashing young ensign (36th Regiment), as good at a cross-country gallop after the fox as he was at a minuet at the Wells. He was but a boy when encamped at Swinley, for he was only sixteen when he was present at Rorica and Vimiera; but he more distinguished himself afterwards in another field as Sir Roderick Murchison. Sir Frederick Ouseley also, the Oriental scholar, in a similar way left his regiment, the 8th Dragoons, after the campaign of 1794, to shine still more in literature. All men were in training then. As early as 1760, Gibbon had been "playing at soldiers" in the Hampshire Militia at Arlesford. They were young in harness in those days. Sir William F. P. Napier was promoted to a lieutenancy at sixteeen.

Less romantic scenes, however, occurred in this long room sometimes; for in August 1800 a certain Captain Bruhl was tried there by court-martial for being drunk whilst on the King's guard at Cumberland Lodge. General Cowell was president. The prisoner pleaded the heat of the weather, among other excuses, but was found guilty. The ballroom, by the bye, did service of another kind at a later period; for in 1827 it was hired for our church service when the old church was demolished, but the Sunday before and the Sunday after the Ascot week were excepted from the hiring. But here for a moment we must halt.

The eighteenth century closed in depression and gloom. The public funds had fallen to a point never before touched; in August 1798 Consols were down to $47\frac{1}{2}$; and after two bad harvests there was a scarcity of bread. When, in 1796, wheat fell 17s. in a fortnight—to between 45s. and 60s.—the people were so rejoiced at Staines and Egham that they set the church-bells ringing.

The nineteenth century opened in anxiety; the nation was fully committed to war. Sunninghill, however, amid the general gloom, was still enjoying a life of exceptional excitement. The coming and going of troops, the reviews, the public breakfasts at the Wells,

---

* *Reading Mercury*, August 27th.

the balls that honoured the arrival or bade farewell to the departing regiments, stimulated its gaiety, and drew to the place a fashionable society. The good families in the neighbourhood kept "open house" to their gallant visitors, and so in its own way did the Wells.

The encampments continued, and more men were quartered round our village than twenty years before the whole forces of the kingdom amounted to. Then, as we have seen, we could not have mustered 20,000 men; now we had over 200,000 under arms. This very first summer of the century, our hills around were bristling with bayonets. In May it was announced that there were to be six regiments of cavalry, of 800 men each, encamped at Swinley, two mounted troops, and a large park of artillery; at Bagshot a very large encampment of infantry, 3000 Guards, and twelve regiments of the line, amounting to about 15,000. The head-quarters of His Royal Highness, the commander-in-chief, were at Bagshot House. At the risk of wearying my readers, I must notice one more incident, as it so well carries us back, and tells of the state of the country when under the apprehension of invasion. On the 17th July 1800, the King reviewed the whole of these encampments, amounting to 32,000 men, on Winkfield Plain and Ascot Heath. Among the ranks there appeared "a small squadron of French emigrants." The Duke of York acted as commander-in-chief, and the Prince of Wales with a large bough of laurel in his hat marched on to the ground at the head of the Guards. The light infantry of the Guards wore "new hats like the Austrians." Swinley was quite the rage. The Princesses appeared in white "with light village cloaks," and they and all the young ladies of fashion adopted "the *Swinley slouch*, ornamented with a small military plume!" The royal family afterwards dined at Cumberland Lodge, and a ball was given there in the afternoon, but it was over at eight, when the King went off to Windsor.* Seldom had there been such a sight, and in order to witness it many had slept the previous night in their carriages. "At the great lodge the entertainment was very splendid;" covers were laid for 330; the tureens in the King's tent, we are especially told, "were of solid gold, the others of silver;" and to heighten the enthusiasm, the trophies of war appeared—"eight magnificent Eastern tents, taken from Tippoo Sultaun, were erected on the lawn."

This excitement lasted yet some years, but at last, in 1814, came peace. The allied sovereigns had been fêted in London, and

---

* See *Reading Mercury*.

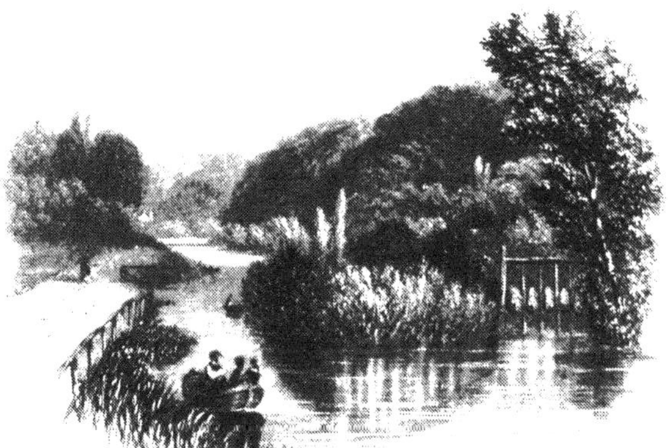

the Duke of Wellington wherever he went. In August he reviewed his fine regiment, the Blues, on Winkfield Plain, in the presence of the young Prince Frederick of Orange and a large staff; and on his return to Windsor was presented with the freedom of the Corporation in a gold snuff-box. To close the gaiety of our neighbourhood, the officers of the Duke's regiment shortly afterwards fêted their local friends at a delightful water-party at Cliefden, the residence of the Countess of Orkney. In September they had some fun chasing the deer out of our forest, and "all went merry as a marriage-bell." These were the sunny hours of the soldier's life, before the storm burst in the great fight at Waterloo, which closed the glorious campaign of the following summer, and ended our little life of excitement.

Of recent encampments, none perhaps is more noteworthy than that of the Highlanders under Sir Colin Campbell in 1853, before they embarked for service on the heights of Sebastopol. The clump of Scotch firs on Chobham Common round which they lay, one of the most conspicuous objects in the neighbourhood, marks the site of their encampment.

CHAPTER XXVIII.

The Great Park and Virginia Water.

THE old park of Windsor is of great antiquity, dating no doubt from Saxon days. It lay then adjacent to the palace of Old Windsor, before the fortress on the hill had been erected. It is said that the earliest notice of a park at Windsor is in the time of Henry I.; its existence, I think, is implied in the Chertsey charters, where mention is made of "the new harbour."* Edward III., we know, among his great works at Windsor, made another park; for in his grant of the office of constable to Helmingo Legette† we read of "Novum parcum de Windsor."

It is of the Great Park only that I propose to speak; and first of that portion of it lying on the east of our parish, comprising Virginia Water.

This, among artificial lakes, is one of the finest in England. It covers about 150 acres, and its length from China Island to the iron gates is said to be two miles and two hundred yards. It is better known, I venture to say, by the stranger, who travels hundreds of miles to see it, than by many who live on its borders; and yet it is a charming piece of water. One cannot expect, of course, the wild beauty of a Highland loch among the lonely hills, but when the woods are bright with the young foliage of spring, or on a fine autumnal evening when glowing in their decay, this Virginia Water of ours is a beautiful lake.

From the high ground of "Hangman's Hill," where the clock-case tower now stands, we get a glimpse through a break or two in the plantations of what was once by far the best view of it, and may realise to perfection the homely beauty of our Berkshire scenery.

---

* Tighe and Davis, Hist. of Windsor, vol. i. p. 30.   † See Cal. Rot. Pat., 43 E1. III.

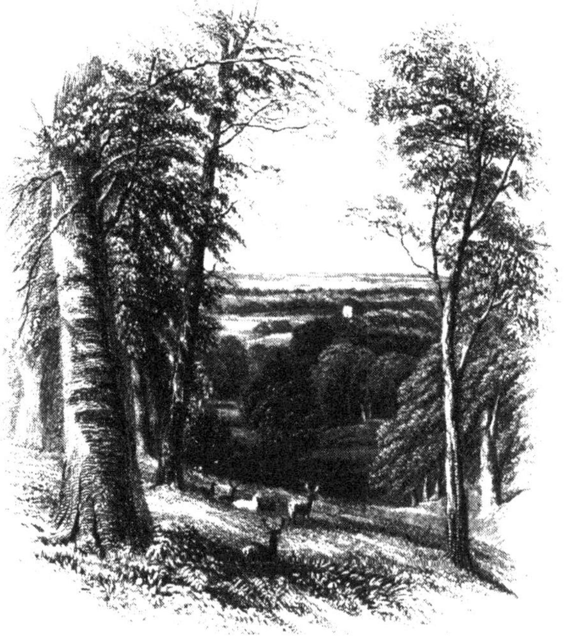

Beneath you lies the Roman road, issuing from its deep cutting on the left, striking across the valley towards the heights of the Belvidere; on the other side, you look down on the sunlit water, which carries the eye along its silver stream towards Sunninghill, where it has its source.

We may trace back this moorland river to its origin among the great oaks of Swinley and the low lands bordering it, whence, after flowing in a rapid current of red waters through our village, augmented by the Blackwick stream, it hurried on to the Lord's Mill, and entered the Great Park near China Island: there it widened in beds of reed and rush, the home of water-fowl of many kinds, and the favourite haunt of the crane and the bittern; becoming still further swollen by the stream from Sunninghill Park, it formed what was afterwards known as the Virginia River; and passing by the ancient manor-house, which stood where the Fishing Temple Lodge is, it finally flowed away over the bank by Harpesford towards the south.

"And so by many winding nooks he strays"

to join the waters of the Thames. It was called the Bourne, and throughout its course it was a beautiful forest stream, open on all sides to the "sullen purple moor," save where, as at the great coppice, it was closed in by the thick foliage of its woods.

But all is now changed. Selmere has lost its wild character, and become deepened into Silwood Lake. It has seen its harvest-fields come and pass away, and the wild deer of the forest are superseded by the tame ones of the park.

Nor, when we enter the royal domain itself, do we find it different. Time has played sad havoc with its old houses and old roads, so that it is extremely difficult to recall its ancient history or identify the present with the past.

In such questions Norden's maps, published 1607, are most valuable, and although we cannot expect in them the accuracy of our modern Ordnance Surveys, they are substantially correct. They enable us, by the aid of certain great natural features, which no time can efface, to clear up our difficulties. We learn from them that there was "a park conjoining the castle, called the Little Park, whereof Mr. Charles Lister is keeper."

In the Great Park, he says, there were four walks, Norries', Langland's, Greene's, and Haybourne's, and moreover, that, "every of theis walks hath a lodge," M. Haybourne also the manor-house." But before I attempt to fix their location, let me refer to those lasting landmarks, the watercourses. The most important, as also the most transformed of these, was what is known now as Virginia Water, of which I need hardly say that "the great lake of olden time," described by Mr. Harrison Ainsworth, had no existence except as a poetic imagination. In Norden's time it was a mere stream running from west to east, of uniform width, except just before it flowed over the bank at Harpesford, where it ran by or through what was called the Green Pond, which it was destined in after time to absorb. Into this Virginia river, at a point since occupied by the Fishing Temple, ran a tributary stream from a piece of water south-west of Cumberland Lodge, called the "Mistle Pond," which ere long expanded into "the Great Lake." From this we get the name of the present "Mezel Hill." It flowed on, forming three other pools in its course. Almost parallel with this, to the west, came another stream from a spring in the hill, above what Norden calls the "Lepperye" or Leper's Pond, and this entered the same river by the China Island. In the angle formed by the first of these stood the

MANOR LODGE,

an old moated house, much superior to the other lodges, with an entrance by a bridge on the west. There is no doubt whatever as to this site.[*] Norden clearly shows it there, as also does a map at Windsor of 1662, and among the drawings in the Royal Library is one by Paul Sandby, showing an old red brick mansion on that identical spot; and another, taken, as it is described, "from the north side of Virginia river near the Manor Lodge," of which I give an illustration.

I have met with allusion to this house so early as the time of Richard II., when Arnald de Brocas was appointed clerk of the works at "the manor and lodge of the King in Windsor Park." We hear of it again shortly afterwards, when, in 1406, Henry IV. was laid up "at the manor in Windsor Park" with an attack of ague, and having suddenly hurt his leg. In the Calender of State Papers, 24 Henry VI., again, mention is made of the repairs of the "bridge in the King's Manor within Windsor Park," and which without doubt has reference to this place.

---

[*] See Norden's Maps, also Map at Windsor 1662; Roque's Map, 1762; Plan de la Forest de Windsor.

We get a curious notice of it in a letter written at Christmas 1558 * by a Mr. Tyle, its then occupier, to Mr. (afterwards Sir William) More, about five weeks after the accession of Queen Elizabeth; it concludes: "My ladie wold be glad to see yo^u and yor bedfellow here this holydayes. Thus I byd yo^u most hartely farewell from the Manner of the great p'ke of Wyndsor this p'sent Saynt Steevens daye. By yo's to com'and, EDWARD TYLE." †

In 1648 Bulstrode Whitelock became the owner of this manor, walk, and lodge, having resigned his High Stewardship of Greenwich to the Earl of Pembroke in exchange for it; ‡ and it is not at all improbable that it was here he came with his friend Sir Thomas Widrington when he fled out of London to avoid giving countenance to the King's trial, and the fatal issue of it, that he knew so well had been determined on. When he began to distrust his great leader, Cromwell, he undoubtedly came to his lonely moorland mansion to ponder over what it was all drifting to, and to enjoy the relaxation of his forest-hunting.

NORRIS'S LODGE

was at the northernmost entrance to the Great Park, towards the town of Windsor, and seems to have been an addition to it, separately impaled. Between this and the Castle were private meadows, and the road to Frogmore and Datchet. It became afterwards known as Lester's or Leicester's Lodge.

Not far to the south, at a spot near the Long Walk, at which there was formerly a mineral spring, stood

LANGLANDS,

or the Middle Lodge; but of these two houses not a vestige now remains. Of *Green's Lodge*, anciently called Guisne's or Guinness's, the precise site is not exactly known. Norden shows it at a spot west of the Great Cumberland Lake, midway between "Mistle"

---

* See Tighe and Davis, Hist. of Windsor, vol. ii. p. 37; Kempe Loseley MSS.

† This gentleman was of an ancient family here, his ancestor, Thomas Tile, having been Lieutenant to Simon Burley or De Beverley in the time of Richard II.; they were parishioners of Winkfield and Windlesham long afterwards.

‡ See Memoirs of Bulstrode Whitelock, by R. H. Whitelock.

Pond and "Lipperye" Pond; a line drawn from the manor-house to Sandpit Gate would pass through it. It was much nearer, however, to the latter place, and almost in the line of Queen Anne's Avenue.

The old pathway to it from Sunninghill crossed the Silwood stream by a bridge still known as Guinness's bridge.

HAYBOURNE'S LODGE

is to us a still more interesting one. It took its name from one Ric. Haybourne, who, in 1529, is styled late yeoman with the Queen, and was probably the keeper of what was called Haybourne's Walk. This was only little less in extent than Green's; it included what was then known as Blackness Beeches, and a large portion of the park to the north-east of it.

Norden shows the old house standing on the edge of the hill, overlooking "Mistle" Pond towards the south-west, exactly on the spot on which Cumberland Lodge now stands. The principal road from the southern entrance of the park at Blackness Beeches led by the Manor Lodge, and then divided in two ways, one leading up what was known as Long hill towards the north-west to Green's Lodge, and so on due north over Snowdon or Snowdown Hill, and the other to the north-east up Breakheart hill to Master Haybourne's, and thence by the old cross and Holme's hill to Langland's.

What Norden shows in this walk as "the lodge" had doubtless been the keeper's house for centuries. It was this lodge, I believe, which was afterwards the site of the "Banqueting House," then became the Ranger's or Great Lodge, and finally

CUMBERLAND LODGE,

of which I will endeavour now to trace the history.

Charles I., we may remember, in the midst of his troubles in 1644, gave to his faithful secretary, Nicholas, a lease of the parks; but it must have been a hollow affair, for the one had virtually no power to give, what the other had certainly no power to enjoy. We next hear of the Great Park being cut up and allotted to the Roundhead soldiers in lieu of pay, and of its being ploughed, as mentioned in another paper. But when the Restoration came, these questionable dealings were set aside. The rights were certainly a little shadowy, and although Sir Edward Nicholas had what would be termed the nominal right, the great folk were crowding round the restored monarch clamouring for places, and in 1660 Abraham Dowcett and his two sons obtained a grant of the Lodge and Paddock Walk; Henry Hyde of the two walks in Cranbourne Chase; and, in reversion to Nicholas, the keepership of the Great Park was given to Lord Mordaunt, who married one of the "Carey heiresses," and was father of that dashing officer who commanded the Horse Guards at the battle of Steinkirk.

In 1661 one Barry was "to be restrained from ploughing up the meadows in the Great Park, and laying open the gardens and orchards of the new house erected there."* This "new house," I believe, was on the site we are describing.

At this time, the worthy Mr. Nicholas having returned, bethought him of his dormant rights, and petitioned Charles II. in 1662 "for a lease of the Great Park, the custody of which was granted to him by the late King in 1644, on a rent of £5 a year, it having been disparked, enclosed, and tenements built thereon during the usurpation, and cannot be re-imparked without great cost. But should His Majesty choose to impark it, he will resign his lease, retaining custody of herbage and pannage only."

The reply to this petition was a warrant, in March 1662, "to dispark 3410 acres in Windsor Great Park, to grant all the deer therein to Secretary Nicholas, to discharge all the keepers; also a grant to Nicholas of the Park, with the houses thereto belonging, on a rental of £200; with a proviso empowering the King to restore the Park and replenish it with deer, if he choose so to do, granting to Nicholas the keepership thereof."

The King evidently resumed his ownership a few years afterwards, for on the 2nd of June 1670 he granted to Sir Edward Nicholas the keepership of it, with its four lodges and lands in Coworth and Sunninghill—in all, 3410 acres.

In June 1671 we learn that "His Majesty was pleased to re-impark yᵉ Great Park of Windsor from 1st October next, and to grant the office of keeper of all the parks (excepting the Paddock Walk) to Baptist May, Esq., during His Majesty's pleasure."† Edward Tyrringham had been keeper of what was called the Middle Walk, and was pensioned with £100 a year on this appointment. As early

---

* Cal. State Papers, Dom. 1661.　　　† See Docket Book at Rolls, 1671.

as 1639, Nicholas had tried to buy up Captain Tyrringham's interest in this walk.

It was then, Mr. Menzies tells us, that the oldest part of Cumberland Lodge was built; but, from what I have said, it may possibly have been ten years earlier than this.

However that may be, the primitive house of Master Haybourne was now removed, and its beautiful site destined for a more imposing edifice. The "new house" of the Restoration may have been converted into the Banqueting House, where the gay monarch and his courtiers enjoyed those *fêtes champêtres*, so much the fashion of the French Court, in which they had recently been guests.

This idea receives some support from the fact that in the map of 1662 only three lodges are mentioned, while in the grant to Nicholas in 1670 four again appear, the former house having possibly been pulled down, and in the meantime rebuilt as the Ranger's Lodge.

A few years pass, and another great change comes. We often hear of the rage for the Dutch style of gardening that William made so fashionable in England; it was developed here in great strength. Sunninghill Park and Cranbourne both attest this, but the rising glories of "the lodge" on the hill tended especially in that direction.

In 1689 William bestowed on his favourite, Bentinck, Earl of Portland, with whom gardening seems to have been a passion, an office which he had created especially for him, and made him inspector of all the gardens of his various palaces, with £30,000 for laying them out afresh.

In 1697 he became Ranger of the parks and all the lodges, and he made this one his residence. He spent a large sum on it, and laid out its grounds in his own favourite style. It was either he, or more probably the Duke of Cumberland, who formed the "Mistle" Pond into the fine piece of water we now see it.

The Docket was prepared especially to give him scope for his hunting pursuits also, and contained a clause directing him "to put in tilth any part of the park near the several lodges, not exceeding three hundred acres, for the better support and increase of the game of pheasants and partridge."

But while he was enjoying the bounty of his patron he managed to offend the young Princess who was to become that patron's successor; and when she ascended the throne the great Dutchman was relieved of his position at Windsor. The *Flying Post* for May 1702 announced that "Her Majesty gave to Sir Edward Seymour

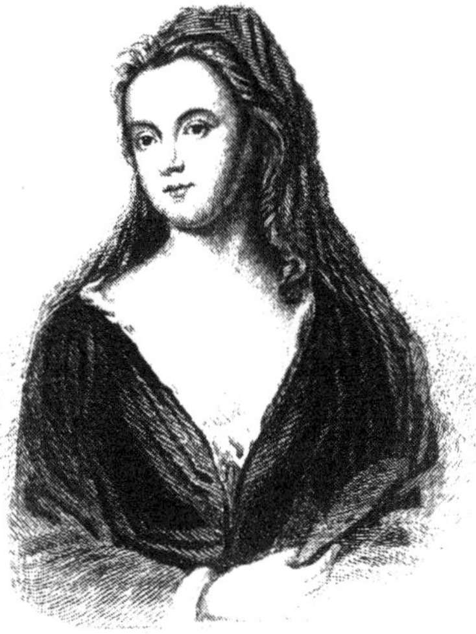

the fine lodge at Windsor, which before belonged to the Earl of Portland." This shows that the little lodge on the hill had by this time become an important mansion.

Miss Strickland imputes this change to the instigation of Sarah of Marlborough, who, she tells us, instantly stepped into the vacated place; but it was not exactly so. The two ladies, no doubt, had their eyes on this pleasant house. Anne wanted to have her favourite near her in "the Great Lodge," the situation of which, in their excursions through Windsor Park, she had repeatedly admired.*

The Queen, in one of her familiar letters (19th May 1702), after alluding to Lord Portland's possession of the house, continues, "Mentioning this worthy person" (whom, by the bye, she especially hated), "puts me in mind to ask dear Mrs. Freeman a question, and that is, if you would have the lodge for your life, because the warrant must be made accordingly."

But for some reason it must have been forgotten, not only by the historian, but by the Queen herself, that she had already bestowed it on Sir Edward Seymour, and it was not until after Sir Edward's death in 1709 that the Duchess " stepped into it."

We may be sure it had been earlier promised, or she would never have had it at all; for this was after that terrible quarrel, when she was told to put in writing what she had to say.

However, she did have it, and it became her favourite residence. On the 18th July 1709,† it was granted to herself and her two daughters, Mary, Duchess of Montague, and Henrietta, Countess of Godolphin, for their lives. The Docket specifies "the Manor Lodge, Hill Lodge, Middle Lodge, and Lower Lodge." Haybourne's little house on the hill had given its name, as we see, to the fine house which Bentinck's lavish expenditure had created. Lysons, a contemporary writer, tells us that "it was built by Charles II., and received many additions and advantages from the late Earl of Portland, and since from the present Ranger, the Duchess of Marlborough."

The Duchess, in one of her angry letters, speaks of the great sums of money she had laid out on her two lodges, meaning, I have no doubt, this and the lower one.

In September 1711, Swift writes of riding out to see Cranbourne, and the Duchess of Marlborough's lodge (which was not far from it),

---

* See Coxe's Memoirs of Duke of Marlborough, vol. i. p. 77.
† See Pat. Roll. 8 Anne, 2nd part, No. 3469.

and speaks of the plantations and of the fine riding on the artificial roads made by the Queen. It must have been to this house he alluded, for the Queen did not make the ride to Frogmore or the Lower Lodge.

The Duchess in 1717 writes sometimes from "the Lodge," and sometimes from "Windsor Park;"* and from one of these, the lower one doubtless, she says in a letter to Mrs. Masham, "Though the house is not large, I am confident you are all so good as to be contented with what there is, and a very hearty welcome."

Although there may be some slight vestiges of Charles II.'s house left, I am inclined to think that the principal part of the present house was erected by the Earl of Portland, and that it was he who laid out its gardens and pleasure-grounds. The Duchess of Marlborough made great alterations and additions to it, as the Duke of Cumberland afterwards did to the gardens and grounds.

Be that as it may, it became the Duchess of Marlborough's favourite residence, and here, in spite of Mrs. Masham and Her Majesty's anger, the old lady enjoyed life as far as was possible to one who took such pleasure in making every one round her miserable. It was here, too, Walpole tells us, that her favourite granddaughter, Diana Spencer, afterwards Duchess of Bedford, was to have been privately married to the Prince of Wales, with a dowry of a hundred thousand pounds, but that Sir Robert Walpole got intelligence of the project and soon prevented it.

But amid all her vexations one great consolation remained to her—the love of her husband; and this opens to us one of the most memorable associations of the place.

It must ever be an object of interest to us, as having been the residence of England's great soldier, John, Duke of Marlborough; and although we cannot, without a passing shudder, think of that imperturbable nature and the avarice of the man, of whom St. John writes to his friend at the Hague, "I am sorry that my Lord Marlborough gives you so much trouble; it is the only thing he will ever give you," and we may smile when we think what anguish it must have been to him to yield up those five hundred sovereigns to the highwayman, we must remember the sweetness of his temper, and have pity on him, the best-tempered man in the kingdom, married to the most ill-tempered woman. When, as we are told,† in a fit of passion she cut off her beautiful locks to annoy him, and flung them

---

* See Letters of Duchess of Marlborough, Brit. Mus.
† Lord Orford's Works, vol. iv. p. 313; and Stanhope's Life of Queen Anne.

in his face, I expect, although history does not record that, he only kissed them.

But we should never think of his avarice without remembering the quiet reproof of Bolingbroke, who, on being reminded of it, merely observed, "He was so great a man, I forgot he had that defect."

His glorious exploits make his memory immortal, and we cannot look upon this red pile without remembering it as the home of one of England's greatest sons.

An erroneous impression seems to have arisen on this subject. It is generally believed that the Duke never lived here. And Roque's map, showing a view of the house at Frogmore, which formerly stood where the dairy is now, and in which it is described as "His Grace the Duke of Marlborough's Lodge," may have been the origin of this error. But it is obvious that this plate can be no authority. The Duke to whom it was dedicated was not the great Duke John, but Charles, the second Duke.

It was certainly to Cumberland Lodge that the Duke retired in disgust on his quarrel with Mrs. Masham.

If any further proof were required that it was here, and not in the Little Lodge, that the Duchess lived, and that the latter was otherwise occupied, I need only refer to a well-known incident, which Walpole tells us of, that not only roused the old lady's wrath, but also no little amusement among the courtiers of the day. She had let her granddaughter, the Duchess of Bedford, and her husband, occupy the Little Lodge, and afterwards she turned them out; and pretending that the young lady and her cousins (the eight Trevors) had stripped the house and garden, she had a puppet-show made with waxen figures representing the Trevors tearing up the shrubs and the young Duchess carrying off the chicken-coop under her arm.*

At Cumberland Lodge, too, worn out by infirmity of body and vexation of mind, a sad wreck, the great soldier breathed his last, on the 16th June 1722.† This fact has not been established as it should have been. The *Daily Post* of the time, I find, announces his death as at Cranbourne Lodge, and the last edition of the "Encyclopædia Britannica repeats that statement. Other authorities give Windsor Lodge as the place, and I find it so stated in a short poem written on the day of his funeral. But I am satisfied it was here at Cumberland Lodge,

---

* See Walpole's Letters.
† See Alison's Life of Marlborough, Ledyard, iii. 496; Universal Mag., 1749, p. 307.

known then as "The Lodge" or the "Great Lodge," and often described as "Windsor Lodge," that he lived and doubtless died.*

The Duchess lived to the age of eighty-five, and died immensely rich in 1744, and it was at this house, only in the autumn before, that the old lady received a visit from Pope and Lord Chesterfield.† Her will, confirming what I have stated, shows that at the time of her death she had both the Lodges, and that the furniture in them belonged to her. She leaves the Rangership of the Great Park for the term of the three lives she had in it, as also the furniture, to her grandson, the Hon. John Spencer (this being the only place under the Crown that he was permitted by the will to accept). It had then become known as "the chief lodge;" and the further to identify it, William, Duke of Cumberland, we shall see, only obtained the Rangership after the death of the Hon. John Spencer on the 20th June 1746. This gentleman is described in the Court Register for that year as Keeper of the Park.

Now as to its Hanoverian period, George II., on the glorious intelligence of the victory of Culloden, gave the Rangership, just then vacant, to his son before his triumphal entry into London in the autumn of 1746.

The Duke was almost at once sent off in command of the army of observation to protect Hanover, and although thus fully immersed in his military occupations, he found time, on his visits to England, for country pursuits and a little landscape-gardening.

We get a contemporary account of his improvements there in the eloquent style of the day, in which we are told "that he greatly improved the natural beauties of the Park, and by large plantations of trees, extensive lawns, new roads, spacious canals, and rivers of water, made this villa one of the most delightful and princely habitations that can be seen." Frederick, the second Duke of Cumberland, died in 1791, when the Park reverted to His Majesty.

VIRGINIA WATER.

Of this I will now resume my account—who made it, and when, and why was it so called.

---

* See *Morning Penny Post*, June 5, 1751, and June 26.
† See Pope's Life, Carruthers.

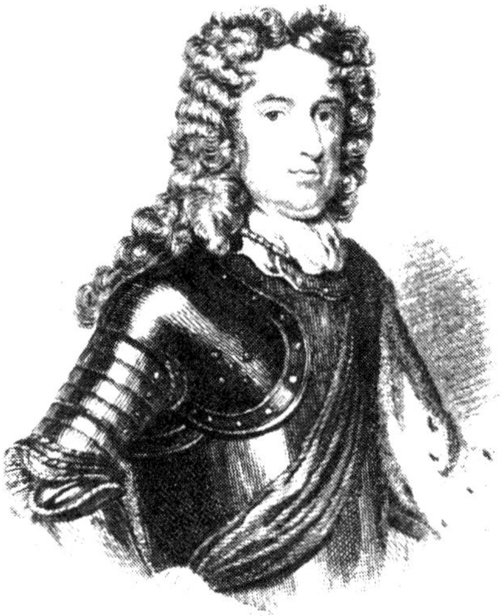

Tradition says the Duke of Cumberland formed the first lake by the aid of some of his disbanded troops after the battle of Culloden. Mr. Menzies, the late forester, on the other hand, tells us that the first lake was formed after 1770, in Mr. John Pitt's time. But to show that this is erroneous, I need only point out that the lake burst its banks two years before that date. As to tradition's account, I always regret having to consign any of her pleasant stories to the basket of historical errors; and in this case she is very near the truth, although I think not quite.

We know the soldiers were here when they came back from Culloden, for I find Lieutenant-General Hawley writing to Lord Albemarle in September 1746,* "The ragged troops of my regiment cross in their way from Berkshire into Sussex, where they are going to ride down the smugglers, who are in a sort of snivelling rebellion, depending upon the two Sussex Dukes; for as long as they live, no Sussex man will be hanged." But the lake was not then begun. Mr. Rawlins,† moreover, says that General Wolfe's regiment was among the troops so employed in 1746, and that they were ordered off in the midst of these works of peace to the assault of Quebec. But as that event occurred in 1759, and, as I shall presently show, the lake was finished in 1753, he is clearly mistaken in this, as he also is in the date of the disaster that destroyed it. The Windlesham Register, moreover, shows that it was in 1756 that Colonel Wolfe's regiment was quartered at Bagshot.

William Augustus, the first Duke, had no authority over the Great Park till after his appointment to the Rangership, to which he was gazetted in the summer of 1746. He then at once made Thomas Sandby, the architect, his draughtsman at Culloden, Deputy Ranger, and very soon after that he may have turned his thoughts to the plantations and the formation of the lake and the roads round it. The necessary excavations, however, must have occupied some years, and I have no doubt the first Virginia Water was formed between 1750 and 1752.

In this latter year they were apparently in full work, and then it was that the brother, Paul Sandby, a water-colour artist, also engaged in the Scotch surveys, gave up his employment there, and came to reside with his brother Thomas at Windsor, to assist him in these works; and the charming sketches of the new water, the lodges

---

* See Earl of Albemarle, "Fifty Years of my Life;" see also Windlesham Parish Registers.
† Virginia Water, by the Rev. F. J. Rawlins, 1886.

and the various interesting spots of the Forest, show well how their leisure hours were spent. One of them, dated 1753, shows that the Belvidere had been built, and also that the first lake had been then finished; for it represents the Duke of Cumberland showing to a youth, not unlikely his nephew, the heir-apparent, the Mandarine Barge, that had been just transported to the new lake. My views are entirely confirmed by a letter of Mr. Hellard of the Office of Woods, who kindly writes me, "I have a copy of a plan by J. Vardy, made in 1750, which shows that then the great part of Virginia Water did not exist, but only a river called the Virginia River;" and as it was finished in 1753, it must have been made during the years 1750-51-52.

Shortly after this, when his Hanoverian campaign collapsed in the defeat at Hastenbeck, he returned to England in October 1757, to so different a reception at the hands of both king and people to that which greeted him on his Scotch triumph, that in disgust he threw up all his military appointments, and sought the retirement of his pleasant home in the Great Park. Here, with his "limner" Maurier,* his draughtsman Schutz, and the two Sandbys, he found a most congenial employment in still further laying out and planting the hill-slopes of this Virginia River, and looking after his horses, and the buffaloes and ostriches he was endeavouring to acclimatise.

Nor can we wonder much that, like the Duke of Grafton, who, under the lash of Junius, about this time, becoming sick of office, and beginning, as Macaulay says, to look wistfully towards the shades of Euston, so the Duke of Cumberland, under the cold shadow of royal disfavour, should seek repose at his beloved Windsor.

The *Gentleman's Magazine* for 1765, at the time of his death, tells of "the large sums he yearly expended at Windsor, and the number of workmen he daily employed there, have rendered that place one of the wonders of England, and makes his loss severely felt in the neighbourhood."

This expenditure was, it seems, from his private purse, so that the payments do not appear in the public records; and it confirms what has been said, that when his funds failed the workmen were dismissed till his coffers were replenished.† His sister, the Princess Amelia, used to assist him, and on one occasion when he applied to her for money,

---

* David Morier, a Swiss painter of battle scenes.
† See Manning and Bray's "Surrey," vol. iii. p. 252.

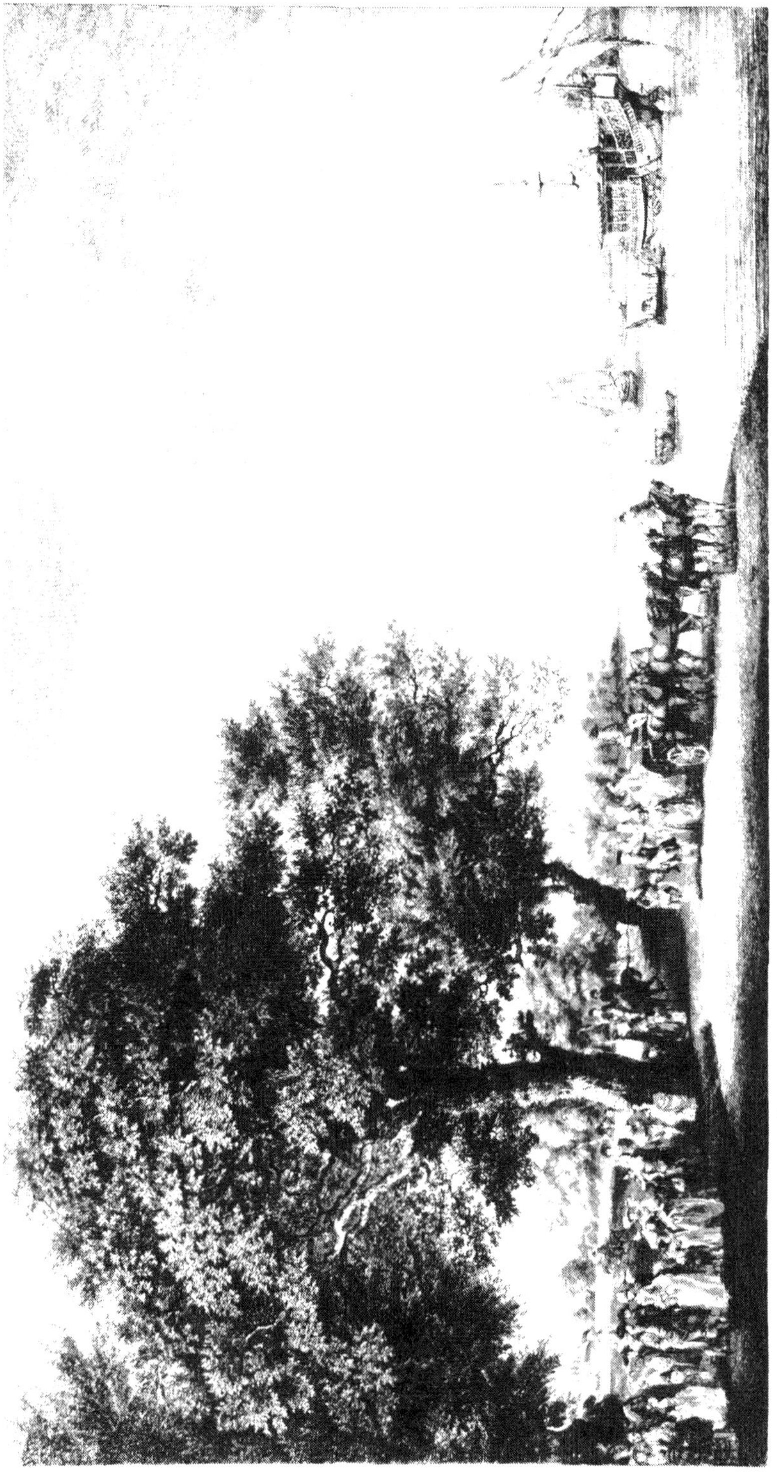

she hinted that he did not want so many workmen. "True," said he, "but they want me." He showed at times a kindly, generous disposition, which makes it difficult to understand the justice of that charge of cruelty in Scotland that has stained his reputation so unfortunately; and without in the least excusing the wanton slaying and burning that disgraced that terrible campaign, I have always thought, surrounded as he was by old and experienced officers, who had been trained in the harsh school of Continental warfare, he, a young man of three or four and twenty, had to bear more than his fair share of the blame.

I am confirmed in this by the publication of the MSS. of John Ramsay,* who says "that the Earl of Ancrum directed a set of wretched men found in a house at Culloden, the day after the battle, to be taken out and shot, as an offering to the manes of his brother Robert, who had fallen in the fight; and that the Duke was so much incensed at this barbarity, that he did not speak to his Lordship as long as he was in Scotland." But the generous toast of the good Lord President Forbes, when he dined with the Duke on his arrival at Inverness, "Now that your Royal Highness has so happily suppressed this unnatural rebellion, allow me to drink a bumper to mercy and peace." fell dead on the company; the Duke and his military grandees drank off their glasses without saying a word.

His letters show no lack of feeling for others, and a staunch loyalty in his friendships. He died in the arms of his constant companion George Keppel, Lord Albemarle, by many beloved and regretted.†

Among the other works here about this time was the erection of an important timber bridge over the Virginia River near the Fishing Temple, long remembered as the High Bridge, and a fanciful Chinese-looking house, not exactly a pagoda, on what ever afterwards became known as China Island. This summer-house and Chinese barge, following a fashion set, it is said, for the first time at Stowe, were probably the very earliest instances of Chinese architecture in England.‡

---

* MSS. of John Ramsay, by Alex. Allardyce; and see *Quarterly Review*, 1888.

† See Memoirs of Marquis of Rockingham and of Earl of Albemarle; also letter from Lord Bolingbroke to Sir Everard Fawkner, mentioned in Memoirs of Lord Chesterfield, vol. i. p. 246.

‡ We knew but little of China until forty years afterwards, when, in 1792, Lord Macartney's embassy to Pekin opened up that country to us, and William Alexander's beautiful drawings brought us the true style. Then it was that Virginia Water, Kew, and other places bristled with genuine Chinese pagodas and summer-houses.

It was not, however, till the time of George IV. that the old manor-house gave place to the Fishing Temple.

One of Paul Sandby's drawings shows this bridge with the island in the distance; on the back of it is a note made by him more than forty years afterwards, "View of the great wooden bridge over the Virginia River in Windsor Great Park, built for His Royal Highness William, Duke of Cumberland, by Mr. Fleatcroft, in the year 1760, which went soon to decay, and an elegant stone bridge was afterwards erected by T. Sandby, Esq. This drawing was made by the two brothers, T. and P. S. Esqs."

The first lake did not extend much beyond where the artificial ruins now stand, at which point a pond-head or dam was thrown across to form the lake, but it was soon afterwards carried away by a great flood, which, as it is described, "drowned" the country.

This disaster occurred not in 1780, but on the 1st September 1768.* A storm which arose in the night deluged London and the country around with torrents of rain for eight hours, such as had hardly been known in the memory of man; and it was then, as the Annual Register tells us, that "the late Duke of Cumberland's fine water-works in Windsor Forest were entirely destroyed; several persons were drowned in different places, as well as horses, oxen, and hogs."

The damage was estimated at £9000, and that it would cost £3000 to repair the mischief done within the Park.

Sandby was not a "fortunate" engineer; he built a bridge at Staines, which almost the first flood afterwards destroyed.

Mr. Rawlins informs us that there was an old coach-road from Windsor to Guildford, which ran from Botany Bay Point to the site of the ruins, thus crossing the middle of the present lake at the junction of the counties; and that when the waters were drawn off, the foundations of the original "Wheatsheaf," a humble roadside inn, were still to be seen half-way across the water. What his authority for this was, I do not know, for neither Norden's map of 1607, nor any subsequent one I have seen, shows any such road. The way from Guildford passed through Chobham down to the "watering-place" where the cascade is now, and so round the Park corner over Wickheath to Windsor. What Mr. Rawlins had described to him as visible in the bed of the lake may have been remnants of

---

* See Annual Register, September 1768.

the first dam and road that skirted it, left after the great inundation of 1768. But to continue.

The lake was restored in the second Duke's time under the direction of Mr. John Pitt, the royal surveyor of woods, who was then residing at the manor-house, Sunninghill. Some time elapsed, however, before the completion of this second work. Indeed, it seems not to have been finished till 1790, at least in its present form; and the reason was, doubtless, the considerable extension of the water then decided on, to enable which it was necessary to negotiate with the parish of Egham for the acquisition of some of the land now forming the eastern end of the lake and its surrounding woods, including what was formerly part of the old Wick Heath.

Norden shows half the present lake as, in his time, not in the Park, nor was it in 1750, as appears from a map by J. Vardy at the Office of Woods, Whitehall.* With the consent of the parishioners of Egham, 109 acres were enclosed in consideration of an annual payment of £5, 5s. by the Crown, for the use of the poor for ever; this negotiation having been advantageously accomplished, the work proceeded, and Virginia Water was doubled in size.

Another old map at the Woods and Forests shows that in the summer of 1789 a number of soldiers, parties of the 23rd Fusiliers, were apparently at work on the dam or pond-head, confirming the above account, and explaining possibly the origin of the earlier tradition to which I have referred. That, too, may have arisen partly from the fact that in Prince Frederick's time, before the Duke of Cumberland's connection with the Park, troops had been employed "smoothing the rugged wilderness," as Somerville tells us, at Ascot and Swinley, and this may possibly have been on their return from Culloden.

Near the iron gates called "the Wick Gate," we are told, there was in the time of Henry VIII. a religious house of some kind. After its suppression it was used as a farmhouse, which was pulled down by the second Duke of Cumberland for the extension of the lake. "Chapel" Wood hard by, and a fine old cherry-tree which long stood in the farmhouse garden, were, a few years since, the only remaining evidences of its existence. As to the name "Virginia," this, it has been said, was merely appropriated by the Duke of Cumberland as representing in miniature the forest scenery of its transatlantic namesake;† but that, I think, was not so. Its origin was

---

* See *Gent. Mag.*, 1763, vol. xxxiii. p. 17.
† See Rev. F. J. Rawlins' Hist. of Virginia Water.

much older, for in the map of 1662 before referred to, there is shown on the south side of Virginia River, before its enlargement, a house somewhere near the spot of the present Wheat Sheaf Inn, and marked "Mr. Fabian's;" but, what is still more interesting to us, slightly west of it, where now stands the under-keeper's lodge, there was a house called "Virginia," from which, I imagine, came the name of the water. Norden did not give this name to the stream, nor does he show this house, which was not probably built in his time, although it must have been shortly afterwards, when I infer it gave name to that part of the Bourne which flowed below, and the river in turn gave its name to the lake. Besides, the Duke's own plans call it Virginia River before he excavated the lake.

Paul Sandby has left a drawing of an important red brick house with two wings, called the Keeper's Lodge, which occupied the site at the middle of the last century, and may possibly have been the veritable "Virginia." Near to it was the spot then known as the Blind Man's Gate.

Near the present cascade there was formerly a grotto, on which Mr. Paul Sandby evidently expended considerable thought, as is shown by the designs he left of it. I have alluded incidentally to the Clock-case Tower; it was erected by the Duke of Cumberland; but although the clock was made, it was never put up, I am informed. At the Duke's death the land was sold and the tower converted into a summer-house. George IV. repurchased it.

I will now add a few words as to the avenues for which this Park is celebrated. The earliest were probably in the Home Park, and were those alluded to by Evelyn when he tells us that in 1670 the King spent much of his time in the Park, which "he was then planting with rows of trees."

The Long Walk was not commenced till later. Messrs. Tighe and Davis say it was begun in 1680, and it was certainly in the course of construction shortly afterwards, for I find an entry in the Audit Office Record Books: "1682.—Making an avenue between the Castle and Great Park." It was laid out 240 feet wide, and was completed by William III. There was formerly in the Long Walk a medicinal spring, which was opened by direction of George IV. in 1823, after it had been closed for thirty years.

Queen Anne's Avenue,[*] as the name of course implies, was planted by her, and was commenced, I think, in the very first year of her

---

[*] See Cal. State Papers, Dom.

reign; for in November 1703 "a new riding," we are told, "was being made in the Great Park through the woods, and to be continued through some part of the forest adjoining to the Park pale." The trees standing in it were then "valued at £70 if they stood till the bark would run [sap?], but if not, at £60."

Of Windsor I do not propose to speak, although I may allude to Peascod Street, a name the origin of which seems never to have been ascertained. The earliest notice of it I can find is 6th July, 34th Elizabeth (1592), when allusion is made to Prescrofte Streete, *alias* Pescod Street.

May it not have been from the early planting there of the laburnum, which was introduced into England at the end of the sixteenth century, just about this time? Gerrard had one in his garden before 1596, and it was then known as the pescod tree, and is so described in Gerrard's Herbal.

The Cowpond Avenue of limes was planted, Mr. Menzies tells us, in 1718.

Frogmore, alluded to in the "Merry Wives of Windsor," was in the Little Park. It was sold, among other Crown lands, in the time of the Commonwealth, or in some way became the property of Dr. Thomas Howell, Canon of Windsor and Bishop of Bristol, who by his will in 1650 left "his farm of Frogmore in New Windsor" equally to his children; but at the Restoration the house was occupied by some of the children of Charles II.,[*] subsequently by the Marlborough family, and ultimately by Sir Ed. Walpole.[†] In 1792 it belonged to the Hon. Mrs. Ann Egerton. She in that year sold it to Queen Charlotte—who rebuilt the house, although in the "Complete Traveller," 1794, it is described as "a handsome house, built by Sir Ed. Walpole."

In the time of George III., Frogmore Green was a great place of festivity, "the play-place" of the townspeople, and famous for its fêtes and sports. The mansion subsequently became the residence of the Princess Augusta until her death in 1840. The Duchess of Kent died there in 1861. It was afterwards occupied by the Prince of Wales, and was the birthplace of his eldest son.

---

[*] See Beauties of England, vol. i.   [†] Walford's Tourist's Guide to Berkshire.

THE MOAT PARK,

which had always been a separate enclosure, was formed, I think, before the time of Edward IV., for I find it mentioned in the first year of his reign. Subsequently Richard Weston, the Nevilles, and afterwards Hugh and Adrian May, were its keepers. In the time of James I., Stafferton held the post; but when "the troubles" came it was mortgaged by King Charles I. to Dr. Christopher Potter for £2000. He was paid off by the Duke of Albemarle, who seems in some way to have acquired the freehold.

In 1673 the Crown appears to have agreed for its purchase at the price of £7000, but for some reason there was difficulty in obtaining a proper conveyance of it, and it was ordered that the collectors of "fyre-hearth and stoves in the county of Southampton pay Christopher, Duke of Albemarle, £300 a year, until he received the purchase-money." It was at once, however, laid into the Great Park, although still remaining private property.* This was in the time of Charles II., and not, as has sometimes been stated, in the reign of William; for in 1675 it had been done.

In 1706 the Crown officers investigated the title, and reported that the Moat Park, the lodge there, and 300 acres of land, belonged to the representatives of the Earl of Albemarle deceased, and Bernard Granville, claiming under him. From the Earl's representatives, I believe it was ultimately acquired by the Crown. It extended southward to part of Cranborne Wood.

Norden shows a good lodge on it, and the moat is especially indicated. Subsequently it had two lodges, one of which afterwards became known as "the Cottage."

Here occurred once an amusing incident—amusing from its very incongruity. James I., about a year before his death, when incessantly annoyed by the Windsor people by reason of their Puritan proclivities and open hostility to his enclosure of the parks, was having a quiet day's coursing in the Moat Park with his son Charles and Buckingham. In the midst of his sport he was "intruded" upon by a deputation, and from Windsor of all places. The poor Vicar, John Martin, had got the Mayor, two Windsor Aldermen, a county magistrate, and others, to present, at that inopportune moment, a petition for an increased endowment of the Vicar-

---

* See Docket Book at Rolls, and Treasury Papers, 1693.   † See Treasury Papers, 1706.

age. Imagine James and Buckingham having their sport spoiled by the men they held in greatest contempt, and for an object they secretly detested!

James stormed at them, ridiculed their prayer, and told them "to go and whip the rogues that broke his parks and stole his wood." This reminds one of Jonson's fulsome address:—

> "Bless him, too, from all offences,
> In his sports as in his senses,
> From a boy to cross his way,
> From a fall or a foul day."

Rather a thinly-veiled satire on one who in his sports seemed never in his senses, and whose particular horror was to have any one cross his path.

I may well close my paper, while in fancy we may still be wandering on the pleasant banks of this royal lake, by recalling the remark of that ferocious republican, who, as some one tells us, once proclaimed his discovery of the reason why, in the mysterious dispensations of Providence, such things as kings and queens were permitted to be; it was to preserve parks and gardens and open spaces for the people. Let us rejoice, then, that in this instance the "masses" are so much indebted to the "privileged classes" for so costly and charming a pleasure-ground!

CHAPTER XXIX.

Cranbourn Tower.

ON one of the loftiest ridges of the Forest stands the old Cranbourn Tower. Although in the midst of woods, it commands the most beautiful views. Towards the north, Windsor Castle seems to lie almost in a valley beneath; on the west spread out the dark heath-lands of Ascot; while southward, in many undulations of hill and dale, the Forest falls towards Sunninghill. But it is rather for its own immediate surroundings and associations that the place is most interesting to us.

There stands the crumbling red-brick tower, like an old way-post with its directions defaced, or like the figure-head of some old fighting ship, with all the scars of time upon it; yet who knows when or by whom it was built? The walls show relation to other walls that are gone, and the sward around is hard with the foundations of some extensive buildings that are no more. On the warm southern slope of the ridge are still the ancient gardens and their walls, and the avenues of lime that sheltered them; in the dells on the north the fish-ponds still remain.

It is always interesting to endeavour to recall the past history of a place where such vestiges of former habitation are strewn about, and stones lie here and there that tell of a life that has fled.

But of this we know but little. Every writer, without exception, who notices it tells us that Cranbourn Lodge was built by Richard, Lord Ranelagh, Paymaster of the Forces in the time of Charles II. This, however, is obviously a mistake; for in 1653 Cranbourn Lodge was much out of repair. The tower was originally built a short time before the reign of Henry VII., and the Lodge in a much handsomer manner rebuilt by Sir George Carteret in 1665. Lord

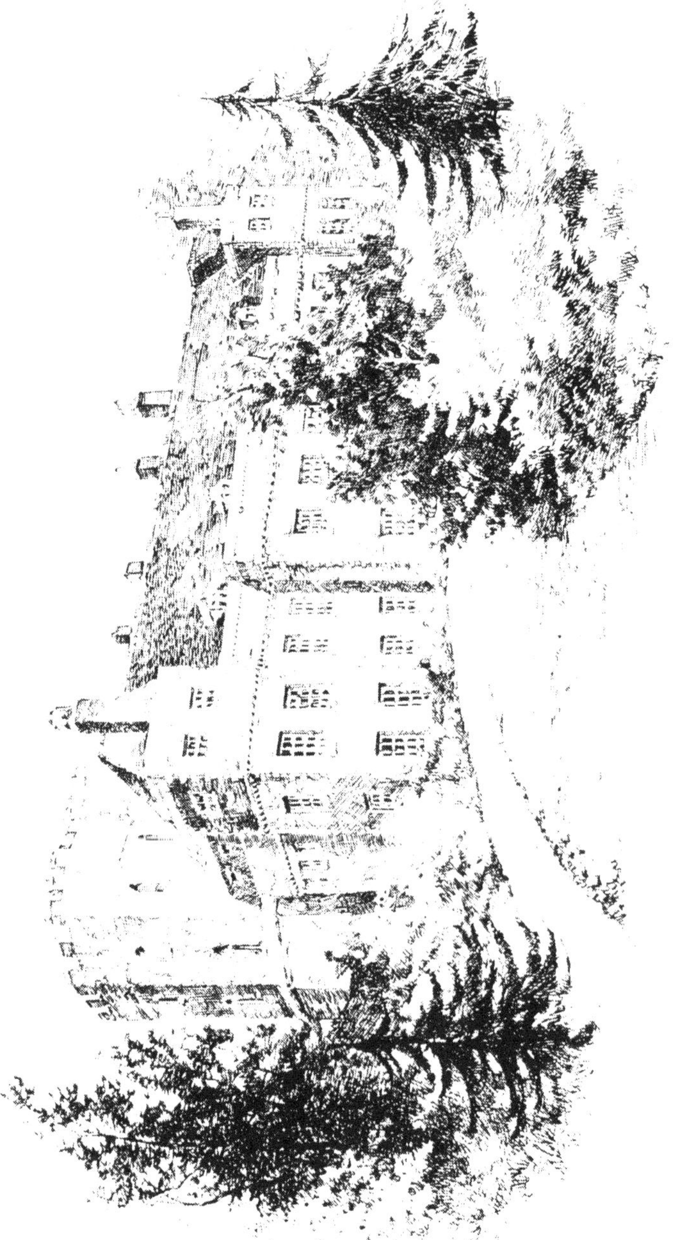

Ranelagh had nothing to do with the place till the time of James II.

It has always been the property of the Crown; in fact, the lodge of the keeper of Cranbourn Chase, which formed part of the bailiwick of Battles. This bailiwick comprised two walks, besides Swinley, which formerly went with it. Over these, separate under-keepers were appointed, and their places were in the gift of the keeper of Cranbourn.

It was rather a coveted post, and was generally granted to some favourite of the sovereign for life or term of years; and in later times a transferable interest seems to have been created, which the keeper might, under certain conditions, dispose of.

The earliest notice I find of it carries us back to the troublous times of Henry IV., when it was evidently in the keepership of one John Parker (whose family we hear of in these parts at a still earlier period); and on the accession of Henry V. he was confirmed in that office for life. In the 5th Henry VI. William Staverton, a member of one of the most ancient of our Forest families, was appointed to this office for life; but for some reason in 1436 John Hynde seems to have superseded him. The terrible wars of the Roses made every man a rebel in his turn; and Staverton probably sided with the Yorkists, and when they triumphed he was reinstated at Cranbourn.

We hear of it in 1476. When Bishop Beauchamp was rebuilding the royal chapel at Windsor, this neighbourhood was laid under tribute for materials; and while, as we have seen, the oaks of Sunninghill were being felled for the timber, " heath stone from Cranbourn Chase" was employed to restore the fabric, which had lain in ruins since the time of Chaucer.

After the battle of Bosworth, when Henry VII. came to the throne, we find him filling up the vacancies in his Forest offices which the change of dynasty had occasioned; and he speaks of Cranbourn, "whiche William Staffertone, our rebelle, late had;" and then, on the 14th July 1486, he grants for life to Gilbert Mawdesley, one of the King's serjeants at arms (upon the surrender of a patent, 21st September, 1 Henry VII.), the offices of keeper of the new park called the Mote Park, in the Forest of Windsor, and keeper of Cranbourn, alias, one of the foresters in the said Forest within the bailiwick of Bateilles bailly, or keeper of the said bailiwick, with the custody as well of *the new tower or lodge called "the toure in the hethe,"* as of the enclosure or grove of Swinley, within the said bailiwick, with emoluments such as John Dethe formerly had, temp. Richard II.

with certain horses and cows, and other privileges therein mentioned, "and a certain dwelling-house for the said Gilbert, as William Stafferton heretofore had." From this we learn that the "toure in the hethe" had then been recently erected, and that the Mote Park was new.

Mawdesley held this appointment during the whole reign, and for some years into the next, when Henry VIII., in 1515, appointed Richard Weston, who had been one of his earliest personal attendants, "to be keeper of the Mote Park in Windsor Forest, with fourpence a day, out of the issues of Oxon and Berks, on surrender of patent 20 Henry VII. granting same, *vice* Gilbert Mawdesley."

Two years afterwards this rising favourite had, among other better things, the appointment of "keeper of the swans in the Thames;" and in the following year Sir Richard Weston, Knight of the body, was keeper of Cranbourn Chase, with fourpence a day out of the issues of Windsor Castle.*

The King had set himself actively to put his Forest lodges in repair, and as soon as he had completed the house in Sunninghill Park, he took Cranbourn and the Mote in hand. For as early as 1518 we find Sir Richard Weston was paid for the repairing of the manor in the Mote Park, the tower in the heath, and the making of a *new lodge* in Cranbourn Chase, £133, 6s. 8d. In 1520 another payment was made to Sir Richard Weston of £79, 17s. 8d. for the new lodge in Cranbourn Chase.

This new lodge, I am inclined to think, is the original of its namesake, the present mansion of Madame Van de Weyer; for one is clearly shown in the old map of Lord Burleigh, of the date of Elizabeth, as standing on that site.

After Sir Richard Weston, Richard Staverton in 1536 had a grant of the reversion of the office, with the new lodge and keepership of the tower, and following him one Thomas Ward, an officer of the household to Henry VIII., had Cranbourn. He held, among other appointments, the important one of "yeoman harbinger"—the purveyor of lodgings. Under his comptrollership in 1535, "Juettes Lodge, le Motte Park, Folyjohn, and Cranbourn Lodge" were repaired. This family of Ward continued long afterwards in the Forest, and I believe still exists in our neighbourhood. They held estates at Winkfield, where a Sir Richard Ward and a Dame Mary Ward were owners of the manor; from them it passed to their son-in-law, Richard Harrison.

---

* Windsor, 15th October, 9 Hen. VIII., del. Westminster, 26th January.

The Staffertons were soon restored to favour; for I find in 1537 the Princess Mary standing godmother to a child of Mr. Stafferton the Ranger, and giving her 67s. 6d. as "the sponsor's present." Long after this, no doubt, the heath extended over all that is now known as Cranbourn, save the small enclosure on which these buildings stood.

The next enclosure that we hear of had a rather curious historical origin. It seems that from one of the stranded vessels of the Spanish Armada a letter fell into the hands of Burleigh containing instructions to the Admiral to be sure to cut down and destroy the Forest of Dean, to prevent its furnishing timber for our navy. He was much alarmed at this, and at once desired a nursery for his timber less accessible to such a blow. Thereupon, in 1580, he stretched his powers over the Forest, and enclosed thirteen acres at Cranbourn, which were fenced into the Great Park pales, to plant with young oaks. This was probably, as Mr. Menzies observes, the first regular plantation ever made in England.

One Richard Day in 1627 presented a petition to James I. proposing to plant acorns in convenient places in the Forest; he there mentions that Burleigh's thirteen acres had then become "a wood of tall young oaks."* These may still be identified. The late Mr. Menzies a few years ago measured one of these trees then standing, and found it 12 feet 3 inches in circumference at 5 feet from the ground. Burleigh, I have reason to believe, lived at Ascot Place, Winkfield, which was called "Burleighs."

Mr. Richard Ward was still at Cranbourn in October 1585, for we find his neighbour, Sir Henry Neville, in a state of excitement writing from Pillingbere to Walsingham, "It is commonly reported that Mr. William Knollys has bought Cranbourn Chase of Mr. Warde; he desires that a new patent be not granted to Knollys till his claim shall have been tried." However that was arranged, Sir Henry Neville (who, by-the-by, had married a cousin of the all-powerful Cecil) was very shortly afterwards the ruling personage here, and had the great house at Sunninghill Park, as so fully mentioned elsewhere, and with it the keepership of the Mote Park, and Riding-forester of Battles Walk.

In 1590 I find a grant of two walks in Cranbourn Chase to Richard Lovelace, and to Richard, his son, for their lives in reversion after the decease of Richard Ward. Here we come upon a name full

---

* Cal. State Papers, 7th July 1627.

of romantic associations. Richard Lovelace, the keeper of Cranbourn, was descended from an old Kentish family of Cavaliers, that had been seated at Bethersden since the days of Edward III. Hever Castle also at one time belonged to them. Of this stock sprang three sons, one of whom, Sir William of Woolwich, was father of Richard Lovelace the poet; another, John, migrated into Berkshire, where he bought the manor of Hurley, just then wrested from the Nunnery, and became the father of our Richard of Cranbourn Chase. The poet, handsome, brave, and intensely loyal, had all the virtues and vices of his class; he shone alike as poet and soldier; now deep in love and love-sonnets, and now still deeper immersed in riot and revelry. He presented, with Sir William Boteler of Barham Court, the famous petition to the House of Commons in 1642, and was imprisoned and bailed in £40,000. He spent his whole fortune in the King's cause, stripped himself even of his ancestral estates, and died in a cellar in London in 1658, sighing out his love to "Althea"—

> "Stone walls do not a prison make,
> Nor iron bars a cage;"

and to "Lucasta" on his going to the wars—

> "I could not love thee, dear, so much,
> Loved I not honour more."

And but for the monument these few lines have wrought for him, we should hardly know him now. How different the fate of our Berkshire branch. John bought Hurley, and his grandson Richard, who was of an enterprising spirit, forsook for a while his hunting the deer of Cranbourn to go off with Sir Francis Drake for a little privateering on his own account under a letter of marque from Elizabeth. "They had the success," as old Fuller says, "to light on a large remnant of the King of Spain's *cloth of silver*, I mean his West Indian fleet, wherewith he and his posterity are the warmer to this day." His share of this splendid prize enabled him to rear his fine mansion of "Lady Place" on the site of the Nunnery of Our Lady at Hurley, where the Thames, as Macaulay tells us, "rolls under woods of beech round the gentle hills of Berkshire." From this Richard, whom Charles I. raised to the peerage as Lord Lovelace of Hurley, descended to his son John his great wealth and handsome person, a still more fiery nature, and greater love of magnificence. It was he who told James II., who accused him of playing a trick, "that he had never played His Majesty or any one else a trick, and whoever has accused me of playing tricks to your Majesty is a liar." In a subterraneous vault that may still be seen in his mansion on the Thames, he plotted against this King in favour of William. We get an amusing account of him almost as soon as he was out of his mother's leading-strings; for in April 1637 he was designedly presented as a suitor to the beautiful Dorothy Sidney, who had just snubbed the young widower Waller. He was not without advantages, a handsome person (her mother called him "pretty"), noble and wealthy; but Lady Leicester had sharp eyes and ears; "he had kept," she heard, "extreme ill companie, and was given to drinking;" and so he went his way. But "whiles we shut the gates upon one wooer, another knocks at the door," and the young lady was soon married at Penshurst to Lord Spencer, and made her home in the stately house at Wormleighton; but in June 1643 he fell at Newbury. Dorothy in her old age met her discarded lover at Woburn near Beaconsfield, and was guilty of that memorable indiscretion of exclaiming, "Well, Mr. Waller, and when shall you address such fine verses to me again?" "When, madam, you are as young again!"

It was doubtless concerning the northernmost of these two walks, in which, as we have seen, a new lodge had been erected, that the King in 1605 wrote to Sir Richard Lovelace, the keeper, about some trouble which Richard Staverton, was giving. "As we would prevent the late spoil of the deer in the New Lodge Walk, we authorise you to call the Verderers and Regarders of the said Forest unto you, and take view what deer are within the said walk, and take especial care of them, signifying to Richard Stafferton that neither he nor any in that place kill any deer before they have acquainted you with it."

In Norden's time Sir Richard Lovelace was keeper of Cranbourn Walk and Stafordton of the New Lodge Walk. This latter seems to have gone with the woodwardenship of Cookham and Bray. Sir Charles Harbord, William Lord Paget, Francis and William Retson, and Sir Charles Howard the elder and the younger, were severally keepers.

In 1604 Cranbourn was given to Thomas Fountain for life, while Richard Harrison and Sir Charles Harbord were afterwards keepers of the New Lodge.

When James I. came to the throne, no part of Cranbourn was in the Park, but he soon began to enclose it; for in the Survey of 1613, Cranbourn Wood, containing 725 acres, and another of 350 acres, and a smaller plot of 25 acres, are described as enclosures. That of 25 acres might be round the tower, and used with the lodge, and possibly included the 13 acres of young oaks. This enclosure by the King was exceedingly unpopular.

In 1616 Sir Francis Steward had this keepership for life; and in 1628 Sir Richard Harrison, Ward's son-in-law, was there; but soon after that, Sir Thomas Aylesbury, who was Master of Requests and Surveyor of the Navy, was living at Cranbourn, and one of his daughters in 1632 married Edward Hyde, afterwards Lord Clarendon. In that year, too, I find Secretary Conway writing to him about the new proposition of Richard Daye for planting there. Sir Thomas Aylesbury, we know, was in the lodge in 1637, for in that year his little grandchild was born there, who became in after time the mother of Queen Anne.

Then came warnings of the Civil War, and a riot took place here, and one hundred deer were killed at New Lodge by the people.

During this period, Anne Hyde, as she herself tells us, lived here till she was twelve, "having in that time seen the ruin of Church and State and the murder of my King." All the existing arrangements were upset and the officers changed; but, as before observed, it only made a Cavalier give up his place to a Roundhead. And accordingly it will not surprise us to find that while Windsor Castle was the seat of the Lord Commissioner Whitelock, Cranbourn Lodge was in the possession of Captain James Whitelock, his son, and afterwards of the Parliamentary officer Colonel Christopher Whichcote.

In a Report made in 1653, Cranbourn Lodge, with the outhouse, is mentioned as much out of repair, and New Lodge also much decayed. One more turn of the wheel of fortune, and we have the restoration of the royal family, and several changes in the keepership of Cranbourn took place before things settled down. Old Sir Thomas Aylesbury died at Breda in 1657 at the age of eighty-one, and in November 1660 the two walks and lodges were granted to his son-in-law, Edward Hyde. Prince Rupert also became interested in the lodge, as he figures as its keeper in 1662.[*]

What a charming retreat the old tower on the heath must have been for him when, after the turmoil of his life, he gave himself up to scientific pursuits, pondering over his discoveries in steel and metal!

At this same time the new lodge was granted to Elizabeth, Viscountess Mordaunt, by her husband, the Ranger, with the magnificent fee of fourpence a day! This lady was the daughter of

---

[*] Cal. State Papers, 1660, grant to Henry Hyde, with reversion for Laurence and Edward Hyde for life.

Carey of Sunninghill Park, and mother of the third Peer, who became as impetuous a Royalist leader, both by sea and land, almost as Prince Rupert himself. He was Marlborough's great opponent. The Mordaunts carried things with a high hand, as I find by a petition in 1662 of one Curtis, an underkeeper of New Lodge Walk, praying restitution to his place, which he had lost during "the troubles," Lord Mordaunt having put his own butler into the post.

I next find that in 1664 Cranbourn was granted to Sir George Carteret, Treasurer of the Navy, during the lives of Lord Cornbury, and Laurence and Edward Hyde, and for thirty-one years after; and thereupon Sir George set about its restoration; indeed, he pulled down the old house, all but one room, which he saved in compliment to the rising greatness of old Aylesbury's little grand-daughter.

Sir George Carteret was the staunch Royalist governor of Jersey, who succeeded in that office his father-in-law, Sir Philip de Carteret; he was the grandfather of that brilliant minister of George I., John Carteret, Earl Granville, of whom Swift says, "He carried away from Oxford more Greek, Latin, and philosophy than properly became a person of his rank." He took there too a temper more sweet even than Marlborough's; and of that, no less than of his wit and power of repartee, the Dean had a wholesome dread. It is of him the story is told that when Swift was kept waiting at the Castle in Dublin in some suspense as to whether the Government intended to prosecute him for some of his writings, he sent into Carteret his complaint—

"My very good Lord, 'tis a very hard task
For a man to wait here who has nothing to ask;"

and had back in reply—

"My very good Dean, there are few who come here
But have something to ask, or something to fear."

We next get a very interesting notice of Cranbourn from the indefatigable Mr. Pepys, who, on the 19th August 1665. paid his chief a visit there, to break out to him that most unpleasant affair, the disaster of our fleet before Bergen. He lost his way in the Forest, was benighted, and obliged to retrace his steps, and was carried to Cranbourn late at night. The old house, he tell us, was new building, and he had to go up a ladder, "and saw Sir George in his bed, told him all this bad news, which troubled him mightily;" but his irrepressible spirits were equal to the strain, "for yet," says he, "we were very merrie and made the best of it." Perhaps they discussed their business over a bottle of good old wine, for which the worthy Secretary had a special weakness. He lay in the Duchess of York's chamber, which had been preserved, and restored himself with a bottle of "strong water" he took with him, "whereof," he says, "now and then a sip did me good." He left us his impressions of Cranbourn, for "the next day I walked forth to see the place, and find it to be a very noble seat, in a noble forest, with the noblest prospect towards Windsor, and round about over many counties that can be desired, but otherwise a very melancholy place, and little variety save only trees."

On the 25th of the following February he paid Cranbourn another visit, travelling from London in a coach-and-four early one Sunday morning to dine with the Carterets, Lord Hinchingbroke, and other friends, at the new mansion by the old tower; had a quiet ramble in the park with Sir George to discuss the subject of Bergen and the sale of Dunkirk, two matters causing them much anxiety. He mentions a remarkable incident of the great fire that had just then left London a heap of ruins. "Lady Carteret," he says, "herself did tell us how abundance of pieces of burnt papers were cast by the wind as far as Cranbourn; and among others, she took up one, or had one brought to her to see, which was a little bit of paper that had been printed, whereon there remained no more nor less than these words, 'Time is it is done.'" As far as Oxford the sun was obscured, and shone, although in a cloudless sky, with a dim reddish light, caused, as Locke, who was living there then, tells us, by the smoke of the burning city, driven that way by an easterly wind.

This old house was the scene of much gaiety about this time. Pepys gives us a sad picture of a gathering here in September 1667, when King Charles came over from Bagshot to spend a happy day with Carteret. It was not a place at which the hospitalities of the age would be wanting. They all frolicked and caroused till their conviviality overpowered them, and then they drank the Duke of York's health on their knees, and in that undignified position also made the King do the same.

Of this "noble seat" I have been so fortunate as to find a pencil drawing, by a copy of which I am glad now to perpetuate its memory.

Evelyn visited Cranbourn in 1674, when Sir Robert Holmes gave a great entertainment there to His Majesty and all the Court. He paid it another visit in 1686, and, with his accustomed grandeur, he travelled in a coach-and-six. He tells us the reason why the one room was spared when Sir George Carteret pulled down the old house was, "because the late Duchess of York was born in it." He also tells us that Cranbourn had then been purchased by Lord Godolphin. It was, however, only a lease of it he bought, for I find (from the Docket Book at the Rolls) that the grant was made in 1688 for thirty-one years only.

I must now speak of one of Cranbourn's most interesting tenants, Richard Jones, Lord Ranelagh, Paymaster to the Army for 1686-87-88. A nephew of Robert Boyle, he had this keepership by assignment, with that also of Bagshot, and several other good appointments in the neighbourhood. He seems to have been a man of some cultivation, or at least had a taste for the cultivation of trees, and he it was, no doubt, who planted the lime avenues leading through Winkfield Plain towards the school, and the fine trees still about Cranbourn Tower, and made the fish-ponds there.* That he had laid out the grounds tastefully, and that it was quite "a show place," I learn incidentally from Swift; for in September 1711 he writes, " I rode out this morning with the Doctor [Arbuthnot] to see Cranbourn, a house of Lord Ranelagh's, and the Duchess of Marlborough's Lodge and the park; the finest places they are for nature and plantations that ever I saw, and the finest riding."

Among the Treasury papers I have fallen upon an interesting letter of Lord Ranelagh's, dated 24th March 1707, in which he pleads most pathetically for the preservation of the beautiful old trees of Cranbourn, twenty of which, as he thought, had already been felled. "It was true they were old, but still growing and making a noble show and shade every summer; their number great, and no young trees could pretend to match them in fifty years; that they would yield a very inconsiderable sum, and that a hundred times that sum could not supply the want of them in that age; and if the destruction be continued," he says, "Cranbourn will look like Bagshot Heath." What a proverb the barrenness of Bagshot was! " The neighbours," he continues, " were sensibly afflicted with the loss of their greatest delight," and ends by "praying his Lordship's pity for old trees, and for his devoted servant, old Ranelagh." Mr. Wilcox, the surveyor, replied to this, implying that his Lordship was really crying out before he was hurt, and that they had cut nothing within a mile of him; and then referring to Mr. Lowen, the keeper of another walk,

---

* Menzies's Hist. of the Great Park.

whom he saw "after his return from New Forest," continues, "If the money designed for the poor inhabitants of Porchester were not raised in Cranbourn, he knows not where it could be raised by wood sales." This allusion to Porchester and the New Forest was puzzling, and made me think at first it must be Cranbourn Chase in Dorsetshire to which the letter referred, and that it was the "Cranbourn Oaks," that Macaulay has made historical, that were threatened; but, on the other hand, Mr. Lowen was keeper of the New Lodge (Madame Van de Weyer's) at that time, having, in July 1701, petitioned "that his house might be repaired, as it had suffered by the severity of last winter's snow and tempestuous weather;" but subsequent search clearly established the fact that it was our Cranbourn. Just at that time it is said a colony of poor distressed people from the Palatinate had been brought over after Marlborough's wars, and housed at Porchester in Hampshire, and Queen Anne, it seems, took pity on them, and was desirous of sending them assistance. But from the Treasury papers I gather it was to rebuild Porchester Church, which had been used by the Dutch prisoners in Charles II.'s time, when they were secured in the castle, and was then set fire to. It became so ruinous that divine service could no longer be held in it, and Queen Anne, either out of compassion for the poor strangers, or for the poor parishioners, who were unable without assistance to restore their church, ordered these wood sales of the "old dotard" trees to furnish the means.* But what is quite conclusive, "poor old Ranelagh" had, with his bodily infirmities, the infirmity of being unable to keep his accounts; he had millions of the public money through his hands, and a good deal of it, instead of going to maintain the soldiers in the Palatinate, had found its way to the gardeners and upholsterers at Cranbourn Lodge. He had evidently over-spent himself, for in 1705 he sold to the Earl of Arran the lease of Bagshot Place, which James II. had granted to James Graham, Esq., and in 1711 he was ordered by his physician to "go to the Bathe" for his health's sake, but "could neither go thither nor anywhere else unless a payment was made to him!" He was questioned in the House as to his accounts, and special allusion was made to his extravagance in laying out and furnishing Cranbourn. At last came the exposure, and he was found a heavy defaulter. He died in 1711, and a special Act of Parliament was passed for the sale of his estates. Ranelagh House, Chelsea, and the office of the "two

---

* See Cal. Treasury Papers, 1705-6.

Walks in the Chase of Cranbourn, within the Forest of Windsor, together with the custody of the Lodge there built," with the custody of the woods, "and the herbage and pannage of Brewswood, and windfalls and dead boughs of trees and the masts, and the *toll or duty of Chiminage*," with all other perquisites and profits thereof, and the furniture, pictures, and goods of the said Earl which were in the said Lodge, were to be sold towards paying his debt to the Crown. The sale was only of the property of Lord Ranelagh, not the estate, which still remained in the Crown, subject to his Lordship's lease.

The Treasurership of the Navy seems to have afforded irresistible temptations, for Lord Ranelagh's predecessor, Carteret, was especially aimed at by the Bill passed in 1666 for examining the public accounts.

In February 1717 a Bill was brought into Parliament for the sale of this estate, but it was rejected. The Crown, it seems, had purchased Lord Ranelagh's furniture.

During the first quarter of the century, several keepers were appointed: Lord Cobham in 1717, the Earl of Carlisle in 1723, and the Duke of St. Albans in 1730. In 1731 the house and keepership, together with the use of the furniture, were bestowed on Miss Henrietta Maria Withers. Cranbourn subsequently became the residence of Charles, Duke of St. Albans; and on his death in 1751 its keepership was conferred on William Augustus, Duke of Cumberland, who removed to it from the Ranger's Lodge in the Great Park, of which he had been Ranger since 1746; and here, the year before he died, he bred the celebrated racehorse "Eclipse" in the paddock adjoining the Tower, and a memorial recording the fact is now to be seen there.

Then came the Duke's nephew, Frederick, brother of George III., subsequently the Duke of York, and afterwards the Duke of Gloucester lived there. In 1768 it was the scene of some gaiety, when, on the 17th September, the King of Denmark paid the Duke a visit. After seeing Eton College, he had been conducted to the Great Park to see a stag turned out, and thence on to Cranbourn Lodge, where he dined.*

In 1778 it was announced that a grant of Cranbourn was being prepared to the Duke of St. Albans and his successors in lieu of their seat at Windsor, which was entailed on that family by King Charles, and which His Majesty had lately annexed to his own house adjoining. However, in 1791, Prince William, son of the

* *Reading Mercury.*

Duke of Gloucester, was appointed Ranger, and in 1794 Charles Knight, in his "Windsor Gazetteer," speaks of Cranbourn as a fine house then in the Duke's possession, and notices especially a spacious room decorated in large panels with representations of the military uniforms of the various European armies.

In 1808, after the death of the Duke of Gloucester, the mansion was put into complete repair; the tower was restored and redecorated, as may still be seen from the ceiling of a room there, and the windows were repointed.*

The Hon. George Villiers was then its occupant for a short time.

I have spoken of the natural beauty of this spot, but there were times, however, when, to the most romantic natures, the beautiful oaks of Cranbourn became as melancholy as they seemed to Mr. Pepys. When poor old Ranelagh walked out of his beloved mansion a bankrupt man, his last gaze on those beautiful trees was not an enviable one; nor was the place enchanting altogether to the forlorn maiden who would not marry the man she did not love, and was therefore sent to compose her outraged feelings (some called it her undutiful heart) amid the silent groves of that old Tudor tower. This unhappy state of things did actually occur here in the year 1814, which I must mention if I am to be true either to history or romance.

The Princess Charlotte, we may remember, was in 1813 rather drawn into a betrothal to the Prince of Orange, although she never liked him; and when, in 1814, Prince Leopold appeared at Court, the Princess, much to her father's indignation, could no longer think of her betrothed; indeed, virtually broke off the engagement. Her father at once dismissed her household and sent her to the Tower— not of London, but Cranbourn, "a solitary house in the Forest of Windsor, to consider her obstinacy; nobody should be allowed to visit her except the Queen-mother once a week." Rather a hard fate; but if this were ever ordered or even threatened, it was certainly never strictly carried out: she may, as was said at the time, have breathed more freely there, but the retirement soon affected her health. The Duke of Sussex brought the matter before the House of Lords, and the *Morning Chronicle* beginning to discuss the subject a little too plainly, she was removed to Weymouth for sea-bathing, and returned to Cranbourn in the autumn.

The popular idea was well expressed by an old man in the Forest, who told me, more than seventy years afterwards, how well

---

* *Gent. Mag.*, vol. lxxix p. 430.

he remembered her being sent to Cranbourn as an "*exile*." She married Prince Leopold in 1816. The old house was pulled down about the end of George IV.'s reign. In H. Walter's map of 1823 it is shown. The materials were sold and carted away to build a house at Ascot; but the drawings here given will enable us on a visit to the place to see exactly the arrangement of it. The chief approaches to the house seem to have been from Winkfield up a gentle ascent to the principal front, which faced west; another led through an avenue from the south still existing, and entered a small courtyard at the back of the mansion. Look on the old tower, and you may see the mark in the brickwork showing where Sir George Carteret's house joined on to it; and in the octagon side, which united the two buildings, may still be seen on each of the first three floors the bricked-up openings which afforded communication between them. The very line of frontage too of the old house may be clearly traced on the grass, and some of its foundation bricks are visible still. On ascending the tower, a magnificent view is obtained of Windsor Castle and Eton College, lying as it were beneath you, and of St. Leonard's Hill, that stands out so boldly in the west.

CHAPTER XXX.

Ascot.

THE parish of Sunninghill in its gradual rise towards the north-west gains its highest point near the Ascot Hotel, and there falls again sharply to its boundary stream.

At this fine elevated spot, the highest within ten miles of Windsor, the well-known heaths of Ascot and Bagshot formerly adjoined; and a more charming country or a healthier can hardly be found. Sunninghill and the dells of Swinley lie to the south, and the Frimley ridges rise up in the distance beyond; towards the west we look down on Englemere, much smaller now than it was once; and northward a fine prospect extends over the broken undulations of Cranbourn, Winkfield, and Bray. The view from here has been much shut in by plantations, and there are men still living in the parish who remember it much more extensive and beautiful. The warm sands, once covered with a carpet of heather and gorse, and the bracing air, leave nothing to be desired in climate. So, doubtless, thought those British and Saxon tribes whose favoured home this was. Two of their barrows still remain on the heath, and scattered around lie the stone implements of a still earlier race. Arrow-heads and celts are picked up here in considerable numbers, as, in fact, they are in almost all the localities known to have been inhabited by British tribes. At Rushmore in Wiltshire, the North Riding of Yorkshire, and in Scotland they have been found in thousands. In the latter place, as Pennant tells us, they were called "Elf-shots," shot by fairies at the cattle, and to which all their diseases were attributed; the touch of one of these flints was supposed to effect a cure. Those found here are said to be of the Palæolithic as well as the Neolithic type; but although that primitive Basque or Iberian people were numerous in the valley of the Thames,* it is doubtless to their successors, the tall fair race, to whom these round barrows belonged. But how changed, during the last half century even, is all this country!

It was once the wildest spot in the Forest. The dark heath over which we are looking was, even to Saxon imagination, a picture of desolation. The great "blacan mor" was the boundary limit towards Sunninghill of the abbey lands of Abingdon, and down through this "blacan mor" courses to this day the Blackmore brook.

Centuries passed before the scene from this British village site became suggestive of any improved civilisation. For although in Saxon days it had long been the habitation of men, it had become again, as we glean from the Chronicles of Abingdon (vol. ii. p. 7), merely a harbour for wild beasts. After the Conquest, it was once more a wilderness. Norman kings afforested its plains, and Norman ecclesiastics ruled their serfs here with difficulty. Within a mile of this spot, in the days of Edward I., stood the dark hillock known as the "Quelmes," the gibbet or place of execution; not the one which for ages formed a forest boundary beyond Virginia Water, but a similar one, the site of which may, I think, be identified with Mr. Ferard's farm and the lodge now known as the Roundabout.

This identical spot is marked in Norden's map as the "Quelmes," and in an ancient purveyance list in Mr. Ferard's possession, we find mention of a place in Winkfield called the "Quelmes, alias the mirhuells mounte" (i.e., the morshill or gallows). I have met with the name "morshull" in other parts here. There were several of these ghastly erections in the Forest, and not far off, in the neighbouring manor of Heywood (as I have mentioned elsewhere), the Abbot of Abingdon hanged a woman in the time of Edward I.

On this hill, close to the schools, were the "conduit heads" mentioned by Norden, seven in number. They were connected with a great work carried out in the reigns of Edward VI. and Queen Mary to supply Windsor Castle with water. The principal supply was brought from Blackmore in 1555. The pipes were laid by way of Frith Lane, now called Free Lane, to Ascot Plain, and thence by the Mote Park to Windsor. John Norris was comptroller of the works, and some of the lead used was brought from the old college at Maidstone, which had just before been suppressed. This same source was again resorted to by George IV. It is now only used for the kennels.

---

* Sir C. Ramsay, p. 552.

As to the tumuli, an excellent account of them is given by Gough in his additions to Camden, where he tells us that until after the middle of the last century there existed "on a hill near the race-ground, about a mile from Sunninghill Wells, on Ascot Heath, four barrows, on the south side of the turnpike road to Oakingham, the nearest not above 300 yards from the road; they stand south-east by south of each other. The trenches round the large ones are about 12 feet wide and 2 deep. About two miles south-south-west of the barrows is Tower Hill, a small irregular hill, very steep on all sides, except the north-north-east, where is the entrance to the entrenchment that runs round the top of the whole hill and follows all its irregularities."

It may be well to record the present condition of these Ascot barrows. They are about 12 feet high; that on the south-east has now no trench, and, measuring from north to south, is about 90 feet across, *i.e.*, about 30 feet up each side, and 30 across the top; measured from east to west, it is rather less, but that may be accounted for by its less perfect form there. The other larger one, about 50 yards to the north-west, is more perfect, but the 12-feet ditch round it has given place to one only 2 feet wide and 1 foot deep, the rest having become filled up, whereby the sides have become slightly lengthened, and give a measurement from north to south of 108 feet, from east to west 105. It was probably not larger than the other originally. A smaller barrow between the two, about 40 feet from the western one, is still to be traced, although fast disappearing; but the fourth I cannot find. These tumuli were probably not earlier than the period known as the Iron Age; but unfortunately, although they are supposed to have been opened, no record has been preserved of their contents, so that their precise date is uncertain. I must not, however, weary my readers with any further notice of these antiquities. The very thought of such vestiges of Palæolithic and Neolithic, or even of Bronze and Iron Ages, is bewildering. But when we enter upon the modern history of Ascot we are still in a dilemma.

Where is Ascot? If it be all those pleasant villas, as they are called, that overlook its famous Heath, it has lost its ancient history. If it be the Manor or the Tithing of Ascot, it has lost its ancient houses. None of any consequence remain. Mr. Waterson, once Vicar of Winkfield, wrote long years ago of that place, "It is remarkable there is not so much as the appearance of a gentleman's house in all the parish of any antiquity;" the good houses have all been built from the ground on former sites.

The Manor of Ascot conferred its name on the beautiful Heath that adjoins it, although nearly all that now exists of that lies in the parish of Sunninghill.

Where the new Ascot stands there was not, at the beginning of the century, a single habitation of any importance, save perhaps the old Queen's Hill Lodge. Fortune favoured the wild spot when Queen Anne selected it for her royal racecourse. Ascot Heath stood sponsor for the famous races, and the races made the place. They made it, however, at first in a very primitive fashion. The old wayside inn, the Wells, was its grand hotel for "the quality;" but of this, as also of its first grand-stand, I have spoken elsewhere.

Two other refreshment places ere long arose; one, at the archway of Ascot Heath House, has been erroneously described as having been built for an approach to the stables and as a stand from which to witness the racing. For this latter purpose it would certainly have been useless. It was really erected by a Mr. Charles Wright as a refreshment place for the higher classes, to enable him more especially to introduce his newly imported champagne, a wine which, although known in England as early as the time of Henry VIII., and drank at the Court of Charles II. and down to Pope's time, had, during the French wars, become almost unknown here. Another, a rustic one of much less pretentious character, was the "Stag and Hounds," still remaining, long kept by Richard Morton, an old cricketer, one of the best bats in England. His predecessor was Thomas Kettle, who, as we are told, exhibited his native wit by hoisting up on a pole forty feet high an old tin kettle by way of sign, so that there might be kettle outside as well as in.

The first agricultural attempt at Ascot was at Englemere farm. The late Mr. Cooper of Windsor, about 1820, having bought up several allotments on the enclosure of the Heath, was induced to build stabling for thirty horses for the use of His Majesty as private racing stables and as an advantage to the sterile soil; but they were so used only for a short time.

Close here, on the hill, to the north-west of the schools, the lines of an encampment may still be traced. It was the camp of 1739, when George II., alarmed by the Pretender, induced Parliament to increase our national forces to the number of 18,000.

Of this Ascot, of course, there can be no archæological history; but, like Coworth and Broomhall, it is so bound up in our fortunes, that we may ramble a little beyond its borders, and find out what we can of the ancient Ascot in Winkfield. Of the very interesting church there, I regret that my space will not allow me to speak.

Winkfield is in the hundred of Ripplesmere, and consists of two tithings, Winkfield and Ascot. These, it seems, were both dependent on the royal manor of Folyjohn. Thus in 1588 I find* a "certificate of rents of the inhabitants and tenants of the manor of Folyjohn, with its members of Hyremere, Winkfield, and Ascot, parcel of the lordship of New Windsor."

Ascot was, as it were, a manor within a manor, and formerly paid to Winkfield 20s. 10d. a year as an acknowledgment of its dependence.

The Chronicles of Abingdon carry us back to the primitive condition of Winkfield as an early clearance in the forest, "in a place which its ancient inhabitants called Wæclesfeld."

In 942 the Saxon King Edmund gave this "Uuinchefeld" with "Swinleie" to a certain Saethrithe, the most religious of women, as the grateful monks record, and shortly after this that lady bestowed it on their Abbey of Abingdon. In 1015 we are told the Lady Eadfleda also gave to the monastery certain lands here.

Domesday states that "in the hundred of Ripplesmere the Abbey itself (of Abingdon) holds Wenesfelle, and always held it." "Four hides of this land are in the King's forest." In the time of William Rufus the Abbey seems to have been interfered with by the Great Forester, Walter Fitz Other, for I find the King by his writ commanded that worthy to permit the abbot and convent to enjoy the land and wood of Winkfield without molestation. In the time of Henry I. the Abbey again had some trouble in their holding, and wanted a confirmation of their title, which the King granted on the same conditions on which they held the lands in the time of his father and brother, and enjoined that the encroachment which Godric, the Reeve of Windsor, had committed by the enclosure there, should remain permanently.

The Nomina Villarum (9 Ed. II.) gives "Wynekefeld and Ascote as belonging to the Abbey of Abingdon," and so they continued till the time of Henry VIII. Folyjohn was in the bailiwick of Bagshot; Ascot in that of Battles. But while in Folyjohn and Sunninghill the timber belonged to the Crown, at Winkfield, after litigation as to the trees at Swinley, it was held to be in the lord.

Folyjohn was an ancient possession of the family of Trussell of Cublesdon, one of whom, Sir William, was cousin-german, as Leland tells us, of that Sir William Trussell who took so important a part in

---

* Cal. State Papers.

the deposition of Edward II. Oliver de Bordeaux, one of that King's Gascon favourites, and gentleman of his chamber, was also interested in lands at Folyjohn.* He was in 1316 permitted to empark his wood of Folyjohn and Hyermere and two years later to enclose and add to it forty acres more of the waste. This would seem to have been the origin of the Folyjohn estate; and how it came to Oliver de Bordeaux appears from a curious entry in the Wardrobe accounts of 10th Edward II. (1317),† in which I find payment of "£2, 10s. for money thrown over the heads of Oliver de Bordeaux and the lady Maud Trussel, during the solemnisation of their nuptials at the door of the chapel within the park at Woodstock;" and it would seem that this young lady, Maud Trussel, was the daughter and heiress of Warine Mainwaring, and the widow, strictly speaking, of Sir William Trussell, who had died in his tenth year, and to whom she had been contracted in marriage. On the death of her second husband, Oliver de Bordeaux, this estate seems to have reverted to her family. I find a grant in 1319 to Oliver de Burdegalia in tail-general of all the hereditaments of Folyjohn and Hiermore, Berks, lately of John Drokenford, Bishop of Bath.‡

The Trussels in 1328 fled from the vengeance of Mortimer and sought an asylum in France; but as soon as he was removed they returned, and in 1336 the estate was restored to a William Trussel, the same probably who in 1356 was governor of Odiham Castle.

Henry Bataille, jun., was forester of the bailiwick of Ascot under Edward III.§ In 1350 that King granted to William Trussell the manor of Eaton Hastings in Berks, in exchange for lands in Folyjohn, Hermere, and Winchmere, Old and New Windsor, Winkfield and Ascot, all which the King rejoined and united to the Castle and manor of Windsor. In 1360 Commissioners, of whom the indefatigable William of Wickham was one, were directed to take these manors in hand. They held an inquiry as to their value, and reported that they had accordingly enclosed certain lands there, and that Folyjohn, with its members Hyremers, Winkfield, and Ascot were worth £30, 14s. 2d, besides the King's manor and park unenclosed. And soon after this William of Wykeham was ordered to deliver these Folyjohn lands to Thomas Cheyne, the constable of the Castle, on the King's behalf. Wickham was extremely active here at this time, and "certain unnecessary houses in the King's manor

---

* Pat. 10, Ed. II., m. 17. † See Archæologia, vol. xxvi.
‡ See 1 Pat. 12, Ed. II., also Brocas Family, by Prof. Burrows, p. 74.
§ See Decimo Regis Ed. III., and 32 Ed. III., Cal. Rot. Pat.

of Ascot" were sold.* On thus becoming a royal manor, it was probably granted to this William Trussel, for we find among the escheats in the Inquisition Post-mortem Rolls (50), "Ed. 3 anno tricessimo nono," "Will'us Trussell de Cublesdon, miles," as being seized at the time of his death, about 1366, of "Eton, Shawe, Windsor Vetus, Merserude purpresture, Assermede, Folye jon maner, Heremere, Winkefelde, and Ascot, terr and ten."

In 1368 the King granted to the tenants of the manor of Folyjon that they should be free from the carriage of the King's goods and have common of pasture in the forest. That it was then in the King's hands we know from the fact of Arnold de Brocas having been appointed in 1385 clerk of the works to the King's manor of Folyjohn.† It is not easy to reconcile these early manorial divisions. The expression the "King's manor of Ascot" must have arisen from its dependence on Folyjohn.

Winkfield was a very extensive manor, comprising nearly the whole parish, including Swinley, Earlywood, and a portion of Bagshot Park. It is rather, however, with its demesne lands that we are most interested. These had been broken up into several parcels; a large tract of over 150 acres had been at an early period bestowed on the Nunnery of Bromhall, and 191 acres at Swinley had been given by the monks of Abingdon to the Church of St. Mary de Stratford at Westham. Of part of this, as we see in the account of Cranbourn, the Crown became occupier as early as the reign of Henry VII., of "the enclosure or grove of Swinley," and of the small keeper's house there, known afterwards as Beard's Lodge.

On the dissolution of Bromhall, Henry VIII. gave "Chawridge alias Winkfield," with its ancient manor-house of Chawridge Place, to St. John's College. And at the later general dissolution in 1540 he bestowed the manor of Winkfield on Anthony Ellis and Sir Richard Warde, the son of his "yeoman harbinger," to be holden in capite by the 20th part of a knight's fee, and a rent of 16s. 7½d. Warde's manorial house, in which Queen Elizabeth visited him, is said to have been an ancient mansion called Godwins, in which Mr. Hatch afterwards resided. In 1600 this manor was in the sole possession of Sir Richard Harrison, Warde's son-in-law, and subsequently of Dame Mary Harrison; and at the beginning of the eighteenth century it belonged to Dame Mary Draper, Anthony Meeke, and Gray Neville in different shares. The old manor-house of Ascot had long been in the hands of other tenants of the

---

* See Roll at Carlton Ride, F. L. H. 943.   † See Brocas Family, by Prof. Burrows.

Abbey. It was for ages the ancient home of the great Norman family of Bataille, who were owners also of lands at Sunninghill, and from them their old mansion took its name of Battles, by which it was known for several generations afterwards. In the Church of Winkfield there is an aisle called the Battle's Aisle, and under a large stone at the east end of it, raised up three feet from the pavement, mouldered their bones. But after being plundered of its brasses, as Mr. Waterson tells us, and much defaced, it was removed to another part of the church. These unfortunate removals are of course unavoidable. The name lingered in the parish several hundred years, and the family seems to have held the rank of gentlemen down to 1599. From one of them it appears the Broughtons were descended, as in like manner some of the Norreyses were from the Lovels,* who were important owners in this part of the Forest in early Norman days.

This Ascot manor-house next became known as Burleighs, from the residence there, doubtless, of the great Lord President in Queen Elizabeth's time; in confirmation of which, I find an old agreement for sale of 1 acre and 3 roods of the waste for planting by the dog-kennels, and in which it is described as in the parish of Sunninghill, adjoining to land called "Burleighs," "alias Ascot Lodge." That he was so resident in the neighbourhood, we have another little piece of evidence, for in 1595 his servant George Wade fell in love with one of our village maidens, and they were married in our Church, he being described as "servant to the Right Hon. Lord President."

Now whether Ascot Place ever belonged to the Norreys I do not know, but the Heralds' Visitation tells us that young Henry Norris was knighted at Ascot. As early as the time of Henry VII., Sir William Norreys had been appointed keeper of Folyjohn; after his decease, his son William in 1510 had a grant of it; and it was certainly held by Henry Norris on his attainder in the Ann Boleyn business.†

Very early in the seventeenth century Ascot must have been in the possession of the Broughtons; for in the Survey of 1613 I find "Broughton, Francis, one fair house called Battles alias Ascot, with seven closes of pasture and meadow ground, 37 acres 1 rood 5 poles," and other lands there.

The Broughtons seem to have come into Berkshire from Broughton in Suffolk, one Francis Broughton having married Margaret, daughter of Ricdi de Warvill in Berks, and it was probably from the

---

* See Nichol's Progresses of Queen Elizabeth, vol. iii. p. 421. † See Cal. State Papers, Dom.

marriage of his son to Agnes, daughter of Henry Battle of Wingfield, that Ascot passed from that ancient family to the Broughtons.* There were several children of this marriage, and among them Humphrey and Francis; the former of whom was, doubtless, Francis Young's under-keeper of Bearwood Walk, who got into trouble with the Council during the Commonwealth about the timber. The ancient fashion of calling places after their owners' names especially prevailed here; we can trace it in this estate from Norman days, for the manor-house, as we have seen, was for centuries called "Battles," then "Burleighs," afterwards, for a hundred years, the residence of the Broughtons, it became known as Broughtons. In 1722 it seems to have been in the possession of Robert Foster, Esq., and was then always called "Fosters;" after this gentleman's death, the Ascot property appears to have belonged to the family of Meeke, with the exception of one-ninth which was in Henry Grey, Esq. (a son of Richard Neville of Billingbere, who had just taken the name of Grey); and in April 1726† it was for sale and the Crown in treaty for its purchase, as it was thought advantageous towards the preservation of the game at Swinley. It was described as possessing a court leet and court baron, and within it was another manor, which paid quit-rents to Winkfield. It included "a small farm or warren, within which were the seven water-conduits from which Windsor Castle was formerly, and might again be, supplied with very good water; also another farm, and several large sluice ponds stocked with carp, valued at 20s. an acre." No mansion, however, is mentioned. Had the old manor-house of Battles been pulled down then? This negotiation having failed, it was ultimately sold to Andrew Lindegren, a foreign merchant in London, who erected the present house on a new site; his executors sold it in 1787 to Daniel Agace, Esq., who was its owner in 1813. On his death in 1828 it passed to the family of the present owner, Charles Ferard, Esq. The old house stood, I have reason to think, nearer to the road, on the eastern side of the lake, on a spot surrounded by fine trees, and still bearing traces of having been the site of an ancient habitation, not improbably moated. The new house was erected on the bank at the other side of the water. Meanwhile the Winkfield manor and Swinley Lodge and enclosure had been separately purchased by His Majesty George III., as his private estate. He retained it till the end of his reign, when in

---

* See Visitation of Berks, Brit. Mus. Add. MS.
† Potes, Les Delices des Châteaux Royaux, 1785. ‡ See Cal. State Papers, 1726.

1819 the manor, but not the Swinley land, was again annexed to the Ascot estate on its purchase by Mr. Agace of Lord Brudenel, His Majesty's trustee.

But returning to modern days, Murray in his "Guide" says, "Adjoining to the cascade in Virginia Water is a sort of grotto formed of stones dug up at Bagshot Heath, and supposed to have been a Druidical circle;" and Colonel Cooper King, I see, in his History of Berkshire, repeats the story. I cannot, however, discover where this circle was, or whether it ever did exist. Let us hope, as I quite believe, it is all a mistake, or what with the circle and the barrows, if the ghost of an ancient Briton should ever wander over the heath to revisit the tombs of his ancestors, he will go away with a sad opinion of eighteenth-century refinement.

Was it this, or was it the levelling of the rabbit warrens at Swinley, that Somerville in "The Chase" thought worthy of especial commendation—

> "When the brazen voice
> Of war is hush'd (as erst victorious Rome)
> T' employ his stationed legions in the works
> Of peace; to smoothe the rugged wilderness."

What were these "works of peace" on which "the stationed legions" were employed? It was not, as elsewhere mentioned, in making Virginia Water, but rather, I believe, literally in "smoothing the rugged wilderness," to render it more suitable for the chase, just then reviving here. In also adding to the roads or ridings, they may truly have "made things smooth" by removing the stones to the grotto; but their prowess was long recorded in Latin as well as English on a monument called "The Soldier's Pillar," erected on one of the tumuli I have described at Bowledge Hill; it mentions the troops engaged in the works, but of this inscription I have been unable to obtain a copy.

To this pillar converged nine of the straight drives. Some of these may have been made in the time of George III., but most of them were constructed by Queen Anne. The one from Bagshot Rails, over Caesar's Camp by Tower Hill, known now as the Nine Mile Ride, was clearly so, as it is spoken of in 1716* (two years after her death) as "the new riding," then requiring repair. In that year also King's Beech Riding across Sunninghill Bog had been just newly made

---

* See Forest Book, Windsor Castle.

Old Patey, the herdsman, told me that the morass was in his time quite impassable except by this road.

Some of my young readers may suppose that the newest thing at Ascot is its cricketing; but that is only a revival; nearly a hundred years ago it was more famous for the game than it is now.* On the 20th July 1815, in the midst of the rejoicings and bell-ringings of the villages round after the great victory of Waterloo, there was played on Ascot racecourse a great match between the Gentlemen of Berkshire and the Gentlemen of Buckinghamshire for two thousand guineas. High stakes were the fashion then. The game generally lasted two or three days; they met at Sunninghill Wells at nine o'clock, and the wickets were pitched at ten. They played near to the spot on which the grand-stand is now, and there, we are told by a writer in the *Windsor and Eton Gazette* for April 1889, he well remembers a great match played between Sir John Cope's Bramshill eleven and the Sunninghill Club. Before concluding, I must not omit to notice the separate ecclesiastical district into which this western corner of the ancient parish has been formed.

In December 1841 Sunningdale was made a separate district, and a new church was erected there, which was afterwards enlarged, and ultimately, under the auspices of its present Vicar, the Rev. J. A. Cree, assisted mainly by the liberality of a parishioner, almost rebuilt in 1888. But this, although bordering on, did not include any portion of our parish. But at Ascot, by Order in Council in 1865, a similar district was created, and a church, built mainly through the exertions of the Rev. Cunningham Ellis, Vicar of Cranbourn, was consecrated in the previous year. It has since been much beautified by its present Vicar, the Rev. B. K. Pearse. The parish boundary-line runs from the intersection of the New Mile Road with that to Ascot, down the hill through the Railway Arch, and thence in a line south-south-west to the boundary stone fixed at a spot west of the newly erected Nunnery. From these additional sources of help much good has unquestionably resulted; and although we cannot find in the old parish or in either of these districts any approach to a model village, that poetic Utopia so much more easily imagined than discovered, we have reason to believe from those who knew the place half a century ago that we have improved, and need not blush at any comparison of the present with the past. But no one acquainted with the social condition of our village can fail to perceive that its one great vice of

---

* See *Reading Mercury* of that year.   † See Order in Council, March 9, 1865.

intemperance still prevails in it, and is the prolific parent of more than half our evils. I believe the unnecessary number of public-houses to be answerable for much of this. Against their baneful influence Church and State alike wage an unequal warfare. Reform in this is certainly required.

CHAPTER XXXI.

Bagshot and Windlesham.

BAGSHOT lies in one of the most beautiful parts of our country, where the counties of Berks and Surrey meet, and in the centre of that wild heath to which it has given its name. This sandy waste, as it used to be deemed, a very proverb of barrenness, extended, at the beginning of the century, for many miles round, and although so bleak and sterile, it lay like a beautiful fringe along the southern border of the Forest. Fringe it was in other aspects; geologically, a strip of open heath-lands of the Bagshot sands skirting the London clay; historically, a fringe or border-line between the Forest with its dread laws, and the bailiwick of Surrey and the law of the land. For ages this was debatable ground, as I have already explained.

Situated in the line of road to Winchester, Salisbury, and the West, it was always famous as a stage for travellers; and soon became, in truth, a village of inns. In the early Tudor days there was a house in the street called "Le Crowne," out of which a rent-charge was payable to the King; and as early as 1515 one of the fraternity had prospered there, for in that year John Rosyer, innkeeper, gave to the chapel of Bagshot a torch, price 3s. 4d., and bequeathed 13s. 4d. from land at Finchamsted, towards the support of a priest for the chapel, and 6s. 8d. for repairing it. Among the Signet Bills of Queen Elizabeth (1575) the hostelry called "the Crowne at Bagshot" is again mentioned.

The "King's Arms" was a very old inn; and Aubrey says it was originally the Chantrey House, and that it showed at the back of the premises its great antiquity.

In 1607 I find "a license to Thomas Baker and Thomas Yeamans to sell wines in the town of Bagshot, Surrey." The next principal

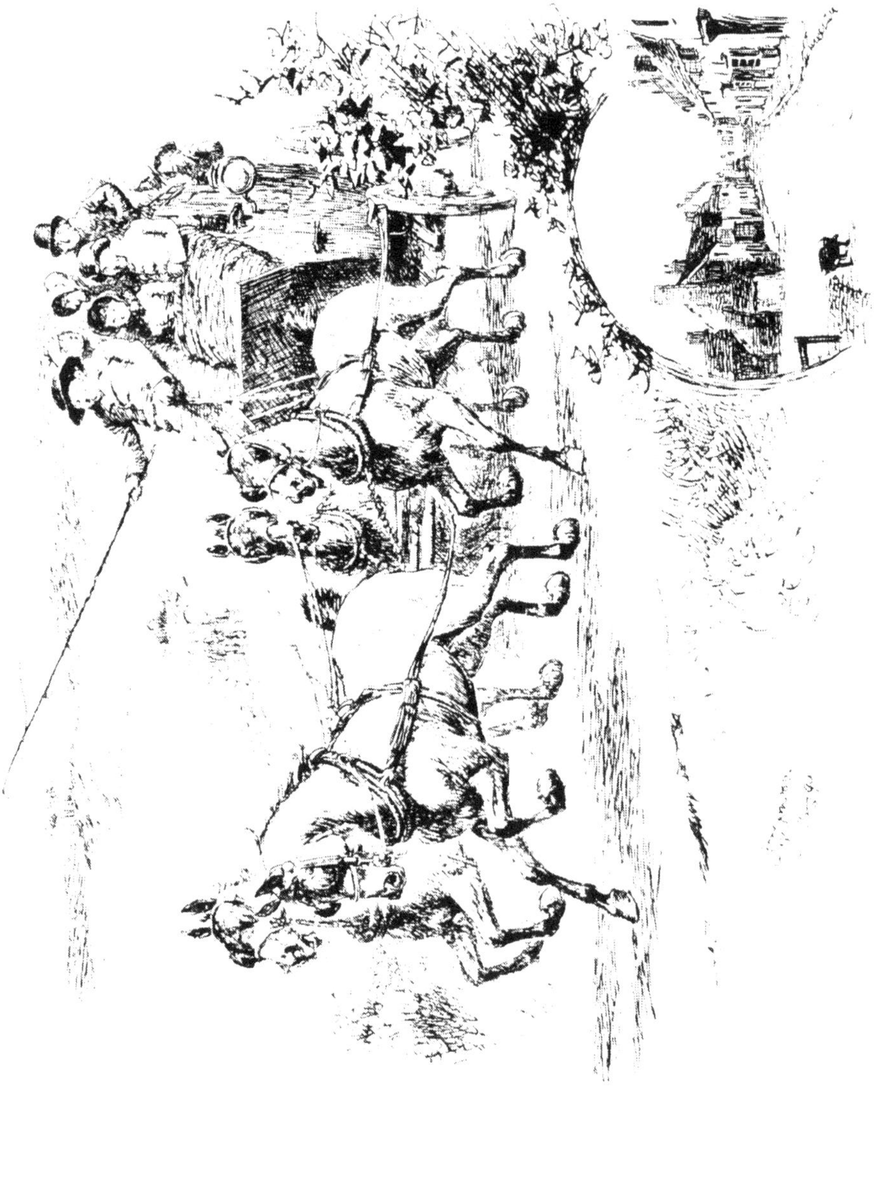

trade of the place was the tanning business, for which at one time it was famous.

It was quite an oasis in the desert, and such indeed it was to the weary traveller who had run the gauntlet of Combe Wood, Hounslow Heath, Shrubshill, and the low stretch of this "black desert," as in 1722 De Foe actually described it.

Although the chivalry of Claude Duval had degenerated into a more commonplace rascality, Bagshot was still notorious as the favourite haunt of that lawless crew that Gay has immortalised in "The Beggar's Opera." That rare picture of low life took by storm the fashionable drawing-rooms of the day, and stamped "Polly's" picture on their choicest fans and screens. The wits said "it made Gay rich, and Rich (the play-manager) gay." But umbrage was taken at the second part of the opera, and for promoting subscriptions to it, the Duchess of Queensberry—Prior's "Kitty beautiful and young"—was forbidden the Court.* But another age succeeded, and found the gentry of the road as active as ever, without being more respectable; but of this I have said enough elsewhere. I will only notice here an amusing incident that occurred on this very Heath in 1722, when two fellows ransacked the Dorchester coach, and carried off the valuables of a whole coach-load of passengers, and all the Christmas presents of turkeys and geese that were coming up from the country.†

These were the days when the Forest track had been transformed into a road, and all the traffic of the West poured through this little hamlet at the foot of the hill; for the present important road through Leatherhead and Guildford was not then practicable for coaches. Here the various "Flying Machines" stopped to change horses and regale their passengers on the far-famed Bagshot mutton.‡ Men now living may remember it as an important stage in their journey to the West. Thirty stage-coaches used to pass through Bagshot daily. One of them in particular was noted for its journeys to Salisbury in the beginning of the century, and was known as "the light Salisbury coach."

Many an adventure, many an affair of honour, has been mourned over or laughed over at the King's Arms, the Crown, and the Fight-

---

* Charles, third Duke of Queensberry, in 1720 married the beautiful and sprightly Lady Catherine Hyde, daughter of the Earl of Clarendon, a great friend and patron of Gay. See Walpole's Letters. *The Beggar's Opera* was produced in 1727; "Polly" was played by Miss Fenton, afterwards Duchess of Bolton.

† See *Post-Boy*, December 27, 1722.   ‡ Brayley's Surrey.

ing Cocks in the street; but probably none more ridiculous than when Wilkes fought a duel with Lord Talbot in the garden of the Red Lion here in 1763. The circumstances that provoked this Quixotic encounter were so comical, I am induced to relate them. At the coronation of George III., Lord Talbot was to officiate as Lord Steward, appearing in Westminster Hall on horseback. His horse had been at numerous rehearsals so assiduously trained to what was thought the most difficult part of his duty, the retiring backwards from the royal table, that at the ceremony itself no art of his rider could prevent the too docile animal from making his approach to the royal presence tail foremost. This ridiculous incident was the occasion of some sarcastic remarks in the *North Briton* of 21st August 1763, which led to an angry correspondence, and ultimately a duel.* Mr. Wilkes proposed that they should sup together that night and fight next morning, but Lord Talbot insisted on fighting immediately. Through this altercation and some delay of Wilkes' in writing letters, it was dusk before they went out; the moon was up, and after a harmless exchange of shots, the parties shook hands, and drank a bottle of claret together at the inn with a great deal of jollity.

But the old times are gone, and as one looks over the transformed little place, memories arise very eloquent of "Auld Lang Syne;" the life and the bustle of the road, which Mr. Hugh Thomson has so admirably recalled in his graphic sketches of that most picturesque of all life's stages, "the stage" of a hundred years ago, are departed. How well he represents the telling little incidents that gave life and humour to the scene. Boniface and Boots at the door, Betsy the chambermaid at the casement, and Ben the ostler at the leader's heads, the gaping rustics everywhere, all in their several orthodox fashions saying adieu to their departing guests; the "insides" and the "outsides" refreshed and snugly re-seated, are rolling away on their "Flying Machine."

Bagshot was in all its glory at the end of the eighteenth century, and looked back, as it were, with a smirk of self-satisfaction on Mother Windlesham up on the hill. But one more turn of the wheel of fortune has left it out in the cold itself; the coaches are all gone, and the passengers find their way into the West by another line; and so here is the old village like an orchestra without its musicians. Almost the first house you come to is empty, and looks as though it had never

---

* See Junius's Letters, vol. ii. p. 212; Walpole's Letters, vol. iv. p. 311; also Memoirs of Marquis of Rockingham, Earl of Albemarle, vol. i. p. 274.

been otherwise; but it has something very like a stable-yard, and, I believe, a deserted "tap;" yet this was once a busy house; it was the old White Hart. On the road the "Cricketers," and the King's Arms in the street remain, with their "best bedrooms" as comfortable as of old, and the sheets no doubt as white as ever; the lavender's perfume has not yet lost its old-fashioned fragrance, nor the mutton-chop its ancient flavour.

Higher up the street, the Fighting Cocks are on the signboard, but fortunately nowhere else.

The royal lodge has given place to a new one, to which, however, the old garden seems hardly to belong; and the old animosities and jealousies between the Forest authorities and the villagers, who always stoutly maintained their freedom from the Forest laws, are buried as things of the past.* But to proceed.

Bagshot is a place of great antiquity. Imagination may point to it as the "seat" or homestead of Bægsecg, the Danish king who was slain in the great battle of Ascecdun, for this was his country; but I am strongly inclined to attribute to it a Danish or Saxon origin. It took its name, I think, naturally enough, from the hill range on which it stands, and which forms so striking a feature of the neighbourhood, being derived, I would suggest, from the Danish *bag*, a back, Saxon *bæc*, synonymous with the Norman *rugge*, a ridge,† a meaning, too, of which we get an instance close by in the well-known Hog's-back. In the Chronicles of Abingdon the name is written "Bacsceat." The termination *shot*, as elsewhere noticed, being the enclosure in the hill corner or angle.

Bagshot is included in a grant to Chertsey Abbey as early as A.D. 993, but, like Sunninghill and Windlesham, it is not mentioned in Domesday. From the Chronicles of Abingdon I find mention of the wood of Bagshot at a date earlier than that of the Survey. All these places were portions of the great Bearroc wood, in which clearances had been made, and farmsteads may possibly have arisen, although not of sufficient importance to be especially named in Domesday. Edward the Confessor held all this district in royal demesne, and bestowed part of it on the monks of Westminster. The Conqueror, however, soon

---

* See Codex Diplomaticus, ccclxiii.

† The old twelfth-century couplet from Tuvedale (p. 289)—

"He saw won stand on the brygge
With a burden of corne on is rygge,"

well exemplifies this meaning.

arranged with them, and it continued in royal demesne throughout the reigns of William I., William II., Henry I., Stephen and Henry II. They treated it as forest until Henry III. was made to disafforest it. Subject to its hunting rights, the Crown granted portions of these wild lands to certain great lords, on the usual rents and services. The family of Otho, and their descendants the Windsors, evidently held estates here under the honourable tenure of castle-guard of the Castle of Windsor; other portions were held in grand-serjeanty.

Bagshot, a hamlet of Windlesham, is said to have been a member of the manor of Woking, but its early history is but little known. It seems doubtful if it was ever properly a manor of itself. The Testa de Neville, however, speaks of it as such; and the Escheator of Surrey in 1486 alludes to a heriot from "the Manor of Bagshot." The inquisition post-mortem of Galfrid, the goldsmith, presently referred to, expressly describes as among his possessions the manor of Woking, but the bailiwick only of Bagshot; and the inquisition also on the death of the Earl of Kent in 1331 tells of his lands there, but not of any manor.

Large part of Windlesham found its way into the possession of the nuns of Broomhall, who held it in frankalmoign till the dissolution of their house in the time of Henry VIII. Bagshot seems to have been reserved for a much more varied history; it saw many vicissitudes and great changes of fortune.

For a while it would seem to have been in the possession of Roger Belet, the Lord of Woking, then of one Heming, and of Ralph, his younger son.[*] The Testa de Nevill says that "in the time of Henry II. one Ralph held this manor (which was of the King's demesne) in fee-farm at 40s. rent; but being in arrear, Henry III. gave it to one Hoypesiort to hold per serjantiam de Valtiæ or Venatriæ,[†] of whom Robert de Basing bought it, and Robert de Basing, heir of Robert aforesaid, now [time of John] holds it. King Henry the elder gave that part of Bacsiet to John Belet, but by what service is not known, and Michael Belet his heir then held it."[‡]

In 15th John (1214) "Robert de London paid £10 to have seizin of 15s. rent in Bacscete, of which he had been disseized for concealment of his service, and going into Ireland without license."

The jurors of the great assize held here in the reign of Henry III. say that "Heming formerly held of Roger Belet, with which Roger the King was so angry by reason of something he had done or omitted about a spar-hawk, that he disseized him of all his lands and 40s. rent; and Ralph, younger son of Heming, had the 40s. of the King's gift to keep his dogs; but soon after he displeased the King by refusing to receive his dogs, and permitting Herbert to eject him."

---

[*] Alanus Basset held the manor of Woking, which was confirmed to him in 1st John 1200. See Cal. Rot. Chart. Rolls.
[†] i.e., the footman who leads the King's dogs.   [‡] Madox Esch.

In 1272 the estate seems to have descended on Alice, or Aliva, the daughter of one of the Bassets, to whose ancestor, Alan, Lord Basset of Wicomb, Richard I. had given the Manor of Woking, which they held for four generations. Her first husband was Hugh Despenser, who was killed at the battle of Lewes. She afterwards married Roger Bigod, Earl of Norfolk, and died in 1281. Whereupon the Earl of Norfolk, to make himself tenant for life by the curtesy, pretended that she left issue by him; but he would not face the jury empannelled to try that fact, and the estates went to Hugh Despenser, the son of Aliva by her first husband, usually known as the elder De Spenser, executed at Bristol in 1326. But there had again been litigation, for I find "Ide Brigges and Alice his wife pray recovery of it, the Earl of Winchester having obtained it through bribery." Then came the younger Spenser, executed at Hereford in 1327, on whose attainder the estates reverted to the Crown. Edward III. in 1329 bestowed it on his uncle, Edmund of Woodstock, Earl of Kent; but he was destined to hold it but a short time, for in 4th Ed. III. (1330), through the intrigue of Mortimer, he was beheaded, and his estates were mostly given over to Geoffrey, Mortimer's son.

The inquisition on the death of Edmund is worthy of notice. It states that he held "one ruinous messuage at Bagshot, with a small garden and eighty acres of arable, eight acres of pasture, and twenty acres of wood, which he held of the lordship of Stanwell by castle-guard to the Castle of Windsor." This lordship of Stanwell was the house of the Lords Windsor, the descendants of the Norman De Otho, and this supports my earlier surmise.

The King next granted this manor, or quasi manor, to Bartholomew de Berghersh; but it very shortly afterwards was restored to the deposed family, and became the property of John, Earl of Kent (next brother of Edmund, who had died a minor). He dying in 1353 without issue, it devolved (not, as some say, "bequeathed," for land could not in those days pass by will), together with the Manor of Woking, on his young sister Joan, the wife of Sir Thomas Holland, knight, and only daughter of the unfortunate Edmund, and better known as the Fair Maid of Kent, afterwards the wife of the Black Prince. Sir Thomas Holland did homage for Woking in 27th Ed. III. He had a son, Sir Thomas, who was created Earl of Kent in 5th Ric. II. Joan and her son, however, held Bagshot subject to Elizabeth's (the brother's widow's) prior right of dower to a third of it. She does not seem to have had possession, but probably made over her interest, as she did that of the Manor of Woking, as to which I find, "Johanna, late Princess of Wales, gave to Alice, who was the wife of Thomas, late Earl of Kent, the Manor of Woking."* This Alice was probably the widow of Sir Thomas Holland, eighth Earl of Kent, who was Joan's son-in-law, and died in 1397. The estate ultimately devolved on Margaret Beaufort, daughter and heiress of John, first Duke of Somerset, who by her first husband, the Earl of Richmond, was mother of Henry VII; but previously to this, on the attainder and execution of Henry, Duke of Somerset, in 1463, it escheated to the Crown. In Henry VII.'s reign it was restored to Margaret Beaufort, and on her death it came to her grandson, Henry VIII. It remained in the Crown until James I. in 1620 granted it to Sir Edward Zouch. The connection of the Windsor family with Bagshot is again shown by the Escheator of Surrey in 1486 being commanded "to deliver to Elizabeth Windsor, on the death of her husband, Thomas Windsor, and then in the hands of the Crown, half a knight's fee, a rent of 3s. 4d. every twenty-four weeks, suit of court every three weeks, and a heriot from the Manor of

---

* Cal. Rot. Chart, 1 Hen. IV. (1399). See also Inq. post-mortem of Thomas de Holand, 20 Ric. II. Manning and Bray's Hist. of Surrey.

Bagshote."* The "Manor of Bagshot" would seem in 1620 to have been the property of Sir Ed. Howard, and to have been given by his will to his "loving brother, Sir Charles Howard."†

Windlesham, Bagshot, and Woking, always so closely connected, were usually included in these devolutions, although they might not all of them have been included in each case; but Bagshot Park, a small strip of which is on the Berkshire side, has from the most remote period been retained by the King in his demesne, and held by his foresters as Bailiffs of Surrey, or, as it was called,

BAGSHOT BAILIWICK,

an office of much consideration, reserved for some personal attendant of the King. The lodge was his official residence.

Galfrid de Bagscete, or Galfrid the Goldsmith, held this important post of bailiff; and in an entry of the Testa de Nevill, under Berks and Oxon, Galfridus de Bakeshet is mentioned as holding half a knight's fee in Bagshot, "of the honor of Wyndel of Thos. de Lasceles, Baron of Wyndel, and other lands also of Wm. de Wyndel." The inquisition post-mortem on the death of this great knight (before referred to) shows him to have been possessed of "Bagshot Ballivat," for which, the jury reported, "he pays to our Lord the King 60s. annually."

This office comprised not only the house or lodge of the forester at Bagshot, but extensive rights and privileges over a large tract of the Forest, and of the chase on the Surrey side, including Windlesham, Egham, Chertsey, Thorpe, Chobham, East and West Horsley, Byfleet, Pirford, Stoke, Woking, Worplesdon, Ash, Wanborough, Frimley, and the Tithing of Tongham in Seale.

Richard de Bataille seems to have succeeded Galfrid as forester, and thenceforward we find a long line of successors, down, I may say, to the present time. Of some of these I will speak as we proceed. In 10th Hen. IV. the King granted to John Hargreen [or Hargreve] for life the office called "Bagshot Ballie, within the Forest of Windsor, in the county of Surrey; the wages, 6d. a day, to be paid by the Sheriffs of Oxford and Berks." Its perquisites and privileges, as well as the enjoyment of the lodge, made it a very enviable post. Henry VI. gave it to John Jenyn and Richard Ludlow, serjeants of his cellar. Edward IV.

---

* Materials for Hist. of Hen. VII.
† See Surrey Archæological Coll., 1888, vol. vi. p. 430.

of course soon changed this, and in the first year of his reign gave it to Ed. Kingdon, and after him came one Thomas Rede. Henry VII., as soon as he came to the throne, " in consideration of the true and diligent service done as well unto us as unto our derrest moder by oure faithfulle lyegeman, Wm. Michell," granted to him "the office of the keeper of the Park of Bagshote."* This is the first mention I find of any park there. This grant is followed by another to him of "wages out of the farm of a messuage called le Crowne in Bagshote, and all other possessions belonging to the Crown in Bagshote and Wynesham, Co. Surrey, and of the fields of Bagshote, and the town and fields of Wynesham." In the same year there was a grant of it to Thomas Stoughton, gentleman, and John Baggar.

Henry VII. left the hunting to be done by his young sons, of whom Henry the younger soon found it a pastime of never-failing interest. He drew round him his companions, and placed them in the various Forest lodges, on their first vacancies. In 1521 he appointed his earliest friends, Sir William Fitzwilliam and Anthony Brown, "Bailiffs of Surrey or Bagshotes Baylies."

It was a very favourite place with James I.

In May 1603 adverse claims to the keepership of the Park arose, and it is mentioned in the direction to the Lord Admiral Chief-Justice in Eyre south of Trent that "Her late Majesty granted to John Lidcott the custody of Bagshot Park. He sold his interest to one Furst, who conveyed it to Sir Henry Guildford, and afterwards sold it again to another; by which double sale great disturbance has grown; and meantime our deer and woods are neglected. As we hold Sir Henry Guildford meetest to have the keeping, and as he has the best right from Lidcott, we require you to order that he be put into quiet possession."

Accordingly in June 1604 there was a formal grant to Sir Henry Guildford for life.† He was succeeded in 1609 by Sir William Harmon, to whom, it seems, he had assigned the keepership. In November of that year there is a warrant to pay the necessary sums for finishing the repairs of the lodge, and in the next year a report was made to Salisbury, with an estimate of the cost. In 1612, on the surrender of Sir William Harmon, Sir Noel de Caron‡ was put in. On his decease in 1624 it was granted to John Baker.

---

* P. S. 22 Sep. No. 216.   † See Treasury Papers, 1604 to 1612.
‡ Sir Noel de Caron was Dutch ambassador to England in the reigns of Elizabeth and James I. He resided in a fine mansion at South Lambeth.

In 1621 James granted to Sir Edward Zouch, the owner of the fine old mansion of Bramshill, "the Manor of Bagshot, and all the waste lands called Bagshot Heath, or Windlesham Heath, within the said manor, containing by estimation 1000 acres;" but out of this grant was especially excepted "the Bailiwick, the Park, and site of the manor, and the house within the Park," which the Crown still retained. By order of the Duke of Buckingham, the keepership of the Park was in 1626 conferred on Thomas Seabrook, with an annuity of £5, 6s. 8d. for life. From him in 1631 it passed to George Drawbridgecourt, and in 1634 Sir Charles Howard was keeper of the Walk; but very soon afterwards Lord and Lady Newburgh were the royal tenants of the lodge.

But now came the restless period that preceded the great revolution. Conflicting agencies were everywhere visible. On the one side an undue stretch of prerogative and tyrannical dealing with the rights of the subject; and on the other resistance, at first justifiable, and afterwards degenerating into lawlessness. The foresters were, as elsewhere described, simmering in insubordination. The King set his unscrupulous Attorney-General to work, and in 1632 the famous Grand Court of Justice-seat was held at Bagshot. The verdicts were all for the Crown, and with the gentry and lower orders alike it left behind a feeling of disgust throughout the Forest. Public opinion was with the "broom-squires" and deer-stealers.

As early as 1624 we find a letter from Secretary Conway to the Justices of the Peace for Surrey, wherein he says he is "charged by the King to instruct them to deal according to law with Taddy Farnwall of Bagshot, charged with killing a hind calf, keeping greyhounds, shooting with guns, &c., and to be careful to inflict condign punishment for offences of that kind."* Now this is somewhat remarkable, for if Bagshot had been in the Forest, the Forest Courts would soon have made short work with Taddy Farnwall without troubling the magistrates.

Amid all his troubles, however, the King was intent on his hunting. He had been at Bagshot when he was interrupted by the serious illness of the Queen. On 29th August 1633 we learn that "His Majesty, finding the Queen out of danger, and bettering hourly, returns to his hunting sports to-morrow to Bagshot at night." This was not long before the birth of Prince James. The lodge was just then very ruinous, and in 1638 its repair was ordered. In the same

---

* Cal. State Papers, Dom.

year an importation of new stock into the Forest was made by a consignment of deer from France to Bagshot.

But the Civil War was approaching, and Bagshot had a good share of its excitements and losses. It saw the King brought through a prisoner; and its woods felled in 1650 by order of the Admiralty Committee. To this spoliation objection was offered, but in vain.

A troop of horse had been quartered on the village to keep order, but at the price of their support the good folk doubtless found the remedy worse than the disease.

That they had a rough time of it is apparent from a petition, at the Restoration, of one Peere Williams, who, in June 1660, prayed "relief in consequence of his irreparable losses sustained through Sir William Waller's troop in Bagshot Park, in which he was keeper. Hopes that a Prince of inexpressible sufferings even from his tender years will graciously reflect on the calamities of his subject's sufferings."

The general disorder that reigned during the Commonwealth is well illustrated by a curious if not nefarious transaction that occurred in relation to Bagshot Park. In 1655 I find one Margaret Barry petitioning that "her husband, Major Samuel Barry, now in Jamaica, joined with Captain Peck in the purchase of Bagshot Park, and conveyed it to John Barry, a lawyer, who was to have half for a £300 debt, and £850 more, which he now refuses to pay,"* and begged that Barry should be called to account.

More light was thrown on this questionable affair a few years afterwards, for they evidently quarrelled over the spoil, and probably over-reached themselves, for in September 1660 came another appeal to a different tribunal, and we have the "case of John Barry touching his purchase of Bagshot Park. That Lieutenant-Colonel Samuel Barry, now an officer in the army, and Captain Peck, both of whom laid down their commissions when the late King's person was seized by Colonel Joyce, were obliged to purchase Bagshot Park for £4000 in lieu of their arrears of pay. John Barry bought it from them for £2000, instead of money due to him from his brother Samuel, and has spent £2000 more on it."

Also John Barry's case "touching Windsor Park, taken for pay by Captain Byfield, whose widow he has married, and left by the Captain for payment of debts and support of his wife and daughter, he having spent £5000 at least in improvments, so that Barry must be ruined if he can neither have the lands nor recompense."

---

* Cal. State Papers, Dom. 1655.

What a state of things this wholesale trafficking with estates shows. The finest properties were sold for anything they would fetch to discharge the arrears of pay to a clamouring soldiery.

But after many days things settled down. The Park pales were set up again, the deer replaced, the old lodge repaired, and the grand folk flaunted about more stately than ever. The people rejoiced to see them back again.

In September 1667 the restored King was at Bagshot for four or five days' hunting, when he had the jovial day at Sir George Carteret's at Cranbourn, of which I speak in my account of that place. Again in the September of the following year he was at Bagshot with his brother and the Court, and Pepys relates an instance of Buckingham's overbearing insolence on that occasion, for he caused Prince Rupert's horses to be turned out of the inn stables to make room for his own. Yet the King supported him in this against the complaint even of the Prince and Duke of York. Then, too, it was that the King paid Sir Thomas Draper a visit at Sunninghill Park.

In 1682 James Graham, Esq., Privy Purse to Charles II., was keeper and ranger of Bagshot Park. In his time the Crown evidently rebuilt the lodge,* for I find in that year an order to pay him £1200, followed in 1686 by another payment of £2688, 9s. 11d. for moneys by him expended in the "building and repairing of His Majesty's house at Bagshot, and impailing the park;"† and in 1687 he had a lease of it (probably a renewal) for thirty-one years. Evelyn paid the Hon. Mrs. Graham a visit there in 1685, when he saw the Park again full of red deer.

This new house, we may well imagine, once more resounded with an old-fashioned revelry; and perchance at times, too, with a melody so sweet and touching as to cause the listener to forget from whose lips it flowed, for as Moll Davies was often residing here, she doubtless sang her song, "My lodging is on the cold ground," as no one else perchance has ever sung it since. Her portrait long hung on the walls at Billingbere, if not still there.

I have alluded elsewhere to one of the favourites of fashion in the eighteenth century. Here we meet with a still more typical one of the seventeenth. Hardly a more romantic life, and certainly not a more sorrowful one, is to be found, than that of old Colonel Graham of Bagshot Lodge, a brave old Jacobite gentleman of the intensest type. Sprung from the wildest of borderland clans, the Grahmes of

---

* Docket Book Rolls 1682. † Clarendon Diary, March 4.

Netherby, he brought from his native hills all the fire and daring of his ancestor "John with the bright sword," or the fair Ellen of young Lochinvar, while he cherished those gentler memories of home inspired by the old hall at Levens and its beautiful vale. But he plunged into a world of intrigue, and clung with an imperishable loyalty to a worthless cause.

Evelyn introduces us to him as a young gentleman desperately in love with his charming ward, the beautiful Dorothy Howard, maid of honour to the Queen, and, in pure pity, spoke a good word for him to her mother. He served in the Duke of Monmouth's Regiment of Auxiliaries in France, and became Privy-Purse to the King, who bestowed on him the rangership of Bagshot. In 1679 Prince Rupert gave him the keepership also of Pirbright.

Here, at Bagshot, he spent some of the brightest days of his life, till 1688, when all his hopes perished in the flight of James. He clung to his master to the last, and was the most trusted of the few intimate friends the broken-down monarch possessed.

On the 4th of March 1688 Clarendon writes—"Cornet Richards came to me from his quarters at Farnham. He told me that a messenger was at Bagshot yesterday to apprehend Mr. Graham, but he was not at home." Nothing could be brought against him, for Lord Clarendon dined with him several times at the lodge in the following year.

When the crisis came with James in October, Graham fled with him to Rochester, and into his name £10,000 East India Stock, and £3000 in the African Company, were transferred by the King—a few crumbs to be saved in that terrible collapse.

Sir Stephen Fox wrote to the Hon. Mrs. Graham at Bagshot Lodge to report her husband's precipitate journey.

He was arrested again in April 1691, but was discharged, never having committed himself sufficiently for any other punishment than that of having to live under continual suspicion.

He lost his sons, and his beautiful Dorothy, but found solace in his old age in the affection of "those silent strings that send no sound to posterity," as old Fuller says—his two daughters, Lady Berkshire and Mary Michel; saw his beloved Levens nearly destroyed by fire in 1703; and at the age of fourscore craved burial with his moss-trooping ancestors at Heversham in Westmoreland.

Pope mentions meeting him in his old age at dinner in 1711. The manorial property which had been granted to Sir Edward Zouch

---

* See Ashtead and its Howard Possessors, by Rev. F E. Paget.

still remained in his family, and a little later in 1695 a report from the Solicitor-General shows that the Manor of Bagshot (among other properties), granted by James I. to Sir Edward Zouch, knight, the grandfather of the then petitioner, James Zouch, Esq., could not be prevented reverting to the Crown on the determination of the estate tail therein.

But the Park, which had been excepted, continued in royal hands, and with the keepership and various offices of profit had been settled by Charles II. on trustees for the notorious Duchess of Cleveland; but when James fled in 1688 there was an indenture of sale between "the Duchess of Cleveland and Charles Young and others, and Charles Duke of Northumberland, natural son of Charles II.,"* conveying to Charles Dartiguenave and Thomas Trussell among other properties "the office of Bagshot Bailiwick and the Collectorship of Chertsey, Chobham, Egham, and other places near in trust for sale." Meanwhile Graham's lease of the Lodge and Park had become vested in Richard, Earl of Ranelagh, our old friend of Cranbourne, who in 1705, however, was obliged to sell it again; and we have a petition of Charles, Earl of Arran, setting out "that he had purchased from Lord Ranelagh his interest in the Park of Bagshot, being the remainder of a lease granted by King James II. to James Graham, Esq., and praying a lease for three lives rather than for thirty-one years." Queen Anne granted him a lease accordingly.

The Earl of Arran continued there some years, and on the termination of his lease it came back to the royal family, and was given by George II. to Lord Albemarle. In 1772 the Hon. George Keppel, Admiral Keppel's brother, died there. We then come to the time of George III., who was reviving the taste for hunting in the Forest, and seems to have been anxious to draw his young son, the Prince of Wales, from his dangerous pursuits in the metropolis, and encourage the more innocent ones of the Forest. In 1781 the Duke of Cumberland gave up to his royal nephew "his delightful villa in the Great Park."† But in April 1783 we are told that the "beautiful seat called Bagshot Park, which was granted to Lord Albemarle by his late Majesty, and continued by promise of the present to Lord Keppel for life, is said by His Majesty's particular request to be appropriated for the residence of the Prince of Wales; and his Lordship is to receive a stipulated annual rent during his life. This most delightful habitation is on Bagshot Heath, and has cost at least £50,000 for improvements since it has been in the Albemarle family." From this we may infer that

---

* *Cal. State Papers, Dom.* † *Reading Mercury.*

the Lodge that has recently been pulled down was mainly rebuilt by Lord Albemarle.

It had been given to the Albemarle family, not, as sometimes stated, by George III. on the taking of the Havannah, but by the Duke of Cumberland, who persuaded George II. to extend his grant of it for three lives, as the Ranger could only give it for one life.*

There was much gaiety here in Lord Keppel's time. On certain days the place was open to the public, and promenades were held, which were much appreciated by the neighbourhood.

In 1786, on the death of Lord Keppel, Bagshot Place reverted to the then Ranger, the Duke of Gloucester, who wrote, it seems, to the Prince of Wales, offering him the use of it as long as he pleased. In 1792 we learn that the King had made a present of Bagshot Lodge, till then occupied by the Prince of Wales, to Prince William of Gloucester. The Prince of Wales's monetary difficulties, and his relations with the King, doubtless led to this change. At the end of 1830, during the riots that prevailed in the southern counties, of which Charles Kingsley gives us so graphic an account, there was great excitement at Bagshot Lodge. Mrs. Sumner (the Bishop of Winchester's mother), who was in the midst of it, writes, "The Duke of Gloucester came to Bagshot to be at the head of his household, who are all armed. The threats have been very dreadful against his residence." †

The Duke was there for many years, and afterwards for a still longer period we hear of it as the residence of the Duchess of Gloucester. After her Sir James Clark had it, and it is now in the possession of their Royal Highnesses the Duke and Duchess of Connaught.

Before I close, I must say a few words more of old Bagshot. Of its ancient chapel we know but little. It was a building of great antiquity, and is shown on an old map which belonged to Lord Burleigh as a more important edifice than either Windlesham or Sunninghill. It has been gone for more than two hundred years. Its ancient site was in the street near the road that leads to Windlesham and Chobham, which I think was the earliest approach to the village.

The manor of Freemantles was formerly given to support a priest in Huglett's chantry in the chapel of Bagshot; and the Commissioners

---

* *Reading Mercury.*
† Life of Charles Richard Sumner, by his son, Rev. G. H. Sumner.

appointed in 2nd Edward VI. reported that the chantry was founded for that purpose, there being no incumbent; that it was worth in land £6; that it had 5¼ ounces of plate, value 25s. 4d., ornaments 6d., bells 26s. 8d.

A successor to this earlier chapel was built on the site of the one so recently pulled down, and to which Aubrey must allude when he tells us that "about half a mile from the street or road stands the church, in which are neither monument nor gravestone," for this could not possibly have applied to Windlesham, which he sadly confuses with it, as he goes on to speak of its destruction by fire in 1676, when the parish church was burnt down. However, the ancient chapel disappeared; and a new and somewhat anomalous building was erected by subscription about 1820, and was finally taken down in 1883.

Of the new church it is unnecessary for me to speak.

The old Lodge, the great house of the place, repaired, and patched, and rebuilt several times, had its last known site near the road at the entrance to the village, a little to the north of the present kitchen-garden, and south of the existing mansion. The ancient road from Sunninghill passed to the north of the house after passing the Gibbet, and a still earlier one ran directly through the Park by the mansion, out into the upper part of the village, at an entrance called the "Crowne Gate." In Norden's map it is shown near the second stream that crosses the street, and opposite to the old Crown Inn, that I have been informed stood there.

The present road was turned through the village only in 1728, when the first Act was passed to improve the highway from Hounslow to Basingstone, on the hill near the Golden Farmer. We get an allusion to Bagshot in 1742 from "The Tour of a Gentleman through England" (written earlier by De Foe), in which he says, "The principal place is the Earl of Arran's, which is a large enclosure, the wood walks and other plantations being upwards of two miles in circumference, and the Park, which runs on the other side of the house, is upwards of three miles. The next seat is that of the Right Hon. the Earl of Anglesea's, which is an ancient house situate very near the church, and almost surrounded with large trees, so that only the front appears to view." This is all gone now, although a new house occupies its site. Another seat was that of the Duke of Roxburgh, in which his Grace used to reside a great part of the summer and autumn for the pleasure of shooting, being very fond of that sport. This was probably the white house in the street, the Cedars, lately occupied by Mr. Waterer.

Of the *parish of Windlesham* my space will not permit of more than a few words about its church and manors. Windlesham was included in the gift of Edward the Confessor to the monks of Westminster, but when or by whom the church was erected is not known. It is said to be older than the time of Edward I., as appears from the Bodleian Valor, and this is confirmed to some extent by the remaining portions of the chancel of the old building, which now forms the south aisle of the present one; in this are three windows, of about that period, I think.

Aubrey records having seen on one of its beams a date,[*] but it was too dark a day for him to decipher it, although he was able to make out the following inscription, written in red "oker" in an old kind of court-hand character:—"William Whitchill was maker of this werke: pray ye for all the werkemen of this precious Werke of this . . . . . of Windlesham. Amen. Quod. R. Marmion." The word "quod" here is evidently an old English form of "quoth," equivalent to "Amen, says R. Marmion."[†]

Philip Marmion was a great warrior in the reign of Edward I., and Robert, his father, may have built this church. They were lords of the great northern stronghold of Werke, as well as of "Tamworth tower and town," and they held the honourable office of royal champion from before the Conquest: this, through a co-heiress of Robert de Marmion, descended to the family of Dymoke, who still hold it.

During the twelfth century the advowson of this church was in the possession of the Priory and Convent of Newark, more anciently known as Aldebury and afterwards as De Novo Loco, a small religious house of Black Canons, which stood, by its seven streams, on a site near Woking in the parish of Sende; it was founded, it has been said, by Rual de Calva and Beatrice de Sande, his wife, before 1204.[‡]

The site of the house, after its dissolution in 1544, was granted to Sir Anthony Brown: the Priory building, as usual, became a stone quarry, and helped to mend the roads; while the great bell found a resting-place, Aubrey tells us, in the church-tower of Woking. This interesting bell, he says, was the third of the peal, and bore on its edge the motto " ✠ En multis annis—Resonet campana Johannis." It

---

[*] Aubrey's Hist. of Surrey.   [†] See prologue to Chaucer, Prioress's Tale.
[‡] See Dugdale's Monasticon; Manning and Bray's Surrey, vol. III. p. 110; Description of England, 1770, p. 93; and *Gent. Mag*, 1840, p. 409.

must have been one of the "V gret bells in the stepull" which the Church-Goods Commissioners of 6th Edward VI. found there.* Here, after a troubled existence, it resounded to the wild winds, in accordance with its founder's wish, for nearly a century longer, when, as appears by the churchwarden's accounts, just published, it was borne away with its fellows to Chertsey, and recast by William Eldridge in 1684. Another was added to the peal in 1766, and they were all re-hung in 1887. Aubrey's account is so precise and circumstantial that I cannot but accept it. Aubrey made his Collections before 1684, so that this old Newark bell must have been one of those recast.†

In the returns for military service ordered by the Parliament of Lincoln, 2nd Edward II., appears "Vill' de Windlesham, hundred de Wokkinge, est D'ni Regis est in manu Vic' ad firman suam." The lords of the manor, or rather manors, were, we are told, "Prioris de Novo Loco" (Prior of Newark), "Rici de ffremantel" (Richard Freemantle). Although a large part of Windlesham was given to the Nuns of Bromhall, they had nothing to do with the church, which seems to have been appropriated to the Priory of Newark in 1262 in the time of Edward I.‡ The church had probably not long been built then. In 1226 I find notice of "the chapelle de Windlesha,"§ a fact quite consistent with its having then been merely a chapel in possession of the monks. It remained in their hands until it was, for some reason, taken from them in 1447,∥ when it seems to have come into lay hands; for in that year, and in 1466, William Skern and Robert Howlett or Hulet (founder of the Bagshot charity) presented to the living; and afterwards Agnes, the wife of Robert Skern, became possessed of it. She and her second husband, Peter Curteis, presented in 1489 and 1493, their right having been established in opposition to the Prior of Newark. John Quinby presented (*pleno jure*) in 1536.¶ William Muschamp, Esq., in 1562, and in 1588 John Attfield (whose family, although in a less important position, still exists in the parish) was patron of the church. He was

---

* See Aubrey's Hist. of Surrey, 1718, and Surrey Archæological Collections, vol. iv. p. 241.
† It is curious to find this identical inscription at Heathfield, Sussex (see "Church-Bells of Sussex," by Daniel Tyssen), as well as on the most important of a very interesting set of bells at Limpsfield Church. The letters are Lombardic, of rather small and peculiar character, and are pronounced to be of date between 1350 and 1400. This bell is unfortunately cracked. The next bears the inscription, "Sancta Mergareta ora pro nobis ☉ T. H. ☉." The third, of date between 1475 and 1525, "✠ Sum Rosa Pulsata—Mundi Maria Vocata."
‡ See Manning and Bray's Hist. of Surrey.
§ Rot. Lit. Clausarum, 10 Hen. III.
∥ See Cert. of Bishop Waynflete to the Exchequer, dated 13th April 1464.
¶ Salmon's Surrey.

owner of one moiety of the manor of Freemantles; but Queen Elizabeth, who had previously granted the other moiety to Reve and Evelyn, retained the patronage, which has ever since been in the Crown.

The old church became much neglected after the Reformation, and the report of the Church-Goods Commissioners of 6th Edward VI. shows it in a very melancholy case. All that was left of its plate and effects, to be handed over to Edward Tile and others, was "an olde cope with a vestment, an old rood clothe, and four littell bells in the tower," "all that lacketh of the former inventory were stolen by thieves when the church was robbyd."

The fabric was destroyed by lightning, January 20, 1676, and was rebuilt in 1680, in the time of John Attfield and Richard Cotterell, churchwardens; but I cannot confirm the tradition. I find noticed in *Notes and Queries* that fifteen other churches in the neighbourhood shared the same fate in that great storm. This building had not much architectural beauty, and fell into great dilapidation before it was superseded by the present edifice. The living is a Rectory in the Deanery of Stoke, and is valued in the taxation of Pope Nicholas at £8, and in the King's books at £10. 9s. 7d. The church is dedicated to St. John Baptist.

As to the manor of Windlesham, there has always been confusion among writers. It is said, for instance, that Henry VIII., after the dissolution of the Nunnery of Bromhall, gave the manor of Windlesham to St. John's College; and Dugdale and others mention it as among their estates; but we are also told that James I. bestowed it on Lord Zouch.

There were, in truth, four manors in the parish—Forsters *alias* Windlesham, Windlesham, a distinct manor of that name, Bromhall, and Freemantles. This last was but a small manor or reputed manor, which included the Hall Grove estate, and seems to have become divided, and, as we have seen, was given to support Hughlett's charity. In 1809, Dare, a nurseryman, possessed it, or a share of it. Forsters comprised the western or Frimley side of the parish, including the hamlet of Bagshot, as well as the Park and Royal Lodge, which James I., however, took great care to except and retain when he granted the manor to Sir Edward Zouch in 1621, and since then I believe it has never been deemed as part of the manor; but it did not touch any portion of the village of Windlesham.

In 1603 it was the property of the Evelyn family, who sold it to James Lynch of Whiteparish, Wilts, from whom it descended to his grandchildren the Gauntletts (children of his daughter), and the hus-hands of two of them in their right, Robert Field and Daniel Moore. In 1705 it was in the possession of Samuel Maynwaring, afterwards of Heneage Finch, Lord Guernsey; it was then sold to John Walter (not Walker, as sometimes stated) of Busbridge in Godalming; and by his descendants in 1752 to Richard, Lord Onslow, in whose family it still remains.

Bromhall occupied the eastern part of the parish, and extended into Sunninghill; it included all the village of Windlesham, and this is what passed to the College together with the separate manor of Windlesham before mentioned.

My space will not allow of my attempting any account of the numerous Rectors of Windlesham, although I may make a passing allusion to one of its curates, young Edward Stanley, who, on leaving college at the beginning of the century for his travels in Italy, was called home to take the command of the Alderley Volunteers when the country was under fear of invasion. He then became curate of Windlesham, and lightened his work in rambles over those wild heaths, indulging his great fondness for ornithology and natural science. In 1805 he was preferred to the family living of Alderley, and in 1837 became Bishop of Norwich. His highly gifted son was the well-known Dean of Westminster.

CHAPTER XXXII.

The Nunnery of Broomhall.

"She was one of those kind of nuns, an' please your honour, of which your honour knows there are a good many in Flanders, which they let go loose."—TRISTRAM SHANDY.

IN the moorland dale at the south-eastern extremity of the parish, where formerly the great Bearroc wood sloped down to the Roman road, stood the ancient Priory of Broomhall, a convent of Benedictine nuns. It occupied a slightly rising ground on the southern bank of the stream, which ran down from a large pond, lately known as Charters Pond (now almost filled up), and so on in a north-easterly direction to Virginia Water.

This stream probably at first formed the northern boundary of the convent grounds, and supplied its mill, but cut it off from Sunninghill, so that the road thither must have required a bridge; and that there was a bridge there I have, curiously enough, found proof in an old charter of the time of Henry III. (1246), which runs "Priorissa de Bromhall Sunninghull, tres acr' terr' extend' versus la Newebrugg." This shows not only that there was such a bridge, but that it was then called the New Bridge; it crossed the stream probably a little eastward of the present one, carrying the road nearer to the Sunningdale Schools, and up over the hill in a straight line towards our village and the church, thus avoiding the awkward corner of the existing road at the farm, which is of course modern. This, I have been told, was the direction of the old bridleway until altered within living memory. The gate-house of the Nunnery, alluded to at the time of the dissolution of the house, stood on the south side of the convent, on the road by which it was approached, and which led through the Forest from Staines to Bagshot. The site was one of those bosky margins of the great wood where it opened out into the sandy waste which stretched away southward, in heath-covered ridges, to Chobham and Chertsey.

The broom, from which, perchance, the place takes its name, grew there then, as it does still, with great luxuriance, and shone in all its golden glory over the dark heath, so as to make even this wild spot in summer-time beautiful. In Saxon times this place was known, not as Bromhall, but "Hertlei;" and at a spot towards the south-east of it, now called Mincing Ride, stood a cross, placed there possibly before any Nunnery arose in the valley. Of this we get an interesting notice in the transcript, made about the time of King Stephen, of the Saxon charter of Fritwald, A.D. 666, wherein the boundary of the Egham lands is described as going "from thorni hulle to Hertleys nuther ende of the menechene rude." This menechene rood or monk's cross has given a name to the place, which it has retained for more than seven hundred years.

The charter rather implies the non-existence of the Nunnery at the date of the transcript, or so important an edifice could hardly have been unnoticed; and this, on the other hand, makes me incline to put the date of the MS. as rather earlier than Stephen's time; more probably that of Henry I.

A question has been raised as to the true site of the Nunnery. Some antiquaries have asserted that it was not at Sunninghill at all, but near Billingbere, on the road to Reading; but if such a doubt still exists, I shall have little difficulty in setting it at rest. The site is as above described beyond all question.

The charter of Henry de Laci, to which I shall presently refer, could hardly have been mistaken for the charter of foundation; its language is very different, and it alludes to our Lady and the Nuns of Bromhall as an existing establishment. It was simply a grant by De Lacy of a tract in the waste of Ashridge. Ashridge Wood lies exactly as described near the royal road (*i.e.*, the public road), between Brackenhale and Reading. That was Old Bracknell before the present town became New Bracknell. But we have only to consider that on the dissolution of the Nunnery all its estates were granted to St. John's College, and that those in Berkshire were described as "Bromehull situs Prioratus," "Bromehall manerium," "Charugge alias Wynkfield manerium," and that to this day the College possesses our manor of Broomhall, and the lands still known as Broomhall farm, and we get a link of devolution which surely establishes the fact beyond dispute. The allusion to the three acres of land in Sunninghill against the "Newe brugg" is also not without bearing on this. If more were required, I would add that Norden's map of 1607 shows no house or building on the Ashridge Wood site, but it does show one on the identical spot at which we place it. It is there called "Bromwell," Nunnery no longer, but an extensive pile, and the "well" remained.

The hunting-man of the last generation and the rustic of the present know the spot, less from its ancient associations than from the little roadside beer-house called "Brummell Hutch" hard by, a place of refreshment of a totally different kind from that to which it probably owed its name—the "hutch" or place where bread was stored and distributed by the nuns.

There can be little doubt that the sisterhood in its early career was a blessing to the rude people it ventured amongst. The house stands near the great Roman road to Silchester, on the more modern Forest way from Staines to Bagshot, and must have been a very welcome resting-place to the traveller over these wild moorlands.

But the first obvious questions that arise are when and by whom was this Nunnery founded? Hakewell, on the authority of Speed, says it was founded by Edward the Black Prince, and so said our Vicar, Mr. Morris. This, however, is entirely a mistake; there are several earlier charters relating to it; but it is worthy of note that in the Inquisition taken on the suppression of the house by Henry VIII., it is stated that the Nunnery was "founded by the King's progenitors."

The learned antiquaries Dugdale, Baker, and Willis, from whom we get nearly all that has been written on the subject, do not enlighten us at all on these points. All they tell us is, that its foundation was earlier than 1199, the first year of King John. They give no reason for this, but the very important charter of King John made in that year is undoubtedly their authority.

Now the Nunnery and church are closely connected both in their origin and history; and from the general suggestions of local and historical facts, to which, as the foundation charter is not forthcoming, we are remitted, I incline to think that the Nunnery was founded in the twelfth century, not by "the good Queen Molde," or Matilda, Henry's first queen, at whose instigation probably the church had been built, but by her daughter Matilda, or by Adeliza of Louvain, his second queen. I am satisfied that the church could not be much later than 1140, and believe it to have been rather earlier—say between 1120 and 1130—and that the Nunnery followed it towards the end of the century. To Henry's Saxon sympathies and the strong religious tendencies of his two queens we owe, I think, the foundation of both church and Nunnery; in this latter having especially the co-operation of the family of De Warrenne, Earls of Surrey, on whose lands the Nunnery itself stood. The site of the house is peculiarly suggestive, for geographically it is in the county of Surrey, on the southern bank of the boundary stream, on a small indentation obviously at some time taken out of Surrey and added to Berkshire, in which county it is always supposed to be. It has been regarded as an isolated portion of the parish of Sunninghill.*

The De Warrennes were closely allied to the royal family. The first Earl William had married Gundreda, Henry I.'s half-sister. They were great benefactors, as Henry himself also was, of the Benedictine Order, and were founders of the Priory of Lewes, the chief Cluniac house in England. Another connection also existed between them, for Matilda's nephew, Prince Henry, son of David I., in 1139 married Ada, daughter of Earl Warrenne and Surrey; and Adeliza, after Henry I.'s death, married William de Albini, on whom she conferred the lordship of Arundel. Matilda, the wife of De Lacy, was also closely connected with the royal family, and became the greatest benefactress of the house.

But whoever founded it, let us now inquire as to its earliest endowments. We can almost trace them from its first erection, when it possessed no more than its actual site. Their first property was probably the manor of Bromhall, on which their house was erected; but they soon increased their possessions, mainly by the piety of benefactors, but also by clearances and encroachments on the Forest.

One of their first acquisitions was what is to us the most interesting of all. King John, in the very first year of his reign, gave to the Nunnery the church of Sunninghill. This important endowment runs:

---

* The seal of this Nunnery, formerly in the Chapter-House, Westminster, the only one known to exist, is now at the Rolls (Chapter-House, box 1, No. 17). It is in white wax, discoloured somewhat by age, and of the pointed oval form. It represents St. Margaret, crowned, with a spear, or doubtless the cross, in her hand, transfixing the Dragon beneath her feet; the heads in profile probably representing St. Peter and St. Paul; they are raised from the surface. The oval form was that usually adopted by religious houses or ladies; and although the white wax, the unusual style of the heads, and the costume rather suggest to me an earlier period, the general character of the seal is not considered to imply a time much earlier than that of Richard II., the date of the document to which it is appended, or Edward III. We could hardly expect the original seal to have been in use after two hundred years. The document was a deed made 16th Richard II. by Eleanor, the Prioress of Bromhale, assuring an annuity of 3s. 4d. per annum to the Dean and Chapter of Lincoln in consideration of a grant to the Nunnery of the church of Northstoke, in that diocese.

THE NUNNERY OF BROOMHALL.

"Anno 1 John, Charter to the Monks of Bromehale.*

John, by the grace of God, &c. Know ye that, moved by divine love, and for the salvation of our souls and of those of our ancestors, we have given and granted to the house of the blessed Margaret of Bromhale, and to the Monks serving God at that place, the Church of Sunninghill and all things pertaining thereto, in pure and perpetual almsgift, to have and to hold to them and to their successors for ever, in war and in peace, freely and quietly and absolutely. Wherefore we will and firmly enjoin that the said Monks do have and hold the aforesaid Church of Sunninghill, and all things to it pertaining in war and in peace as is before mentioned.

"T. W. LONDON, Bishop, &c.

"Given under hand, S. Archdeacon Welln and J. de Gay, Archdeacon of Gloucester, at Alton, 23 day of April, the year, &c."

This is conclusive that both the Nunnery and the church existed before 1199.

The next fact we have is the grant by the same King† of a virgate of land in Windsor (Old Windsor lay close to the Nunnery on the east). On this it would seem a rent of forty pence was at first reserved, but was afterwards released in 9th Henry III. The farm of Windsor was charged in favour of the sisterhood with a payment of 8s. 2½d., and the halfpenny per day which they also had was afterwards raised to twopence.‡

In 1227 we get a statement of what their properties then were.

"*The Monks of Bromhale.*

"Fifty acres of the marsh of the Manor of Windsor in Laverset above the water of Bagshot.

"Hartley, thirty acres of marsh land in Hurley under Chabeham.

"Twenty acres of marsh of the Manor of Tottenhurst in the parish of Sunninghill assarted."

In the 23rd Henry III. this is written "Tetenhurst," and the quantity is increased to thirty acres. The thirty acres at Hartley was the homestead of Bromhall, known then as Hertley under Chobham.

In 1231 Henry III. granted to the Prioress of Bromhall in perpetuity pannage for the hogs in the King's forest at Windsor.§

---

* See Rot. Chart. at Rolls, 1 John. † Rot. Chart. 6 John, m. 12.
‡ Rot. Chart. 9 Hen. III., A.D. 1225; 11 Hen. III., A.D. 1227; 12 Hen. III. m. 7, m. 31.
§ Rot. Patentium, 16 Hen. III.

We afterwards learn from the Hundred Roll of encroachments on the royal demesne made by the Prioress, and of her having torn up two hundred oaks and more, to the great damage of the Crown; and we also learn that the Prioress held by gift of the King's father, Henry III., 150 acres of the forest at Winkfield. This, doubtless, was the manor of Chawridge.*

But one of the most important of their acquisitions was the benefaction of Henry de Lacy and his wife Margaret, who appears to have been a daughter (illegitimate) of Henry II.

The charter itself is worth transcribing, if only to show how little alteration seven hundred years have made in the essential language of a grant of land in this country; the words would pass an estate in the present day. Translated it runs, I think, thus:—

"*The Priory of Bromhale in Berkshire.*

"The Charter of Henry de Lacy,† Earl of Lincoln, of 100 acres of land of his waste of Asseridge.

To all to whom this writing shall come.

"Henry de Lacy, Count of Nichole and Constable of Chester, Lord of Ros and Reweynnok, and Margaret his wife, salute you. Know that for the salvation of our souls, and for the salvation of those of our ancestors and our heirs, we have released, and for all of them and ourselves and our heirs quit claim to God and our Lady of Bromhale, and her Nuns in that place serving her, 100 acres of land of our waste of Asseridge, with their appurtenances, measured by the perch of twenty feet,‡ which lies between Pillingbere and the royal way which leads from Brackenhale to Redinge, to have and to hold of us and our heirs as aforesaid, to the Nuns and their successors in free, pure, and perpetual almsgift for ever, &c. In testimony of which thing to this writing we have set our seals; and these are the witnesses: Monsire Roberd, the Bishop Roger, Monsire Peter de Maulley, Monsire William de Vavasur, Monsire Roberd de Maulley, Monsire John de Cresakre, uncle of our Senechal, Monsire Gefray de Picheford, Monsire Willame de Estopham, Knights, and others."§

---

* See Cal. Rot. Ed. I., anno 11, grant of a hundred acres.
† Henry de Lacy, knighted in 1272; see Gale, vol. ii. p. 226.
‡ It was customary in measuring Forest land to use a rod of 20 feet; see Elton's "Tenures of Kent," p. 129.
§ This charter was confirmed 13 Ed. I.; see Cal. Rot. Pat. Hallam says the appellation Sire was applied to Barons; Bannerets being distinguished only by that of Monsieur.

Henry III. was evidently well disposed to our Nunnery. In the 26th of his reign he says: "Pay out of our treasury to Brother John, our Almoner, to feed the poor for the soul of the Empress formerly our sister, £8, 6s. 8d., to feed two thousand poor persons, to wit, one half at Ankerwick, and the other half at Bromhal."

The Empress was Eleanor, wife of the Emperor Frederick II. of Germany. In 1268 a certain Agnes was Prioress, and Isabella de Sonninges presided over the house in 1295.

This Isabella is the lady alluded to in the Hundred Roll of Edward I., from which it seems she fell out with one of her neighbours. "They say," it informs us, "that when Joan, who was the wife of John de W"lveley, complained of Isabella of Sunninghill, Geoffrey de Picheford came and took ten beasts of the said Isabella, and detained them for a fortnight against sureties and pledges, until upon petition to the Queen they were restored. Nevertheless, Phillips, the porter of the Castle of Windsor, took seven shillings from the said Isabella for the keep of the said beasts."

About this time the sisterhood suffered a great calamity; their house was destroyed by fire or much damaged; for I find a record of Walter de Cantilupe, Bishop of Worcester, addressing a pastoral letter to all the abbots, priors, archdeacons, &c., within his diocese that they might collect alms from the faithful for the Prioress and nuns of St. Margaret of Brumhale, "nuper combusto."* In 1392 the sisterhood acquired the church of Northstoke in Lincolnshire.

It was not long before this that the general depravity of these institutions evoked Robert Langland's satire, that most remarkable prophecy in Piers Ploughman:—

> "And there shal come a king, and confess you religious;
> And beate you, as the bible telleth, for breaking your rule;
> And amende monials, and monks, and chanons,
> And put hem in her penaunce ad pristinum statum ire." †

In 1404 an unpleasantness arose in this establishment; for in Archbishop Arundel's Register at Lambeth may be seen a commission for inquiring into the conduct of Juliana Bromhale, a nun, who, it

---

* These briefs or licenses for collections were at first issued by or under the authority of the Pope; but when his authority was abrogated in England, the King adopted the same course, and they were called "King's Letters."
† See White's Selbourne, Lord Selbourne's Edit., vol. ii. p. 214.

was alleged, had much injured the Convent's reputation and her own. But we will not pursue that.

Dugdale, relying chiefly on Baker's MS.,* gives the following list of the Abbesses, to which I make a few additions.

1266. *Agnes was Abbess.*
1268. Agnes occurs 53rd Henry III. Cole, in two of his MS. vols., calls her Agnes de Sancto Edmundo. [*On inspection of the Liber Evidentiarum at Salisbury (398), I find there was a grant of tithes to Agnes, the Prioress, in 1266.*]
1281. Margery de Wycumbe was elected November 9.
1295. Isabella presided 24th Edward I. [*This was Isabella de Sonninges; she resigned in 1310, and the petition of the Nuns for license to elect her successor is among the Tower letters, temp. Edward II.*]
1310.
1321. Matilda de Burgton, and 1324. [*I suggest 1310 as the date of her election.*] She is elsewhere called Broughton.
1336. Gunilda occurs also in 1348, 10th and 23rd Edward III., soon after which last date she was succeeded by
1348. Isabella de Hougheforde, who also occurs in 1350.
1358. Alicia de Falle occurs, as also in 1363.
1373. Alienora, as also in 1385 [*and* 1393]. Willis thinks she might possibly be the same person with
1402. Eleanor Burton, whose name he met with at this date. Juliana Dunne was the next Prioress, upon whose resignation
1405. Thomasia or Thomasine Bodington was elected. She occurs also in 1413 and 1419, and again in 1430.
1437. Alice Burton presided, and she occurs again in 1445.
1461. Isabella Beale occurs in the reign of Edward IV., between the years 1461 and 1483, in which last year she was succeeded by
1483. Anne Thomas, on whose promotion to the Priory of Wintney, Hampshire, after 1489,
1484. [*Alice would appear from the records of the Manor of Bray, as quoted in Kerry's History of Bray, and also by the Rev. W. Cole in his Notes on the History of Burnham, to have been Prioress in 1484, and Anna in 1492.*]
1492. [*Anna. See "Collectanea Topographica et Genealogica," vols. v., vi., British Museum.†*]
Elizabeth Lewkenor.
1511. Joan Rawlins occurs 3rd Henry VIII., and surrendered August 9, 1521, according to Willis. [*I think there was no surrender; the Nuns were simply expelled.*]

Time rolled on, and great changes came. The monasteries had abused their high trust; the dawn of a brighter day was breaking, and they could not bear the light. The first blow to the old order of things was the suppression of the alien monasteries by Henry V., a measure based, no doubt, on sound policy. No home monastery had, however, been touched till Alcock, Bishop of Ely, made the first

---

* Willis, Mit. Ab., tom. xi. App. p. 3; Baker's MSS. Brit. Mus. † Cole's MS. Brit. Mus.

example of the demoralised St. Radegund at Cambridge, and on its site and with its revenues he founded Jesus College. On the thoughtful mind of the master of Michael House in that town, John Fisher, this example made a lasting impression. Singularly enough, he came shortly afterwards to dwell in this neighbourhood, and entered the household of Margaret Beaufort, Countess of Richmond, mother of Henry VII., who in her old palatial manor-house at Woking was tending the sick and needy, and giving herself up to charitable works.

Here, only a few miles across the common, she and her chaplain were working out their views to supplant the old and effete, and establish the new. This was at the opening of the century; but whether, at that early period, they had looked down upon our Nunnery in the dale below with thoughts of ever bringing that within the range of their policy, I know not; but they soon determined to extend their operations to Cambridge again, and Christ's College arose on the site of a monastery of which with some difficulty they had obtained the dissolution.

They were dealing in like manner with the house of the Austin Canons there when the Countess died in 1509. Fisher, her executor, carried out her directions after considerable difficulty and delay; and St. John's College was opened at last in 1516. Only a few years elapsed when Fisher became Bishop of Rochester, and close to him there he found the Nunnery of Higham, an establishment of a very doubtful reputation. It must be suppressed! It was then his thoughts reverted to the little house at Sunninghill; and that too was doomed. The floodgates were now opened, and a precedent established. What the pious and zealous Churchman had initiated, the more ambitious and powerful genius of Wolsey was not slow to take advantage of. He was dreaming of his great foundations at Ipswich and Christ's Church, Oxford.* Henry's will too, as we know, was very strong, and his exchequer very empty. Wolsey and Cromwell were made the unscrupulous instruments by which, in a flagrant fashion, was worked out perhaps the most extensive reform that has ever been achieved in this country. Different motives in the first instance actuated the two great workers in this. Wolsey saw the vast change that was coming over society, and his ambition was stimulated by the opportunity it afforded him of enriching his rising colleges. Henry too had views of his own. He had scarcely

---

* See Hook's Lives of Archbishops, vol. 1. New Series, p. 64.

perhaps yet dreamt of any scheme of general confiscation; but he was pondering an aggressive measure against Rome in the extension of his regal authority in ecclesiastical matters. Reform soon became spoliation.

The scheme at first was full of danger; but how cautiously it was begun! If a feather was required to be thrown up to see which way the wind blew, poor little Bromhall was exactly the feather they wanted. Friendless and helpless, for the King was himself the patron, it could be made away with more easily than most. So the wicked sister and the forlorn one—Higham and Bromhall—were manacled together. Wolsey lent the aid of his legatine authority; the scruples of Fisher were satisfied, and Audley of Sarum readily succumbed to the King's vehemence. The bishops were slow, but the King soon " quickened their paces," as Baker tells us.

This case of Bromhall is one, I think, worthy of more notice by the historian than it has hitherto received.* It was perhaps the very first instance of a purely tyrannical suppression of a religious foundation (other than the alien Priories), and of property impressed with religious uses having been violently, and without consideration, transferred to lay hands. The few earlier cases at Oxford and Cambridge had been more tenderly dealt with; the properties had been acquired with at least a show of right; but here there was no scrupulousness. It shows, too, the extreme caution and sagacity of the great actors in the movement. In their first cases they acquired the rights, and had only the religious scruples of the world to overcome. Here they move a step farther, and touch the benefactions of others, but of which they alone were the guardians. Had there been any instance then of the suppression of a foundation of a purely religious character that had an independent powerful patron? It was the cautious opening of a great game.

Thus, long before February 1536, when the King gave "directions" to the Parliament to suppress the lesser monasteries, Wolsey had been preparing and extending his plans. The great Lords were sounded, and even staunch Catholics such as Fitzwilliam found it impossible to resist the promised plunder. He and his family were afterwards loaded with it. The Priory of Newark, near Woking, was one of the smaller plums.

As early as 1521 Bromhall was suppressed. Dugdale and Willis say it was "surrendered" to the King on the 9th of August of that

---

* See Life of Margaret Beaufort, by C. A. Halsted, also C. H. Cooper's Life of same.

year; but that could hardly be, I think. It was not until the 20th of October that the Bishop's Visitation was authorised. Wolsey on that day wrote to the Bishop of Sarum, Edmund Audley, "By our power of legation, we be contented that ye act as our deputy, to visit the nunneries of the diocese, and proceed against such as are guilty of misgovernance and slanderous living. The nuns are to be removed unto other places of that religion, where ye can best and most conveniently bestow them."

Then comes a letter dated "Bromhall, 4th December," from Richard, archeprieste:—"*With much ado* the nuns are removed from Bromhall. My Lord will not give up the evidences until he can see the King's grant." *

On the 13th of December, Henry, writing to the Bishop of Sarum, "thanks him for the care he has taken in *suppressing* the Nunnery of Bromhall, for such enormities as was by them used. The Bishop is to deliver to the bearer the 'evidences' of the house now in his hands. Richmond, 13th December, 13th Henry VIII."

On the 6th February 1522, the archpriest Richard writes from Ramsbury "that he had sent for the resignations of the ladies, late of Bromhall."

On the 3rd of March 1522, an inquisition was taken at Windsor before William Moleyns, escheator, when the following facts were found:—"That a Priory of Nuns of St. Benedict's Order, dedicated to St. Margaret, at Bromhall, was founded by the King's progenitors, and under the authority of the Bishop of Salisbury; that Joan Rawlins, Prioress, resigned on the 12th September last; that two nuns were there, who on the 5th December, with Rawlins, left the Priory as a profane place, which is consequently dissolved; that the convent was seized of the Church of St. Margaret, the churchyard, and of the site and grange of the monastery, which latter included a mansion, manor, water-mill, gate-house, gardens, &c. The church and churchyard are of no value, because set apart for divine service; the rest are worth 4s. a year. The convent was also seized of the manors of Bromhall [and] Chawrig, alias Wingfield [Berks]."

A strange valuation this of 4s. a year for a mansion, manor, water-mill, and gardens. Our church, too, is dedicated to St. Michael and all Angels, and I believe has always been so. It was doubtless erroneously named as St. Margaret in this document because of the dedication of

---

* Baker's Hist. of St. John's College. Baker, MSS. Harleian Collection, No. 7028, vol. 1. Tiddes, c. p. 123.

the Nunnery; but I presume it was a clerical error. Besides these possessions in Berks, the Convent also had " the manor of Windlesham, and the manor of Egham, and land at ' Potenhall,' and Knoll Hill and Thorpe, and at ' Mynchynreyde,' Surrey."

On this important document I must make a few remarks. In the first place, I think Dugdale must be in error in giving the 9th August as the date of the "surrender," for the Visitation was not authorised till the 20th October, and had there been any earlier inquiry, we should surely have heard of it. Besides, the finding on the Inquisition is precise to the fact that the Prioress "resigned on the 12th of September," which she could hardly be said to have done had she already "surrendered" in August. That, however, is but of little consequence. The more important point is the manner of her leaving. Baker says the Prioress Jane Rawlins resigned "voluntarily;" but as to that, notwithstanding the fact of her having had a pension assigned her, I think no impartial judgment can imagine that she was a free agent. There was no surrender of the Nunnery beyond that purely constructive one of which the Inquisition tells us, "its being left" on the 5th December "as a profane place, and which is consequently dissolved." The King had determined on the suppression, urged the Bishop to it with indecent haste, and thanked him for the care he had taken in "suppressing" the Nunnery for "such enormities as was by them used." This implies a previous inquiry, and is quite inconsistent with a voluntary surrender in August. The whole thing seems to have been a transparent concoction. The real truth, I believe, was, that the three lone women were threatened, possibly so early as August, with the proposed Visitation, and terribly frightened. The Prioress and the two nuns clung to their beloved home till the last moment, and fled from it only on that dark December day, thrust out by Archdeacon Richard and his myrmidons when no longer permitted to remain. What can show this more clearly than that worthy's own letter, written from the Convent that very afternoon, "With *much ado* the nuns are removed from Broomhall." This does not sound like a voluntary surrender; much more like a surrender at the point of the bayonet. It is not unlikely that at a later date the Prioress, seeing all was lost, accepted the annuity as the only alternative she had for support.

Then as to the evidences, by which of course are meant the charters and title-deeds, what became of them? Although I could not find them either at St. John's or Salisbury, it is clear they were delivered to the College; for on the 9th of January 1522, Archdeacon Richard writes to Dr. Metcalfe of St. John's, "My Lord is contentyd ye come or send for the evidences of Bromhall at what tyme ye will." And on the 13th there is an "acquittance by Randall Hall, servant to Dr. Metcalfe, to Bishop of Sarum, on receipt of the evidences and *seal* of Bromhall." Thus was this little Forest house made one of the very earliest victims of the new policy. Helpless as it was, its fall was easy, and the Pope's bull and the King's bribes satisfied the conscience of the orthodox Catholic party.

When the tools had done their work they were cast aside, and there is every reason to believe, as Baker suggests, that at the time of Wolsey's fall Fisher felt remorse at the part he had been made to play, and became out of favour by being disaffected to the King's proceedings.

A very few years after this, it was one of the express charges against Wolsey on his disgrace that he had in many cases asserted "that the religious persons so suppressed had voluntarily forsaken their said houses, which was untrue."

Apropos of this, I came upon a curious entry at the Record Office. In 31st Elizabeth legal proceedings were instituted for the purpose of ascertaining whether, soon after William Symonds was Mayor of New Windsor, he was punished for perjury, "and did ride with a paper in his hat or cap with one Dr. London in the town of Windsor, with their faces to the horses tayle."

This infamous Dr. London, who had been so zealous in his persecution of the religious bodies, and who boasted of how he had defaced the various Friars' houses, and churches, was publicly punished as above described.*

It is very humiliating to see how, when, at a subsequent date, the Parliament sanctioned the destruction of the lesser monasteries, every one endeavoured to conciliate the great upstart Secretary, "Thomas the Mauler," who was distributing the plunder: the spoils of the Forest, as well as of the Kentish orchards, were laid as peace-offerings at his feet. Sir William Fitzwilliam, one of the most powerful men of his time, wrote to Cromwell on 3rd July . . . . from Byflete in this very neighbourhood: "My wife hath sent unto you at this time a dishe of fowle of her own fatting." "By Sundaye at night I trust to send you a piece of a reddere." This from so great a man makes us but little wonder that Thomas Goldwell, Prior of Canterbury, should write with his little present also: we may imagine what his real feelings were towards his dear friend. "We have one fruit growing here, with us in Kent called a Pome riall. He is a very good apull, and good to drynke wyne withall."

To resume. The estates of the Nunnery in several counties having

---

* See also Ellis's Original Letters, 307.

been adjudged escheats to the Crown, were by letters patent dated 21st October 1522, through the interest of Bishop Fisher and the Cardinal, granted, with the Rectory and advowson of Sunninghill, to St. John's College, Cambridge, in whose possession the advowson of the church and the manor of Bromhall have remained ever since.*

In 1524, 28th September, there was a Bull of Clement VII. suppressing the Nunneries of Bromhall and Higham, and confirming the conditional donation to the College.

As soon as this Bull arrived in England, the College set about appointing a local receiver for their newly acquired estates, and Thomas Warde of Winkfield, the King's "gentleman harbinger," was selected to act for them. They let the manor of Chawridge on lease to Richard Warde, clerk of the poultry to the King; and Bromhall to one Oliver Lowthe, yeoman. He was succeeded by Henry Atlee and Anth Batlie, husbandmen. Then came a tenant of a very different class; for in 1564 the manor of Bromhall was let for forty years, at the rent of £7, 6s. 8d., to "Roger Askam of London, gentleman, the Queen's Latin Secretary," the learned scholar of St. John's, who had become a Fellow of that College before he was nineteen years of age. This was at the close of his life, when we can imagine that a good bargain and a little amateur farming would be agreable, and a relaxation after his laborious life of study.

In an old Terrier of 1634 a list is given of things belonging to the church, and therein is included "one annuity or set portion of money per annum 40s., paid half yearly out of a certain farme called Bromhall, which ye College of St. John of Cambridge hath lying neare unto our church, *and is of our parish in all taxes and rates whatsoever, though not in our parish.*"

This somewhat anomalous state of things excited the suspicions of our neighbours at Egham, it seems, and litigation resulted from it. In 1730 came threats, and our Vestry-book contains an entry authorising resistance. "Resolved that if the parish of Egham make any distraint on Broomhall farm or commence any lawsuit thereupon, this parish do defend the said lawsuit." They did go to law, and Sunninghill won the day, as there follows an entry, "April 7th, 1735, Paid ringers for ringing the bells after the tryall 5s., and £8 towards the law expenses of John Baber, Esq. Mr. Aldridge, £8."

---

* Tanner in his "Monasticon" says the grant to the College was on the 21st October, the year after the Inquisition; that would be in 1523.

THE NUNNERY OF BROOMHALL.

In 1736 the accounts contain entries, "Two days ringing 6s." What a rejoicing it must have been! three times as much as for Gunpowder treason! Then came the victors' extra expenses to be defrayed two years afterwards, "Paid John Baber, Esq., towards his expenses concerning y^e lawsuit with Egham parish £10. Paid Mr. John Aldridge towards his father's expenses £10."

In 1766 Thomas Baber was tenant of Tittenhurst and Broomhall.

CHAPTER XXXIII.

The Roman Road.

OF all the antiquities of our neighbourhood, there is none more interesting than the Roman road that traverses the Forest.

It was the great highway between Londinium and Aquæ Sulis, the beautiful city of the springs, over which the British deity Sul and the Roman Minerva jointly presided, and to which it owed its name. It was the Akemanceaster of the Saxons. Along this highway numerous fragments of pottery, coins, and building material have been discovered, and earthworks are still to be seen, all reminding us of Roman occupation; while the camps that command the route show how stubbornly our Forest was defended, and how step by step only its conquest must have been achieved.

It is pleasant to study these evidences of the past, but it must be done with caution. For the last hundred years they have been the subject of considerable discussion, and we can hardly be too grateful to our old writers, Camden, Herne, Aubrey, Guest, and others, for the records they have left us of their earlier explorations.

Towards the end of the last century, however, the study of this subject was greatly stimulated by the discovery, as was asserted, of an Itinerary of Richard of Cirencester, published by Charles Julius Bertram, Professor of English in the Academy of Copenhagen. It first appeared there in 1758. Dr. Stukeley and John Whitaker received it in raptures; and Omerod, Lysons, Sir R. Colt Hoare, Gough, and even Lingard and Gibbon, gave it their support. Conybeare, Dr. Guest, and some few others refused to accept it, and denounced it as fraudulent.

It professed to bring to light another lost station, and to us Berkshire folk a most interesting one, because it was supposed to be close to us. Bibracte, the capital of the ancient British tribe of the Bibroci, an offshoot, we are told, of a colony of the Ædui in Gaul, who dwelt near Autun, where Cæsar gained one of his great victories.[*] Bray was at once adopted as its site. Over this new treasure the learned wrangled, I fear, not a little; and that which should have cleared up all our doubts only introduced fresh complications and inconsistencies. But after puzzling our antiquaries for many years, and leading them so cruelly astray, this precious document (the original of which, by the bye, had never been produced) has been proved to be an elaborate fraud.[†] Mr. F. C. Wex and Professor J. B. Mayor have severally analysed this imaginary work, "De Situ Britanniæ," and demonstrated its spuriousness. But many recent writers, and among them some of the latest who have touched on our country, instead of giving us the benefit of their own researches and local study, are content simply to fall back on their predecessors, and repeat what they had built up on this hollow foundation; they talk of Bibracte as though it were a well-established place, and do not even allude to the fraud that brought it into prominent existence. The name is not even mentioned in the Antonine Itinerary, nor in Hübner; nor does the learned author of "Roman Britain" (Mr. Prebendary Scarth) allude to such a place.[‡] The idea was caught, no doubt, from Camden, who threw out as a conjecture that Bibrax or Bibracte was the name of Bray; but it will be seen on careful study, that had the spurious record been genuine and the distances given in it correct, Bibracte could not possibly have been Bray. So its very existence must for the present be ignored, and Mr. Edgell's stone at Egham, that so boldly proclaims its location, must, in this respect at least, remain a monument of error. In such inquiries if we proceed on the few established facts we possess, and build on these only, we shall avoid much confusion.

Perhaps the most interesting fact we can vouch for is that at Silchester, on a fine elevated plateau, are still to be seen the vestiges of an ancient Roman stronghold; on the site, doubtless, of a still more ancient British one. On the north and north-east lay the marshes, augmented by the confluence of the Kennet, the Loddon, and the Thames; a low swampy district, in which Reading, not then existing, has since arisen. We find that this great Bath road in its eastward direction declined a little southward towards this important fortress; a place of the first importance, as is shown not only from

---

[*] Cæsar, Bell. Gall., i. 23, vii. 55.
[†] Mayor's Edit. of Richard of Cirencester, Introd.
[‡] See Burton's Edit., also Corpus Inscript. Hen. VII. C. F. Baxter, Glossarium Antiq. Brit., 41.

the buildings it possessed, its forum, amphitheatre, and baths, but especially from the great roads that radiated from it. It covered a larger area than Aquæ Sulis itself, was the key of the west, and the centre of, as I think I can establish, seven military roads: one through Basingstoke to Venta Belgarum (Winchester), and thence through Clausentum to Regnum (Chichester), as well as to Bittern on Southampton Water and the Isle of Wight, in its first stage called by the rustics the "Broad Way;"* another to the great fortress of Old Sarum (Sorbiodunum) by what is known as the Port-way; this Berkshire road of ours to Londinium through Pontes, known as the Imperial way, and which was continued out of the western gate to Spinas and on to Aquæ Sulis; one issuing out of its northern gate to Streatley on the Thames and Dorchester, a portion of the Ikenild Street way; a sixth probably south of Reading towards Bray; and lastly, one other (which I cannot doubt the existence of) from the southern gate to Vindomis, an important station uniting the south-eastern with the western and south-western roads.

Calleva stood on the site of an earlier British stronghold, which Camden thought was Caer Segont, the capital of the Segontiaci; and the discovery there in 1732 of a stone bearing the inscription "Deo Herculi Sægontiacorum," although by no means conclusive, is very suggestive of that fact. Nennius, writing in the ninth century, speaks of their chief town as Caer Segeint. The Segontii, however, doubtless possessed this place, and seem to have been driven out by the Attrebates from Gaul, who held it till the Romans dispossessed them; it then became their Calleva Attrebatum. When they abandoned Britain, it fell before the assaults of the Saxon hordes, who burnt it to the ground. Some think that when holding out for Allectus in 294 it was besieged and burnt by Asclepiodatus. Henry of Huntingdon states that Caer Segont was destroyed and all its inhabitants were put to the sword about A.D. 493 by the Saxon chief Ella, in his march from Sussex (where he landed) to Bath, after burning Caer Andred (Pevensey).† It then became, as Horsley suggests, the "Sel" castra, or Silchester, the great camp.‡

And there on the breezy uplands remain to this day the ruins of the ancient city. Its walls are standing; they are about 13 feet

---

* This is not the place to discuss the site of Clausentum. It was not, I think, Bittern.

† See United Service Journal, 1836; Archæological Journal, vol. viii.

‡ When Hearne paid the place a visit in 1714, he describes the walls as almost entire, except where the four gates were, and still six or seven yards in height in some places, and that the ditch all round the walls was about forty yards in breadth.

high and 8 feet thick, a mile and a half in circuit, and enclose about 102 acres. Beyond this wall is an outer defence of a rampart or ditch; the foundations of its public buildings and its streets lie all open to our view. Here were found the hoards of a money-changer, and there the debris of an oyster-shop; while hard by on the tiles, impressed for all time, are the sharp footprints of a deer and fawn chased by a wolf; and on another, scratched by some Roman potter, are words, of which one, "Puellam," may still be clearly seen, telling us of that "old, old story," as fashionable then as it is now. A fine bronze eagle of a Roman standard, now at Strathfieldsaye, was also found there.*

The Rev. Mr. Joyce informs us that the Ordnance Surveyors in 1872 were requested to show the direction of the London road, and where its line would strike the wall. At the exact point excavations were made, and there the foundations of the eastern gate were discovered.

But where are all the ruins gone? For here and there only vestiges of some of the carved Corinthian capitals and columns remain; we have scarcely what Camden describes as "the dead carcass of an ancient city," but little more than its bones.

What a quarry it must have been for ages in a country naturally devoid of building-stone! Much of the material went to build the Abbey of Reading, that centuries afterwards rose up so stately within sight of those blackened ruins. A few more hundred years elapsed, and that noble pile was a quarry in its turn, and these stones were borne down the river to be utilised once more in the poor knights' houses at Windsor. Queen Elizabeth gave two hundred loads of "fine stone from the Abbey" to the Corporation of Reading.

The next fact is that in the midst of our Forest, on the line of this road, called by the Berkshire rustics "the Devil's Highway," we find the remains of a Roman town or village at Wickham Bushes, where Roman pottery and coins are constantly found; and nearly a mile to the north of this, crowning a ridge there, are the extensive earthworks called Cæsar's Camp, a fortress apparently of British origin, adopted by the Roman generals on account of its excellent site. It commanded the road between Londinium and the great city before described; it was well supplied with water, a large pond existing on the north-east side of it, which is now nearly dried up. The area of the camp is

---

* Archæologia, vol. ii. p. 333.

spacious; and, according to the Roman method of encamping, would accommodate, it is said, as many as nine thousand men.*

Still travelling eastward, we come to Rapley Farm, evidently a Roman station, as we shall presently see; and pursuing the same direction, we have another camp on a steep eminence to the north, known as Tower Hill, and two or three miles beyond that, on the south, lay the large hill entrenchment at Sunningdale or Mincing Ride. Then ascending the heights of Egham, one looks down upon the Thames, with Staines and the low marshes of Wraysbury on the north-east, and on the south Walton and Shepperton, where there were the remains of a Roman camp twelve acres in extent. From Walton a rampart or vallum and ditch extended as far as St. George's Hill. On St. Ann's Hill, the Eldebury of the Saxons, are also traces of a camp. At Bray, and Waltham, and Maidenhead Thicket, as well as at Sunningdale close by us, we find evidences of Roman occupation; while nearer to London were the remains of camps on Hounslow Heath.

But perhaps the most important fact of all is that we can trace a well-constructed and skilfully designed road all the way from London to Bath. Here and there, of course, sections of it have been effaced by cultivation and alterations of the surface; but when the missing link or next portion of it is found, the line is continued in an almost undeviating course to the great western capital.

Dr. Stukeley traced the road as leaving London by way of Oxford Street through Tyburn, Turnham Green, and Hounslow, by the north of Ashford Church to Staines; from this place and from Egham are traces of roads communicating with the fortresses of Wraysbury, Laleham, and Shepperton.

From a point on the river close to Staines, the road is clearly traceable to Silchester, and fortunately this section of it in our immediate neighbourhood has been admirably surveyed by the officers of the Royal Military College at Sandhurst.†

They trace the way issuing from the eastern gate of the ancient town (Silchester) near the church, through Strathfieldsaye to Westcourt House, directly through the avenue to the mansion, thence northward of Finchampstead Church, pursuing an unbroken line along the level country to Easthampstead Plain by Wickham Bushes, near Cæsar's Camp, which it leaves more than half a mile to the north;

---

* It is stated to be about 560 paces in length and 280 in width at nearly the middle of it; but it conformed entirely to the very irregular shape of the hill.

† See Surrey Archæological Collections, 1858. Art. by Lieut.-Col. M'Dougall.

thence to Duke's Hill in the vicinity of Bagshot,* where the eastern direction terminates, as its course thence forms an angle of about 25 degrees north of east. It then passes by Charter's Pond to the Sunninghill Road, where it is extremely well defined; thence by the Belvedere its line of direction cuts Virginia Water, in the construction of which it was doubtless interfered with, and passing through the yard of the inn, it touches at Bakeham House in the same line of direction, where, on the brow of the hill which forms the east end of the elevated plain called Engelfield Green, Roman works and traces of the road were discovered in 1835. The road then crosses the Thames between Magna Charta Island and Staines. To this I may add, that the point of crossing was almost exactly in the line of the famous London Stone. This spot was just between sixteen o seventeen English miles from Hyde Park Corner.†

In our immediate neighbourhood the road traverses the plantation of Mr. Kemp-Welch, late Forbes, passing over the hill by the "Fireball Clump," to the southern margin of Charter's Pond, which was probably formed or enlarged by its embankment, and thus afforded a convenient water supply to the Roman wayfarer and troops (a point never neglected by their engineers); then rising again through the property of Count Gleichen, whose house stands almost on the site of the road, it passes through Dr. Girdlestone's garden, where it is supposed to have been struck upon, as I shall presently mention. But when was this road made? ‡

What the Romans themselves have told us is unfortunately very meagre; the principal authority is the Itinerary of Antonine.

The places named in this record as marking the several stages on the road are not very numerous, and are mostly now identified by modern archæologists, with the exception of one, "Pontes," but that one is to us the most important of all. They are, so far as our present

---

* It passed between the two westernmost of four ponds, which lie south of Rapley Farm. Here the water, by neglect or by design, has been allowed to cut through the roadway, thus forming one pond instead of two. (Colonel Cooper King, Note to Prof. Rupert Jones's paper. Geo. Ass., 1880.)

† United Service Jour., 1836. Archæologia, vols. xvi., xix, p. 96, and xxvii. 412.

‡ The interesting fortification at East Hampstead is an instance of the common error of attributing every Roman camp in the country to Cæsar (meaning Julius of the Commentaries); but that Cæsar undoubtedly never saw this camp; he did not enter Berkshire. It was not until the time of the Emperor Claudius, A.D. 43, that Aulus Plautius or his general Vespatian penetrated our Forest district. Then the four Legions, the 2nd, 9th, 14th, and 20th, with their cavalry, advanced to this fortress, afterwards known as Calleva, and thence pushing on to Cirencester (Corinium) and back by the British trackway (the Icknild way) to Streatley and Wallingford. It was about this time that the great road we are describing was constructed.

inquiry is concerned, Londinium, Pontes, and Calleva. But others, Spinas, Cunetionem, Verlucionem, and Vindomis, are incidentally interesting.

Pontes is said to have been equidistant from Londinium and Calleva, twenty-two miles from each of those places. Calleva was described as fifteen miles from Spinas.

These are all-important facts, and are the keystones to our speculations; for thus having shown the road, or, better still, the road having shown itself, we must not ignore it for any theories; and we can hardly admit that any of the stations mentioned in this Iter of the Itinerary can be placed elsewhere than upon it, or upon a branch connected with it.

Where, then, was Calleva, and where Pontes?

Now exactly fifteen miles from Spene (Spinas) is the ancient city already described at Silchester.* Yet Mr. Pearson places Calleva at Wallingford, Mr. Horsley at Reading, and he is followed by Dr. Becke, since by Mr. Reynolds and others, and quite recently by the writer on Berkshire in the "Encyclopædia Britannica." Mr. Chute, too, in his history of the Vyne, adopts the same view, and I cannot but think that, in endeavouring to identify it with Vindomis, he injures his otherwise charming account of the place. Mr. H. F. Napper, a Sussex archæologist, has also just revived this old idea with amusing confidence. He discovered some Roman coins at a spot two or three miles from Reading, known as Calvepit Farm, and from this fanciful suggestion he builds up a theory that there he found the site of Calleva. The learned German geographer on whom he relies probably took Dr. Becke's account, having no local knowledge of his own. All these writers seem to adopt as their authority Dr. Becke's paper in the Archæologia. But he wrote before the Sandhurst Survey was made; half his account, too, was based on the spurious Itinerary of Richard of Cirencester; and as the other half would not fit in with the distances of the Roman account, he simply proposed to alter the Roman figures. He places Calleva 36 miles from Venta Belgarum (Winchester), to make it reach Reading, instead of 22, as the Itinerary states, and which would bring it exactly to Silchester. From Spinæ, again, we are told by the Roman account it was 15 miles to Calleva; but to Reading it would be 20, while to Silchester it is the 15 exactly. Another writer suggests Streatley as Calleva; but a little consideration, I venture to think, will show these views to be quite unten-

---

* Historical Maps, Britannia Romana Archæologia, 1806.

able. Streatley, and much more Wallingford, must be discarded as not conformable to the Roman accounts either in distance or direction. Reading is several miles out of the line of road traced to London, and does not accord at all with the Itinerary. Moreover, there are not, as admitted by Mr. Coates in his history of that town, any traces of a Roman road there, nor have fragments of pottery or coins or remains to any extent been found there to give colour to Roman origin or occupation. It seems to have been named as fitting in with theories otherwise not maintainable. To support these, all the stations on the Bath side must be rearranged to accommodate them; while a little investigation shows places on the actual road more in accordance with the Roman distances. Thus, the advocates for Reading are obliged to make Spinæ Thatcham, which is off the line, while Spene near Newbury, which is on it, agrees in name and distance more accurately; and there is great extraneous support for Spene in the well-known fact that it was a Roman station of importance. Camden writes, "From thence the River Kennet comes to Spinæ, the old town mentioned by Antoninus, which retaining still its name, is called Spene; but instead of town, is now a poor little village, scarce a mile from Newbury, that had its rise out of the ruins of it, for Newbury is as much as the 'New Borough,' that is, in regard to Spinæ, the more ancient place." There can be no question, I think, that Spene was "Spinæ." Marlborough, or rather, as is now generally admitted, Follyfarm, close to Marlborough, was "Cunetio." And after considering the best modern opinions, I hold it beyond doubt that Silchester was "Calleva." Has it ever occurred to those who deny to Silchester this identity to tell us the Roman name of that great city, and what road it was that we trace so distinctly from it to Staines?

But as to "Pontes," the station most interesting to us, where was that? We ought to look for it at a place where there were two or more bridges. It must be on the road which has been so clearly traced, and twenty-two miles from London. We at once conclude that no spot answers these requirements so well as that at which this road crossed the Thames near the London Stone.* The passage of the

---

* The exact point of crossing, important as that is, has not been fixed with certainty. Rickman thought it was at old Staines bridge, which was about 150 yards east or lower down the river than the present one. Colonel Cooper King, following apparently the Sandhurst Survey, places it at the small island in the Thames south of the London Stone; but the Sandhurst Survey does not support this statement. The map places it a third of a mile above the bridge, which carries it westward of the island some distance. Besides, although the island would give a tempting

Thames and the Colne, however, would have required at least two bridges; thus explaining "Pontes" in the plural. The distance of seventeen English miles from Hyde Park Corner, plus three more to the miliarium stone in the City, would hardly give us twenty-two Roman miles (as near London they were nearly equal to our present miles); but of this I will speak presently. A most important fact, however, is that there are no other streams on this road that would comply with the required distance so closely as these. Altogether, I feel convinced that here at this point of the crossing at Staines was the site of "Pontes" (the bridges) of the Roman account. Wraysbury is too far from Silchester, and Colnbrook still farther, and too near to London to be admitted. If we consider the local circumstances of the case, and try to realise what the river was in those days, we shall see why this spot was chosen by the Roman engineers for their crossing.

We have good reason to believe that the bed itself of the Thames has changed,* and that when its waters were augmented by those of the Colne, they spread out in a much greater volume than now. Its very name is supposed by some to be derived from the Saxon *tame* or *tam*, broad or spreading, from this characteristic. Here it formed, as it were, a great lagoon, in which Chertsey was an island. Leland

---

suggestion of the two or more bridges, which the name "Pontes" requires, unfortunately for this theory, there can be little doubt that in Roman times the island did not exist; as an island, it is of comparatively recent formation. I think the real point of crossing was nearly half a mile above the bridge, in a line with the London Stone. In this line both the Sandhurst map and the straight continuation of the road from Virginia Water and Bakeham House indicate it. The continuation from the London Stone was probably by the church, and so through the town by the Brewery, which stands on a Roman burial-ground. This route was skilfully chosen, as here the Colne and the Wyrardsbury unite, so that one stream only had to be crossed, while at any point north of this two branches of the Colne as well as the Wyrardsbury would have been encountered.

* To show how important these changes have been, the channel, now a mere creek eastward of the island alluded to, was a hundred years ago the main river-bed, while what is now the principal stream west of the island was then only a reach. But much more violent changes are clearly traceable here. A considerable piece of Staines parish now lies on the west or Surrey side of the river, as also at Egham a portion of Bucks is on that side. Indeed, I have but little doubt that in Roman times Egham itself was mostly under water. The Thames swept round to the south-west, much nearer to the Egham hills than now, and was probably broader and shallower, so that the "bridges" would be nearer to the Egham hills than now. We get some historic evidence of much later changes. A great inundation about three hundred years ago, it is said, changed the river's course at places, and destroyed Walton Church. (See Description of England, 1770, vol. v. p. 86.) A still more interesting instance of this is to be found in the historic Cowey Stakes. This is now on the southern side of the river, although anciently it formed its northern bank. The question was not long ago elaborately investigated on a legal inquiry as to whether it was in Surrey or Middlesex. Professor Ansted clearly showed that the river had once been four hundred yards wide there, while now it was only about ninety, and that at one time it washed the bank of Oatlands Park. (See the Queen v. County of Middlesex at Maidstone.)

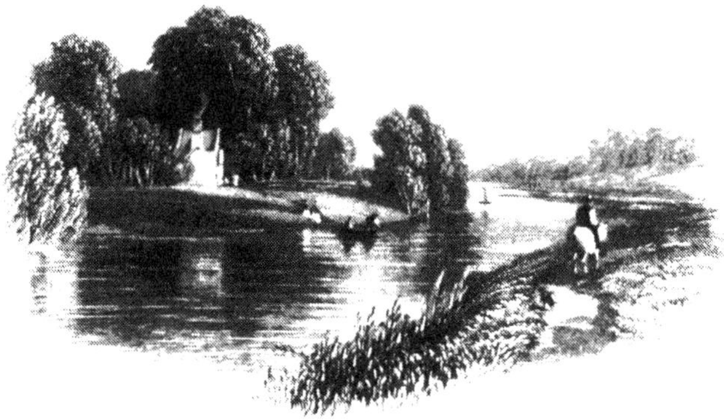

calls it "Cervi insula," and Bede "Ceroti insula." Aubrey, as late as the seventeenth century, tells us "that the causeway from Staines to Egham keeps off the water from Chertsey and Thorpe, both which parishes would," he says, "be otherwise overflowed by the Thames." The waters that thus inundated that district rose very high at times, and were uncertain, and even in summer left it a morass, to have travelled which would have been a work of considerable difficulty and risk. At Staines the river had probably been from the earliest British times crossed by a ford or ferry as the treacherous waters subsided from time to time after periods of inundation. The ancient history of the causeway would further confirm this, I think. It was originally made, we are told, in the time of Henry III.,* by one Thomas de Oxenford, a merchant, for carriage of his wool. A great litigation afterwards ensued upon the question of its repair, which the good folk of the place endeavoured to throw on the Abbot of Chertsey. The case was tried in 24th Edward III. (1351), and again in 42nd Edward III. (1369), at New Windsor, and subsequently at Westminster, when it was proved that there was no causeway before the time of Henry III., "but there was a *More through which none could pass in winter*."† On the morrow of All Souls, therefore, the Abbot was acquitted. The Abbot seems to have been indicted again in 15th Edward IV. (1476), but found not liable. Before the causeway was formed the road lay by the ferry of Redwynde at Chertsey, where in the 2nd Henry IV. the good men of Chertsey had license to build a bridge.

For these reasons I can hardly imagine the existence of a bridge at Laleham, nor lower down the river than where it actually crossed at Staines; for in winter it would most likely have been swept away by the floods. The ford at Staines might have been aided, as in some parts of the country is still customary, by large stones in the river-bed, and from these "stones," rather than from the Druidical circle which seems formerly to have stood on the bank, the place may possibly have taken its name. The hills of Egham and its dry uplands were, we have reason to believe, the seat of an important town or native settlement; and here is traceable to this day the road which the Roman engineers constructed crossing the river beneath. A better spot could not have been chosen. From Egham westward a British road also may have passed by the tumuli on Ascot Heath and Tower Hill to Cæsar's Camp, and on to Silchester. Now, although

---

* Manning and Bray, Hist. of Surrey. † Records, 24 Ed. III.

Pontes was not necessarily a town or village, but simply a place at which were bridges, here, I think, it was both.*

But if we assume "Pontes," the bridges (limiting that word to its strict meaning), to have been at the point of crossing near Staines, to which the road has been traced, we hastily conclude that we have solved the difficulty, and place the lost station at Staines, on the peninsula formed by the Thames and the Colne. But unfortunately there would still remain one objection: it is rather too near to London, and too far from Silchester, to comply with Antonine's account; and we have no right to ignore this because we cannot reconcile it with any particular theory.

After much consideration, I come to the conclusion, anomalous though it may seem, that Pontes, the Roman station to which Antonine's measurements were made, was not on the river at all, but on the hill commanding it, a mile or a mile and a half off, but in Roman times probably not so far; and, contrary to general authority, I place it at Egham. The bridges were over the Thames and the streams on the Middlesex side of it, but so important a passage was doubtless guarded by a body of troops, and where better than on the hills overlooking the bridges could they be stationed? And here, on this dry healthy spot, where the foundations of a tower and other Roman remains have been discovered, and where a British town already existed, the Roman generals appropriated the site and established their own station,† calling it Pontes after the bridges below; and what more likely than that the measurement was to the station of Pontes rather than to the bridges themselves? This would make the distance from London exactly right, as also that from Silchester, and agree precisely with the Roman account. In fact, no spot round the bridges nearer than this would have been habitable, as the marshes were nearly half the year under water.‡

---

* There were others in England, one on the Watling Street Road, in respect to which surely Mr. Wheatley must be in error; for in his article "Middlesex" in the "Encyclopædia Britannica," he speaks of the three stations on the Watling Street Road as Londinium, Sulloniacæ, and Pontes, and then alludes to the doubt as to whether this last was at Staines or Old Windsor. But the Pontes there referred to were over the Colne, not far from St. Alban's, a place next after Sulloniacæ, which was at Brockley Hill, on the road to St. Alban's, and not near our Pontes.

† See Paper read by Lieut.-Col. P. L. M'Dougal before Surrey Archæological Society, May 1854.

‡ Staines itself does not seem to me to have been more than a post for troops, not a residential place, or at least not until a late period of Roman occupation. All the skeletons discovered have been those of men. No temples or villas have been met with; money is constantly found all over the town, but always of a late date. In those days the site of the town could

There is one feature, however, in this road which must strike every one who will follow its course on the map. I mean the angle of 25° N.E. which at Duke's Hill, near Rapley's Farm, Bagshot, it strikes off towards Egham. For so remarkable a divergence in a Roman road we know there must have been good reason, such as the avoidance of some natural obstacle, or attainment of some particular object. Had the road thence pursued its eastern direction after passing Duke's Hill it would have gone over Chobham Common by the Roman Camp at Sunningdale, and crossed the river about Chertsey or Laleham; and although it strikes off, as we have seen, there it did go, as I shall show.

It may be fairly asked if Pontes was the best practicable crossing place, why did not the road go to it in a straight line from Cæsar's Camp, so as to avoid the angle at Duke's Hill?

This opens up a very interesting question, and one, I think, very easily solved. Duke's Hill was the point at which the Silchester road struck into another still more important to us—the Winchester and Chichester road. Here we get the key of our position. The Roman engineers, from their commanding post at Egham, looked westward over the Forest with two objects especially to achieve. First, to reach the important station with its great encampments near Farnham, which lay within twenty miles to the south-west of them; and so on to Winchester and their ports at Chichester and Bittern, near Southampton. Secondly, to work out their great western road to Silchester and Bath. These they accomplished with considerable skill. They perceived that the first section of about seven miles might be conveniently formed to be common to both routes, thus saving themselves five or six miles of difficult road, and they accordingly struck it exactly midway between the two points of destination; and at Rapley Farm they parted one due west towards Silchester, passing about a mile south of Cæsar's Camp, to which a short branch went off; the other in a south-westerly direction to Farnham, as described.

Rapley's Farm * was not only the junction of the Farnham and

---

hardly have been dry land. Even recently, when a cemetery was required, only three places could be found where a common grave could be dug seven or eight feet without coming to water.

* At Rapley Farm in 1784 was a spot called the Roundabout, surrounded by a deep fosse and important earthworks; and in a field still called Roman Down the plough came upon some crockery, and the poor ignorant farmer merely altered his ploughshare to go a foot deeper and drove through a rich mine of treasures. Fifty or sixty urns and other pottery were crushed to pieces. Very few fragments were preserved. (Archæologia, vol. vii. p. 199.) The junction of the roads was at some distance east of the farm-buildings, but starting from them towards the north-west a road has been traced leading directly to Cæsar's Camp.

Silchester roads, which met again, as we shall see, at Winchester, but it was also a station on the road connecting Cæsar's Camp at East Hampstead with the fortresses on St. George's Hill, Weybridge, and Wimbledon, a link of which we get a very ancient notice. It was the "antiqua fossa," known in Saxon days as the old "mule dich" and the "olde herestræt," which struck away from Weybridge towards Rapley. Charles Kingsley pointed it out as passing about a mile south of the Sunningdale encampment.

Now although the officers of the Sandhurst Survey could find no trace near Rapley Farm of such a road to Farnham, I have not the slightest doubt that one existed; and through the kind assistance of my friend the Vicar of Bagshot, and of Mr. Morris, the Surveyor of Woods, I believe I have found it. Having pointed out the direction I wanted to survey, Mr. Morris remembered having seen a Roman urn and other debris dug up on that particular line, and on visiting the spot we found, I cannot doubt, the object of our search—a broad road track, almost overgrown with heather, running close by from Rapley Farm in a straight line through the Poor's Allotment over the hill north of the Old Golden Farmer towards Farnham. It is about thirty feet wide, and scales the hill with a better gradient than it could elsewhere have obtained. This road continued its course over the open heaths to Frimley by Sign Farm, Farnborough Green, Cove Common, Aldershot Common, towards another Cæsar's Camp there, and so on to Alton, and, as I think, by Crondall to Winchester.

Defoe in 1742 describes the section between Alton and Arlesford as particularly well defined. Dr. Stukeley had traced it throughout its course from Winchester to Farnham, and indeed as far as Farnborough, where it branched off, he says, into two roads—one to Guildford and Dorking, where it joined the Stane Street coming from Chichester, and the other to Staines. The only link not completely established is this one from Rapley to Farnborough, which Stukeley mentions as having been visible in his time, and on the line of which, at Frimley, coins have been found, and near Bagshot the remains I have described.

Thus may we not only solve the difficulty, as it appeared, of the angle at Rapley, but it will help to fix more clearly the site of Vindomis.

Mr. Chute's idea that it was on his estate of the Vyne cannot be entertained for a moment. For although there was a road from Winchester northward through Stratton and Worting by the Vyne and Basingstoke straight to the southern gate of Silchester,* we are not told that Vindomis was on this road. And indeed it could not possibly be, for its whole course is but about three and twenty miles, while Vidomis is said to have been fifteen miles from one terminus and twenty-one from the other!

The Iter of Antonine merely shows that it was on some road leading from Calleva to Venta, and as it occurs in a different Iter, it is fair to assume it was on a different road. Whitchurch, on the Salisbury and Andover road, has sometimes been thought of as its site, but that is out of the question, as it is only about fourteen miles from Venta instead of twenty-one. Assuming Silchester to be Calleva, we get a clue to the locality of Vindomis. It was twenty-one miles from Venta Belgarum and fifteen from Calleva. Now if we take a map (allowing about one-seventh for winding of roads) and draw a circle say with a radius of about thirteen miles from Silchester, and another at eighteen from Winchester, those circles will cut one another at two points—between Ashmandsworth and Beacon Hill on the west, and near Lower Froyle on the east. The first is in the wrong direction, while everything points to the latter spot between Froyle and Crondall, or at least in that neighbourhood, as the site of Vindomis.

Large encampments are shown to have existed there, on Badley Pound Farm and in an adjoining field. Mr. Woodward tells us in his history of the county that important Roman remains have been found on the site of this road; on Castle Hill are vestiges of a fosse; and a house near the Church is built mainly of Roman materials.

Besides all this, its geographical position makes this locality a most important one, as having been that at which the great south-eastern route from Chichester through Guildford struck into and formed a junction with Silchester and the west, as also with Winchester. I cannot doubt that Vindomis was on this Farnham route. Thus does our Bagshot link elucidate the others, and render more complete our knowledge of these southern roads. That there was, moreover, a road from Silchester to Vindomis in the neighbourhood of Farnham, probably through Odiham and Wanborough or thereabouts, I look upon as certain.

---

* Of the existence of this road we get very interesting proof; for in 1415, William Brocas, who obtained the Beaurepair Estate, and wished to impark this country, sought means to take in the old Roman way. This early instance of "road-stopping" was accomplished with all due formality. An inquisition ad quod damnum was held, which tells us that William Brocas, Esq., "includere et tenere possit quondam viam in Sherburne Bromleghque se ducit ab dea villa usq. Silchester per medium parci W. Brocas sibi et hered suis." (See Old Roads, by T. W. Shore, Archæological Review, Ap. 1889.)

Returning to Sunninghill, I must not omit to mention that the road there has been struck upon, and its foundations laid bare in several places, in one case especially, during some excavations on Dr. Girdlestone's property. Trees, of which I have been favoured with specimen pieces, were dug up beneath three feet of gravel (of a kind not commonly met with there), at a spot certainly on the line of the Roman road, and with them were found fragments of a Roman urn, with some bricks and tiles. Of these facts I am satisfied; but the wood was in almost too wonderful a state of preservation to justify the belief that it was thrown in by the Roman workmen, as suggested, to form a foundation through the swamp; and cogent as the evidence seems to be, it is hardly, I fear, absolutely conclusive. One piece was a branch of oak almost as dark and hard as iron, although, I am told, it was soft when first taken out; another was birch, the timber of which was crumbling in decay, but the bark was quite perfect, as is often the case; a third piece was not easily made out, till Sir Joseph Hooker kindly inspected it for identification, and pronounced it to be a species of plane.

I must in fairness observe, that it was at a place where the troops that were encamped here a century ago might have found it necessary to construct a road crossing this Roman way; and we know that thereabout heaps of Roman bricks and tiles lay ready to their hands; some are there still; and it would be difficult to answer the suggestion that they might have placed the trees there, and used this ancient debris to cover them and form their road. I must leave this question for time and further investigation to elucidate. Near to this spot, when the railway was made, a fragment of a Roman pavement was found; it was of bluish-grey black and white tesselated work, and about a yard square.

I will, lastly, refer to what has been termed an interesting Roman statue of a gladiator standing in Mr. Waterer's Nursery at Bagshot, found, as we are told, in Charter's Pond; the more interesting because that was in the line of the Roman road. But, unfortunately, I must destroy this tradition. My first inspection impressed me with surprise that it could ever have been mistaken for the representation of a gladiator; its costume is that of a Roman general with the victor's crown of leaves. Then, again, it was not found in Charter's Pond, but, as I have satisfied myself from local inquiry, in a swampy place by the highroad near Brummel Hutch, afterwards formed into a nursery; a very important difference in such a matter as this.

Having a suspicion of the genuineness of the statue, I have had it photographed, and submitted to the best authorities at the British Museum; they pronounce it to be a work unquestionably later than the sixteenth century, and fix the latter part of the seventeenth as its probable date. So, much to my regret, I must destroy the interesting fancy that has been suggested of its having been cast into the pond in a moment of panic or during the Saxon invasion, or left, as others have thought, on its way to decorate the Forum of Calleva. It might quite possibly have been cast into the roadside ditch when a troop of Roundhead cavalry were coming along, or when William of Orange was approaching Windsor, and his father-in-law was flying from it. It was a well-known fashion to import these Italian figures (and it is said to be of Italian stone) to adorn the gardens of this period. Of Roman work there is no instance of a large statue having been found in the South of England; the few large ones that have been discovered were in the North.

CHAPTER XXXIV.

Ockwells.

"Who has not known the hush, the peace which lingers
In halls where, years agone, the spirit came
Of the old middle age? His dreamy fingers
Have touched the walls, the ceilings, and the same
Weird charm, the same imperious silence, lies
Upon them in our time of haste and change."
—S. W. JOHNSON, *Erule.*

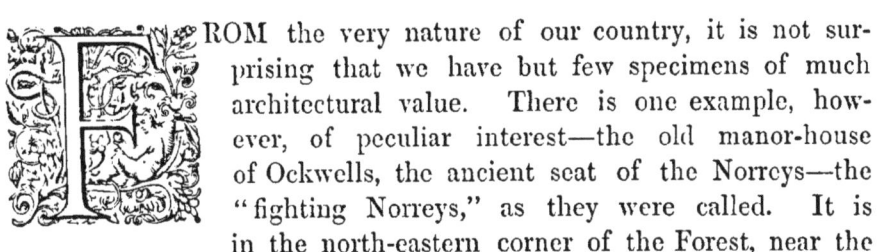

FROM the very nature of our country, it is not surprising that we have but few specimens of much architectural value. There is one example, however, of peculiar interest—the old manor-house of Ockwells, the ancient seat of the Norreys—the "fighting Norreys," as they were called. It is in the north-eastern corner of the Forest, near the quaint pleasant village of Bray, about midway between our parish and its parent manor of Cookham. There, surrounded by its orchards and green meadows, we may still see the crumbling shell of this once important mansion, a perfect gem of a fifteenth-century manor-house. But it is now fast perishing; here a window-frame hangs only by a rusty nail, and there lies a door fallen altogether from its hinges; the rose peeps in smiling on its carved image on the ancient panels, and the young tendrils of the vine entwine themselves through the unglazed casements; while the swallow flies in and out the vacant chambers. In one room a huge pair of jack-boots, and a lump of rusty metal, which, on inspection, proved to be a very ancient shirt of mail, were carelessly lying about when I recently paid it a visit; in the hall an old dining-board was still to be seen. But what makes this the more especially interesting is its untouched genuine condition; for, wreck though it may be, it gives us a perfect representation of a house of that period, now becoming year by year more scarce. And what a charming picture it makes! How rich in

ORWELLS, BERKS.

colouring! Its grey brickwork glows here and there with warm tones of red, and the ancient oak, silvered with age, is spotted with lichens of the brightest green.

The plan of the house is very characteristic. The entrance porch, with the porter's room on the left and the great hall on the right, leads into a glazed corridor which surrounds a small courtyard, now almost filled up by the late sixteenth-century staircase; this corridor is repeated on the upper floor. But the chief glory of the house was the great hall, a beautiful apartment, in length about 40 feet, including the minstrels' gallery, which occupies about 6 feet of it; in width it is about 24 feet; in addition to which is a fine bay oriel window at the end, covered by the smaller of the gables.

Mr. Hudson Turner in his "Domestic Architecture" speaks of the timber roof as open at the time he wrote; it is now covered up by a plaster ceiling; but he is surely in error when he tells us that the whole side of the hall was originally glazed. It was never more so, one would think, than now; the great oak beam on which the top lights rest shows the present arrangement to be original; and besides, at the date of this house it was not customary to glaze, but to panel the lower sides of the dining-halls. With its oak roof, however, and windows rich in the glory of its fine stained glass, it was indeed a noble hall.*

The house was evidently much altered about a century and a quarter after it was built, as the classic designs at places show; and it was then, doubtless, that a new staircase was inserted in part of the inner court. The approach to it was through an outer courtyard, the northern side of which was formed by a loopholed fortified wall, still standing, and the southern by the chapel, which,

---

* These glazed panels were removed by the owner, Mr. Grenfel, to his own residence, Taplow Court, and were the subject of litigation in October 1887. They consisted (as I learn from an article by Charles Baily, Esq., published in the Surrey Coll., vol. iv. p. 293) of the arms of King Henry VI., with the antelopes, his supporters, and the motto, "Dieu et mon droit;" of his Queen, Margaret of Anjou, with her supporters, the antelope and the eagle, and motto, "Humble et loyall;" of Norreys, with beavers for supporters, and motto, "Feythfully serve;" of the Abbey of Westminster (I thought those of Abingdon were there); of Beaufort, Duke of Somerset; of Edmund, Earl of March; of Henry, Earl of Warwick; of De la Pole, Duke of Suffolk; of Sir William Beauchamp; of Lord St. Amand; of Sir William Lacon of Bray, Chief-Justice of the King's Bench; of the Lord Wenlock; of Sir Richard Nanfan, Captain of Calais; of Sir John Pury, Knight of Chamberhouse Castle, Thatcham, Berks; and of Bulstrode quartering Shobingdon. The last was probably intended for Richard Bulstrode, Esq., one of the builder's executors. The royal arms were surmounted by highly bowed crowns; the others, by crests and lamberquins. The mottoes were several times repeated in old text character in diagonal lines across the window lights, and the quarries of the background being powdered with yellow flowers.

as we shall see, John Norres in his will left directions for the building of, and which I find was destroyed by fire in 1778. Two doorways and three window openings still indicate the site of this chapel. The large northern gable was originally flanked by two smaller ones; that remaining over the fine oriel window of the great hall, and another which must have been pulled down after Mr. Twopeny made his drawing for the "Domestic Architecture" in 1827, now in the British Museum. The southern gable was, I think, similarly flanked, the small one surmounting the picturesque entrance porch having had its counterpart in the garden, forming the southern termination of the house. In the large upper chamber of the great gable a doorway still appears, which must have opened into this lost wing; it is now blocked up, and a chimney-stack was subsequently erected in the garden against the outer wall.

George IV., it is said, was so much struck with the beauty of the front of this house, that he wished to become a purchaser of it, and it afterwards furnished the design for the King's Cottage in Windsor Great Park.*

Our interest in this place is the more increased by our being able to fix so closely the date of its erection. Mr. Hudson Turner pronounces it a perfect timber house of the time of Henry VII.; but it was built by John Norreys, Esq., early in the reign of Edward IV., about 1464. It was hardly then finished, for by his will, made in 1465 and proved in 1467, direction was given for its final completion.

This John Norreys was of one of the most ancient of our Forest families, and owner of extensive estates in our neighbourhood, including the manorial property of Sunninghill. He was Sheriff of Berkshire and Oxfordshire (formerly united) in 1438.

It has been said that this place has no history; but the place has more reason to say it has no historian. It has plenty of history, if we only knew it. Mr. Joseph Nash has done his best to restore it to life, at least by his pencil; and a little research into the records of history will add reality to his imaginative scenes.

This ancient family sprang, as many another noble race has done, from the royal kitchen.† Richard le Norreys was cook to Eleanor, Queen of Henry III., and received a grant of the Manor of Ockholt in

---

* Letter in *Standard*, 22nd February 1888.
† In 5th Edward I. we meet with a grant by way of confirmation to Guiccardo de Charon and Isabella his wife of all the lands which were Gilbert le Norreys' "cum molendino aquatico" and other possessions in Thame, granted to him by the Bishop.

Bray in 1267 ; not improbably as in payment of overdue wages, when money was scarce with his royal mistress. We must not, however, look upon this menial office as derogatory in days when the great head of the Neville family was the King's cowherd, and yet ranked with the highest nobles. The grant runs: "52 Hen. III. Rex concessit Rico de Norreys, Coco Reginæ, in feudo purpresturam in Forestæ de Windsor vocat Ocholt pro anno reddit quadragint' solid' 62." We hear of this Richard in the Manor Court Rolls as paying threepence for the pasturage of his cattle in the Frith near Ockwells in 1334. He died in 1337, leaving a son William.

In the time of Edward I. we find mention of a William de Ocholt and Alicia, his wife, who had a son John.*

The Norreys continued through many generations at Ockholt, and distinguished themselves in the French wars and the Scotch, as also in Spain, and brought back, no doubt, to their old home rich spoils from abroad.

Sir Henry Norres of Speke in Lancashire chose his two wives from Cheshire, and left behind him, through his first marriage with Alice Erneis of Chester, a long line of descendants, who became the Norreys of Fifield in Bray; by his second alliance with Cecilia, the daughter of Hamon Massey of Puddington, a maiden of a family as ancient and honourable as any in Cheshire (where some of their descendants are still living), he left a posterity of warriors equally celebrated. They were known in history as the "fighting Norreys," and stand out as almost the last examples of that rude type of chivalry and physical courage that had to yield ultimately to the levelling influence of gunpowder.

From this Cecilia in a few more generations Ockwells became vested in John Norres, Esq., a wealthy commoner and "faithful" servant of Henry VI., and Master of his Wardrobe. This young Berkshire cavalier brought home as his first bride Alice of Yattendon, the sole heiress to a good estate, which thus became added to the family possessions. He married twice afterwards, and probably was persuaded that the older house at Ockholt was hardly grand enough for him, and so, about 1464, he set about building a new one, and this new house is the old Ockwells of to-day. He died in all the "odour of sanctity" and in great wealth in 1466. Day after day the bells of Bray tolled for him in orthodox fashion, as he had directed by his will. He bequeathed "to the full bilding and making uppe of the

---

* See Inquisition Post-mortem, William de Okholt, 13 Ed. I., and Rot. Fin. 13 Ed. I., m. 19.

chapell with the chambers adjoynyng within my manoir of Okholt in the p'issh of Bray aforesaid not yet finished xl. li."* He bequeathed to the high altar there, for the "tithes and offerings withdrawen and forgotten, a hundred shillings," but on condition also that "the vicarie of the said church devoutley pray for my soul." They had a separate legacy "to pray for the souls of Alice, Alianore, and Margaret,† sometime my wifes."

The motto of the family was "Feythfully serve," and it is strange to see what a peculiar type of fidelity Bray seems to have produced. The famous Vicar of Bray, whose strong point, we know, was inconsistency, was evidently not the first exponent of the virtue; for while old John Norres glazed his fine dining-hall with the arms of Henry VI. and Queen Margaret, his stalwart son William, who was living at his mother's old house of Yattendon, supported the arms of Edward, and for his aid in crushing his father's patron at the battle of Northampton was knighted, as some authorities say on the field, in July 1460, although I should rather incline to think it was on Edward's ascending the throne in the following March.

On Edward IV.'s march from York in 1471, Sir William Norreys and others repaired to him, and here the curious Norreys notion of "fidelity" was singularly displayed; they always fought for the King, but which was the King they didn't care; and now they would not fight for Edward till he had proclaimed himself as such, saying "they would serve no man but a King."

Sir William, who was now reigning in his father's stead at Ockwells, married first into the great family of Neville, and afterwards into that of De Vere, the powerful Earl of Oxford; was Esquire of the Body to Edward IV.; and ere long threw his sword into the opposite scale, and, under Henry VII., showed his prowess as a commander of the King's forces at Stoke, and was rewarded for his good and "faithful" service. His son Edward, as valiant as himself, was also knighted on that field, or, as some say, at the King's coronation.

What rejoicings the old hall must have seen when the father and son returned thus laden with honours! But the picture had its reverse. While Sir Edward and his followers were revelling in the hall, his lady was in her chamber stifling her grief. This lady was Frideswide Lovell, sister of the illustrious Viscount Lovell, who had lost at Bosworth a peerage which his family had held from the days of

---

* See Kerry's Hist. of Bray, wherein the year of his death is given as 1467.
† This Margaret was the Duchess of Norfolk.

Richard I., and, with all his vast possessions confiscated, he had been a wanderer, hiding in the Fens of Lincolnshire and Norfolk for some months, till he got across into Flanders; but now, having returned with John De la Pole in support of Lambert Simnel, to stake once more his fortunes at Stoke, the throw failed, and he lost everything. Some thought he was slain on the field, but others maintained that he had escaped and sought concealment at his mansion of Minster Lovell. The herald at the time speaks not of his death, but that he had fled.* In support of this idea, the Duke of Rutland in 1708 mentioned the curious fact, that during some excavations at Minster Lovell, in a vault behind a chimney a skeleton was found at a table, as though death had occurred while writing there, starved, as was suggested, either by accident or design of those above. The rumour of his hiding in the Fens is mentioned at the time in the Paston Letters, which goes to show that he certainly was not slain on the field.

Mr. Hepworth Dixon, in his Lives of the two Queens, alludes to this union of the White Rose and the Red in the Norreys family, but he confuses their pedigree, I think. "Little Harry" was the son, not of Sir William, as he asserts, but of Sir Edward; Sir William was his grandfather.†

But at no time were their fortunes more flourishing than in the next generation, when young Henry Norreys became the favourite of Henry VIII. Many a joyous day's hunting round the new mansion at Ockwells and over Ascot Heath and Sunninghill had Henry and his faithful attendants, Norreys and Weston, before that fatal time when Mistress Ann, having undermined the great Cardinal's influence, became for awhile the central figure of those pleasant hawking-parties here about 1526. But

> "'Tis the bright day brings forth the adder,
> And craves wary walking."

What could be more ominous of evil than the following minute instructions:—"1526—No other [than Norreys] of the six gentlemen to enter the bed-chamber, unless called by the King." "The persons of the privy chamber to keep secret all things done there. Not to inquire in the King's absence where he is going, or talk about his pastimes." Henry Norreys, this most favoured of all the grooms,

---

* See Lingard, vol. v. p. 290; Lel. Coll., 214; Banks, "Dormant Peerages"
† Fuller's Worthies, and Cal. State Papers, Dom. S., 1510; and Heralds' Office Pedigree; also Manor Rolls of Bray; Kerry's Hist. of Bray.

was just then at the height of his prosperity. Among other good things, he had a grant in 1530 of the wardship of Richard, the infant heir of his neighbour, Edward Fiennes (his wife's brother or cousin probably), and possession of all his estates.

But suddenly a dark cloud burst upon the family and involved them all in disaster. Norreys was required to pander to the tyrant's will and admit a false charge against the Queen; and this, like an honourable gentleman as he was, he persistently declined to do. "Hang him up then; hang him up," said the tyrant; and, as the Heralds' Visitation afterwards quaintly expresses it, "he was attainted 8th June, 28th Hen. VIII., being hanged for Queen Ann Boleyn, whom said King was jealous of for him." There was no escheat, as the jury found that he left no estate. His elder brother was living. Henry Norreys was at the time a widower; his deceased wife was Mary, daughter of Lord Dacre of the South, from that fine old castle of Hurstmonceaux in Sussex. He was just then courting Madge, Ann Boleyn's cousin, but hung back unfortunately, so as to give colour to Frank Weston's impudent speech, that he came more into the royal chamber to see the mistress than the maid.

Poor Norrey's fate was a sad one, but common enough then were such fluctuations of fortune; he had seen worse cases than his own. The great Buckingham had died for a fault hardly less trivial; and the fall of a greater one still must have been fresh in his memory. This very Norreys it was whom the King sent after Wolsey when journeying from Putney on his mule, the most abject of men, so lately the mightiest in Europe! Norreys was to deliver a ring to him from the King, a trifling salve of conscience as he gloated over the houseful of treasure the Cardinal had that morning been expelled from.

But soon the clouds passed away, and the sun shone out upon the family more brightly than ever. The unfortunate Ann's great daughter was now on the throne, and it was not likely that young Henry Norreys, the heir, who inherited on the death of his uncle, would be forgotten. In the fourth year of the Queen's reign he served the office of Sheriff, was afterwards knighted at Ascot, and in 1572 was created Baron Norris of Ricot, Berks. He died in 1601.

The neighbouring branch of the family at Fifield was equally flourishing. Almost the first thing Elizabeth did on coming to the throne was to summon a few of her most faithful friends to come to her in council. John Norris was one of them. It was he of

Fifield who set out with Raleigh into the Low Countries, and was afterwards with Drake.* To Lady Margaret Norris on the death of her son the Queen wrote a most affectionate letter of sympathy, addressing her quaintly enough as "my own crow," so called from her black complexion; a colour, says Fuller, which no whit unbecame the faces of her martial issue. "No county in England," continues that facetious writer, "can present such a brace of families, contemporaries, with such a bunch of brethren in either for eminent achievements; so great their states and stomachs, that they often jostle together, and no wonder if Oxfordshire wanted room for them, when all England could not hold them together." Well might they be termed the "fighting Norreys." Of Lord Norrey's six children, nearly all died in battle. Their great enemies were the Knowllys, who were connected with Elizabeth through the Boleyns. "Elizabeth loved the Knowllys," says Fuller, "for themselves; the Norrises for themselves and herself, as needing such valiant men in her service." "The Norrises get more honour abroad; the Knowlls more profit at home, conversing constantly at court; and no wonder if they were the warmest who sate next to the fire.† There was once a challenge past between the two families at certain exercises, the Queen and their aged fathers being the spectators and judges, till it quickly became a flat quarrel between them, and they soon fell to it in earnest with sharps indeed."

It was John Norris of Fifield to whom I have elsewhere alluded as holding an important office in the Park in the time of Edward VI., and superintending during Queen Mary's reign the works for supplying the Castle with water from Blackmore Park, Winkfield, completed in 1555; and from him doubtless we get the name of Norris' Lodge in the Great Park. It was he, too, who was one of Elizabeth's captains, called to her aid to repel the attack of the Spanish Armada, and afterwards served in Ireland; but he had the old Norris fire in him, and when one of the opposite faction was put over his head as Lieutenant of Ireland, he was so filled with grief and anger that he went up to his chamber and died, 1597.

On the death of the Lord Norris in 1601, Elizabeth did all honour to his memory, and although then herself showing signs of failing, she set out on a progress from Windsor to Reading to attend his funeral. Her first stage was at Mr. Richard Warde's, thence on to Reading, where she knighted Mr. Warde and dined with Sir Edward

---

* Morley's Eng. Lit., p. 396.   † Fragmenta Regalia, Knowlls.

Norris at Englefield. One of his servants, Abraham Boulton, writing to Dudley Carleton at Paris, tells him all that was going on. "The funeral," he says, "was very honourably performed, and the Queen was well pleased with her entertainment, and gave many gracious speeches to my master and lady, and bestowed knighthood on Mr. John Norris and Mr. Reed Stafford." This was Norris of Fifield.

But the fire of the family burnt itself out at last. We are told that Francis, the second Baron Norris, succeeded his father in 1601. That, however, is not quite correct, I think. He succeeded his grandfather, the first Baron; William, the father, had previously died at Berwick; and, moreover, it could not have been in 1601, but 1603, as is shown by a letter from Sir Thomas Edmunds to the Earl of Shrewsbury.*

Francis seems to have been of a quarrelsome disposition. In 1610 he fought with Peregrine Willoughby, and hurt him dangerously in the shoulder; and in 1620, soon after he had been raised to the title of Viscount Thame and Earl of Berkshire, he had a quarrel with Lord Scrope in the passage of the House of Lords, for which he was committed to the Fleet, "and bore the indignity so ill," that he went home to Ricot and mortally wounded himself with a cross-bow, and died in a few days. The title became extinct, but in 1682 a descendant of the family was created Earl of Abingdon.†

Elizabeth had also knighted —— Fittiplace, a descendant of Thomas Fettiplace, who married Elizabeth, the sister of that Sir Edward Norris who was the husband of Frideswide Lovell, and who is shown by the Manor records to have died seized of "Okeplace, lying in Altewoodde," in 1507. In this ancient family Ockwells probably remained till the middle of the seventeenth century, when it passed to the Days of Eton; for we find one Ralph Day residing there in 1661, and his son, Thomas Day "of Ockwells," was baptized in 1667, and was buried in 1749. In 1768 some maiden ladies of the

---

* Nicholl's Progress of James I., vol. i. p. 447, note; Lodge's Illustrations of Brit. Hist., vol. iii. p. 200.

† This Francis, second Baron Norris, married Lady Bridget de Vere, daughter of the Earl of Oxford, and had an only daughter, the Hon. Elizabeth Norris, who married Edward Wray or Ray, Groom of the Chamber to James I., and was mother of an only daughter, Bridget Wray or Ray, who married the Hon. Edward Sackville, second son of Edward, fourth Earl of Dorset; and secondly, Montagu, Earl of Lindsey, by whom she had the Hon. James Bertie, who was summoned to Parliament in 1675 as Baron Norreys of Rycote, and Earl of Abingdon in 1682. The Berties were of the family of Robert Bertie of Bearsted, Kent, living in the fifteenth century.

family were residing there. A story is told that Farmer Day of Ockholt was knighted by Queen Anne for his politeness in opening his gates for her; but it is not correct.

The family of Finch of Hertfordshire, it is said, became possessed of it in 1679, and in 1786 sold it to Penyston Portlock Powney, Esq. It is now the property of Charles Pascoe Grenfell, Esq.

CHAPTER XXXV.

The Ascot Races.

IN a previous paper I have alluded to the great interest which the Princess Anne and her husband Prince George, took in our Forest sports. They showed an especial passion for horse-racing, which at once became fashionable. She was a true Stuart in this taste; for racing, although known for centuries before the Stuarts came to England, may almost, in its present form, be said to have been introduced by them from Scotland. Races, it is true, had been practised on the Roodee at Chester in 1512; and in 1540 a silver bell, valued at "3s. 6d. or more," was substituted for the wooden ball adorned with flowers which had previously been the prize.

James I. gave great encouragement to the pastime, of which he was very fond; it was in his reign that Captain Dover appeared in one of His Majesty's old suits as master of the ceremonies of the celebrated Cotswold games, of which racing formed a part. Nichols tells us of the King's presence at Lincoln in 1617, "at a great horse-race on the heath for a cupp;" the course was a quarter of a mile long. At Gatherley Forest, near Richmond, in Yorkshire, a golden ball, afterwards changed for a little golden bell, was the trophy raced for. It is from this, by the bye, that we get the poetical expression "bearing away the bell." A bell-course, in fact, was the ordinary expression for a race-ground. Gervase Markham, writing of "the Turkie horse," says, "they are of great courage and swiftnesse, for I have seen them used at our English bell-courses."

Epsom, Newmarket, York, Enfield Chase, and Banstead Downs became our chief racing places. Doncaster races had been established in 1703, the year after Queen Anne came to the throne.

ASCOT RACES.

From the original picture by Paul Sandby.

The Derby and Oaks were long after Ascot, dating only from 1779 and 1780.*

The cares of State on Queen Anne's accession did not interfere much with her recreations. She and her royal spouse both ran horses in their own names. "Pepper," "Mustard," and "Star" were hers. Godolphin, the great patron then of the sport, and owner of the celebrated Godolphin Barb, was living close by at Cranbourn Lodge, and was so keen a sportsman that he forgot to make money as a minister,—a rare thing in those days.

"Now just at this time," says Luttrell in 1705, "the royal couple seemed mightily given to racing; the Queen has appointed horse-races to be at Datchet, after her return from Winchester to Windsor." The same author notes, "1709, 25th August—Yesterday was a great horse-race at Datchet. Colonel Moreton won the Queen's Plate, and the Earl of Bridgewater that of the town of Windsor."† So plates were run for at this period.

In 1710 the first gold cup is said to have been given by the Queen; it was won by "Bay Bolton."

But when were these famous races instituted?—a question very often asked, but never correctly answered. In an elaborate article in the *Quarterly Review*‡ it is asserted that the Ascot Races were founded by William Augustus, Duke of Cumberland, uncle of George III., and almost every writer since that day has echoed the statement, until it has been accepted as an undisputed fact. The author of the most recent history of Berkshire states that they were instituted by the Duke, and that the first meeting took place on the 4th July 1751; but more careful research has convinced me that these accounts are altogether incorrect. The races were not founded by the Duke of Cumberland at all. It can be shown that there was racing at Ascot long before his time.

In Cheney's "Racing Calendar," which preceded Weatherby's, it is stated that there was racing at Ascot prior to 1727. But in Mr. Ashton's interesting work, the "Social Life of Queen Anne" (p. 305), is the conclusive statement that in 1713 a gold plate was run for at Ascot Heath on August 12th,—the first mention, he says, that he can find of any racing there. I was therefore led to the conclusion that it was to Queen Anne that Ascot was indebted for its races, and that they were instituted about 1711 or 1712, nearly twenty years

---

* See article on Horse-Racing in the *Encyclopædia Britannica*.
† Vol. vi. p. 481.   ‡ Vol. xlix. pp. 409, 410.

before the Duke of Cumberland was born. This appeared the more probable because of her fondness for Ascot. She had opened up that country by her new drives, which had become the favourite riding-grounds of her courtiers, and she built, as I have said, the kennels there. She doubtless thought it would be much more convenient to have a racecourse on her own "demesne" than continue to patronise an outside place, as Datchet Mead was, for her favourite sport.

Since writing the above, I have succeeded in fixing the exact date of the making of the course. Stumbling upon a letter from Swift to Stella, dated August 10, 1711, I read, "While at Windsor, Dr. Arbuthnot, the Queen's physician and favourite, went out with me to show me the places; we overtook Miss Forester, a maid of honour, on her palfrey, taking the air; we made her go along with us; we saw a place they have made for a famous horse-race to-morrow, where the Queen will come." And he goes on to say that he had that day ridden a dozen miles. Now this place was not Datchet, or he would have said so, but some other place, then without a name, or at least unknown to him, some six miles off, which is exactly the distance of Ascot. On the 13th there was racing again there, for under that date he says, " I missed the race to-day by coming too late when everybody's coach was gone, and ride I would not." Why? Because, wonderful walker as the Doctor was, he was a miserable rider; and says he, "I felt my last riding three days after." So we establish the fact, I think, beyond dispute, that the course which they had been making during the summer of 1711 was on Ascot Heath, and that the first race ever ridden on it was that "famous" one of the 11th August 1711, in the presence of Queen Anne and a fashionable gathering; for Swift tells us that much company came overnight to Windsor to attend it. All doubt on the subject is removed by reference to the *London Gazette* of the time, to which a Review of my Pamphlet in the *St. James's Gazette* of 8th June 1887 called attention.

On the 12th July 1711 it was advertised "that Her Majesty's Plate of 100 guineas will be run for round the new heat on Ascot Common near Windsor, on Tuesday the 7th of August next, by any horse, mare, or gelding, being no more than six years old the grass before, as must be certified under the Hand of the Breeder, carrying 12 stone, three Heats; to be entered the last day of July at Mr. Hancock's at Fernhill, near the Starting Post."

Another plate of fifty guineas was to be run for round the same "Heat" on Monday, 6th August.

It seems that these events, for some reason, were postponed from the 6th and 7th to the 11th and 13th August.

We even learn from the accounts of Charles, Duke of Somerset,

Master of the Horse, that the sum of £558, 19s. 5d. was paid "to sundry workmen employed in making and perfecting the round heat on Ascot Common in the months of July and August 1711." So after all we owe something to poor "Est il-possible," although he did not live to see the course.

From that day the Ascot Races have continued to draw together, for one week in the year, not only the best patrons of the turf, but the *élite* of fashionable society; fair faces and all that is perfect and elegant in toilette have been there displayed year after year to the most fastidious criticism. The newest fashions have always been reserved for the wild Berkshire Heath. At the very opening meeting, it may interest the ladies to know that "quite a new thing" in costume was exhibited. The riding habit as now worn was then almost for the first time introduced; for Swift tells us that his stylish young friend Miss Forester "was dressed like a man."

The beautiful course was admirably selected, as he who has in some fine day in June viewed it from the lofty stand will fully admit; the Heath lies beneath, and far away the blue distance extends over many undulations of the Surrey and Berkshire hills; the white towers of Windsor stand out shining on the eastern horizon, and north and south stretch wide wastes and woodlands.

On the first establishment of these races there were two meetings in the year, one in May or June, and the other in August or September; and this continued to be the practice in 1753. In 1797 and 1798 the racing was continued on the Saturday.

When the Duke of Cumberland, on his return from Culloden, was appointed to the Rangership of the Great Park, he infused new life into the Ascot racing, which had probably languished during the reigns of George I. and George II., and the meeting of July 1751, hitherto generally regarded as the first, may for some reason have been on a grander scale than usual.

The Duke about this time became a great breeder of horses, and to him we owe some of the most remarkable of our Stud-book celebrities. It was in this neighbourhood, at Cranbourn Lodge, he bred a colt which was foaled in April 1764, that "bore away the bell" from all compeers; it was on the day of an eclipse of the sun, and "Eclipse" the ugly white-footed colt was named. He turned out to be of unsurpassed speed. The story is well known of the old woman who had seen him in one of his practice gallops; on being asked which was first, said the white-stocking one left all the others behind; and later, when Mr. O'Kelly became his owner, he wagered he would place the horses, and did so in his memorable declaration, "'Eclipse' first, and the others nowhere." He won a plate at Ascot in 1769.* The Duke was the breeder also of another fine horse, "Herod," in 1758.

In 1766 His Royal Highness Prince Henry met with a serious accident at the races.

We may be curious to know what the first Grand Stand was like. It stood under two lofty beeches which grew near to the site of the present building. I am permitted to give an engraving of this most interesting drawing of Paul Sandby's from the royal collection at Windsor. It would seem from the costumes to have been painted rather later than the middle of the century. It strikes one as strange, when we consider all the ceremony and formality of that age, to see so primitive a structure. The hooped petticoats of nearly half the nobility of the country were here wont to find accommodation from time to time in a rough wooden stand that would hardly now do honour to a country fair or a suburban tea-garden! The present Grand Stand was first opened to the public in 1839, and the funds to erect it were raised by a hundred shares of £100 each, of which £5 were to be repaid every year, so that at the end of twenty years the Stand was free from debt.† Near this site was the old cricket-pitch.

A drawing of "Baronet's" victory shows a concourse of spectators very different from that which assembles on the Heath on similar occasions now. We could hardly in these days spare room for carriages with four horses harnessed standing lengthwise against the ropes opposite the royal enclosure.

These races continued to be the most fashionable gatherings of the day. Prince George, while residing at Bagshot, joined the turf in 1785, when twenty-three years of age, and in that year was given (possibly in honour of the event) the Royal Hunters' Plate. In 1786, however, he sold off most of his horses on account of financial difficulties; but in 1788 the *Reading Mercury* announced that the presence of their Majesties and the patronage of the Prince of Wales promise to make the Ascot of this year superior to anything since the time of the late Duke of Cumberland. Three years after this the Prince won the Derby with "Sir Thomas," and the valuable

---

* Wildman, it is said, only gave forty-five guineas for "Eclipse," and afterwards sold him to O Kelly for 1700 guineas.

† See the *Field*, June 20, 1888.

Oatland Stakes at Ascot in June 1791 with "Baronet." On the Prince winning this race, Wraxall tells us, the King was present, and offered his congratulations in a very characteristic style, riding up to his son, "Your Baronets," said he, "are more productive than mine. I made fourteen last week, but I got nothing by them. Your single Baronet is worth all mine put together." The Prince's winnings were over £17,000, it is said.

It is indeed an ill wind that blows no one good. An incident occurred towards the end of this year which contributed indirectly to the advantage of Ascot. The Prince preferred Newmarket to all other courses, but his connection with it came to a very abrupt end in October 1791.* A charge was made against Samuel Chifney, the Prince's rider, and the Jockey Club, after investigating the facts, intimated to the Prince that if he were ever allowed to ride again, no gentleman would send a horse to the post against him. It would seem that the sole ground for this was that the horse was beaten on one course by others which he beat on another course the next day—by no means an uncommon occurrence. The Prince, to his credit, stood by his servant, and never visited Newmarket again. His action throughout this business was that of a gentleman.

I may here observe that the ceremony of the royal visit was quite an imposing feature in the proceedings of the meeting. Thus in 1797 we are told, "Tuesday, June 20th, their Majesties honoured the races here to-day, and again on Thursday and Saturday. After the first heat the Royal Family rode in procession up and down the course. His Majesty was on horseback, and the Queen and Princesses in sociables. On their return home they were caught in a tremendous storm.

In 1807 the Gold Cup was first offered, and it at once became the great prize of the meeting. From 1845 to 1853 it was known as the Emperor's Plate, it having been during that period provided by the Emperor of Russia. The war, however, caused it to revert in 1854 to its original title of the Ascot Gold Cup. The Queen's Vase was given in 1838, and the Royal Hunt Cup in 1843. In 1865 was added the Alexandra Plate.

The irrepressible Mr. Greville makes frequent allusion in his Memoirs to these races, at which, of course, he was a constant attendant. On the 24th June 1829 he tells us he was at Stoke for the races, "there was such a crowd to see the cup run for as never was seen before. The King was very anxious and disappointed. I bought the winner

---

* *Quarterly Review*, October 1885.

for Chesterfield two hours before the race." Again, in 1831, on the 5th June, he was at Fernhill, on the same pleasure bent. "The Royal Family came to the course the first day with a great cortége, eight coaches and four, and other carriages;" but he adds, "The reception was strikingly cold and indifferent; not half so good as that which the late King (George IV.) used to receive. William was bored to death with the races, and his own horse broke down." "On Thursday he was more cheered." The King dined, it seems, at the Castle each day, and invited the neighbouring gentry to dine with him.

William IV., in fact, tried to patronise the meeting, but did not know how to do it. He made a present, it has been said, to the Jockey Club of the hoof of "Eclipse" mounted in gold; but what has become of this trophy no one knows.

In 1832 there was an unpleasant occurrence on the Heath, and to use Mr. Greville's own words, "the event of the races was the King's having his head knocked with a stone; it made very little sensation on the spot" (rather a vague expression), "for he was not hurt, and the fellow was a miserable-looking ragamuffin." But it afterwards produced a burst of loyalty in both Houses of Parliament.

In 1833 Greville was at "a place called Buckhurst, eating and drinking and playing again." We know the place under a less glaring light than that which shone on the card-tables half a century ago.

This is a convenient halting-place to reflect for a moment on the social aspect of the subject. It is curious to note how time and fashion change the social habits of a people, and to trace the way in which from age to age we pursue our pleasures. We get glimpses of the manner in which our forefathers enjoyed themselves. Our little inn on the Heath might tell strange tales.

Ascot has always attracted a distinguished company. How in the eighteenth century did they demean themselves? They wagered and swore like "real gentlemen;" the women vied with the men in gambling; and, in the true spirit of the age, the latter finished their day's pleasure with a prize fight on the Heath, or a cocking match at some neighbouring inn. Thus, at the very first meeting that took place here, it was advertised in the *London Gazette* that on the race-days, beginning at eight o'clock in the morning, there will be back-sword playing for pieces of plate; and in 1798 the *Reading Mercury* for June tells us that "during Ascot Races will be fought the great main of cocks at the Crown Inn, Egham, between the gentlemen of Surrey and Middlesex against the gentlemen of

Kent and Sussex, for five guineas a battle and fifty the odd. Five days!" If right honourable gentlemen delighted in such pastimes, little wonder that rude foresters and simple clods relished their bull-baitings at Oakingham or their rude sports on the village green. Sunninghill, by-the-bye, was noted for its efficiency in boxing. Where Fir Grove now stands was once a butcher's shop, kept by a sporting character and well-known trainer of prize-fighters, who afterwards took an inn at Egham. Our ancestors worked hard at their pleasures, racing all the morning, with refreshments; a battle of some sort in the afternoon, with refreshments again; dinner later on, with more refreshments; and very thirsty play all night! I am not romancing, for at one of the great houses of the day the entertainment for the Saturdays and Mondays throughout the summer is thus described by one of the guests:—"We dine at eight, and sit at table till eleven. In about a quarter of an hour after we leave the dining-room, the Duke sits down to play at whist, and never stirs from table as long as any one will play with him." "The stakes he prefers is fives and ponies" (*i.e.* £5 points and £25 on the rubber (*sic*)). "The Duchess generally plays 2s. 6d. whist." Of the morality of the turf itself there is little to choose between the present and the past. "Pulling" was practised as much then as now. A very flagrant case occurred in 1769, when a horse was pulled as he was winning the "give-and-take race." The petty thefts and swindling on the ground were punished in a very rough-and-ready way indeed; the pickpocket or cheat, when detected, was unmercifully thrashed off the course, and then dragged down to Englemere Pond, and well ducked; and local tradition adds to this, that, as a culminating degradation, a small piece of the culprit's ear was cut off, that he might be known ever after.

Since the act of "Welshing" was dignified by a decision of our judges in full court in December 1887, and found to be *larceny* (by a trick), the offence is hardly likely to hold its ancient importance among turf delinquencies.

In 1813 the Enclosure Act passed, and this Ascot course was especially assigned as part of His Majesty's share of the allotments, subject to the important provision contained in the Act, that it "should be kept and continued as a racecourse for the public use at all times, as it has usually been."

In 1837, during the first week in June, Mr. Greville was at Buckhurst again. There was an immense party at the Castle notwithstanding the King's illness; "he was bad, but not alarmingly ill," although, in fact, he never recovered.

Of 1838 he writes, "June 16th, at Hillingdon for Ascot Races. A great concourse of people on Thursday; the Queen tolerably received; some shouting, not a great deal, and few hats taken off. This mark of respect has quite gone out of use, and which neither her station nor her sex procures. We are not the nearer a revolution for this; but it is ugly. All the world went on to the royal stand, and Her Majesty was very gracious and civil, speaking to everybody." Yes, this good old custom has gone out of fashion; but happily that young Queen, "so gracious and civil," has transformed the niggard offering into what is now an ovation.

This reminds me that we cannot write in allusion to the morals or manners of the nineteenth century—and especially in connection with Ascot Races—without acknowledging how much we owe to her under whose particular patronage those races are conducted. In an earlier chapter I have traced in outline the history of the Forest, and shown how one sovereign after another has taken delight in it. I should be unjust if I failed to acknowledge that of the long line of sovereigns who have held sway in their Castle of Windsor, there has never been one so honoured or beloved as its present owner. By none of them has a higher example been set to the people. She came, a young girl, to rule over a Court of which we will say no more than that she has transformed it; and being nobly aided by the refinement of her deeply-lamented Consort, has waved over the land a magic wand refining and purifying, supplying in truth a higher tone and standard of excellence to our national life.

CHAPTER XXXVI.

The Geology of the District.

MY space will not allow of my giving any scientific account of the Geology of our country, even were I able to do so. All I will attempt is a sketch of some of its more striking physical features, interesting to my younger readers, and at the same time ucidating the important question of our water supply.

What makes our country especially healthful is its soil, made up of dry porous sands and gravels with a large amount of peat, to the powerful antiseptic properties of which it is to a great extent owing that where it prevails, however damp and marshy the situation may be, malaria is unknown. Nor must I altogether ignore another cause, to which some authorities attribute an important influence;—the ozone generated by the pine woods with which our country abounds. The hygienic principle common to the pine and eucalyptus is, as we are told by chemists, "the evolution of the peroxide of hydrogen and camphoric acid," arising from naturally secreted oils.[*] The delightful aroma of our woods, drawn forth by the light and warmth of the summer sun, tells of the existence of that principle of "terpene" to which we owe these salutary advantages.

But as to the soil, an able geologist has said[†] of the Sandhurst neighbourhood, that the "whole of the well-water of the district, which common human experience pronounces wholesome, is obtained from the upper ferruginous sand" of the Bagshot series; "and that from a well about fifty feet deep, reaching the water-bearing level of the passage beds between the middle and upper Bagshots (the water being held up by the clayey strata which occupy a high horizon in the

---

[*] See Works of T. F. Bond, M.D., B.A., London, and C. T. Kingzett.
[†] Rev. Dr. A. Irving's paper, Geological Journal.

middle series), the water was so pure and soft that he could only compare it with water from the crystalline rocks of the Alps above the glaciers; while some of the shallow well-waters are putrid by reason of their shallowness, and the presence so near the surface of the peaty and decayed vegetable matter of the old Forest district."

Happy man who drinks of his own cistern from the upper sands! Now, although the district spoken of lies within our Forest bounds, I am glad to say that Sunninghill and Ascot are not within this questionable circuit. They are so near to it, however, that it behoves us to work the question out a little. The Bagshot sands comprise a vast area of Tertiary deposits of nearly 300 square miles in extent, upon the northern margin of which Sunninghill and Ascot stand. They extend from Esher to Winkfield in one direction, and from Ascot to Aldershot in the other, and they attain an altitude above the Ordnance datum level of between 400 and 500 feet. They form what geologists term the middle and upper division of the Eocene strata, and rest on the London clay, which is included in the lower division. The whole series occupies a wide depression of the Chalk, lying, as it were, between the ranges of the Hogsback and the Surrey hills on the south, and the chalk hills of Berks and Buckinghamshire, parallel with the river Thames, on the north.* Their history has been pretty accurately traced by geologists, but to enable us to realise the great truths they have laid open requires almost the language of romance.

When the lower Bagshot bed was deposited on the London clays, a warm climate prevailed here, and in the steaming deltas flourished a verdure of tropical luxuriance; while far away on the drier grounds rose forests of pine. An age followed especially characterised in some parts of the world by volcanic agencies, producing great changes in the earth's crust, and remarkable oscillations in its climate. This Tertiary period becoming more temperate, its flora approached nearer to that of our time, and its fauna was assuming a higher development; its life-energy may be said to have been peculiarly mammalian.† But gradually, after a long "day" of existence, from causes which astronomers may best be able to explain, our climate became arctic; the lion gave place to the musk-sheep and reindeer; and, incredible as it may seem, over our once verdure-covered plains, in which tree-

---

* See Professor Rupert Jones' paper, Geological Association, 1881.
† In contrast to the molluscan and reptilian types, which preceded it, and to the newer forms to which in due time it was destined to give place.

ferns had luxuriated, down from the north-west huge glaciers worked their slow way, amid the stillness of perpetual snow; the land subsided, sinking gradually beneath the sea; the floating ice stranded on the rocks, and scored them all over as it grated along, leaving behind in many places an accumulation of boulder-clay and mud transported from their northern home. Over all this, in the glacial period were deposited the superficial gravels, beds of which still remain capping the hill-tops, where the curious formation of the iron "pan" has preserved them from destruction; or, as Professor Rupert Jones has explained it, "as this extensive gravel-flat or submarine plain came nearer to the surface, and finally appeared above it, the shallowing water becoming sea-creeks, ate out the rising plateau, with the aid of winter ice, and roughly carved out the present valleys." The valleys were deepened and widened by rain and snow. The heavy rainfall of the Pluvial period cut out the spurs and ridges more definitely, and formed lakes in the line of drainage having gravel lips or beaches. "Certain portions of the plateau-gravel obstinately resisted denudation, being fortified by the hard compact ferruginous character of the lower layer."

While these great changes were going on, depression, denudation, and erosion were playing their various parts; and when the snow and ice, and the glaciers and their moraines and icebergs, had done their work, the climate again became milder; the arctic fauna and flora, which had come south, now receded; as the mists and icy vapours cleared away, the land lay open, if not to a warmer sunshine, at least to a sunshine that could be felt, and beneath the influence of increased light and warmth the hill-tops, which had borne up the shells of those tiny inhabitants of the ancient seas and the fossilised remains of an extinct flora, became carpeted with a new verdure; grass grew upon the mountains, and the earth in the calm that succeeded was left much in its present state.

But during those great Tertiary revolutions in many places the water had become land, and the land water, stultifying our modern proverbs, "Firm as a rock" and "Fickle as the sea,"* by proving that it is the sea only is constant, and that

"Time writes no wrinkles on its azure brow;"

while the land is never permanent. Far truer is the poet when he tells us—

---

* Geikie's History of a Boulder.

> "There rolls the deep where grew the tree ;
> O Earth, what changes hast thou seen !
> There, where the long street roars, hath been
> The stillness of the central sea."

Here, at Sunninghill and Ascot, we are living on the site of an important Eocene river, an affluent, probably, of the larger estuary in which these sands were deposited on the London clay.* The lower bed, which is essentially a fresh-water fluviatile deposit, consists of pale yellow or buff sand or loam, with layers of pipe-clay and occasional lines of pebbles. It contains no organic animal remains, but a copious subtropical vegetation. It has been thought that a few mollusca could be traced in it, but this is very doubtful.

The middle bed is one of delta and lagoon deposits, the lagoon having been partially saline, perhaps by occasional intrusions of the sea, and by percolation through fringing shingle terraces. It consists of a series of green sands and clays with rubble beds. On this rests the upper bed, a deposit of a marine estuary covering up the middle series, and laying down upon it in the first place an accumulation of pebbles composed here and there of rolled black flints, forming a characteristic line of demarcation between the middle and upper beds. Upon that came a layer of fine yellow sand, in which a salt-water fauna is met with.

These facts evidence the great changes of sea and land at the time the beds were formed. At Ascot we find on the hills a capping of the upper sands, the base of which stands at 300 feet O.D. At Sunninghill, which is about 225 to 250 O.D., this does not appear.†

To the south of us may be seen an instance of simple valley erosion, along the floor of which even the lower sands are but thinly represented. At Sunningdale not more than 30 feet of the lower sands appear above the London clay.

Our barren sandy ridges, so beautifully covered with heather, run mostly from N.E. to S.W. That on which our village is situated extends in that direction from Egham to Ascot. At Easthampstead plain the upper beds are seen cropping out again, still remaining visible on the heights on each side of the valley. Charles Kingsley

---

* Geol. Jour., vol. xliii., 1887.
† Mr. Gerome Harrison (Geology of the Counties) states that a well sunk at Wokingham passed through London clay 263 feet, Reading beds 54 feet, sand 16 feet, and pierced the chalk for 64 feet, obtaining a good supply of water.

THE GEOLOGY OF THE DISTRICT.

took much interest in this country, and his list of the strata (including, however, a rather wider area) virtually agrees with the above. He describes them as—

1. Gravel dust.
2. Upper Bagshot sands.
3. Bracklesham clays (or Middle Bagshot).
4. Lower Bagshot sands.
5. Lower drift (not recognised now).
6. London clay.

He calls attention to a beautiful section of ice-formation to be observed in the railway cutting close to our village (now, however, much less clearly defined than formerly), and says, "Now I am certain as I can be of any earthly thing, that the whole of these Windsor Forest flats were ages ago ploughed and harrowed over and over again by ice-floes and icebergs, drifting and standing in a shallow sea."

Over the surface lie, here and there, thin sheets of ice-borne gravel, with layers of clay and small patches of loam of various thicknesses; and so variable are they, that one may have gravel and no clay, while his adjoining neighbour may have clay in abundance, but not a patch of gravel, and are more or less so intermingled that ponds may be formed almost anywhere with but little difficulty, and often without puddling.

It is to the loam that we owe our fine timber.

The highest point in our parish is the Ascot Hotel, which has an elevation of 309 feet O.D. The main road falls from this spot more than 100 feet to the lower part of Sunninghill by the Wells Inn. The Ascot Station road leaves the main road at an elevation of about 252 feet, and the station itself stands at about 227 feet.*

To return now to the water supply of our immediate neighbourhood. It may be taken generally that by sinking through the strata before described, water may be obtained, and in most places in unfailing quantity, at depths varying, according to the elevation of the place, between 50 feet and 120 feet. Between 50 and 70 feet would lie the average depth hereabouts at which it would be reached. But there are other small local water-bearing strata formed by the patches or basins of clay that yield a supply at from 15 to 20 feet. This, however, is not in quality good, or in quantity at all to be depended on. The main supply is from a running sand at its junction

---

* See Ordnance Survey. Dr. Ballard's Report, Local Government Board, 1878, and *Quarterly Review*, 1876.

with the blue clay of the London basin. The grit of the former, I may observe, is terribly biting to the metal of all pumping apparatus.

A well was sunk here a few years since, near to the New Inn and not far from the church, at a spot about 235 feet O.D., and it may be instructive to furnish the analysis of its water. Some of the immediate neighbours were supplied from the higher level of 20 feet, and when this was missed, it was at first a disappointment, and the sinking had to be continued to a depth of 55 feet where water was met with in a shifting sand on the blue clay before spoken of; but what was thought a misfortune proved a blessing. Dry summers seriously affected the higher level supplies, but never exhausted this lower one; and although not more than two or three feet of water ever stood in the well, that always does stand in it, however great the demand is.* The following is a copy of the analysis:—

Physical Characteristics.

Colour when examined in a tube two feet long,	Yellowish green
Suspended matter,	Very heavy
Smell when heated to 100° F.	None
Taste do. do.	None
Hardness before boiling 4°,	6
Hardness after boiling 4°,	6

Chemical Results. — Grains per gall.

Total solid matter,	13.16
Loss on ignition, after deducting combined carbonic acid,	4.48
Total mineral matter,	8.68
Chlorine, equal to chloride of sodium,	2.62
Lead and copper,	None
Iron in solution,	None
Phosphoric acid,	None
Nitrogen as ammonia,	None
Nitrogen as albuminoid ammonia,	.0008
Oxygen absorbed by organic matter from solution of permanganate of potash at 80° F. in two minutes,	None
Do., do., do., in four hours,	.0140

---

* This well was sunk at an altitude of about 235 feet O.D. The great Ascot boring was at a spot about 250 feet O.D.; and inasmuch as the London clay in the former case was met with at a depth of 55 feet, while in the latter they pierced it only at 118 feet, it shows that the London clay-bed at that part of Ascot lies at an altitude of 132 feet O.D., while at Sunninghill it rises to 180 feet, thus indicating a dip eastward from us.

Valuation according to Wigner's valuation scale.

According to which values below 35 indicate first-class water, and samples having a value above 75 are unfit for drinking.

The London waters generally average a value of about 30, and the best public supplies 10 to 15. The valuation of this water is 28, it is therefore a first-class water.

Remarks.—This is a good water: there is no indication of pollution with sewage or drainage matter.

The suspended matter is heavy, and consists of oxide of iron. This should be removed by settlement or filtration; it would then be an excellent water for drinking and domestic purposes. ALLEN & HANBURYS.

The water of course is not everywhere of equal quality; it varies considerably. The great peculiarity is the quantity of iron it contains—not in solution, but in suspension; but as our sands are clean and pure, our general water supply is good, and if not rivalling that from "the crystalline rocks of the Alps," is far removed from that of the shallow wells of our neighbourhood. All our surface waters are exposed to the same injurious peaty impurities that spoil those of our neighbours at Sandhurst; but we need never draw our supply from these sources. We have only to go down a little lower through the sands to find an unfailing store of excellent water in the London clay. Dr. Irving's proposition, that no wholesome water is to be obtained in the Sandhurst district except from the upper ferruginous sand of the Bagshot series, is indeed startling. I have shown practical proof, I think, of the excellence of water yielded by the *lower* sands of that series in our country. The Doctor gives us a case of a well not 30 feet deep, and one could hardly expect such a supply to be free from risk. Over the whole district these superficial sources are dangerous. My own experience is in accord with Professor Rupert Jones' opinion when he says, "The Lower Bagshots resting on the London clay form a good reservoir of water, although they may not be good everywhere." There is one fact, however, I must not forget, that water arising from peaty moorlands, wherever situated, is liable to generate "humus" acid: this dissolves lead, and thereby acquires a poisonous character. Leaden pipes should, therefore, be discarded in favour of iron ones. The cost of raising our water is moderate; and if the influence of the iron on the pipes is deemed an inconvenience, we have the alternative of resorting to the Company's water, which has recently been brought from a distance.

But passing from the water to the land again, we have a few natural features that must not be entirely passed over. The first must have struck every one who has crossed our sandy heaths, or endeavoured to bring them into cultivation. I mean the frequent occurrence there of large boulder stones, "grey-wethers" or "Sarsen" stones, as they are called. They are masses of consolidated sand, so heavy as to excite our wonder as to what the agency was that deposited them. It was long thought that it was in floating ice-bound masses that they were brought here; but modern geological opinion does not support this theory. They are now generally considered to be portions of those sandy Tertiary strata which once covered the districts where they occur; while the softer portions of these strata have been washed away, others, increased in hardness probably by exposure, and held together by a silicious cement, have been let down, as it were, and remained behind as "grey-wethers."

They are mostly derived from the Bagshot sands, although also found numerously spread over the chalk downs of the South and West of England.

Another feature of this district is worthy of special notice, as the physical aspect of our country has been greatly affected by it; it has helped to mould the hills around us, and add the charm of variety to their undulations. I allude to that curious formation underlying the surface here for many miles called locally the "pan," a seam of irony conglomerate about six inches thick, varying much in hardness, which lies hereabouts between two and three feet below the surface, although at some other spots much lower. No crop can be hoped for until this cold impervious layer is broken up; and it is this, to a great extent, to which we owe our wide uncultivated wastes, as it has rendered the country so stubborn to reclamation. The ordinary steam "cultivator" will not always reach it, and trenching is very costly; while at the same time (as before described) we owe to it also the upholding of many of our gravel-capped spurs and ridges.

This "pan" is in reality accumulated iron-rust (aggregation of iron oxide), washed by rain and streams down through the gravel or sandy gravel till it rests on the next impervious surface, which in this district is sand choked with fine particles of clay and rust. It varies in colour and consistency; about Windlesham it is nearly pure iron oxide—bog-iron ore; in the gravels it forms a conglomerate with the pebbles; it is ruinous to vegetation, and can only be thrown out to be reacted on and disintegrated by the weather.[*]

I am not aware whether the pebble-bed spoken of as the line of division between the upper and middle of this series has ever

---

[*] See Dr. Irving's paper, 1884, Geological Journal, H. W. Monckton's paper, vol. xxxix., 1883.

been used for building; but we find in the gravels an iron-cemented conglomerate, which, owing to the complete state of oxidation, is of a very hard and durable character. Our forefathers well understood its building value. Archbishop Beauchamp fetched "heath-stone" from Cranbourn to build his chapel at Windsor, and it is this which the old Norman builders used for the erection of our church. The chancel, just pulled down, shows it hanging together to this day, as hard as when it was placed there; and some large slabs of it are to be seen in the walls of Silchester, as sound as when placed there by the Roman masons.

Before I conclude, I must allude to a curious natural deposit to be met with in Sunninghill Bog and other similar localities. It was the cause of the failure of the drainage system adopted here a few years ago. The surveyor, in spite of the proverbial "craft of the clouted shoe," discarded the old practice of open drains or ditches for the modern plan of sunk tile-drains, but it was a failure; in two or three years the pipes were stopped with a yellow ferruginous-looking fluid of about the consistency of thick soup. It was supposed to be of mineral nature and produced from the bog-ore, but it would seem to be of a vegetable character. Ehrenberg found it abundant in the marshes round Berlin, and although, after evaporation of the water, it looked exactly like oxide of iron, under the microscope it was found to consist of slender articulated threads or plates, partly silicious and partly ferruginous, of what he considered an animalcule—Gaillonella ferruginea—but which most naturalists now regard as a plant.*

The rainfall here, by which alone our springs are fed, is put by some authorities at 23 inches for the year; but I think a better average fall would be between 24 and 25. At Aldershot it is stated to be only 16½, while Woolmer Forest is given as nearly 27.†

---

* See Sir C. Lyell, Prin. Geol., 9th edit., p. 722.
† Encyclopædia Britannica, "England," vol. viii. p. 217.

CHAPTER XXXVII.

The Fauna.

LET me now say something of our furred and feathered friends, dwellers in the Forest, of whose habits it is always refreshing to speak. The wild ox no longer roams over our plains, nor is the wild boar to be found in the dense thickets of Swinley; the yellow-breasted marten, so prized for its fur, dwells with us no more; the red and fallow deer, too, are gone. They were all of them once denizens of our Forest, and so, too, was the wolf. The great bustard* at a comparatively recent period might have been seen trooping over our sandy ridges, and the boom of the bittern was often heard at evening over the swamps.†

Civilisation, with its increasing population, its field-cultivation, and enclosure, has waged an unequal warfare with the wild beasts and birds of the Forest. Against arms of precision they have but a poor chance; and while our fair friends covet for their adornment the bright plumage of the birds, the beautiful kingfisher has a hard fight for survival. One by one our rare animals disappear; but not, it is to be hoped, like the great copper butterfly, that hovered like a burnished speck over the marshes of the great Bedford Level ere the centrifugal pump sounded its doom of extinction. It is not now to be met with elsewhere in the world, I believe.

But what proof is there that we ever had all these wild animals in our Forest?

First, as to the wild ox; not the colossal *Bos urus* or Primi-

---

* The great bustard, Mr. Kennedy tells us, was met with on Lambourn Downs in this county up to 1802, but has not occurred there since.

† The last bittern that was shot in Sunninghill Bog was in 1843, and was in the possession of Mrs. Round of Weston-super-Mare. One was killed near Wargrave in 1855, and another near Cookham in 1867. See Kennedy's "Berkshire Birds."

genus, for although it is stated * he was here in Roman times, we had better consider him only as prehistoric. His remains have certainly been found in the Thames and Kennet Valleys, showing his existence there in early ages. The small deer-like *Bos longifrons*, however, which Cæsar found domesticated amongst us, can fairly be claimed as having been a wild occupant of our woods, for its bones have on several occasions been found among Roman remains, especially at Farringdon in 1850. Our modern cattle would seem to be descendants of the Continental Urus, introduced by the Saxons, which became again established as a wild race in our forests.

Matthew Paris speaks of the district through which Abbot Leofstan, in the time of Edward the Confessor, cut his road from the edge of Siltria (the Chilterns) towards London, as abounding with "spatious woods, the habitation of various beasts, wolves, boars, forest bulls, and stags;" and again, Fitz Stephen, describing the country round London in 1174, says, "Close at hand lies an immense forest, woody ranges, hiding-places of wild beasts, of stags, of fallow deer, of boars, and of forest bulls." †

It is difficult to imagine that when the reindeer was still lingering in the North of Scotland, the famous Southdown flocks were grazing those thymy pastures to the south of us, still so famous for them.‡ The sheep can show, we are told, a line of pure descent from a time anterior to the Conquest; while the reindeer is mentioned in one of the Norse Sagas as having been hunted in Caithness as late as the twelfth century; and, as Mr. Boyd Dawkins admits, its bones have been discovered in the refuse-heaps of the Pictish Burghs.§

But of all the denizens of our Forest, the little roebuck, the smallest of British cervidæ, was perhaps the most interesting.‖ This beautiful little stag was in Roman times quite common in the South of England; indeed, it was as numerous, if not actually more so, than the red-deer. This is well established by the explorations which General Pitt Rivers has so ably carried on in the Romano-British villages round Rushmore, Wilts. There he found the bones of the roedeer in much larger quantity than those of the red-deer, proving perhaps, not so much that they were more abundant than the others, as that the stone arrow-heads of the British hunter were more effective against them than against the wilder and larger stags. They were

---

* See Recent Origin of Man, by J. C. Southall.
† See also Placita Corum Rege. Domestic Arch., Hudson Turner, vol. i. p. 105.
‡ See *The Field*, January 1888.   § J. C. Southall, Recent Origin of Man.
‖ A full-grown one stands not above 26 inches high at the shoulder.

plentiful on the Welsh mountains; but they have been gradually driven northward, and in the middle of the last century were not to be found south of Perthshire.

Pennant, in his Scotch Tour in 1769, writes, that "near Invercauld the little roebucks were perpetually bounding before us, the black-game often sprang under our feet, and the mountain-tops swarmed with grouse and ptarmigan."

Roedeer are not now to be seen save in the wild fastnesses of the Scotch Highlands, and that but rarely. Considering how little they possess the shy, wary nature of the red-deer, the wonder is how one remains alive. They are quite children of the woods, and will die out with the forests.

The wolf was undoubtedly very common in England once. The Saxon Chronicle speaks of

> "That grey beast
> The wolf in the weald."

And that they were numerous in this very Forest of ours in Roman times, and daring even round the habitations of man, I find an interesting fact in the remains of Silchester, affording cogent proof. Across the prepared clay the wolves chased a deer and fawn, and there in the baked tiles we may see the sharp claws of the "grey beast" and the footprints of its victim as clearly defined as when they were impressed 1600 years ago. They were not exterminated in England, we are told, till the time of Edward I., but they abounded long after that in Scotland. Between 1690 and 1700 four old wolves and several whelps were killed there—the last in Sutherlandshire; the den was in the narrow Glen of Loth.*

The beaver once abounded here; and I have seen an old map in which Sunninghill Park is marked as Beaver Park.† In a charter of 944 mention is made of a Beaver Island in the Kennet. The otter has always been very plentiful here. The Chertsey Abbey charters give the "Ottershaghe" as a boundary point, of which Ottershaw Park still reminds us.

The wild boar was common at a much later date. In "Guy of Warwick" we read ‡—

---

* See Scrope's Days of Deer-Stalking, p. 374.
† Also in *Windsor Gazette*, 1794, so called. See Dawkins' Cave-Hunting, p. 76.
‡ Ritson's Ancient Songs and Ballads. Wild White Cattle of Brit., Rev. J. Storer, p. 56. Encyclop. Brit., vol. x. p. 341.

"In Windsor Forest I did slay
A boar of passing weight and strength;"

showing at least that there in the writer's imagination was its favourite haunt.

In many of the old Forest charters giving the right of hunting, and more often than not to the monks of some neighbouring abbey, the species of game which they were permitted to take was carefully specified. In several of them I find the privilege thus limited: "capere vulpem, leporem, tessonem et cattum;" and in one instance "murelegum" occurs. "Tessonem" was the badger, a Latinised form, from the old French *taisson* and *tesson*, Lat. *taxus, tassonis*; "murilegum," the cat, literally "mouse-catcher." For this explanation I am indebted to an eminent naturalist, who adds, "The wild cat was hunted formerly, not only for diversion, but for the sake of its skin, which was much used as trimming for dresses." In Archbishop Corboyle's Canons, 1127, it is ordained "that no abbess or nun use more costly apparel than such as is made of lamb's or cat's skins;" and as no other part of the animal but the skin was of any use, it grew into a proverb that "you can have nothing of a cat but her skin." "Cattum" or "catum," from *catus*, is of course a post-classical word.

The crane (*Grus communis*), as the old ballad of the King and the Shepherd shows, was a common bird here in the time of Edward III.,[*] Chaucer also numbers it among our native birds—

"The crane (the geant) with his trumpe's soun;"

and in 1555 Turner mentions it as breeding in our fens. In Michael Drayton's time we know "here stalked the stately crane;" but when Pennant wrote, it was quite unknown in England.

Macaulay alludes to the rare yellow-breasted marten as not uncommon in the time of Queen Anne. I have met with an interesting notice of it by Evelyn, who, writing to Aubrey in February 167¾, says, "In the sandy banks about Albury do breed the trodgladytic martines, who make their burrows in the earth."

This was evidently *Mustella martes* to which Aubrey alludes, not *M. foina*, for that breeds wholly in trees, but the yellow-breasted marten or pine-weasel, so called because of its especial fondness for the tops of pine trees. It has a yellow breast and throat, and a much finer fur than the other species, and is found only in large forests. Mr. Alston's investigations go to show that the beech-marten (*M. foina*) is not, and probably never

---

[*] See also Ancient Laws of Wales, and *Edinburgh Review*, January 1887.

was, found in the British Isles; and the pine-marten (*M. martes sylvatica*), although once common, is now rarely met with in England. A beautiful specimen was shot while climbing a tree at Woodcot, Oxon, in November 1794,* and one was taken in Surrey in 1847; and so lately as May 1889 one was shot in a Scotch fir plantation in Suffolk as it was carrying off a full-grown young wood-pigeon.†

But let us not, while we recall the past, forget the present. Wildfowl of several sorts still haunt and breed in our moorland ponds, and snipe and woodcock are plentiful. A few coveys of black game have still lingered on Bagshot Heath, or, having been reintroduced, are every year to be met with there. In Hampshire they abounded in 1826, and Lord Malmesbury shot a blackcock on the spot where St. Peter's Church, Bournemouth, now stands.

I cannot find that we ever had the red grouse on our moors, although it is native in the British Islands, and found nowhere else.

Heath poults or grey hens, however, are spoken of in Prince Rupert's Book of the Forest as then common game; and in the Ascot Manor papers is an old entry that "in ancient times there was a great store of game there, particularly heath poults." In 1665 the King alludes to them always having been in Windsor Forest, but then of late had been much destroyed, and appeals to the gentlemen of Surrey to help him to preserve them. They were never shot before the 1st of August.

The French partridge, a recruit of doubtful advantage, is still found here in its earliest haunts. It was first brought into England in the time of Charles II., and turned out in the fields near Windsor.

Peewits are numerous, and to the wanderer over the moors their wild cry in the spring-time is still a pleasure. I witnessed an interesting sight once on Chobham Common. While loitering there one bright day in April (it was the 17th), a fox came running close by me, with ears back, at the top of his speed, as though for very life; three peewits alternately swooped down upon him, flapping their wings above his head, and uttering the most plaintive cries, driving him, as they fancied, from their nests, he, poor beast! the while hurrying on, without waiting to resist. In another moment the music of the pack, not heard at all before, arose, and in full cry the dogs came surging in a dense phalanx over the hill, down as straight as a line on the poor flying beast; the whole field followed, but he reached the enclosed country and got away.

---

* *Reading Mercury*, November 10, 1794.
† See *The Field*, July 1889; but it is being driven northward, and the Lake District, North Wales, and parts of Scotland are its best remaining haunts. It is more rare even than the wild cat, and is likely soon to become quite extinct in Britain.

Although foxes still abound, the badger (*Males taxus*), or grey, as it was called, although at one time very common, is scarce now. It will be a pity to lose it altogether, for it is said to be the oldest of al existing British mammals.

But perhaps the most interesting of ancient notes on the ornithology of this neighbourhood is that made by John Norden in the time of James I. On the back of No. 13 of his beautiful maps, referring to Byfleet, Surrey, he writes, "The hooping bird, vulgarlie held ominous, muche frequenteth this parke muche." It is uncertain what this "hooping bird" was. Some say it was the nightjar, the ominous character of which is well known to this day. Not long since, one of our neighbours met on the Common one evening a superannuated old gamekeeper, well known to him; he was not looking well, and my informant said, "I'll go and get you something to drink." On his return the old man seemed much agitated, "A very bad thing," said he, "has happened, sir, since you left; one of them jar-birds has flown against me, and almost knocked my hat off, and that's a very bad sign." He was greatly depressed, went home, and very soon died. These birds are still very numerous here. The able authority before referred to has kindly written, "The only two birds I know which can properly be said to 'hoop' or whoop are the wild swan or whooper, and the hoopoe (*Upupa*), both so named from this note. The former, not being a Forest bird, is not likely to be mentioned in a Forest charter; the latter, a summer visitor to the British Islands, and somewhat uncommon, can hardly be the bird referred to. It is much more likely to be the green woodpecker or yaffle, which has a loud laughing cry." But who could find it in his heart to call that "loud laughing cry," the delightful alarm-note of our woodland favourite, a hoot or whoop? And besides, it was never considered ominous. I must here, however, observe, that the ornithologist referred to hardly had the local circumstances of the case sufficiently laid before him, so that without presumption I may be permitted to form an independent judgment. I must reject the nightjar, because it does not whoop; and the yaffle, because it neither whoops nor is ominous. The hoopoe, though held in great veneration by the Egyptians, can hardly be said to be a bird of particular omen; and although it is an uncommon visitor here, I find Ray, singularly enough, mentioning it as seen sometimes, although rarely, in two places in England—in Northumberland and in Surrey; the very part we are speaking of; and much more recently it has been shot in this neighbourhood.

The owl certainly might contend with some reason that he conforms in both particulars; he hoots, and has ever been "vulgarlie held ominous." Among all nations this poor bird's note of alarm or love has been always heard with dread. But to none of these, I think, did Norden allude; they are all, with the exception of the hoopoe, extremely common in our district; and he might almost as well have said that the robin redbreast or the rook frequented this place much: he surely meant a bird that was not so numerous elsewhere in the Forest.

I have no doubt the bird Norden spoke of was the wild swan, which has always been called the hooper: the sound from a large flock of them is very musical when heard from a distance; it is very like the word "hoop" repeated ten or a dozen times; when made over a dead comrade, it is the melody of the dying swan of the poets. The swan was a bird undoubtedly ominous, but of good omen generally.

The expression "frequenteth," moreover, implies that the bird was a visitor, not a constant resident. As to its not being a Forest bird, the locality was exactly suited to the wild swan. Through Byfleet Park ran the river Wey, in Norden's time doubtless a larger stream than now; it opened close by into the Thames, and the whole district was one of rivers and lakes and pools.* Lord Malmesbury, speaking of his home, Heron Court, near Christchurch, says, "Every sort of wildfowl, from the hooper to the teal, frequents our three rivers and the ponds on the heath." This locality is not more than forty miles from us—and even of late years the hooper has frequently been shot round Chertsey and Cookham. In truth, that they are not with us now is only owing to the incessant persecution of them when they do appear. I am glad to hear that in October 1886 a dozen of them were seen sailing quietly on the extensive water called Petersfield Pond, Hants.

Speaking just now of the nightjar, how pleasant is that vibrating note of his, reminding us of the first warm evenings of June. They arrive here about the second week in May, and hatch their young in July. This is the only reason of their visit to us, and exemplifies the curious law that influences the breeding haunts of migratory birds; they are almost always in the coldest regions to which the birds ever resort.

The nightingale is much less common here than it was. To the bird-catcher it is a tempting prize, and most easily snared.

---

* In this very park, in 1770, there was a decoy, the first in this part of England.

How comes it to pass that the beautiful old Cornish song, "The sweet nightingale," or "Down in those valleys below," should be almost peculiar to a country in which the nightingale is never heard? It raises the question, was it always a stranger to those western valleys?*

In such a country as this, all the ordinary woodland and heath-loving birds of course are common. Who in the early summer has been among those furze patches on the wilder spots of the heath, and not noticed the pretty little black-velvet headed, white-throated bird, the stonechat? If you look sharp enough, you will soon find in the thorny bush its nest, full of bright blue eggs. As you walk on, you may notice on the topmost spray of the highest Scotch fir a bird somewhat larger than the yellow-hammer; he greets us with his quiet, long-drawn note, shifts to another tree, and repeats it, but does not fly far away: this is the bunting.

Among the rarer birds that remain still with us is the sturdy hawfinch, which builds in this neighbourhood. During one or two hard winters it visited the shrubberies here, where the chicken-food was the attraction; it fed close to the house for some days. But a more interesting ornithological fact is that a flock of crossbills (*Loxia curvirostra*) has for many years taken up its quarters during autumn and winter in the larch and Scotch firs at King's Wick. In 1882 a few were observed remaining on into the spring; and a nest was shortly afterwards discovered, about thirty feet high, in an overhanging branch of a lofty Scotch fir, which fairly puzzled our most experienced bird-nesters, either to identify the nest, or, fortunately, get at it. It excited some curiosity; it was a large nest, loosely built of dried grass, moss, and shavings. On the 18th of the following May a young crossbill, scarcely able to fly, was taken on the lawn: they had built and brought up their young here; the hornbeam seeds as well as the fir cones doubtless attracted them.

Darwin, to prove that any organ normally developed in any unusual degree tends to be highly variable, adduces as an example the variable bill of this bird, but hardly with his usual logical force; for he omits to tell us that the bird varies as much in its general size as it does in the form of its bill.

---

* Since writing this I find it stated (see *Temple Bar*, October 1887), that in the Welsh district tradition avers that the nightingale is never heard beyond the red sandstone defile, the Bwlch Hill of tourists, leading from the Vale of Crickhowell to that of Brecon; and that in former days they have been found farther west, as the names of many Welsh places testify, *e.g.* Nanteous (the nightingale's brook), in Cardiganshire; and Llwyngreos (the nightingale's grove), in more than one part of Carmarthenshire. I did not know it was ever found so far west; but if so, it confirms my surmise.

I must here note another fact, still more rare probably, that the woodcock, common enough during the winter in the moist dells of our wilder heathlands, has been known to stay the summer and nest here: its eggs were taken in 1888, and are now in the possession of the Vicar of Bagshot.

Among the rarest of our winter migrants, I must not omit to record the waxwing (*Bombycivora garrula*) or silk-tailed chatterer, whose visit to us our neighbour Sir Joseph Hooker has kindly communicated to me as having been noticed by Mr. Symonds in January 1886. It was observed several times feeding on the berries of a shrub at the Camp. Snow lay for some days on the ground at the time, and large flocks of them had been observed in Germany during that inclement winter. This interesting bird is most uncertain in its visits. Ray mentions large flocks coming to England in 1685; Gilbert White had one brought to him as a rarity in 1767, and Bewick records them in 1789-90 and in 1828. They were noticed in 1866 and 1867, and would probably be found every snowy winter if closely looked for. Surrey is a favourite county for them, on account of the prevalence of the mountain ash and hawthorn, of the berries of which it is especially fond. It is not migratory in the proper sense of the term, being driven south only by inclement snowy seasons; a thaw soon sends them back. They are not gregarious in summer.

At the same time an unusually large number of redwings was observed in our shrubberies close to the house, evidently hard driven for food. Fortunately the hollies were full of berries, on which the redwings feasted for several days, and almost cleared them all off before the snow vanished. It was a pretty sight to watch the birds in the bright sunshine scrambling for the berries; the bushes seemed alive with them.

A rarer and still more beautiful bird must be claimed as an occasional visitor to this district, the golden oriole. A friend, who assures me he knows the bird well, saw it near the station at Sunningdale. The possibility of his mistaking for it the great green woodpecker, whose plumage in high condition looks very golden, was suggested, but he knew the oriole, he said, too well to doubt about its identity. Mr. Brigg also records its having been seen at Billingbeare, in our Forest.

Of birds of prey this wooded country is very rich. The horned owl builds with us, and a wood at Bagshot has been almost from time immemorial the haunt of a pair of carrion crows. Every year they rear their progeny, and in due time drive them off, and themselves continue to rule the wood, curiously enough, in perfect harmony with two or three species of hawks and owls, but to the dread of all else of the feathered race. On one occasion a heron, disturbed on the mere close by, was seen to soar away over the wood, but was immediately assailed by the pair of crows. A desperate battle ensued, in which the retreating heron was terribly punished by his powerful foes. Previously a constant visitor there, he never again entered the crows' domain. A pair of the Royston crows (*Corvus cornix*) has been seen near Cumberland Lodge, picking over a piece of a dead sheep, which they were very loth to leave.

Many kinds of hawks abound here. Indeed, almost every British species of the Falconidæ has at one time or other been met with in the Forest. A splendid specimen of the white-tailed eagle (*Haliaëtus albicilla*, Selby) was shot at Bagshot Park so lately as the winter of 1887. The fine hen-harrier is not unfrequently seen coursing over the open common on Bagshot Heath in pursuit of its prey; it will carry off a full-grown partridge very easily. One, to my great regret, fell a victim to the gun of a rustic in June 1885. This bird was unfortunately too much damaged for preservation.

The kite, so common once, is hardly now to be met with. It seems strange to read that the Bohemian Schaschek, who visited England about 1461, had nowhere seen so many kites as round London Bridge.

The following incident, now that we are on the subject of hawks, proves how wonderfully the wisdom of Providence is shown in its works. The bailiff on the land before referred to at Bagshot found the sparrow-hawks, as he said, "terrifying" the young partridges; but he had been told not to kill them. He soon very adroitly reported that a green woodpecker had been their victim, and of the exciting chase he had seen of a kingfisher, a prime favourite, screaming along the lake, pursued by the hawk. The veto was reluctantly withdrawn, and the hawks were soon disposed of. Sad to say, as it afterwards appeared, their parental instincts were made the means of their destruction. Two or three young nestlings were placed in a cage near the nest, and the old birds were both soon caught. When taken to the cage, there appeared a heap of something close to it, which proved to be dead mice, brought as food for the young. When carefully counted, there were twenty-three mice and one small bird. All these had been brought to them between the hours of one o'clock and eight in the evening; many had, of course, during that time been consumed by the birds. It turned out, as one would expect from this, that he had killed a pair of kestrels, not sparrow-hawks at all. Such an exploit will not occur there again; he knows now that he killed his best friends. A field of oats close by showed the ravages of the mice, and how full the bank was of their holes. It is curious, however, that within a fortnight of this massacre another pair of kestrels appeared " to reign in their stead."

A large pond there is every year the resting-place, in their migrations, of a few of the common sandpiper (*Tringa hypoleucos*), the Willie wet-feet of the Scotch children. In April they arrive from the south, flying apparently in the night, rest for a day or so, and proceed northward. In August or September they return in rather augmented numbers, though never numerous, rest again, and go south. I have seen them in the Scotch Highlands in July after the nesting. They haunt the waterside, and may be seen running over the stones or mud, flirting the tail up and down, or skimming over the lake like a swallow, only with bent wings and zigzag flight, then rising and wheeling away high up in the air. Half a dozen of them were seen one morning resting on a raft, as though after a long flight.

The Pici are well represented; in fact, every British variety has been shot in the Forest, even the great black woodpecker occasionally; and the great spotted woodpecker (*Picus major*), called sometimes the French pye, was seen at King's Wick in January 1887, and several times since in March and April his loud peculiar note was heard resounding in the Cranbourn woods. But very numerous is that chiefest glory of the district, the great green woodpecker, the "garnet-headed yaffingale," or, as in old Berkshire dialect he was called, the "yelpinggale," whose loud laughing notes when disturbed are so pleasing to the ornithologist as he wanders among our fragrant pine-woods. They stay the winter with us, and early in the morning often come close to the house. So brilliant is their plumage in the spring, that a servant has been known to run in to tell her mistress that there was a parrot on the lawn! They built for several seasons in a hole in a decayed cherry-tree in the King's Wick meadow.

The Tits of all kinds, and the charming little golden-crested Wrens, are very abundant. But for them probably our fir trees would be entirely destroyed. It is not for nothing that you see them with head now up now down (it is quite indifferent to them which way it is), searching every spray and crevice of your conifers. You may see one, as it seems, vigorously attacking a tender shoot: watch and afterwards examine the spot of his tiny energies, and you will find just at the root of that shoot the cocoon-bed, now emptied of its maggot; that was the *bon bouche* of our little friend, not the shoot itself. Often one sees the trees almost destroyed by this insect pest, the succulent shoots hanging limp, and ultimately falling off, owing to this maggot. These beautiful little birds are thus working out their destined service in the great system of which they form part. The ring-ousel has been frequently seen near Cumberland Lodge. The Dartford warbler has been found nesting at Bagshot, and the reed-warbler at Sunninghill.

Of polecats, weasels, and such "small deer" we have still plenty. In the time of James I. a pension was granted to a poor man for destroying vermin in Windsor Forest, and so late as 1754 "the vermin-killer" appears in the Forest books as a regular salaried officer, as the "sparrow-catcher" does in the parochial ones.

The history of our legislation on the destruction and preservation of wild animals, and the popular views which from time to time have induced them, are extremely curious. What one age seeks to destroy, another does its utmost to preserve. The Wild Birds' Protection Act of the present day, and the statutes relating to the preservation of our commons, show a strange reversal of the policy of our forefathers. When our powers of destruction were less perfect, the wild life of the forest and the plain was superabundant, and the aid of the Legislature was sought to diminish it.

In the days of Queen Elizabeth a price was set on the heads not only of "ould crowes, pyes and rokes," but also on those of the rare Cornish chough, as it is called now, when, almost exterminated, it lingers only among the wild cliffs of Cornwall and Devon, and on such inaccessible spots as Beachy Head; and then the rustic was paid "for the heads of every three of them one penny!" *

The cormorant was common then far inland. "For the hawke (our friend the kestrel included), the buzard, the king-tayle, the mold kite," the parish officers would pay 2d. a-piece. "For every rauen, kyte [the common one], or wood owle 1d." "For every want [mole] one halfpenny." But think of the bullfinch being associated with the kingfisher at 1d. each! The nineteenth century, after all, is but little worse than the sixteenth!

What will the naturalist say when he learns that in 1705 one Gloucestershire parish paid for the destruction of 230 tomtits, and, worse by far, "2s. for woodpeckers"?

For a fox or a grey they gave a shilling, but in some places in the seventeenth century the price was as high as 5s. In the sixteenth they gave "for a falchen, polecat, weasell, slow faire badger, or wild cat only a penny." Imagine a falcon for a penny! But to have taken such a bird in our Forest would have been a terrible offence. The next item in the same register is rather anomalous. "For a otter or hedgehog 2d." In Cartmel, Lancashire, they paid in 1675 for the first time for killing "mould warpes:" this was the old Saxon form of the word "warpe," cast—the mould-caster. In Sutherlandshire and Caithness so late as 1824 half a sovereign was paid for an old eagle, and in seven years 295 were killed, and 1143 wild cats, martens, and polecats were destroyed.

But on all this a better culture has thrown a much pleasanter light; it tells us that the poor proscribed kestrel is one of the farmers' best friends, and that to spare the "want" is better than to have

---

* See Parish Register, Dursley, Gloucestershire. J. H. Blunt's Hist.

the wire-worm. The wood-owl with its noiseless flight is no longer a terror to us; the little restless tit has its beneficent side; and the hedgehog is no longer such a useless "noysome varmint" as he was formerly considered.

The fox was doubtless at that time so numerous as to carry alarm into every homestead; he was fair game.

> In 1677 the Squire of Cartmel shot an old fox, gave it to a labourer, who took it to the parish officers, explained the facts, and received 5s. for it. In 1708 in a single parish thirty foxes were brought in under "Justices warrant." How would the Justices look now upon a rat-catcher who brought them a trapped fox? But in 1722, at a public meeting in the same parish, it was resolved that no Churchwarden thenceforth should pay for a fox without a lawful order of a Justice of the Peace.

What did the fox owe this tenderness to? No longer trapped like a felon, or taken by nets as of old, a revival of the taste for hunting him in a gentlemanly way now set in, and the "varmint" of the seventeenth century became a favourite beast of chase in the eighteenth and nineteenth, and we hear no more of his being "run in" under Justices warrant. The poor rooks were in no slight danger when, in 1626, we find so intelligent and influential a personage as Mr. Henry Hyde writing to his brother, Mr. Nicholas Hyde, urging that a statute be passed to compel the destruction of rooks, "the wildest and most unprofitable varmin," says he, "that is in my opinion, and easiest to be destroyed."

The Registers of Sunninghill show nothing of such a warfare as this against the wild birds and beasts of the Forest. The explanation probably is, that no one had a right to molest them in the Forest without the King's license, and that until quite lately we had no grain to protect.

In these days of domestic poultry fancying, it is not uninteresting to note any accession to our original stock. In the time of Charles I., John Nicholas, Esq., of Winterbourne Earles, Wiltshire, Secretary Nicholas's father, was a great poultry connoisseur, and in 1637 we find him promising to send to Dr. Nicholas (another son) two Muscovy ducks. On another occasion he writes of a *new kind* of fowl of the "bastard pheasant breed," the famous game bird of our time probably. His neighbour at Christchurch, the eccentric Mr. Hastings, was also taking great care of his birds of the same kind — evidently rarities.*

---

* See Cal. State Papers, Dom. 1634; and Lecroix, Manners of the Middle Ages.

About the same year Sir John Pennington promised to get for Mrs. Nicholas, while then at Sunninghill, "some guinea-fowls, as soon as any came from Barbary or Guinea." They must then have been rare in England, and the importation to Sunninghill is likely to have been one of the earliest introductions of them to this country.

CHAPTER XXXVIII.

The Flora.

"Lo! in the middle of the wood
The folded leaf is woo'd from out the bud
With winds upon the branch, and there
Grows green and broad, and takes no care,
Sun-steeped at noon, and in the moon
Nightly dew-fed; and turning yellow,
Falls, and floats adown the air."—TENNYSON.

IN considering either the fauna or the flora of the Forest, we cannot overrate the influence on both which drainage and enclosures have had: they have materially affected the physical aspects of the country, as well as its climate. Whenever a district like this is enclosed, and the deer and cattle roaming over it are prevented from cropping the tender shoots and destroying the young trees, the whole country silently becomes forest. The oak, the beech, the birch, and above all the Scotch fir, seed themselves rapidly in our warm soil, and every year add to its woodland character. What an interesting account of the influence of the animal on the vegetable kingdom Darwin gives us. On the unenclosed commons round Moor Park, he says, not a tree was to be seen for miles; while, on looking closer into the heather, he saw tens of thousands of young Scotch firs (thirty in one square yard), with their tops nibbled off by cattle. "One little tree three inches high appeared by its rings to be twenty-six years old!" *

Among these self-sown trees I must especially notice the Spanish chestnut, as it is rather a botanical curiosity to find it growing wild, as it does on our hills. It thrives in the deep sands and gravels of Bagshot and Windlesham. This is rarely the case in England,

---

* Darwin's Life, vol. ii. p. 99.

although we have so many noble planted specimens; and even in parts of France they are not known to reproduce themselves in this way.

But a still more important change has been brought about by drainage; we meet everywhere with evidences that tell plainly of the existence of a much greater extent of swamp and marsh formerly than now.

The Roman road shows by its foundations places that were marshy and are now dry; old deeds and charters speak of fords where none now exist, and of mills on streams which now scarcely run at all, save after heavy rains in winter; while the best crops of corn are standing on what once were ancient marshes. Sunninghill Bog could at one time be crossed only by the causeway through it, and in its depths an ancient forest was buried. I have been assured by a neighbour that often, when a boy, he has seen black oak stems taken out by the villagers.*

The numerous morasses with which the Forest as well as the Great Park were studded held the winter rains as in natural storehouses, to be distributed in more uniform continuous streams throughout the year. In the hottest summers the uplands were green where now, as the water runs off rapidly ere the summer comes, they are parched with drought. Many of these pools and meres, once the favoured haunts of wild-fowl and the hawking-grounds of our ancestors, are now dried up or shrunk to insignificant proportions. The continual breaking up of the "pan" and letting the water through, may have an important influence on our streams and ponds.

Yet still to the botanist or the lover of wild nature how lovely are the green and golden mosses of these moorland swamps, and the plants and grasses which conceal their treacherous depths, still dangerous at times to man and cattle. The white-tufted cotton-grass waves over every peaty hollow. To the botanist, however, our immediate neighbourhood does not yield a very rich harvest; and although he will not despise the simple beauty of those

"Blue-bells trembling by the forest ways,"

but would rather believe, with Crabbe, that

"Bog, and marsh, and fen
Are only poor to undiscerning men,"

---

* This confirms Gilbert White's contradiction of Dr. Plott's remarkable statement, "that there never were any fallen trees hidden in the mosses of the southern counties." White had often seen cottages on the verge of Wolmer Forest whose timbers consisted of a black hard wood, looking like oak, which the owners assured him they procured from the bogs by probing.

he must wander on until he reaches the chalk hills to the south of us for rarer treasures. But of that beauty which our wild heaths show throughout the summer, when "all golden with the never bloomless furze," and rosy with the ling, the wide landscape spreads out its wealth of colour, we may well boast. Three kinds of heather grow here in great profusion, *Calluna vulgaris*, and *Erica tetralix* and *cinerea*. We find on our sandy hills the marsh gentian (*Gentiana pneumonanthe*), with its pretty blue flowers, a rare British plant. The butterfly orchis, both large and small (*Habenaria bifolia*, and *H. albida*), so sweet-scented, are common with us at places. The green-winged orchis (*Morio*), is also common here, although evidently a child of the South; it is unknown in Scotland; and save in these southern counties, it seems rare in England. The curious twisted spiked orchis (*Spiranthes autumnalis*) has also, but not commonly, been found here; it is a chalk-loving species. We have the sundews, both common and oblong (*Drosera rotundifolia* and *longifolia*), on our heaths. The beautiful little bog pimpernel (*Anagallis tenella*), with its pale pink flowers, may be met with on Chobham Common and Bagshot Heath, with the bright scarlet *A. arvensis*, that most common but interesting plant, the poor man's weatherglass, which never opens on a rainy day, and closes its petals on the approach of a shower. This sensitive flower, Dr. Seeman tells us, was taken in, however, once, when there was an eclipse of the sun at noonday, for it was then found folded up as at midnight.

Of the rarer plants, *Erysimum orientale*, although mentioned by Bentham as scarcely permanently established in Britain, and not included in Sir Joseph Hooker's "Flora," has been found by Mr. White about Windlesham in some number. The little white-flowered *Draba incana* (although not so rare as *D. hirta*, which is only to be found in Britain on the high summits of the Scotch and Irish mountains) has been discovered here. As it is generally found only in the North of England and Scotland, it is curious to see such an inhabitant of the bleak hills a denizen of ours in the south. It is very rare, however. *Pyrola minor*, again, is like a wanderer from the North which has lost its way down here; it is a local plant. On our sandy soils it is not so strange to find *Hypocharis glabra*, although it is decidedly uncommon. In *Euphorbia esula* we have a plant of great interest and variety. Bentham thinks it not really indigenous in Britain, although said to have established itself on the banks of the Tweed, and in a few localities of Southern Scotland. Mr. White has found it in one or two places. *Claytonia perfoliata* is a naturalised weed almost. It is interesting to find so arctic a plant as the lichen *Cladonia rangiferina*, the reindeer-moss, that clothes the frozen plains of Lapland and Iceland, and when the heath-fires lay bare those dreary regions for miles, springs up at once to cover the burnt surface with its verdure, spread over our sandy ridges in the south. On the hill-tops of Windlesham, Bagshot Heath, Ascot, and Sunninghill this grey antler-like moss is very common.

The Fungi of our neighbourhood are very beautiful, and well worthy of more particular notice than my space will allow.

On the hills round the Roman Camp the bilberry (*Vaccinium myrtillus*), commonly known as the whortleberry, carpets the fir woods in the early summer with its bright green foliage, to be followed with its black glaucous-bloomed berries. Miles of the hills to the south are covered with this plant. On Hindhead, near Haslemere, it is a very pretty sight, on some bright morning of July, to see the groups of little rustics gathering these berries—"blackhearting," as they call it in the New Forest. In this country, curiously enough, the natives call them "hurts," but in Somersetshire they are still, as they were in olden time, known as "worts." Chaucer, when he wished to show the lowly station of his heroine Griselda, makes her resort to the moors, as the poor children do to this day—

> "And whan sche com home sche wold brynge
> Wortis and other herbis tymes oft."

The crowberry (*Empetrum nigrum*), with its black fruit, so relished by grouse, was, according to some authorities, to be met with here; and certainly the cranberry (*Oxycoccus palustris*), with its delicate rose-coloured blossoms, may still here and there be found on our swamps, where it was once more plentiful. Here too we find common enough that most aromatic of shrubs, the sweet gale (*Myrica gale*). Aubrey, writing of Windlesham, says, "At Lightwater Moor grows great store of a plant about a foot and a half high, called by the inhabitants gole, but the true name is gale, it has a very grateful smell, like a mixture of bays and myrtle, and in Latin it is called *Myrtus brabantica*; it grows also in several places of this heathy country, and is used to be put in their chests among their linen; it is a dwarf-willow."

The earliest study of botany was doubtless to discover the medicinal virtues of plants, and the ladies in their still-rooms in after-ages were its chief followers. Well skilled were they—

> "In every virtuous plant and healing herb
> That spreads her verdant leaf to the morning ray."

It is amusing to find some of our most eminent men having faith in such "simples." Thus in 1671 Sir Hans Sloane writes to Ray with specimens of a plant from our neighbourhood that we quite neglect now, because, I suppose, we lack the faith he had in its "admirable virtue in curing the bites of mad dogs." It grew, he said, on Newmarket Heath and in Surrey, and was called "the Star of the Earth;"* "one of his Majesty's huntsmen having proved it a great many times, gave the King his way of using it, which was an infusion of wine with treacle and one or two more simples." Ray in reply said he thought the plant was *Sesamoides salamanticum magnum* of Clusius or *Lichnis viscosa flore muscoso* of C. B. Sir Philip Skippon, in a letter to the same eminent person, alludes to a practice—a frail adornment of beauty—hardly suited to rough times. "Hedge-sparrows' eggs emptied," he says, "fair ladies wear at their ears for pendants."

Some of these old writers thought the wild camomile (*Anthemis nobilis*) a sufficiently rare plant to be worthy of notice; and tell us that north-east of Virginia Water is a hill called Camomile Hill on that account; and Aubrey speaks of it as growing at Purbright "very common and wild." Evelyn was surprised to find how the waters at Swallowfield were flagged about with *Calamus aromaticus* (*Aconis calamus*), "with which," he says, "my lady has hung a closet, that retains the smell very perfectly."

In its trees this neighbourhood is singularly rich. It attracted the notice of Mr. Pepys; and when Scott spoke of "Windsor's oaks," he was only echoing their proverbial fame. "Cranbourn's oaks," of which Macaulay sings the praises, are hardly so beautiful as those of the Cranbourn of our Forest, over the threatened destruction of which poor old Lord Ranelagh mourned. Of one of these patriarchs Mr. Frith's picture of "An Old English Merrymaking" will preserve to us a lasting portrait.†

Another giant of the woods is mentioned by Jesse‡ as having a stem 38 feet in circumference; and there are two other magnificent ones near Cranbourn Lodge, one just within the park paling, about 300 yards from the Lodge, and the other at the point of the road leading up to it; the former at six feet from the ground measures 38 feet round; the other is 36 feet in circumference at four feet from the ground. Mr. Menzies, however, the surveyor, at a later date says that an old pollard oak at Forest Gate is about the largest in the Forest, being in circumference at five feet from the ground

---

* The common avens, *Geum rubanum*, was known in olden time as "the Star of the Earth," and was thought to possess great medicinal virtues; but it grew on roadsides and near woods rather than on open heath-lands; while *Plantago coronopus* was also known as "the Star of the Earth," and does grow on dry sterile soils, as described.

† Frith's Reminiscences, vol. i. p. 123.

‡ Jesse's Gleanings, p. 201.

26 feet 10 inches, and he gives its probable age as 800 years! An oak in the shrubbery at Sunninghill Park is remarkable for its lofty stem, which, with a circumference of 13 feet, rises up 70 feet without a branch. But none of these are so grand and picturesque as some in Swinley, where there are four or five near the Lodge of wonderful size and beauty, telling us what the Forest was generally before its destruction. I measured one 26 feet 6 inches in circumference three feet from the ground; at five feet it was 24 feet.

When we come to discuss the age of English trees, we touch a subject on which the most learned authorities are at variance, and as delicate as that of the possible longevity of the human race. Unfortunately, there is no satisfactory rule or method of ascertaining the age of a tree, so much depending on the soil in which it is growing; and even when cut down, the rings can only tell us the years of its growth, not of its decay. Mr. Menzies, and many other writers whose opinions are entitled to much respect, are advocates of a very great age for the oak as well as the beech, and, like Tom Moore, tell you of trees "superannuated" centuries ago, or a more modern poet, who talks of "huge trees, a thousand rings of Spring in every bole." Other naturalists, equally able, hold a different opinion; and while the former attribute to William the Conqueror's Oak in Windsor Forest a growth of 1200 or 1500 years, some eminent authorities declare that there is not an oak in England 500 years of age. Of the yew, of course, nothing is said, for that every one admits to be capable of great antiquity. Between these extremes probably the truth lies. There are oaks, surely, in England that can be shown to have existed over five centuries, not by tradition merely, but by actual documentary evidence. The oak, still standing, I believe, in Burleigh's Coppice at Cranbourn, supplies us with a very interesting and authentic example; that tree is 12 feet 3 inches in circumference at five feet from the ground, and its age by a well-known rule* should be about 312 years: it was actually planted in 1580.

The Sawyer's Lodge beech had been dying long before Strutt sketched it, but nearly a hundred years after that, when drawn by Jesse, it was not dead: an oak would be much longer in its decay, and as long in its growth and maturity. These are only local instances, and our soil is warm and moist in places, conditions that invariably promote rapidity of growth.

---

* Which gives 12 to 15 inches of growth to an inch of radius (which we may put in this case at 13).

We may remember Macaulay's allusion to the gigantic oak at Magdalene College, "older by a century, men said, than the oldest college in the university!" This was the tree that William of Wainfleet gave directions for Magdalene College to be built near in 1458, describing it then as "the great oak."* It fell suddenly in 1788, and out of it as a memorial the President's chair was made. It could not therefore have been less than 500 or 600 years old, for it thus had a recognised existence of more than three centuries after it had become known as "the great oak;" and allowing a couple of centuries for it to have attained that exceptional size, it must have been more than 500 years old when cut off, as it were, by a violent death, still a vigorous tree, while two more centuries of vitality would probably have been left in it.

But the beeches are not less beautiful or less fine than the oaks. We have no particulars of the King's Wick beech, under which the highwayman was shot, although it was evidently a well-known object. Mr. Strutt, in his "Silva Britannica," speaks of that at Sawyer's Gate, Sunninghill, as presenting remains of surpassing grandeur, and evidently of great antiquity. "Its rugged projections and twisted roots give it on one side the appearance of some rude mass of broken architecture, whilst on the other it is entirely hollow." Mr. Jesse, speaking of the same tree in 1845, gives us as its measurement 36 feet round at six feet from the ground; and continues, "It must once have been hollow, but the vacuum has been nearly filled up; one might almost fancy that liquid wood, which had afterwards hardened, had been poured into the tree." It was blown down about fifteen years since.

Near Holly Grove, not far from the entrance into the Park, on the right of the road to Windsor, stands a remarkably fine beech in the full splendour of its growth; it measures at a yard from the ground 25 feet 6 inches; and a very beautiful and conspicuous one, called sometimes the Queen of the Forest, may be seen near the Swinley deer-paddock of 20 feet 5 inches.

One of the grandest pieces of woodland scenery in England is that of the well-known Burnham Beeches, anciently on the verge of the Forest of Windsor. The trees are pollards of great size; and they again may be cited on the question of the age of trees; for I think the truth of the tradition can be established which ascribes their

---

* J. A. Farrar, *Longman's Magazine*, September 1883.

being pollarded to Cromwell's soldiers, and then, nearly 240 years ago, they were large trees.

In Sunninghill Park there are trees of great beauty. Two Spanish chestnuts near the house are especially remarkable. The largest measures 36 feet in circumference at three feet from the ground, one of the finest in the kingdom. The limes at King's Wick, a hundred feet in height, have already been noticed. The elms in the playing fields at Eton are well known. They are about 300 years old. One is spoken of as 15 feet in circumference.

The silver birch, everywhere plentiful, adds greatly to the effect of all our woodland scenery; its loveliness rather than its longevity has usually been its boast, but when dead, its timber, if kept moist, is very durable, and its bark almost indestructible. Is it not this the Anglo-Saxon poem speaks of when it tells us that the

> "Beorc is beautiful in its branches;
> It rustles sweetly in its leafy summit,
> Moved to and fro by the breath of heaven"? *

The mountain ash, too, the rowan-tree,† is everywhere conspicuous here; in summer bright with blossom, and in autumn with its clusters of coral berries, such a boon to the birds, and in superstitious ages to the human race too; for as a protection against evil a branch of it was often hung over the byre,‡ because the

> "Rowan-tree and red thread
> Haud the witches a' in dread."

Not fifty years ago in Morayshire the cattle all went out to their May pastures with a red cord round their tails to guard them from witches.§

Of the Scotch pine (*Pinus silvestris*), to those who know the proportions to which it attains in favourable positions in its native valleys of Scotland, we must not boast of ours; but, for the south, one in the meadow at Grove Place, Windlesham, is a splendid tree. No more picturesque specimens can be found in this part of England than those on the border of our Forest at Eversley, that most charming of English Rectories, that has had so pleasant a hold on our memories ever since

---

* Anglo-Saxon poem on the names of the Runes by Hickes.
† Supposed to have been derived from the Norse "runa," a charm. It was held in great veneration.
‡ Johnston in East Bord.
§ See Religious House of Pluscardyn, by Macphail.

Kingsley lived there, to which we may well add the noble trees in Pope's garden at Binfield.

When the Scotch pine was first introduced into this part of the country is not known with certainty. Kingsley gives it as a tradition that they were first planted at Bramshill, Eversley, in the time of James I.; but it is not at all a clearly established fact. That it was then hardly known here, we have reason to believe. Robert Church, who was Norden's assistant in his Survey early in that reign, says, "The firre tree is rarely found in England." Did he mean the Scotch pine, then often called the fir, although the distinction was well known then, as shown in Spencer's "Faerie Queene." Even so lately as the end of the last century, when Mr. Agace planted some Scotch firs at Ascot Place, they were considered as rarities.

It may have been reintroduced in the time of James I., but I cannot but believe it flourished in the South of England at a much earlier period of its history; was destroyed and replanted. It is so striking a feature of our country, however, now, and so remarkable a link between the present and past ages, that its history is worthy of special consideration.

Its ancient home was in the great Scandinavian forests, from which it probably spread to North Britain in that remote age when as yet it formed part of the European continent. There, whether its native place or home of its adoption, it has flourished for some thousand years; and now, after seeing its parent forests utterly decay, it still clothes the mountain valleys of Perthshire and Argyleshire with trees of great luxuriance.

In the middle of the last century Pennant describes those in the forest of Delmore as the finest natural pines in Europe: some he saw were 4½ feet in diameter at the lower end, while at Gordon Castle is still preserved a remnant of "the Lady of the Glen," which stood in the Forest of Glenmore, 5 feet 5 inches broad, probably the largest tree ever cut down in Scotland.

We find *Pinus silvestris* as a fossil in the sandstone of Craigleith and Granton, and we see it lying in its lignite state many feet below the surface in most of the peat-bogs and mosses of Scotland, in all stages of preservation.

But the natural forests of this grand tree are doomed; they are dying out slowly but inevitably. These magnificent remnants of natural wood at Invercauld, Braemar, and a few other places are the isolated representatives of the vast forest tracts of more ancient days. But for the protection of exclusive private ownership, not a single tree would Scotland now possess of these noble old forests. Yet there it lingers still, as in its last stronghold of Western Europe. In Denmark they are quite gone, for although they lie thickly imbedded in the mosses, not a tree has grown there for centuries. Lewis, Orkney, and Caithness, and several of the storm-swept valleys of the Western Highlands, show the existence of ancient forests, although they are now quite bare. In Ireland too they are no more.

The Romans describe Caledonia as consisting almost entirely of pine forests and morasses; and they are accused of making terrible havoc with the woods; and doubtless for the use of their armies in so inclement a climate, and for strategic purposes, they did fearful destruction to them. In the time of Boethius the "horrida silva Caledoniæ"

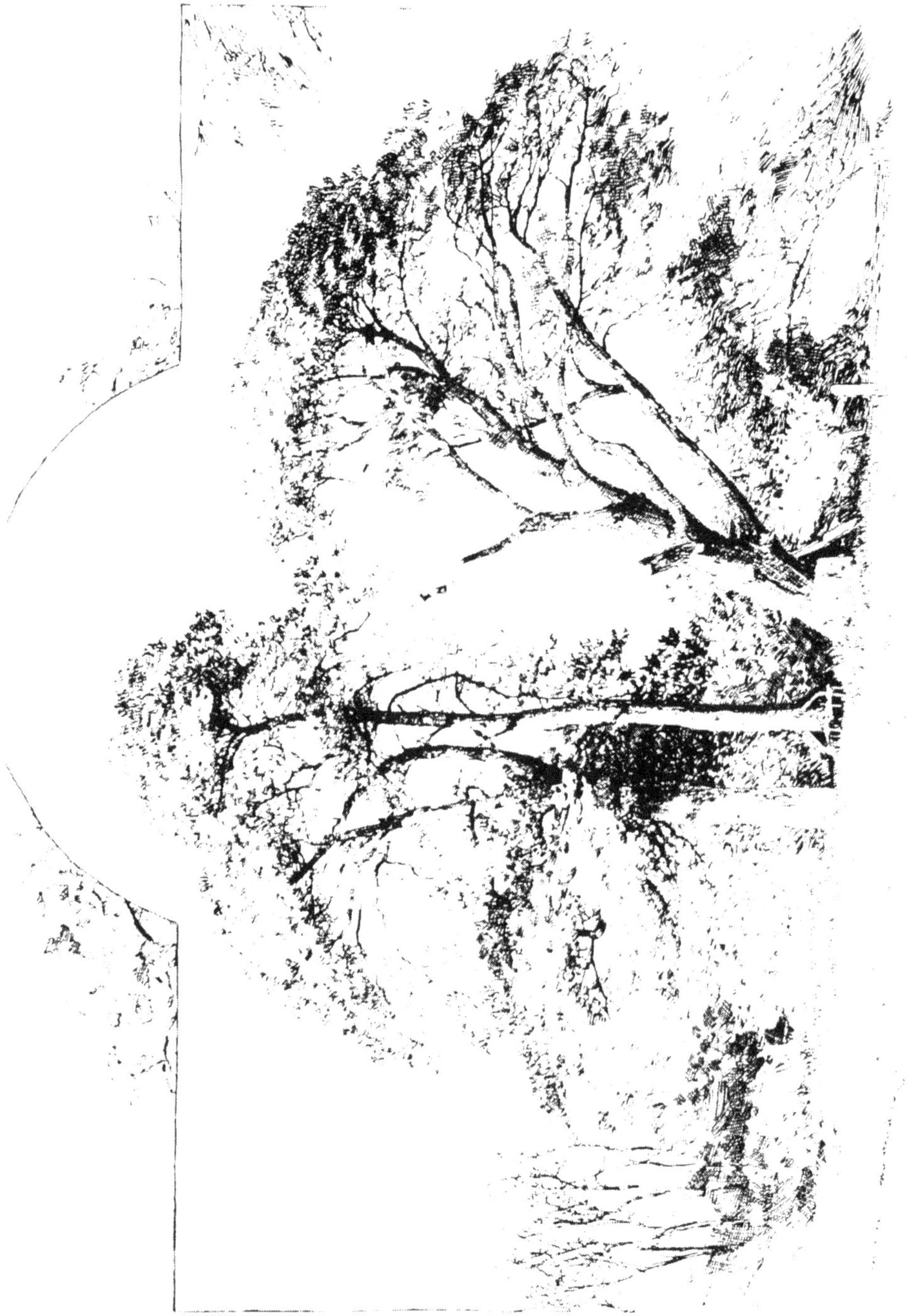

had become mere matter of history. Fifeshire, once well wooded, was then bare, and the metals of Isla could not be wrought for want of fuel.

In the fifteenth century the decay of the woods was the subject of alarm, and James I. and II. of Scotland enacted laws for their preservation; and the Parliament of 1503 again addressed itself to the same object, and to compel planting.

On the south side of Ben Nevis a large pine forest, which extended from the western Braes of Lochaber to the black water and mosses of Rannach, was once burned to expel the wolves; and another near Loch Sloy, nearly twenty miles in extent, was consumed for the same purpose. Pennant in 1769 tells us that the pine forests had even then become very rare. Glen Urcha, about a hundred years ago, was divested of a superb forest by some adventurers. Rothiemurchus, which once covered sixteen square miles, Glenmore and Rannach have lost all their ancient trees; the latter was "unmercifully slaughtered," as Sir T. D. Lauder tells us.

The closing of the Baltic ports during the great French war, by raising the price of timber, gave a final blow to these noble woods.

In the South of England, I cannot doubt the pine once abounded, although never perhaps so universally as in Scotland.

Cæsar was clearly wrong when he said that it did not grow in Britain, for its wood has been frequently dug up with Roman remains. At Hatfield Chase, Yorkshire, where the Roman general Ostorius cut down the forest in the time of Vespatian, as also in Goole Moor, it was found in large numbers; stems 90 feet long have been dug up there. Some of the trees showed marks of the ancient flint axe; others had been felled by means of fire.* Sir John Lubbock notices† the finding of *Pinus silvestris* in the Lake dwellings. It has also been discovered in the peat-bogs of Bournemouth,‡ and in Ireland also. Indeed, Professor Geikie says that pine in the bogs of the South of England compares favourably with the best timber of the old pine forest of Rothiemurchus.

But while their fate in the North has been a struggle for existence, in the South they succumbed ages ago. I doubt whether, before its reintroduction about the sixteenth century, a single tree of ancient forest descent was to be seen here.

How have they disappeared? Professor James Geikie attributes it to change of climate; but surely its own particular nature and its peculiar aptitude for man's service are amply sufficient to account for its destruction. It could hardly be due to climate, for they were here in pre-glacial times, when the climate was warm, and are flourishing still in the South of Europe; and now that they are replanted here, we see Nature reproducing them around us in the greatest profusion. And as to quality, there are specimens on the Bagshot Sands as fine as any in Scotland, save in those famous districts I have spoken of. No tree is so convenient as timber to a primitive people as the Scotch pine, with its long straight stems, nor is any tree so easily worked. At the same time, no tree is so exposed to the incessant assaults of Nature. A storm has often been known to destroy a whole forest, and heath-fires to sweep away miles of the noblest woods. Besides all this, we must never forget that a natural reproduction of the pine is difficult where cattle have access to the young plants.

Whether this tree has been an ancient inhabitant of our country, destroyed and replaced, I leave others to decide; it has certainly found

---

* Davis and Lees, West Yorkshire. J. C. Southall, Recent Origin of Man, p. 460.
† Prehistoric Times.
‡ Evans and J. C. Southall. Dr. Page, Advanced Text-Book, p. 419. Arthur Young's Irish Tour. Lyell's Principles of Geology, p. 746, 1853.

here a very congenial soil for quantity, if not for size of growth; the seed everywhere sowing itself in the direction of the generally prevailing westerly wind; so that but for man and beast Nature would of this tree alone soon form a forest of the sandy tracts of Surrey and Berks. To our own particular district they are giving a peculiar charm, and almost a distinctive character. I say charm, for they are not vast enough in their plantations to frighten us with the horrors of

> "Those matted woods, where birds forget to sing,
> But silent bats in drowsy clusters cling,"

although to each of those facts our pine woods certainly bear testimony. How silently and yet unceasingly does Nature work out her great changes! We may see it in our fir woods, beneath whose branches a sunless gloom prevails; the cones lie all around, but never one germinates; not a young tree ever comes up. But in the open glades at the edge of the woods, nurseries of young Scotch are rising as thick as they can grow; the woods, in fact, are moving eastwards, and as the old trees die, they are succeeded by young oaks and beeches. This precise order is found in Norway. Geology proves the existence there of three distinct forests, one above the other; first the pine, with its accompanying stone implements; then the oak, with bronze ones; and lastly, the beech, still living.

We all know the aroma of this tree that "incense of the Spring," so noticeable on entering a wood of them on a fine day in June, when the hot sun drives you there for its shade, and then rewards you with its perfume. There, while you are listening to the tiny explosions of its bursting cones, quite audible in the fierce noon-day heat, you may inhale the vapour of the oil which the tree distils. Commerce has taken the hint and given us its sanitas.*

I must not, while on this subject, omit to mention a very successful experiment in raising fallen trees. On the 14th October 1881 a fearful storm of wind occurred, and the trees, still laden with their full foliage, suffered terribly. Two fine limes at King's Wick, between 80 and 90 feet in height and of great breadth, came down. When pollarded, it was decided, notwithstanding the high authority against such an attempt, that their stems should be raised and set up again. It was first tried with an iron chain and windlass, but the chain

---

* This hygienic principle, common to the fir-groves and the eucalyptus, is the evolution of the preoxide of hydrogen and camphoric acid, emitted by the naturally secreted oils. The "terpene," or principle of turpentine, is that which produces the aroma, and gives to it its salutary character.

snapped like a thread of silk. Two jacks were then employed, and inch by inch they rose, till, after four days' labour, they stood in their old positions. The largest stem was 27 feet long, and averaged 3 feet 3 inches in diameter. Their age must have been over two hundred years. Unfortunately, in falling, all their large roots on one side were torn away; and in raising them their stems shot back too far, and the roots on the other side then snapped one by one with quite loud reports, leaving only the fibrous roots enclosed in the ball of earth torn up with them. The next year they put out shoots, and are now, after several years, established thriving pollards, and will soon become handsome trees. This successful operation is the more noteworthy because of the adverse opinion of some eminent authorities as to its possibility.

The great oak in the Plestor at Selborne, under whose branches so many generations of the young people of that village had danced, was blown down in the memorable storm of 1703. The Vicar and inhabitants, at considerable expense, did their best to set it up again, but it was a failure. After sprouting for a time it died. In the Annotations to White's "Selborne," Mr. Menzies, referring to an oak which had been blown down, says, "That no tree which fell in this way, if of any size, can be put up again and live. I have frequently been consulted, but never advise it; the case is hopeless."

Referring to these limes, records extending over thirteen years show that the fall of the leaf is much more uniform than its opening. During this period they have varied in the time of falling hardly more than a week—sixteen days once, as an exceptional case. They fall generally about the last week in October; but in their opening the divergence has been nearly a month. The difference of temperature and moisture in our English springs sufficiently accounts for this, while in the autumn the variation is much less.

I may here allude to the storm of the 26th December 1886, the most disastrous to the Forest trees of this neighbourhood that has occurred within the memory of man; it was remarkable chiefly for the coincidence of causes which together only could work such destruction; it was all done in two or three hours. The snow fell in a half-melted state, and adhered to the branches, and their freezing, weighted them with lumps of ice; at the same time a hurricane of wind made every branch, as it were, a pendulum. Fine oaks were split, and main branches a foot in diameter were twisted into all possible contortions, and wrenched off as is hardly ever seen. Swinley Forest was in a sad plight; the old keeper said there had never been such havoc there during the forty years he had known it.

I must here notice the two famous vines in this neighbourhood, but little inferior in size to the great one at Hampton Court, which was planted about 1768, and which Mr. Rose, formerly the gardener at Frogmore (writing about twenty years ago), tells us was at the surface 2 feet 10 inches in circumference, and at three feet was a yard. It covered an area of 1950 feet, and yielded 600 to 800 pounds of grapes annually.

Of ours, the first is at Cumberland Lodge. It was planted by a Mr. Tidy, the foreman and manager there; and I find from a notice in the *Reading Mercury* for September 1815 that it must have been about 1802; it had then 1100 bunches of grapes.

At the time of the above measurement of the Hampton Court vine, this measured* at the surface 3 feet in circumference and at two feet 2 feet 10 inches, covering an area of 2553 feet, producing from 600 to 1200 bunches of grapes.

The next remarkable tree is at Silwood; it was a cutting from that at Cumberland Lodge, and was planted about twenty years later; its girth at the surface is 2 feet 4 inches, it occupies an area of 1500 feet, and produces about 800 pounds of fruit annually.

---

* See W. Thompson's Vine Culture.

APPENDIX.

I.

CHARITIES AND ENDOWMENTS.

No. 1.—THE CHURCH HOUSE AND GREEN.

THE most ancient gift to our parish was that known as the Church House and Green; it consisted of a building and half an acre of land lying directly opposite to the Cedars, and adjoining to the churchyard on the north. We have no knowledge as to how or when this property was acquired. It was an ancient clearance from the Forest, held at a quit-rent of 4d., payable to the King as lord paramount of the manor.

It became vested in trustees for all the parishioners of Sunninghill. It was exchanged with the Hon. John Yorke, owner of the Cedars, for fourteen acres of land at Chobham, which were sold by order of the Poor Law Commissioners in 1841, and the money so produced was laid out in building cottages.

No. 2.—PARISH COTTAGES.

Another of our old possessions was that dealt with by a deed of 4th December 1665, a small enclosure called "Old Thomas May's," near the present police-station, in respect of which the Enclosure Award gave to the churchwardens and overseers of Sunninghill, as trustees for the poor, an allotment, No. 96, containing 30 poles, and the two together made up the 1 rood 18 poles which are designated in the parish map as Nos. 385 and 386.

Two old cottages upon it, mere hovels according to our present ideas, became ruinous beyond repair, and were condemned by the sanitary authorities. The vacant land was recently sold to Mr. George Walker for £100. This sum was invested in consols, in the name of the official trustee, for the use of the parish.

No. 3.

The next property to be noticed was a cottage and garden, containing 1 rood, more or less, abutting on Mill Lane, near Lord's Green, dealt with by deed of 12th June 1680. At the time of the enclosure it was exchanged by the trustees with Mr. Vernon, who lived at Buckhurst, for a parcel of land and a cottage thereon near the old workhouse. This plot, with a cottage on it recently occupied by Widow Dentry, and two others occupied by Widows Pither and Curtis, was sold, with the consent of the Charity Commissioners, about five or six years ago, to Sir Cowel Stepney for £500, and the money invested in consols. The Commissioners at the time suggested that the dividends from this should be distributed in small sums or doles at Christmas. The trustees, however, strenuously opposed this view, and induced the Commissioners to consent to its reinvestment in cottages for the poor; and accordingly four cottages were ultimately built on the site of old Stevens' hovel in Sunninghill Bog, belonging to the parish.

These cottages are let to deserving parishioners at a rent of 1s. a week—a form of charity, in the judgment of the trustees, superior to that of doles, and peculiarly adapted to the special circumstances of this neighbourhood.

No. 4.

The parish land in Sunninghill Bog, on part of which are the four new cottages just referred to. The parish anciently possessed a small plot of land adjoining Sunninghill Park called Pound Hill Plat. Allusion was made to this in the last century, when timber was to be taken from it to make a new gate for the Church Lane. It is referred to in deeds of 12th June 1680 and 6th January 1706, as being held for all the poor parishioners.

This, at the time of the enclosure, was exchanged with Mr. G. H. Crutchley for 1 a. 3 r. 27 p. of land in Sunninghill Bog, and adjoining to which lay 7 a. 12 p. allotted to the parish under the enclosure, No. 73; these together make up the 8 a. 3 r. 39 p. shown in the Tithe map as No. 294. From this, 2 a. 1 r. 11 p. were sold to the Staines and Wokingham Railway in 1855, and thus left belonging to the parish trustees 6 a. 2 r. 28 p. The money received for this land sold to the railway in 1855—amounting to £111, 1s.—was in 1859 laid out in rebuilding the new double cottage at Cheapside, for a long time in the occupation of Widows Kidd and Turner.

No. 5.

The parish has another small plot of land containing 1 a. 14 p. adjoining this last, and to the Fuel Allotment, No. 251 in the Tithe map. It also possessed other plots, Nos. 260, 320, 366, 367, and 294, in the same map. Of these, 260, 320, and a portion of 294 were, as before observed, taken by the railway in 1855, and Nos. 366 and 367 were, it is believed, disposed of many years ago, probably by order of the Poor Law Commissioners, as in 1841 I find that, besides the Poorhouse and garden, containing 1 a. 3 r. 27 p., were also at the same time sold one cottage and 38 p. of land south-east of Queen's Beech Hill (on the southern side of the Ascot Road), and also one cottage and garden near the Bog.

No. 6.—Lane's Charity.

Edward Lane of Coworth left by will in 1714 a rent-charge of £2 per annum to the poor of the parish of Sunninghill not receiving relief. This was chargeable on the Coworth estate, and has always been paid at Easter by the owners thereof. It seems to have been distributed for the first time in 1733.

No. 7.—Moody's Charity.

The Parliamentary Returns of 1786 state that Samuel Moody left to the poor a rent-charge of £1 per annum, and the table of benefactions in the church states that there was such a rent-charge payable out of a cottage at Blackness Gate.

In 1803 this cottage came into the possession of a pauper in consequence of the long-continued absence of the reputed owner.

About five years previously to 1836, when this report was made, the cottage was sold, and as no document could be produced to substantiate the claim, the rent-charge was disregarded. The cottage was eventually sold to the Crown and pulled down, and the £1 rent-charge lost by non-claim.

No. 8.—Mrs. Ann Palmer's Charity.

Ann Palmer, by her will, directed a sum of £50 to be given for the poor of the parish of Sunninghill, and the interest thereof laid out in bread, and distributed amongst the poor by the churchwardens and overseers every Easter Sunday after divine service in the afternoon. This sum was laid out in the purchase of an acre of land called Crab Acre, in Northfield, Winkfield, and two half acres lying also in Northfield, with another acre lying in Millfield, and "two small plats or doles" of meadow-land in Millfield. Under the powers of the Enclosure Act these lands, which lay dispersed in the open fields, were exchanged for two allotments, the first in Millfield, and the second near Engelmore Pond, bounded by the Windsor and Bagshot Road on the east side.

In the inquiry made by the Charity Commissioners in or about 1836, this last allotment is asserted to be of "very little value!" It would be of very considerable value now. These lands appear to have been sold in 1855, and the purchase-money invested in £360, 8s. 2d. consols, which now stand in the name of the official trustee for the purposes of the trust, yielding a dividend of £10, 16s. 2d.

No. 9.—Mrs. Elizabeth Squire's Charity.

Elizabeth Squire, of St. Margaret's, Westminster, by her will, dated 4th May 1733, gave for the poor of the parish of Sunninghill the sum of £200, to be given "to old people and those that were visited with sickness," and made Elizabeth Northcote sole executrix. This sum was laid out in the purchase from William May of nine acres of land, lying near the Millpond in Winkfield, on which it abutted towards the south, and on the north and east on the waste called Cranbourn Wood. On condition that so long as the said William May and his heirs should pay in the church porch of Sunninghill the yearly rent of £7 at the Feast of St. John the Baptist and St. Thomas the Apostle, by equal payments, free from all taxes and charges whatsoever, parliamentary or otherwise, they should enjoy the lands and take the rents for their own use.

The land originally belonged to William May, and now to Mr. Savory. It lies on the margin of our parish, and near what was formerly known as Lord's Mill, and now forms part of Buckhurst Park. The distribution belongs to the churchwardens and overseers.

No. 10.—Mrs. Ann Dawson's Charity.

Mrs. Ann Dawson, of Sunninghill, who died in 1831, "bequeathed to the minister and churchwardens, for the time being, of the parish of Sunninghill

£100 sterling, to be invested in the public stocks of Great Britain, and to lay out the dividends in the purchase of blankets and warm clothing, and distribute the same, on the 17th September in each year, among such of the resident poor of the parish as they shall think most deserving."

She created a similar trust of £100 in favour of the school.

The two sums produced £204, 4s. consols, or for this charity £102, 2s., which now stands in the name of the official trustee, yielding annually about £3, 1s. 2d, payable half yearly.

No. 11.—Lucas Hospital.

This parish is entitled in turn to have one inmate in Lucas Hospital at Chapel Green, Wokingham, under the terms and provisions of that charity.

No. 12.—Stables' Charity.

John Stables, of the Wilderness, Ascot Heath, by will in 1856, left £333, 6s. 8d. Consols in trust, to apply the dividends in the purchase of warm clothing for the benefit of five deserving old men and five deserving old women of the parish, to be selected by the Vicar and churchwardens, such clothing to be distributed on the 13th of December every year.

No. 13.

The parish trust estate also comprises four (formerly five) cottages at Cheapside and 172 poles of land, distinguished in the Tithe map as

Nos.	a.	r.	p.
521	0	0	24
522	0	2	26
523	0	0	34

These cottages were built out of moneys from time to time accruing to the parish, including the purchase-money of the 14 acres of land at Chobham, sold in 1841, £105 received in 1793 for a plot of land sold to His Royal Highness the Duke of Cumberland near the Kennels at Ascot, and also the before-mentioned sum of £111, 1s. 0d. received from the railway in 1855 for the land in Sunninghill Bog.

No. 14.—The Fuel Allotment.

Of this important property I have fully spoken in the account of the enclosure of the Forest.

II.

From the tombstones in our church and churchyard the following extracts are set out for their better preservation, as time, accident, or neglect soon render the inscriptions illegible, and the very stones themselves, after many years, perish or disappear. Want of space prevents my setting out these inscriptions in full.

Mr. JOHN ALDRIDGE, late of this parish, departed this life the 27 April 1737, aged 66 years.

SARAH ALDRIDGE, his daughter, died Feb. 26, 1737, aged 35 years.

MARY ALDRIDGE, his daughter, died Nov. ye 24, 1740, aged 23 years.

ELIZABETH, his daughter, ob. 25 Aug. 1744, æt. 29.

ELIZABETH, his wife, ob. 27 July 1745, æt. 67.

JOHN, his son, late of Doctors Commons, London, gent., ob. 26 April 1747, æt. 45.

Mr. JOHN ALDRIDGE (only son of the late Mr. Henry Aldridge), died Nov. 16, 1782, aged 36 years.

Also Mr. HENRY ALDRIDGE, died Nov. ye 17, 1703, aged 43 years.

Mrs. SARAH ALDRIDGE, wife of Mr. Henry Aldridge of this parish, died March ye 31, 1752, aged 27 years.

Also SARAH ALDRIDGE, daughter of ye above, died June 5, 1754, aged 6 years.

Mr. JOHN ATTLEE, of this parish, died March ye 10, 1740, in the 64 year of his age.

And also MARY, his beloved wife, died June 15, 1765, in the 78 year of her age.

(On the south wall of chancel.)

Near this place lies THOMAS DRAPER BABER, Esq., late of Sunninghill Park, who died 27 of April 1783, aged 72 years.

On the outer side of this wall lie the remains of CHARLOTTE D. BABER, spinster, second daughter of Thomas Draper Baber, Esq., and Barbara his wife. She died 10 Sept. 1814, aged 71 years and 3 months.

BARBARA BABER, relict of the late Thomas Draper Baber, Esq., departed this life 15 June 1794, aged 86 years.

MELVILLE ELIZABETH, the beloved daughter of GEORGE and CAROLINE ELIZABETH BARTLETT, of the Royal Kennels, Ascot, departed this life April 27, 1863, aged 14 years and 10 months.

JAMES BARWELL, Esq., of Coworth Manor Farm, in the county of Berks, fourth son of William Barwell, Esq., formerly Governor of Bengal, died the 24 Nov. 1811, aged 63 years.

FREDERICK ADOLPHUS BOISSIER, died March 1, 1829, aged 10 months 16 days.

HENRY RICHARD, second son of CHARLES CLEMENTS BROOKE, Esq., died May 2, 1844, aged 1 year.

ELIZABETH, wife of CHARLES CLEMENTS BROOKE, Esq., of Laurel Cottage, Winkfield, departed this life June 5, 1845.

(At the eastern corner of the north aisle, on the floor.)

PETER EVERARD BUCKWORTH, Esq., died Jan. 14, 1840, aged 71 years.

ANNA MARIA BUCKWORTH, formerly of Park Place and afterwards of Engelfield Green, spinster, died 4 April 1840, aged 83. She was buried in a vault in this church.

Also PETER EDWARD BUCKWORTH [as above], buried in the same vault.

Also JOSEPH FRANCIS BUCKWORTH, late of Wooton House and Sandy Place in the county of Bedford, died 31 Dec. 1845, aged 75, and buried at Sandy in the county of Bedford. The above were three of the children of Charles and Elizabeth Buckworth of Park Place.

(In the south aisle.)

FRANCIS BUCKWORTH, the second daughter of Charles Buckworth, Esq., of Bishopgate, Berks.

Also in the churchyard is a record to GEOFFRY BUCKWORTH, who died an infant.

CHARLES BUCKWORTH, Esq., son of Sir John Buckworth, Bart., of Sheen, in Surrey. He married Elizabeth, the only surviving daughter of Peter Silakerley, Esq., of Somerford, in the county of Chester, by whom he left three sons and two daughters, and departed this life Aug. 22, 1783, aged 50 years.

And also ELIZABETH, relict of the above Charles Buckworth, Esq., late of Engelfield Green, Berks, died Sept. 27, 1811, aged 73 years.

The LADY GEORGIANA CATHCART, widow of the late General the Hon. Sir George Cathcart, K.C.B., died 12 Dec. 1871. Hear my prayer.

The infant son of Sir Reginald and Lady Cathcart, born and died January 16, 1882.

JOANNA CHURCHILL, eldest daughter of Sir Patrick Murray, 4th Baronet of Ochtertyre, Co. Perth, N.B., and widow of Charles Churchill, Esq., grandson of Sir Robert Walpole, 1st Earl of Oxford, and grand-nephew of John Churchill, 1st Duke of Marlborough, departed this life May 14, 1846, aged 95.

Also in the same vault are interred the remains of MARY HELEN CHURCHILL, only daughter of the above Joanna Churchill, departed this life Dec. 1, 1850, aged 52.

APPENDIX.

CHARLES NELSON COLE, Esq., died Dec. 18, 1804, in the 82 year of his age.
Also the remains of Mrs. ANNE HESTER COLE, relict of Charles Nelson Cole, and youngest daughter of Sir Wm. Abdy, Bart., of Chobham Place, Surrey. departed this life Dec. 28, 1805, aged 70 years.

EDWARD COOK, died Sept. 20, 1860, aged 91 years.
Also MARY, widow of the above, died Feb. 11, 1861, in her 79 year.

JAMES CRAUFURD, Esq., departed this life on the 17 Feb. 1816.
Also MARY, his wife, died on 28 June 1837, aged 79 years.

Mrs. MARY CRIDLAND (wife of Mr. Henry Cridland of Fulham in MDX.), died March 25, 1784, aged 79 years.

Beneath this urn are deposited the remains of GEORGE HENRY CRUTCHLEY, of Sunninghill Park, who was born Oct. 24, 1778, and died Jan. 25, 1868, aged 89.
And also those of JULIANA, his wife, daughter of Sir William Burrell, Bt., who was born July 11, 1782, and died Dec. 24, 1856, aged 74.

CAROLINE DALLAS, only daughter of Lucy and the late Robert William Dallas, died 28 Sept. 1865.

Mr. SAMUEL DALTON, departed this life June 24, 1863, aged 61 years.
LOUISA EMILY DALTON, Aug. 15, 1869, aged 23 years.

MARIANNE, the beloved wife of JOHN HOWELL DAVIES, Esq. ob. 23 Oct. 1837, aged 42 years.
Also JOHN HOWELL DAVIES, Esq., of Tittenhurst Lodge, in this parish, died 8 April 1856, in his 55 year.
CHARLES DAVIS, Royal Huntsman, Ascot, died 26 Oct. 1866, aged 78 years, and MARY, his wife, died 6 May 1856, aged 66 years.

(On a small black marble tablet, in capitals, on the north wall of chancel, removed in 1889 to the north aisle.)
Hic jacet GEORGIUS DAWSON, A.M. et hujus ecclesiæ vicarius per XXXVII. annos.
Qui suâ sorte contentus
Fretus tamen spe melioris.
Abiit obiit A.D. M.D.CC., ætatis suæ LXIII. Prope jacet ANNA, uxor, quæ obijt 26 Nov. anno 1711.

MICHAEL DUFFIELD, Esq., died 18 Feb. 1820, aged 85 [?]. He left two sons George Henry Crutchley and Thomas Duffield, and   daughters.
Also ALICE DUFFIELD [?], Michael Duffield, Esq., died 11 January —— aged 81.

JANE, the beloved wife of WILLIAM EDWARDS of Windsor (daughter of the late Mr. George Sharpe), died Feb. 8, 1872, aged 78.

Also WILLIAM EDWARDS, of Trinity Place, Windsor, husband of the said Jane Edwards, died Sept. 2, 1875, aged 86.

GEORGE ELLIS, Esq., born 19 Dec. 1754, died 7 April 1815.
Also ANN, his widow, born 3 May 1773, died 26 Aug. 1862.

(On the eastern wall of the north aisle is a tablet.)

To the memory of GEORGE ELLIS, many years an inhabitant of this parish. With rare talents, with incomparable industry, and with a tried capacity for great affairs which eminently qualified him for public station, he had the wisdom and the fortitude to decline the allurements of ambition, and while yet in the vigour of his age and intellect, sought and found his happiness in the tranquillity of private life, devoting himself in this chosen retirement to the pursuits of elegant learning. He investigated and displayed with admirable sagacity and taste the progress and refinement of our national language and poetry. His knowledge was various, profound, and accurate; and he imparted it without effort or ostentation. His wit illuminated every object which it touched, but its brilliancy, though powerful, was unoffending. In the maturity of literary excellence he listened with the humility of a learner, and amidst the severest studies he could relax into the playfulness of a child. He was exemplary in the discharge of all social duties; in his temper singularly placid; in his affections enthusiastically warm. His name will long be cherished by the lovers of English literature. The void which he has left in society can never, to those who knew him, be supplied.

Mrs. JANE FARRELL departed this life the 19 May 1774, aged 25 years. She was the wife of Walter Edward Farrell, of Highgate, in the County of Middlesex, Esq.

(On the tomb of General R. Fitzpatrick in the churchyard, written by himself.)

THE RIGHT HONOURABLE RICHARD FITZPATRICK, second son of John, Earl of Upper Ossory, and Evelyn Leveson Gower, his wife, General of His Majesty's Forces, Colonel of the 47th Regiment of Foot, Privy Councillor in both Kingdoms, and at different times Member of Parliament for the borough of Tavistock and the county of Bedford. He twice held the important office of Secretary at War, and once that of Secretary to the Lord-Lieutenant of Ireland, and was during forty years the intimate friend of Mr. Fox. He was an inhabitant and proprietor in this parish. Born 30 Jan. 1749, died 25 April 1815.

My own Epitaph.

Whose turn is next? This monitory stone
Replies, vain passenger, perhaps thy own.
If idly curious, thou wilt seek to know
Whose relics mingle with the dust below.
Enough to tell thee that his destined span
On earth he dwelt—and like thyself a man.
Nor distant far th' inevitable day
When thou, poor mortal, shalt like him be clay.
Through life he walk'd unemulous of fame,
Content if friendship o'er his humble bier
Drop but the heartfelt tribute of a tear;
Though countless ages should unconscious glide,
Nor learn that ever he had lived or died.

MICHIE FORBES, Esq., of Silwood Park, in this parish, and Crimond, Aberdeenshire, born 16 May 1779, died 24 Aug. 1839.

MARY, wife of the above Michie Forbes, born 31 Aug. 1795, died 16 May 1874, in her 79 year.

And also JAMES SIDNEY, fifth and youngest son of the above, born 5 Sept. 1827, died 7 Jan. 1861, in his 34 year.

Sir WILLIAM ADOLPHUS FRANKLAND, 9th Baronet of Thirkleby, Colonel Royal Engineers, born 12 Aug. 1837, died 29 Nov. 1883.

FREDERICK WILLIAM GREY, Admiral, G.C.B., third son of Charles, 2nd Earl Grey, born Aug. 23, 1805, died May 2, 1878.

In peace.

(On floor of chancel.)

Mr. ROBERT HANCOCK, who departed this life the 25 day of Aug. Ano. Dñi. 1667, ætatis suæ 50.

On the erection of the new chancel in 1889 this stone was removed into the churchyard, and laid down at the north-east corner of it.

Mr. THOMAS HATCH, of Coworth, in the parish of Old Windsor, departed this life Jan. 31, 1736, aged 34.

Also JANE, his wife, died Nov. 3, 1739, aged 46.

Mrs. MARY HATCH, wife of George Hatch, Draper, of Windsor, in the county of Berks, departed this life Nov. 1, 1790, aged 55 years.

Mr. GEORGE HATCH, Senior Alderman and many times Mayor and Justice of the Borough of New Windsor, died Nov. 1, 1799, aged 78 years.

Also Mrs. MARY HATCH, died 20 Jan. 1837, aged 71 years.

Also JOHN HATCH, Esq., son of the first-named Mrs. Mary Hatch and Mr. George Hatch, died Feb. 3, 1838, in the 77 year of his age.

CHARLOTTE, widow of Rear-Admiral HARDYMAN, C.B., departed this life April 19, 1872, aged 91.

ADMIRAL HARDYMAN, died in London, April 17, 1834, aged 63.

MARIAN ELIZA, died June 23, 1836, aged 19.

LUCIUS HEYWOOD, died Jan. 6, 1842, aged 25, children of Lucius and Charlotte Hardyman.

In affectionate remembrance of THOMAS HOLLOWAY, born Sept. 22, 1800, died Dec. 26, 1883.

In affectionate remembrance of JANE, the beloved wife of THOMAS HOLLOWAY, born Nov. 1, 1814, died Sept. 26, 1875.

ANNE JANE HORT, relict of Thomas Hort, Esq., departed this life at her residence, Ascot Lodge, in this parish, Dec. 18, 1842, in the 73 year of her age. She was bereaved of her husband, who fell a victim to yellow fever in the West

Indies, in 1806. They had issue, Richard, Kitty-Jenkyn, and Annette-Jane, who died young in 1810, and was buried at Malling, in the county of Sussex.

LOVEL THOMAS, third son of Richard, above mentioned, died young at Ascot Lodge. Their remains are interred in a vault near this church.

JOHN INGALTON, of Eton, died Aug. 23, 1823, aged 22 years.

Lieut. FRANCIS JEFFERSON, of the Royal Navy, departed this life 13 Jan. 1855.

Also ELEANOR JEFFERSON, widow of the above, died 6 Nov. 1868, aged 78 years.

MARY, the beloved infant daughter of JOHN and MARY ANN JEFFERSON, died May 13, 1856, aged 13 months.

(On east wall of north aisle.)

In a vault underneath this porch are deposited the remains of Mrs. ANN JOHNSTON, of the parish of St. James, Westminster, who departed this life May 12, 1802, aged 56 years.

WILLIAM HARRIS JOHNSTON, Esq., son of the above, died 20 Sept. 1809, aged 43 years.

General Sir THOMAS KENAH, K.C.B., died 26 March, A.D. 1868, aged 86.

ELIZABETH AMELIA KENAH, wife of Colonel Thomas Kenah, C.B., departed this life 27 May 1838, in the 49 year of her age.

HENRY KING, Royal Huntsman, departed this life Dec. 30, 1871, in the 57 year of his age.

Also JANE KING, relict of the above, died Jan. 21, 1877, in the 67 year of her age.

(Elias Ashmole says) " In Sunninghill, on the south side of the churchyard, on a black marble tomb raised on brick.

"Here lieth the bodies of Mr. EDWARD LANE of Coworth, and ELIZABETH, his wife. The said Elizabeth departed this life on 22 June 1661, aged 33. The last Edward on the last day of October 1714, in the 98 year of his age."

RICHARD LANE, of Fir Bank, Ascot, third son of Richard Lane, late of Limpsfield, Surrey, died on 25 May 1880, aged 85 years.

Lieut.-Col. GEORGE LYON, late H.M. 2nd Life Guards, died at Sunninghill, 24 Oct. 1879.

JOHN MACBRIDE, Admiral of the Blue, and URSULA, his wife, eldest daughter of Wm. Ffolkes, Esq., of Hillington Hall, Norfolk, who departed this life in Dec. 1796; he Jan. 14, 1800.

Mrs. SARAH MAN, wife of James Man, Esq., of this parish, died 8 April 1804, aged 44 years.

APPENDIX.

Mr. WM. MAY, Alderman of Windsor, and late of this parish, died April 10, 1761, aged 63 years.

Also Mrs. ANNE MAY, wife of the said Mr. Wm. May, died July 14, 1755, aged 49 years.

WM. MAY, of Fir Grove, Sunninghill, died Feb. 1, 1862, aged 82 years.

Mr. FREDERICK MUMFORD, died 14 Dec. 1859, aged 51 years.
CAROLINE SOPHIA, wife of the above, died Feb. 10, 1880, aged 70 years.

Sir WILLIAM NORRIS, late Chief Justice of Ceylon and Recorder of Penang, born 7 Nov. 1793, died 7 Sept. 1859.
JAMES THOMAS NORRIS, Lieut. 27 Reg. B. N. I., born 7 Nov. 1833, fell 2 Aug. 1857 in the mutiny at Kolapore.

JAMES PAINE, Esq., died 7 May 1829, aged 83 years.
Also ELIZABETH, died 18 Feb. 1864, aged 91 years.

JOSCELINE WILLIAM PERCY, second son of George, 5th Duke of Northumberland, born 17 July 1811, died 25 July 1881.

WM. PITHER, died Oct. 20, 1871, aged 65 years.
Also ELISABETH PITHER, widow of the above, June 16, 1887, aged 71 years.

(On a column with a square base is recorded)
"Buenosayres"

In memory of Rear-Admiral Sir HOME RIGGS POPHAM, K.C.B., K.C.G., K.M., F.R.S., who died at Cheltenham, Sept. 11, 1820, aged 58 years.

Affection's fondest terms are found too weak to state his conduct as a husband or a father, and as a friend 'twere difficult to do him justice. Yet memory retains what language fails t'express.

His public services were great and various; but those let history tell. This page posthumous has to record still nobler triumphs. These his great success excited envy, and envy persecution, but they both were foil'd in their attempts upon his character, for Truth was umpire, and Justice found the verdict. While he added most feelingly, this last, this best, this strongest confirmation—Forgiveness.

(On east side of base.)
"Cape of Goodhope."

(On west side.)
"Copenhagen."

(On north side.)
"North Coast of Spain."

Here also rests the remains of LADY POPHAM, widow of Sir Home, she died at her residence, 2 Portland Place, Bath, on 12 March 1866, in her 95th year, having survived her husband 45 years.

Also to the memory of CATHERINE MARY, eldest daughter of Admiral PACKENHAM, and grand-daughter of Sir Home and Lady Popham, died April 5, 1878, aged 60.

SAMUEL GROVE PRICE, Esq., of Taynton, in the county of Gloucestershire, late Fellow of Downing College, Cambridge, barrister-at-law and Member for Sandwich, Kent, born June 17, 1793, died June 17, 1830.

Also MARIANNE, his wife, daughter of Wm. Page, Esq., member of Council, Bombay, born Oct. 23, 1805, died Aug. 1, 1868.

Also of LETTSOM GROVE PRICE, eldest son of the above, born 11 Feb. 1832, died 18 March 1880.

To the memory of HARRIETT, widow of the late RICARDO, Esq., who departed this life October 5, 1844, this monument is erected by her children.

STEPHEN ROUND, Esq., departed this life 2 Sept. 1818, aged 69 years.

MARIA, wife of WHINFIELD S. ROUND, Esq., of Kingsbeech Hill, died 27 Dec. 1832, aged 48 years.

PENNINGTON ROUND, second son of Whinfield Round, Esq., of Kingsbeech Hill, died Feb. 13, 1842, aged 20 years.

HENRIETTA, the daughter of Stephen Round, Esq., departed this life 11 Sept. 1818, aged 19 years.

JAMES ROUSE, Esq., died at the Wilderness, Sunninghill, Nov. 12, 1868, aged 43 years.

JULIUS SANDEMAN, died Sept. 20, 1877.

WILLIAM SEAGRAVE, M.R.C.S.E., of this parish, born Dec. 21, 1815, died April 23, 1886.

Mrs. DOROTHEA SCHUTZ, wife of Spencer Schutz, born 22 Sept. 1728, died 20 Dec. 1803.

AUGUSTUS SCHUTZ, Esq., of Sunninghall, for many years a resident in this parish, and an active magistrate of the county of Berks. He was a man of cultivated mind, sound understanding, unaffected piety, unblemished integrity, and enlarged benevolence. His earnest desire to promote the established religion of the country, and the religious instruction of all around him, is manifested by his munificent donations for the enlargement of this Church, and his benefaction to the school of this parish. He died on 5 Nov. 1830, aged 57.

Also ELIZABETH, his wife (daughter of General Sir David Lindsay, Bart.), died on 19 June 1827.

CHARLES PATRICK STEWART, born 27 May 1823, died 7 July 1882.

CHARLES STRUTTON, of the Grange, Ascot Heath, and Princes Street, Lambeth, died Oct. 17, 1877, aged 65 years.

APPENDIX.

JOHN THACKER, Esq., departed this life 27 Nov. 1863, aged 71 years.
Also JANE THACKER, his wife, departed this life 3 June 1866, aged 71 years.

SAMUEL TOLLER, of Beech Grove, in this parish, eldest son of the late Samuel Toller, of Benhall, in the county of Suffolk, gentleman, born July 2, 1795, died May 16, 1860.

JOHN TOLLER, his brother, of Beech Grove, in this parish, born June 23, 1797, died November 2, 1878, and ANNE GERTRUDE, his wife, born June 2, 1803, died May 10, 1887.

GEORGE EDWARD TOWRY, Esq., of Harewood Lodge, in this parish, died at East Cowes, and was buried at the Parish Church, Whippingham, Oct. 24, 1857, aged 54.

In the vault beneath are deposited the remains of ELEANOR, daughter of WILLIAM URQUHART, Esq., of Craigston, Aberdeenshire, born 1769, died 5 March 1848.

In the vault beneath are deposited the mortal remains of JANE, daughter of WILLIAM URQUHART, Esq., of Craigston, Aberdeenshire, and widow of FRANCIS GREGOR, Esq., of Fruarthenick, late M.P. for the county of Cornwall, born 1770, died 6 May 1851.

MARY, the wife of JOHN VERNON, Esq., died 3 Aug. 1823, aged 47 years.
The above-named JOHN VERNON departed this life on 30 April 1825, aged 72.

Hic jacet quod mortale est ALEXANDRI MALCOLM WALE, B.D., hujus parochiæ vicarii cum Carolina conjuge, communi sepulchro, communi fide Christi, conjunctissimi. Dominus dedit: Dominus ademit: Domini nomini benedicatur.
C. W., a. d. X. Kal. Sep. MDCCCLXVII. Nat. LXV. annos.
A. M. W., a. d. VII. Kal. Jun. MDCCCLXXXIV. Nat. LXXXVII. annos.

THOMAS CHARLES FRANCIS WALE, died Jan. 1843.

Near this place lieth the body of CATHERINE, wife of THOMAS WATTS, Esq., of Beaumont Lodge, in this county. She died July 3, 1781, aged 40.

The remains of FRANCES LADY WENTWORTH, wife of Sir John Wentworth, Bart., are here deposited. Springing from an unblemished family in New England, and married to John Wentworth, Esq., Governor of New Hampshire, she encountered, with a resolution not to be excelled, the tempest of a furious revolution, until driven by the rage of civil war from the land of her nativity, she found refuge with her only child in the bosom of the parent country. . . . A most affectionate mother and unblemished wife, she rendered up her soul to God through Christ, in the principles of the Established Church of England, A.D. MDCCCXIII.

3 K

Rev. THOMAS WHATELY, M.A., Rector of Chetwynd, Salop, and formerly Vicar of Cookham, died May 10, 1864, aged 91 years.

ISABELLA SOPHIA WHATELY, died April 21, 1870, aged 84 years.

HENRY NORTON WILLIS, Esq., died Aug. 13, 1819, aged 73 years.

MURRELL WRIGHT, of Brook Cottage, died 18 Oct. 1865, aged 81 years.

Also MARY WRIGHT, wife of the above, died 27 June 1862, aged 78 years.

MATTHEW WYLIE, born 7 October 1815, died 18 April 1872. This monument is erected by his loving and disconsolate widow.

INDEX.

ABBOT of Chertsey, keeper of the peace, 14.
Adam Gurdon, the outlaw, 63.
Anne, Queen, 72, 73, 308.
Anne Boleyn, incident on her committal, 44.
Ascot, 312; racecourse and races, 85, 385, 386.
Ashurst, Sir Henry, 137, 250.
Avenues in Great Park, 294.

BAGGESET, GALFRID DE, 108.
Bagshot, 13, 16, 37, 324, 332.
Ballad of the King and the Shepherd, 64.
Bangor Lodge, 258.
Barwell, James, 249.
Battaille family, 109.
Beech Grove, 240.
Beggar's-Bush Heath, 95
Berroc-wood, 97.
Bibroci, kingdom of, 5.
Black Act, origin of, 19, 81.
Blackman, an early Saxon name here, 107.
Blackwick Hill, King's Beeches, 147.
Broomhall Nunnery, 100, 106, 139, 343; suppression of, 352.
Broughton family, 319.
Brocas family, 35.
Brown, Sir George, 8.
Buckhounds, Mastership of, 70, 74, 82.
Buckhurst Park, 254.
Bulstrode, Whitelocke, 55

CALLEVA, 360.
Camps, military, 269.
Carey arms, 201; pedigree, 206.
Carter, Mrs. Elizabeth, 229.
Carteret, Sir George, 305.
Cedars, the, 233.
Cæsar's Camp, 6, 272.
Charles I., journey through the Forest a prisoner, 53.
Charities and endowments. *See* Appendix.
Charters, 253.
Chertsey land boundaries, 98.
Chiminage, 32, 309.
Church, Sunninghill, 91, 167; church-house and green, 93, 173; Norman door of, 177; gift of, to Broomhall, 171, 178; bells and plate, 183; Windlesham, 339.

Claude Duval, his house, 15.
Climate, Sir James Clark's opinion, 13.
Cobbett, 11, 147.
Commonwealth, Sunninghill during, 125; disorders of, 333.
Coworth, 108, 245.
Cranbourn Tower and Lodge, 298, 311.
Crutchley family, 210.
Cumberland, Duke of, 78, 141, 288; Lodge, 283.

DERIVATIONS of local names, 97.
Dick Turpin, 16.
Domesday Survey, Sunninghill, 104.
Dornford, 115.

EASTHAMPSTEAD, Roman camp at, 5
Edward the Confessor, 30.
Ellis, George, 234.
Evelyn, 6; journey through the Forest, 57

FARRANT family, 118, 218.
Fauna of district, 402.
Fitzpatrick, General Richard, 240.
Flora of district, 416.
Forest, in its technical sense, 26; its people, 14; boundaries of, 34, 50; "walks" in, 39; destruction of timber, 54; traditions of, 60; enclosure of, 80; hunting, 69, 76; privileges of, 86.
Frith, the, 28.
Frogmore, 295.

GAY, 9.
Geology of district, 393.
George III., his hunting, 78.
Gipsies, 21.
Graham, Colonel James, 308, 334
Great Park, Windsor, 278.
Great storm, 134.
Gwynn at Sunninghill, 93, 128.

HALL GROVE, Windlesham, 8.
Harewood Lodge, 256.
Haybourne's Lodge, Great Park, 282.
Henry VIII.'s love of sport, 43.
Herne's Oak, 61.
Highway robberies, 16, 132.
Hundreds, the seven, 92.

INDEX.

JAMES I., his hunting, 48.
Justice-seat at Bagshot, 37.

KING'S beeches, 252.
Kingsley, Charles, account of country, 12.
King's Wick, 95, 114, 223; the avenue, 225.

LA CNAPPE, derivation of, 100.
Lammas lands, 116.
Land, its increase in value, 151.
Lane, family of, 247.
Langland's Lodge, Great Park, 282.
Lecky's allusion as to Waltham Blacks, 19.

MAIDENHEAD Thicket, 20.
Marlborough, Duke of, 287; Duchess of, 7, 286.
Manor Lodge, Windsor Park, 280.
Mill at Sunninghill, 113.
Moat Park, 296.
"Molly Mog," Gay's ballad, 10.

NEVILLE family, 120.
Nicholas, Secretary of Navy, 6, 126.
Norris, family of, 247, 376; Lodge, Great Park, 281.
Noy, Attorney-General, at Bagshot, 49.

"OAKS, the," 257; Cranbourn's Oaks, 307.
Ockwells, 374.

PEPYS, SAMUEL, 6; journey to Cranbourn, 72.
Poor laws, 139.
Pope, his love of Nature, 8; much at Sunninghill, 8; Pope's wood, 9; trees before his house, 9.
Pontes, 364.
Porter, Endymion, 227.
Potnal Park, 38.
Prince Arthur's journey through the Forest, 41.
Prince de Beauvau born at Sunninghill, 231.

QUELMES, 100, 313.

RACKETT, Mrs, Pope's sister, 8, 146.
Rainfall, 6, 401.
Ranelagh, Lord, 307.
Rapley Farm, a Roman station, 369.
Richard II.'s queen, Miss Strickland's mistake about, 110.
Roads, 158; British, 160; Roman, 160, 358; church, 163; to Windsor, 165.

Roman camp, Easthampstead, 5; Roman road, 358.

SCOTCH fir, seeding, 6; introduction here, 424.
Scott, Sir Walter, 235.
Shot as a termination, derivation of, 101.
Shrubshill, 21, 101.
Sibbald family, 221.
Silchester, 359.
Silwood, 116; Park, 214.
Staines, "Stane's Wood," 4; Bridge, 161.
Swift here, 9.
Swinley Forest, 26, 48; Lodge, 76.
Strickland, Miss, mistake as to Sunninghill, 110.
Sunninghill, description of, 1, 11, 16, 91; its people, 136, 148; under Commonwealth, 125; social condition, 142, 149; registers, 146; in Domesday, 105; manor, 110; rating, 153; population, 154; charities, 145.
Sunninghill Park, 200.
Sunningdale Park, 255.

TETWORTH, 257.
Thistlethwaite, Rev., 142, 198.
Tithing-men, 138.
Traditions of neighbourhood, 2; of Forest, 60.
Trees, age of, 421.

VESTRY, 139.
Vicars and Vicarage, 187.
Virginia Water, 280, 289, 321.
Vindomis, 370.

WALE, Rev. A. M., 199.
Waltham Blacks, 17; Lecky's mistake as to, 19.
Wells Inn, 260.
Wheat, price of, at beginning of century, 23.
William the Conqueror, 30; his oak, 31.
Windlesham, 324; Church, 339.
Windsor Castle, 29; Forest character of country, 4; inhabitants, 14; Blackstone's error as to origin of, 46; coal in, 58.
Winkfield, 316.
Winwood, M.P. for Windsor, meeting Cromwell, 130.
Wokingham, bull-baiting at, 22.

YEOMEN prickers, 77 *note*, 85.

PRINTED BY BALLANTYNE, HANSON, AND CO., EDINBURGH AND LONDON

LIST OF SUBSCRIBERS.

His Royal Highness the Duke of CONNAUGHT.
The ROYAL LIBRARY, Windsor Castle.
ST. JOHN'S COLLEGE, Cambridge.
His Grace the Duke of WESTMINSTER, K.G., Eaton Hall, Cheshire.
Lord NAPIER AND ETTRICK, Thirlstane, Selkirk.
Lord HARLECH, Tetworth, Sunninghill.
Sir JOSEPH DALTON HOOKER, The Camp, Windlesham.
Sir GEORGE RUSSELL, M.P., Swallowfield Park.
Sir CHARLES RYAN, Ascot.
General CRUTCHLEY, Sunninghill Park.
Major CRUTCHLEY, Scots Guards.
Mrs. H. L. GIBBS.
Colonel BLUNDELL, M.P., Ashurst, Sunninghill.
F. T. BARRY, Esq., M.P., St. Leonard's Hill
General MICHAEL, Bangor Lodge.
T. CORDES, Esq., Silwood Park.
The Rev. J. SNOWDON, Vicar of Sunninghill.
The Rev. B. K. PEARSE, Rector of Ascot.
The Rev. J. A. CREE, Vicar of Sunningdale.
WM. BARR BROWN, Esq., Ascot.
Lady EMILY PEPYS, 75 Victoria Street, Pimlico.
Miss FOWLER, Brunswick Terrace, Brighton.
Mrs. THOMAS, Park House, Englefield Green.
EDMUND CALVERLEY, Esq., Oulton Hall, Yorkshire.
Mrs. EADEN, King's Farm, Shelford.
CLAUDE LYON, Esq., Malta.
Mrs. MATTHEW WYLIE, The Mains, Sunninghill
THOMAS BRANKSTON, Esq., Blackheath, Kent.
Mrs. BRANKSTON, Blackheath, Kent.
Mrs. ASHBURNER (two copies), St. Remo, Italy.
E. LAURENCE, Esq., King's Ride, Ascot.
Miss DURNING SMITH, King's Ride, Ascot.
Mrs. BURTON PHILLIPSON, Rome.
ALFRED FAGG, Esq., Arundel Street, London.
The Hon. C. STONOR, South Ascot.
J. K. FARLOW, Esq., Egham.
Mrs. BOLTON, Cottage Hospital, Egham.
G. R. THOMPSON, Esq., Lynwood, Sunningdale.
Miss MINNIE MARTIN, Upton Grey House, Odiham, Hants.

[*Over.*

LIST OF SUBSCRIBERS.

Mr. J. Pither, Sunninghill.
The Rev. J. Freshfield, Rector of Windlesham.
Major R. R. Holmes, Royal Library, Windsor Castle.
E. T. Hall, Esq., Moorgate Street, London.
The Rev. Pendarves Lory, Vicar of Bagshot.
E. Hughes, Esq., Warbleton, Sussex.
Miss Margaret Thacker, Queen's Hill, Ascot.
C. F. Dowsett, Esq, 3 Lincoln's Inn Fields.
Joseph Savory, Esq., Buckhurst Park.
Wm. Farmer, Esq., Coworth Park.
The Rev. H. Sargent, Rector of East Wittering, Sussex.
C. D. Kemp Welsh, Esq., Broadlands, Ascot.
Sir G. Martin Holloway, Tittenhurst, Sunninghill.
Miss Driver, Tittenhurst, Sunninghill.
Vere L. Oliver, Esq., Sumner Grange.
Miss J. D. Langlands, 4 Strathearn Place, Edinburgh.
A. G. Lacy, Esq., Sunninghill.
Charles Ferard, Esq., Ascot Place, Winkfield.
Miss F. C. Fairman, Frognal, Sunninghill.
J. K. J. Hichens, Esq, Beech Grove, Sunninghill.
Colonel the Hon. C. R. Hay, Harewood Lodge, Sunninghill.
C. G. Barnett, Esq., King's Beeches, Sunninghill.
Ed. Hamilton, Esq., Charters, Sunninghill.
C. Reginald Hargreaves, Esq, Remenham, Wraysbury.
Miss Louisa Wale, Bagshot Hall.
Captain F. G. Vigor, The Hut Encampment, Pembroke.
Charles Peel, Esq., Fair View, Sunninghill.
Ed. Bell, Esq., F.S.A, Hampstead, Middlesex.
G. Noble Taylor, Esq.
R. F. Scott, Esq., St. John's College, Cambridge.
The Rev. Dr. Irving, Wellington College, Wokingham.
George Hudson, Esq., Whiteheather, Sunninghill.
The Rev. Canon Savory, Binfield Rectory, Bracknell.
Edward Pott, Esq., The Cedars, Sunninghill.
Miss Blundell, Ascot Cottage, Winkfield.
Mrs. Entwistle, The Oaks, Sunninghill.
The Rev. W. Goodchild, Wellington College, Wokingham.
Hy. Pigé Leschellas, Esq., Highams, Bagshot.
M. Kempson, Esq., Stout's Hill, Uley, Dursley.
The Misses Hardyman, Silwood Cottage, Sunninghill.
Colonel Victor Van de Weyer, New Lodge, Windsor Forest.
Albert Chancellor, Esq., M.S.A., Ascot, Berks.
James Wm. Chalmer, Esq., 66 Gloucester Place, Portman Square.

Lightning Source UK Ltd.
Milton Keynes UK
UKHW032017291020
372463UK00012B/145